FOURTH EDITION

2

Series Director: **Diane Larsen-Freeman**

Grammar Dimensions

Form • Meaning • Use

Lesson Planner

Ingrid Wisniewska

THOMSON

HEINLE

Australia • Canada • Mexico • Singapore • Spain • United King

THOMSON

HEINLE

Grammar Dimensions 2: Form, Meaning, and Use
Lesson Planner
Series Director: Diane Larsen-Freeman
Ingrid Wisniewska

Editorial Director: *Joe Dougherty*
Publisher: *Sherrise Roehr*
Consulting Editor: *James W. Brown*
Acquisitions Editor, Academic & Adult ESL: *Tom Jefferies*
VP, Director of Content Development: *Anita Raducanu*
Director of Product Marketing: *Amy Mabley*
Executive Marketing Manager: *Jim McDonough*
Senior Field Marketing Manager: *Donna Lee Kennedy*

Senior Development Editor: *Michael Ryall*
Senior Content Project Manager: *Maryellen Eschmann-Killeen*
Senior Print Buyer: *Mary Beth Hennebury*
Development Editor: *Sarah Barnicle*
Production Project Manager: *Chrystie Hopkins*
Production Services: *Pre-Press PMG*
Cover Designer: *Studio Montage*
Printer: *RR Donnelley*

For more information contact Thomson Heinle, 25 Thomson Place, Boston, Massachusetts 02210 USA, or you can visit our Internet site at http://elt.thomson.com

For permission to use material from this text or product, submit a request online at http://www.thomsonrights.com

Any additional questions about permissions can be submitted by email to thomsonrights@thomson.com

ISBN 10: 1-4240-0357-1
ISBN 13: 978-1-4240-0357-0

CONTENTS

Unit 4   Asking Questions   48

Opening Task   48

Unit 5   Modals of Probability and Possibility   70

Opening Task   70

Unit 6   Past Progressive and Simple Past with Time Clauses 88

Opening Task   88

A Word from Diane Larsen-Freeman, Series Director

Before *Grammar Dimensions* was published, teachers would ask me, "What is the role of grammar in a communicative approach?" These teachers recognized the importance of teaching grammar, but they associated grammar with form and communication with meaning, and thus could not see how the two easily fit together. *Grammar Dimensions* was created to help teachers and students appreciate the fact that grammar is not just about form. While grammar does indeed involve form, in order to communicate, language users also need to know the meaning of the forms and when to use them appropriately. In fact, it is sometimes not the form, but the *meaning* or *appropriate use* of a grammatical structure that represents the greatest long-term learning challenge for students. For instance, learning when it is appropriate to use the present perfect tense instead of the past tense, or being able to use two-word or phrasal verbs meaningfully, represent formidable challenges for English language learners.

The three dimensions of *form*, *meaning*, and *use* can be depicted in a pie chart with their interrelationship illustrated by the three arrows:

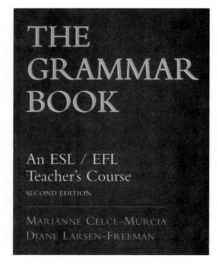

How is the grammar structure formed? (accuracy)

form

What does the grammar structure mean? (meaning)

meaning

use

When or why is the grammar structure used? (appropriateness)

Helping students learn to use grammatical structures accurately, meaningfully, and appropriately is the fundamental goal of *Grammar Dimensions.* It is consistent with the goal of helping students to communicate meaningfully in English, and one that recognizes the undeniable interdependence of grammar and communication.

THE GRAMMAR BOOK

An ESL / EFL Teacher's Course
SECOND EDITION

MARIANNE CELCE-MURCIA
DIANE LARSEN-FREEMAN

To learn more about form, meaning, and use, read *The Grammar Book: An ESL/EFL Teacher's Course,* Second Edition, by Marianne Celce-Murcia and Diane Larsen-Freeman. ISBN: 0-8384-4725-2.

To learn about theory that has informed *Grammar Dimensions,* consult *Teaching Language: From Grammar to Grammaring,* also by Diane Larsen-Freeman. ISBN: 0-8384-6675-3.

Enjoy the Fourth Edition of Grammar Dimensions!

Grammar Dimensions

Welcome to *Grammar Dimensions,* Fourth Edition!

The **clearest**, most **comprehensive** and **communicative** grammar series available! The fourth edition of *Grammar Dimensions* is more **user-friendly** and makes teaching grammar more **effective** than ever.

GRAMMAR DIMENSIONS IS COMPREHENSIVE AND CLEAR.

Grammar Dimensions systematically addresses the three dimensions of language— form, meaning, and use—through clear and comprehensive grammar explanations and extensive practice exercises. Each unit methodically focuses on each students' dimension and then integrates what they have learned in end-of-unit activities. In addition, grammatical structures are recycled throughout the series allowing students to practice and build upon their existing knowledge.

GRAMMAR DIMENSIONS IS COMMUNICATIVE.

Grammar Dimensions includes a large variety of lively communicative and personalized activities throughout each unit, eliciting self-expression and personalized practice. Interactive activities at the start of each unit serve as diagnostic tools directing student learning towards the most challenging dimensions of language structure. Integrated activities at the end of each unit include reading, writing, listening, and speaking activities allowing students to practice grammar and communication in tandem. New research activities encourage students to use authentic Internet resources and to reflect on their own learning.

GRAMMAR DIMENSIONS IS USER-FRIENDLY AND FLEXIBLE.

Grammar Dimensions has been designed to be flexible. Instructors can use the units in order or as set by their curriculum. Exercises can be used in order or as needed by the students. In addition, a tight integration between the Student Book, the Workbook, and the Lesson Planner makes teaching easier and makes the series more user-friendly.

GRAMMAR DIMENSIONS IS EFFECTIVE.

Students who learn the form, meaning, and use of each grammar structure will be able to communicate more accurately, meaningfully, and appropriately.

New to the Fourth Edition

■ **NEW and revised grammar explanations** and examples help students and teachers easily understand and comprehend each language structure.

■ **NEW and revised grammar charts and exercises** provide a wealth of opportunities for students to practice and master their new language.

■ **NEW thematically and grammatically related Internet and *InfoTrac®College Edition activities*** in every unit of books 2, 3, and 4 develop student research using current technologies.

■ **NEW Reflection activities** encourage students to create personal language goals and to develop learning strategies.

■ **NEW design, art, and photos** make each activity and exercise more engaging.

■ **NEW Lesson Planners** assist both beginning and experienced teachers in giving their students the practice and skills they need to communicate accurately, meaningfully, and appropriately. All activities and exercises in the Lesson Planner are organized into step-by-step lessons so that no instructor feel overwhelmed.

SEQUENCING OF *GRAMMAR DIMENSIONS*

In *Grammar Dimensions* students progress from the sentence level to the discourse level, and learn to communicate appropriately at all levels.

	Grammar Dimensions Book 1	*Grammar Dimensions* Book 2	*Grammar Dimensions* Book 3	*Grammar Dimensions* Book 4

Sentence level   Discourse level

	Book 1	**Book 2**	**Book 3**	**Book 4**
Level	High-beginning	Intermediate	High-Intermediate	Advanced
Grammar level	Sentence and sub-sentence level	Sentence and sub-sentence level	Discourse level	Discourse level
Primary language and communication focus	Semantic notions such as *time* and *place*	Social functions, such as *making requests* and *seeking* permission	Cohesion and coherence at the discourse level	Academic and technical discourse
Major skill focus	Listening and speaking	Listening and speaking	Reading and writing	Reading and writing

Guided Tour of *Grammar Dimensions*

"Unit Goals" **provide a roadmap** for the grammar points students will work on.

"Opening Task" can be used as a **diagnostic warm-up** exercise to explore students' knowledge of each structure.

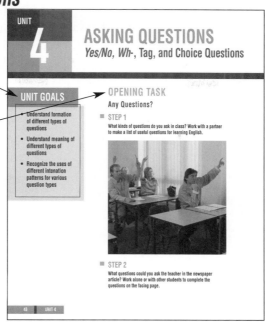

ASKING QUESTIONS
Yes/No, Wh-, Tag, and Choice Questions

UNIT GOALS

- Understand formation of different types of questions
- Understand meaning of different types of questions
- Recognize the uses of different intonation patterns for various question types

OPENING TASK
Any Questions?

■ STEP 1
What kinds of questions do you ask in class? Work with a partner to make a list of useful questions for learning English.

■ STEP 2
What questions could you ask the teacher in the newspaper article? Work alone or with other students to complete the questions on the facing page.

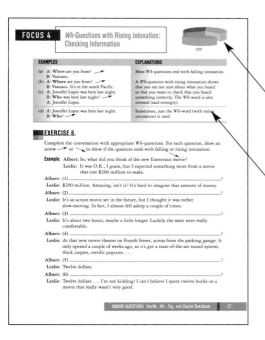

"Focus" sections present the **form, meaning, and/or use** of a particular structure helping students develop the skill of **"grammaring"**—the ability to use structures accurately, meaningfully, and appropriately.

Clear grammar charts present rules and explanation preceded by examples, so teachers can have students work inductively to try to discover the rule on their own.

Purposeful exercises provide a wealth of opportunity for students to practice and personalize the grammar.

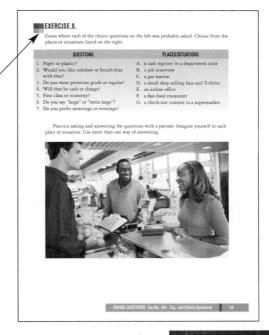

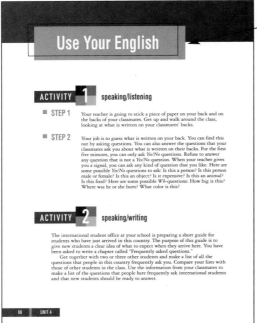

"Use Your English" (fondly known as the purple pages) offer communicative activities that **integrate grammar with reading, writing, listening, and speaking skills.** Communicative activities consolidate grammar instruction with enjoyable and meaningful tasks.

Engaging listening activities on audio cassette and audio CD further reinforce the target structure.

Research activity using *InfoTrac®College Edition* and the Internet encourages students to read articles on carefully selected topics and use this information to reflect on a theme or on information studied in each unit. *InfoTrac® College Edition*, an Online Research and Learning Center, appears in Grammar Dimensions 2, 3, and 4 and offers over 20 million full-text articles from nearly 6,000 scholarly and popular periodicals. Articles cover a broad spectrum of disciplines and topics—ideal for every type of researcher. Instructors and students can gain access to the online database 24/7 on any computer with Internet access.

Reflection activities help students understand their learning style and create learning strategies.

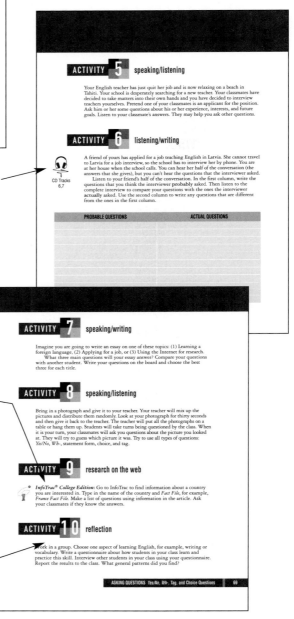

Supplements

These additional components help teachers teach and student learn to use English grammar structures accurately.

The Lesson Planner

The lesson planner facilitates teaching by providing detailed lesson plans and examples, answer keys to the Student Book and Workbook, references to all of the components, and the tapescript for the audiocassette activities. The Lesson Planner minimizes teacher preparation time by providing:

- Summary of main grammar points for the teacher
- Information for the teacher on typical student errors
- Step-by-step guidelines for every focus box, exercise, and activity
- Suggested correlations between exercises and activities in the Use Your English pages
- Suggested timing for each exercise and each lesson
- Lead-in suggestions and examples for focus boxes
- Suggestions for expansion work follow most exercises
- Balance of cognitive and communicative activities
- Explanation for the teacher of the purpose of each activity, in order to differentiate cognitive from communicative emphasis
- Occasional methodology notes to anticipate possible procedural problems.

Assessment CD-ROM with ExamView Test Generator

The Assessment CD-ROM allows instructors to **create customized quizzes and tests** quickly and easily from a test bank of questions. Monitoring student understanding and progress has never been easier! The answer key appears with instructor copies of each quiz or test created.

Audio Program

Audio cassettes and CDs **provide listening activities for** each unit so students can practice listening to **grammar structures.**

Workbook

Workbooks **provide additional exercises** for each grammar point presented in the student text. Also offers editing practice and questions types found on many language exams.

Web Site

Features additional grammar practice activities: elt.thomson.com/grammardimensions.

Empirical and Experiential Support for the *Grammar Dimensions* Approach

Opening Task Activities

The approach to teaching grammar used in the *Grammar Dimensions* series is well-grounded empirically and experientially. The Opening Task in each unit situates the learning challenge and allows students to participate in and learn from activity right from the beginning (Greeno 2006). In addition, students don't enter the classroom as empty vessels, waiting to be filled (Sawyer 2006). By observing how students perform on the Opening Task, teachers can analyze for themselves what students know and are able to do and what they don't know or are not able to do. Teachers can thus select from each unit what is necessary for students to build on from what they already bring with them.

Consciousness-Raising Exercises and Focus Boxes

Many of the exercises in *Grammar Dimensions* are of the consciousness-raising sort, where students are invited to make observations about some aspect of the target structure. This type of activity promotes students' noticing (Schmidt 1990), an important step in acquiring the grammar structure. The Focus Boxes further encourage this noticing, this time very explicitly. Explicit formulations of the sort found in the Focus Boxes can lead to implicit acquisition with practice (DeKeyser 1998). Moreover, certain learners (those with analytic learning styles) benefit greatly from explicit treatment of grammar structures (Larsen-Freeman and Long 1991).

Productive Practice and Communicative Activities

However, noticing by itself is insufficient. In order to be able to use the grammar structure, students need productive practice (Gatbonton and Segalowitz 1988; Larsen-Freeman 2003). Therefore, many of the exercises in **Grammar Dimensions** are of the output practice sort. Furthermore, each unit ends with communicative activities, where attention to the grammar is once again implicit, but where students can use the grammar structure in "psychologically authentic" or meaningful ways. Psychological authenticity is very important in order for students to be able to transfer what they know to new situations so that they can use it for their own purposes (Blaxton 1989) and so they are not left to contend with the "inert knowledge problem," (Whitehead 1929) where they know about the grammar, but can't use it.

The Three Dimensions of Grammar: Form, Meaning, and Use

Finally, applied linguistics research (Celce-Murcia and Larsen-Freeman 1999) supports the fundamental premise underlying **Grammar Dimensions:** that knowing a grammar structure means being able to use it accurately, meaningfully, and appropriately. Form focus or meaning focus by itself is insufficient (Larsen-Freeman 2001); all three dimensions—form, meaning, and use—need to be learned.

References

Blaxton, T. (1989). Investigating dissociations among memory measures: Support for a transfer-appropriate processing framework. *Journal of Experimental Psychology: Learning, Memory, and Cognition 15 (4): 657-668.*

Celce-Murcia, M. and D. Larsen-Freeman. (1999). *The grammar bbook: An ESL/EFL teacher's course.* Second Edition. Boston: Heinle & Heinle.

De Keyser, R. (1998). Beyond focus on form: Cognitive perspectives on learning and practicing second language grammar. n C. Doughty and J. Williams (eds.), *Focus on Classroom Second Language Acquisition.* Cambridge: Cambridge University Press, 42–63.

Gatbonton, E. and N. Segalowitz. (1988). Creative automatization: Principles for promoting fluency within a communicative framework. *TESOL Quarterly 22 (3):* 473–492.

Greeno, J. (2006). Learning in activity. In R. K. Sawyer (ed.), *The Cambridge handbook of learning sciences.* Cambridge: Cambridge University Press, 79–96.

Larsen-Freeman, D. (2001). Teaching grammar. In M. Celce-Murcia (ed.), *Teaching English as a Second or Foreign Language.* Third edition. Boston: Heinle & Heinle, 251–266.

Larsen-Freeman, D. (2003). *Teaching language: From grammar to grammaring.* Boston: Heinle & Heinle.

Larsen-Freeman, D. and M. Long. (1991). *An introduction to second language qcquisition research.* London: Longman.

Sawyer, R. K. (2006). Introduction: The new science of learning. In R. K. Sawyer (ed.), *The Cambridge handbook of learning sciences.* Cambridge: Cambridge University Press, 1–16.

Schmidt, R. (1990). The role of consciousness in second language learning. *Applied Linguistics 11 (2), 129–158.*

Whitehead, A. N. 1929. *The aims of education.* New York: MacMillan.

Acknowledgments from the Series Director

This fourth edition would not have come about if it had not been for the enthusiastic response of teachers and students using all the previous editions. I am very grateful for the reception *Grammar Dimensions* has been given.

I am also grateful for all the authors' efforts. To be a teacher, and at the same time a writer, is a difficult balance to achieve . . . so is being an innovative creator of materials, and yet, a team player. They have met these challenges exceedingly well in my opinion. Then, too, the Thomson Heinle team has been impressive. I am grateful for the leadership exercised by Jim Brown and Sherrise Roehr. I also appreciate all the support from Anita Raducanu, Amy Mabley, Sarah Barnicle, Laura Needham, Chrystie Hopkins, Mary Beth Hennebury, and Crystal Parenteau of Pre-Press PMG. Deserving special mention are Amy Lawler and Yeny Kim, who never lost the vision while they attended to the detail with good humor and professionalism.

I have also benefited from the counsel of Marianne Celce-Murcia, consultant for the first edition of this project, and my friend. Finally, I wish to thank my family members, Elliott, Brent, and Gavin, for not once asking the (negative yes-no) question that must have occurred to them countless times: "Haven't you finished yet?" As we all have discovered, this project has a life of its own and is never really finished! And, for this, I am exceedingly grateful. Happy Grammaring all!

A Special Thanks

The series director, authors, and publisher would like to thank the following reviewers whose experienced observations and thoughtful suggestions have assisted us in creating and revising *Grammar Dimensions*.

Michelle Alvarez
University of Miami
Coral Gables, Florida

Edina Pingleton Bagley
Nassau Community College
Garden City, New York

Jane Berger
Solano Community College,
California

Mary Bottega
San Jose State University

Mary Brooks
Eastern Washington University

Christina Broucqsault
California State Polytechnic
University

José Carmona
Hudson Community College

Susan Carnell
University of Texas at Arlington

Susana Christie
San Diego State University

Diana Christopher
Georgetown University

Gwendolyn Cooper
Rutgers University

Julia Correia
Henderson State University
Arkadelphia, Arkansas

Sue Cozzarelli
EF International, San Diego

Catherine Crystal
Laney College, California

Kevin Ccross
University of San Francisco

Julie Damron
Interlink at Valparaiso
University, Indiana

Glen Deckert
Eastern Michigan University

Eric Dwyer
University of Texas at Austin

Nikki Ellman
Laney College
Oakland, California

Ann Eubank
Jefferson Community College

Alice Fine
UCLA Extension

Alicia Going
The English Language Study
Center, Oregon

Molly Gould
University of Delaware

Maren M. Hargis
San Diego Mesa College

Penny Harrold
Universidad de Monterrey
Monterrey, Mexico

Robin Hendrickson
Riverside City College
Riverside, California

Mary Herbert
University of California, Davis
Extension ackow

Jane Hilbert
ELS Language Center,
Florida International
University

Eli Hinkel
Xavier University

Kathy Hitchcox
International English
Institute, Fresno

Abeer Hubi
Altarbia Alislamia Schools
Riyadh, Saudi Arabia

Joyce Hutchings
Georgetown University

Heather Jeddy
Northern Virginia
Community College

Judi Keen
University of California,
Davis, and *Sacramento*
City College

Karli Kelber
American Language Institute,
New York University

Anne Kornfield
LaGuardia Community
College

Kay Longmire
Interlink at Valparaiso
University, Indiana

Robin Longshaw
Rhode Island School of Design

Robert Ludwiczak
Texas A&M University
College Station, Texas

Bernadette McGlynn
ELS Language Center, St.
Joseph's University

Billy McGowan
Aspect International, Boston

Margaret Mehran
Queens College

Richard Moore
University of Washington

Karen Moreno
Teikyo Post University,
Connecticut

Gino Muzzetti
Santa Rosa Junior College,
California

Mary Nance-Tager
LaGuardia Community
College, City University of
New York

So Nguyen
Orange Coast College
Costa Mesa, California

Karen O'Neill
San Jose State University

Mary O'Neal
Northern Virginia
Community College

Nancy Pagliara
Northern Virginia
Community College

Keith Pharis
Southern Illinois University

Amy Parker
ELS Language Center, San
Francisco

Margene Petersen
ELS Language Center,
Philadelphia

Nancy Pfingstag
University of North
Carolina, Charlotte

Sally Prieto
Grand Rapids Community
College

India Plough
Michigan State University

Mostafa Rahbar
University of Tennessee at
Knoxville

Dudley Reynolds
Indiana University

Dzidra Rodins
DePaul University
Chicago, Illinois

Ann Salzman
University of Illinois at
Urbana-Champaign

Jennifer Schmidt
San Francisco State
University

Cynthia Schuemann
Miami-Dade Community
College

Jennifer Schultz
Golden Gate University,
California

Mary Beth Selbo
Wright College, City Colleges
of Chicago

Mary Selseleh
American River College
Sacramento, California

Stephen Sheeran
Bishop's University,
Lenoxville, Quebec

Kathy Sherak
San Francisco State
University

Sandra E. Sklarew
Merritt Community College
Oakland, California

Keith Smith
ELS Language Center, San
Francisco

Helen Solorzano
Northeastern University

Jorge Vazquez Solorzano
Bachillerato de la Reina de
Mexico
S. C., Mexico, D. F.,
Mexico

Christina Valdez
Pasadena City College
Pasadena, California

Danielle Valentini
Oakland Community College
Farmington Hills,
Michigan

Amelia Yongue
Howard Community College
Columbia, Maryland

Welcome to the *Grammar Dimensions* Lesson Planner

To the Teacher

This newly revised Lesson Planner for *Grammar Dimensions* (4th edition), Book 2 provides the teacher with a comprehensive guide to using the *Grammar Dimensions* student book. Its aim is to facilitate lesson planning by suggesting step-by-step guidelines for each task, focus chart, exercise, and activity. It also provides suggestions for supplementary expansion exercises and variations on the current exercises. In addition to the new guidelines, methodology, language, pronunciation, culture, and grammar notes integrated throughout the lesson plans may help to answer questions often asked by students. In addition, there are unit-by-unit examples of typical student errors for each grammar point that may be used by the teacher to predict student problems, identify areas of difficulty, and create supplementary materials.

The Lesson Planner is *not* intended as a blueprint to be followed closely in every detail. We hope that as you use *Grammar Dimensions*, you will continue to explore and discover new ways of adapting the material to suit the needs of your students, as well as your own teaching style. It is hoped, however, that by providing more detailed teachers' notes, the Lesson Planner will help guide teachers who are using *Grammar Dimensions* for the first time and provide additional ideas and activities for those have already used the book many times.

OPENING TASK

Each unit starts with an Opening Task. The aim of this task is to help you, the instructor, find out what your students know and don't know. This information will enable you to target the material in the unit. You may decide to omit sections of the unit material that are already well understood by your students. You may decide to add extra exercises to the sections that present difficulty. The best way to find out the extent to which your students are able to use a particular structure correctly is to put them into a situation or context where they need to use it. This is what the Opening Task aims to do. Each task has been constructed so that students will need to use the target structures in order to complete it.

When using these tasks, we ask you to focus students' attention on understanding and completing the task. They should not be made to feel that this is a test of their linguistic knowledge. While their attention is focused on completing the task, you will be able to listen and take note of their language use. This diagnostic approach is quite different from communicative tasks that are used to practice a given structure. The purpose here is to allow students the opportunity to make mistakes as well as to use the target structures correctly. Only by allowing them the freedom to do this, will you be able to understand which aspects of the grammar points cause difficulty and which aspects of meaning, use, and form need most attention. You may, however, decide to come back to the Opening Task, once the grammar has been studied in more detail, and use this task to practice the given structures.

The Opening Tasks are designed so that, after initially setting up the task and explaining the steps, they may be carried out by students independently in pairs or groups. This will allow you to circulate among the students with your notebook, "eavesdropping" on their conversations, and taking notes of problems in meaning, form, or use that will be useful for you later in the unit. While you are listening, try to visualize the "form, meaning, and use" pie chart in your mind and see if you can determine where they have been successful, and where they need help.

At this point, it is probably better if you avoid error correction and assistance with the grammar of the task. The tasks are designed to encourage students to work meaningfully without concern that they will be interrupted, evaluated, or corrected. The only exception might be the need to remind students to work in English if they are using another language.

In this new edition, we have recognized the importance of allowing some time for students to become familiar with the topic of the task in Step 1. Some topics may be culturally unfamiliar, for example, the topic of fortune telling in Unit 3. Sometimes the vocabulary may need reviewing, for example, words for geographical features in Unit 21. In these cases, it is worth spending a little time talking around the topic in order to generate increased motivation for the task. We hope that the pictures and drawings will also help to engage students visually. (You may wish to supplement them by bringing in more pictures of your own.) In general, however, if students seem comfortable with the topic and the vocabulary, we recommend moving on to Step 2 as soon as possible.

In this new edition, we have also tried to focus more explicit attention on the target structure in the final step of the task. This final step can be used to make sure all students have recognized the link between the target language and the task. If some students have been using the target structures successfully, they can share this knowledge with the class. If no one has been able to use the structures, the teacher may use this opportunity to bridge to the first focus chart through direct instruction.

In many cases, the Opening Task is referred to at later points in the unit. If you collect examples of students' performance in the Opening Task, you may also find yourself referring back to these examples as you reach the relevant explanation or practice exercise later in the unit. For this reason, we do not recommend omitting the Opening Task. But, if you are short of time, you might want to shorten or omit either Step 1 or the final step.

FOCUS CHARTS

The focus charts present the form, meaning, and use of the target structure with examples and explanations that are appropriate for the level. Each aspect of the unit grammar is presented separately and is followed by exercises providing controlled practice. The focus charts allow students to develop step-by-step a better understanding of, and an ability to use, the structure accurately, meaningfully, and appropriately. The pie chart at the top of the focus chart indicates whether the box focuses on the form, meaning, use or combination of these to examine the target structure.

A new feature of this revised teacher's edition is the step-by-step guidelines for using the focus charts. As with all suggestions in this Lesson Planner, they are intended for guidance only. Teachers will use the focus charts in different ways depending on the needs of their students and their own teaching style.

The notes for each focus chart start with a *Lead-in* suggestion. We have tried to include a variety of presentation styles in the Lead-in, such as using student examples, using diagrams or pictures, creating information gaps, and other ideas that may help to vary the presentation format of the chart. We hope that you will experiment with different ideas and find the best way to present each grammar point, noting only that any student (and teacher) may get tired of repeatedly using the same presentation format.

In some cases, we have suggested asking students to look at the examples and try to work out the rules. You may find this takes longer, but the increased engagement of the learner and the greater time investment involved may result in greater retention. If you prefer a more deductive approach, you may ask students to read the information in the chart and come up with further examples of their own. A variation on this is to ask students individually or in pairs to present the information in a focus chart to another pair of students, or even to the whole class, adding a few new examples of their own. Teaching something to others is a great way to learn, helping students to understand if they truly understand a point!

Another possible way of using the focus charts is not to present them at all, but rather to assign students the exercises that go along with them. The focus charts can be used for reference purposes as the students work their way through the exercises. In this way, the material becomes more meaningful to students because they will need to understand it in order to complete the exercise.

■ EXERCISES

At least one exercise follows each focus. There is a wide variety of exercises in *Grammar Dimensions*. Comprehension exercises work on students' awareness and understanding. Production exercises develop students' skill in using the structures. The step-by-step teacher's notes for each exercise begin with an introductory sentence explaining which grammar point is being practiced and whether the purpose is to practice the form or use of the target structure.

Some exercises continue the theme of the Opening Task and some introduce students to new themes and vocabulary in order to provide variety and to foster students' ability to transfer their learning to new contexts. There are also many personalized exercises, in which students use their own background knowledge or opinions to answer questions.

As with the focus charts, there is a variety of different ways in which you may decide to use the exercises. Depending on your class length, you may decide to assign some exercises for homework and go over the answers in class. You may do the exercises in class using pairs or groups, perhaps assigning one section of the exercise to one set of groups and pairs, and another section of the exercise to the others. You may do the exercise orally in class and ask students to write the answers for homework.

Reviewing Exercises

There are also many options for how exercise answers can be checked. For example:

1. You can circulate while students are doing an exercise in class and spot-check.
2. You can go over the exercise afterwards as a whole class with each student being called on to supply an answer.
3. Exercises can be done individually and then pairs of students can get together to check their answers with each other. Where a difference of opinion occurs, you (or another pair of students) can act as a referee.

4. Different students, pairs, or groups of students can be assigned different parts of an exercise. For example, the first group does 1–5, the second group does 6–10, etc. The groups post their answers on newsprint or butcher block paper and everyone circulates at the end noting the answers and asking questions.

5. A variation of number 4 is to have one student from each group present to the other students the exercise answers that his or her group came up with.

6. You can prepare a handout with the answers, and each student corrects his or her answers individually.

7. You can collect the written work, and make a list of common errors. You can put the errors on an overhead transparency and show it to the students during the next class and have them correct the errors together.

Many exercises require students not only to choose the best answer, but also to explain the reasons for their choices. We believe that this ability to justify and explain the reasons for grammatical choices will enhance students' ability to use grammar accurately, meaningfully, and appropriately.

TIMING AND LESSON PLANS

In this new edition, we have made suggestions for the estimated time needed to complete each unit as well as timing for each exercise and activity. Most of the units are divided into two distinct lessons of 90 minutes each. A few units are not long enough for two 90 minute lessons, but they always contain at least an hour's worth of work. The length of a lesson will vary depending on the degree of difficulty your students have with this structure, whether they have previewed the exercise for homework, and other factors such as the size of your class. The time length given for exercises and activities is only a rough estimate of the minimum time needed to complete the exercise in class.

WORKBOOK

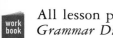

All lesson plans have been correlated with the additional exercises provided in the *Grammar Dimensions 2* Workbook. The workbook provides extra practice with each grammar point and its form, meaning, or use designation. Every three units, the workbook examines the grammar points covered as well as editing skills gained through a summarizing quiz.

ASSESSMENT

ExamView
Test Generator
For further pre-assessment, unit assessment, and end of semester assessment of student skills, the instructor is reminded at the end of each unit to use the *Grammar Dimensions 2 ExamView* which provides a bank of relevant grammar questions that can be modified or grouped with questions from other units. These quizzes developed may be saved for future use and individualized per class need.

USE YOUR ENGLISH ACTIVITIES

The Use Your English activities section at the end of each unit offer a range of activities where students can apply the language discussed in the unit to wider contexts and integrate it with the language they already know. Many activities give students more freedom than the exercises do and offer them more opportunities to express their own points of view across a range of topics. Most of the activities lend themselves to being done with structures covered in the unit, but they do not absolutely require their use.

The activities section is also designed to give instructors a variety of options. As you will probably not have time to do all the activities, you might select the ones you think would be most beneficial, or ask your students to choose ones that they would prefer. Perhaps different groups of students could do different activities and then report on their experience to the whole class. We suggest that the activities should be interspersed throughout the unit (as well as at the end of the unit) in order to provide variety and also to allow you to assess students' ability to use the target structures in natural contexts. In the Lesson Plans, therefore, we have suggested correlations between the exercises and the activities, keeping in mind that these are entirely optional. Also, it may be useful to go back to a previous unit and do an activity for review purposes. This is especially useful at the beginning of a new, but related, unit.

Skills

You will notice that the activities section provides activities in the four major skill areas (reading, writing, listening, speaking), some skills in combination and some skills practiced exclusively. In addition to these four cornerstone language skills, students will have the opportunity to practice research on the Internet and through InfoTrac (See more on these sections below.). Students are also guided to reflect on the learning process by examining the why's and how's of their own language learning experience.

If you are teaching in a skill-based program, you might want to collaborate with your colleagues and distribute the activities among yourselves. For example, the writing teacher could assign the activities that involve a written report, the teacher of listening could work on the listening activities during his or her class periods, or the teacher of speaking could work with students on activities where students are supposed to make an oral presentation.

The activities are an integral part of each unit because they not only provide students with opportunities to stretch their language use, but, as with the opening task, they also provide you with the opportunity to observe your students' language use in action. In this way, activities can be informal holistic assessment measures encouraging students to show you how well they can use the target structures communicatively. Any problems that still exist at this point can be noted for follow-up at a later time when students are more ready to deal with them.

Internet and InfoTrac® Activities

 This new edition includes a "research on the Web" activity at the end of each unit. The purpose of this Internet search activity is to provide a natural context for using the target grammar. An additional purpose is to encourage students to share strategies for finding information on the Internet. Internet search engines are suggested but instructors are encouraged to assist students in looking for information in a discriminating manner.

 In some cases, the research activity is based on using *InfoTrac® College Edition*, a resource of over 20 million articles accessed online by means of an individual password bound into each student book. Once the students establish a link to InfoTrac they are able to access over 6,000 academic journals and newspapers. It is highly recommended for *Grammar Dimensions* Book 2 users that instructors provide a suggested list of sources to read through via *InfoTrac* or provide specific keywords to assist students in finding level-appropriate articles.

Reflection Activities

Also new to this edition is the addition of a *reflection* activity towards the end of each unit. These activities provide an opportunity for students to use the target structures of the unit while reflecting on their language learning. Many of these activities can be done as pair or group activities in class. Others can also be assigned for homework. In this case, you may consider it a good idea to ask students to keep a learning journal. As well as providing you with firsthand feedback on your students' progress, it is also a good way to encourage reflection and self-evaluation that can facilitate language learning. In addition to the reflection activities, here are some suggested topics to include in a learning journal:

- Which grammar points do you find difficult, confusing, or easy—and why?

- Which grammar points are similar to or different from your native language?

- Which learning activities did you enjoy most in this unit and why?

- Which learning activities would you like to do more of or less of?

- What aspect of your learning did you feel most proud of when doing this unit?

Other Features

 • Correlations to Audio CD Tracks are noted in the student books as well as in the lesson plans. (Audiotape cassettes are also available.) In the Appendix of this Lesson Planner are the printed audioscripts, which instructors might wish to read through prior to the lesson or to photocopy for student use and review if needed.

• An Answer Key for the *Grammar Dimensions 2* Workbook exercises is provided in the Appendix.

As you can see, *Grammar Dimensions* is meant to provide you with a great deal of flexibility so that you can provide quality instruction appropriate for your class. We encourage you to experiment with different aspects of the material in order to best meet the needs of your unique group of students.

SIMPLE PRESENT
Habits, Routines, and Facts

UNIT GOALS

- Know when to use simple present tense
- Form simple present tense correctly
- Understand the meanings of various adverbs of frequency
- Place adverbs of frequency in correct sentence position

OPENING TASK
How Do You Learn Grammar?

■ **STEP 1**

How do you prefer to study grammar—in a group with other students, or individually at home?

■ **STEP 2**

What do you usually do to learn grammar? Read each statement and say how often often you do each of these things.   1 = never   2 = rarely   3 = sometimes   4 = often   5 = always

1. If I don't understand a new grammar point, I . . .
   a. look it up in a grammar book.   1 2 3 4 5
   b. look it up on the Internet.   1 2 3 4 5
   c. ask my teacher.   1 2 3 4 5

2. If I want to practice a new grammar point, I . . .
   a. write some example sentences.   1 2 3 4 5
   b. try to use it in conversation.   1 2 3 4 5
   c. look for examples in a book or a newspaper. 1 2 3 4 5

3. In order to improve my grammar, I . . .
   a. ask my teacher to correct my mistakes.   1 2 3 4 5
   b. ask my friends to correct my mistakes.   1 2 3 4 5
   c. don't worry about mistakes.   1 2 3 4 5

4. I prefer to practice new grammar by . . .
   a. working in a group with classmates.   1 2 3 4 5
   b. listening to and reading grammar explanations. 1 2 3 4 5
   c. making my own examples.   1 2 3 4 5

■ **STEP 3**

Compare your answers with another student. Explain the reasons for your answers. Do you like to learn English grammar in the same ways? In what ways are you similar and in what ways are you different? Write a few sentences about how you learn grammar.

Example: *I use the Internet to look up grammar rules, but my partner goes to the library.*

■ **STEP 4**

Tell the rest of the class how you and your partner learn English grammar.

LESSON PLAN 1

UNIT OVERVIEW

Unit 1 provides practice with the simple present tense and includes an overview of how adverbs of frequency can be included in present tense statements.

GRAMMAR NOTE

The *present tense* can be expressed in English by using either progressive or simple aspect. The *simple aspect* conveys a view of an action or event as something that happens regularly, habitually, or is always or usually true. Some languages do not have different forms for simple and progressive aspects and it may be difficult to understand the difference in meaning. Some languages have both progressive and simple forms, but they correspond to different uses. Students may be able to form the tense correctly, but they may not be able to use it appropriately.

UNIT GOALS

Some instructors may want to review the goals listed on this page after completing the Opening Task so that students understand what they should know by the end of the unit. Other instructors may want to discuss these at the end of the unit as students may not grasp the terms used at the start of the unit.

OPENING TASK [30 minutes]

Please read the general introduction to the purpose and use of the Opening Tasks throughout this book, see To the Teacher, Lesson Planner (LP) page xxii.

Setting Up the Task

STEP 1

Use this step as an introduction to the theme of learning styles, as well as a contextualized way of using the simple present. Ask questions about the pictures. What are these people doing? What are the differences between these study environments? Ask students to describe their ideal study environments.

Conducting the Task

STEP 2

1. Introduce the questionnaire by asking for students' reactions to the word "grammar." Do they like it/dislike it/think it's useful/difficult/ boring, etc.? At this stage you may want to discuss the importance of rules in language learning, and how understanding those rules can help us to avoid making mistakes.

2. Read the instructions and explain the rating system for the answers. Model the first question using your own response as an example.

3. Have students work individually to complete the questionnaire. Emphasize that there are no wrong or right answers.

4. You can also do the questionnaire, based on your own experiences as a language learner.

5. Students who finish early can pair up with each other and proceed to Step 3.

STEP 3

Students work in pairs or groups of three to compare their answers. Encourage students to give reasons for their choices—for example, why they more often use the Internet than a grammar book, and which is easier or more reliable. Walk around the class and observe use of the simple present and adverbs of frequency, but resist suggesting responses. Take notes of typical errors. These can help you when you focus on accuracy of form, meaning, or use later in the unit.

STEP 4

Bring the class together to share and compare findings. You may want to start off by sharing your responses to the questionnaire, expanding and elaborating on them with examples from your own experiences as a language learner. Ask for a few volunteers from each pair of students to report on the similarities and differences in their responses.

CULTURE NOTE

Students' perceptions of the best way to learn grammar may vary greatly according to their cultural background and learner training. In some cultures, memorization and repetition may be the norm. In other cultures, translation may be the most common teaching/learning tool. It is important to respect the validity of these perceptions, and also to realize that such learning habits are hard to change. You can use this task to open up alternative complementary paths to learning grammar that will expand students' existing learning styles.

Closing the Task

As a wrap-up, you can conduct an informal poll of learning preferences based on the questionnaire. Answers can be recorded on the board, on poster paper, or on an overhead projector (OHP) transparency.

GRAMMAR NOTE

Typical student errors (form)

- Omitting the 's' in third person singular verbs, e.g. * *She go to town every Saturday.* (Instead of: *She goes to town.*)
- Using statement forms with rising intonation instead of questions forms, e.g.* *He works in a bank?* (Instead of: *Does he work in a bank?*)
- Omitting the auxiliary do/does in negative statements, e.g. * *He not go to school on Mondays.* (Instead of: *He doesn't go to school on Mondays.*) and in questions, e.g. * *What time you get up?* (Instead of: *What time do you get up?*)
- Placing the frequency adverb before the verb 'be' * *I usually am late on Mondays.* (Instead of: *I am usually late on Mondays.*)

(Grammar Note continues on LP page 5.)

FOCUS 1

Verbs in the Simple Present Tense

use

Habits and Routines

EXAMPLES	EXPLANATIONS
(a) I ask questions when I do not understand.	*Ask, do not understand,* and *uses* are simple present verbs.
(b) Elzbieta **uses** English as much as possible.	Use the simple present to talk about habits (things you do again and again).
(c) Our classes **start** at 9:00 A.M. (d) Daniela **goes** to school five days a week.	Use the simple present to talk about everyday routines (things you do regularly).

EXERCISE 1

Go back to Step 2 of the Opening Task on page 1. Underline all the simple present verbs you can find. Compare your answers with a partner.

FOCUS 2

Simple Present Tense

form

STATEMENT		NEGATIVE		QUESTION		SHORT ANSWER			
I You We They	work.	I You We They	do not/don't work.	Do	I you we they	work?	Yes,	I you we they	do.
He She It	works.	He She It	does not/doesn't work.	Does	he she it	work?	Yes,	he she it	does.
							No,	I you we they	don't.
							No,	he she it	doesn't.

EXERCISE 2

Look at what you wrote in Step 3 of the Opening Task on page 1. Underline all the simple present verbs that you used. Did you use them correctly? Check your answers with a partner and then with your teacher.

EXERCISE 3

STEP 1 What are some *other* things you do and do not do to learn English grammar? Complete the following, using full sentences.

Some things I do:

1. I usually write an example sentence in my notebook.
2. I ___
3. I ___

Some things I don't do:

1. I ___
2. I ___
3. I ___

STEP 2 Get together with a partner, and tell each other about things you do and do not do to learn English grammar. Then, without showing your answers to each other, write about what your partner does and doesn't do.

My partner, (name) ___ ,

does several different things to learn English grammar. (She/He) ___

STEP 3 Now get together with a different partner. Ask each other what you do to learn English grammar (*Do you . . . ?*). Together with your new partner, decide on the three most useful ways to learn English grammar. Share your ideas with the rest of the class. Write them here:

1. We ___
2. We ___
3. We ___

ANSWER KEY

Exercise 1 1. understand, look up   2. want, write, try, look for   3. improve, ask, ask, worry   4. prefer

Exercise 2 Answers will vary. Possible answers are: like/likes/don't like/doesn't like, prefer/prefers, study/studies, memorize/memorizes; read/reads, etc.

Exercise 3 It is impossible to predict answers here, as they will obviously depend on students' own experiences.

FOCUS 1 [10 minutes]

This focus chart introduces students to the concept of using the simple present to describe habits and routines. Discussion of the form is presented in Focus 2.

1. **Lead-in:** Write two examples of these different uses of the simple present on the board and ask students to find the difference between them. For example: *I usually study grammar in the library. I go to school at 9:00 AM every day.* (The first is a habit, something you usually do. The second is a routine, something that happen at the same time every day, week, etc.) You may ask questions to give clues: Is it something that is happening now? Is it something that happens regularly? Or something that happens often?

2. Read the examples and explanations in the chart.

3. Ask students to give other examples of each use. Write some examples on the board, using real information about your students. For example,

Habits: *Leo corrects his grammar mistakes with a red pen. Milan and Kim use the Internet to look up grammar rules.*

Routines: *Peter leaves home at 7:45 every morning. His classes start at 8:30 AM He doesn't go to school on the weekend.*

4. Write or ask volunteers to write full sentences on the board, underlining simple present verbs.

EXERCISE 1 [5 minutes]

Turn back to the questionnaire on Student Book (SB) page 1. Check the answers together as you go through the questionnaire.

For more practice, use *Grammar Dimensions 2* Workbook page 1, Exercise 1.

FOCUS 2 [10 minutes]

Focus 2 illustrates the form of the simple present. Explain that the chart is for reference and can be used throughout the unit as necessary.

1. **Lead-in:** You can introduce this chart by starting with a review of the grammatical terms used in the chart: statement, negative, yes/no questions, *wh*-questions (questions starting with *where, when, why, who, what, or how*), and short answers. Also review the meaning of *auxiliary verbs* and *contractions*. This will help students to interpret charts throughout the book.

2. Model the pronunciation of the examples in the chart, focusing on contractions: *don't* and *doesn't* and word blends: *do you* and *does he/does she.* You may want to add further practice with *wh*-questions in the simple present.

EXERCISE 2 [5 minutes]

If students wrote sentences in Step 3 of the Opening Task, have them check their sentences. If not, have them write two or three sentences now.

For more practice, use *Grammar Dimensions 2* Workbook page 1, Exercise 2.

EXPANSION [20 minutes]

Use Activity 1 on SB page 13 for further practice of simple present for daily routines.

EXERCISE 3 [20 minutes]

In this exercise students will have a chance to focus more explicitly on the simple present, using affirmative, negative, and question forms. This exercise will also help students share their ideas for learning grammar.

STEP 1 Have students complete Step 1 individually. Walk around the class to observe their work.

STEP 2 Have students work in pairs to complete Step 2.

STEP 3 Have students find a new partner to complete Step 3.

Ask volunteers to report their answers to Step 3. Ideas from the whole class can be collected and displayed as a poster.

For more practice, use *Grammar Dimensions 2* Workbook page 2, Exercise 3.

METHODOLOGY NOTE

As you get to know your students' language levels, you may want to think about how you'd like them to pair up. Some teachers find that pairing up weak and strong students is beneficial to both. Others like to match up students according to similar level. Some teachers like students change seats with someone on the other side of the room, so they work with a different partner each time. You may want to vary these strategies as you go through the exercises in this book.

EXPANSION [20 minutes]

Ask students to make a list in their notebooks of strategies for successful language or grammar learning. As time passes, they might want to add to their repertoire of strategies.

Use Activity 9 (Reflection) on SB page 17 as a homework task following this exercise. Please read the general introduction to the purpose and use of Reflection activities throughout this book (see To the Teacher, page xxii).

FOCUS 3

Showing How Often Something Happens

form ● meaning

Adverbs of Frequency

EXAMPLES	EXPLANATIONS
(a) Kazue **often** uses a dictionary, but Florian **never** uses one. Most Often (100%) ⬆ always usually often sometimes seldom rarely hardly ever ⬇ never Least Often (0%)	*Often* and *never* are adverbs of frequency. They show how often something happens. For more information on adverbs of frequency, see Unit 18, Focus 5.
(b) I **usually** get up early. (c) He **never** calls me.	Where to put adverbs of frequency: **before** the main verb (b and c)
(d) She is **always** happy. (e) They are **rarely** late.	**after** the verb *be* (d and e)

EXERCISE 4

Which of these things do you do to practice English? Tell your partner. Add some more ideas of your own. Use an adverb of frequency from the chart.

- Use a dictionary?
- Read a grammar book?
- Use the Internet?
- Write in your journal?
- Read the newspaper?
- Play games?
- Write words in a vocabulary notebook?
- ....
- ....
- ....

Example: **Student A:** *Do you use a dictionary to help you study?*
Student B: *I rarely use my dictionary in class, but I often look up new words at home.*

EXERCISE 5

STEP 1   Describe a typical day for students in each of these photos. Use the words in the box.

sit in rows	take notes	work in groups
work in pairs	ask questions	raise your hand
answer questions	listen carefully	use computers

1   use computers

2   work in groups

3   raise your hand, ask questions, answer questions

4   sit in rows, take notes, listen carefully

SIMPLE PRESENT Habits, Routines, and Facts   5

ANSWER KEY

Exercise 4   Answers will vary.

Exercise 5   Answers will vary. Possible answers are listed above.

LESSON PLAN 1

FOCUS 3 [10 minutes]

This focus chart presents an overview of different adverbs of frequency used with the simple present.

1. **Lead-in:** You can introduce the different adverbs of frequency by drawing a scale on the board. Write "always" at one end of the scale and "never" at the other end. Then give examples of things that you do frequently or rarely, and ask students to suggest the correct adverb. For example, *I get up at 7 a.m. every day.* (always), *I don't take the train to work.* (never), *I go to the mall once a year.* (rarely) etc.

2. Have students read the examples and the explanations in the chart. You may assign approximate percentages to each of the points on the scale, but point out that there are no set answers. For example, "sometimes" may mean 1 out of 3 times (33%) or it may mean half of the time (50%). Ask students for their estimates and see if you agree.

3. Ask students to give true sentences about themselves for each of the adverbs. Have other students question them about what they mean. For example, if a student says, *I rarely go shopping,* does "rarely" mean once a week? Once a month?

4. Point out the different word order with the verb *be* and with other main verbs.

EXERCISE 4 [10 minutes]

This exercise provides extra practice with using adverbs of frequency with the simple present and extends the theme of learning grammar to language learning skills in general.

1. Have students work in pairs to talk about each of the topics.

2. Walk around the class to observe their progress.

3. Invite volunteers to give examples of their learning strategies. Try to get at least one example of each different adverb.

EXPANSION [20 minutes]

If you have asked students to keep a learning journal, you may ask them to write a summary of their responses in class or in their journal for homework.

EXERCISE 5 [20 minutes]

This exercise provides another opportunity for students to become aware of their own learning styles, and for you to understand their assumptions and expectations about classroom learning.

STEP 1

1. Ask volunteers to describe what a typical school day is like for the people in the pictures. If students start to use the present progressive to describe the pictures, you may want to mention that the present progressive is used for actions happening now, but the focus here is on what their typical school routine is like.

2. Encourage students to make interpretations about what these students and teachers usually do, using adverbs of frequency. For example, *They usually listen and take notes. They hardly ever ask any questions.*

3. Have students write short descriptions of each picture in their notebooks. If you wish, divide the class into groups, and assign each group just one of the pictures. Then have a representative from each group read their description aloud.
   (Exercise 5 is continued on Lesson Planner page 7.)

GRAMMAR NOTE

(Continued from LP page 1.)

Typical student errors (use)

- Using the simple present for something that is happening now, e.g. * I go to work now. (Instead of: *I am going to work now.*)
- Using present progressive for habits or routines, or facts, e.g. * I am swimming every morning. (Instead of: *I swim every morning.*)
- Using simple present for future time, e.g. *I see you tomorrow.* (Instead of: *I'll see you tomorrow.*)
- Using the simple present for events that started in the past e.g. * I study in the U.S. since April. (Instead of: *I have studied/have been studying in the U.S. since April.*)

EXERCISE 6

STEP 1 Complete the chart about students and teachers in your country and in the United States. The first one about teachers in your country has been done for you as an example. If you do not have enough room to write your answers on the chart, copy the chart into your notebook.

	TEACHERS IN YOUR COUNTRY	STUDENTS IN YOUR COUNTRY	TEACHERS IN THE UNITED STATES	STUDENTS IN THE UNITED STATES
Usually	*stand in front of the class*			
Sometimes				
Hardly ever	*walk around the class*			
Never				

STEP 2 Get together with another student from another country, if possible. Ask this partner questions about teachers and students in his or her country.

Example: *Tell me about teachers in your country. Do they usually give a lot of homework? Do they sometimes tell jokes in class?*

STEP 3 Look at the information from your chart and from your partner's chart. Use the information to make as many true sentences as you can.

Example: *Students in my country usually stand up when the teacher comes into the room.*

STEP 2 Read the descriptions below and match each description to a picture on page 5. Write the number of the picture under each description. Compare your answers with a partner.

A We sit in rows, and the teacher stands at the front. The teacher explains grammar rules, and the students listen and take notes. Students sometimes practice their writing in class.

____4____

B Our English classes are always very relaxed. We usually work in pairs or small groups and often play games in class to practice our English. These games are a lot of fun and we sometimes laugh a lot. We don't feel nervous about speaking English when we play games.

____2____

C We often work on special projects in our English class. We use computers to find information about a topic or we interview people to see what they think. Then we make a presentation about our topic to the rest of the class.

____1____

D The students in my English class are very enthusiastic. Every time the teacher asks a question, everybody wants to answer it. We always raise our hands and hope that the teacher will choose us.

____3____

STEP 3 How are the classes in the photographs like (or unlike) classes in your country? First, discuss this question with your partner. Then be ready to tell the rest of the class.

ANSWER KEY

Exercise 5 **Step 3:** Answers will vary. Sample responses: *Students in my country rarely work in groups. Students in my country don't have access to computers. Students in my country sit in rows and listen to the teacher.*

Exercise 6 **Step 3:** Answers will vary depending on the cultural backgrounds of your students. Possible answers are: *Teachers in my country hardly ever talk to students outside of class. Students in my country never ask questions in class. Teachers in this country usually give homework. Students in this country sometimes call their teachers by their first names. Teachers in my country stand in front of the class.*

LESSON PLAN 1

EXERCISE 5   (Continued from Lesson Planner page 6.)

STEP 2

1. Allow some time for students read the descriptions on SB page 6 and match them with the pictures on SB page 5.

2. Compare answers as a class.

STEP 3

1. Using the photographs as a starting point, ask volunteers to describe typical classes in a school in their country, or in another country they know about.

2. Encourage students to ask you about other educational settings that you are familiar with.

3. Discuss some of the differences between academic norms in other countries and in the United States. Some possible topics are:

- Student participation is an important part of one's learning progress. In United States classrooms, students are expected to participate in discussions and ask questions.

- Discussion and debate are seen as valuable ways of learning to express oneself and learn about others' opinions. There isn't always a correct answer. The teacher's opinion isn't always right.

- Plagiarism is strictly forbidden. All material taken from other sources must be carefully acknowledged.

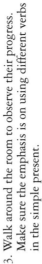

For more practice, use *Grammar Dimensions 2* Workbook page 3, Exercise 4.

EXPANSION [20 minutes]

To expand this topic further, have students interview each other about a typical school day in their country (or another country they know). They may present their information in the form of a chart.

	In the United States	In _____
School start/finish time		
Typical classroom activities		
Typical homework activities		
Typical after-school activities		
Typical end-of-semester activities		

VARIATION

You may also use this type of chart to compare high school and college in the same country.

EXERCISE 6 [15 minutes]

This chart provides further practice in the use of simple present for routines and habits.

STEP 1

1. Introduce the chart and clarify the meaning of "my country" and "this country." (This is intended for students who are currently studying in a country different from their native country). You may find it better for students to choose another country they are familiar with. Cross out "this country" in the chart and substitute a country that you or your students know about. Alternatively, you may wish to compare differences between high school and college in the same country.

2. Have students work individually to complete the charts.

3. Walk around the room to observe their progress. Make sure the emphasis is on using different verbs in the simple present.

STEP 2   Pair students up with someone from a different country. If this isn't possible, have them discuss their own country together.

STEP 3   Have students write sentences based on the information in their chart.

For more practice, use *Grammar Dimensions 2* Workbook page 5, Exercise 6 and 7.

EXERCISE 7

STEP 1 Get together with a partner. Quickly look at the occupations in the box below.

OCCUPATIONS		
a student	a police officer	a businessperson
an administrative assistant	a flight attendant	a bartender
a mechanic	a teacher	a nurse
an architect	a bus driver	a restaurant server

STEP 2 Read the job descriptions below. Can you match them with the occupations in the box? Write the occupation on the line next to each description.

1. He wears a uniform and usually travels many miles a day. He serves food and drinks, but he hardly ever prepares them himself. ___a flight attendant___

2. She works in an office, but she often takes work home with her. She generally earns a high salary, but often feels a lot of stress. She sometimes entertains clients in the evening. _a businessperson_

3. He usually wears a uniform and always carries a gun. He leads a dangerous life, so his job rarely gets boring. _a police officer_

4. He often works at night and meets many different people. He serves drinks and gets tips when people like his service. _a bartender_

5. She wears a uniform and drives many miles a day. She never serves food and drinks. _a bus driver_

6. He spends many hours in the classroom and asks questions. He always has a lot of work to do and sometimes writes on the board. _a student (or teacher)_

7. She often wears a uniform and walks many miles a day. She works very hard and does not earn very much money, although she sometimes gets generous tips. _a restaurant server (or waitress)_

8. He spends a lot of time in the classroom and likes to ask questions. He often writes on the board. _teacher (or student)_

STEP 3 Now write similar descriptions for the jobs in the box that are not described above. What do these workers do?

9. _____

10. _____

11. _____

12. _____

STEP 4 On your own, think of two more jobs and write a short job description for each one.

13. _____

14. _____

STEP 5 Get together with another student and read your descriptions to each other. Ask and answer questions until you guess the jobs your partner described in Step 4. For example: *Does he or she . . . ? Is he or she a . . . ?*

EXERCISE 8

Sam is looking for a roommate to share his apartment, and Dave is looking for a place to live. They are trying to find out if they will get along as roommates. Complete their conversation, using verbs that fit the meaning of the sentences. Sometimes more than one answer is possible.

Sam: What do you usually do on weekends?

Dave: Well, I usually (1) _wake up_ early, about 5:30, and then I (2) _walk/run/jog_ by the river for an hour or so before breakfast.

Sam: Yeah? And what (3) _do_ you _do_ next?

Dave: After breakfast, I (4) _take_ a cold shower, and then I usually (5) _ride_ my bike, or I sometimes (6) _play/watch_ tennis for a couple of hours. What (7) _do_ you _do_ on Saturday mornings?

Sam: I like to relax on weekends; I (8) _stay_ home and (9) _read_ the newspaper and (10) _watch_ TV.

Dave: All weekend?

Sam: No. On Sundays, I often get in my sports car and (11) _drive_ to the beach.

Dave: Great! I like swimming, too. It's a habit that I learned from my brother. He (12) _swims/surfs_ in the ocean every day of the year, even in the winter.

Sam: Well, I rarely (13) _swim_ in the ocean. I usually (14) _sit/stay/lie_ on the beach and try to get a good suntan. Then I (15) _meet/call/visit_ some of my friends, and we go to a nightclub and dance.

Dave: Don't you ever exercise?

Sam: Well, I (16) (not) _don't go/belong_ to a health club or gym, but every Saturday night I go to a nightclub, and I (17) _dance_ for hours. That's my idea of exercise.

Dave: Look, here's the phone number of a friend of mine. He (18) _likes_ dancing and nightclubs, just like you. Why don't you give him a call and see if he wants to be your roommate?

ANSWER KEY

Exercise 7 Step 3: Answers will vary. Possible answers are: an administrative assistant: They work in offices. They answer telephones, type letters, and make appointments for their bosses. They are usually very organized people. An architect: She plans buildings where people work or live. She is good at math and drawing.

Step 4: #13 and #14 depend on what occupations students list.

Step 5: Answers will vary.

Exercise 8 Some answers may vary.

LESSON PLAN 2

EXPANSION 1 [20 minutes/homework]

You can use Activity 7 (Writing) on SB page 17 in class or as a homework task following this exercise.

EXPANSION 2 [20 minutes]

Have students write a list of sentences to describe what happens in your classroom. For example:

- Students ask questions, and the teacher answers them.
- Students talk in pairs and the teacher listens.
- Students write sentences and the teacher corrects the mistakes.

VARIATION

1. Have students work in groups to write "False" sentences about what happens in the classroom.
2. Have groups exchange their sentences and "correct" them so that they are true.
3. Display the "corrected" sentences on the wall.

EXERCISE 7 [15 minutes]

This exercise provides practice of the simple present as used on descriptions of people's occupations.

STEP 1 Preview the words in the Occupations box by asking students to describe what each of these people do in their daily jobs.

VARIATION

Ask students to describe what the person does, and the others will guess which job it is.

STEP 2

1. Read item 1 together as a class. Have students work individually to complete the rest of the matching exercise. Set a time limit of three to five minutes.
2. Check the answers as a class.

STEP 3

1. Set a time limit of five minutes for students write job descriptions for the four jobs not mentioned in Exercise 7 (administrative assistant, mechanic, architect, nurse). If you wish, you can divide the class into four groups and assign one job to each group.
2. Have students read out their descriptions and ask the other students to evaluate if they are accurate and what they would add or change if they are not.

STEPS 4 AND 5 Have students write descriptions of two other jobs. The descriptions can be a little ambiguous (like the ones in Step 2) so that their partners will have to ask some questions to clarify what the job is.

LANGUAGE NOTE

There are several job titles that are now considered *sexist* or *ageist* and are gradually being replaced. Although some of these terms are still used in common speech, many states now require employers to advertise these jobs using the new gender-neutral terms. Below are a few examples:

server—previously waitress (female) or waiter (male)

administrative assistant—previously secretary

flight attendant—previously stewardess or steward

police officer—previously policeman or policewoman

homemaker—previously housewife

EXPANSION 1 [20 minutes]

You can use Activity 2 on SB page 13 as an expansion exercise following Exercise 7. Students can interview each other about their real or imaginary jobs. You can also assign this for homework.

EXPANSION 2 [15 minutes]

1. Write the names of jobs on small separate pieces of paper, one for each student.
2. Hand out the papers, and have students stick the job names on each others' backs using sticky tape.
3. Have students walk around asking each other *Yes/No* questions to find out what their job is. For example, *Do I work in a hotel? Do I serve food?*
4. When students have discovered what their job is, they can sit down.

EXERCISE 8 [15 minutes]

This exercise provides practice of the simple present used in a natural conversational context.

1. Introduce the idea of college roommates. (This usually means two or more college students sharing an apartment.) Ask for suggestions as to what kinds of questions you would ask a potential roommate.
2. Have students work individually to complete the conversation. Sometimes more than one verb is possible.
3. Have students compare answers with a partner.
4. Check the answers as a class.
5. Have students read the conversation aloud in pairs, concentrating on wordlinking and appropriate intonation.
6. Choose one pair of students to perform the conversation for the class.
7. If you have time, have students adapt the conversations using their own information.

FOCUS 4

Talking About Facts

use

EXAMPLES

(a) The sun **rises** in the east and **sets** in the west.
(b) Brazilians **speak** Portuguese.
(c) Water **boils** at 100° C.

EXPLANATIONS

Use the simple present to talk about facts (things that are true).

EXERCISE 10

STEP 1   Match the pictures to the animal names in the box.

spider

bear

bat

swan

horse

elephant

scorpion

horse	antelope	elephant	spider	bat
bear		swan	scorpion	antelope

What do you know about these animals? Be ready to tell the rest of the class anything that you know.

EXERCISE 9

STEP 1   Talk to your partner about your daily routines. Complete the chart using adverbs of frequency. Would you make good roommates, or not?

	YOU	YOUR PARTNER
Wake up early		
Sleep late		
Go to bed early		
Stay up late		
Go running		
Go to a nightclub		
Play tennis		
Relax at home		
Watch TV (not "a lot")		
Have friends over		
Read quietly		

STEP 2   Change partners. Tell your new partner about your previous partner.

ANSWER KEY

Exercise 9   *Steps 1 and 2:* Answers will vary.

LESSON PLAN 2

EXERCISE 9 [15 minutes]

This exercise provides further practice of questions and statements in the simple present in a more personalized context.

1. Remind students of the adverbs of frequency studied on SB page 4 (Focus 3).

2. Have students work individually to complete the middle column of the chart.

3. Then have students work in pairs to complete the right column.

4. When they have finished, have them report to the class on whether they would make good roommates or not, and say why. For example, *Serena and I always get up early and usually go to bed early, so we would be good roommates.*

METHODOLOGY NOTE

There are a number of strategies you can use to handle errors in the simple present tense. For example, you can give students the opportunity to correct themselves, or you can ask other students: *Was the sentence accurate? Were there any errors?* You can correct errors immediately, or write them down for use in an error correction activity later on.

EXPANSION [20 minutes]

You can use Activity 6 on SB page 16 as an expansion exercise following Exercise 9.

FOCUS 4 [10 minutes]

This focus chart presents the use of the simple present for facts, or things that are always true.

1. **Lead-in:** Read some examples of facts (see below) to the class and ask if they are true or false.

• The sun rises in the west. (**false:** it rises in the east)

• The sun sets in the west. (**true**)
• Water boils at 212 degrees Fahrenheit (100 degrees Celsius) (**true**)
• Water freezes at 0 degrees Fahrenheit (32 degrees Celsius) (**false:** it freezes at 32 degrees Fahrenheit (0 degrees Celsius))
• The Earth goes around the sun once every thirty days. (**false:** it takes approx. 365 days)
• The moon goes around the Earth about twelve times in one year. (**true**)

3. Read the examples and explanations in the box.

4. Ask students for some further examples of scientific facts.

EXERCISE 10 [15 minutes]

Have students first guess the names of the animals in the pictures (they should cover the word box with another book or a piece of paper).

STEP 1

1. Have students work individually to complete the matching exercise.
2. Check the answers as a class.
3. Ask students to tell the class anything they know about each of the animals.
4. Ask volunteers to write their sentences on their board.

STEP 2 Have students work in pairs to match the animals and the facts.

STEP 3 When they have finished, they can compare answers with another pair.

STEP 4 Brainstorm a list of unusual animals and any facts that students know about them.

For more practice, use *Grammar Dimensions 2* Workbook page 4, Exercise 5.

EXPANSION 1 [20 minutes]

Assign Step 4 as a short written exercise. Students can work together on their chosen animal, pooling information and writing 3–5 sentences for each animal. This can also be assigned as a homework task.

EXPANSION 2 [20 minutes]

Have students work in groups to develop a general knowledge quiz. If you wish, have students select an area in which they have some specialist knowledge, e.g., geography, medicine, etc. When they have written the quiz, they can exchange them with other groups to answer the questions and comment on the use of the simple present.

UNIT GOAL REVIEW [10 minutes]

Ask students to look at the goals on the opening page of the unit again. Help them understand how much they have accomplished in each area. Ask students to give examples of the use of the simple present for habits, routines, and facts. Ask them to make sentences that contrast different adverbs of frequency (e.g., *never* and *always*) and explain the differences in meaning. This is also an opportunity to ask students to identify which areas they would like more practice with and to point out that different verb tenses are covered in other units of this book. You may want to allow time for reviewing the relevant focus charts.

 For assessment of Unit 1, use *Grammar Dimensions 2 ExamView®*.

Use Your English

STEP 2
Get together with a partner and draw lines connecting the animals in Column A with appropriate information about them in Column B. Don't worry if you are not sure of all the answers. With your partner, decide what you think is probably the best match for each piece of information.

A	B
Horses	live for about two years.
Bats	sometimes go for four days without water.
Scorpions	stay with the same mates all their lives.
Elephants	use their ears to "see."
Swans	have twelve eyes.
Antelopes	sleep during the winter months.
Bears	sleep standing up.
Spiders	run at 70 miles per hour.

STEP 3
Get together with another pair and compare your answers. When you are ready, compare your answers with the rest of the class. As a class, decide on what you think are probably the best answers. Then check your answers on page A-14.

STEP 4
Do you know any other unusual facts about these animals or any other animals? Tell the rest of the class about them.

ACTIVITY 1 speaking/listening

The purpose of this activity is to prove or disprove the following statements about your classmates. Stand up, walk around the room, and ask your classmates questions to see if the following are true (T) or false (F).

1.	Most of the people in this room do not eat breakfast.	T	F
2.	Women drink more coffee than men.	T	F
3.	Fifty percent of the people in this room watch TV at night.	T	F
4.	Somebody in this room wears contact lenses.	T	F
5.	More than three people read a newspaper in English every day.	T	F
6.	More than 50 percent of the people in this room drive a car.	T	F
7.	Nobody likes opera.	T	F
8.	More than two people here come to school by bike.	T	F
9.	Everybody gets more than six hours of sleep a night.	T	F
10.	Most of the people in this room have a sister.	T	F

ACTIVITY 2 speaking/listening/writing

Interview someone about his or her job. Find out three things he or she sometimes does, often does, and never does. Write a description of the job based on your interview. What is your opinion of the job? Is it different from or similar to what you expected?

ANSWER KEY

Exercise 10 **Steps 2 and 3:** Horses sleep standing up. Bats use their ears to "see." Scorpions have twelve eyes. Elephants sometimes go for four days without water. Swans stay with the same mates all their lives. Antelopes run at 70 miles per hour. Bears sleep during the winter months. Spiders live for about two years.

Activity 1 Answers will vary.

USE YOUR ENGLISH

The Use Your English activities at the end of the unit contain situations that should naturally elicit the structures covered in the unit. For a more complete discussion of how to use the Use Your English activities, see To the Teacher, page xxii. While students are doing these activities in class, circulate to see if they are using the structures accurately. If an activity is to be completed outside of class, review the resulting projects for appropriate use of the structures or ask students to report the results to the class. Make note of structure use for future review.

ACTIVITY 1 speaking/listening
[20 minutes]

You can use this activity after Focus 2 on SB page 2.

The aim of this activity is to practice the use of the simple present for routines and habits.

1. In this activity, students will walk around the room asking each other questions and making notes of the answers.

2. Read the instructions aloud and check comprehension by asking questions, *Are you going to walk around the room? What are you going to say? What are you going to do?* etc.

3. Model the activity with one student by asking *Do you eat breakfast?* Make a note of the answer in your notebook.

4. Explain that each statement must be turned into a question. Go through all the statements if appropriate.

5. Observe the students as they walk around the class. Make notes of errors for future use.

6. When they have finished, have students report the results. For example, *The first sentence is false because everyone in the class eats breakfast.*

VARIATION

Turn this into a research/interview project by asking research teams of four to six students to find out about a certain group of people. Instead of all the students in the room they can find out about: family members, people of a particular age (example: 25 and over/under), students in another class (ESL classes might want to combine classes occasionally and work together), all the students they know from a particular place/region/country, people that live together (e.g., a student dormitory) etc. Students can pool their information and prepare a short written or oral report.

ACTIVITY 2 speaking/listening/writing
[20 minutes]

You can use this activity after Exercise 6 on SB page 7.

The aim of this activity is to take the language learning experience outside the classroom. Students can interview a friend or a family member, or someone in the school. Students can read their descriptions to the class.

ACTIVITY 3 speaking/listening

The purpose of this activity is to find out what people usually do on certain special days.

STEP 1

Form a team with one or two other students, and choose one of the special days from the chart below.

STEP 2

Tell the rest of the class which special day your team has chosen. Make sure that there is at least one team for each special day.

STEP 3

With your team, interview three different people (native speakers of English if possible). Find out what they do or what they think usually happens on this special day. Make notes on the chart below or in your notebook. If possible, record your interviews.

STEP 4

After doing your interviews, use your notes to tell the rest of the class what your team found.

New Year's Eve _____

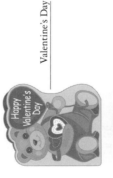

Valentine's Day _____

Halloween _____

Thanksgiving Day _____

STEP 5

Listen to your recorded interview, or use your notes to identify and write down any sentences that contain the simple present tense or adverbs of frequency.

ACTIVITY 4 listening

STEP 1

Listen to the audio of people describing what they do on certain special days. Which special days do you think each speaker is talking about? Write your answers under "Special Day" in the chart below.

SPEAKER	SPECIAL DAY	VERBS IN THE SIMPLE PRESENT TENSE
Speaker 1	Halloween	*makes, go around, give, dress up, decorate*
Speaker 2	Thanksgiving	*gets together, have, eats, don't give*
Speaker 3	Valentine's Day	*gets, don't get*

🎧 CD Tracks 1,2,3

STEP 2

Listen to the audio again. On the right side of the chart, write down as many examples of verbs in the simple present tense as you can.

ACTIVITY 5 speaking/listening

Prepare a short talk for your classmates, describing a special day or holiday that people celebrate in your country, city, or region. Talk about what people usually do on this day and how they celebrate. Don't forget to include an introduction to your talk. For example: *I am going to tell you about a very special holiday in my country. The name of the holiday is. . . .* If possible, record your talk and listen after class.

USE YOUR ENGLISH

ACTIVITY 3 speaking/listening [20 minutes]

You may want to use this activity (and the following Activities 4 and 5) before doing Focus 4 on SB page 11.

The aim of this activity is for students to listen to the simple present being used in natural everyday conversational English.

1. Read through the list of special days. Find out what students already know about each of them.
2. Brainstorm a list of questions that students may ask to find out about habits and customs on these special days. Questions may include: *What kinds of food do you eat? What kinds of clothing do you wear? Do you celebrate this day with your friends or with your family? What do you usually say or do?*
3. If students do not have access to native English speakers, students can interview people who speak English proficiently and/or who have lived in English-speaking countries.

VARIATION

You can use also this activity as an in-class interviewing activity. If you have students of different cultures in your class, have them choose holidays that are popular in their culture and interview each other about them. If your students are all from one culture, you can substitute holidays that are more familiar to your students and have them find out about any differences between ways of celebrating them. The results can be displayed on a classroom poster and illustrated with pictures or drawings.

METHODOLOGY NOTE 1

If it is not possible to record the interviews, be sure to have more than one student conducting the interview. Research teams of two or more people have an advantage since you can allocate responsibilities: one person asks the questions, one person asks for clarification or elaboration if necessary, one person focuses on what specific words are used (in this case, what form of the verb), etc.

ACTIVITY 4 listening [20 minutes]

CD Tracks 1,2,3

This activity is a nice follow-up to Activity 3, since it validates and confirms the "findings" of the interviews conducted on this topic. Students can copy the chart into their notebooks if they want more room for notes.

1. Explain that students will hear someone talking about three different holidays. They will listen and try to identify the holiday. (Hint: the holidays discussed are some of those pictured in Activity 3.) Then they will listen again, and write down examples of verbs in the simple present.
2. Play the audio. Use audio CD tracks 1, 2, and 3 for this activity. The audio script is on page S-1.
3. Have students make guesses about each holiday. What were the clues? Try to identify the key words.
4. Play the audio again. Have students make notes of the verbs in the simple present.
5. Have students compare answers in pairs.
6. Play the audio again if necessary.

LANGUAGE NOTE

If students in your class have not been exposed to native-speaker English, encourage them to talk about the differences between spoken and written English. Ask: *What do you notice about how the speakers said things? Is there anything about the talk that surprised you, or was hard to understand?* (Likely answers: *They speak quickly. Their words "run together". They always use contractions. Sometimes you can't hear certain syllables or words*.) You can explain that words in "native speaker" or "fluent" English are linked together smoothly, and that reduced forms, contractions and ellipses are common.

ACTIVITY 5 speaking/listening [20 minutes]

Use this activity as a follow-up to Activity 4.

1. Have students write a short description (in class or for homework) of a popular holiday in their country or in another country.
2. Ask volunteers to read their descriptions aloud.
3. The other students will ask questions for more details about each one.
4. You can follow this activity with Web Research Activity 8 on SB page 17.

VARIATION

Introduce information about some other popular U.S. holidays, or ask students to research what usually happens on those holidays. Examples: Father's Day, Mother's Day, Independence Day, Labor Day, Memorial Day, Columbus Day, St. Patrick's Day. You may want to divide students into groups and have each group research one of the holidays.

METHODOLOGY NOTE 2

If it's not possible to record students giving their talks or presentations, assign students from the "audience" to be note-takers who focus specifically on simple present tense usage. After each talk, have the listeners/note-takers give feedback to the speaker. They can provide examples of speakers' sentences with simple present tense usage and can query any errors that the speaker made.

ACTIVITY 6 speaking/listening/writing

STEP 1

Complete the following with information that is true about yourself. Write complete sentences.

Something I usually do in summer

Something I often do on weekends

Something I rarely do in this country

Something I sometimes do on Fridays

STEP 2

Memorize these four sentences about yourself.

STEP 3

Walk around the room. When your teacher tells you to stop, find the nearest person. Tell the person your four sentences and listen to that person's sentences. Then memorize each other's sentences.

STEP 4

Walk around the room. When your teacher tells you to stop, find a different person. Tell this new person about the last person you spoke to. Then listen to that person's sentences. Do not talk about yourself. Memorize what he or she tells you.

STEP 5

Find someone different. Tell him or her the information the last person told you. Listen to the new person's sentences. Memorize what he or she tells you.

STEP 6

Now find someone new. Continue the process for as long as possible. Remember, you always pass along the information the last person tells you. Try to speak to as many different people as possible.

STEP 7

At the end, tell the rest of the class the information you heard from the last person. Is all the information true?

ACTIVITY 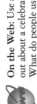 7 writing

Write a description of a typical high school classroom in your country. For example, what does the room look like? Where do the students sit? Where does the teacher sit? Is there any special equipment in the room? What is on the walls? What do teachers and students usually do when they are in the classroom?

ACTIVITY  8 research on the web

On the Web: Use an Internet search engine such as Google® or Yahoo® to find out about a celebration or holiday in another country. When does it take place? What do people usually wear/eat/do? If you want, you can research one of these examples: Mardi Gras (Brazil), Obon (Japan), Inti Raymi (Peru), Songkran (Thailand).

ACTIVITY 9 reflection

Think of one study skill that you would like to improve. Describe in detail how you usually practice this study skill. Try to break your description down into several different steps. Read your description to your partner.

Example: Writing an essay: First, I get out my notebooks, dictionary, and grammar book. Then I find some sheets of rough paper. I sharpen all my pencils. Then I . . .

ANSWER KEY

Activity 8   Answers will vary. In their answers, students should use capital letters for the beginning letter of a sentence, the pronoun I, the name of a person, a place, a day, and a month.

USE YOUR ENGLISH

ACTIVITY 6 · speaking/listening/writing
[30 minutes]

You can use this activity after Exercise 9 on SB page 10.

The aim of this activity is to practice the simple present for routines and habits. If your class is large, consider dividing the class into groups. Let each group stay together through the whole process. If you want, you can regroup and share the results of Step 7.

■ STEP 1 Students write sentences individually. You can walk around to provide help if needed.

■ STEP 2 Students memorize their sentences.

■ STEP 3 Divide students into groups if appropriate (see note above). Arrange a signal that will tell students when to stop walking, e.g., clap your hands, or ring a bell, or switch the lights on or off. You could also play some music and stop the music when you want to stop students to stop walking and start talking.

■ STEP 4 Tell students to walk around the room. At the signal, they will stop and tell their sentences to their partner, and memorize their partner's sentences. Set a time limit for this step.

■ STEP 5 At the signal, students will resume walking again. When they stop the next time, they must tell the new sentences to another partner.

■ STEP 6 Continue this procedure for as long as the energy level in the class is high.

■ STEP 7 Have students sit down and tell the class about the last person's sentences. Is the information correct? What is different?

ACTIVITY 7 · writing
[20 minutes or after class]

You can use this activity after Exercise 6 on SB page 7.

You may start brainstorming ideas for this task in class and set the writing as homework. Encourage students to recycle some of the vocabulary you have been using in Exercises 4, 5, and 6. If you have asked students to keep a learning journal, you may ask them to write about how their learning styles have changed in the transition from high school to college.

EXPANSION [15 minutes]

Make this into a peer editing activity, in which students exchange descriptions with each other.

1. Students read each other's descriptions for content. Are all statements clear? If not, they can ask the writer of the description for clarification or elaboration where necessary.

2. Students check each other's descriptions for the grammar targeted in this unit. Did they use the simple present tense accurately and appropriately?

ACTIVITY 8 · research on the web
[After class]

See To the Teacher, page xxii for the purpose and use of the Web activities throughout this book.

You can use this activity instead of or in addition to Activity 5 on SB page 15.

The purpose of this Internet search activity is to provide a natural context for using the simple present. An additional purpose is to encourage students to share strategies for finding information on the Internet. After talking about these different

festivals, encourage students to share tips on how to obtain this information. What Web sites were most useful? What keywords did they use?

ACTIVITY 9 · reflection
[30 minutes]

See To the Teacher, page xxii for a more detailed explanation of the function and use of the reflection activities throughout this book.

The dual aim of this activity is to use the simple present to talk about habits and routines, and to raise awareness of study skill strategies. You may have asked students to keep a record of their learning journal throughout this course as suggested in the To the Teacher, page xxii. This reflection activity will be part of that learning record. Alternatively, you can use this activity as a way of brainstorming study skills strategies that will benefit the whole class.

PRESENT PROGRESSIVE AND SIMPLE PRESENT
Actions and States

UNIT GOALS

- Know when to use present progressive
- Form present progressive correctly
- Choose between simple present and present progressive
- Know which verbs are not usually used in the present progressive

OPENING TASK

What's Happening?

STEP 1

A typical day at the office includes short conversations. Look at the picture. Where is this conversation happening? What are they discussing?

STEP 2

Work with a partner. Student A will look at picture A on the next page. Student B will look at picture B on page A-14. There are ten differences between the pictures. What are they?

Example:

Student A: *The woman at the front is opening a letter.*

Student B: *No, she isn't. She's writing a letter.*

Picture A

ANSWER KEY

Opening Task

Step 2: Differences between Pictures A and Picture B (Picture A/Picture B):

1. The woman on left is talking on the phone and holding some papers/her hand is on the desk.

3. Man reading the newspaper at desk on left is wearing/not wearing a suit jacket.

4. Man at file cabinets is wearing a gray suit/a dark brown suit.

5. The woman at the front desk is

6. Receptionist is talking on the phone/to a visitor.

7. Man with red tie is writing a letter/drinking coffee. He isn't/is wearing glasses.

8. Woman at desk on right is reading/typing.

9. The man at the back desk is sitting and writing/ is standing and holding files next to the woman in green.

10. Man on the couch is talking on his cell phone/is reading a newspaper.

UNIT OVERVIEW

Unit 2 provides practice with the present progressive, contrasts the present progressive with the simple present, and includes an overview of major verbs not usually used in the progressive.

GRAMMAR NOTE

The *present tense* can be expressed in English by using either progressive or simple aspect. The *progressive aspect* conveys a view of the action or event as temporary or incomplete, such as actions or events at or around the moment of speaking. Many languages do not have a different form for progressive and simple usage. Some languages have these two forms, but they correspond to different meanings.

UNIT GOALS

Some instructors may want to review the goals listed on this page after completing the Opening Task so that students understand what they should know by the end of the unit. These goals can also be reviewed at the end of the unit when students are more familiar with the grammar terminology.

OPENING TASK [30 minutes]

The purpose of the Opening Task is to create a context in which students will need to use the present progressive to describe actions in progress. The problem-solving format is designed to show the teacher how well the students can produce the target structures implicitly and spontaneously when they are engaged in a communicative task.

Setting Up the Task

▪ STEP 1

Use this step as an introduction to the theme of work and daily activities, as well as a contextualized

way of using the present progressive. Ask questions about the photograph. Who are these people? What are these people doing? What are they discussing? Is this a good place to work?

▪ STEP 2

Divide students into pairs. Student A will look at Student Book (SB) page 19. Student B will look at SB page A-14. Explain that each student has a slightly different picture. They should not look at their partner's picture. The aim of the task is to find the differences between the two pictures by asking questions.

Suggestion: Before starting this task, you may want to review some useful expressions for describing location, such as: *on the left/right, in the middle/center, at the front/back, next to, between, in front of, behind* etc.

Conducting the Task

1. While students work in pairs, you can circulate and listen to get an idea of students' current use of the present progressive. Do not correct; accuracy is not important at this stage.

2. Take notes of typical errors. These can help you when you focus on accuracy later in the unit.

3. Take notes of correct uses of the present progressive. You can use them when you debrief the task.

4. If some students finish early, ask them to write a list of the differences in their notebooks.

Closing the Task

1. Bring the class together so that students can compare their ideas.

2. Invite a volunteer to act as secretary and make a list of the differences on the board. Refer to the answer key on Lesson Planner (LP) page 18.

3. When all ten differences have been listed on the board, ask students to check the sentences for errors in form or use. Do not go into explanations at this stage.

4. Use these points to lead into Focus Chart on SB page 20.

GRAMMAR NOTE

Typical student errors (form)
(See Focus Chart 2.)

- Omitting the auxiliary verb, * *Where you going?*
- Omitting the –ing ending, * *She is go to the bank.*
- Misspelling of the participle, * *writting,* * *rainning,* * *takeing*

Typical student errors (use)

- Using the present simple for something that is happening now, * *Why do you leave?* (Instead of: *Why are you leaving?*) (See Focus Chart 1.)
- Using present progressive for something that happens regularly, * *What time are you starting work every day?* (See Focus Chart 3.)
- Using present progressive instead of present perfect, * *She is living here for two years.*
- Using progressive forms with non-progressive verbs, * *I am believing you.* (See Focus Charts 4 and 5.)

SPELLING NOTE

Notice the North American spelling conventions for adding -ing:

write → writing (drop -e)

bit → bitting (double consonant in 1-syllable words with one vowel)

travel → traveling (single consonant in 2-syllable words with first syllable stress)

rebel → rebelling (double consonant in 2-syllable words with second syllable stress)

The reason for doubling the consonant is to show that the vowel is short. Compare, for example, the pronunciation and spelling of *hoping* and *hopping.*

FOCUS 1 — Present Progressive: Actions in Progress

use

EXAMPLES	EXPLANATIONS
(a) Right now, I *am sitting* on the couch and my brothers *are cooking* dinner.	*Am sitting* and *are cooking* are present progressive forms.
(b) It *is raining* and Oscar *is waiting* for the bus.	Use the present progressive to describe an action that is in progress and happening at the time of speaking.
(c) This semester, I *am taking* three math classes.	Use the present progressive for an action that is happening **around** the time of speaking, but not happening **exactly** at that time.
(d) Their baby **is waking up** very early these days.	These time expressions are often used with the present progressive.
At time of speaking:	Around time of speaking:
right now	*this year*
at the moment	*this semester*
today	*this week*
at present	*these days*

EXERCISE 1

STEP 1 Read the following statements about picture A in the Opening Task. Without looking back at the picture, which statements are true (T) and which ones are false (F)?

1. Two women are talking on the phone. (T) F
2. Three men are wearing jackets. (T) F
3. Two people standing. T (F)
4. Two men are reading. T (F)
5. Three people are talking. (T) F
6. One man is drinking coffee. T (F)

STEP 2 Now look at picture A and check your answers. How many of your answers were correct?

---

form

FOCUS 2 — Present Progressive

To form the present progressive, use *be* + present participle (*-ing*) of the main verb:

STATEMENT	NEGATIVE	QUESTION	SHORT ANSWER
I am (I'm) working.	I am not (I'm not) working.	Am I working?	Yes, I am. No, I'm not.
You are (you're) working.	You are not (aren't) working.	Are you working?	Yes, you are. No, you aren't. (No, you're not.)
She/He/It is (She's/He's/It's) working.	She/He/It is not (isn't) working.	Is she/he/it working?	Yes, she/he/it is. No, she/he/it isn't. (No, she's/he's/it's not.)
We are (We're) working.	We are not (aren't) working.	Are we working?	Yes, we are. No, we aren't. (No, we're not.)
They are (They're) working	They are not (aren't) working.	Are they working?	Yes, they are. No, they aren't. (No, they're not.)

EXERCISE 2

Study the picture on page 19 for one minute. Close your book and, from memory, write as many sentences as possible to describe what is happening in the picture. Compare your sentences with those of the rest of the class. Who can remember the most?

ANSWER KEY

Focus 2—LP Expansion Answer Key—(delete final *e*) hope, phone, take, live, bite, smile   (1-syllable verbs that double final consonant) win, sit, bet, stop, hop, plan   (1-syllable verbs that don't double final consonant) beat, break, book, rain   (2-syllable verbs that double final consonant) rebel, begin, refer, upset   (2-syllable verbs that don't double final consonant) travel, label, open, offer, develop, visit

Exercise 2   Answers will vary.

PRESENT PROGRESSIVE AND SIMPLE PRESENT

LESSON PLAN 1

FOCUS 1 [10 minutes]

This focus chart introduces students to the concept of using the progressive to describe actions in progress. Discussion of the form is presented in Focus 2.

1. **Lead-in:** Write two examples of these different uses of the present progressive on the board and ask students to find the similarity and the difference between them.

   Maria is studying ballet. (around the time of speaking)

   Maria is reading a book. (right now)

2. Read the examples and explanations in the chart.

3. Ask students to give other examples of each use. Write some examples on the board using real information about your students. For example,

   Actions in progress right now: *Leo is looking out of the window. Milan and Kim are writing in their notebooks.*

   Actions in progress around the time of speaking: *Tranh is living with his sister this semester. Prem is looking for a roommate.*

4. Review the list of sentences written on the board from the Opening Task.

5. Ask students to identify examples of the present progressive in the list. Help students to infer which use of the present progressive this is (action in progress).

6. If some verbs are in simple present, invite students to make changes, or explain their reasons for not changing them.

EXERCISE 1 [10 minutes]

In this exercise students will have a chance to focus more explicitly on the present progressive, using affirmative, negative, and question forms. This will lead into Focus Chart 2 on SB page 21.

1. Ask students to remember facts about the picture on SB page 19. When they have finished, they can check their answers by turning back the page. See answer key on LP page 18.

2. To extend this activity, ask students to make further true or false sentences about the picture and test each other's memory.

3. This activity can be done as a class or in pairs.

For more practice, use *Grammar Dimensions 2* Workbook page 6, Exercise 1.

EXPANSION [20 minutes]

The following exercises can be used to provide further practice of the present progressive for activities that are happening right now.

1. Work in pairs. Close your eyes and take turns to describe what your partner is wearing.

2. Look around the classroom and write three sentences about what is happening right now.

3. Think of some people (friends or family members) who are not in your English class. What are they probably doing right now? Write three sentences.

4. When students have finished, have them share their answers with the class.

FOCUS 2 [10 minutes]

1. **Lead-in:** You can introduce this chart by starting with a review of the pronunciation and spelling of contractions. Write or say the full forms and ask volunteers to write the contractions on the board. Remind students of the alternative forms for negative contractions. Point out when contractions are and are not used.

2. Model the pronunciation of the examples in the chart, focusing on contractions and word blends such as *Is she* and *Is be.* You may want to add further practice with *Wh-* questions in the present progressive.

3. Select individuals to repeat the examples after you.

4. Explain that the chart is for reference and can be used throughout the unit as necessary.

EXPANSION [20 minutes]

1. Write or dictate a list of common verbs that exemplify the different spelling rules (see below). Say the infinitive form of the verb. Students will write the *-ing* form.

2. Check the answers by asking volunteers to write the *-ing* forms in a chart on the board (see answer key below).

List of verbs:

beat	label	sit	begin
live	smile	bet	offer
stop	bite	open	take
book	phone	travel	break
plan	upset	develop	rain
visit	hop	rebel	win
hope	refer		

EXERCISE 2 [10 minutes]

This exercise returns to the Opening Task and focuses on accurate production.

1. Have students work individually to write as many sentences as they can.

2. **Suggestion:** Instead of asking students to write sentences, have them work in pairs to ask and answer questions about the picture. Student A can look at the picture and ask questions, for example, *Is the woman on the left reading a book?* Student B cannot see the picture and gets a point for every correct answer.

The Exercise 2 expansion follows on LP page 23.

For more practice, use *Grammar Dimensions 2* Workbook page 6, Exercise 2.

FOCUS 3

Simple Present or Present Progressive?

use

EXPLANATIONS

EXAMPLES	Simple Present	Present Progressive
(a) Philippe **watches** six TV programs a day.	For an action that happens regularly, again and again. (See Unit 1.)	
(b) A: Where's Philippe? B: In his room. He's **watching** TV.		For an action that is in progress **at the time of speaking**.
(c) Leanne can't come to the phone right now because she's **taking** a shower.		
(d) Philippe **is watching** more TV than usual these days		For an action in progress **around the time of speaking**.
(e) Audrey **is learning** Greek this semester.		
(f) Carmina **lives** in Mexico City.	For facts, situations, and states that we do not expect to change.	
(g) The sun **rises** in the east.		
(h) Mark always **reads** the sports section of the newspaper first.		
(i) Angela **is living** with her mother for the time being. (Someday she will move into a house of her own.)		For situations and actions that are temporary and that we expect to change.
(j) Matt will start college next year. Until then, he **is working** at Fat Burger.		
(k) Cell phones **are becoming** more popular these days.		For situations and actions that are changing.

EXERCISE 3

Check (✓) the sentence (*a* or *b*) that is closest in meaning to the first statement. Compare your answers with a partner.

1. I live in New York now.
   - (a.) New York is my home.
   - b. I expect to move very soon.

2. I'm staying with a friend.
   - a. I'm at my friend's house right now.
   - (b.) I won't stay at my friend's house for long.

3. I start work early in the morning.
   - (a.) I usually start work early every day.
   - b. I start work earlier than usual these days.

4. I'm walking to work these days.
   - a. I'm walking to work right now.
   - (b.) I started walking to work recently.

5. I'm writing to you on my computer at work.
   - (a.) I am writing at this moment.
   - b. I usually write letters on my computer.

6. Oh, no! The boss is coming over to my desk.
   - a. The boss is walking towards my desk right now.
   - b. The boss visits my desk quite often.

7. Many students are using wireless Internet in cafés.
   - a. Many students are using computers in cafés these days.
   - b. Many students are using computers in cafés right now.

8. The receptionist makes the coffee at work.
   - (a.) He makes the coffee every day.
   - b. He is making the coffee right now.

EXPANSION [20 minutes]

The aim of this activity is to give students the opportunity to use the target structures in an appropriate context, focusing on language use.

1. Bring in pictures from a magazine, or ask students to bring them. Ask students to study the picture for one minute before turning the picture over. Have students write as many sentences as they can, using the present progressive. Then look at the picture again to check their answers.

2. This activity can also be done using questions and answers (see Suggestion in Exercise 2, above).

You may want to use Activity 2 on SB page 30, or use the suggested Variation for Activity 2 on LP page 31 in class.

FOCUS 3 [10 minutes]

This focus chart contrasts the different uses of the present progressive and the simple present.

1. **Lead-in:** You can introduce the contrast between these two tenses by presenting an example in the context of a story or a picture. You might present an example of something you do regularly and something you are doing right now. For example, *I talk to students every day. I'm talking to my students now.* Similarly, you might show a picture of a person and make sentences about him or her that illustrate the meanings of both tenses. For example, *She starts work at 8am every day. She's working right now.*

2. Have students read the examples and the explanations in the chart.

3. Ask students for additional examples for each category using real information. For example, *Michaela drinks a cup of coffee every morning. Berta is studying in the library right now. I'm learning to drive this semester. We live in (California). Susanna is living with a host family. People are doing more shopping online these days.*

VARIATION

You may also start this section doing Exercise 3 as a way of checking students' understanding of the concepts before looking at the Focus 3.

EXERCISE 3 [20 minutes]

This exercise helps students gain skills in talking about meaning, and about how meaning and form are linked. The aim of this exercise is to understand and explain the reasons for the correct choice in each case.

1. Have students work individually to complete their answers.

2. When they have finished, they can compare their answers with a partner.

3. Have students explain the reasons for their choices to each other.

4. Invite volunteers to explain the answer for each question to the class. See answers on LP page 22.

EXPANSION [20 minutes]

In this exercise students will practice explaining reasons for grammatical choices.

1. Give students some additional examples of sentences where either present progressive or simple present could be used, but with a change in meaning.

Nina's practicing the piano. (=right now)/*Nina practices the piano.* (=every day)

Are you having trouble with your car? (=right now)/*Do you have trouble with your car?* (=usually)

What language is she speaking? (=right now)/*What language does she speak?* (=usually)

Kristen's getting really good grades. (=Her grades are better than usual.)/*Kristen gets really good grades.* (=She always gets good grades.)

Terry's wearing a suit. (=Terry seldom wears a suit.)/*Terry wears a suit.* (=Terry usually wears a suit.)

2. Write the sentences on the board.

3. Students work in pairs to explain the difference.

4. Invite volunteers to explain answers to the class.

5. If there is time, have students create mini-dialogs incorporating these sentences.

EXERCISE 4 [20 minutes]

This exercise provides an opportunity for students to use contractions in an everyday conversational context. Ask students to look at the example done for them in the text. How can they change the example to be more like spoken English? *She is taking.* → *She's taking.*

1. Students work individually to complete the conversation.

2. In pairs, ask students to practice reading the conversation, being sure to use contracted forms.

3. Point out that using full forms gives emphasis:

Q: *Katarina says you're not going to work today.*

A: *Actually, I am going.*

4. See answers on LP page 24.

5. After the exercise, elicit or point out how the choice between present progressive and simple present depends on the factors presented in Focus 3 – whether the action happens regularly, is happening now, is changing, or is expected to change.

6. You may want to use Activity 1 on SB page 30 (listening) and Activity 4 on SB page 32 as follow-up activities for this section.

For more practice, use *Grammar Dimensions 2 Workbook* page 9, Exercise 3 and Exercise 4.

(The Exercise 4 Expansion follows on LP page 24.)

EXERCISE 4

Complete the following sentences using either the simple present or the present progressive. Use a form of the verb in parentheses. The first one has been done for you.

Melissa: Hello?

Chris: Oh hi! Is Angie there?

Melissa: Hi, Chris. It's Melissa. Angie's here, but she (1) _is taking_ (take) a shower at the moment. How are you? What (2) _are_ you _you doing_ (do) these days?

Chris: I (3) _am studying_ (study) business management this semester. How about you?

Melissa: I (4) _am taking_ (take) computers and Spanish. I _am working_ (work) part-time at the computer store for a few weeks.

Chris: I (5) _speak_ (speak) Spanish, but I'm terrible at computers. In fact, I _am having_ (have) trouble with my computer right now.

Melissa: I could help you, if you like.

Chris: Sure! (6) _Do_ you _do_ you _have_ (have) time today? What time (7) _finish_ (finish) work?

Melissa: At around 3 P.M. on Saturdays, but I usually (8) _don't get_ (not, get) home till around 4.

Chris: OK, let's meet at 4:30.

EXERCISE 5

When people send text messages by phone, they often use just the first letters of each word to make the messages shorter. Can you translate the following into written English? Write your answers below.

Key:
B = believe, C = see,
D = don't, H = hear,
I = I, it
K = know, L = later, love
M = mean, N = next,
O = or, N = not,
R = are, S = so,
T = think, U = you,
W = what, welcome

1. CUL _See you later_
2. IHU _I hear you_
3. KWIM? _Know what I mean?_
4. ILU _I love you_
5. IDTS _I don't think so_
6. IDK _I don't know_
7. BION _Believe it or not_
8. URW _You are welcome_

You can find the answers on page A-14.
Now underline all the verbs from your answers. Write them in the appropriate boxes below. The first one has been done for you.

VERBS THAT EXPRESS EMOTIONS AND FEELINGS	VERBS THAT EXPRESS SENSES AND PERCEPTIONS	VERBS THAT EXPRESS COGNITION: KNOWLEDGE THOUGHTS, AND BELIEFS
love	see	mean
	hear	think
		know
		believe
		are welcome

Which verb does not fit these categories? _____

LESSON PLAN 1

PRONUNCIATION NOTE

Some students may think that contracted forms are bad English, but they are part of the normal sound pattern of spoken English. When native speakers talk naturally, the words with *meaning* (such as nouns, adjectives, and main verbs) are emphasized, while the words that express the grammar (auxiliary verbs, articles, and prepositions) are not generally stressed. Therefore, the contraction of the auxiliary verb *be* in the present progressive follows the rules of English pronunciation. Contractions, however, are not normally used in formal written work.

EXPANSION [15 minutes]

Have students work in pairs to make up similar conversations based on the following situations. Encourage them to use present progressive and present simple forms at least twice in each conversation. Invite volunteers to role-play the conversations for the class.

Situation 1: Phone your friend to find out if she can come with you to the movies tonight. Your friend is busy right now and cannot come to the phone, so you talk to her sister instead. Find out about her sister's studies, hobbies, and what she usually does on the weekend.

Situation 2: Phone your friend to find out if he can help you with your homework right now. Your friend is busy right now. Ask about his or her daily routine to find out when he or she can help you.

Situation 3: Your friend works at Billy's Fast Food. Phone your friend at work and find out what he or she is doing right now. You work at Sam's Shop and Save Supermarket. Tell your friend about what you are doing now. Talk about your daily routines and find out who has the most interesting job.

Situation 4: You are at school right now. Your friend is in a different class. Phone your friend and find out what he or she is doing right now. Tell your friend about what you are doing now. Talk about your classes and find out which ones are more interesting.

EXPANSION [15 minutes]

1. Draw the chart on the board. Have students work individually to complete the chart with true information.

Things I'm doing now (temporarily)	Activities I usually do

2. Tell each other sentences based on the chart and continue to ask further questions on the same topic.

Example: A: I usually go to school by bike, but this week I'm taking the bus.

B: Why's that? Is your bike broken?

A: No, I lent it to my sister.

EXERCISE 5 [15 minutes]

This exercise will prepare students for the next focus chart. The aim of this exercise is to elicit verbs that do not use the progressive, but avoid explanations of this until after students have completed the exercise.

1. Introduce the topic of text messaging. Ask how many students send text messages. What kinds of abbreviations do they use?

2. Demonstrate how to use the key to 'translate' the messages. Use the first one as an example.

3. Have students work individually to work out the meanings of the messages.

4. Invite a volunteer to be secretary and write the answers on the board.

5. Draw the chart on the board and ask students to tell you which verbs go in which category. See answers on LP page 24.

6. Ask if students can think of any other verbs which can go into these categories. Check the answers by going to Focus Chart 4 on SB page 26.

For more practice, use *Grammar Dimensions 2* Workbook page 10, Exercise 5.

work book

FOCUS 4
Verbs Not Usually Used in the Progressive

meaning

EXAMPLES

(a) He **loves** me, but he **hates** my cat.

(b) NOT: He is loving me, but he is hating my cat.

(c) I **know** your sister.

(d) NOT: I am knowing your sister.

(e) Hugo **likes** opera, but his girlfriend **prefers** ballet.

(f) Those flowers **smell** wonderful!

(g) I **think** the President has some interesting ideas about health care, but many people **believe** he is wrong.

(h) Please be careful with that vase. It **belongs** to my aunt.

(i) A: Are you going to buy that radio?
B: No, it **costs** too much.

EXPLANATIONS

Some verbs are not usually used in the progressive. The reason is that they describe states or situations that we do not expect to change. They do not describe actions.

Common nonprogressive (stative) verbs:

- Verbs that express feelings and emotions:
  love   prefer   hate   like   appreciate   want   dislike

- Verbs that describe the senses:
  see   hear   taste   smell

- Verbs that express knowledge, opinions, and beliefs:
  think   believe   know   understand

- Verbs that express possession:
  have   belong   own   posses

- Other common nonprogressive verbs:
  be   seem   owe   exist   need   appear   cost   weigh

EXERCISE 6

Complete the following with the simple present or the present progressive, using the verbs in parentheses.

Technology (1) _is changing_ (change) the way we communicate. Today, more and more people (2) _own_ (own) a cell phone right now? Cell phones many people (3) _are using_ (use) a cell phone right now? Cell phones (4) _give_ (give) us a feeling of safety. We never (5) _feel_ (feel) lonely. Cell phones (6) _are becoming_ (become) popular with teenagers, too. They often (7) _send_ (send) hundreds of text messages every day. They (8) _think_ (think) they will be unpopular if they (9) _don't have_ (not, have) a cell phone. People (10) _are talking_ (talk) to each other more these days, but have) a cell phone. People (10) _are talking_ (talk) to each other more these days, but (11) _do_ they _understand_ (understand) each other better?

use

FOCUS 5
States and Actions

EXAMPLES

(a) I **love** you.

(b) I **hate** my job.

(c) She **knows** a lot about the history of her country.

State	Action
(d) I **weigh** 120 pounds.	I **am weighing myself** (to see if I've gained weight).
(e) Mmm! Dinner **smells** great!	I'm **smelling** the milk (to see if it smells fresh).
(f) This soup **tastes** good.	He is **tasting** the soup (to see if it needs salt).

(g) David **is** very polite.

(h) Tanya **is** a little shy.

(i) We **have** two cars.

(j) NOT: We are having two cars.

(k) We **are having fun.**

(l) We always **have fun** on vacation.

(m) I can't talk to you right now because I **have** a really sore throat.

(n) NOT: I am having a sore throat.

(o) Sandy **has** a headache and a high fever today. Maybe she **has** the flu.

(p) NOT: Sandy is having a headache and a high fever today. Maybe she is having the flu.

EXPLANATIONS

Nonprogressive verbs usually describe a state or quality that we do not expect to change. They do not describe actions.

Some verbs describe both a state **and** an action. If the verb describes a state, use the simple present. If the verb describes an action, use the present progressive.

Do not use *be* in the progressive when it describes a state or quality you do not expect to change.

Do not use *have* in the progressive to describe possession.

However, you can use *have* in the progressive to describe an experience. Use the progressive if the experience is in progress at or around the time of speaking (k). Use the simple present if the experience happens again and again (l).

Common expressions using *have* to describe an experience:

have fun	*have a good time*
have problems	*have trouble with*
have difficulty with	

Do not use *have* in the progressive to describe a medical problem or physical discomfort.

FOCUS 4 [10 minutes]

This focus chart introduces the difference between *stative* verbs (verbs that describe states) and *action* verbs. Verbs describing states that we don't expect to change do not use the progressive form. This topic is discussed further in Focus 5. Also, see grammar note below.

1. **Lead-in:** Read two or three of the examples in the chart. Ask students to explain why using the progressive would be incorrect in each of these examples.

2. Write these headings on the board and dictate the verbs in the chart, asking students to write them under the correct heading in their notebooks.

feelings and emotions	senses	knowledge, opinions, and beliefs	possession	other

3. Invite volunteers to the board to fill in the chart. Students can then discuss and check their answers.

4. Other examples of verbs that do not usually take the progressive are: imagine, see (=understand), suppose, wish, mean, promise, surprise, depend, involve, realize.

GRAMMAR NOTE

There are times when English speakers *do* use these verbs in the progressive. These uses usually show a change in state:

I'm feeling sick . . . I think I need some air.

OR

When I first started playing the guitar, I loved it, but lately I'm hating it more and more because it takes too much practice.

EXERCISE 6 [15 minutes]

This exercise gives students the opportunity to combine the information from the previous focus boxes in this unit and check their hypotheses in context.

1. Discuss the topic of cell phones. How many students have cell phones? What are the advantages and the disadvantages for them?

2. Have students read the text and complete individually.

3. When they have finished, invite volunteers to explain the answers.

4. Encourage students to refer back to the explanations in previous focus charts to justify their choices.

5. It may be helpful to make a copy of the passage on an overhead transparency and review the answers together.

6. You may want to use Activity 3 on SB page 31 as a follow-up activity for this section.

workbook — For more practice, use *Grammar Dimensions 2 Workbook* page 11, Exercise 6.

EXPANSION [20 minutes]

This exercise will expand students' opportunity to talk about changes happening in the world right now using the present progressive.

1. Write the following sentence stems on the board.

The world's population is . . . .
The world's climate is . . . .
Health coverage is . . . .
Computers are . . .
Teenagers these days are . . .
The world's forests are . . .
The price of gas is . . . .
Air travel is . . . .
Older people are . . . .

2. Have students work individually to complete the sentence stems with their own ideas about what is happening to each of them.

3. Have students work in pairs to construct dialogues incorporating their sentences.

4. Invite volunteers to perform their conversations.

5. The other students will listen for uses of the present progressive and the simple present.

FOCUS 5 [10 minutes]

This focus chart looks more deeply at the issue of using stative vs. action verbs.

1. **Lead-in:** As a way of introducing the information in this chart, give some examples of verbs which have different meanings in progressive and simple forms (examples d, e, and f in the chart). See additional examples below.

2. Write the examples on the board

3. Ask students to explain the difference in meaning of the verbs in the two sentences, or to describe contexts where these sentences might be said.

4. Read the other examples and explanations in the chart.

5. Ask students to give further examples of each of the categories listed in the chart.

6. You can use Activity 3 on SB page 31 after this focus chart.

EXERCISE 7

Work with a partner or in a small group. You need a die and a small object (like a coin) to represent each person. Each person will also need a piece of paper and a pen or pencil.

STEP 1 Take turns throwing the die. The person who throws the highest number starts.

STEP 2 Put your coins (or objects) on the square marked "Start" on the following page.

STEP 3 Throw the die and move your coin that number of squares.

STEP 4 Complete the sentence in the square you land on by saying the answer out loud. If everyone agrees with your answer, you may write it on a piece of paper with your name and take another turn. If the class is not sure, the teacher will be the referee. If you make a mistake or do not know the answer, the next person gets a turn. The winner is the first person to reach the final square.

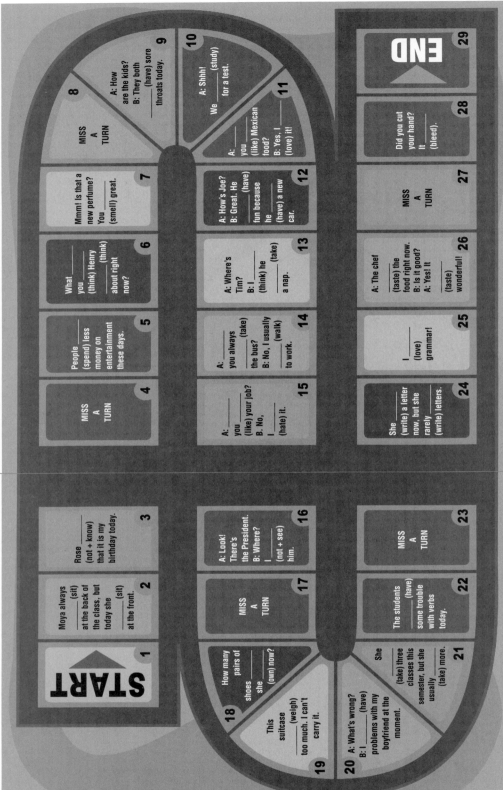

ANSWER KEY

Exercise 7

Note: Not every number requires an answer.

2. sits; is/'s sitting 3. does not/doesn't know 5. are spending 6. do you think; is/'s thinking 7. smell
9. have 10. are/'re studying 11. Do you like; love 12. is/'s having; has 13. think; is/'s taking 14. Do take;
walk 15. Do you like; hate 16. do not/don't see 18. does she own 19. weighs 20. am/'m having 21. is/'s
taking; takes 22. are having 24. is/'s writing; writes 25. love 26. is/'s tasting; tastes 28. is/'s bleeding

EXPANSION 1 [20 minutes]

Here are some additional examples of verbs that change their meaning in simple and progressive forms.

- Think: *What are you thinking about?* (=what is in your mind right now?)/*What do you think of the new book?* (=what is your opinion?)

- See: *I'm seeing a doctor about my headaches.* (=I'm consulting a doctor)/*I see what you mean.* (=I understand.)

- Feel: *I'm feeling sick* (=my physical or emotional state right now)/*I feel it is right to make this decision.* (=my opinion)

- Look: *What are you looking for?* (=search)/*He looks like Brad Pitt.* (=appearance)

1. Write the sentences on the board.

2. Ask students to work out the differences in meaning from the context.

3. See if students can work out a general pattern or rule from the examples. (Progressive uses of the verb tend to describe an action, or a state that is likely to change.)

EXPANSION 2 [20 minutes]

Bring in newspapers to class, or have students bring them in. Search for uses of the present progressive. Write some examples on the board. Decide which grammar explanation best fits the examples. Can the verb be changed from the progressive to the simple form? How does the meaning change?

EXPANSION 3 [30 minutes]

You may use Activity 5 (journal writing) or Activity 6 (research on the Web) as a follows-up in class for this section. Or assign them for homework and review answers at the beginning of the next class.

EXERCISE 7 [30 minutes]

This exercise uses a board game to practice and review the different uses of the present progressive presented in this unit.

Materials needed: one die for each group, a small counter for each student (students can provide their own).

1. Divide students into groups.

2. Explain the purpose of the game.

3. Use one group to demonstrate the rules of the game.

4. Each group should appoint one secretary to keep note of points that were disputed.

5. After the game is completed, review those items that caused disagreement among students.

EXPANSION [20 minutes]

To extend the use of this game and increase its relevance to student needs, take some examples of correct and incorrect sentences from previous exercises or activities. Write each sentence on a separate card and have students use the game to discuss whether they are correct or not.

METHODOLOGY NOTE

Some students may think that playing a board game is not a serious way of learning. For this reason, it may be a good idea to explain that the purpose of the game is not to win, or complete the game as quickly as possible. The purpose is to use the questions to discuss and clarify the grammar points covered in this unit. The process of discussing and clarifying concepts is the most valuable part of the game.

UNIT GOAL REVIEW [10 minutes]

Ask students to look at the goals on the opening page of the unit again. Refer to the pages of the unit where information on each goal can be found.

For a crossword that practices Unit 2 grammar and vocabulary, use *Grammar Dimensions 2 Workbook* page 12, Exercise 7.

ExamView® Test Generator   For assessment of Unit 2, use *Grammar Dimensions 2 ExamView®*.

Use Your English

ACTIVITY 1 listening/writing

CD Track 4

In this activity, you will hear a teacher describe a Resource Center.

■ **STEP 1** Before you listen, write down three things that you expect students to be doing in the Resource Center.

■ **STEP 2** Listen to the audio again. Write down examples of simple present and present progressive verbs in the chart below.

SIMPLE PRESENT	PRESENT PROGRESSIVE
keep, prepare, have, learn, come, do, is, need	going on, filling out, practicing, using, doing, checking

ACTIVITY 2 writing/listening

Go to a crowded place where you can sit, watch, and listen to what is happening around you. Look carefully at everything that is happening. Pretend you are a journalist or a radio or television reporter. Describe in writing everything that you see. Do not forget to include everything you hear as well.

ACTIVITY 3 speaking/listening

Do you know how to play tic-tac-toe? In this activity, you will be playing a version of this well-known game. Work with a partner or in teams.

■ **STEP 1** Copy each of the following onto separate cards or different pieces of paper.

she/speak	she/dance (?)*	you/live
we/hear	we/sing	I/see
I/understand	they/work (?)*	
they/eat	he/believe	
they/think about	you/write (?)*	(?)* = make a question

■ **STEP 2** Place the cards face down on the table in front of you.

■ **STEP 3** Player or Team X chooses a square from the box below and picks up a card from the pile. The player must make a meaningful statement that includes the word(s) in the square and the word(s) on the card. If the card has a "?" on it, the player must ask a question. Each statement or question must contain at least four words, not including the words in the square. Use the simple present or present progressive.

every day	today	usually
this week	occasionally	right now
often	at the moment	sometimes

■ **STEP 4** If everyone accepts the statement, Player or Team X marks the square with an X.

■ **STEP 5** Player or Team O then chooses a different square and takes a new card. The Player or Team O makes a statement. If the statement is correct, Player or Team O marks the square with an O.

■ **STEP 6** The first person or team to have three Xs or three Os in a straight line wins. You can play this game again and again by erasing the Xs and Os at the end of each round, or by writing them on small pieces of paper and covering the squares with these. Good luck!

USE YOUR ENGLISH

The Use Your English activities contain situations that should naturally elicit the structures covered in the unit. For a more complete discussion of how to use the Use Your English Activities, see To the Teacher, page xxii. When students are doing these activities in class, you can circulate and listen to see if they are using the structures accurately.

ACTIVITY 1   listening/ writing
[30 minutes]

You can use this activity after Exercise 4 on SB page 24.

The aim of this activity is to recognize and identify uses of the present progressive and the simple present.

1. Introduce the context of a Resource Center. If students are not familiar with this concept, explain that it is a kind of study center where students can access books, computers, CDs, and information about, for example, exam preparation, and sometimes career choices. Students can go there to study, to borrow materials, and to get help and advice.

2. Ask students to suggest two or three things they would be interested in using a resource center for.

3. Play the audio. Ask students to take notes in the chart.

4. Ask for a few suggestions for the chart. Or ask how many items they have managed to fill in.

5. Play the recording again.

6. Compare answers with the audio script on page S-1.

7. See answer key on LP page 30.

EXPANSION

This audio provides a natural context for uses of both the present simple and the present progressive. You may ask students to role-play other similar contexts,

for example, showing someone around the school, the library, or around their place of work. If possible, have students make audio or video recordings of their role-play and play them to the class

ACTIVITY 2   writing/listening

You can assign this activity for homework after Exercise 2.

1. The first part of this activity should be done outside the classroom. Students can choose a place they normally go to, such as a coffee shop, the library, or the train. They should take notes in a notebook of what people are doing and write them up later in paragraph form. If you have asked your students to keep a journal, this may be assigned as a journal task.

2. Have students exchange descriptions and check their work for correct use of the present progressive.

3. Read out the most interesting descriptions, or display them on the classroom wall.

4. Have students listen and draw a picture to go with the descriptions.

5. For an in-class activity, see the variation suggested below.

VARIATION

Bring a video to class. Be sure the scene you show includes a lot of activity (action films and comedies like *Mr. Bean* are good examples). Students work in pairs, with Student 1 facing the video screen while Student 2 has his/her back to the scene and acts as secretary. Turn the volume all the way down and have Student 1 describe what s/he sees to Student 2. Students then rewrite the notes together or present them orally to the class.

ACTIVITY 3   speaking/listening
[30 minutes]

You can use this activity after Focus Chart 5 on SB page 27.

The aim of this activity is to practice making sentences with verbs that take the progressive and verbs that do not take the progressive form.

To play this activity, it is helpful to have an overhead transparency of the chart, as well as a copy of the chart for each group. It is also helpful to prepare the small cards with phrases beforehand and have one set for each group.

1. Explain and demonstrate the game of tic-tac-toe on the board.

2. Draw the chart on the board (or use an overhead transparency) and play one round of the game as a whole class.

3. Divide the class into groups.

4. Give each group a copy of the chart and a set of cards (or have them prepare their own).

5. Have each group appoint a secretary to keep a note of the sentences made by the group.

6. At the end of the activity, discuss any disputed sentences as a class.

EXPANSION [10 minutes]

This activity can be used as a review at the beginning of the next lesson. You may want to organize this as a team competition activity.

1. Make a list of the sentences created by the students (some correct and some incorrect).

2. Write them on the board or on an overhead transparency.

3. Ask students to vote on which sentences are correct.

4. If they are incorrect, ask students to explain why.

ACTIVITY 4 speaking/listening/writing

STEP 1

Go around the classroom and try to find a different person for each of the situations in the chart below. Write the person's name in the box marked *Name* and add more information in the box marked *Information*. We have given some suggestions here, but you probably have more ideas of your own.

SITUATION	NAME	INFORMATION
. . . is reading a book in English		*Title? His/her opinion?*
. . . regularly reads a newspaper from his/her country		*Why?*
. . . reads more than one book a month (in any language)		*Favorite books?*
. . . usually goes to the movies several times a month		*How often? Favorite movie?*
. . . is wearing an article of clothing made in the U.S.A.		*Describe it.*
. . . regularly plays a musical instrument		*What kind? How often?*
. . . is wearing perfume or cologne at the moment		*What kind? Describe it.*
. . . has a pet		*What kind? How old?*

STEP 2

Look at all the information that you collected. Choose three or four of the most interesting or surprising things that you learned about your classmates and write about this information. Remember to include an introduction. For example: *I interviewed some of my classmates and I learned several new things about them. First, I learned that Maria likes to read. In fact, she is reading a book in English that she is enjoying very much. . . .*

Read your report to a partner. Ask your partner to listen first to count the examples of the **simple present** and then listen again, doing the same for the **present progressive**.

ACTIVITY 5 writing

Journal Entry: What things are changing in your country? What things are getting more popular? What things are disappearing? How do you feel about it?

ACTIVITY 6 research on the web

On the Web: Use an Internet search engine such as Google® or Yahoo® to find out about events that are happening right now in your town or neighborhood. Type the name of your city or town and "current events." Choose one event that you like and tell your class or a partner about it.

ACTIVITY 7 reflection

How do you use technology in your studies? How are your study habits changing because of technology? Write a journal entry about how you feel about these changes.

USE YOUR ENGLISH

ACTIVITY **4** — speaking/listening/writing [30 minutes]

You can use this activity after Exercise 4 on SB page 24.

The aim of this activity is to practice using the present progressive and the simple present appropriately.

To do this activity, students will need to move around the room with their textbooks and a pen or pencil, making notes in their books as they talk to each student. It may be helpful to have an overhead transparency of the chart to demonstrate how to complete each section.

1. Read the chart and check that students understand all the vocabulary.

2. Model the activity with one or two students. Explain that they should make questions using the correct tense. Examples: *Are you reading a book in English? Do you regularly read a newspaper from your country?*

3. If the answer is no, they should move on to another student. If the answer is yes, they should follow up with some extra questions.

4. They should only ask each student one question (but if your class is small, they may ask the same students again after asking some other students first).

5. Invite volunteers to report on the most surprising and interesting things they learned about their classmates.

6. Students can do the writing part of this activity in class or as homework.

EXPANSION [20 minutes]

You can review these tenses by using a class survey activity.

1. Write each of the following questions on a separate piece of paper (or think of other questions more appropriate to your group).

2. Give each student one question.

3. Students will walk around the class and ask everyone in the class their question, taking notes of the answers.

4. Students report back to the class on the results.

   How many people in the class . . .

   . . . are reading an English book?

   . . . regularly read a newspaper?

   . . . go to the movies every month?

   . . . are learning another language besides English?

   . . . use text messages to keep in touch with their friends?

ACTIVITY **5** — writing [30 minutes]

You can assign this activity as homework after Exercise 6 on SB page 26.

This activity provides a context for students to use the present progressive when talking about changes in the United States or in their country. You may want to brainstorm a few ideas with the students before they write. Here are some possible topics: technology, fashion, food, music, TV, advertising, leisure activities, communication, jobs, values, lifestyles, beliefs. This is a good opportunity for students to express themselves on complex and abstract topics, as well as giving concrete examples to explain and justify their opinions.

ACTIVITY **6** — research on the web

The purpose of this Internet search activity is to provide a natural context for using the present progressive. An additional purpose is to encourage students to share strategies for finding information on the Internet. After talking about events that are happening in your town or city, encourage students to share search tips. What Web sites were most useful? What keywords did they use?

ACTIVITY **7** — reflection

You may have asked students to keep a record of their learning in a journal throughout this course as suggested in To the Teacher, see page xxii. This reflection activity will be part of that learning record. Alternatively, you can use this activity as a group learning activity online. One way of doing this is to create an "e-mail tree" where groups assign numbers to each of their members. The first student sends an e-mail message to the second student who adds a comment and forwards it to a third student, and so on until all members of the group have contributed their ideas. The final member of each group prints out the contributions and brings them to class to exchange with other groups.

TALKING ABOUT THE FUTURE

Be Going To and Will

UNIT GOALS

- Form statements and questions about the future using *be going to* and *will*

- Know the uses of *be going to* and *will*

- Choose between *be going to* and *will*

OPENING TASK
Telling Your Future

Some people believe that you can see your future in the lines of your palm. Palm reading is the art of telling your future by looking at your palm. What is your opinion of palm reading?

■ STEP 1

Read the meanings connected with each line on page 35.

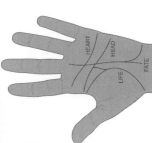

Life Line:

Does a line cross your life line? You will have a big change in your life. You are going to move, change schools or jobs, or marry.

Does your life line split into two branches? Your life will be full of adventure.

Does it bend towards your little finger? You are going to have a pleasant and quiet life.

Head Line:

Does it go straight across? You will be a lawyer, a doctor, or a scientist.

Does it curve down? You will be an artist, a musician, or a dancer.

Heart Line:

Is it close to your head line? You will have a few close friends.

Is there a wide space between your heart and head lines? You will be friends with many different people.

Fate Line:

Is it a straight downward line? You will achieve all your goals.

Does it bend towards your first finger? You are going to be successful.

■ STEP 2

Use the information to make predictions about each person's future.

■ STEP 3

Look at your partner's palm. Make predictions about your partner's future.

ANSWER KEY

Opening Task   Answers will vary. Sample response: Steve will be friends with many different people. He will be successful. Pam will have a few close friends. She will achieve all her goals.

3 LESSON PLAN 1

UNIT OVERVIEW

Unit 3 provides practice with the future *be going to* and *will* and contrasts their uses for making predictions, decisions, and promises.

GRAMMAR NOTE

The future tense is expressed in English by using *will* and *be going to*, as well as present tense forms with future meaning. The difference in meaning between the different structures is not always easy to explain. In some contexts, there is no difference in meaning. This unit identifies some of the main differences between *will* and *be going to*, focusing in general on whether the future event has been previously planned or is decided at the moment of speaking.

UNIT GOALS

Some instructors may want to review the goals listed on the opening page of the student book unit after completing the Opening Task so that students understand what they should know by the end of the unit. These goals can also be reviewed at the end of the unit when students are more familiar with the grammar terminology.

OPENING TASK [30 minutes]

The purpose of the Opening Task is to create a context in which students generate talk about the future that naturally uses *be going to* and *will*. The problem-solving format is designed to show the teacher how well the students can produce the target structures implicitly and spontaneously when they are engaged in a communicative task. For a more complete discussion of the Opening Task, see To the Teacher, Lesson Planner (LP) page xxii.

Setting Up the Task

Introduce the topic of palm reading by asking questions about the picture. What are they doing? Do you believe in palm reading? Have you ever had your palm read? Why do people want to know their future?

■ STEP 1

1. Divide students into pairs and have them read the explanations.
2. Students can look at their own palms (left hand) to see if the lines correspond.
3. Check comprehension of any difficult vocabulary.
4. Have students expand on the possible meanings of some phrases such as "a life full of adventure" (What kind of adventures?) and "a pleasant and quiet life" (Will it be boring and dull? Will you stay at home and not travel anywhere?).

Conducting the Task

■ STEP 2

1. Have students continue to work in pairs to solve the problem. There may be some disagreement about the answers. This is good as long as students are actively using the target structures.
2. Check the answers together. See answers on LP page 34.

■ STEP 3

1. Have students "read" their partner's palms and tell their future. Encourage students to be creative and predict interesting and exciting futures for each other!
2. Take notes of errors in meaning or use, but do not correct them at this stage. Exercise 1 returns to the Opening Task and gives students the opportunity to write their predictions from Step 3, thus focusing on accuracy.

GRAMMAR NOTE

Typical student errors (form)
(See Focus Chart 2.)

- Using full forms instead of contractions, e.g. * I *will see* you. (Instead of: *I'll see you.*)
- Omitting the verb *be* from *be going to*, e.g. * *You going to be here tomorrow?* (Instead of: *Are you going to be here tomorrow?*), *We not going to have a test next week.* (Instead of: *We are (We're) not going to have a test next week.*)

Typical student errors (use)

- Using *be going to* for decisions that are made at the time of speaking, e.g. * *That's too heavy for you. I am going to help you.*
- Using *will* for events that have been planned beforehand, e.g. * *I'll go to Florida next week. I bought the tickets and booked the hotel already.*
- Using *will* for events that are about to happen immediately, e.g. * *Help! I will fall.*

FOCUS 2 — *Will* and *Be Going To*

Will does not change to agree with the subject:

STATEMENT

I You We They She He It	will 'll	leave.

NEGATIVE

I You We They She He It	will not won't	leave.

QUESTION

Will	I you we they she he it	leave?

Be going to changes to agree with the subject:

STATEMENT

I 'm	am going to leave.
You We 're	are going to leave.
They	
She He It 's	is going to leave.

NEGATIVE

I	am not 'm not going to leave.
You We	are not aren't going to leave. 're not
They	
He She It	is not isn't going to leave. 's not

QUESTION

Am	I	going to leave?
Are	you we they	going to leave?
Is	he she it	going to leave?

EXERCISE 2

STEP 1 Imagine our world 100 years from now. Write yes/no questions about what life will be like.

Example: Will we live in houses with solar energy for electricity?

1. _____
2. _____
3. _____
4. _____

FOCUS 1 — Talking About the Future with *Will* and *Be Going To*

EXAMPLES

(a) Your life is going to be full of adventure.
OR
Your life will be full of adventure.

(b) Your life will be full of adventure.

(c) You are going to be sucessful.
OR

(d) You will be sucessful.

EXPLANATIONS

Use either *be going to* or *will* to make a prediction or talk about the future.

EXERCISE 1

Write predictions about yourself and your partner using the information from the Opening Task.

Example: *My partner's life will be full of adventure.*

1. _____
2. _____
3. _____
4. _____
5. _____
6. _____

Check your sentences. Did you use *will* and *be going to* correctly?

ANSWER KEY

Exercise 1   Answers will vary.

Exercise 2   Answers will vary.

FOCUS 1 [5 minutes]

This focus chart introduces students to the concept of using *will* and *be going to* for the future. Discussion of the form is presented in Focus Chart 2. Discussion of differences in the use of *will* and *be going to* will be presented later in the unit.

1. **Lead-in:** Draw a chart on the board and have students either copy the chart in their notebook and complete it individually, or come to the board and write their ideas in the appropriate column.

tomorrow	next week	next year

2. Have students make sentences about their future using *will* and *be going to*.

3. Read the examples and the explanations in the box.

EXERCISE 1 [10 minutes]

1. Have students return to Step 3 of the Opening Task on Student Book (SB) page 35 and write some of their predictions.

2. Have students edit each other's sentences. If there are errors in form, they will be a bridge to the next focus chart.

For more practice, use *Grammar Dimensions 2* Workbook page 14, Exercise 1.

EXPANSION [20 minutes]

You may want to use Activity 2 on SB page 45 as a follow-up to this exercise. This activity can be a fun

---

way to help students remember the use of *will* for predictions.

FOCUS 2 [5 minutes]

Focus 2 illustrates the forms of *will* and *be going to*.

1. **Lead-in:** You can introduce this chart by talking about the use of contractions and the differences between formal written English and spoken English.

2. Dictate some sentences using contracted forms and have students write the full forms. Note that the pronunciation of *we're* and *they're* might lead students to omit the verb *be* (or think that it is omitted in rapid speech).

3. You may want to add your own examples of *Wh-* questions using *will* and *be going to*, or ask students to think of examples.

LANGUAGE NOTE

Contractions of will (*'ll* and *won't*) and of *be going to* are commonly used in spoken English and in informal written style (e.g., letters, e-mails, etc.). In very informal spoken style, *going to* is pronounced *gonna*, as in *I'm gonna leave. What are you gonna do?* It's a good idea for students to use contractions if they want to sound natural and fluent.

Another difference between full and contracted forms is that the full forms are used for emphasis, as when giving an order or a command (e.g., *You will listen to me! You will not leave this room till you have done your homework. I am going to the party tomorrow!*).

EXERCISE 2 [20 minutes]

This exercise provides practice with the question forms, and affirmative and negative statements.

STEP 1

1. Introduce the topic of describing our world 100 years from now. Brainstorm a list of ways in which our world will be different. Write the topics on the board. Some examples are: *housing, food, medicine, technology, clothing, cars, communication.*

2. Have students work individually to write five questions about the future. Set a time limit of 5 minutes. They can use *Wh-* or *Yes/No* questions forms. They can use the topics on the board or their own ideas.

3. Walk around the classroom as students are writing in order to monitor their work.

4. Ask volunteers to read a few example questions aloud.

STEP 2   Ask your partner the questions from Step 1 and write down his or her answers. Think of what things we are going to have and also things we are *not* going to have.

Example: No. We aren't going to live in houses with solar electricity. We will live in
houses under the sea. _____

1. _____
2. _____
3. _____
4. _____

use

FOCUS 3

Making Predictions: *Will* or *Be Going To?*

EXAMPLES

(a) Be careful! That chair **is going to** break.
(b) NOT: Be careful! That chair will break!
(c) Oh no!! That little boy **is going to** fall off the bridge
(d) NOT: Oh no!! That little boy will fall off the bridge.

(e) *Babysitter to child:* Your mommy's **going to** be very angry about this.

(f) *Student to professor:* **Will** the test be difficult?

Professor: It **will** be tough, but I don't think you **will** have too many problems with it.

EXPLANATIONS

It is better to use *be going to* for actions or events that you think will happen very soon or immediately

When the future event or action will not happen immediately:

It is better to use *be going to* in informal situations (relaxed and friendly situations, with family or friends). In informal speech, *going to* is usually pronounced *gonna*.

It is better to use *will* in more formal situations.

EXERCISE 3

For each of the following, decide on the best form to use: *be going to* or *will*. In some sentences, it is possible to use both. The first one has been done for you.

1. Quick! Catch the baby! I think he _is going to_ roll off the bed.

2. Excuse me, Mr. President. Do you think unemployment _will_ decrease in the foreseeable future?

3. Oh, no! Look at those clouds. It _is/'s going to_ rain.

4. I predict that you _will/are going to_ meet a tall, dark, and handsome stranger, and you _will/are going to_ fall in love and get married.

5. One day _will/'ll/are going to_ look back at all this and laugh.

6. I don't believe it. Look at Paula! I think she _is/'s going to_ ask that guy to dance with her.

7. A: What do you think about my son's chances of getting into Harvard, Dr. Heath?

   B: I don't think he _will/'ll_ have any problems at all, Mrs. Lee.

8. Meteorologists predict that the drought _will_ end sometime this fall.

FOCUS 4

Future Plans and Intentions: *Be Going To*

use

EXAMPLES

(a) What are you **going to** do this summer?
(b) We're **going to** spend the month of August in Italy. We bought the tickets last week, and we're **going to** leave on August 2nd.

EXPLANATIONS

It is better to use *be going to* to talk about a future plan or an intention (something you want to do in the future). This shows that you made the decision to do this **before** speaking.

EXERCISE 4

In this exercise, you need to get information from one of your classmates. Use *be going to* or *will* in your answers, as appropriate.

1. Get together with a partner and find out three things he or she intends to do after class:

   My partner _____

2. Now find out three things he or she does not intend to do after class:

   My partner _____

ANSWER KEY

Exercise 3   *Answers will vary. Possible answers are listed above.*

Exercise 4   *Answers will vary.*

LESSON PLAN 1/LESSON PLAN 2

STEP 2

1. Have students work in pairs to ask each other their questions from Step 1.
2. Walk around the room to monitor their progress.

VARIATION

You can have students do Step 2 verbally first, then, after gathering some of their ideas on the board, have them write the most interesting answers in their books.

3. Ask volunteers to read aloud examples of their answers.

For more practice, use *Grammar Dimensions 2* Workbook page 15, Exercise 2.

EXPANSION [20 minutes]

Exercise 2 is a good way of brainstorming ideas for the writing activity in Activity 3 on SB page 45. You can start this activity in class and have students continue their writing for homework.

FOCUS 3 [5 minutes]

1. **Lead-in:** Using a book, notebook, or other unbreakable object, demonstrate the difference between *It's gonna fall!* and *It'll fall!*. With the first, the implication is *right now!* You can exaggerate by expressing urgency in your voice and actions (louder volume, a display of nervousness, etc.). With the second, the implication is *if . . . I push it a little farther* (off the edge of a desk), or *move it closer to the edge.* You can contrast this with *It'll fall!* said in a more calm tone of voice, and with a rising and falling intonation.
2. Read the examples in the chart, using appropriate intonation.
3. Read the explanations in the chart. Point out that *be going to* is so commonly used that some people wouldn't see the difference in register—how

informal or formal it's considered. For example, some would say that it would be appropriate to use *Is the test going to be difficult?* in (f), especially considering that classrooms in the United States are typically quite informal.

4. Here are some additional examples. Ask students if they are events that will happen very soon or not. If both are possible, ask students to explain the contexts.

get pizza after class   take the pronunciation class

move to California next year   ask the teacher your question

For more practice, use *Grammar Dimensions 2* Workbook page 15, Exercise 3.

EXPANSION [20 minutes]

Bring in pictures to provide further practice of *will* and *going to*. The pictures should provide scenes of people involved in various activities, so that students can practice *will* and *going to* for what they think will happen next.

EXERCISE 3 [10 minutes]

This exercise provides practice with examples that contrast different uses of *will* and *be going to*. The emphasis is on understanding the reasons for each use in each context.

1. Read the first item together and go over the reasons for the answer.
2. Have students work individually to complete the answers.
3. Have students compare their answers in pairs, explaining the reasons for their choices.
4. Have students read their answers aloud (using contractions as appropriate).
5. Check the answers as a class, referring back to Focus Chart 3 as necessary. See answers on LP page 38.

LESSON PLAN 2

FOCUS 4 [5 minutes]

This focus chart contrasts with the use of *will* for quick decisions presented in Focus Chart 5.

You may want to introduce this focus chart by using Activity 1 on SB page 44. Students can talk about their plans and intentions during this activity. Later, they can reflect on their use of future forms with reference to the focus chart.

1. **Lead-in:** If, as suggested above, you have used Activity 1 to introduce this lesson, you can lead into this focus chart by reading aloud some examples of students' sentences from the activity and asking what these sentences all have in common. (They all imply some element of pre-planning, a plan that you have already thought about.)
2. Read the examples and explanations in the focus chart.
3. Use examples from the activity (or other examples relevant to your students' context) to contrast the use of *will* and *be going to*. Point out that using *will* instead of *be going to* sounds like at the moment of speaking you got the idea to do this; you hadn't planned to do this before speaking. This topic also serves as a link to Focus Chart 5.

EXERCISE 4 [20 minutes]

This exercise provides practice of *be going to* for events that have already been planned and *will* for those that have not been planned yet.

1. Have students work in pairs and ask each other questions to complete questions 1, 2, and 3.
2. They should take notes of the answers in full sentences.

(Exercise 4 is continued on Lesson Planner page 41).

use

3. Now find out three possible plans that he or she has for this weekend:

My partner _____

Finally, look back at what you have written in this exercise. Where did you choose *be going to* and where did you choose *will*? Why did you make these choices?

FOCUS 5

Two More Uses of *Will*: Making Quick Decisions and Serious Promises

EXAMPLES	EXPLANATIONS
(a) A: I think there's someone at the front door. B: I'll go and check	Use *will* for quick decisions or for something you have decided to do at that moment.
(b) A: Telephone! B: OK. I'll get it.	The contracted *'ll* is usually used in these situations.
(c) A: I need someone to help out at the recycling center. B: Oh, I will!	Do not use *'ll* in short answers.
(d) I will always love you.	Use *will* to make a serious promise.
(e) I'll give you my homework tomorrow, I promise!	
(f) A: Remember, this is top secret. B: I won't tell anybody. You can count on me.	*Will* + *not* = *won't*

EXERCISE 5

Read the following conversation between two friends carefully and decide if the use of *be going to* or *will* is more appropriate. Check (✓) the sentences you think are acceptable. Correct the sentences you think are unacceptable.

A: (1) ✓ What are you going to do next year? (2) ✓ Are you going to go to college?

B: (3) ✓ Yes! I'm going to go to college in California. I sent in my application six months ago. (4) _____ I'll study nursing.

A: (5) ✓ Fantastic! You'll be a very good nurse.

B: Thanks. What are your plans?

A: I'm not sure. (6) ✓ I'm going to wait until I get my exam results. (7) _____ I'll work during my vacation. I already have a part-time job at the sports center.

B: That sounds good. Did you hear the news about Stan? (8) ✓ He's going to get married!

A: That's wonderful news! (9) _____ Is he going to invite us?

EXERCISE 6

Complete the following, using a form of *be going to* or *will*, as appropriate. The first is an example.

A: What (1) _are you going to_ (you) do tonight?

B: The World Cup Final (2) _will_ be on TV at 6:30. Julie (3) _is going to_ come over and watch it with me.

A: Oh really? Who do you think (4) _will_ win?

B: The newspapers say Brazil (5) _will_ win. But I think Mexico (6) _will_ give them a good match. What (7) _are you going to_ (you) do tonight?

A: I (8) _am going to_ go to the movies with Fran. I (9) _are you going to_ be home around 11.

B: You'd better take your umbrella. It looks like it (10) _will_ rain any minute.

A: Thanks. Can I take yours? I promise I (11) _will not/won't_ lose it!

B: Sure. I (12) _will/'ll_ go look for it in the closet.

ANSWER KEY

Exercise 4 Answers will vary.

Exercise 5 Answers will vary. Possible answers are listed above.

Exercise 6 Answers will vary. Possible answers are listed above.

LESSON PLAN 2

EXERCISE 4 [20 minutes] (Continued from Lesson Planner page 39)

3. Have students work in pairs to reflect on their choice of *will* or *be going to* in their answers.
4. Walk around the room and make notes of students who are able to give effective explanations of their choices.
5. Ask selected volunteers to summarize the results of their discussion.

EXERCISE 5 [15 minutes]

The following exercise provides more structured practice of the choice of future forms.

1. Read the first item together and explain the answer with reference to the focus chart (the speaker is asking about plans that have been made).
2. Have students work in pairs to complete the blanks.
3. Walk around the room and encourage explanation and justification of grammar choices.
4. Check the answers as a class. See answers on LP page 40.
5. You may also want to assign this exercise as homework and check it in class next lesson.

[workbook] For more practice, use *Grammar Dimensions 2 Workbook* page 16, Exercise 4.

EXPANSION [15 minutes]

You may want to use Activity 6 on SB page 47 after this exercise, or between Exercises 4 and 5.

FOCUS 5 [10 minutes]

You may already have touched on some of these explanations when discussing the contrast with *be going to* in the previous focus chart.

1. **Lead-in:** Read aloud the examples below. Ask students to try and work out why *be going to* is *inappropriate* in each of these examples.

1. (in a restaurant)
   A: *Are you ready to order?*
   B: *Yes, I'm going to have the fish. Oh no, I think I'll have the salad instead.*
2. (in a school)
   A: *Where's the library?*
   B: *I'll show you the way.*
3. (in a classroom)
   A: *I don't understand the homework.*
   B: *I'll help you.*
4. (in a library)
   A: *You can't bring your CD player in here.*
   B: *It's OK. I won't disturb anyone.*
5. (in a classroom)
   Can I borrow your pencil? I'll bring it back in five minutes.

2. Explain that *will* (or *'ll*) is used for decisions that are made at the moment of speaking (not previously planned). This includes the use of *will* for offers and promises.
3. Read the explanations and examples. Ask students to describe the possible contexts. (In example (d) you may want to point out the use of *will* for a more serious context such as wedding ceremony.)
4. Point out that *will* cannot be contracted in short answers.

EXERCISE 6 [10 minutes]

This exercise provides further practice in distinguishing contexts where *will* and *be going to* are appropriate.

Have students work individually to complete their answers.

Have students work in pairs to read their dialogues aloud, focusing on fluent and natural use of contractions.

Ask volunteers to perform their dialogue for the class. Check the answers, asking for explanations on any points of disagreement. See answers on LP page 40.

EXERCISE 7

With a partner, look at these situations and decide on ways to respond using *will* or *be going to*.

1. You look out of the window and notice there are a lot of stormy, black clouds in the sky. What do you say?

   Example: _We are going to need an umbrella._

2. Your friend Oscar is interested in music and in physics, but he can't decide which one to major in next year. After a lot of thought and discussion, he has finally decided to major in music. What does he say to his family?

   (I've decided) I'm going to major in music next year.

3. Your friend is organizing an international potluck. She needs people to bring food from different countries. You want to help. What will you promise to do? What are you going to bring or cook?

   I'll bring . . . to the potluck (if you think that sounds good).

4. It's 6:30 A.M. You have to drive to the airport to pick up your uncle at 7:30 A.M., but your car won't start. Your roommate offers to lend you hers, but she needs to have it back by 9:00 A.M. to get to work. What do you tell her?

   I'll (be sure to) bring the car back by 9:00.

5. You are standing in line in the campus cafeteria. You notice that the backpack of the student in front of you is open and all her books are about to fall out. What do you tell her?

   (It looks like) your books are going to fall out of your backpack.

6. One of your classmates is sick and has to go to the doctor's office. He is very worried about missing his history class. You are also in that class. What can you say to reassure him?

   I'm going to go to class today, so I'll take notes for you (if you'd like).

7. Your friend is giving you a ride home. Suddenly you notice a little boy who is about to run into the road. Your friend hasn't seen him. What do you say?

   (Watch out! Slow down or) you'll/you're going to hit that little boy!

8. Your friend Frank loves ballet. He has just bought the last ticket for a special gala performance of *Swan Lake* next Saturday night. You ask him about his plans for the weekend. What does he say?

   I'm going to go to Swan Lake.

9. You have promised to do the dishes and clean up the kitchen after dinner. Just before you get started, you receive an unexpected phone call from a friend whose car has broken down, and he urgently needs your help. As you are leaving, your roommate comes into the room and asks, "What about the dishes?" What do you say?

   I'll do them later. (I've got to go help my friend.)

10. Madame Cassandra is a fortune-teller who makes exciting predictions about the future. Your teacher is consulting Madame Cassandra. What does Madame Cassandra tell your teacher?

    You will/You're going to...

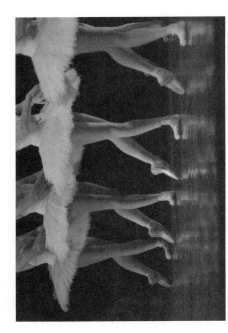

ANSWER KEY

Exercise 7   *Answers will vary, depending on students' responses. Possible answers are listed above.*

LESSON PLAN 2

EXERCISE 7 [20 minutes]

This exercise reviews all the uses of future forms presented in this unit.

1. Divide students into pairs. These may be "same-level" pairs, or "mixed-level" pairs (see Methodology Note on LP page 3).

2. Set a time limit for students to read through the situations and come up with possible solutions. Encourage them to think of two or three possible answers for each situation.

3. When students have finished, have them find a new partner and compare their answers.

4. Check the answers as a class. See answers on LP page 42. Refer back to the relevant focus charts as necessary.

VARIATION

Have students say their answers. Ask the other students to guess which situation it goes with.

work book

For more practice, use *Grammar Dimensions 2* Workbook page 17, Exercise 5.

EXPANSION 1 [20 minutes]

Have students choose one of the situations and create a conversation incorporating as many future forms as possible.

EXPANSION 2 [50 minutes]

You may want to use Activity 4 and Activity 5 on SB page 46 after this exercise. Activity 5 can be done as homework or as an in-class interviewing activity (see Variation on LP page 47).

UNIT GOAL REVIEW [10 minutes]

Ask students to look at the goals on the opening page of the unit again. Help them understand how much they have accomplished in each area. Ask students to make sentences that use *will* and *be going to* and explain the differences in use. This is also an opportunity to ask students to identify which areas they would like more practice with and to point out that different verb tenses are covered in other units of this book. You may want to allow time for reviewing the relevant focus charts.

work book

For a crossword puzzle reviewing Unit 3 grammar and vocabulary, use *Grammar Dimensions 2* Workbook pages 18 and 19, Exercise 6.

work book

For a grammar review quiz of Units 1–3, refer students to pages 20–22 in the *Grammar Dimensions 2* Workbook.

Exam*View* Test Generator
For assessment of Unit 3, use *Grammar Dimensions 2 ExamView®*.

Use Your English

ACTIVITY 1 speaking/listening/writing

The purpose of this activity is to collect as much information as possible about the future plans and intentions of your classmates. Look at the chart below. Complete as many squares as you can by finding the required information. *Maybe* and *I don't know* are not acceptable answers! Write the information in the appropriate square as well as the name or names of the people who gave you the information. The first person to get information for three squares in a row in any direction is the winner. Good luck!

Find someone who is going to take the TOEFL® test* soon. When is she or he going to take it?	Find three people who are going to cook dinner tonight. What are they going to cook?	Find two people who are going to go to the library after this class. What are they going to do there?
Find two people who are going to play the same sport this week. What sport are they going to play?	Find someone who is going to move to another city within a year. What city is she or he going to move to?	Find someone who is going to go to the movies today. What movie is she or he going to see?
Find someone who is going to get his or her hair cut in the next two weeks. Where is she or he going to get it cut?	Find two people who are going to watch TV tonight. What are they going to watch?	Find two people who are going to celebrate their birthdays next month. What are their birth dates?

*TOEFL is a registered trademark of the Educational Testing Service (ETS). This publication is not endorsed or approved by ETS.

ACTIVITY 2 writing/speaking

STEP 1
Write predictions about the future for your teacher and five of your classmates. Write each prediction on a small slip of paper, and give each one to the appropriate person.

STEP 2
The people who receive predictions will read them aloud, and the rest of the class will decide if they think the predictions will come true.

ACTIVITY 3 writing

What are your predictions for the next ten years? What do you think will happen in the world? What do you think will happen in your country?

STEP 1
Write a brief report on your predictions. Your report should include a short introduction to your topic. It is not necessary to use *will* and *be going to* in every sentence you write!

STEP 2
When you finish writing, read your report carefully and check your use of *will* and *be going to*. Remember, it is often possible to use either one.

We have written the beginning of a report to give you some ideas, but you probably have better ideas of your own.

LIFE IN THE FUTURE

Nobody knows exactly what will happen in the future, but in my opinion, there will be many important changes in the world in the next ten years. Some of them will be good and some of them will be bad. In this short report, I am going to talk about some of my predictions for the future of the world, as well as the future of my country.

First, let me tell you about my predictions for the world ...

USE YOUR ENGLISH

The Use Your English activities contain situations that should naturally elicit the structures covered in the unit. For a more complete discussion of how to use the Use Your English activity section, (see To the Teacher, LP page xxii). When students are doing these activities in class, you can circulate and listen to see if they are using the structures accurately.

ACTIVITY 1 speaking/listening/writing [20 minutes]

You may want to use this activity as an introduction to Focus 4 on SB page 39.

1. Preview this activity by playing a quick game of Tic Tac Toe with simple Xs and Os on the blackboard. It's best if you can find a student who has played this to volunteer to play it with you.

2. Explain that this activity uses the same concept, since they are trying to answer a line of three squares in any direction—vertically, horizontally, and diagonally.

3. Tell students that they will walk around the room and ask each other questions.

4. Read aloud the information in the first square. Ask: "What question will you need to ask to find the answers?" (*Are you going to take the TOEFL® Test soon? When are you going to take it?*) Demonstrate asking and answering this question with one or two students and making notes of their answers.

5. Go through the other squares if necessary.

6. As students collect information from each other, circulate, noting any errors in the use of *be going to*.

7. When students have finished, ask for volunteers to report on their answers. Ask for additional details if appropriate.

8. Think about how (and if) you want to address possible student errors. For example, do you want to read the statements with errors and have the students find and correct them? Do you want to review Focus 2?

ACTIVITY 2 writing/speaking [20 minutes]

Use this activity after Exercise 1 on SB page 36.

1. You may want to prepare small pieces of scrap paper ahead of time for use in this activity, or have students tear scrap paper into strips.

2. Students should write five predictions each, for five different people.

3. Allow a couple of minutes for students to walk around and hand out their "predictions".

4. Have students read their predictions aloud and say if they think it will come true or not.

METHODOLOGY NOTE

This activity is meant to be light and humorous, but in case any predictions are inappropriate, you might want to add the additional rule that if anyone is uncomfortable with his or her fortune, for any reason, they can "pass"—they don't have to read their fortunes aloud to the rest of the class.

VARIATION

1. Have everyone write a prediction for themselves on a piece of paper. (They should not write their names on the papers.)

2. Collect the papers and mix them up.

3. Have each student take a paper (not their own!) and try to guess whose prediction it is.

ACTIVITY 3 writing [30 minutes]

Use this activity after Exercise 2 on SB page 37. You can also follow this activity with Web Research Activity 7 on SB page 47.

1. Introduce the topic of describing our world 100 years from now. Brainstorm a list of ways in which our world will be different. Write the topics on the board. Some examples are: *housing, food, medicine, technology, clothing, cars, communication.* (You may already have done this as part of Exercise 3 on SB page 39.)

2. Have students work in groups to write a plan for their essay, with key points and minor points in outline form. If they have studied writing a descriptive essay (in your class or in another class), this may be a chance to remind them of the key points of good essay planning.

3. Point out that they can talk about future changes in their country (if appropriate), the United States, or in the world.

EXPANSION

Make this into a peer editing activity, in which students exchange descriptions with each other.

1. Students read each other's descriptions for content. Are all statements clear? If not, they can ask the writer of the description for clarification or elaboration where necessary.

2. Students check each other's descriptions for the grammar targeted in this unit. Did they use the future tense accurately and appropriately?

ACTIVITY 6 listening/speaking

In this activity, you will create a chain story about your teacher's next vacation.

■ **STEP 1**   Your teacher will start by telling you where he or she is going to go for his or her next vacation and one thing he or she is going to do:

Teacher: *I'm going to go to Hawaii for my vacation, and I am going to climb a mountain.*

■ **STEP 2**   The next person repeats the first part and adds another statement about the teacher's vacation until everyone in the room has added to the description.

Student 1: *Ms. O'Neill is going to Hawaii. She is going to climb a mountain. She is going to swim in the ocean, too.*

ACTIVITY 7 research on the web

 **On the Web:** Choose one type of technology that you are interested in: for example, cameras, cars, computers, music players, or video games. Use an Internet search engine such as Google® or Yahoo® to research new developments. How will this type of technology be different in the future? How will it affect our lives?

ACTIVITY 8 reflection

Think of three ways you would like to improve your study skills. Write an action plan. What skills are you going to improve? How are you going to work on them?

ACTIVITY 4 speaking/listening

CD Track 5

■ **STEP 1**   Listen to the audio of an interviewer and three students talking about their goals and future plans. About how old do you think each speaker is? Take a guess. Take notes on what each speaker says in the chart below

SPEAKER	AGE	FUTURE PLANS AND GOALS
Student 1		
Student 2		
Student 3		

■ **STEP 2**   Think about your own goals and future plans. Are they similar to those of any of the three speakers? Explain to a partner.

■ **STEP 3**   Listen to the audio again. Write down all the examples you hear of the future with *will* and *be going to.*

ACTIVITY 5 speaking/listening

■ **STEP 1**   In this activity, you will interview several people about their goals and future plans. Interview at least three young people who are at different stages of their lives: college students, high school students, and children. Find out what they are going to do when they leave school. Take notes about their goals and plans or, if possible, record your interviews.

■ **STEP 2**   Make a list of the most interesting plans and share them with the rest of the class. Report your findings to the class.

■ **STEP 3**   (Optional) If you recorded the interviews, listen to the recording and take note of the different ways these native speakers talk about the future. What verb forms do they use to express the future?

ANSWER KEY

Activity 4   *Check audio script on page S-1 of this book for answers.*

USE YOUR ENGLISH

ACTIVITY 4 — speaking/listening [30 minutes]

Use this activity after Exercise 7 on SB page 42. The script for this listening activity appears on LP page S-1.

CD Track 5

STEP 1
1. Read the instructions for Step 1. Check that students understand by asking questions: What are you going to hear? What are you going to write?
2. Play the audio.
3. Give students time to fill in their notes. Then play the audio again.

STEP 2
1. Have students compare their answers and continue with Step 2 in pairs.
2. Gather and check answers for Steps 1 and 2. See answers on LP audio script page S-1.

STEP 3
1. Play the audio again while students listen and write down uses of the future. Again, refer to audio script on LP page S-1.
2. Discuss the answers and the reasons for the different uses of the future.

ACTIVITY 5 — speaking/listening [20 minutes]

Use this activity after Exercise 7 on SB page 42.

This is an opportunity to take grammar and use it outside the classroom setting. For situations where there is little or no access to native or non-native English speakers, students can conduct interviews in their own languages and then do the other steps in English.

1. Have students think about whom they will interview and describe them. They should try to interview three people of different age groups.
2. As a class, brainstorm the kinds of questions they will need to ask. For example, *What are your plans and goals for the next year? the next five years? the next ten years? What are you going to do when you leave school? graduate college? retire?*
3. If students cannot record their interviews, have students conduct their interviews in pairs or groups of three (see Methodology Note 1 on LP page 14).
4. In the next class, have students give presentations about their findings and say what they found most surprising or interesting about their interviews.

VARIATION

Have students interview each other about their future goals. You may want to help them focus their questions by working on a chart identifying and classifying their goals according to career, life, family, study, health, etc.

ACTIVITY 6 — listening/speaking [15 minutes]

Use this activity after Exercise 5 on SB page 40.

1. This activity can be done as a whole class or in groups. (The larger the group, the more difficult it is!)
2. Model the activity first with a small group.
3. Make up a sentence about your next vacation, or use the one on SB page 47.
4. Have five students in turn repeat and add a piece of information.
5. The last student gets a round of applause.
6. Have students continue the activity in groups.

ACTIVITY 7 — research on the web

See To the Teacher on LP page xxii for the purpose and use of the Web activities throughout this book. Use this activity to supplement or follow Activity 3 on SB page 45.

The purpose of this Internet search activity is to provide a natural context for using the future. An additional purpose is to encourage students to share strategies for finding information on the Internet. After talking about future changes in these different uses of technology, encourage students to share tips on how they obtained this information. What websites were most useful? What keywords did they use?

ACTIVITY 8 — reflection

See To the Teacher, LP page xxii for a more detailed explanation of the function and use of the Reflection activities throughout this book.

The dual aim of this activity is to practice using future forms and to raise awareness of study skill strategies. You may have asked students to keep a record of their *learning journal* throughout this course as suggested in To the Teacher (see LP page xxii). This reflection activity will be part of their learning record.

4

ASKING QUESTIONS
Yes/No, Wh-, Tag, and Choice Questions

UNIT GOALS

- **Understand formation of different types of questions**
- **Understand meaning of different types of questions**
- **Recognize the uses of different intonation patterns for various question types**

OPENING TASK

Any Questions?

■ STEP 1

What kinds of questions do you ask in class? Work with a partner to make a list of useful questions for learning English.

■ STEP 2

What questions could you ask the teacher in the newspaper article? Work alone or with other students to complete the questions on the facing page.

South City College 2006 Teacher of the Year!

Congratulations to Elena Dominguez, who was named Teacher of the Year. Elena was born in Venezuela and now lives in South City. She came to South City College five years ago to complete her Masters in Education. She started teaching Spanish here three years ago.

Elena is married and has one daughter. She speaks Spanish and is planning a study trip to Mexico with her students next spring. She likes jogging and cycling. Her favorite food is pineapple. She loves teaching because she learns something new every day.

Teacher of the Year

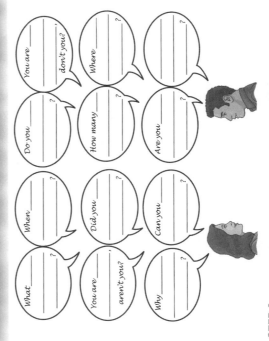

What _____ _____ ?

When _____ _____ ?

You are _____ _____ don't you?

You are _____ , aren't you?

Do you _____ _____ ?

Did you _____ _____ ?

How many _____ _____ ?

Where _____ _____ ?

Why _____ _____ ?

Can you _____ _____ ?

Are you _____ _____ ?

■ STEP 3

With a partner, role-play the conversation between you and Elena Dominguez.

ASKING QUESTIONS *Yes/No, Wh-*, Tag, and Choice Questions

ANSWER KEY

Opening Task   Step 1: Possible questions are: How do you spell . . . ? How do you say . . . ? What does . . . mean? What is the past form of . . . ? What is the opposite of . . . ? etc.

Step 2: Possible questions are:

When did you start teaching at South City College?

Where are you from? Where were you born? Where do you teach? Where do you live?

Do you like cycling? Do you teach ESL?

You're a teacher, aren't you? You're from Venezuela, aren't you?

You teach ESL, don't you? You like jogging, don't you?

Why did you come to South City College? Why do you like teaching?

Can you cycle? Can you speak Spanish?

Did you finish your Masters degree?

Are you married? Are you planning a study trip with your students?

UNIT 4

LESSON PLAN 1

UNIT OVERVIEW

In this unit, students are introduced to a variety of question forms using different grammatical structures. They are also introduced to the pronunciation and intonation patterns for different question types.

GRAMMAR NOTE

English has a variety of question forms. These include: Yes/no questions (where the expected answer is Yes or No), Wh- questions (which start with a question word such as why? or what?), choice questions, also known as alternative questions (where the answer is one of two or more choices), and tag questions (where a statement is turned into a question by adding a tag such as Isn't it? or Doesn't it?). Questions can also be formed by adding rising intonation to a statement, or a single word or phrase, e.g., On Friday? OK? This unit deals with all of the above question types.

UNIT GOALS

Some instructors may want to review the goals listed on the opener page after completing the Opening Task so that students understand what they should know by the end of the unit. These goals can also be reviewed at the end of the unit when students are more familiar with the grammar terminology.

OPENING TASK [30 minutes]

The purpose of the Opening Task is to create a context in which students will need to use the form and use of questions. At this level, students should already have some familiarity with forming questions. The problem-solving format is designed to show the teacher how well the students can produce the target structures implicitly and spontaneously when they are engaged in a communicative task. For a more complete discussion of the purpose of the Opening Task, see To the Teacher, LP page xxii.

Setting Up the Task

STEP 1

The aim of this task is to elicit a variety of different questions types and to encourage students to ask questions in the classroom. Have students discuss the photograph in pairs or groups. What questions do they think the students in the picture might have for their teacher? Brainstorm a list of questions and write them (or ask students to write them) on the board.

Conducting the Task

STEP 2

1. Read the article aloud.
2. Don't ask any questions about it. Ask your students to ask Elena questions.
3. Write two or three of their ideas for questions on the board.
4. Explain how these examples could fit into the balloons on this page.
5. Have students continue to fill in the other balloons with questions. They can work in pairs or individually.
6. They can use whatever question forms they like for the last two question balloons.

Completing the Task

STEP 3

1. Have students work in pairs to role-play the conversation between Elena and the journalist.
2. They can make up answers for any questions that are not answered in the text.

3. Ask volunteers to perform the conversation for the class.
4. Take notes of any errors in form, meaning, or use for reference later in the unit.

FOCUS 1

form
meaning

Review of Yes/No Questions

EXAMPLES

EXPLANATIONS

(a) *Question:* **Are** you Brazilian?

When you ask a *Yes/No* question, you expect the answer *yes* or *no*.

Answer: Yes, I am./No, I'm not.

(b) *Question:* Do you understand? ↗
Answer: Yes, I do./No, I don't.

Yes/No questions end with rising intonation.

	subject	*be*	
(c) *Statement:*	He	is	tired.
	be	*subject*	
Question:	**Is**	he	tired?

Yes/No questions with *be*:

Invert the subject and the verb (move the verb in front of the subject).

(d) **Are** you ready to go?
(e) **Am** I too late for dinner?
(f) **Was** the plane on time?
(g) **Were** they mad at me?

	subject	*verb*	
(h) *Statement:*	They	speak	Turkish.

Yes/No questions with other verbs:

	do	*subject*	*base verb*	
Question:	**Do**	they	**speak**	Turkish?

(i) NOT: Speak they Turkish?
(j) **Does** the bus **stop** here?
(k) **Do** you **take** credit cards?
(l) **Did** the President **know** about this?

Put the appropriate form of *do* in front of the subject. Put the base form of the verb after the subject.

	subject	*be*	*verb + -ing*
(m) *Statement:*	They	are	leaving.
	be	*subject*	*verb + -ing*
Question:	**Are**	they	**leaving?**

Yes/No questions with verbs in the progressive:

Invert the subject and *be* (move the *be* verb in front of the subject). Put the -ing form of the verb after the subject.

(n) **Is** your computer **working** today?
(o) **Am** I **meeting** you tomorrow?
(p) **Was** it **raining** there?
(q) **Were** her parents **visiting?**

For information on *Yes/No* questions with present perfect and past perfect, see Units 13–14, and 19.

EXAMPLES

EXPLANATIONS

	subject	*modal*	*base verb*
(r) *Statement:* It		will	rain.
	modal	*subject*	*base verb*
Question: **Will**	it		rain?

Yes/No questions with modals:
Invert the subject and the modal (put the modal in front of the subject). Put the base form of the verb after the subject.

(s) **Would** you repeat that?
(t) **Can** you help me?

(u) *Statement:* She asked him out. ↗
Question: She asked him out? ↗

Statement form of *Yes/No* questions:
A statement said with rising intonation is also a type of *Yes/No* question. This type of question is common in informal conversation.

(v) You're from England?
(w) Sasha can come?
(x) He's 40 years old?
Yes, he is.

When a statement form question is used, the speaker usually expects the listener to agree.

EXERCISE 1

Get together with a partner and make a list of five *Yes/No* questions you could ask your teacher. Write them here or in a notebook. You will have an opportunity to ask these questions later in the unit.

1. _____

_____

2. _____

_____

3. _____

_____

4. _____

_____

5. _____

_____

4 LESSON PLAN 1

FOCUS 1 [10 minutes]

1. **Lead-in:** Choose some *Yes/No* questions from the Opening Task to introduce this focus chart. Ask your students:

   Is Elena from Brazil? Does she teach Spanish? Is she going to Mexico? Does she like jogging and cycling?

2. When they have answered *yes* or *no* to several of these questions, explain that these are all examples of *Yes/No* questions.

3. Ask students for a few more examples. Choose one question with *be* and one question with *do*. Write them on the board. Ask students to explain how these questions are formed. This will highlight the need to introduce the auxiliary *do* with main verbs.

4. Model the intonation by reading the examples in the box. Students can read along with you or repeat after you.

5. This can also be done in pairs, with their partners determining if they sound "interested" or not. Students repeat their sentences until their partner is satisfied.

LANGUAGE NOTE

Some students may have difficulty with the use of the auxiliary verb *do* with present simple verbs (except for *be*). Once students recognize that *do* is the simple present auxiliary (or "helping") verb, the subject-auxiliary inversion for *yes/no* questions is regular:

They <u>are</u> Slovak. → <u>Are</u> they Slovak?
They (<u>do</u>) speak Slovak. → <u>Do</u> they speak Slovak?
They <u>are</u> speaking Slovak. → <u>Are</u> they speaking Slovak?
They <u>can</u> speak Slovak. → <u>Can</u> they speak Slovak?

If you find some students using subject-verb inversion with *have* as the main verb (as with *be*), you can point out that in American English this form is rarely used:

NOT: Have you the time? → Do you have the time?

If they have studied British English, they may have encountered this structure.

PRONUNCIATION NOTE

Many languages use rising intonation for question forms, so this concept is often not a problem. Some languages, however, use a "flatter" tone than English, which may make students sound disinterested or bored in English.

Using a greater range in rising intonation is especially important when turning statements into questions, as in (u)–(x). Over-use of this question form can sound unnatural in English.

EXERCISE 1 [15 minutes]

This exercise provides practice of the form and meaning of *Yes/No* questions.

1. Ask students for one or two suggested *Yes/No* questions they want to ask you and write them on the board.

2. Have students continue to think of other questions in pairs.

3. Encourage students to help each other correct errors.

4. While they are working, you can circulate around the room to note some of their errors for later discussion.

5. When they have finished, write some of their questions on the board or overhead projector for class editing.

6. You do not need to answer the questions at this stage as this will come up later in Exercise 14 on SB page 64.

   Suggestion: Pass around one or two sheets of paper and have each pair of students write at least one question on it (questions must not be repeated). You can use this later at the "press conference" in Exercise 14.

For more practice, use *Grammar Dimensions 2* Workbook page 23, Exercise 1, and page 24, Exercises 2 and 3.

EXPANSION 1 [20 minutes]

Activity 1 on SB page 66 is a fun walk-around activity that can be used to practice *Yes/No* questions following this exercise.

EXPANSION 2 [20 minutes]

The following exercise can be used to provide further practice of *Yes/No* questions.

1. Ask students to imagine that they are new students coming to class on the first day. They meet a student who has attended class here for some time. What questions would they ask? The rules are that they can only ask *Yes/No* questions, and they should try to alternate *be* verb questions with other verbs.

2. Have students make a list of ten questions in their notebooks.

3. Have students work in pairs to ask and answer their questions.

4. Circulate while students are doing this and take notes of errors.

5. Correct errors together as a class by writing them on the board and asking students to correct them.

FOCUS 2

form meaning

Review of Wh-Questions

EXAMPLES

(a) Q: What is your name?
A: Elena.

| Who | What | When | Where |
| Why | Whose | Which | How |

(b) Where do you come from?
(c) When did you arrive?
(d) How many languages do you speak?

(e) Q: Why are you late?
A: Because I missed the bus.

| Wh-word | be | subject |

(f) **Where** | **is** | the restroom?
(g) **What** | **was** | her name?
(h) **Who** | **are** | his friends?
(i) **What's** | | the time?
(j) **Where's** | | my car?

(k) Q: When did she get here?
A: Just a few minutes ago.

| Wh-word | do | subject | base verb |

(l) Who(m) | do | you | love?
(m) What | does | a judge | do?
(n) Where | did | Nicole | live?

(o) Q: What time can you leave?
A: As soon as this class is over.

| Wh-word | modal | subject | base verb |

(p) How long | can | I | stay?
(q) When | will | she | come?

EXPLANATIONS

A Wh-question usually begins with a Wh-word and expects the speaker to give information rather than yes or no in the answer.

Wh-questions usually end in falling intonation.

Wh-questions with be:

Choose a Wh-word. Invert the subject and the verb.

In informal speech, is is often contracted to 's in Wh-questions.

Wh-questions with other verbs:

Choose a Wh-word. To form a question, follow the Wh-word with a form of do.
In informal speech, use who instead of whom.

Wh-questions with modals:

Choose a Wh-word. To form a question, put the modal directly after the Wh-word and before the subject.

EXERCISE 2

Get together with a partner and write down five Wh-questions you could ask your teacher. Write them on a piece of paper or in your notebook. You will have an opportunity to ask them later in the unit.

EXERCISE 3

Bruno and Ken are friends. Bruno has just introduced Ken to his cousin, Marta. Ken is very interested in getting to know more about her, so now he is asking Bruno all about her.

Get together with a partner and look at the answers that Bruno gave. What questions do you think Ken probably asked? Write them in the appropriate place.

Ken: (1) *Does she live alone/go to school/have a car/have a job* ?

Bruno: Yes, I think she does.

Ken: (2) *Does she smoke/go school/have a car* ?

Bruno: No, she doesn't.

Ken: (3) *What time does she usually go to sleep* ?

Bruno: Usually around midnight.

Ken: (4) *Do you see her very often* ?

Bruno: Not usually.

Ken: (5) *Where does her family live* ?

Bruno: In Buenos Aires.

Ken: (6) *How often does she talk with them* ?

Bruno: Three times a week, I think.

Ken: (7) *Is she married* ?

Bruno: No, she isn't.

Ken: (8) *Was she ever married* ?

Bruno: Yes, I'm pretty sure she was.

Ken: (9) *When did she get divorced* ?

Bruno: Last year, or maybe the year before. I can't remember exactly.

Ken: (10) *Do you think she'd be interested in going out with me* ?

Bruno: I have no idea. You'll have to ask her that question yourself.

Now change partners. Read the questions that you wrote while your new partner reads Bruno's answers. When you finish, change roles to read your partner's dialogue. Compare your questions with a partner's questions. Does Marta seem like a different person? In what ways?

ANSWER KEY

Exercise 2 Answers will vary. Possible answers are listed above.

FOCUS 2 [15 minutes]

This focus chart reviews the form and meaning of questions that start with *Where, When, Why, Who,* and *How.* Further discussion of these question forms is given in Focus charts 3 and 4.

1. **Lead-in:** Choose some *Wh-* questions from the Opening Task to introduce this focus chart. Ask your students:

   Where is Elena from? What does she teach? Where is she going?

2. When they have answered several of these questions, explain that these are all examples of *Wh-* questions.

3. Ask students for a few more examples. Choose one question with *be* and one question with *do.* Write them on the board. Ask students to explain how these questions are formed. This will highlight the word order of verb and subject after the question word, and the need to introduce the auxiliary *do* with main verbs.

4. Model the examples in the box, focusing on intonation.

5. Have students repeat or practice in pairs.

PRONUNCIATION NOTE

Aside from the difference in expected response, the intonation of these questions also differs from those in Focus 1.

While you should avoid discussing this issue at this point, be sure to stress the importance of the use of falling intonation, as rising intonation in *Wh-* questions indicates the need for clarification or shows surprise:

   What time is it? ↘ (general request for information)
   What time is it? ↗ (checking information or indication of surprise)

The use of falling intonation often takes some practice, as in many languages falling intonation is reserved for statements. The use of rising intonation is discussed in Focus chart 4.

EXERCISE 2 [15 minutes]

This exercise provides practice of the form and meaning of *Wh-* questions.

1. Ask students for one or two suggested *Wh-* questions they want to ask you and write them on the board.

2. Have students continue to think of other questions in pairs.

3. Encourage students to help each other correct errors.

4. While they are working, you can circulate around the room to note some of their errors for later discussion.

5. When they have finished, write some of their questions on the board or overhead projector for class editing.

6. You do not need to answer the questions at this stage as this will come up later in Exercise 14 on SB page 64.

7. **Suggestion:** Pass around one or two sheets of paper and have each pair of students write at least one question on it (questions must not be repeated). You can use his later at the "press conference" in Exercise 14 on SB page 64.

EXERCISE 3 [15 minutes]

This exercise provides practice in forming both *Yes/No* and *Wh-* questions.

1. Read (or ask a students to read) the introduction to the exercise.

2. Point out the difference between answers to *Yes/No* questions and *Wh-* questions by comparing number 1 and number 3. Ask: *Do you think this is a Yes/No questions or a Wh- question? Why?*

3. Read the first question, and ask for possible alternatives. (*Does Marta work in a bank? Does Marta go to school every day?* etc.) For number 1, all questions must be in the simple present, and not use a *be* verb.

4. Have students work in pairs to complete the exercise.

5. Circulate to provide help and advice.

6. When they have finished, have them change partners to complete the second part of the exercise.

7. Discuss possible questions as a class. See suggested answers on Lesson Planner (LP) page 53.

For more practice, use *Grammar Dimensions 2* Workbook page 25, Exercise 4; page 26, Exercise 5; or page 27, Exercise 6.

EXPANSION [20 minutes]

You may want to use Activity 1 on SB page 66 again, this time focusing on both *Yes/No* and *Wh-* questions. Or you can use Activity 8 on SB page 69, which is a fun way to use visuals to practice questions.

FOCUS 3

Wh-Questions That Focus on the Subject

form ● meaning

EXAMPLES

(a) Q: **Who(m)** did you call?
   A: I called Tony.
      object

(b) Q: **Who** called you?
   A: Martin called me.
      subject

Wh-word Verb

(c) Q: **Who** lives here?
   A: Shan lives here.

(d) Q: **Who** told you?
   A: Herb did.

(e) Q: **What** annoys her?
   A: Everything.

(f) Q: **What** music annoys her?
   A: Rock music.

(g) Q: **What** bands annoy her?
   A: Aerosmith and Bon Jovi.

EXPLANATIONS

This question asks about the object. *Who* is more common in informal speech. *Whom* is very formal.

This question asks about the subject.

For *Wh*-questions about the subject, put the appropriate *Wh*-word in front of the verb. Do not use *do* in the question.

Use *what* to ask a general question about something.

Use *what* + a noun when you want a more specific answer. Make the verb singular or plural to agree with the noun.

EXERCISE 4

Get together with another student or someone in your class for this exercise. First read the report on the next page. Next, think of the questions you need to ask your friend in order to complete the report. Write the questions in the "Question Box." Ask your partner all of the questions without showing them to him or her. Finally, use the answers that your friend gives you to complete the report.

Report:

My friend (1) _____ is from (2) _____ and speaks
(3) _____ languages: (4) _____. He/she was born in
(5) _____ and he/she has (6) _____ brothers and sisters.
His/her favorite subjects in school were (7) _____. He/she is taking this
class because (8) _____. In his/her free time, he/she likes to
(9) _____. His/her favorite (10) _____ is/are
(11) _____. When he/she first came here, (12) _____
surprised him/her. After he/she finishes school, he/she hopes to (13) _____.
(14) _____ make(s) him/her happy, but (15) _____ make(s)
him/her angry. Finally, there is one more thing I'd like to tell you about my friend:
(16) _____.

QUESTION BOX

1. What is your name _____ ?
2. Where are you from _____ ?
3. How many languages do you speak _____ ?
4. What languages do you speak _____ ?
5. Where were you born _____ ?
6. How many sisters and brothers do you have _____ ?
7. What were your favorite subjects in school _____ ?
8. Why are you taking this class _____ ?
9. What do you like to do in your free time _____ ?
10. What are your favorite (foods/sports/movies, etc.) _____ ?
11. See Question 10. _____ ?
12. What surprised you when you first came here _____ ?
13. What do you hope to do after you finish school _____ ?
14. What makes you happy _____ ?
15. What makes you angry _____ ?
16. What is one more thing you'd like to tell me _____ ?

ANSWER KEY

Exercise 4 *Question Box:* For items 10, 11, and 16, answers will vary. The other likely answers are listed above.

LESSON PLAN 1

FOCUS 3 [10 minutes]

This focus chart presents the differences in form and meaning between questions about the subject and the object.

1. **Lead-in:** Write the following sentences (with the blanks) about your students on the board. (You may extend this list with sentences appropriate to your class.)

_____ sits next to (Julie)? (name

of a student in your class)

_____ works in a (bank)?

_____ helps you (sleep) better?

2. Have students ask you *Wh-* questions to fill in the blanks. They will need to ask questions about the subject.

3. As they try to form these questions, point out the difference in form from questions about the object (see Language Note below).

4. Read the examples and the explanations in the focus chart.

LANGUAGE NOTE

There are some differences between questions about the subject and the object. For instance, if the question is about the subject, the *Wh-*word replaces the subject and there is no inversion.

Q: *Who sits next to you?*
A: *Jan sits here.* -or- *Jan does.*

However, when the question is about the object, there is inversion.

Q: *Who are you talking to?*
A: *I'm talking to Ali.*

Whom is also worth noting when discussing questions since the object form whom is rarely used in spoken English. It is most often used in formal contexts such as academic writing. In formal written English, whom is optional when referring to an object, but you must use whom when it follows a preposition—e.g., Who(m) were you talking to? To whom were you talking?

EXERCISE 4 [20 minutes]

This exercise provides practice in making *Wh-* questions about the subject and the object of a sentence.

1. The exercise has three steps: (1) reading the report; (2) writing the questions; (3) asking questions and filling out the report.

2. Read the first sentence of the report and ask students to provide the questions that will be needed to fill in the first two blanks. (1. What is your name? 2. Where are you from?)

3. Explain that these are to be written in the box below the report (or in their notebooks).

4. Have students work individually to write the other questions. See suggested answers on LP page 55.

5. Circulate to provide help and advice.

6. When they have finished writing, have students work in pairs to ask each other the questions and fill out the report.

7. Ask volunteers to read their report to the class.

8. Go over the questions together, focusing on the difference between subject and object questions.

work book

For more practice, use *Grammar Dimensions 2* Workbook page 27, Exercise 7; and page 28, Exercise 8.

EXPANSION [40 minutes]

You may want to use Activity 5 (speaking) and Activity 6 (listening) on SB page 68 to provide further practice of *Wh-* and *Yes/No* questions.

EXERCISE 5

Chris is talking to Robin about his next vacation. Read their conversation below and write a question to go with each of Chris's answers. When you're finished, compare your questions with other students' in class.

Robin: (1) _Where are you going for your next vacation_ ?

Chris: I'm going to Borneo for two weeks.

Robin: (2) _Have you been to Borneo before_ ?

Chris: No, it'll be my first trip to Borneo.

Robin: (3) _What interests you about Borneo (Or: Why do you want to go there?)_ ?

Chris: The unique wildlife really interests me.

Robin: (4) _Who are you going with_ ?

Chris: I'm going with two environmentalists on a study trip.

Robin: (5) _Where/When did you meet them_ ?

Chris: I met them on a summer course last year.

Robin: (6) _What equipment are you taking with you_ ?

Chris: We're taking backpacks and camping equipment.

Robin: (7) _What worries you most about the trip_ ?

Chris: They have some poisonous snakes there, which worries me a little.

Robin: (8) _When are you leaving_ ?

Chris: We're leaving on Sunday morning.

Robin: (9) _How long does the journey take_ ?

Chris: It takes twenty hours by plane.

Robin: (10) _What time do you/does the flight leave_ ?

Chris: The flight is at 4 P.M.

FOCUS 4

use

Wh-Questions with Rising Intonation: Checking Information

EXAMPLES	EXPLANATIONS
(a) A: **Where** are you from? ↗ B: Vanuatu.	Most *Wh*-questions end with falling intonation.
(b) A: **Where** are you from? ↗ B: Vanuatu. It's in the south Pacific.	A *Wh*-question with rising intonation shows that you are not sure about what you heard or that you want to check that you heard something correctly. The *Wh*-word is also stressed (said strongly).
(c) A: Jennifer Lopez was here last night. B: **Who** was here last night? ↗ A: Jennifer Lopez.	
(d) A: Jennifer Lopez was here last night. B: **Who?** ↗	Sometimes, just the *Wh*-word (with rising intonation) is used.

EXERCISE 6

Complete the conversation with appropriate *Wh*-questions. For each question, draw an arrow ↗ or ↘ to show if the question ends with falling or rising intonation

Example: Albert: So, what did you think of the new Eisentraut movie? ↗

Leslie: It was O.K., I guess, but I expected something more from a movie that cost $200 million to make.

Albert: (1) _How much did it cost_ ↗ ?

Leslie: $200 million. Amazing, isn't it? It's hard to imagine that amount of money.

Albert: (2) _What's the movie about_ ↗ ?

Leslie: It's an action movie set in the future, but I thought it was rather slow-moving. In fact, I almost fell asleep a couple of times.

Albert: (3) _How long is it_ ↗ ?

Leslie: It's about two hours, maybe a little longer. Luckily the seats were really comfortable.

Albert: (4) _Where did you see it/Where was it playing_ ↗ ?

Leslie: At that new movie theater on Fourth Street, across from the parking garage. It only opened a couple of weeks ago, so it's got a state-of-the-art sound system, thick carpets, terrific popcorn. . . .

Albert: (5) _How much was the ticket/How much did it cost_ ↗ ?

Leslie: Twelve dollars.

Albert: (6) _How much_ ↗ ?

Leslie: Twelve dollars . . . I'm not kidding! I can't believe I spent twelve bucks on a movie that really wasn't very good.

EXERCISE 5 [15 minutes]

This exercise provides practice with *Yes/No*, *Wh-*, subject, and object questions.

1. Read (or ask a students to read) the introduction to the exercise.
2. Point out that the clues to the type of questions are in the answer (as before in Exercise 3).
3. Read the first question, and ask for possible alternatives.
4. Have students work in pairs to complete the exercise.
5. Circulate to provide help and advice.
6. When they have finished, have them read the conversation aloud.
7. Discuss possible questions as a class. See suggested answers on LP page 56.
8. **Suggestion:** This exercise may also be set as homework and checked in class.

For more practice, use *Grammar Dimensions 2* Workbook page 28, Exercise 8.

EXPANSION 1 [30 minutes]

You may want to use Activity 2 on SB page 66 as a follow-up to this exercise.

EXPANSION 2 [20 minutes]

1. Use the questions generated by students in Activity 2.
2. Have each student write one question on a piece of paper.
3. Collect the papers, mix them up, and redistribute them.
4. Students now have to write the answers on another piece of paper.
5. Give each student a number. They should write the number on their answer paper.

6. All students will now pin their answers around the walls of the classroom (not the questions).
7. Everyone then walks around reading the answers and trying to work out what the questions were.
8. When they have finished, you can check the answers by asking students to say the number and the question, and check this with the original owner of the question.

FOCUS 4 [10 minutes]

Point out the importance of the proper use of intonation, as misunderstandings can easily occur.

1. **Lead-in:** Show the use of intonation to signal a difference in meaning by reading the following dialog:

Initial Question:
Q: *Where are you from?* ↘
A: *Seattle.*

Follow-up Question:
Q: *Where?* ↗ (rising intonation for checking information)
A: *Seattle.* (old information clarified)

or

Q: *Where?* ↘ (falling intonation for further information)
A: *Just northeast of downtown.* (new information)

2. Model the examples in the box and have students repeat.
3. Read the following examples, and have students identify whether you are checking information (rising) or asking for further information.

A: *I saw* Pirates of the Caribbean.
B: *What film did you see?* ↗
A: Pirates of the Caribbean.
A: *I went to the movies last night.*
B: *What film did you see?* ↘
A: Pirates of the Caribbean.
A: *I went to Florida last week.*
B: *Where did you go?* ↘

A: *I went to Florida.*
A: *I went to Florida last week.*
B: *Where did you go?* ↗
A: *To Miami.*

PRONUNCIATION NOTE

Intonation refers to the rise and fall of the voice to add a layer of meaning. Although there are individual as well as regional variations in the use of intonation, every language has certain fixed intonation patterns. In Spanish, for example, all questions are accompanied by a rising intonation. In English, this can make all *Wh-* questions sound is if the speaker is checking information. Speakers of some other languages may find it difficult to make their voice rise and fall. Point out that a very slight rise or fall is sufficient to show the intended meaning, but if their intonation is constantly flat, it may signal boredom, lack of interest, or lack of enthusiasm.

EXERCISE 6 [20 minutes]

This exercise provides practice in recognizing when to use appropriate intonation with questions.

1. Do the first questions together with your students.
2. Have students work individually to complete the exercise.
3. Check the answers. See suggested answers on LP page 57.
4. Have students practice the intonation in pairs. You may find it helpful to have them exaggerate their intonation at first.
5. Ask volunteers to perform the conversation for the class.

FOCUS 5

Choice Questions

form

meaning

use

EXAMPLES	EXPLANATIONS
(a) A: Are you a **graduate student or a professor?** B: I'm a graduate student.	A choice question has two or more possibilities, or options. The speaker expects you to choose one of these options in your answer. You can add more information in your answer if you want.
(b) A: Do you live in a **dorm or an apartment?** B: I live off campus, in an apartment.	
(c) Does Tina walk ⟋ to school or take ⟋ the bus?	Choice questions have a different intonation pattern from *Yes/No* questions. *Yes/No* questions have rising intonation at the end; choice questions have rising intonation in the middle and falling intonation at the end.
(d) A: Are you from Malaysia or from Indonesia? B: Neither. I'm from Singapore.	
(e) A: Would you like coffee or tea? B: I'll have some tea, please.	Choice questions are often used to get information quickly or to make offers (please see Unit 16 for more information on making offers with *Would . . . like*).
(f) A: (Do you want) paper or plastic? B: Paper, please.	In informal conversation, the first part of the question is sometimes dropped. Answers to choice questions are often very short. Adding *please* to your answer makes it more polite.

EXERCISE 7

Thongchai is a new student from Asia. You want to find out some information about him. Complete the following choice questions with options that are similar in meaning and form.

1. Are you from Thailand or _____?

2. Do you speak Chinese or _____?

3. Do you eat noodles or _____ for breakfast?

4. Do you live _____ or _____?

5. Are you going to study _____ or _____?

6. Do you walk to class or _____?

7. Do you like to play tennis or _____?

Practice asking and answering the questions you completed with a partner.

EXERCISE 8

Guess where each of the choice questions on the left was probably asked. Choose from the places or situations listed on the right.

QUESTIONS	PLACES/SITUATIONS
1. Paper or plastic?	A. a cash register in a department store
2. Would you like coleslaw or french fries with that?	B. a job interview
	C. a gas station
3. Do you want premium grade or regular?	D. a small shop selling hats and T-shirts
4. Will that be cash or charge?	E. an airline office
5. First class or economy?	F. a fast-food restaurant
6. Do you say "large" or "extra large"?	G. a check-out counter in a supermarket
7. Do you prefer mornings or evenings?	

Practice asking and answering the questions with a partner. Imagine yourself in each place or situation. Use more than one way of answering.

ANSWER KEY

Exercise 7 *Answers will vary.*

Exercise 8 1. *G* 2. *F* 3. *C* 4. *A* 5. *E* 6. *D* 7. *B*

LESSON PLAN 1

FOCUS 5 [10 minutes]

This focus chart presents the form and meaning of questions where the answer is one of two or more choices given in the question, as well as the intonation patterns associated with them.

1. **Lead-in:** Describe some situations where choice questions are common—e.g., in a restaurant (eat-in or take-out?), in a department store, (debit or credit?), at a supermarket check-out (paper or plastic?). Have students suggest different types of questions common in these situations.
2. Write one or two questions from the box on the board. Ask a volunteer to come to the board and draw the intonation pattern above the words as you are speaking.
3. Model all the examples in the box and have students repeat.
4. Read the explanations and ask students for some additional examples.

PRONUNCIATION NOTE

In English, choices are indicated by rising pitch on each item until the last item on the list, which is indicated by falling pitch. Ending the final item on a rising pitch often indicates that the listener is able to add more items to the list. For example:

Q: *Do you want coffee ↗ or tea ↘ ? (indicates two choices)*
A: *Tea, please.*
OR
Q: *Do you want coffee ↗, tea ↗ juice ↗ . . .? (indicates there may be other possibilities)*
A: *Actually, I'll just have some water.*

EXERCISE 7 [20 minutes]

This exercise provides practice with the formation and intonation of choice questions.

1. Have students work individually to complete the questions (adapting the questions as appropriate to their partner).
2. Circulate and provide help and advice.
3. Have students work in pairs to read the questions and provide feedback to each other on their intonation.
4. Encourage alternative versions of the questions using two or more choices.
5. Ask volunteers to read their questions.

For more practice, use *Grammar Dimensions 2* Workbook page 29, Exercise 9.

EXPANSION [20 minutes]

You may want to use Activity 4 on SB page 67 as a follow-up to this exercise.

EXERCISE 8 [10 minutes]

This exercise is a helpful activity for contextualizing the places where we are likely to hear choice questions.

1. Have students cover the right-hand side of the chart with a piece of paper or another book.
2. Ask them to work in pairs and try to guess where each question might be asked.
3. Check the answers as a class. See answers on LP page 59.
4. Have students work in pairs to think of other similar questions in these or other contexts.
5. Ask volunteers to read out their questions. The other students will guess where it was asked.

EXPANSION 1 [30 minutes]

You may want to use Activity 10 on SB page 69 after this exercise. This activity can be used to follow

up Exercise 8 by having students focus on asking choice questions in their questionnaire—e.g., *Do you prefer to study in a group or on your own? Do you check your spelling in a dictionary, or on the Internet?*

EXPANSION 2 [20 minutes]

For a different perspective on using questions, you may want to use Activity 7 on SB page 69. This activity provides practice in using questions to develop ideas for the content of an essay and may be adapted to suit an essay topic that they have recently been assigned in your or another class.

FOCUS 6

Tag Questions

form

meaning

EXAMPLES

statement	*tag*
(a) He is nice,	isn't he?
(b) She isn't here,	is she?
(c) We're late,	aren't we?
(d) They like it,	don't they?
(e) NOT: They like it,	like they?
(f) You didn't go,	did you?

statement	*tag*
affirmative +	*negative*
(g) They play tennis,	don't they?
(h) The car was hot,	wasn't it?
(i) NOT: The car was hot,	was not it?
(j) Our teacher will help,	won't he?
(k) She is sleeping,	isn't she?
(l) We can wait,	can't we?
(m) I am right,	aren't I?
(n) NOT: I am right,	amn't I?

statement	*tag*
negative +	*affirmative*
(o) Your friends don't drive,	do they?
(p) It wasn't hot,	was it?
(q) You won't help,	will you?
(r) The baby isn't sleeping,	is she?
(s) We can't wait,	can we?

(t) Q: You're not cold, are you?	
A: No, I'm not.	
(u) NOT: Yes, I'm not.	
(v) Q: You're cold, aren't you?	
(w) A: Yes, I am.	
(x) NOT: No, I am.	

EXPLANATIONS

A tag question is a statement, followed by a short question (a tag).

Tag questions are often used in conversation.

The speaker expects a *yes* or *no* answer.

The verb in the tag agrees with the subject.

An affirmative statement has a negative tag.

The speaker thinks that the answer will probably be *yes.*

The verbs in negative tags are contracted.

A negative statement has an affirmative tag.

The speaker thinks that the answer will probably be *no.*

The verbs in affirmative tags are not contracted.

When you answer a tag question, respond to the statement, not to the tag.

If you agree with the statement:

Answer *no* to a negative statement.

Answer *yes* to an affirmative statement.

EXPLANATIONS

It's not always necessary to use the words *yes* or *no* in your answers.

EXAMPLES

(y) Q: She left, didn't she?
A: (Yes,) she did.
OR Right. OR I think so.

(z) Q: They won't call, will they?
A: (No,) they won't.
OR I doubt it. OR Probably not.
OR I don't think so. OR No way.

No way is very informal.

EXERCISE 9

Ivana is talking with her school's career counselor. Complete the counselor's questions with an appropriate tag.

1. You are studying business and computers, _aren't you_ ?

2. Computer skills are very important nowadays, _aren't they_ ?

3. You won't finish until next June, _will you_ ?

4. Your grades aren't final yet, _are they_ ?

5. You also speak Russian, _don't you_ ?

6. That's a difficult language, _isn't it_ ?

7. And you worked as a store manager in your vacations, _didn't you_ ?

8. You don't want to work in a large company, _do you_ ?

9. Those jobs can be very stressful, _can't they_ ?

10. But you want a job with good career opportunities, _don't you_ ?

11. There are a lot of different possibilities, _aren't there_ ?

12. We'll meet again and talk some more about it next week, _won't we_ ?

LESSON PLAN 1

FOCUS 6 [15 minutes]

Examples (a) to (s) deal with the formation of tag questions. Examples (t) to (z) deal with answering tag questions. The intonation of tag questions is discussed in Focus chart 7.

1. **Lead-in:** Write a chart on the board with three columns headed: **Sure, Not sure,** and **Don't know.** Tell students you are going to ask them some questions and they will tell you if they are sure or not sure about the answer. Start with some easy questions about yourself which you are sure they will be able to answer. For example, where they live, or where you were born, or what languages you speak. Your dialogue may go like this:

You: *Do you know where I was born?*

Student: *Were you born in Hawaii?*

You: *Are you sure or not sure?*

Student: *Not sure.*

You: *So how would you check this information? What questions could you ask?*

Student: *Are you from Hawaii?*

You: *That's good if you don't know the answer. But let's say you think I was born in Hawaii, and you want to check that. What could you ask?*

Student: *You're from Hawaii?*

If students can't come up with the tag question (*You're from Hawaii, aren't you?*), provide the model and continue to practice using other facts about yourself or about students in the class.

2. Have students read the examples in the box and see if they can come up with any rules about the formation of tag questions.

3. Check their guesses by reading the explanations sections of the box. (They may come up with some extra rules or queries, see Language Note below).

LANGUAGE NOTE

The key issues concerning question tags are:

• Auxiliary verbs must match in the statement and tag (but note irregular use of *are* after the first person singular as in example (m) *I'm right, aren't I?*)

• Negative tags go with affirmative statements, and affirmative tags go with negative statements. (Note that it is possible to have an affirmative tag after an affirmative statement—e.g., *So you're going to college, are you?* This point is not dealt with in this unit.)

• Other points not mentioned in this focus chart: The subject may be omitted in informal speech—e.g., *Nice day, isn't it?* Negative words used in an affirmative statement require an affirmative tag—e.g., *He's never late, is he?* When the statement uses *everybody, somebody, nobody,* the tag uses the subject *they*—e.g., *Everybody is here today, aren't they?*

• The answer to a tag question corresponds with the statement that is being verified. If you agree with an affirmative statement, the answer is *Yes.* If you agree with a negative statement, the answer is *No.* Speakers of some Asian languages may agree with a negative statement by saying *yes,* e.g., Q: *You haven't finished yet, have you?* A: * *Yes.* (=Yes, that's right, I haven't finished.)

EXERCISE 9 [10 minutes]

This exercise provides practice with correct formation of tag questions.

1. Read the introduction to the exercise to establish the context. Explain that all the questions are asked by the career counselor and they are all tag questions.

2. Do the first question together.

3. Set a time limit for students to complete the questions individually.

4. Check the answers. See answers on LP page 61.

5. If necessary, go over the questions again by asking students to close their books. Read each statement and select a student to supply the appropriate tag.

EXPANSION 1 [20 minutes]

You can provide further practice of question tags by using the following exercises.

1. Have students work in pairs. One student closes the book, the other will read the statements from the examples in the focus chart. The first student will supply the appropriate tag. Then they swap roles.

2. Have students work in pairs to create a "test" similar to Exercise 9. They should try to cover all the different types of auxiliaries. Have pairs exchange tests with each other.

3. Extend this practice by focusing on the correct answers to tag questions. Model one or two examples of questions that require a clear *Yes* or *No* answer. For example,

Q: *Katrin wasn't absent yesterday, was she?*

A: *No, she wasn't.*

Q: *Tomorrow's class meets at 9:00, doesn't it?*

A: *Yes, it does.*

For more practice, use *Grammar Dimensions 2* Workbook page 30, Exercise 11.

Then have students work in pairs to write three *Yes* and three *No* questions. Select students to read them to the class. The class will provide the appropriate answer.

EXPANSION 2 [30 minutes]

You may want to use Activity 3 on SB page 67 as a follow-up to this exercise.

EXERCISE 10

Deb and Sylvie are talking on the phone and making plans for their friend Bouzid's birthday.

Work with a partner. Fill in the blanks with an appropriate tag question and then put the conversation in order. Write the order of the conversation on the next page. We have done some of them for you.

DEB

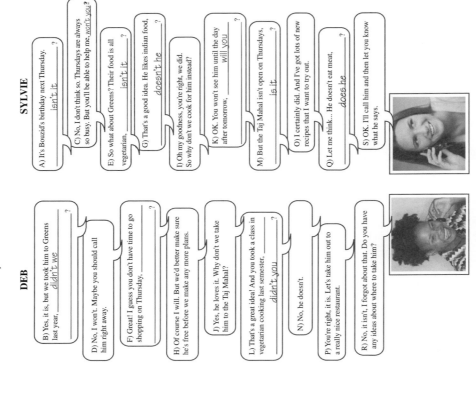

B) Yes, it is, but we took him to Greens last year, _didn't we_ ?

D) No, I won't. Maybe you should call him right away.

F) Great! I guess you don't have time to go shopping on Thursday, _____ ?

H) Of course I will. But we'd better make sure he's free before we make any more plans.

J) Yes, he loves it. Why don't we take him to the Taj Mahal?

L) That's a great idea! And you took a class in vegetarian cooking last semester, _didn't you_ ?

N) No, he doesn't.

P) You're right, it is. Let's take him out to a really nice restaurant.

R) No, it isn't, I forgot about that. Do you have any ideas about where to take him?

SYLVIE

A) It's Bouzid's birthday next Thursday. _isn't it_ ?

C) No, I don't think so. Thursdays are always so busy. But you'll be able to help me. _won't you_ ?

E) So what about Greens? Their food is all vegetarian, _isn't it_ ?

G) That's a good idea. He likes indian food, _doesn't he_ ?

I) Oh my goodness, you're right, we did. So why don't we cook for him instead?

K) OK. You won't see him until the day after tomorrow, _will you_ ?

M) But the Taj Mahal isn't open on Thursdays, _is it_ ?

O) I certainly did. And I've got lots of new recipes that I want to try out.

Q) Let me think... He doesn't eat meat, _does he_ ?

S) OK. I'll call him and then let you know what he says.

---

1. _A_
2. _P_
3. _G_
4. _J_
5. _M_
6. _R_
7. _Q_
8. _N_
9. _E_
10. _B_
11. _I_
12. _L_
13. _O_
14. _F_
15. _C_
16. _H_
17. _K_
18. _D_
19. _S_

You can find the answers to this exercise on page A-15.

FOCUS 7   Tag Question Intonation

use

EXAMPLES

(a) Q: His name is Tom, isn't it? ↗
    A: Yes, it is.

(b) Q: It's not going to rain today, is it? ↗
    A: No, it isn't.

(c) Q: His name is Tom, isn't it? ↘

(d) Q: It's not going to rain today, is it? ↘

EXPLANATIONS

Falling intonation in tag questions shows that the speaker is fairly sure that the information in the statement is true. The speaker is also sure that the listener will agree.

A person making an affirmative statement with falling intonation (a) expects the answer *yes*. A person making a negative statement with falling intonation (b) expects the answer *no*.

Rising intonation in tag questions shows that the speaker is not sure if the information in the statement is true.

EXERCISE 11

Go back to the conversation in Exercise 10. With a partner, draw arrows ↘ or ↗ to show falling or rising intonation in the tags. One of you will take Sylvie's part and the other will take Deb's. Read the exercise aloud to practice intonation. Finally, get together with another pair and listen to each other's performances.

EXERCISE 12

Your teacher will ask some tag questions. Circle **Y** if you think the expected answer is yes and **N** if you think the expected answer is no.

1. Y	N	4. Y	N	7. Y	N
2. Y	N	5. Y	N	8. Y	N
3. Y	N	6. Y	N	9. Y	N

ANSWER KEY

Exercise 11 Answers will vary depending on how sure the speaker is of the information.

Exercise 12 Refer to the page 63 Lesson Plan for questions. Answers will vary.

LESSON PLAN 1

EXERCISE 10 [15 minutes]

This exercise provides further practice in the correct formation of different types of tag questions.

1. Read the introduction to the exercise to establish the context.

2. Have students work in pairs to read the conversation and fill in the missing tags.

3. When they have finished they can put the conversation in the correct sequence.

4. Check the answers as a class. See answers on LP page 62.

5. Students can read the conversation aloud if they want, but they will come back to this exercise to read it aloud in Exercise 11 after studying intonation in Focus Chart 7.

EXPANSION [10 minutes]

Have students adapt the conversation using their own information.

FOCUS 7 [10 minutes]

1. **Lead-in:** Check that students are able to identify the difference between rising and falling intonation. If you wish, you may review some of the *Wh-* questions from Focus Chart 4 on SB page 57.

2. Model the examples in the box. Falling intonation show that the speaker expects an agreement (which can be *Yes* or *No*). Rising intonation shows that the speaker is not sure what the answer will be.

3. Read the explanations.

EXERCISE 12 [20 minutes]

This exercise provides you with a good opportunity to make sure students understand that expected answers agree with the **statement**, not the tag.

1. Read the following questions to the class. Adapt the information in the questions to suit your context. **Use falling intonation for all the questions** (meaning that you expect agreement). Your students will have to decide whether the agreement is *Yes* or *No.*

2. Students can complete the answers in their books or out loud.

1. *He's late, isn't he?* (Expected answer: *Yes.*)
2. *You live in (Oregon), don't you?* (Expected answer: *Yes.*)
3. *We're having a test tomorrow, aren't we?* (Expected answer: *Yes.*)
4. *You're not leaving, are you?* (Expected answer: *No.*)
5. *It's (Friday) tomorrow, isn't it?* (Expected answer: *Yes.*)
6. *They won't come, will they?* (Expected answer: *No.*)
7. *You eat meat, don't you?* (Expected answer: *Yes.*)
8. *You don't understand, do you?* (Expected answer: *No.*)
9. *These are difficult, aren't they?* (Expected answer: *Yes.*)

LANGUAGE NOTE

Intonation in tag questions shows how certain the speaker is of his or her information. Since a person using falling intonation with a tag question expects the listener to agree with his/her statement, the listener should be more careful to "soften" the disagreement. For example,

Q: *You're from Kuwait, aren't you?* ↘
A: *Actually, I'm from Qatar.* OR A: *Well, no, I'm really from Qatar.*

Q: *Summers in New Orleans are cold, aren't they?* ↘
A: *Sorry, but I think summers in New Orleans are really hot!*

Depending on the culture(s) you work with, you may need to point out that it **is** possible to disagree with the speaker, depending on the formality of the situation, and provided that the listener is polite in his or her response.

EXERCISE 11 [10 minutes]

This exercise provides practice of the use of intonation in tag questions.

1. Go back to Exercise 10.

2. Have students work in pairs to draw arrows over each question tag.

3. Students can read the conversation aloud in pairs. The swap roles and read it aloud a second time.

4. Circulate and provide help.

5. Ask volunteers to perform the conversation for the class.

EXERCISE 13

Read each tag question aloud, using the intonation as marked. For each question, tell whether the speaker expects a certain answer, and if so, what the speaker expects the answer to be, *yes* or *no*. Answer the question the way you think the speaker expects it to be answered.

	(a) Is the speaker fairly sure what the answer will be?	(b) If *yes* to (a), answer the question.
1. It's going to rain today, isn't it? ↗	No	
2. You don't know where my umbrella is, do you? ↗	yes	*Yes, you are.*
3. You're driving today, aren't you? ↗	No	
4. It's not my turn to drive, is it? ↗	No	
5. You made lunch for me, didn't you? ↗	yes	*Yes, you are.*
6. I didn't forget to thank you, did I? ↗	No	
7. I'm pretty forgetful, aren't I? ↗	yes	*Yes, you are.*

EXERCISE 14

Your teacher has been nominated for a "Teacher-of-the-Year Award" and will appear at a press conference to answer questions from journalists and reporters. You and your classmates are all newspaper reporters. You need to write a profile of your teacher for your paper and want to get as much information from him or her as possible.

STEP 1 Get together with two or three other students. As a group, choose eight questions that you would most like to ask your teacher at the press conference. You can use some of the questions you wrote in Exercise 1, Exercise 2, and the Opening Task if you want to, or you can make completely new questions. Important note:

- Two questions must be *Yes/No* questions.
- Two questions must be *Wh*-questions.
- Two questions must be *tag* questions.
- Two questions must be choice questions.

ANSWER KEY

Exercise 14 *Answers will vary.*

STEP 2 When you have decided on your questions, your teacher will hold the press conference, but he or she will only answer your questions if they are correctly formed and if the intonation is appropriate. If another group asks a question that your group wanted to ask, you must ask a different question (your teacher will not answer the same question twice). Write your questions and the answers below. If possible, record the "press conference" and listen to the recording to check your intonation and your teacher's answers.

QUESTIONS	ANSWERS

LESSON PLAN 1

EXERCISE 13 [10 minutes]

This exercise provides practice in using the correct intonation with tag questions, and understanding the expected answer.

1. Select students to read the questions aloud. You may want to model the questions and have students repeat after you.

2. Have students work in pairs to practice reading the questions aloud and fill out the chart.

3. Check the answers as a class. See answers on LP page 64.

4. You can also make an overhead transparency of the chart to discuss it as a class.

EXERCISE 14 [20 minutes]

Exercise 14 gives students the opportunity to use a range of question types in a creative role-play.

1. Remind students of the article in the Opening Task. Ask them to imagine that you have won a similar "Teacher of the Year" Award. They are to play the role of newspaper reporters.

2. Ask students to look back at the questions they wrote in Exercises 1 and 2. You may already have collected some of these questions as suggested in the Teacher's Notes for Exercises 1 and 2.

3. Have students work in a group to list the questions they want to ask. They can only ask six questions, but they should have some questions in reserve, in case their question is asked by another group.

4. Circulate to help with problems or questions.

CULTURE NOTE

Some students may find it inappropriate to ask the teacher personal questions in this exercise. On the other hand, some may ask questions that are too nosy! If you would rather avoid these possible potential problems, you can assign different topics to different groups, for example, questions about your job, your students, or your hobbies and favorite sports, etc. You may also want to reserve the right to "pass" on questions that you feel are too personal.

5. You may want to set up your "conference" by changing your normal classroom seating pattern. Seat yourself at a table at the front of the class, for example, or in the center of the class, with students gathered around you.

6. You can appoint a "secretary" to take notes of all the questions you are asked.

7. Decide ahead of time how you will handle incorrect questions. You can shake your head, or say *incorrect*, or just ignore the question and move on the next questioner.

8. Each student can ask a question and they should take notes of the answers. They will use their notes later to write a group report.

9. Start the conference.

10. When all the questions have been asked, have students return to their seats and write an article about you (similar to the one in the Opening Task) in class or for homework.

11. You can also go over some of the incorrect questions and ask students to correct them.

UNIT GOAL REVIEW [10 minutes]

Ask students to look at the goals on the opening page of the unit again. Together, find the pages of the unit where information on each goal can be found.

ExamView® Test Generator — For assessment of the Unit 4, Use *Grammar Dimensions 2 ExamView®*.

EXPANSION [20 minutes]

Make a 4-column chart on the board or overhead projector (see below).

Yes/No	Wh–	Choice	Question Tags

2. Ask students for examples of each of the different question forms and write them in the chart.

3. Practice saying some of them with different intonation, asking them what the different intonation patterns mean.

Use Your English

ACTIVITY 1 speaking/listening

STEP 1

Your teacher is going to stick a piece of paper on your back and on the backs of your classmates. Get up and walk around the class, looking at what is written on your classmates' backs.

STEP 2

Your job is to guess what is written on your back. You can find this out by asking questions. You can also answer the questions that your classmates ask you about what is written on their backs. For the first five minutes, you can only ask *Yes/No* questions. Refuse to answer any question that is not a *Yes/No* question. When your teacher gives you a signal, you can ask any kind of question that you like. Here are some possible *Yes/No* questions to ask: Is this a person? Is this person male or female? Is this food? Is it expensive? Is it an object? Is this an animal? Is this a person? How big is this? Where was he or she born? What color is this?

ACTIVITY 2 speaking/writing

The international student office at your school is preparing a short guide for students who have just arrived in this country. The purpose of this guide is to give new students a clear idea of what to expect when they arrive here. You have been asked to write a chapter called "Frequently asked questions."

Get together with two or three other students and make a list of all the questions that people in this country frequently ask you. Compare your lists with those of other students in the class. Use the information from your classmates to make a list of the questions that people here frequently ask international students and that new students should be ready to answer.

ACTIVITY 3 speaking/writing

Work in a group. You are going to play the role of career counselor to one person in your group. Make a list of 10–15 questions that would help that person decide what kind of career to choose. Write the questions on a sheet of paper. When you are ready, choose one person to answer your questions (you can add further questions during the interview!). Then change roles.

ACTIVITY 4 writing/reading

STEP 1

In this activity you cannot speak, but you can write. Sit down next to a student that you do not know very well. Spend a couple of minutes thinking about some of the things you would like to know about this person. Take a piece of paper and write **one** question for your partner to answer. Pass the question to your partner. Read the question that your partner gives you. Without speaking, write your answer to the question and write another question for your partner to answer. **Do not speak at all.**

STEP 2

Exchange papers with your partner. Read your partner's answer to your question and answer his or her question to you. Continue writing questions and answers to each other until your teacher tells you to stop. Now you can speak!

Optional: With your partner's permission, share some of the information from your silent interview with the rest of the class.

STEP 3

Look back over the questions that you and your partner wrote. Were you able to use any of the kinds of questions discussed in this unit?

USE YOUR ENGLISH

These Use Your English activities are designed to provide more communicative practice of the grammatical structures in this unit. While you can note errors to provide feedback later, the emphasis in these activities is on more natural communication. You may find it helpful to recap and discuss some of the errors you hear at the end of the activity.

ACTIVITY 1 speaking/ listening [20 minutes]

You may want to use this activity after Exercise 1 on SB page 51, and again after Exercise 3 on SB page 53. This activity is especially helpful in practicing *yes/no* questions, but can be used to include *Wh-* questions.

1. Choose a group of words that are all of a similar category—e.g., animals, jobs, furniture, items you find in a kitchen. Be sure to choose items you think your students are likely to be familiar with. You can use pictures instead of words.

2. Write each word separately on a small piece of paper. You will need one piece of paper for each student.

3. Hand out the papers to your students and have each student stick a paper on their neighbor's back (without showing it to them). The best way to stick things on students' backs is to use self-stick notes or index cards with sticky tape.

4. Model the activity by asking a student to stick an item on your back. Ask questions to find out what your item is.

5. Have students walk around the class and ask each other questions to find out what their item is. They can only ask each person one question before moving on.

6. At the end of the activity, if there are some people left who cannot guess their items, other students can give helpful hints. If some students guess their items very quickly, give them a second item to guess.

ACTIVITY 2 speaking/ writing [30 minutes]

You may want to use this activity after Exercise 5 on SB page 56. This activity provides students with the opportunity to create their own questions using their knowledge of student life.

1. Read the description of the activity with your students.

2. Check that they understand they will be writing questions from the point of view of people in the United States asking questions from other countries. If you are in a non-U.S. context, students can think of questions that visitors from the United States or other countries might ask them.

3. Circulate and take notes of any errors to go over with the class.

4. Ask volunteers to role-play a few of the questions and answers for the class.

VARIATION

If you have access to the Internet, you can have students access a university's website to log on to its student services page. Be sure to find a site that has a list of "FAQs" (Frequently Asked Questions) first. They can write their FAQs from the international student perspective.

ACTIVITY 3 speaking/ writing [30 minutes]

You may want to use this activity after Exercise 9 on SB page 61. This activity continues the theme of career counseling from Exercise 9 and can be used to provide either further practice of *Yes/No* questions, or a variety of different question types.

1. Read the description of the activity with your students. Ask if students have ever met with a career counselor and ask for some suggestions for possible questions.

2. Tell students what kinds of question types you would like them to practice (*Yes/No* questions, or a variety of different question types).

3. Have students work in small groups of four of five students to create a list of 20 questions.

4. When they have finished, they will choose one person in the group to answer all the questions.

Suggestion: One person in each group can move to another group to answer their questions.

6. Circulate and take notes of errors if appropriate. Select and mention some of the most interesting questions.

ACTIVITY 4 writing/ reading [20 minutes]

You may want to use this activity after Exercise 7 on SB page 58. This activity focuses on accuracy as all questions have to be written. It can be used for all question types.

1. Have students walk around the room and sit down next to a student they do not know well. (They will need to bring pen and paper with them.)

2. This activity is like a silent conversation. Each student can write just one question, exchange it with a partner, and write the answers to their partner's questions.

3. You can set a time limit of 10 minutes, and make it into a competition to see who can ask and answer the most (correctly formed) questions.

4. At the end of the "conversation," they should have a list of written questions and answers.

5. Ask students to edit their work, or exchange papers with another pair for peer editing.

6. Circulate and take notes of recurring errors.

VARIATION

If you have a class discussion list or your students have e-mail accounts, you can do this activity via computer, rather than on paper.

ACTIVITY 5 speaking/listening

Your English teacher has just quit her job and is now relaxing on a beach in Tahiti. Your school is desperately searching for a new teacher. Your classmates have decided to take matters into their own hands and you have decided to interview teachers yourselves. Pretend one of your classmates is an applicant for the position. Ask him or her some questions about his or her experience, interests, and future goals. Listen to your classmate's answers. They may help you ask other questions.

ACTIVITY 6 listening/writing

CD Tracks
6,7

A friend of yours has applied for a job teaching English in Latvia. She cannot travel to Latvia for a job interview, so the school has to interview her by phone. You are at her house when the school calls. You can hear her half of the conversation (the answers that she gives), but you can't hear the questions that the interviewer asked.

Listen to your friend's half of the conversation. In the first column, write the questions that you think the interviewer **probably** asked. Then listen to the complete interview to compare your questions with the ones the interviewer **actually** asked. Use the second column to write any questions that are different from the ones in the first column.

PROBABLE QUESTIONS	ACTUAL QUESTIONS

ACTIVITY 7 speaking/writing

Imagine you are going to write an essay on one of these topics: (1) Learning a foreign language, (2) Applying for a job, or (3) Using the Internet for research.

What three main questions will your essay answer? Compare your questions with another student. Write your questions on the board and choose the best three for each title.

ACTIVITY 8 speaking/listening

Bring in a photograph and give it to your teacher. Your teacher will mix up the pictures and distribute them randomly. Look at your photograph for thirty seconds and then give it back to the teacher. The teacher will put all the photographs on a table or hang them up. Students will take turns being questioned by the class. When it is your turn, your classmates will ask you questions about the picture you looked at. They will try to guess which picture it was. Try to use all types of questions: *Yes/No*, *Wh-*, statement form, choice, and tag.

ACTIVITY 9 research on the web

 InfoTrac® College Edition: Go to *InfoTrac* to find information about a country you are interested in. Type in the name of the country and *Fact File*, for example, *France Fact File*. Make a list of questions using information in the article. Ask your classmates if they know the answers.

ACTIVITY 10 reflection

Work in a group. Choose one aspect of learning English, for example, writing or vocabulary. Write a questionnaire about how students in your class learn and practice this skill. Interview other students in your class using your questionnaire. Report the results to the class. What general patterns did you find?

ANSWER KEY

Activity 6 Check audio script on page S-2 of this book for actual questions.

Activity 9 Possible answers for France, for example, include: How large is France? What is the capital? What is France famous for? What is the population of France?

USE YOUR ENGLISH

ACTIVITY 5 speaking/ listening [20 minutes]

You may want to use this activity after Exercise 4 on SB pages 54–55. This activity provides an opportunity to apply their knowledge of question forms to using questions in a real-life context.

1. Read the description of the activity with your students.

2. Brainstorm a few possible questions and write them on the board (include some *Yes/No* and some *Wh-* questions).

3. You may want to suggest possible topic areas—e.g., qualifications, teaching experience, future goals, etc.

4. Have students work in pairs or groups to create a list of questions.

5. Ask a volunteer to play the role of job applicant.

6. **Suggestion:** If your class is large, this might be intimidating for one student, so divide your class into two groups, and have each group work independently. It may help to change the seating arrangement so that all students are seated facing or gathered around the job applicant.

ACTIVITY 6 listening/ writing [20 minutes]

CD Tracks 6 and 7

You may want to use this activity after Exercise 4 on SB pages 54–55. It is a good follow-up to Activity 5.

1. Read the description of the activity with your students.

2. Explain that in their first listening, students will hear only the job applicant's half of the conversation. They have to guess what the questions are. In the second listening, they will hear both sides of the conversation and can check their guesses.

3. Play the first part of the audio.

4. Allow students some time to compare their answers (do not check answers at this stage).

5. Play the second part of the audio.

6. Check their answers. See audio script on p. S-2.

7. As a class, discuss some of the questions students came up with, noting some of the variations.

ACTIVITY 7 speaking/ writing [20 minutes]

You may want to use this activity after Exercise 8 on SB page 59. This activity provides practice in using questions to develop ideas for the content of an essay and may be adapted to suit an essay topic that students have recently been assigned in your or another class.

1. Choose one of the essay titles (or another title that they have been assigned) and brainstorm a few possible questions on the board.

2. Ask students to choose a title and write a list of questions for their topic.

3. You may want to specify whether these titles are for descriptive, argument, or process type essays. Alternatively, you can wait to see what kinds of questions your students come up with and categorize them as a way of wrapping up the activity.

4. Discuss and compare questions as a class.

ACTIVITY 8 speaking/ listening [20 minutes]

You may want to use this activity after Exercise 3 on SB page 53. This activity can be used to practice all questions types, or to focus on one specific question type.

1. During the class before this, ask students to bring in one photograph each. You may prefer to bring in the photographs yourself, especially if your class has been working on a particular theme, such as travel or the environment.

2. Collect the pictures, mix them up, and hand them out again. (Make sure no one gets their own picture back again.)

3. Set a time limit of 30 seconds for students to look at their picture and remember all the details.

4. Collect the pictures and spread them out on a table.

5. Have students gather round the table.

6. Each student in turn has to answer questions about their picture. The other students have to work out which picture it is.

7. Make notes of interesting and creative questions.

ACTIVITY 9 research on the web

This activity directs students to use InfoTrac. See p.vi for more information about this web resource. They will use InfoTrac to locate an article containing facts about their chosen country. They will take notes of the most interesting facts and turn these facts into questions to ask their classmates. If your students have trouble accessing InfoTrac, this activity can also be done on the web.

ACTIVITY 10 reflection

This activity encourages students to use questions to reflect on their different learning styles. You may want to refer them to the questionnaire about grammar in Unit 1, page 1 for an example. Students may use multiple choice, *Yes/No*, *Wb-*, or choice questions. This activity can be done in class or for homework.

5

MODALS OF PROBABILITY AND POSSIBILITY

Could, May, Might, Must, Couldn't, and Can't

UNIT GOALS

- Use *could, may, might, must, couldn't,* and *can't* to show how certain you are about a present situation

- Form statements and questions to describe probability and possibility in the present and past

- Use the progressive with modals of probability and possibility

- Use *could, may, might, will/be (probably) going to, may not,* and *might not* to talk about future probability and possibility

OPENING TASK

Identify the Mystery Person

One evening toward the end of March, a New York taxi driver found that someone had left a briefcase on the back seat of his cab. When he opened it, he found that the briefcase was empty, except for the things you can see on the next page.

■ **STEP 1**

With a partner, examine everything on the next page carefully. Can you find any clues about the identity of the owner of the briefcase? Use the chart to write down your ideas and to show how certain you are about them.

HOW CERTAIN ARE YOU?

GUESSES

	Name	Sex	Age	Marital Status	Occupation	Likes and Interests	Family and Friends	Habits	Recent Activities	Future Plans	Anything else?
Less than 50% certain (it's possible)											
90% certain (it's probable)											
100% certain (it's certain)											

STEP 2

Now get together with a group and share your ideas about the identity of this mystery person, showing how certain you feel about each one.

Example: *He might be a businessman.*

ANSWER KEY

Opening Task Step 1: Answers will vary, but some likely answers regarding the owner's identity are:

The owner's name must be Chris Murray.

His sex must be male.

He might be middle-aged or older.

He must be married.

He might be a businessman.

He might be learning Japanese.

He must like sports (golf, tennis).

He could like the movies.

He could like chess.

He might like opera and theatre.

He must be planning a trip to Japan.

He visited Paris for a business meeting.

He ate at a French restaurant.

He stayed at a hotel in Paris.

He must like to travel.

5 LESSON PLAN 1

UNIT OVERVIEW

Unit 5 provides practice with modals of probability and possibility: *could, may, might, must, couldn't, and can't.*

UNIT GOALS

Some instructors may want to review the goals listed on this page after completing the Opening Task so that students understand what they should know by the end of the unit. These goals can also be reviewed at the end of the unit when students are more familiar with the grammar terminology.

OPENING TASK [20 minutes]

The purpose of the Opening Task is to create a context in which students will need to use the modals *could, may, might,* and *must.* The problem-solving format is designed to show the teacher how well students can produce the target structures implicitly and spontaneously when they are engaged in a communicative task. For a more complete discussion of the purpose of the Opening Task, see To the Teacher, page xxii.

Setting Up the Task

1. Introduce the topic by looking at the picture and talking about things that people usually carry in their purses, wallets, backpacks, or briefcases.

2. Hold up your own purse, briefcase, or wallet and invite guesses about what is probably inside. Ask a volunteer student to do the same. The aim is to show that we can often guess something about the owner of the purse or wallet from its contents.

3. As students make guesses about what is in your purse/wallet, you can prepare them for the chart by asking: *Are you certain? Are you really certain? 100 percent certain? Are you 50 percent certain? Not very certain? Don't worry*

about modal use at this point since the focus here is on preparing students for the chart.

4. Look at the picture and make guesses about this person.

Conducting the Task

STEP 1

1. Check that students understand the situation: A briefcase was found in a taxi and they are trying to guess the identity of the owner by looking at the contents.

2. Go through the chart, checking that students understand what they are to do. If they are 100 percent certain that the mystery person is male, they write "male" in the 100% row. If they are less than 50 percent certain that he or she is 40 years old, they write "40" in the Less than 50% row, and so on. They do not need to write full sentences, just the relevant piece of information. Encourage them to examine everything very carefully before completing the chart.

3. Have students work in pairs to examine the clues and fill out the chart.

4. Take notes of possible errors in form, meaning, or use, but do not correct at this stage. Students will get an opportunity later to focus on accuracy, converting the information into full sentences. Exercises 2, 4, 9, and 11 also revisit the task.

5. Circulate to provide help if needed. Encourage students to speculate and think of alternatives.

6. There is no right or wrong answer to this task. It all depends on whatever ideas the students come up with.

Closing the Task

STEP 2

1. Bring the whole class together to share ideas and to establish how certain students are about each item on the chart.

2. You can make an overhead transparency of the blank chart or write the headings on the board and fill in the different ideas that students contribute.

3. Use this chart as a springboard for the information in Focus 1, by building on students' own ideas to weave in or elicit possible modal uses.

GRAMMAR NOTE

The following errors should not be presented to students. Rather, they are presented for teacher reference. The asterisks (*) indicate sentences that contain errors.

Typical student errors (form)

- Using the infinitive after must, e.g. * *They must to speak English.* (Instead of: *They must speak English.*)

- Use of auxiliary do ro make questions and negatives with modals, e.g. * *Where did she could go?* (Instead of: *Where could she have gone?*)

- Using third person with modal verbs, or with the accompanying main verb, e.g. * *He mights know him.* * *Jack could lives here.*

Typical student errors (use)

- Confusion between the different meanings of *must* for obligation and probability.

- Confusion between the different meanings of *can and can't* for permission, ability, and probability.

- Use of present tense modals to talk about the past, e.g. * *She should take the test yesterday.* (Instead of: *She should have taken the test yesterday.*)

- Use of *can* as a modal of probability, e.g. * *She can be sick today.* (Instead of: *She could/might/may be sick today.*)

FOCUS 1

Using *Could, Might, May, Must, Couldn't,* and *Can't* to Show How Certain You Are about the Present

EXAMPLES	EXPLANATIONS
Situation: He's got a baseball hat on.	*Could, might, may,* and *must* show how certain or not you are about a present situation.
Less Certain ⟷	**Possible (less than 50% certain)**
(a) He **could** play baseball.	Use *could, might,* or *may* to express possibility
(b) He **might** play baseball.	(to show that you believe something is
(c) He **may** play baseball.	possible, but you are not very certain if it is true or not). You are making a guess.
More Certain	*May* shows that you are a little more certain
Situation: She is wearing a white coat.	that something is true.
Less Certain ⟷	
(d) She **could** be a doctor.	
(e) She **might** be a doctor.	
(f) She **may** be a doctor.	
More Certain	
Situation: He's wearing a baseball hat. He's carrying a baseball glove.	**Probable (about 90% certain)** Use *must* to express probability (to show that you believe something is probably true).
(g) He **must** play baseball.	
Situation: She is carrying a stethoscope.	You are **almost** certain that this is true. You are drawing a conclusion, based on what you know.
(h) She **must** be a doctor.	
(i) He **couldn't** be a soccer player.	Use *couldn't* and *can't* to show that you are almost certain that something is **not** true.
(j) She **can't** be a teacher.	
Situation: It's the middle of a baseball game. He is throwing a ball to his teammate.	**Certain (100% certain)** These are facts. You are completely certain about these situations. Do not use *could, might, may,* or *must.*
(k) He **plays** baseball.	
Situation: She performed heart surgery on my mother in the hospital and saved her life.	For information on other ways of using *could, might, may,* and *must,* see Units 10, 11, and 17.
(l) She **is** a doctor.	
(m) She **isn't** a nurse.	

EXERCISE 1

Look at the situations below and complete the sentences to show how certain the speaker is about each one.

SITUATION	POSSIBLE
She always wears a purple hat.	**Less Certain**
	⟷ 1. She _could_ like purple.
	2. She _might_ like purple.
	3. She _may_ like purple.
	More Certain
Situation	**Probable**
She always wears a purple hat and a purple coat.	4. She _must_ like purple.
Situation	**Certain**
She always wears purple clothes, she drives a purple car, and lives in a purple house surrounded by purple flowers.	5. She _likes_ purple.
Situation	**Possible**
He's carrying a French newspaper.	**Less Certain**
	⟷ 6. He _could_ be French.
	7. He _might_ be French.
	8. He _may_ be French.
Situation	**More Certain**
	Probable
He's carrying a French newspaper and he's speaking French to the people with him.	9. He _must_ be French.
Situation	**Certain**
He's carrying a French newspaper and he's speaking French to the people with him. He was born in France and has a French passport.	10. He _isn't_ British.
	11. He _is_ French.

Compare your answers with a partner's and then check what you have written with the information in Focus 1.

GRAMMAR NOTE

Modal verbs are special kinds of auxiliary verbs used before other verbs to add meaning, for example, probability, possibility, certainty, or obligation. In the present form, modal verbs are not used with other auxiliaries to form questions or negatives. In questions, they invert with the subject. In negatives, they are followed by *not*. They are not followed by an infinitive using *to* but by the base verb alone.

Modal verbs can have a number of different meanings. For example, *must* and *can't* are used for obligation and permission, as well as for different degrees of probability as explained in this unit. For this reason, modal verbs can be deceptive. They look familiar, but can present a variety of problems on the level of meaning, as well as of form.

FOCUS 1 [15 minutes]

1. **Lead-in:** Bring in a selection of pictures of people. Ask students to make guesses about the pictures, for example, *What is his or her job? What country is it? What season?* Each guess must be based on a fact about the picture. Write their statements on the board, categorizing them according to whether they are facts (e.g., *It's snowing.*) or guesses (e.g., *It must be winter.*). For guesses, ask students to estimate how sure they are and write an approximate percentage next to each one. At this point it is not necessary to use modals, but if students come up with them, you can use them as a bridge to the next step.

2. Copy the arrow onto the board (or on an overhead transparency) labeling the top with "Less Certain" and the bottom as "More Certain," as in the diagram.

3. Read the situations from the left-hand column. Then read the sentences and ask students where they go on the arrow.

4. Write each statement up in the appropriate place along the arrow, as in (a)–(c) and (d)–(f). See Language Note.

LANGUAGE NOTE

There is very little difference in meaning between *could* and *might*, although *may* expresses a slightly stronger possibility. There is, however, a big jump in meaning between all of these and *must*.

- *Might* is not the past tense of *may* when used as a modal of probability. *Might* represents a lower probability than *may*.
- The opposite of *must* is *can't*, not *mustn't*. *Mustn't* is reserved for modals of prohibition.
- *Can* is not used as a modal of probability in the affirmative.

Note that future tense modals *could*, *might*, and *may* have the same form as the present—e.g., *It might rain tomorrow.* The future meaning is shown by time markers, or by context. Future probability and possibility with modals are presented in Focus Chart 5.

Situation (continued): *He smells like an ashtray.*
Response: *He must smoke.*
Situation: *He's puffing on a cigarette. He always has a cigarette after dinner.*
Response: *He definitely smokes!*

work book For more practice, use *Grammar Dimension 2* Workbook page 31, Exercise 1.

EXPANSION 1 [20 minutes]

You may want to use Activity 1 on Student Book (SB) page 84 as a follow-up to this activity.

EXPANSION 2 [20 minutes]

Activity 2 on SB page 84 is an extension of Activity 1 and provides further practice of present tense modals.

EXERCISE 1 [10 minutes]

This exercise provides students with practice in making deductions using *could, might, may, must, couldn't,* and *can't.*

1. Read the first situation together with your students and ask for suggested answers.

2. Have students work individually to complete the rest of the chart.

3. Circulate to see if there are any problems, questions, or errors.

4. Check the answers as a class. Refer to the answer key on Lesson Planner (LP) page 73.

5. Go over any problems, referring back to Focus Chart 1 if necessary.

Suggestion: For further practice, use the situation below or make up others.

Situation: *He's got a box of matches in his pocket.*

Responses: *He could smoke. He might smoke. He may smoke.*

FOCUS 2

form

Modals of Probability and Possibility

EXAMPLES	EXPLANATIONS
subject + modal + verb	**Affirmative Statements**
(a) Jack **could** live here.	Modals come before the base form of the verb.
(b) NOT: Jack could lives here.	
(c) Alex **might** know him.	Modals have only one form. They do not take *s*.
(d) NOT: Alex mights know him.	
(e) Shirley **may** be at home.	
(f) NOT: Shirley maybe at home.	*Maybe* is not a modal.
subject + modal + not + verb	**Negative Statements**
(g) She **must not** like cats.	*May not, might not,* and *must not* are not usually contracted when they express possibility or probability.
(h) Bo **might not** know that.	
(i) That's impossible! Ron **couldn't** be in Las Vegas. I saw him just a few minutes ago. He **can't** be there.	*Couldn't/can't* show that you strongly believe that something is impossible.
	Couldn't/can't are usually contracted. However, *could* expresses very weak certainty. It shows that you are not very certain if something is possible.
modal + subject + verb	**Questions**
(k) **Could** Sid be in Reno?	*May* and *must* are not used in questions about possibility and probability.
(l) **Might** Cathy know about this?	
Question: *Answer:*	**Short Answers**
(m) Does he take the train? I'm not sure. He **might.**	Use the modal by itself in short answers.
(n) Does Sue like Thai food? She **may not.** She doesn't like spicy food very much.	
(o) Is Jay at home? He **might be.** He's not in his office.	Use the modal + *be* in short answers to questions with *be*.
(p) Is Tom busy right now? He **might not be.** I'll ask him.	Use the modal + *not* for negative short answers.

EXERCISE 2

Turn back to the Opening Task on pages 70–71. Make statements about the owner of the briefcase. Use *must, may, could, might, couldn't,* or *can't* to show how certain you feel. Share your opinions with your classmates and be ready to justify them as necessary.

Example: Name: *In my opinion, the owner of the briefcase might be called Chris Murray because this name is on the boarding pass. However, this boarding pass could belong to somebody else.*

1. SEX: In my opinion, the owner of the briefcase _____

   because _____

2. OCCUPATION: I believe he or she _____

   because _____

3. MARITAL STATUS: This person _____

   I think this because _____

4. LIKES AND INTERESTS: _____

5. HABITS: _____

6. AGE: _____

ANSWER KEY

Exercise 2   Answers will vary depending on the inferences students made in the Opening Task.

LESSON PLAN 1

FOCUS 2 [10 minutes]

1. **Lead-in:** Have students cover the right side of the chart. Allow some time for them to read the examples in pairs and try to work out the rules for the formation of modals.

2. Discuss their answers as a class.

3. Let them uncover the right side of the chart and compare their rules with those in the book.

4. Model the pronunciation of some of the examples (see Pronunciation Note below).

5. Point out that (j) through (o) are Yes/No questions and should end with rising intonation.

6. Have students practice the pronunciation by repeating after you or by working together in pairs.

PRONUNCIATION NOTE

Both words in the modal + negative "pairs" —*must not, might not, may not*—are stressed and not reduced or contracted in speech.

EXERCISE 2 [15 minutes]

This exercise provides an opportunity for students to review their sentences in the Opening Task, this time focusing on accuracy.

1. Turn back to the Opening Task chart on SB page 71.

2. Have students go through the chart, using the information to make statements using *could, might, may, must, couldn't,* and *can't.* Each deduction should be supported by a fact.

3. Students can work in pairs or write their sentences individually.

4. When they are ready, ask volunteers to read their statements aloud.

5. Ask other students to try and contradict each statement read aloud by making other logical guesses based on the information.

Student A: *He might be French because he stayed in Paris.*

Student B: *I think he must be American because he received a letter at his address in New York.*

Student C: *He could be a French man who lives in New York.*

Student D: *But he doesn't have a French name. And his Japanese book is in English. He must be American.*

6. Try to keep the discussion going as long as possible. The focus here is on meaning.

7. Make a list on the board of the deductions most people agree on. Now you can focus on accuracy. Answers to some of the questions may come up in the focus charts later in this unit.

For more practice, *use Grammar Dimension 2* Workbook page 32, Exercise 2.

EXPANSION 1 [30 minutes]

You may want to use Activity 6 on SB page 87 as a follow-up to this activity.

EXPANSION 2 [20 minutes]

Activity 7 on SB page 87 is an extension of Activity 6 and provides further practice of present tense modals in the context of writing a description.

FOCUS 3

Modals of Probability and Possibility in the Past

EXAMPLES	EXPLANATIONS
subject + modal + have + past participle	**Affirmative Statements**
(a) Vi **may have left.**	Choose the appropriate modal + *have* + past participle to show how certain you are about something that happened in the past.
(b) I'm not sure how Liz went home last night. She **could have taken** a cab.	
(c) There's nobody here; everyone **must have gone** out.	
subject + modal + not + have + past participle	**Negative Statements:**
(d) I **may not have seen** him.	Choose the appropriate modal + *not* + *have* + past participle to show how certain you are that something did not happen in the past.
(e) Selena **might not have been** in town last week.	
(f) Darius **couldn't have robbed** the store. He was at home with me all evening.	
modal + subject + have + past participle?	**Questions:**
(g) **Could** she **have known?**	Choose the appropriate modal + subject + *have* + past participle to ask about possibility and probability in the past. Remember that *must* and *may* are not usually used in questions about possibility or probability.
(h) **Might** the police **have followed** the stolen car?	
(i) Q: Did Jerry talk to Kramer last night?	**Short Answers:**
A: I'm not sure. He **may have.**	Use the appropriate modal + *have* in short answers.
(j) Q: Did Bernadette remember to go to the store?	
A: She **must have.** The refrigerator is full of food.	
(k) Q: Was Vinny depressed?	Remember to use the appropriate modal + *have* + *been* in short answers to questions using *be.*
A: It's hard to say. He **might have been.**	
(l) NOT: He might have.	

EXERCISE 3

Add an appropriate short answer to the questions in these conversations. The first one has been done for you. Several responses are possible.

A: Where's Mike? Is he at lunch?

B: I don't know. He (1) _____ might be./may be _____

A: Do you know if he speaks Turkish?

B: Yes, he (2) _____ might/may _____. He lived in Turkey for ten years.

A: Do you think he has time to help me translate this letter?

B: I'm not sure. He (3) _____ might/may not _____ (not). He'll be in meetings all day today.

A: Do you know if he'll come back here later?

B: He (4) _____ might/may _____, but I don't really know.

A: Will he be here tomorrow?

B: He (5) _____ might/may not be _____ (not). I think he is planning to work at home tomorrow.

A: If I leave a message, will he call me? It's very urgent.

B: Well, he (6) _____ might/may _____, but I can't say for sure.

ANSWER KEY

Exercise 3 *Answers may vary. Possible answers are listed above.*

EXERCISE 3

This exercise provides practice in using short answers with and without *be* (see *Short Answers* in Focus Chart 2).

1. Look at the picture and ask students to suggest what *might be going on.*

2. Allow some time for students to work individually to read the conversation and fill in the missing answers.

3. Have students compare answers by reading the conversation in pairs.

EXPANSION [10 minutes]

To provide further practice of short answers, you can use a short drill. Use real information about your students if appropriate. For example:

You: *Is she at home?*
Students: *She might be.*
You: *Do they speak Spanish?*
Students: *They might.*
You: *Does Carrie come to school on Fridays?*
Students: *She might not.*
Etc.

FOCUS 3 [15 minutes]

1. **Lead-in:** Since these modals require the use of the past participle, it may be a good idea to review the past participles of some common verbs. Choose some of the verbs used in the chart and create a short drill based on these verbs. For example:

You: *leave*
Students: *may have left*
You: *take*
Students: *may have taken*

You: *must*
Students: *must have taken*
You: *go*
Students: *must have gone*
You: *could*
Students: *could have gone*
You: *see*
Students: *could have seen*
You: *couldn't*
Students: *couldn't have seen*
Etc.

2. Ask individuals to take turns reading the examples (a) through (k). Ask students to suggest contexts for each one to make clear that they are about the past.

3. After each example, have students explain why they think that modal was used. Answers should be in terms of *how certain* they are.

4. Then ask why *have* + past participle was used. Answers should be along the lines of: *because the situation was in the past.*

LANGUAGE NOTE

The negative form of must (*mustn't have*) is not usually used in the past. It occurs in some regional variations of spoken English with the same meaning as *can't have (done)*, but is not commonplace in current American English.

form

Modals of Probability and Possibility with the Progressive

EXAMPLES

subject + modal + be + verb + -ing

(a) He **might be sleeping.**

(b) Q: What's Lisa doing these days?
A: I'm really not sure. She **may be working** in Latvia.

(c) Something smells good! Albert **must be cooking** dinner.

(d) You **must know** the Van Billiard family. They live in Amherst.

(e) NOT: You **must be knowing** the Van Billiard family.

subject + modal + have been + verb + -ing

(f) He **may have been sleeping.**

(g) Mo **must have been working** on his car; his hands are really dirty.

EXPLANATIONS

Use modals with the progressive to make a guess or draw a conclusion about something in progress at or around the time of speaking.

Remember that some verbs cannot be used in the progressive. For more information, see Unit 2.

Use this form to make a guess or draw a conclusion about something that was in progress before the time of speaking.

EXERCISE 6

Look back at the situations in Exercise 5. Can you make any statements about the people in these situations using *must, may, might,* or *could* with a progressive form? Use present forms (to talk about what you think they might be doing now) or past forms (to talk about what you think they might have been doing before now). For example: *Someone may be watching to see how many people try to pick up the $20 bill.* Compare your ideas with a partner.

EXERCISE 4

Turn back to the Opening Task. Make statements showing how certain you are about the person's past activities. Use *must, may, could, might, couldn't,* or *can't + have + past participle* to show how certain you feel. Be ready to share and justify your opinions.

EXERCISE 5

Read the following situations. Can you figure out what happened? Think of as many possible explanations as you can. Then compare your ideas with a partner.

Example: You are walking along the street when you see a $20 bill on the ground.
Someone must have dropped it. Someone might have put it there as a trick.

1. A boy is crawling on the ground looking for something. He is crying.
He must have lost something. He may have lost his watch or his key.

2. A car has stopped in the middle of the road. A bicycle is on the ground next to the car.
The car must have crashed into the bicycle.

3. There is a big hole in the front window of the bank.
There might have been a robbery.

4. Your train is twenty minutes late.
There might have been an accident.

5. A man and a woman are sitting in a restaurant. The woman is holding a diamond ring. She looks surprised.
The man might have just proposed to her. She must have gotten a surprise birthday gift.

6. A man is standing outside a house. He is wearing pajamas and slippers. He is holding a newspaper and ringing the front door bell.
He must have left his key inside. He must have locked himself out.

7. A man is standing in line at the bus stop. His coat is completely wet.
He must have forgotten his umbrella. He might have left his umbrella at home or at work.

ANSWER KEY

Exercise 4 *Answers are completely dependent on the inferences students make in the Opening Task.*

Exercise 5 *Answers will vary. Answers will vary, depending on what students said in Exercise 5. answers are listed above.*

Exercise 6 *Answers will vary. The choice of modal depends on the speaker's certainty. Possible*

EXERCISE 4 [15 minutes]

This exercise focuses on accuracy in the use of past tense modals.

1. Turn back to the chart in the Opening Task on SB page 71.
2. Have students make statements using *could have, might have, may have, must have, couldn't have,* and *can't have.* Each deduction should be supported by a fact.
3. Students can work in pairs or write their sentences individually.
4. When they are ready, ask volunteers to read their statements.
5. Ask other students to try and contradict this statement by making other logical guesses based on the information.

Student A: *He must have been in Japan on vacation because he traveled there with his wife.*

Student B: *He might have gone on business because his pamphlet says "Japanese for Business."*

Student C: *His wife could have stayed with him while he was working there on business.*

6. Try to keep the discussion going as long as possible. The focus here is on meaning.
7. Make a list on the board of the deductions most people agree on. Now you can focus on accuracy. Answers to some of the questions may come up in the later focus charts in this unit.

EXERCISE 5 [20 minutes]

This exercise provides further practice in the form and meaning of past modals of probability.

1. Explain that for each situation, students will try to guess what happened and must try to think of as many possible explanations as they can.
2. Read the first situation with your students and see if they can add any additional possible explanations. Encourage the use of different modals.
3. List the sentences on the board in order of probability.

4. Have students work in pairs to continue with the other situations.
5. Circulate to provide help and advice.
6. Take notes of creative solutions, as well as errors.
7. Ask volunteers to read their answers aloud.

Suggestion: Have students vote on the best/most convincing/most original/funniest answer for each item.

For more practice, use *Grammar Dimensions 2* Workbook page 33, Exercise 3.

[workbook]

METHODOLOGY NOTE

This may be a good time to think about various ways of handling errors.

1. If students are working in pairs, ask the listener to notice any errors in form, pointing any out to the person who made the statement.
2. If students are reading statements aloud to the whole class, open this listening-for-errors exercise up to anybody in the class.
3. You might want to allow students who make the error the first opportunity to correct it. Or allow the person who notices the error this opportunity.

LESSON PLAN 2

FOCUS 4 [15 minutes]

This focus chart presents the form of modals of probability and possibility used to talk about the events in progress at the time of speaking, and events that were in progress at a past time.

1. **Lead-in:** Review modals for different degrees of certainty from the previous lesson. Introduce a few situations where deductions can be made about events in progress. For example:

Situation 1: You: *A man is sitting in the armchair. His eyes are closed. He's snoring.*

Answer: *He must be sleeping.*

Situation 2: You: *The cooker is on. I can smell food.*

Answer: *Someone might be cooking dinner.*

Situation 3: You: *There's a lot of noise next door. People are singing. There's loud music.*

Answer: *They might be having a party.*

2. See if students can add any more situations of their own.
3. Ask volunteers to read the example sentences in the box.
4. You may want to refer back to Unit 2 and the use of the present progressive to clarify when to use simple or progressive forms.
5. To clarify the use of the past progressive, you may want to add a few more examples and ask what students think they may have been doing. For example:

Situation 1: You: *Her clothes are covered with dust.*

Answer: *She might have been cleaning.*

Situation 2: You: *His hands are covered in paint.*

Answer: *He must have been painting.*

Situation 3: You: *They look very tired.*

Answer: *They must have been working a lot.*

EXERCISE 6 [10 minutes]

This exercise provides an opportunity to practice the present and past progressive forms presented in Focus Chart 5.

1. Turn back to Exercise 5.
2. Do the first example together again. Ask students for additional suggestions.
3. Allow some time for students to go over the other situations and make at least one sentence for each situation.
4. Ask volunteers to read them aloud.
5. See if the rest of the class agrees that they are (a) logical and (b) accurate.

For more practice, use *Grammar Dimensions 2* Workbook page 34, Exercise 4.

meaning

FOCUS 5

Future Probability and Possibility with Modals

EXAMPLES	EXPLANATIONS
(a) There are a few clouds in the sky; it could / might / may rain later.	Use *could*, *might*, or *may* to express future possibility.
(b) Cheer up! She **might** call tomorrow.	*May* shows that you are a little more certain that something will happen.
(c) We **may** see them next month.	
(d) Q: Where's Anna? A: She'll **probably** get here soon.	Use *will* or *be going to* with *probably* to show that you are almost certain that something will happen in the future. Do not use *must*.
(e) NOT: She must get here soon.	
(f) Q: What's Jim going to do after he graduates next year? A: He's **probably going to** travel around the world on a motorcycle.	
(g) NOT: He must travel round the world on a motorcycle.	
(h) Look! The sun's coming out. It **may not** rain after all.	Use *may not* or *might not* to show that it is possible that something will not happen. Do not use *could not*.
(i) NOT: It could not rain after all.	
(j) Fran **might not** come to the airport with us tomorrow.	
(k) NOT: Fran could not come to the airport with us tomorrow.	

EXERCISE 9

Work with a partner and turn back to the Opening Task. From the evidence given, what can you say about the person's future plans? Use *probably will/be going to*, *may*, *could*, *must*, or *may not/might not* as necessary. Be prepared to share and justify your answers.

EXERCISE 7

The police are investigating a murder. What might Sherlock Holmes conclude about the following pieces of evidence? Get together with a partner to come up with a theory about what happened. After that, share your conclusions with the rest of the class, using *must*, *may*, *could*, *might*, or *couldn't/can't* to show how certain you feel. Finally, take a vote to decide who has the most interesting theory. How probable do you think this theory is?

Police Report:

The victim was found in her bedroom on the second floor of her house. The front door and her bedroom door were locked from inside. There were two wine glasses on the table in her room; one was empty, the other was full. There was an ashtray with several cigarette butts in it. The victim had a small white button in her hand and several long, blond hairs. Her watch was found on the floor; it had stopped at 11:30. The drawers of the victim's desk were open, and there were papers all over the floor. Nothing appeared to be missing.

EXERCISE 8

You are a reporter for your local newspaper. The editor has asked you to report on the murder described in Exercise 7. Explain what you think happened and why you believe this to be so. Make a headline for your report. Display your headline and your report so that your classmates can compare the different theories about the murder.

MODALS OF PROBABILITY AND POSSIBILITY *Could, May, Might, Must, Couldn't,* and *Can't*

ANSWER KEY

Exercise 7 Answers will vary but the most likely theory is: The victim knew the murderer well (no sign of forced entry) and may have drunk wine with him or her in her room. The full wine glass suggests that the murderer may have drugged or poisoned the victim by putting something in the wine. The murderer didn't drink from the other glass because he or she knew it was poisoned. The murderer may have long, blond hair and might have worn a shirt or jacket with white buttons. They must have fought or struggled violently at around 11:30 (button, hair, smashed watch). After killing her, she must not have found them or might have had to leave before finding what he or she was looking for. The murderer must have left the house by the victim's window. (The doors were locked from the inside.)

Exercise 8 Answers will vary, depending on students' responses in Exercise 7, and/or on new "twists."

EXERCISE 7 [15 minutes]

This story is open to a range of interpretations and is guaranteed to bring out the "Sherlock Holmes" in every student (if it exists!).

1. Read the introduction together with your students.
2. Allow some time for students to read the story in pairs and come up with their theories.
3. Ask students to share and discuss the reason for their explanations.
4. See suggested solution below.
5. Your students' theories about why and how the crime occurred might be even more interesting.

The most likely theory:

The victim knew the murderer well (no sign of a forced entry) and may have drunk wine with him or her in her room. The full wine glass suggests that the murderer may have drugged or poisoned the victim by putting something in the wine. The murderer didn't drink from the other glass because he or she knew it was poisoned. The murderer may have long, blond hair and might have worn a shirt or jacket with white buttons. They must have fought or struggled violently at around 11:30 (button, hair, smashed watch). After killing the victim, the murderer might have searched for information or documents in her desk, but he or she must not have found them or might have had to leave before finding what he or she was looking for. The murderer must have left the house by the victim's window. (The doors were locked from the inside.)

EXPANSION [30 minutes]

You may want to use Activity 8 on SB page 87 after this exercise. Activity 8 centers on real-life mysteries, and asks students to do some independent research on the Internet to come up with explanations for them.

EXERCISE 8 [20 minutes]

This exercise provides an opportunity to use modals of probability in written work. You may want to set this exercise for homework after Exercise 7.

1. Brainstorm ideas for a headline for this article. Point out how headlines only keep the "essential" words, dropping articles *the* and *a*, prepositions, and other "function words" and keeping the "content words"—nouns, verbs, adjectives, and adverbs.
2. Have students work in pairs or groups to start writing the article. They can finish it for homework.
3. Read aloud the best versions or display them in the classroom.

FOCUS 5 [15 minutes]

1. Lead-in: Give some examples contrasting future probability/possibility with past and progressive usage (Focus Charts 3 and 4). For example:
   1a. *He might be cooking dinner.* (right now)
   1b. *He might cook dinner tomorrow.* (in the future)
   2a. *She must work on Saturdays.* (usually)
   2b. *She must be working on Saturdays.* (temporarily)
2. Have students cover the right-hand columns and read the examples.
3. Ask them to work out the rules.
4. Uncover the column and compare their ideas with those in the chart.
5. Read the following example sentences and ask students to say if they are future, past, or present.
   He could go to college. (future)
   They couldn't be from Italy. (present)
   They must have a car. (present)
   They may go to Brazil. (future)
   I might pass the exam. (future)

You'll probably be late. (future)
You couldn't have seen the movie yet. (past)
I may see you again soon. (future)
She can't have any friends. (present)
He may not have got your message. (past)

EXERCISE 9 [10 minutes]

This exercise gives students the opportunity to use modals with future meaning.

1. Turn back to the Opening Task on SB pages 70–71.
2. Have students work in pairs to make two or three guesses about what this person may, might, or could do in the future.
3. Share the answers as a class, focusing first on meaning and then on accuracy.

EXPANSION [20 minutes]

You may want to use Activity 5 on SB page 86 after this exercise. Activity 5 provides a chance for students to use future modals to describe pictures.

EXERCISE 10

Work with a partner and choose the best way to complete each sentence. Bubble in the correct answer. Discuss the reasons for your choice. Share your reasons with the rest of the class.

1. A: Where's Rose?
   B: I'm not sure. She _____ in the library.
   ○ *is*   ● *might be*   ○ *must be*

2. A: My daughter just got a scholarship to Stanford!
   B: You _____ be very proud of her.
   ○ *could*   ● *must*   ○ *might*

3. A: How does Sheila get to school?
   B: I don't really know. She _____ the bus.
   ● *might take*   ○ *takes*   ○ *must take*

4. A: It's really cold in here today _____ the window open.
   B: Yes. Somebody _____
   ○ *must leave*   ○ *might leave*   ● *must have left*

5. A: I wonder why Zelda always wears gloves.
   B: I don't know. She _____ some kind of allergy.
   ○ *may have bad*   ○ *bas*   ● *may have*

6. A: Have you heard the weather forecast?
   B: No, but look at all those dark clouds in the sky. I think it _____ rain. *(preferable to could here because "dark clouds" suggests a greater probability of rain)*
   ○ *could*   ○ *must*   ● *is probably going to*

7. A: Did my mother call while I was out?
   B: I'm not sure. She _____
   ● *might have*   ○ *might*   ○ *did*

8. A: Ellen gave a violin recital in front of five hundred people yesterday. It was her first public performance.
   B: Really? She _____ very nervous.
   ○ *could have been*   ○ *must be*   ● *must have been*

9. A: Are you coming to Jeff's party?
   B: I'm not sure. I _____ go to the concert instead.
   ○ *must*   ○ *will*   ● *might*

10. A: Can I speak to Professor Carroll?
    B: She's not in her office, and she doesn't have any more classes today, so she _____ home.
    ○ *might go*   ● *must have gone*   ○ *will probably go*

11. A: Jenny's sneezing again.
    B: Yes, she _____ a terrible cold.
    ● *must have*   ○ *must be having*   ○ *must have bad*

12. A: Look, Maynard's sitting outside his own apartment. Isn't that weird?
    B: Not really. He _____ his keys, and now he's waiting for his wife to come home.
    ○ *may be losing*   ● *may have lost*   ○ *may have been losing*

13. A: Is Myrna working in the city today?
    B: She _____ I'm not sure.
    ○ *could*   ○ *could have*   ● *could be*

14. A: I can hear the water running in the bathroom.
    B: Yes, Bira _____ another shower.
    ○ *must take*   ○ *must have taken*   ● *must be taking*

15. A: What's up? You look worried.
    B: I am. My dog's sick. I think he _____ eaten some poison.
    ○ *may be*   ○ *may have been*   ● *may have*

16. A: Have you heard? Mel's father died last night.
    B: Poor Mel. He _____ feeling terrible. They were very close.
    ○ *must*   ● *must be*   ○ *must have been*

17. A: Dean has just won a million dollars in the lottery.
    B: He _____ He never buys lottery tickets.
    ○ *must not have*   ○ *could not*   ● *couldn't have*

18. A: Does Isaiah still share a house with his sister?
    B: I don't know. He _____
    ○ *might be*   ● *might*   ○ *might have*

EXERCISE 11

Look back at the Opening Task. Who do you think the "Mystery Person" is? What do you think happened to him or her? Complete the following newspaper article with your ideas about what might have happened. Remember to use *must, may, could, might,* or *couldn't/can't* to show how certain you feel.

MISSING MYSTERY PERSON

It has been a week since New York taxi driver Ricardo Oliveiro found a briefcase on the back seat of his cab. It has been a week of guessing and speculation: Who is the owner of this briefcase and where is he or she now? Several different theories have been proposed, but so far the most interesting is the one which follows . . .

ANSWER KEY

Exercise 11   *Answers are dependent on the inferences students made in the Opening Task.*

EXERCISE 10 [20 minutes]

This exercise reviews all the uses of modals for probability and possibility presented in this unit.

1. You may decide to assign this exercise for homework, or for class time. If in class, you can ask all students to complete all questions, or assign certain questions to certain pairs of students.

2. Allow time for students to read the mini-dialogues and choose their answers.

3. Have students practice reading aloud the conversations in pairs, using appropriate intonation, contractions, and wordlinking.

4. Select pairs of students to read out their conversations.

5. Check the answers as a class. Refer to the answer key on LP page 82. Ask students to explain the reasons for their answers.

For more practice, use *Grammar Dimensions 2* Workbook page 37, Exercise 5.

EXPANSION 1 [40 minutes]

You may want to use Activity 3 and Activity 4 on SB pages 85 and 86 after this exercise. Activity 3 provides an opportunity for students to use various tenses of modals to tell a story. You can follow this with the listening activity for Activity 4.

EXPANSION 2 [20 minutes]

Use the *Expansion* after Activity 3 on LP page 85 as a way of extending this activity.

EXERCISE 11 [20 minutes]

This exercise is a way of reviewing the different modals presented in this unit. By returning to the

Opening Task, students can see how much they have learned since the beginning of the unit.

1. Read the instructions and the opening paragraph.

2. Have students start writing the article in class and finish it for homework.

3. In the next class, have students read over their individually completed newspaper articles, underlining any use of modals + verb, and revising if necessary.

4. Ask students to exchange papers with a partner, reading over each other's articles first for content and meaning and then for accuracy.

5. Have students ask the writer any questions needed to help clarify meaning. Example: *I didn't understand the statement ———. Can you try to say it in another way so that I understand?* (or *What does ——— mean?*)

6. Have students point out any errors and explain their observation and justify their opinion. (It's possible that there is no error, in other words.)

7. Go over problematic items and/or good examples with the whole class, or ask students for these. You might also ask students to explain their revisions: What was wrong with the original statement?

UNIT GOAL REVIEW [10 minutes]

Ask students to look again at the goals on the opening page of the unit. Help them understand how much they have accomplished in each area. This is an opportunity to review some of the meaning distinctions of the different modals and to describe possibility and probability using different time frames. This is also the time to ask students to identify which areas they would like more practice with. If you feel that they are still challenged by some of the points in this chapter, allow plenty of time for the activities and exercises.

ExamView® Test Generator   For Unit 5 assessment, use *Grammar Dimensions 2 ExamView®*.

Use Your English

ACTIVITY 1 speaking/listening

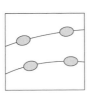

Can you guess these objects? Get together with a partner and see how many different possibilities you can come up with for each picture. Classify your interpretations as "Possible," "Probable," and "Certain." Compare your answers with the rest of the class. (You can find the answers on page A-15.)

ACTIVITY 2 speaking/listening

▪ STEP 1
The purpose of this activity is to confuse your classmates. Form teams and create five different drawings of familiar things seen from an unusual point of view. One example is shown below.

▪ STEP 2
Exchange papers with another team. As a team, see how many different interpretations you can make of each drawing. Write each guess beside the appropriate drawing, showing how probable you think your interpretation is.

▪ STEP 3
When you have made your guesses, exchange papers with another team until all teams have had a chance to "interpret" all the drawings.

It could be a donut.
It might be a hat from above.
It could be an eyeball.

Which team got the most "correct" interpretations? Which team had the most interesting or unusual interpretations?

ACTIVITY 3 speaking/listening

Get together with a partner and examine the pictures below. What's going on? Who are the people? Imagine this story happened yesterday. Create a newspaper story telling what you think might have happened. You can use the photographs in any order that you like. Compare your story with those of your classmates. In what ways do their interpretations differ from yours?

USE YOUR ENGLISH

The Use Your English activities at the end of the unit contain situations that should naturally elicit the structures covered in the unit. For a more complete discussion of how to use the Use Your English activities, see To the Teacher, page xxii. When students are doing these activities in class, you can circulate and listen to see if they are using the structures accurately.

ACTIVITY 1 speaking/listening [20 minutes]

You may want to use this activity after Exercise 1 on SB page 73. It's fun to do this activity "out of the blue," with no warning, before students have a chance to look up the answers (on SB page A-15) or to talk about their ideas with others. You may get some curious answers!

1. Look at the first picture all together as a class. Brainstorm a few ideas of what it *might be, could be,* or *must be.*

2. Have students work in pairs to work out the other pictures.

Suggestion: You could make this into a competition to see who comes up with the most suggestions, or the most creative and original ideas.

ACTIVITY 2 speaking/listening [20 minutes]

This is an extension of Activity 1. The first three steps of this activity can be assigned as homework as it sometimes takes a little time to come up with well thought-out drawings.

1. Ask for some suggestions for other objects that might look unusual when seen from close-up or from another angle. Suggestions: *a paper clip, a drawing pin, a teabag* etc.

2. **Suggestion:** If you wish, you could prepare of list of these items on pieces of paper. Mix them up in a bag and have students choose one.

3. Ask students to draw their object. (This step can be done as homework.)

4. Have students exchange drawings and make guesses about what they *might, must,* or *can't be.* Or pin them up on the board with numbers and have students walk around writing down their guesses about each object.

5. Collect the answers as a class, focusing on using different types of modals *may, might, must, can't,* and *couldn't.*

ACTIVITY 3 speaking/listening [30 minutes]

You may want to use this activity after Exercise 10 on SB pages 82 and 83. This activity can be used to practice a range of modals in different tenses including present, present progressive, past, and future. The emphasis is on finding different possible versions of the story.

1. Ask students to describe some of the things in each picture. Brainstorm some ideas about what is going on.

2. Have students work in groups of five. Taking one picture each, they can tell the story in any order they like.

3. Ask each group to tell their story to the class.

4. You can vote on which stories are the "best" in various categories of your choice (most outlandish, funniest, etc.).

Suggestion: For follow-up accuracy work, record students as they are presenting their stories. Play the recording and stop it after each statement, checking for accuracy in the use of the appropriate modal and tense.

EXPANSION [30 minutes]

Use this optional extra activity to provide further practice in storytelling using modals of probability and possibility.

1. Choose about 10 minutes of a video which has a lot of drama and quite a lot of dialogue. It might be from a soap, a movie, or a TV advertisement.

2. Explain that you will show the video with the sound turned off. Students will take notes of the events and make speculations about what happens. Speculations can be about why these events happened, what they are saying or feeling, the motives for their actions, etc.

3. Discuss the different opinions as a class.

4. Then play the video with the sound on so that students can check their versions.

ACTIVITY 6 speaking/listening

In the Opening Task, you looked at the contents of somebody's briefcase and made guesses about his or her identity. The purpose of this activity is to create your own "mystery person." Form groups and collect a number of items that somebody might carry in his or her pockets (tickets, bills, photographs, business cards, etc.). Choose six items, collect them in a bag, and bring them to class. Exchange bags with another group. With your group, examine the contents of the new bag and try to decide on the possible identity of the owner, using the same categories as in the Opening Task. When everyone is ready, share your conclusions with the rest of the class, showing how certain you are. Remember, your classmates might ask you to justify your conclusions, so be ready to justify each one.

ACTIVITY 7 writing

Write a profile of the "mystery person" your group presented to the class in Activity 6. Make sure you write an introductory sentence and that you provide evidence to support your conclusions. When you finish writing, read your profile to see how much of the language discussed in this unit you were able to use.

ACTIVITY 8 research on the web

On the Web: Look up one of these mysteries on the Internet using a search engine such as Google® or Yahoo® and make notes about what happened: 1) Stonehenge 2) the statues of Rapa Nui 3) the Mayan civilization. What is mysterious about them? Tell your classmates and ask them for suggestions about what might/may/could have happened.

ACTIVITY 9 reflection

Make a list of five things to do before taking an exam. Say what may/might/could happen if you don't follow this advice.

Example: *Don't stay up late the night before an exam, otherwise you might feel tired or sleepy during the exam.*

Activity 8 Possible answers are: Stonehenge might have been an ancient observatory or a temple. Visitors from another country or civilization could have built it and then disappeared.

ACTIVITY 4 listening

CD Track 8

■ **STEP 1**
Listen to the audio of two different people talking about the pictures on page 85. As you listen to their stories, number each picture to show which one comes first, second, and so on. Which story is the most likely, in your opinion? Speaker 1's story or Speaker 2's story?

■ **STEP 2**
Listen to the audio again and write any sentences with *may, might, could,* or *must* that show how certain the speaker feels.

ACTIVITY 5 speaking/listening

■ **STEP 1**
Look at the pictures below. What events are going to happen in each picture? What are you certain will happen? What is possibly going to happen? What are you not sure about?

■ **STEP 2**
Show the pictures to a friend. Ask him or her to tell you what he or she thinks might happen next. Take notes or record the answers he or she gives. Review your notes or listen to your recording and make notes. Do students have different ideas about the photos? Which ones are the most interesting? Tell your classmates.

ANSWER KEY

Activity 4 Students should refer to pictures by letters; pictures are lettered left to right, top to bottom.

Step 1 **Speaker 1:** 1) A 2) D 3) E 4) C 5) B **Speaker 2:** 1) B 2) D 3) A 4) C 5) E

Step 2 Check audio script on LP page S-Z for answers.

USE YOUR ENGLISH

ACTIVITY 4 — listening [20 minutes]

CD Track 8

This activity is a follow-up to Activity 3 on SB page 85. Students will be especially motivated to listen if they recorded some of their own stories, suggested in the teacher's notes for Activity 3.

1. Explain that students will hear a recording of two different people talking about the pictures on SB page 85. Each person will tell a different version.
2. Play the audio while students write their answers. See audio script on LP page S-2.
3. Students may find this activity easier in pairs: one student opens the book at SB page 85 to look at the pictures, and the other opens the book at page A-9 to look at the chart.
4. Check the answers. Refer to the answer key on LP page 86. Discuss any differences between these and your students' versions.
5. Play the audio again and have students write down any uses of modals. Then check the answers. Refer to the answer key on LP page 86.
6. Ask students to explain the degree of certainty for each one. Point out that modals are one way of understanding how speakers feel in terms of certainty. Other ways of doing this are with words like *maybe, probably, very*; a person's tone of voice; how loud their voice is; how they emphasize their words (volume, pitch, intonation); and so on.

ACTIVITY 5 — speaking/listening [20 minutes]

You may want to use this activity after Exercise 9 on SB page 81. This activity provides practice with using modals to talk about the future.

1. Review uses of modals to talk about the future from Focus Chart 5 on SB page 81.
2. Brainstorm ideas about the picture: the people, what they are doing, why they are there.
3. Have students work in groups of four to discuss the pictures.
4. Assign one picture to each person in the group and have them take notes of the other students' opinions.
5. Have students share their ideas with the class, justifying their guesses by referencing facts in the pictures.

EXPANSION [20 minutes]

Have students interview a native English speaker about the pictures. Record the interviews if possible. Compare their versions of the story and discuss what kinds of modals they used.

ACTIVITY 6 — speaking/ listening [30 minutes]

You may want to use this activity after Exercise 2 on SB page 75. This activity provides practice with using modals to talk about the present and the past.

1. Have students form groups of five or six. Each person in the group can contribute an item to the bag of mystery objects.
2. Each group exchanges bags with another group.
3. Turn back to the chart in Opening Task on SB page 71. Have students complete the chart about this new "mystery person."
4. Select a spokesperson from each group to summarize their description of the person.
5. If you have a large class, you might want to form several groups, or choose fewer items.

ACTIVITY 7 — writing [30 minutes]

This activity is a follow-up to Activity 6 but can also be done at the same time or immediately after completing Activity 6, or for homework. Assign this writing activity for individual, pair, or group work, or for homework. Next, have students exchange descriptions and edit each other's work, focusing on the accuracy of the structures targeted in this unit.

ACTIVITY 8 — research on the web

You may want to use this activity after Exercise 8 on SB page 80.

1. Ask students if they have ever heard of any of these mysteries and what they already know about them. Ask students to each select one of the mysteries to investigate, making sure all three mysteries are chosen. Assign the research for homework or for in-class computer work.
2. Have students present the results of their research to the group of students who also studied this mystery. One student can then make the main presentation for each mystery to the class, and others can add information or ask questions after each presentation has concluded. Share suggestions about useful sites or search tips connected to this topic.

ACTIVITY 9 — reflection

This activity encourages students to give themselves advice about exam preparation. Students can use imperatives, followed by modals, to talk about possible or probable future events.

PAST PROGRESSIVE AND SIMPLE PAST WITH TIME CLAUSES
When, While, and *As Soon As*

UNIT GOALS

- Choose between past progressive and simple past

- Form past progressive correctly

- Understand the meaning of *when, while,* and *as soon as*

- Form clauses with *when, while* and *as soon as*

OPENING TASK
Miami Murder Mystery

Last night Lewis Meyer died at his home in Miami. Phil Fork, a police detective, was the first person to arrive at the house after Mr. Meyer died. This is what he found:

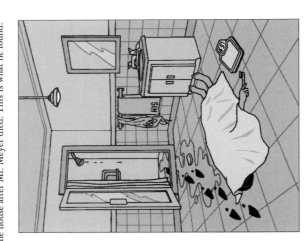

Mr. Meyer's wife, Margo, told Fork: "It was an accident. My husband took a shower at about 10:00 P.M. After his shower, he slipped on a piece of soap and fell down."

Do you believe her? What probably happened? Look at the picture and work with a partner. Decide whether the following statements are **probably true** (T) or **probably false** (F). Be ready to share your answers with your classmates and to explain your choices.

1. Mr. Meyer died after Phil Fork arrived.	T	(F)
2. Mr. Meyer died when Phil Fork arrived.	T	(F)
3. Mr. Meyer died before Phil Fork arrived.	(T)	F
4. Mr. Meyer brushed his teeth before he died.	T	(F)
5. Mr. Meyer was brushing his teeth when he died.	(T)	F
6. Mr. Meyer was taking a shower when he died.	T	(F)
7. Mr. Meyer took a shower before he died.	T	(F)
8. Mr. Meyer died when he slipped on a piece of soap.	T	(F)
9. Somebody hit Mr. Meyer over the head while he was brushing his teeth.	(T)	F
10. The murder weapon is still in the bathroom.	(T)	F

You are the detective. In your opinion, how did Mr. Meyer die?
With your partner, use the picture and your answers above to try to solve the mystery. Make as many guesses as you like. For example: *We think somebody killed Mr. Meyer while he was brushing his teeth. This is how it happened.* . . . Be ready to share your ideas with the rest of the class. Write your ideas here:

WHAT REALLY HAPPENED:

(Solution to the Opening Task on page A-15.)

ANSWER KEY

Opening Task Solution: Mrs. Meyer killed her husband. She entered the bathroom while he was brushing his teeth, and she hit him over the head with the bathroom scale. Then she turned on the shower and put soap on the floor. How do we know this?

- From the toothbrush: He was brushing his teeth, not walking out of the shower.

UNIT OVERVIEW

This unit provides contrasting practice of past progressive with simple past, using the time expressions *when*, *while*, and *as soon as*.

GRAMMAR NOTE

The past progressive and simple past tenses express two ways of looking at past events. The simple past focuses more on the *completion* of the event, while the past progressive emphasizes the *continuous nature of* the activity. These two tenses are often used in one sentence in order to contrast a background event with a more important event. Many languages do not have a different form for progressive and simple usage. Some languages have these two forms, but they correspond to different meanings.

UNIT GOALS

Some instructors may want to review the goals listed on this page after completing the Opening Task so that students understand what they should know by the end of the unit. These goals can also be reviewed at the end of the unit when students are more familiar with the grammar terminology.

OPENING TASK [20 minutes]

The purpose of the Opening Task is to create a context in which students will need to use past progressive and simple past structures. The problem-solving format is designed to show the teacher how well the students can produce the target structures implicitly and spontaneously when they are engaged in a communicative task. In working to solve the mystery, students are more likely to focus on communicating than on grammatical accuracy. For a more complete discussion of the purpose of the Opening Task, see To the Teacher, Lesson Planner (LP) page xxii.

Setting Up the Task

1. Have students describe the picture. To provide students with background for the task, you could talk with them about some well-known detectives in fiction, film, or TV, for example, Sherlock Holmes, Miss Marple, Hercule Poirot. Or to a TV crime series such as *Law and Order* or *CSI* (*Crime Scene Investigation*).

2. Provide and elicit key vocabulary, such as:

murder	evidence
murderer	accuse
victim	murder weapon
guilty	suspicious
innocent	crime scene
clue	investigate

3. Ask students what they think may have happened. (You may find that students use some of the target structures used in this unit.) Explain that all the clues for solving the murder mystery are in the picture and that the true/false questions on the next page will help in finding the solution.

Conducting the Task

1. Read the introduction to the task with your students.

2. Have students work in pairs to decide which of the sentences are probably true or probably false. Students may discuss the differences in grammar between the different sentences. This will help them to engage with the grammar presented in this unit. Don't offer any grammar explanations at this stage. The aim is to raise their awareness of the grammar points involved.

3. Check the answers as a class and try to reach a group consensus on which ones are **probably true** or **probably false**. Refer to the answer key on LP page 88.

Closing the Task

1. In pairs or groups of three, have students discuss their opinions of how Mr. Meyer died, recording their answers in the box provided.

2. If you run out of time in class, this can be assigned for homework as paragraph writing.

3. Remind students that there is no "correct" answer. A number of different theories generally emerge, and discussion can be heated.

4. Discuss their theories as a class. Don't worry about accuracy at this point. Make note of errors in meaning, form, or use in order to focus on those problems later.

GRAMMAR NOTE

Typical student errors (form)

- Errors in third person singular, e.g. * *They was listening to music.* (See Focus Chart 2.)
- Using past participle instead of present participle, * *I was lived in Australia for one year.* (See Focus Chart 2.)
- Incorrect use of commas (see Focus Chart 4.)

Typical student errors (use)

- Using past progressive with verbs that do not take the progressive form, e.g. * *She was hearing a loud noise.* (See Unit 2, Focus Chart 4.)
- Using simple past for temporary or uncompleted events in the past, e.g. * *When I went outside, a fire burned in the next house.* (See Focus Chart 1.)
- Incorrect sequence of tenses, e.g. * *When I was living in Australia, I was studying English.* * *When I watched TV, I heard a loud noise.* (See Focus Chart 3.)
- Misunderstanding the sequence of events in time clauses. (See Focus Charts 3 and 4.)

FOCUS 1 Past Progressive and Simple Past

use

EXAMPLES	EXPLANATIONS
(a) Phil Fork **arrived** at 10:30.	Use the simple past for an action that started and finished in the past. For a list of irregular past forms, see Appendix 5 on page A-13.
(b) Mrs. Meyer **drank** several cups of black coffee.	
(c) Phil Fork **was eating** dinner at 10:00.	*Was eating* and *was brushing* are past progressive.
(d) Mr. Meyer **was brushing** his teeth at 10:00.	Use the past progressive for an action that was in progress at a specific time in the past.
(e) Mr. Meyer **was brushing** his teeth when the murderer entered the room.	Use the past progressive with the simple past to show that one action began first and was still in progress when the second action happened. It is possible that the first action continued after the second action finished.
(f) Phil Fork **was eating** dinner when he heard about the murder.	
(g) Mrs. Meyer **was talking** on the phone while her husband **was taking** a shower.	Use the past progressive with the past progressive to show two actions in progress at the same time.
(h) Phil Fork **was reading** a newspaper while he **was eating** dinner.	

EXERCISE 1

Look back at what you wrote in the Opening Task on page 89. Did you use the past progressive and the simple past? If you did, underline all of your examples of the past progressive, circle all examples of the simple past, and check with your teacher to see if you used them correctly. If you didn't use these forms at all, write three sentences about Mr. Meyer's murder using the past progressive and the simple past. Check with your teacher to see if you used these forms correctly.

1. _____
2. _____
3. _____

FOCUS 2 Past Progressive

form

STATEMENT	NEGATIVE	QUESTION
I / She / He / It **was sleeping.**	I / She / He / It **was not sleeping.** (wasn't)	**Was** I / she / he / it **sleeping?**
We / You / They **were sleeping.**	We / You / They **were not sleeping.** (weren't)	**Were** we / you / they **sleeping?**

EXERCISE 2

Get together with a partner and complete this newspaper report of Mr. Meyer's murder. Use information from the Opening Task on page 88 and your own ideas about what happened to help you.

DAILY NEWS

BATHROOM MURDER

"I am innocent!" says Mrs. Meyer.

Last night police arrested Margo Meyer for the murder of her husband, Lewis. On her way to the police station, Mrs. Meyer told reporters: "I am innocent. I loved my husband very much. I didn't kill him."

According to Mrs. Meyer, on the night of his death, her husband ___ was crossing/walking across the bathroom floor ___ when ___ he slipped on a piece of soap, hit his head, and died ___.

However, Detective Phil Fork and his colleagues have a different theory about how Mr. Meyer died. According to them, ___ somebody killed him ___ while ___ he was brushing his teeth ___.

ANSWER KEY

Exercise 1   Answers will vary.

Exercise 2   Answer will vary. Possible answers are listed above.

UNIT 6

LESSON PLAN 1

FOCUS 1 [10 minutes]

1. **Lead-in:** Ask students to tell you about their weekend. Make a list of things that different students did last weekend. Then ask them to tell you what they were doing at specific times of the day. Your conversation may go something like this:

   You: *What did you do last weekend?*
   Student 1: *I rode a bike.*
   Student 2: *I saw a movie.*
   Student 3: *I went shopping.*

   You: *These actions started and finished in the past, so we use the simple past. What happens if I ask: What were you doing at 10 A.M.?*

   Student 1: *I was taking a shower.*
   Student 2: *I was watching TV.*
   Student 3: *I was eating breakfast.*

   You: *We use the past progressive for an action that was in progress at a specific time in the past.*

2. Read the examples and the explanations in the focus chart.

3. You may want to draw a diagram to show the difference between completed actions and actions in progress.

Yesterday

→	→	→
10 A.M.	1 A.M.	3 A.M.

4. Now contrast the use of the two different tenses in one sentence using *when* (as in examples (e) and (f)). Give some extra examples using class situations. For example, *When I arrived today, Jaro was reading the newspaper and Palo was opening the window.*

EXERCISE 1 [5 minutes]

This exercise gives students a chance to review their work from the Opening Task.

1. Have students look back at their sentences or paragraphs from the Opening Task and identify the different tenses, underlining the past progressive and circling the simple past.

2. Rather than correct their errors directly, you could ask the class which sentences are incorrect and how they would correct them.

EXPANSION [15 minutes]

You can use the following exercise to provide further practice of the past progressive.

1. Ask your students to work in pairs.

2. Have them take turns to ask each other about what they were doing at every hour of the day yesterday and make a list of all the things they were both doing at the same time.

   Student A: *What were you doing at 6:00 AM yesterday?*

   Student B: *I was sleeping.*

   Student A: *So was I.*

3. Ask volunteers to report the results.

   Student: *We were both sleeping at 6:00 AM yesterday.*

For more practice, use *Grammar Dimensions 2* Workbook page 38, Exercise 1.

FOCUS 2 [5 minutes]

This focus chart illustrates the form of the past progressive, including contractions.

1. **Lead-in:** Review the spelling rules for making the present participle in Unit 2, LP page 21.

2. Give a quick spelling test of some of the more troublesome verbs if you have time.

3. Read the examples in the focus chart and add some more examples of *Wh-* questions in the past progressive.

EXERCISE 2 [10 minutes]

Exercise 2 gives students a chance to practice both the form and use of past progressive and simple past.

1. Have students work in pairs to complete the newspaper report.

2. To review their answers, you could have each pair compare their answers with another pair and later discuss their disagreements as a class.

3. See suggested answers on LP page 90.

Suggestion: Make a copy of the exercise on overhead transparency and fill out the news report together, using different pairs' examples. You can correct errors as you write, or point out the errors and ask the class to make corrections.

For more practice, use *Grammar Dimensions 2* Workbook page 40, Exercise 2, and page 41, Exercise 3.

EXPANSION [30 minutes]

You may want to use Activity 2 on Student Book (SB) page 100 to provide further practice of the past progressive for events that were in progress at a certain time in the past.

FOCUS 3

When, While, and As Soon As

meaning

EXAMPLES	EXPLANATIONS
(a) **While** Mr. Meyer was getting ready for bed, Mrs. Meyer drank several cups of black coffee. OR (b) Mrs. Meyer drank several cups of black coffee **while** Mr. Meyer was getting ready for bed.	*When, while,* and *as soon as* give information about time. You can use them **either** at the beginning of a sentence **or** in the middle. *While* introduces an action in progress. It means "during that time." It is usually used with the past progressive.
(c) Mrs. Meyer called the police **when** she found the dead body. OR (d) **When** Mrs. Meyer found her husband's body, she called the police.	*When* introduces a completed action. It is usually used with the simple past. In (c) and (d), *when* introduces the action that happened first: **First** Mrs. Meyer found the body and **then** she called the police.
(e) Mrs. Meyer came to the door as soon as Phil Fork arrived. OR (f) **As soon as** Phil Fork arrived, Mrs. Meyer came to the door.	*As soon as* introduces a completed action and means "immediately after."

EXERCISE 3

Make meaningful statements about Mr. Meyer's murder by matching information from A with information from B. The first one has been done for you.

A

1. Mrs. Meyer called the police
2. While she was waiting for the police to arrive
3. As soon as Phil Fork heard about the murder
4. When Fork asked to see the body
5. While Fork was searching the bathroom for clues
6. He saw that Mr. Meyer died
7. When Fork accused Mrs. Meyer of murder.
8. A crowd of news reporters tried to interview Mrs. Meyer

B

she said that she was innocent.
Mrs. Meyer took him to the scene of the crime.
as soon as her husband died.
while the police were taking her to jail.
while he was brushing his teeth.
she placed a bar of soap on the bathroom floor.
he rushed to the Meyers' house.
he became suspicious of Mrs. Meyer's story.

EXERCISE 4

Look again at the sentences you created in Exercise 3. For each one, underline the part of the sentence that gives information about time. This is the part of the sentence that answers the question "When?"

Example: *Mrs. Meyer called the police as soon as her husband died.*

ANSWER KEY

Exercises 3 and 4 (Answers to Exercise 4 are underlined) 2. *While* she was waiting for the police to arrive, she placed a bar of soap on the bathroom floor. 3. *As soon as* Phil Fork heard about the murder, he rushed to the Meyers' house. 4. *When* Fork asked to see the body, Mrs. Meyer took him to the scene of the crime. 5. *While* Fork was searching the bathroom for clues, he became suspicious of Mrs. Meyer's story. 6. He saw that Mr. Meyer had died *while* he was brushing his teeth. 7. *When* Fork accused Mrs. Meyer of murder, she said that she was innocent. 8. A crowd of news reporters tried

FOCUS 3 [15 minutes]

This focus chart introduces the meaning and use of the time expressions *when*, *while*, and *as soon as*. Further discussion is provided in Focus 4 on SB page 94.

1. **Lead-in:** Describe the following imaginary situation to your class. You were at home watching TV and eating potato chips when suddenly there was a loud noise and all the lights went out. You opened the front door to see what was going on and you saw a fire in the house next door. So you called the fire department right away.

Make some example sentences based on your story. Ask students to help you finish them.

> *While I was watching TV, . . . (I heard a loud noise).*
>
> *The lights went out while . . . (I was watching TV and eating potato chips).*
>
> *When the lights went out, I . . . (opened the front door).*
>
> *As soon as I saw the fire, I . . . (called the fire department).*

2. Go over these sentences with your students, asking them if it is possible to substitute *while* or *when*, or change the order of clauses for each one and if the meaning changes. In this way, you may be able to elicit most of the rules explained in Focus Chart 3. (Note that use of commas is explained in Focus 4.)

3. Read the examples and the explanations in the focus chart. Refer back to your examples.

4. Ask students to think of a sudden event that happened to them, and of what they were doing at the time. If time allows, have students write their own example sentences. If not, choose two or three suggestions from the group and write their sentences on the board.

LANGUAGE NOTE

When, *while*, and *as soon as* are conjunctions that show the *temporal* relationship between two clauses. The clause introduced by *when*, *while*, and *as soon as* is a dependent (or subordinate) clause. A dependent clause is less important than the main clause and cannot stand alone.

While shows that two events happened simultaneously. *While* introduces the "background" event that was going on when something else (the main focus) happened. (*When* is sometimes used in the same way, especially in conversation.) *When* introduces the "background" event that happened before the main event. *As soon as* is similar to *when*, but shows that the first event happened *just* before the main event. **Note:** The terms *dependent* and *independent* clauses are introduced in Focus Chart 4.

EXERCISE 3 [10 minutes]

This exercise uses all three time expressions at different locations in each sentence. Students will build on this exercise in Exercises 4 and 5.

1. Set a time limit for students to read the sentences in the chart individually.

2. Have students work in pairs to match the sentence halves.

3. Answer questions about any new vocabulary items (*innocent*, *jail*, *accused*, *suspicious*).

4. Check the answers as a class. Refer to the answer key on LP page 92. (Note that students will write the complete sentences in Exercise 5.)

VARIATION

An alternative way of doing this exercise is to write the sentence halves on strips of paper. Give one

---

strip to each student. Have them walk around the classroom and try to find their partner. Read the sentences aloud in the best order.

EXERCISE 4 [5 minutes]

In this exercise, students analyze the sentences in Exercise 3, noticing the position of the time marker.

1. Have students re-read the sentences from Exercise 3 and underline the part of the sentence that answer the question *when*?

2. Check the answers as a class. Refer to the answer key on LP page 92.

3. You may want to assign Focus 4 and Exercises 5 and 6 on the next page for homework.

For more practice, use *Grammar Dimensions 2* Workbook page 42, Exercise 4.

EXPANSION 1 [40 minutes]

You may want to use Activity 4 (speaking/ listening/writing) and Activity 5 (listening) on SB pages 101 and 102 to provide further practice of the past progressive for events that were in progress at a certain time in the past. Activity 4 can be used as an in-class interviewing activity (see Variation on LP page 101) or for homework.

EXPANSION 2 [30 minutes]

You may want to extend this activity to talk about events relevant to your students' personal experience. Ask students to close their eyes and think of their earliest memory, their first day at school, or the first time they met a significant other. Have students work in pairs.

FOCUS 4

Time Clauses with When, While, As Soon As, Before, and After

form

EXAMPLES

Dependent Time Clause	Main Independent Clause
(a) When Amy returned home,	everyone ran out to greet her.
(b) While my father was cooking dinner,	our guests arrived.
(c) Our guests arrived while my father was cooking dinner.	

EXPLANATIONS

A time clause is a **dependent** clause; this means that it is not complete by itself. It needs the rest of the sentence (**the main or independent** clause) to complete its meaning.

In order to understand *When Amy returned home,* we need more information.

A time clause can come at the beginning of a sentence (b) or at the end (c). If the time clause comes at the beginning of the sentence, use a comma between the time clause and the main clause.

When ~~~~~~, ~~~~~~

If the main clause comes at the beginning of the sentence and the time clause comes last, do not use a comma between the two clauses (c).

~~~~~~ when ~~~~~~

EXERCISE 5

Turn back to the sentences you created in Exercise 3. Write them below and add commas, as necessary.

1. _____
2. _____
3. _____
4. _____
5. _____

6. _____
7. _____
8. _____

EXERCISE 6

Check (✓) the sentence—(a) or (b)—closest in meaning to each statement.

1. While Mr. Meyer was brushing his teeth, someone entered the room.
   ___ a. Mr. Meyer finished brushing his teeth, before someone entered.
   ✓ b. Mr. Meyer was alone when he started brushing his teeth.

2. When he got Mrs. Meyer's call, Phil Fork left his office and drove to her house.
   ✓ a. Mrs. Meyer called before Phil Fork left his office.
   ___ b. Mrs. Meyer called after Phil Fork left his office.

3. As soon as he got into his car, he took out a cigarette and lit it.
   ___ a. He was smoking when he got into the car.
   ✓ b. He started to smoke after he got into his car.

4. While Fork was driving to the Meyers' house, he was listening to his favorite opera on the radio.
   ✓ a. He drove his car and listened to the radio at the same time.
   ___ b. He turned on the radio when he reached the Meyers' house.

5. When he got there, a number of police officers were searching the house for clues.
   ✓ a. They started when he got there.
   ___ b. They started before he got there.

6. As soon as Fork started to question Mrs. Meyer, she burst into tears.
   ✓ a. She was crying when he started to question her.
   ___ b. She started to cry when she began to question her.

7. Phil Fork carefully reviewed all his notes when he went home.
   ✓ a. He went home first.
   ___ b. He reviewed his notes first.

ANSWER KEY

Exercise 5 *See Answer Key for Exercises 3 and 4, LP page 92, for comma placement.*

FOCUS 4 [5 minutes]

This focus chart provides further information on the use of the time expressions introduced in Focus 3, concentrating on their form.

1. **Lead-in:** Write the example sentence on the board. (*When Amy returned home, everyone ran out to greet her.*) Ask: Which half of the sentence can stand alone as a complete sentence? (*Everyone ran out to greet her.*) Use this to explain the difference between dependent and independent clauses.

2. Read the examples and explanations in the focus chart. Emphasize the use of the comma in the two forms.

EXERCISE 5 [10 minutes]

This exercise builds on Exercises 3 and 4 and focuses on accuracy of form. If you have assigned this exercise for homework, go to Step 3.

1. Refer students back to the work they completed in Exercises 3 and 4.

2. Set a time limit for students to work individually to write all the complete sentences.

3. Students can compare answers in pairs.

4. Check the answers as a class. Refer to the answer key on LP page 94.

For more practice, use *Grammar Dimensions 2* Workbook page 43, Exercise 5.

EXPANSION 1 [20 minutes]

You may want to use Activity 7 on SB page 102 after this exercise. You can assign this for homework or as a class activity (see Variation on LP page 103).

EXERCISE 6 [10 minutes]

This exercise tests students' understanding of the time expressions and verb forms used. There is only one correct answer for each statement. If you have assigned this exercise for homework, go to Step 3.

1. Do the first question together as a class.

2. Set a time limit for students to complete the exercise individually.

3. Students can compare answers in pairs.

4. Check the answers as a class. Refer to the answer key on LP page 94.

EXPANSION 2 [20 minutes]

Use this exercise for further practice in recognizing the sequence of events in time clauses.

1. Write or dictate the following pairs of sentences, and ask students to explain the differences between them.

1(a) *When Dad came home, we ate dinner.*
1(b) *When Dad came home, we were eating dinner.*
2(a) *I was calling my sister when I heard the crash.*
2(b) *I called my sister when I heard the crash.*
3(a) *As soon as Mike finished work, he went to the library.*
3(b) *When Mike finished work, he went to the library.*
4(a) *When I arrived, they did their homework.*
4(b) *When I arrived, they were doing their homework.*

2. Ask students to complete the following sentence stems:

1. *While I was waiting for the bus, ...*
2. *When he saw the accident, ...*
3. *As soon as she finished the exam . . . .*
4. *I was doing my homework when . . . .*
5. *I was listening to music while . . . .*
6. *I called my friend as soon as . . . .*

EXERCISE 7

Work with a partner and write down five things you know about John Lennon.

Here is some more information about John Lennon's life. The wavy line (〰) indicates an action in progress. X indicates a completed action.

1. attend high school〰	2. attend high school〰
X	X
his mother dies	meet Paul McCartney
3. study at art school〰	4. perform in clubs in Liverpool〰
X	X
form the Beatles	sign his first recording contract
5. tour America〰	6. live in London〰
X	X
appear on the *Ed Sullivan Show*	fall in love with Yoko Ono
7. work for peace and write new songs〰	8. leave his apartment〰
X	X
die〰	one of his fans shoots him

Use this information to finish the short biography below. Fill in the blanks, using the simple past or the past progressive. The first one has been done for you as an example.

John Lennon was one of the most famous singer/songwriters of his time. He was born in Liverpool, England, in 1940, but his childhood was not very happy.

(1) _His mother died_ while _he was attending high school_. Life was difficult for John after his mother's death, but after a time things got better.

(2) _He met Paul McCartney_ while _he was attending high school_. Soon Paul introduced him to George Harrison, and they began to play in a band together. After John left high school, he became an art student. (3) While _he was studying at art school_, _he formed the Beatles_. After forming the Beatles, John married his first wife, Cynthia, and they had a son, Julian. (4) _He was performing in clubs in Liverpool_ when _he signed his first recording contract_. John and the Beatles moved to London and became very famous. They traveled all over the world. (5) While _they were touring the United States_, _they were on The Ed Sullivan Show_, a popular television show at the time.

(6) _He fell in love with Yoko Ono_ while _he was living in London_. A couple of years later, the Beatles split up. John and Yoko got married and moved to the United States, where their son Sean was born. John (7) _was working for peace and writing new songs_. On December 8, 1980, (8) _he died_ while _he was leaving his apartment_ when _one of his fans shot him_.

John Lennon died in 1980, but he still has lots of fans all over the world.

EXERCISE 7 [20 minutes]

This exercise introduces the use of different tenses in telling a continuous narrative of someone's life.

1. Look at the picture and ask students what they know about John Lennon. The goal of the first part of this activity is to activate background knowledge on John Lennon through brainstorming. This activity works well in pairs or groups. Don't worry if students do not use accurate grammar at this point. Possible answers include:

   He was born in Liverpool, England.

   He was a member of the Beatles.

   His second wife was Japanese.

   He was killed by one of his fans in New York City.

   He believed in peace and love and was against war.

   His sons Julian and Sean are singers.

2. After the brainstorming session, discuss their information as a class, writing some of the facts on the board.

3. Have students read the information in the chart and combine the two pieces of information in the orange box, using *when* and *while* as indicated.

4. Check the answers as a class.

5. Using the information in the chart, students fill in the blanks on SB page 97. Refer to the answer key on LP page 96.

Suggestion: If you do this activity as a class, copy the exercise on an overhead transparency to fill in students' answers.

EXPANSION 1 [30 minutes]

You may want to use Activity 1 on SB page 99 to provide further practice of past tenses and time clauses. Activity 1 is an information-gap activity based on a fictional life story.

EXPANSION 2 [30 minutes]

To extend this activity and personalize it, you can follow Activity 1 by using Activity 3 on SB page 101. This activity asks students to draw timelines for their own lives, exchange them with a partner and write a life history based on the information.

EXERCISE 8

Complete the sentences in the story below using the words in parentheses. Use the simple past or the past progressive. The first one has been done for you.

1. Wangari Maathai ___received___ (receive) the Nobel Peace Prize in 2004.

2. While Wangari ___was growing up___ (grow up) in Kenya, the land around her home ___had___ (have) plenty of trees and water.

3. While she ___was studying___ (study) biology in college in the United States and at the University of Nairobi, she ___realized___ (realize) the importance of plants and animals to the environment.

4. When she ___returned___ (return) home, she ___found___ (find) that large companies ___were destroying___ (destroy) the forests. Many of the trees and rivers were already gone.

5. When she ___asked___ (ask) poor women from her village about their problems, they ___told___ (tell) her how they walked many miles every day to get firewood and water.

6. So she ___worked___ (work) with these women to plant trees and ___created___ (create) the Green Belt Movement in 1977. In thirty years, they planted 30 million trees.

7. Before she ___started___ (start) to work with the women, they ___didn't feel___ (not + feel) they had any power to change their lives.

8. Some people ___attacked___ (attack) her, and she was injured while she ___was planting___ (plant) trees in the Karura Public Forest in Nairobi, Kenya.

9. The Kenyan Government ___arrested___ (arrest) her many times.

10. When Wangari ___received___ (receive) the Nobel Peace Prize in 2004, she ___made___ (make) a speech. She said that wars start because of unequal distribution of resources: "A healthy environment is the path to peace."

Use Your English

ACTIVITY 1 speaking/listening/writing

Nan Silviera has just written her first book:

As you can see below, the author's life story on the back of the book is not complete. Work with a partner to finish writing it.

■ **STEP 1** Student A: Turn to page 103. Student B: Turn to page A-16.

■ **STEP 2** You both have information about Nan's life, but some of the information is missing. Do not show your pages to each other, but ask each other questions to get information about the parts marked "?".

■ **STEP 3** Write down the information your partner gives you so that when you finish, you will have the complete story.

■ **STEP 4** Use the information from your chart to write the story of Nan's life. You can use the biography on the back of her book to begin writing.

■ **STEP 5** When you finish writing, check your work to see if you have used time clauses and the past progressive and simple past tenses appropriately.

JOURNEYS By Nan Silviera

JOURNEYS By Nan Silviera

About the author
Nan Silviera graduated from Arizona State University. In 1991 she sailed solo across the Pacific. After that she...

EXERCISE 8 [15 minutes]

This exercise continues practice in the correct use of tenses to sell someone's life story.

1. Brainstorm what students already know about Wangari Maathai or about the Nobel Peace Prize.

2. Have students work in pairs to complete the sentences. Circulate to provide help if necessary.

3. Check the answers as a class. Refer to the answer key on LP page 98.

4. If students want to find out more about Wangari Maathai, assign this for homework (or see Internet research activity for Activity 6 on SB page 102).

EXPANSION [30 minutes]

You may want to use Activity 6 on SB page 102 to provide further practice of past tenses and time clauses to tell a narrative. You can assign this for homework and use class time for students to make their presentations.

UNIT GOAL REVIEW [10 minutes]

Ask students to look at the goals on the opening page of the unit again. Help them understand how much they have accomplished in each area by eliciting answers from a few examples.

1. Use examples from some of the focus charts that illustrate the differences between the two structures, asking students why they think the writer chose that particular structure there.

2. To test their knowledge of the past progressive form and of the conjunctions *when*, *while*, and *as soon as*, write a few examples of incorrect use (perhaps taken from errors they have made earlier

in the class or homework) on the board. Ask some students to correct the errors.

ExamView®
Test Generator

For assessment of Unit 6, use *Grammar Dimensions 2 ExamView®*.

work book

For a grammar quiz review of Units refer students to pages 44–45 in the *Grammar Dimensions 2 Workbook*.

USE YOUR ENGLISH

The Use Your English activities in this section at the end of the unit contain situations that should naturally elicit the structures covered in that unit. For a more complete discussion of how to use the Use Your English activities, see To the Teacher, LP page xxii). When students are doing these activities in class, you can circulate and listen to see if they are using the structures accurately. Errors can be corrected after the activity has finished.

ACTIVITY 1 speaking/listening/writing [25 minutes]

You may want to use this activity after Exercise 7 on SB pages 96 and 97. This activity has two main phases. The first phase is speaking when students exchange information from their timelines. The second stage is writing, where they use the information to write a paragraph.

1. Divide students into pairs. Students turn to the appropriate page and read their information.

2. Students work in pairs to complete the missing information.

3. When they have finished, students work individually to write their paragraphs.

4. Ask volunteers to read their completed paragraphs aloud.

5. Select typical errors for class correction.

Suggestion: You may want to follow this activity with Activity 3 on SB page 101, which asks students to draw their own timelines.

METHODOLOGY NOTE

Students must complete this activity in pairs, since each of them has incomplete information. If you have an odd number of students, have some students work in groups of three, and assign one student to act as "secretary."

ACTIVITY 2 speaking/listening/writing

In this activity, you will be gathering information about your classmates' lives by asking what they were doing at the times shown below. In the last box on the chart, add a time of your own choice (for example, on your last birthday, last New Year's Eve, etc.). Do not write information about yourself.

STEP 1 Think about the different students in your class. Can you guess what they were doing at these times? In the box marked *Guesses*, write what you think different people were doing at each time.

STEP 2 Go around the room and talk to as many people as possible to find out what they were really doing.

STEP 3 Write this information in the box marked *Facts*.

NOTE: Copy the chart into your notebook if you need more space to write. If you don't want to give information about a certain time, you can say, "I'm sorry but I'd rather not talk about that time." If you can't remember, you can invent something.

TIMES	GUESSES	FACTS
at 8:30 P.M last Sunday		
in May 1993		
five years ago		
ten years ago today		
????? (you choose a time)		

STEP 4 When you finish, review the information you collected. Choose the most interesting or surprising facts and make a short report (oral or written). Report on the facts, not on your original guesses. For example:

I asked my classmates about certain times in their lives. For example, at 8:30 P.M. yesterday, Sam Wu was working on her homework, and Tran was at home watching TV.

ACTIVITY 3 speaking/writing

STEP 1 Take a large sheet of paper and make a time line for your own life like the one used on page 103. Bring your time line to class and describe the story of your life to your classmates.

STEP 2 Exchange your time line with a partner. Use his or her time line to write the story of your partner's life. How many differences and similarities can you find between your partner's life history and yours?

ACTIVITY 4 speaking/listening/writing

On December 26, 2004, a huge tidal wave—called a tsunami—hit many countries of Southeast Asia including Indonesia, Thailand, Sri Lanka, and India. The giant wave—up to 100 feet high in some places—was caused by an earthquake under the Indian Ocean off the coast of Sumatra. The tsunami killed about 275,000 people and was one of the worst natural disasters in modern history. The tsunami is sometimes called the Boxing Day Tsunami because it took place on December 26, which is a holiday called Boxing Day in many countries. Do you remember what you were doing when you heard about the Boxing Day Tsunami?

STEP 1 With a partner, interview one or two people about what they were doing when they heard the news of the Boxing Day or Asian Tsunami. If possible, record your interviews. Before the interview, get together with your partner to make a list of possible questions. You can use the questions below or make other questions of your own, if you prefer.

STEP 2 Share the results of your interviews with the class.

STEP 3 Listen to your recording and write down any sentences with the simple past or the past progressive. Underline any time clauses in these sentences.

- What were you doing when you heard the news of the Boxing Day Tsunami?
- Where were you living at that time?
- Who were you with?
- What did you do after you heard about it?
- How did you feel?
- Add your own questions.

USE YOUR ENGLISH

ACTIVITY 2 speaking/listening/writing [30 minutes]

You may want to use this activity after Exercise 2 on SB page 91. This activity allows students to practice the past progressive by talking about events relevant to their own lives.

1. Read the chart with your students.
2. **Suggestion:** You may wish to modify the chart so that it is more appropriate to your students' context.
3. Decide if you want to do this activity as a class or in small groups (see Note below).
4. Have students fill in the last box with their own idea. Some examples are: *in December 1996; this time three weeks ago; right before class.*
5. Set a time limit of 5 minutes for students to fill in the "Guesses" column.
6. Set a time limit of 15 minutes for students to fill in the "Facts" column.
7. Circulate to provide help and monitor errors. Students should be asking questions in the past progressive (either *Yes/No* or *Wh-* questions.)
8. Ask volunteers to make a short verbal report about what they found out.

METHODOLOGY NOTE

You can do this activity as a class walk-around activity, or as group work. If you do this as group work, each student will only make guesses about the other people in the group. If you do this as a whole class, you can make sure all students are included by writing students' names on separate slips of paper. Make sure each student's name appears three or four times. Distribute several slips to each student.

ACTIVITY 3 speaking/writing [30 minutes]

You may want to use this activity after Exercise 7 on SB pages 96 and 97. Activity 3 allows students to share information about themselves while naturally using the structures covered in this unit. Step 2 is especially helpful in practicing the third person forms.

1. Remind students of the time line in Activity 1. If you did not do Activity 1, ask them to look at SB page 103 to see what a time line looks like.
2. Provide large sheets of paper for students to draw their time lines. Note: If students are shy about talking about their early lives, they can restrict their time lines to events since they started college, or since they came to the United States.
3. Set a time limit of 10 minutes for students to draw their timelines.
4. When students are finished, they can exchange timelines with a partner.
5. Allow time for students to ask questions at this stage to clarify any points that are unclear.
6. Students can write a paragraph about their partner's life, or present an oral report to the class.

ACTIVITY 4 speaking/listening/writing [30 minutes]

You may want to use this activity after Exercise 4 on SB page 93. This activity can be done as homework or as an in-class interviewing activity (see *Variation* below).

1. Read the introduction to the activity together with your students. Make sure they understand the event that is being described. **Note:** Boxing Day refers to December 26, the day after Christmas Day.

2. Read the questions and ask students to add a few more questions of their own.
3. Assign the interviews for homework.
4. Have students report on the results of their interviews.
5. Write up some examples of past tense time clauses.

VARIATION 1

You may wish to adapt this activity to an event that is more memorable to your students personally, perhaps something that was in the news recently.

VARIATION 2

You can also do this as an in-class interviewing activity, making sure that the events chosen are ones that all students find memorable. If you have access to recording equipment, you can record one or two of the interviews (perhaps sending one pair outside to record their interview in a quiet place, while the others are still busy). You could also record one or two of the presentations.

ACTIVITY 5 listening

For this activity, you will hear three conversations with people being interviewed about what they were doing when they heard about the Boxing Day Asian Tsunami.

CD Tracks 9,10,11

STEP 1 Listen to the audio and take notes in the chart below.

CONVERSATION	PLACE	WHAT WAS THIS PERSON DOING?	WHAT DID THIS PERSON DO AFTER THAT?
Speaker 1	at home in Florida		
Speaker 2			
Speaker 3			

STEP 2 Listen to the audio again and write down any examples of the past progressive or simple past.

ACTIVITY 6 research on the web

On the Web: Think of a famous person you want to know more about. Go to the Internet and use a search engine such as Google® or Yahoo® to find information about his or her life. Type the name of the person and *biography*. Draw a brief time line of the main events in his or her life. Show the time line to your classmates and explain the sequence of events.

ACTIVITY 7 reflection

Think of three key events in your life. What happened? Why were they important? Make sentences using time clauses to describe these events. Try to use the different time clauses you learned in this unit.

Activity 1 (from p.99)
Student A

| 1990 | 1991 | 1992 | 1993 | 1994 | 1995 | 1996 | 1997 | 1998 | 1999 | 2000 | 2001 | 2002 | 2003 | 2004 | 2005 | 2006 |

Travel in Asia and India
Work in Paris
Study journalism at University of Oregon

Go to France
Return to USA
Have a baby
Begin to write a book
Finish book
Win Pulitzer Prize for her book

Graduate from Arizona State University
Sail across the Pacific alone

Activity 5 **Step 2:** *Check audio script on page S-3 of this book for answers.*

Activity 6 *Possible answers are:*
Martin Luther King, Jr.
- 1929, born in Atlanta, Georgia
- 1948, receives a divinity degree at Crozer Theological Seminary in Pennsylvania
- 1953, marries Coretta Scott
- August 28, 1963, makes a famous speech, "I have a dream"

Activity 5 **Step 1:**

Speaker	Place	What were they doing?	What did they do?
Speaker 1	At home in Florida	Sitting down to lunch	Sent a check to the Red Cross
Speaker 2	At a church in New York	Clearing up after dinner	Asked his friends if they knew anyone over there
Speaker 3	At her parents'	Getting ready to drive	Sent some money and some

USE YOUR ENGLISH

ACTIVITY 5
listening
[30 minutes]

CD Tracks 9,10,11

This activity works best if used after Activity 3 on SB page 101.

1. Remind students of the tsunami which was described in the introduction to Activity 4.

2. Explain that they will hear three different speakers talking about what they were doing when they heard about the Boxing Day Tsunami.

3. Play the audio. See audio script on LP page S-3.

4. Allow time for students to compare answers in pairs.

5. Play the audio again.

6. Check the answers as a class. Refer to the answer key on LP page 102.

ACTIVITY 6
research on the web

You may want to use this activity after Exercise 8 on SB page 98.

If you have a computer lab, you can assign one famous person's life or biography for the whole class to study. Assemble the information gathered in a timeline on the board. If you assign this as homework, it may be more interesting to assign different famous people to different groups and have groups present their timeline to the class.

ACTIVITY 7
reflection
[30 minutes]

You may want to use this activity after Exercise 5 on SB page 94.

This activity provides an opportunity for students to use the target structures of the unit while reflecting on their language learning progress. You may have asked students to keep a record of their learning journal throughout this course as suggested in To the Teacher (see page xxii). This reflection activity will form part of that learning record. You can also ask students to focus on something that happened to make them choose their life path.

VARIATION

This activity can be also used as a group activity to discuss events that happened to them in your school or college. What happened on their first day? Or in their first class? Were there any misunderstandings? Were there any amusing incidents?

SIMILARITIES AND DIFFERENCES
Comparatives, Superlatives,
As . . . As, Not As . . . As

UNIT GOALS

- **Use comparatives and superlatives to express differences**
- **Understand the meaning of *as . . . as* and *not as . . . as***
- **Form sentences with *as . . . as* and *not as . . . as***
- **Use *as . . . as* and *not as . . . as* to make tactful comparisons**

OPENING TASK

Friends

■ STEP 1

Can you guess the names of the people in the picture? Work by yourself or with a partner. Use the information in the chart and the list of clues to identify each person. Write their names in the correct position on the picture.

The Left   The Right

Diana

NAME	AGE	OCCUPATION	HAIR	HEIGHT
LINDA	75	doctor	short, white	5'9 1/2"
BOB	21	student	medium-length, brown	5'9 1/2"
SUSAN	25	student	long, blond	5'1"
FRANK	43	artist	short, gray	6'4"
CARLA	28	singer	medium-length, black	5'5"
GEORGE	44	writer	bald	5'10"
DIANA	58	engineer	medium-length, brown	5'10"

Clues

1. The oldest person is next to the youngest person.
2. The tallest woman is in front of someone thirty years younger than she is.
3. The shortest person is in front of someone with white hair.
4. The tallest man is next to the tallest woman.
5. The 28-year-old is in front of the youngest person.
6. The man with short wavy hair is not quite as tall as the person next to him on the right.
7. The man on the right of the youngest person is behind the tallest person.
8. The youngest person is as tall as the person next to him on the left.

When you finish, check your answers with the rest of the class to see if you all agree. You can find the solution to the Opening Task on page A-16.

■ STEP 2

Work in pairs. Describe one person in the picture by comparing him or her with the other people. Your partner will guess which person you are describing.

Example: *She's taller than Susan, but has shorter hair than Diana.* (*Answer:* Linda)

UNIT 7 LESSON PLAN 1

UNIT OVERVIEW

Unit 7 provides a review of comparative and superlative forms with adjectives, nouns, and verbs. It also presents and practices structures *as . . . as*, and *not as . . . as*.

UNIT GOALS

Some instructors may want to review the goals listed on this page after completing the Opening Task so that students understand what they should know by the end of the unit. These goals can also be reviewed at the end of the unit when students are more familiar with the grammar terminology.

GRAMMAR NOTE

Comparatives are used to compare one thing (or person) with another thing (or person). Superlatives are used to compare one thing with a group of other things (or people). Most languages have one main way of forming comparatives and superlatives, so it can be confusing that English has two different forms, using either *-er/-est* or *more/most*. The structure *isn't as . . . as* is more commonly used than in spoken English than the structure *less than* and may not easily be recognized as a comparative form.

OPENING TASK [30 minutes]

The purpose of the Opening Task is to create a context in which students will need to talk about similarities and differences using comparative structures. The problem-solving format is designed to show the teacher how well the students can produce the target structures implicitly and spontaneously when they are engaged in a communicative task. For a more complete

discussion of the purposes of the Opening Task, see To the Teacher, Lesson Planner (LP) page xxii.

Setting Up the Task

■ STEP 1

1. Draw the chart on the board. Have students copy it into their notebooks. It is enough to make lines or spaces (or oval head-shapes) for the seven positions.

2. Explain that this task is a puzzle. Students will have to work out the names of the people in the picture by using the clues on the next page.

3. Have students work alone or in pairs to read the chart, read the clues, and then work on the puzzle.

Conducting the Task

1. While students are working, you can circulate and listen in order to get an idea of their current use of *not as . . . as*, *as . . . as*, comparative, and superlative structures. Note the structures that seem to be problematic.

2. When students have completed reviewing the information individually or with a partner, they should check their answers with the rest of the class or in groups. The aim is now to encourage everyone to talk as much as possible. Students may naturally use comparative structures while trying to solve the puzzle.

Closing the Task

■ STEP 2

1. For each of the seven positions in the Opening Task, you can have a student or a pair of students give one statement that supports their answer.

2. Write these statements on the board.

3. If they are inaccurate, allow students time to reformulate them. Don't attempt to explain errors

at this stage, but see if students can spontaneously correct their errors once they have been pointed out. For example,

Student: *The most tallest people are standing next to each other.*

You: *the most tallest?*

Student: *the tallest*

4. Check the answers as a class. See answers on Student Book (SB) page A-16.

GRAMMAR NOTE

Typical student errors (form)

(See Focus Chart 2.)

- Using *more* or *most* with *-er* or *-est* forms, e.g. * *She is more nicer than me.* * *The most tallest person is on the left.* (See Focus Chart 1.)
- Omitting the definite article with superlatives, * *He is tallest in the class.* (See Focus Chart 1.)
- Omitting the comparative form of the adjective, * *Your book is difficult than mine.* (See Focus Chart 1.)
- Errors with irregular forms, e.g. * *The situation is getting more bad/badder.* (See Focus Chart 1.)
- Errors with use of *than*, * *Linda is taller from Bob.* * *Linda is as tall than Bob.* (See Focus Chart 1.)
- Using *much* with countable nouns, e.g. * *He doesn't have as much friends as I do.* (See Focus Chart 3.)
- Errors with pronouns, e.g. * *I speak better than she.* * *Her hair is longer than me.* (See Focus Chart 3.)

Typical student errors (use)

- Not recognizing comparative forms, e.g. * *Is this book cheaper? No, it isn't cheap.*
- Using comparisons that can seem impolite, e.g. * *You are fatter than her.* (See Focus Chart 4.)

FOCUS 1

Expressing Difference: Comparatives and Superlatives

form → meaning

EXAMPLES

Susan   Frank

(a) Susan is **the shortest**, and Frank is **the tallest**.

Carla   Linda   George

(b) George is **taller than** Linda.
(c) Carla is **shorter than** George.

	Comparative	Superlative
young	younger than	the youngest
easy	easier than	the easiest
difficult	more/less difficult than	the most/the least difficult
carefully	more/less carefully than	the most/the least carefully
weigh	weigh more/less than	weigh the most/the least
money	more/less money than	the most/the least money

(d) George sings **better** (**worse**) than I do.
(e) Carla is the **best** (**worst**) singer in the family.

EXPLANATIONS

The tallest and *the shortest* are superlatives. Superlatives show extremes of difference among people or things. They show which has the greatest amount of a certain quality in a group of people or things.

Taller than and *shorter than* are comparatives. Comparatives show differences among people or things, but they do not show extremes of difference.

Comparatives and superlatives can be used with all parts of speech:
- adjectives with one syllable
- adjectives with one syllable + -*y*
- adjectives with two or more syllables

- adverbs

- verbs

- nouns

Some comparative and superlative forms are irregular. Examples (d) and (e) use irregular comparative and superlative forms of *good* and *bad*.

EXERCISE 1

First fill in the blanks with a word or word ending, and then use the information from the Opening Task to decide if the statements are true (T) or false (F).

1. The oldest woman is taller <u>than</u> the oldest man.   T   (F)
2. George is tall<u>er</u> than the person beside him.   (T)   F
3. Diana is young<u>er</u> <u>than</u> the woman beside her on the right.   T   (F)
4. George is tall<u>er</u> <u>than</u> Frank.   T   (F)
5. The singer is several years older <u>than</u> the person behind her.   T   (F)
6. The doctor is <u>the</u> old<u>est</u> _____.   T   F
7. Bob is old<u>er</u> <u>than</u> the person in front of him.   T   (F)
8. The young<u>est</u> woman is in front of <u>the</u> old<u>est</u> woman.   (T)   F
9. Frank is <u>the</u> tall<u>est</u> man, but he isn't <u>the</u> old<u>est</u>.   (T)   F
10. <u>The</u> old<u>est</u> man is short<u>er</u> <u>than</u> the young<u>est</u> woman.   T   (F)

Now write three statements about the people in the box found in the Opening Task. They can be True (T) or False (F). Show them to your partner. Your partner will decide if they are true or false.

Example: *The doctor is taller than Carla.* (False)

EXERCISE 2

Work with a partner. Read the information at right about working hours and vacation times. Ask your partner questions about each person, using the comparative and the superlative. Or, write down the questions and share them with a partner or the class.

NAME	WORKING HOURS	VACATION TIME
LINDA	8 A.M.–5 P.M.	4 weeks
BOB	9 A.M.–4 P.M.	12 weeks
SUSAN	9 A.M.–4 P.M.	12 weeks
FRANK	6 A.M.–1 P.M.	none
CARLA	9 P.M.–2 A.M.	6 weeks
GEORGE	7 A.M.–3 P.M.	3 weeks
DIANA	9 A.M.–5 P.M.	2 weeks

Examples: **A:** *Who starts work the earliest?*
    B: *Frank does.*
    A: *Who finishes work later, Susan or Linda?*
    B: *Linda.*

ANSWER KEY

Exercise 2   *Answers will vary.*

UNIT 7 LESSON PLAN 1

FOCUS 1 [15 minutes]

This focus chart explains the difference between comparatives (with *-er*) and superlatives (with *-est*). It also gives examples of comparatives and superlatives in different parts of speech. Examples (d) and (e) use irregular forms. (Comparatives and superlatives are typically presented in lower levels of English instruction so this should be review for most students.)

1. **Lead-in:** Draw a picture on the board of five people in order of height, age, and weight. Write the name, age, and weight under each person. Use the drawing to elicit comparatives and superlatives using adjectives: tall, short, old, young, heavy. Have students ask questions (*Who is the tallest?*) and practice sentences (*Linda is the shortest*).

2. Read the examples and explanations in the first two sections of the box. Check that students understand the difference in meaning between comparative and superlative forms.

3. Check that students understand the difference in form between short and long adjectives, and the rules for making the *-er* form of short adjectives. (See Language Note below.) You can do this by dictating a few adjectives and having students write the comparative and superlative form, or by drawing the following chart on the board and having students copy the chart and complete it in their notebooks.

Adjective	Comparative	Superlative
big		
nice		
friendly		
interesting		
important		

4. Review comparatives and superlatives with adverbs, verbs, and nouns by reading the examples in the box. Make additional examples using information from your students if appropriate. For example:

Who woke up the earliest?
Did you wake up earlier/later than (name)?
Do you drive carefully?
Do you drive more carefully than (student name)?
Who had the biggest breakfast this morning?
Who drank the most coffee/tea?

Was your breakfast bigger than (student's name)'s?
Did you drink more coffee than (student's name)?
Who traveled the farthest to get to class this morning?
Did you travel farther than (student's name)?

LANGUAGE NOTE

Rules for forming comparatives and superlatives of short adjectives: Most short adjectives add *-er* and *-est*. Adjectives ending in *-e* add *-r* and *-st*, e.g. *nicer, nicest*. Adjectives ending in one vowel and one consonant double the consonant, e.g. *bigger, biggest*. Adjectives ending in *-y* change to *-ier* and *-iest*, e.g. *heavier, heaviest*. The comparative/superlative forms of the adjectives/adverbs *good/well* and *bad/badly* are the same: *better/best, worse/worst*. Other irregular forms are *far, farther/further, farthest/furthest* and *old, older/elder, oldest/eldest*.

EXERCISE 1 [10 minutes]

In order to do this exercise, you will need the information from the Opening Task. The answers here all use regular comparative and superlative forms.

1. Turn back to the Opening Task and remind students of the answers to the puzzle. If any students were not present for the Opening Task, pair them up with someone who has the answers, or have them do the Opening Task individually now.

2. Do the first question together as a class.

3. Have students complete the remaining questions individually.

4. Compare answers as a class. Refer to the answer key on LP page 10.

EXERCISE 2 [10 minutes]

This exercise provides practice with the comparative and superlative forms with adverbs, verbs, and nouns.

1. Read the chart with your students.

2. Elicit two or three questions from the students and write them on the board.

Who starts work the earliest/latest?
Who finishes the earliest/latest?
Who starts work earlier, Bob or Frank?
Who has the shortest/longest vacation?
Who has a longer vacation, Linda or Susan? etc.

3. Have students work in pairs to ask and answer questions about the chart.

For more practice, use *Grammar Dimensions 2* Workbook page 46, Exercise 1; page 48, Exercise 2; and page 49, Exercise 3.

EXPANSION 1 [15 minutes]

Use this exercise to provide further practice of comparative and superlative forms with adverbs, verbs, and nouns.

1. Have students conduct a group survey to find out who gets up the earliest/latest, works the longest/shortest hours, drives the longest/shortest distance to school, etc.

2. Have students draw a chart in their notebooks similar to the one on SB page 107 using the names of their group members. The group can choose what facts they want to survey.

3. Circulate as the groups conduct their survey and take note of any errors.

4. Ask volunteers to report on the results of their survey.

EXPANSION 2 [20 minutes]

You may want to use Activity 8 on SB page 119 after this exercise to provide further practice of comparative and superlative forms.

meaning

FOCUS 2

Similarity and Difference: *As . . . As* and *Not As . . . As*

EXAMPLES

Linda is about 5'9". Bob is about 5'9".

(a) Linda is **as tall as** Bob.
OR
Bob is **as tall as** Linda.

(b) George is **exactly as tall as** Diana.
OR
Diana is **exactly as tall as** George.

George is 5'10". Bob is 5'9 1/2".

(c) Bob is { almost / not quite / nearly / practically / just about } as tall as George

George is 5'10". Bob is 5'9 1/2".

(d) Bob is **not as tall as** George.

Susan is 5'11". Diana is 5'10".

(e) Susan is { nowhere near / not nearly / not anywhere near } as tall as Diana.

EXPLANATIONS

To show similarity among people or things, you can use *as . . . as.*

To show that people or things are the same, you can add *exactly.*

To show that people or things are very similar, add: *almost, not quite, nearly, practically,* or *just about.*

To show differences among people or things, you can use *not as . . . as.*

To show a great amount of difference, add: *nowhere near, not nearly,* or *not anywhere near.*

Nowhere near and *not anywhere near* are only used in very informal conversation with friends.

EXERCISE 3

Get together with another student. Think of all the ways that you are similar and all the ways that you are different. You have five minutes to make as many sentences as you can, using *as . . . as* and *not as . . . as* to show these differences and similarities. Share your sentences with the rest of the class.

Example: *Fernando isn't quite as tall as I am.*

EXERCISE 4

Use the information in the Opening Task to write complete sentences about the following people. You can use a comparative, a superlative, *as . . . as,* or *not as . . . as* in each sentence. Show the amount of difference or similarity as necessary.

1. Linda/Bob/height
   Linda is as tall as Bob.

2. Susan/Frank/height   *Susan is not as tall as Frank./Susan is shorter than Frank./Frank is taller than Susan.*

3. Linda/Diana/height
   Linda is almost/nearly/not quite/practically as tall as Diana.

4. Linda/Carla/height
   Carla is not as tall as Linda./Linda is taller than Carla./Carla is shorter than Linda.

5. George/Susan/height and age
   George is (both) older and taller than Susan.

6. Bob/George/height
   Bob is almost/nearly/not quite/practically as tall as George.

7. Frank/George/age
   Frank is almost/not quite/nearly/practically as old as George.

8. Diana/Linda/age
   Diana is not as old as Linda./Diana is younger than Linda.

9. Frank/height
   Frank is the tallest.

10. Linda/age
    Linda is the oldest.

11. George/Diana/height
    George is exactly as tall as Diana./Diana is exactly as tall as George.

ANSWER KEY

Exercise 3 *Answers will vary.*

LESSON PLAN 1

FOCUS 2 [5 minutes]

1. **Lead-in:** Draw a picture of two people the same height and age on the board. Write their names and elicit sentences about them such as *Marta is as tall as Maria, Marta is as old as Maria*, etc. (You may also get sentences such as *Marta is the same height/age as Maria*. These sentences are also correct, but not presented in this section.)

2. Examples (b) and (c) show how to qualify and add finer distinctions to this structure. If students are still struggling with the basic structure, you can teach these additional points for recognition only. Emphasize the information in (e)—that these phrases are very informal, and rarely used in formal writing.

3. Encourage students to draw pictures in their notebooks to illustrate the new grammar points in this focus chart.

METHODOLOGY NOTE

Encourage students to use visuals in their notebooks to help them remember grammar examples. Some students may find it childish to draw pictures. Others might say they just don't know how to draw. It may be helpful to explain something to them about different learning styles, and how exercising different parts of our brain by using different styles can improve our learning capacity. Pictures can last longer in our memory than words, and badly drawn or humorous pictures sometimes last even longer! As always when giving advice to students, it is more convincing if you can lead by example and draw pictures on the board.

EXERCISE 3 [10 minutes]

This exercise provides students with an opportunity to personalize the grammar presented in Focus Chart 2.

1. Divide students into pairs, preferably with someone they don't usually work with.

2. Set a time limit of 5 minutes for students to find as many similarities and differences between them as they can. **Suggestion:** In order to target the structures in Focus Chart 2, it may help to focus attention on adjectives that describe personality. You might want to brainstorm a list of personality adjectives before starting the exercise.

3. Have students report on the number of *as . . . as* sentences they made.

4. The pair who made the most can share their sentences aloud with the class.

5. Give 1 point for each sentence that is correctly formed and factually true.

6. Students who are listening should determine whether the sentences are correctly formed. If not, they can correct them, and no points are assigned.

EXERCISE 4 [15 minutes]

This exercise provides practice in all of the comparative and superlative structures studied so far. Students can use the phrases in Focus 2 examples (c) and (e), to talk about *amounts* of differences. If these finer differences of meaning are still confusing, they can still do this exercise with the basic *as . . . as* structure. You may want to assign this exercise as homework.

1. Remind students of the information in the Opening Task.

2. Ask students to present their answers orally.

3. Then allow some time for students to write the answers.

4. Check the answers as a class. Refer to the answer key on LP page 108.

For more practice, use *Grammar Dimensions 2 Workbook* page 50, Exercise 4.

EXPANSION [20 minutes]

You may want to use Activity 7 on SB page 118 after this exercise to provide further practice of comparisons using adjectives, adverbs, nouns, and verbs.

FOCUS 3

Using As . . . As and Not As . . . As

form

EXAMPLES	EXPLANATIONS
(a) Susan is **not as** tall **as** Carla. (b) Frank does not work **as** quickly **as** George. (c) Linda does not have **as** much money **as** Diana. (d) Diana does not have **as** many friends **as** Carla. (e) George **works as** much **as** Linda.	*As . . . as* and *not as . . . as* can be used with all parts of speech: • adjectives • adverbs • noncount nouns • count nouns • verbs
(f) Susan works as hard as Carla works. (g) Carla is not as tall as Linda is. (h) Susan works as hard as Carla does. (i) Susan works as hard as Carla. (j) Carla is not as tall as her younger sister. (k) Susan works as hard as I/you/he/she/we/they.	In sentences using *as . . . as* or *not as . . . as*, the second *as* can be followed by: • clauses • reduced clauses • noun phrases • subject pronouns
(l) Susan works as hard as he works. OR (m) Susan works as hard as he does.	In sentences where the verb is repeated after the second *as*, you can use a form of *do* instead.
(n) Susan works **as hard as he.** OR (o) Susan works **as hard as him.**	The same verb does not need to be repeated a second time. Using the subject pronoun (*he, she, I, we, you, they*) here is very formal. The object pronoun (*him, her, me, us, you, them*) is very common in conversation and informal writing.
(p) Susan's hair is not as short as mine.	Remember to use a possessive pronoun where necessary.
(q) Susan's hair is as long as mine. (r) Susan's hair is as long as me.	In examples (q) and (r), both sentences are correct, but there is a big difference in meaning!

EXERCISE 5

Correct the mistakes in the following sentences.

Example: Miriam is more serious ~~as~~ *than* her sister, Hester.

1. All her life, Hester has been ~~lucky~~ *luckier* than her sister, Miriam.

2. Hester is not *as* intelligent as Miriam, but she was always more successful than Miriam in school.

3. For example, Hester's grades were always better than ~~Miriam~~. *Miriam's*

4. Both sisters are pretty, but many people believe that Miriam is prettier ~~that~~ *than* her sister.

5. However, Miriam does not have as many boyfriends ~~than~~ *as* her sister does.

6. They both have excellent jobs, but Miriam thinks her job isn't as interesting as her *sister's* ~~sister.~~

7. They both travel as part of their work, but Hester goes to more exciting places *than* Miriam ~~is~~ *does*.

8. In spite of these differences, Miriam thinks that she is happier ~~that~~ *than* her sister is.

9. However, Hester thinks that good luck is *more* important than good looks and intelligence.

What do **you** think is the most important: good luck, good looks, or intelligence? Why do you think so? Share your ideas with your classmates.

LESSON PLAN 2

FOCUS 3 [10 minutes]

1. **Lead-in:** Review the meaning of *as . . . as* from Focus Chart 2. Check the answers to Exercise 4 if you assign this as homework.

2. Give a short drill with this structure by providing prompts in the comparative form, for example:

   You: *Carla is taller than Susan.*

   Students: *Susan is not as tall as Carla.*

   You: *George works more quickly than Frank.*

   Students: *Frank doesn't work as quickly as George.*

   You: *Diana has more money than Linda.*

   Students: *Diana doesn't have as much money as Linda.*

   You: *Diana has more friends than Linda.*

   Students: *Diana doesn't have as many friends as Linda.*

3. Read the examples and explanations in the focus chart.

4. Point out the alternative forms in example (f).

   Susan works as hard as I. (formal)

   Susan works as hard as I do. (neutral)

   Susan works as hard as me. (informal)

5. Review possessive pronouns in examples (p) and (q): *mine, yours, his, hers, ours, theirs.*

LANGUAGE NOTE

Many problems with forming comparative and superlative structures in English are caused by interference from the first language. If many or most students in your class share the same first language, it may be helpful to make an explicit comparison between comparative/superlative structures in both languages. This can help to identify the cause of some of the most frequent errors. You may want to use Activity 10 on SB page 119 at some point in this unit to raise students' awareness of this issue.

EXERCISE 5 [15 minutes]

This exercise focuses on grammatical accuracy in using *(not) as . . . as* structures. It also practices editing skills.

1. Correct the first sentence together with the class.

2. Divide the class into pairs or small groups.

3. Have one student come to the board, while the other students dictate the answers to him or her.

4. If there are disagreements, allow students time to defend and justify their answers.

EXPANSION [20 minutes]

You can follow this exercise with further practice in writing a description.

1. First, provide a description of you compared to a family member or a colleague. For example,

   My sister and I look a lot alike, people tell us, but we're really quite different. I'm not as organized as she is. I'm not as good at keeping track of expenses (as she is), my house isn't as clean (as hers is), my car isn't as new (as hers is), and my clothes aren't as nice (as hers are).

   Note: Notice that the second *as* phrase (in parentheses, above) is optional when the context has been established and it is clear what is being compared to what.

2. Then ask students to think of a family member or a friend and think of ways in which they are similar or different.

3. They can fill out a chart like this:

	You	Your friend
personality		
interests		
clothes		
habits		

3. Tell their partner about the differences using *as. . .as* structures if possible.

4. You can use this exercise as a way of brainstorming ideas for a description essay. Assign the essay for homework.

[workbook]

For more practice, use *Grammar Dimensions 2 Workbook* page 50, Exercise 5.

use

Making Tactful Comparisons with As . . . As and *Not As . . . As*

Sometimes it is important to be tactful (more polite and less direct) when you are making comparisons. The adjective you choose can show how tactful your comparison is.

EXAMPLES

Some adjectives commonly used in making comparisons:

Express "MORE":	Express "LESS":
tall	short
old	young
large	small
fast	slow

(a) Linda is as tall as Bob.

(b) Linda is as short as Bob.

(c) Patricia is as old as Virginia.

(d) Patricia is as young as Virginia.

Bob   Frank

(e) Bob is not as tall as Frank.

(f) Frank is not as short as Bob.

(g) Otis is not quite as smart as Rocky.

(h) His latest book is not quite as good as his earlier ones.

EXPLANATIONS

When you use *as . . . as*, it is more common or usual to use an adjective that expresses "more." When you use an adjective that expresses "less," you draw special attention to it because it is an unusual use.

In (a), the use of *tall* is usual. It does not make us think about how tall or how short Bob and Linda are, but only that they are the same height.

In (b), the use of *short* is unusual. It makes us think that both Bob and Linda are very short.

In (c), the use of *old* is usual. It shows only that they are the same age.

In (d), the use of *young* is unusual. It therefore puts special emphasis on *young*.

Both (e) and (f) show that Frank is taller than Bob. However, the use of *short* in (f) is unusual, so it draws special attention to the fact that Bob is short. It is more tactful and more polite to choose (e).

When you want to be really polite and tactful, you can use *not quite as . . . as*.

EXERCISE 6

Work in a group to create a problem like the one in the Opening Task. First use the picture and blank chart below to record your information and then write the clues. Each clue must contain at least one of the following: a comparative, a superlative, *as . . . as*, or *not as . . . as*. Finally, exchange your problem with that from another group and see if you can solve each other's problems.

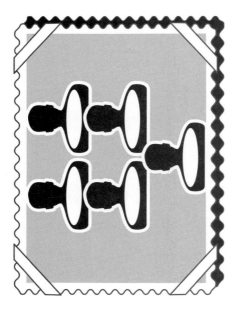

NAME	AGE	HEIGHT	OCCUPATION	WORKING HOURS

Clues

_____

_____

_____

_____

ANSWER KEY

Exercise 6   *Answers will vary.*

LESSON PLAN 2

EXERCISE 6 [30 minutes]

This is a highly productive exercise, always much enjoyed by students, and is well worth the time it takes to construct the problem. Students should be encouraged to create people of their own rather than using information based on the people in the Opening Task. Many students will choose to write about their classmates or about famous people.

1. Turn back to the Opening Task and remind students of how they worked out the identity of the people by reading the clues.

2. Explain that students will now create their own puzzle, using different descriptions of people.

3. Divide the class into small groups. The task is divided into four steps.

   a. Select a group of people (students, famous people, or imaginary people).

   b. Write their names on the picture and their descriptions in the chart.

   c. Write the clues (using comparative and superlative forms).

   d. Exchange clues with another group who will fill in a blank picture.

4. Students can copy the chart into their notebooks, making sure that they have enough space for all the people shown in the picture and enough lines for their clues.

Suggestion: If there is not enough time to solve each other's problems, students could turn the completed problems in to you, and you can try to solve them for "homework."

FOCUS 4 [15 minutes]

1. **Lead-in:** Introduce the topic by contrasting comparisons about height and age.

   She's as tall as I am.   Do you think the speaker is tall or short? (We don't know.)

   She's as short as I am.   Do you think the speaker is tall or short? (Probably short.)

He's as old as I am.   Do you think the speaker is old or young? (We don't know.)

He's as young as I am.   Do you think the speaker is old or young? (Probably young, or used ironically to mean *old*.)

2. In these examples, the use of *tall* or *old* is usual. Using *short* or *young* draws attention because it is unusual.

3. Ask students to think of some other examples using *large/small* (e.g., your house, your office) and *fast/slow* (e.g., your motorbike, your car).

4. Introduce examples (g) and (h) by talking about some comparisons that might be considered impolite in different cultures. For example, it is more tactful to say, *He isn't very smart,* than to say, *He's stupid.*

5. Think of some other pairs of adjectives that can be used in this way.

Negative	Positive
nasty	nice
fat	slim
messy	neat
dirty	clean
homely	beautiful
boring	interesting

6. Ask for examples of polite comparisons using these adjectives.

7. Alternatively, you can provide prompts for a short drill which will also help students prepare for Exercises 6 and 7.

   You: *My older sister is fatter than my younger sister.*

   Students: *My older sister is not as thin as my younger sister.*

   You: *Her home is messier than mine.*

   Students: *Her home is not as neat as mine.*

   You: *Her clothes are dirtier than mine.*

   Students: *Her clothes are not as clean as mine.*

   Etc.

EXERCISE 7

You are the manager of a large company. A smaller company wants to do business with you but there are several problems to discuss. They will have to improve their overall performance before you are willing to do business with them.

Use the adjectives in parentheses with *not as . . . as*. Add *not quite* if you want to be even more tactful. The first one has been done for you.

1. Your company is smaller than ours. (large)
   Your company is not as large as ours.

2. Your factories are more old-fashioned than ours. (modern)
   Your factories are not (quite) as modern as ours.

3. Your workers are lazier than ours. (energetic)
   Your workers are not (quite) as energetic as ours.

4. Your products are less popular than ours. (well known)
   Your products are not (quite) as well known as ours.

5. Your advertising is less successful than ours. (effective)
   Your advertising is not (quite) as effective as ours.

6. Your designs are more conservative than ours. (up-to-date)
   Your designs are not (quite) as up-to-date as ours.

7. Your production is slower than ours. (fast)
   Your production is not (quite) as fast as ours.

8. The quality of your product line is lower than ours. (high)
   The quality of your product line is not (quite) as high as ours.

9. Your factories are dirtier than ours. (clean)
   Your factories are not (quite) as clean as ours.

10. Your factories are more dangerous than ours. (safe)
    Your factories are not (quite) as safe as ours.

EXERCISE 8

Omar is president of the International Students' Association at an American college. He wants to write an article for the college newspaper about international students' reactions to life in America. He made a survey of the international students. Help him to write the answers in a more tactful and polite way.

1. Children in America watch more TV.
   Children in my country don't watch as much TV as they do in America.

2. People have dinner very early in America.
   People in America do not eat dinner as late as they do in my country.

3. People eat more fast food in America.
   People in my country don't eat as much fast food as they do here.

4. Food is cheaper in America.
   The food here in America is less expensive than it is in my country.

5. Americans work longer hours than people in my country.
   The people in my country don't work as long hours as Americans do.

6. People change jobs more easily in America.
   The people in my country can't change jobs as easily as people here can.

7. Cities are cleaner in America.
   The cities at home aren't as clean as the cities here.

8. People drive longer distances in America than in my country.
   People in my country don't drive as long distances as they do in America.

Do you agree or disagree with these comments? Do you have any comments of your own that Omar could include in his article? Add them here:

114   UNIT 7
115   SIMILARITIES AND DIFFERENCES Comparatives, Superlatives, *As . . . As, Not As . . . As*

ANSWER KEY

Exercise 8   *Some answers will vary. Possible answers are listed above.*

LESSON PLAN 2

EXERCISE 7 [15 minutes]

This exercise provides practice in using *as . . . as* to make tactful comparisons. The setting is an example of one where cultural differences in making tactful comparisons could make a lot of difference to the success of negotiations.

1. Read the introduction.
2. Read the example sentence.
3. Have students work in pairs to complete the rest of the exercise.
4. Invite one student to come to the board and have the rest of the class dictate the answers.
5. If you do this exercise in small groups, have one representative from each group read a rewritten sentence to the class.
6. The other students can judge whether the rewritten sentences are more tactful or not.

EXPANSION 1 [20 minutes]

You may want to use Activity 4 and Activity 5 on SB page 117 after this exercise.

EXPANSION 2 [20 minutes]

You may want to use Activity 6 on SB page 118 (listening) after this exercise as it continues the theme of working for a (small or large) company.

EXERCISE 8 [15 minutes]

1. This exercise provides practice in using *as . . . as* to make tactful comparisons.
2. As a variation from the previous exercise, you can do this exercise in small groups.
3. Have students rewrite the sentences and discuss whether or not they agree with them.

4. Bring the class together and have one representative from each group read a rewritten sentence to the class and report whether or not they think the sentence is true.
5. The other students can judge whether the rewritten sentences are more tactful or not, and whether they agree with their opinion.
6. Allow some time for students to write their own (tactful) comments about life in America.
7. Ask volunteers to read their comments and see if the others agree or not.

workbook For more practice, use *Grammar Dimensions 2* Workbook page 51, Exercise 6.

EXPANSION 1 [30 minutes]

Activity 1 on SB page 116 continues the cross-cultural theme of this exercise.

EXPANSION 2 [30 minutes]

Activity 2 on SB page 116 asks students to write a letter on a similar theme. Show students a basic letter outline for an American-style friendly letter including indenting and placement of date and signature. Review greetings and ways to close friendly letters.

CULTURE NOTE

This may be a good time to talk about cultural stereotypes, how they influence us, and how we can avoid them. If students come up with sentences that sound rather negative, try to think of ways to make them positive, or suggest they give more background information. For example:

Because some of us come from places where lots of spices and herbs are used in cooking, some of us feel that American food is not as tasty as the food in our own countries.

UNIT GOAL REVIEW [10 minutes]

Ask students to look at the goals on the opening page of the unit again. Refer to the pages of the unit where information on each goal can be found.

ExamView Test Generator — For assessment of Unit 7, use *Grammar Dimensions 2 ExamView®*.

Use Your English

ACTIVITY 1 speaking/writing

STEP 1

Work in groups. Imagine that someone from your country (or a country that you know well) is going to stay with a family in America. Discuss and make notes about the differences in culture and customs they may find surprising. Include information about the best places in town for international students to meet new people and to practice English.

STEP 2

Divide your group into small groups of two or three people. One small group will write a brief guide for the American host family. The other pair will write a guide for the visiting student. Be tactful where necessary!

ACTIVITY 2 writing

You are staying with an American family for the summer. Write a letter to your own family describing some of the differences you have experienced between life in America and life in your country. Before you start, make a list of interesting, surprising, or reassuring topics.

ACTIVITY 3 speaking/listening

There are many common idioms in English that use the construction *as . . . as*. Some common idioms are:

- as strong as an ox
- as stubborn as a mule
- as quiet as a mouse

Interview several speakers of English and ask them to tell you as many idioms as they can remember. Write the idioms in your notebook and also write an example of when they might use each idiom. Choose one of these new idioms to explain to your classmates.

ACTIVITY 4 speaking/listening

The purpose of this activity is to think of as many differences as possible between two objects. Your teacher will tell you what you are to compare. Form teams. You have five minutes with your team to make a list of as many differences as possible. After five minutes, the teams take turns sharing their differences. The team with the most differences scores a point. Your teacher will then give you the next two objects to compare. The team with the most points is the winner.

STEP 1

To score a point, your comparison must be meaningful and accurate.

STEP 2

You cannot repeat a comparison that another team has already given. However, you can express the same idea, using different words. For example:

Team A says: *A Harley Davidson motorcycle is more expensive than some cars.*

Team B can say: *Some cars aren't as expensive as a Harley Davidson.*

Team C can say: *Some cars are cheaper than a Harley Davidson . . .* and so on.

If possible, try to record your team as you play this game. Afterwards listen to the recording and see how many comparative, superlative, and *(not) as . . . as* forms you used.

ACTIVITY 5 speaking/listening

STEP 1

Choose one set of objects that you compared in Activity 4. Ask three different people outside of class to compare these two objects and record their replies. Listen to the recording. Did they make more comparisons than you did? Or did you make more comparisons than them? Compare your findings with classmates.

STEP 2

Listen to your recording again and write down any sentences with examples of comparative, superlative, and *(not) as . . . as* forms.

USE YOUR ENGLISH

The Use Your English activities in this section at the end of the unit contain situations that should naturally elicit the structures covered in the unit. For a more complete discussion of how to use the Use Your English activities, see To the Teacher, LP page xxii. When students are doing these activities in class, you can circulate and listen to see if they are using the structures accurately. Errors can be corrected after the activity has finished.

ACTIVITY 1 speaking/writing [30 minutes]

You may want to use this activity after Exercise 8 on SB page 115. This activity is a way for students to use their experience to help other students and host families.

1. Read the description of the activity and check that students understand the instructions by asking questions: *What are you going to write? Who is going to read it?* Etc.
2. Brainstorm a list of possible topics on the board. For example: food, accommodation, clothing, greetings, dating.
3. Divide students into groups of four. You may want to group students from similar cultural backgrounds together. If all students are from one culture, then you might want to assign different topics to different groups.
4. Set a time limit for students to come up with as many ideas as they can.
5. Collect ideas and suggestions from the group and invite class comment and discussion.
6. Students can ask clarification questions, such as: *Do you mean that there aren't as many . . . in* (country being described) *as there are here?*
7. Divide groups into pairs and have each pair write about the same topic, one from the host family's point of view, and one from the student's point of view. You can assign this writing as homework.

ACTIVITY 2 writing [20 minutes]

This activity can be used after Exercise 8 on SB page 115 instead of or as a follow-up to Activity 1.

1. Ask students to imagine that they are staying with an American family for the summer. What kind of differences would they encounter?
2. If your students have never been to the United States, or if they have never stayed with an American family, you may want to adapt this topic to staying in another country they know well, or leaving home for the first time to stay in a dorm or a summer camp.
3. Brainstorm a list of topics.
4. Remind students they should try to be tactful in their comparisons.
5. Have students start writing in class and finish for homework.

ACTIVITY 3 speaking/listening [20 minutes]

You may want to use this activity after Exercise 4 on SB page 109.

1. Ask students if they are familiar with any other similar idioms in English. Do they have similar idioms in their native languages? What other idioms do they have?
2. Assign the research/interviewing activity for homework, and have students report on their findings in the next class.
3. **Variation:** If students do not have access to native speakers of English, have them interview several students about the possible meanings of these idioms and compare them with the explanations in the dictionary.

ACTIVITY 4 speaking/listening [20 minutes]

You may want to use this activity after Exercise 6 on SB page 112. This activity provides further practice of all comparative structures.

1. Read the instructions and the example.
2. Divide the class into two teams.
3. Arrange a start and stop signal, such as ringing a bell, or switching the lights on and off.
   a. Some ideas for objects to compare are:
      an apple and an orange
      a car and a bicycle
      a VW and a Ferrari
      a pizza and a hot dog
   b. The best comparisons are ones that have some kind of personal relevance to students.
      two celebrities known to all the class
      two places known to all the students
      two different classes they are taking
      two books/movies they all know, etc.
4. If you are not comfortable using competitive games in your classroom, consider doing this activity in teams but without scoring.
5. You could record the statements containing differences, and review them afterwards for accuracy and to see how many varieties of forms were used.
6. Use Activity 5 as a follow-up to this activity.

ACTIVITY 5 speaking/listening [20 minutes/homework]

This activity is a good follow-up to Activity 4. Students will be more motivated to find out if other people think of the same comparisons or not.

1. Choose one or more sets of objects from Activity 4. Assign one pair of objects to each group of students.
2. Have each group member interview three different people about these objects. This can be assigned for homework.
3. Reassemble the groups and have them combine the information from their interviews.
4. One member of each group can present the results to the class.
5. Ask for examples of the target structures from their interviews.

ACTIVITY 6 — listening/speaking

CD Track 12

STEP 1

Before you listen to the audio for this activity, get together with a partner. Make a list of all the differences you can think of between working for a small company and working for a large company. Write them on the left side of a chart in your notebook.

What are the differences between working for a small company and a large company?

DIFFERENCES: _____ (partner) and I	DIFFERENCES: TERRY AND ROBIN
A small company is friendlier than a large company.	

STEP 2

Listen to the audio. You will hear two people, Terry and Robin, compare working for a small company and working for a large company. Add the differences they describe to the right side of the chart. How many differences did you and your partner find? How many did Terry and Robin find?

STEP 3

Now listen to the audio again, and write down any sentences with comparative, superlative, or *(not) as . . . as* forms in them.

ACTIVITY 7 — speaking

STEP 1

Think of two jobs that you had in the past. Tell your partner about them. Say which one you liked better and why. Report to the class about your partner's jobs.

STEP 2

Make a list of adjectives or adverbs you used in your report. Group the words according to those that use *-er* or *-est*, those that use "more" or "most," and other words that show similarity or difference. Can you find a pattern?

ACTIVITY 8 — speaking/listening

We sometimes honor people with special awards for achievements in different fields. For example, the film industry presents Oscars every year for "the best picture," "the best director," and so on. This year, your school will give several special awards for different achievements. You and your classmates are on the committee that will decide who should get these awards.

STEP 1

In small groups, make a list of awards you would like to give. For example, you can give awards for "the best dressed student," "the most talkative student," "the most creative dancer," "the student who is the most likely to become president of his or her country," and so on. Decide on who should receive these awards. You can also give awards to other people on campus or to places that you like in the community, for example, "the teacher who gives the most homework," "the best hamburger," "the quietest place to study," "the best place to meet other students."

STEP 2

Hold a class awards "ceremony" to announce the winners and present the awards.

ACTIVITY 9 — research on the web

InfoTrac® College Edition: Go to *InfoTrac* to read facts about two countries: for example, Russia and the United States. Type: "Compare facts: Russia and the United States" Write five sentences comparing these two countries and tell the class. What explanations can you think of for the similarities and differences you found?

ACTIVITY 10 — reflection

What similarities or differences are there between English and your first language (or another language you know well)? Which one is easier or more difficult and why? Make a list of differences and similarities and present your list to the class.

ANSWER KEY

Activity 6 **Step 2:** You (sometimes) get a bigger expense account in a large company. You (sometimes) get paid better in a large company. You (sometimes) have to work harder in a large company. The managers/People are (sometimes) friendlier in a small company. The atmosphere is (sometimes) friendlier in a small company.

Step 3: Check audio script on LP page S-3 for answers.

Activity 9 Answers will vary depending on choice of comparison country. *Possible answers: Russia is larger than the United States in area, but smaller in population. Russia has fewer people under age 15. Americans have a longer life expectancy.*

USE YOUR ENGLISH

ACTIVITY 6   listening/speaking
[30 minutes]

You may want to use this activity after Exercise 7 on SB page 114 as it continues the theme of working in a (large or small) company

1. Have students work in pairs to list all the differences between working in a small and a large company.
2. Ask students to copy the chart into their notebooks.
3. Play the audio. See audio script on LP page S-3.
4. Compare answers in pairs.
5. Play the audio again.
6. Check answers as a class.
7. Compare the speakers' opinions with those of your students from Step 1.
8. Play the audio again and have students raise their hands when they hear any examples of the comparative forms.

ACTIVITY 7   speaking
[20 minutes]

You may want to use this activity after Exercise 4 on SB page 109.

1. Have students work in pairs to tell each other about two jobs they have had in the past. (If your students have not worked, they may choose any two jobs that might interest them in the future.)
2. Ask volunteers to summarize what their partner told them.
3. Have students make a list of adjectives.
4. Draw a chart for long and short adjectives on the board and have students come up to the board (all at the same time) and write their adjectives in the correct column. **Note:** Some adjectives take both long and short forms. See Language Note on LP page 107.

VARIATION

Categorize the comparisons according to whether they use adjectives, adverbs, verbs, or nouns (see Focus Chart 1).

ACTIVITY 8   speaking/listening
[30 minutes]

You may want to use this activity after Exercise 2 on SB page 107.

1. Introduce the idea of an awards ceremony, or talk about the Oscars and the various categories of awards.
2. Explain that students will think of their own award categories for other members of the class.
3. Divide students into groups and allow 10 minutes for students to come up with at least five categories. You can make it a rule that all categories must be positive.
4. Organize the awards ceremony with students making a short speech to announce the category and the winner, and winners coming to the front of the classroom to receive their "prizes" (perhaps bring in a bag of candies for this class?).

ACTIVITY 9   research on the web
[15 minutes/homework]

The purpose of this activity is to provide a natural context for using comparisons. An additional purpose is to encourage students to learn to use *InfoTrac® College Edition* as a resource. See To the Teacher, LP page xxii for tips on how to use InfoTrac.

ACTIVITY 10   reflection
[20 minutes/homework]

This activity provides an opportunity for students to use the target structures of the unit while reflecting on their language learning progress. You may have asked students to keep a record of their learning in a journal throughout this course as suggested in To the Teacher (see LP page xxii). This reflection activity will form part of that learning record. Alternatively, you can use this activity to raise awareness of some common errors that may be caused by first language (L1) interference. This may enable students to widen their range of learning strategies.

MEASURE WORDS AND QUANTIFIERS

UNIT GOALS

• Understand special
  measure words used
  with foods

• Use measure words
  with count and
  noncount nouns

• Know how to use
  common quantifiers

OPENING TASK

Getting Ready for a Potluck Dinner

■ STEP 1

Jim has been invited to a potluck dinner—a meal where each
guest brings a dish. The hostess asked him to bring cookies and a
salad for six people. Look at the picture of Jim's kitchen. Can you
name the different foods? How much does he have of each food?

■ STEP 2

Jim wants to make everything himself. He already has these ingredients in his kitchen.

INGREDIENTS	
mustard	chocolate chips
sugar	tomatoes
salt	flour
lettuce	olive oil
hard-boiled eggs	butter
cheese	eggs
vinegar	garlic

Help Jim decide which ingredients he can use in each dish. Write each ingredient in the box
below.

SALAD	SALAD DRESSING	CHOCOLATE CHIP COOKIES
lettuce	mustard	sugar
hard-boiled eggs	salt	salt
cheese	vinegar	chocolate chips
tomatoes	olive oil	flour
	garlic	butter
		eggs

■ STEP 3

How much of each ingredient do you think Jim should use? Write an amount beside each
ingredient. Remember, there will be six people at the party.

■ STEP 4

Are there any other ingredients you would include? Add them to the boxes above, with
suggested amounts.

ANSWER KEY

Opening Task   *Steps 3 and 4:* Answers will vary.

UNIT 8

LESSON PLAN 1

UNIT OVERVIEW

Using recipes and cooking as the main theme, this unit introduces students to the form, meaning, and use of measure words (such as containers, portions, and shapes) and quantifiers (including *all*, *much/many*, and *few/little*). It also reviews the concept of count and noncount nouns.

GRAMMAR NOTE

Count nouns are those whose individual parts can be easily counted. *Noncount nouns* cannot easily be separated from the whole, either because they are mass nouns (rice, soup, flour, milk) or concepts (information, advice, sadness). Note that while many other languages have this distinction, they often do not share the same idea of what is and isn't countable. For example, in some languages, "information" is countable, while in English it is not.

UNIT GOALS

Some instructors may want to review the goals listed on this page after completing the Opening Task so that students understand what they should know by the end of the unit. These goals can also be reviewed at the end of the unit when students are more familiar with the grammar terminology.

OPENING TASK [30 minutes]

The purpose of the Opening Task is to create a context in which students will need to use measure words. The problem-solving format is designed to show the teacher how well the students can produce the target structures implicitly and spontaneously when they are engaged in a communicative task. For a more complete discussion of the purpose of the Opening Task, see To the Teacher, Lesson Planner (LP) page xxii.

Setting Up the Task

1. Introduce the topic of this unit by asking students if they enjoy cooking. Ask students to stand in two groups: Group A for those who enjoy cooking, and Group B for those who dislike it or don't care much about it. (You may need to adjust these categories in order to get two equal groups, e.g. those who hate cooking, or those who don't usually cook.)

2. Have students from group A match up with students from Group B in pairs or small groups. They should try to persuade each other to agree with their point of view. (The aim is to mix students who are more likely to know measure words with those who are not.)

STEP 1

1. Read the introduction to the task and look at the picture. What is a potluck dinner? Have any students been to one?

2. Have students try to name all the food items they can see in the picture.

Conducting the Task

STEP 2

1. Compare the list of ingredients with the picture on SB page 121.

2. Have students work in their groups to decide which ingredients go with which recipe.

3. Check the answers as a class. Refer to the answer key on LP page 120.

STEP 3

Ask students to write the amounts needed for each food item. Don't offer any help at this stage. Let students try to learn from each other and work out how to describe the quantities by themselves.

STEP 4

1. Break students into three groups, with each group focusing on one of the three recipes. If your class is of a lower level or less knowledgeable about cooking, you could focus only on the salad recipe, which is the simplest.

2. Circulate around the room to make sure that everyone is involved in the group work. Take notes of typical errors.

Closing the Task

1. Have groups choose a speaker and share their recipes with the class.

2. Members of other groups can discuss how their recipes differ or if they think ingredients have been left out.

3. To draw their attention to the language being practiced, ask the class to list some of the ways they described the amount of food for each ingredient.

GRAMMAR NOTE

Typical student errors (form)

- Errors in using of with quantifiers, e.g. * *a couple boxes of cereal*, * *a dozen of eggs*, * *most of people*
- Errors in using count or noncount quantifiers, e.g. * *too many money*, * *a few time*, * *a little people*

Typical student errors (use)

- Using incorrect quantifiers, e.g. * *I'd like a piece of lettuce.* * *How much sugar would you like?* A few.
- Misunderstanding the difference between *few/a few* and *little/a little*. (See Focus Chart 3.)

FOCUS 1

Measure Words with Food

meaning

CONTAINERS

Some measure words are **containers** that we can find in a store.

a bottle of (soy sauce, ketchup)

a jar of (peanut butter, mustard)

a box of (cereal, crackers)

a bag of (potato chips, flour)

a carton of (milk, eggs)

a can of (tuna fish, soup)

PORTIONS

Some measure words are **portions**. They describe food items as they are commonly served.

a slice of (bread, cheese)

a scoop of ice cream

a piece of (cake, candy)

a cube of sugar

a strip of bacon

MEASUREMENTS

In North America, these **measurements** are common in recipes:

a cup of (water, rice, flour)

a tablespoon of (salt, sugar, water)

a teaspoon of (salt, sugar, water)

a pinch of (pepper, salt)

LESSON PLAN 1

FOCUS 1 [15 minutes]

Using pictures, this focus chart illustrates the meaning of some English measure words used with food. This topic is continued in Focus Chart 2.

1. **Lead-in:** Bring in some examples of empty food packaging, e.g. a carton of eggs, a package of cookies, a can of tuna. Teach or review the container words from Focus Chart 1. If possible, bring in a set of measuring spoons and a measuring jug. Ask students if they know the measurements and what kind of food is usually measured with them.

2. Look at the illustrations on student book (SB) pages 122–124. Model and practice the pronunciation of each (see Pronunciation Note).

See if students can add one more food item to each measure word list. For example, *a can of . . . (tuna fish, soup), peas, spaghetti, tomato sauce . . .*

3. Choose some pairs of terms that might be confused (e.g., *bottle and jar, box and carton, slice and piece, tablespoon and teaspoon*). Ask students to describe the differences between them. For example, jars and bottles can both be made of glass or plastic, but a bottle has a narrow neck while a jar has a wider neck.

4. If students are out of their home country, have them describe the differences between the ways food is packaged or prepared in their country and where they are studying. For example, in some countries, milk comes in a bag, bread is only sold in loaves, and recipes are measured in grams and milliliters.

PRONUNCIATION NOTE

Prepositions and articles are generally reduced in spoken English. The phrase *a(n) . . . of . . .* is usually reduced in everyday conversation.

It's a piece of cake. (Sounds like: *It's a piece-a cake.*)
It's not my cup of tea. (Sounds like: *It's not my cuppa tea.*)

You may need to explain that these reductions are not "bad English" but are regular pronunciation patterns of spoken English.

SHAPES AND TYPICAL STATES

Some measure words talk about the shape or appearance of the food item.

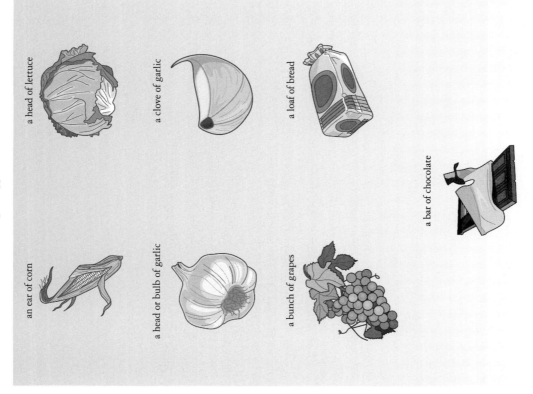

an ear of corn

a head of lettuce

a head or bulb of garlic

a clove of garlic

a bunch of grapes

a loaf of bread

a bar of chocolate

EXERCISE 1

Turn back to the Opening Task on page 121. Look at the ingredients and the amounts. Did you use the right measure words? Make any necessary corrections.

EXERCISE 2

Turn back to the Opening Task and look carefully at the ingredients. Some of these are count nouns (tomatoes) and some are noncount nouns (flour). Write C beside each count noun and NC beside each noncount noun.*

FOCUS 2

Measure Words with Count and Noncount Nouns

form

Measure words express specific quantities. They also allow us to make noncount nouns countable.

three bottles of water

six pounds of coffee

two scoops of ice cream

three cartons of milk

*For more information on count and noncount nouns, see *Grammar Dimensions* Book 1, Unit 4.

ANSWER KEY

Exercise 1 Answers will vary.

Exercise 2 mustard (NC) sugar (NC) salt (NC) lettuce (NC) hard-boiled eggs (C)
cheese (NC) vinegar (NC) chocolate chips (C) tomatoes (C) flour (NC) olive oil (NC)
butter (NC) eggs (C) garlic (NC)

UNIT 8 LESSON PLAN 1

These expansion activities may be done before or after Exercise 1 on SB page 125.

EXPANSION 1 [15 minutes]

1. Find out what kinds of food items your students most frequently buy (in addition to the ones already mentioned in Focus Chart 1).
2. Make a list on the board.
3. Identify what measurement or container words are used with each item.
4. How much do your students usually buy of each food item?

Some other common container words:

a basket	a case	a dish
a bowl	a jug	a mug
a bucket	a tray	a tube

EXPANSION 2 [20 minutes]

Use this picture dictation activity to review the vocabulary presented in Focus Chart 1. The hardest part of this activity is drawing the pictures, but the funnier the drawings are, the more they will help students to remember.

1. Prepare two different shopping lists, one for each group of students.
2. Place the shopping lists on your desk with all items covered except one.
3. Divide your class into two groups.
4. Two people at a time, one from each group, will run to your desk, read the item, go back and draw the item from the list for their team. (They cannot say or write the name of the item.)
5. When the group has guessed the answer, they must write it down, and send the next team member for the next item. You should make sure that the list stays covered except for the next item so that no one gains the advantage.
6. The group that recreates their shopping list correctly first is the winner.

Shopping list 1
Three cans of tomatoes
Two boxes of crackers
One carton of milk
One bag of sugar
One loaf of bread
Two heads of lettuce
One bunch of grapes

Shopping list 2
One box of cereal
One bottle of oil
Two packages of tea
Three cans of tuna
One jar of jam
Four ears of corn
One head of garlic

EXERCISE 1 [5 minutes]

This exercise gives students the chance to go back to their Opening Task recipes and modify the measurements they used to match those from Focus Chart 1.

1. Have students work in their original groups or pairs.
2. Go over the items in their recipes and match them with the measure words in Focus Chart 1, correcting any errors.
3. If they did not complete all the recipes in the Opening Task, they can do so now.
4. Check the answers as a class. Refer to the answer key on LP page 124.

work book For more practice, use *Grammar Dimensions 2* Workbook page 52, Exercise 1, and page 53, Exercise 2.

EXERCISE 2 [10 minutes]

This exercise provides a bridge to the grammar in Focus Chart 2.

1. Turn back to the Opening Task and have students identify which nouns are count nouns and noncount nouns.
2. Compare count and noncount with vocabulary on pages 122–124 and review how the word can be both count and noncount (lettuce NC; a head of lettuce C).

3. Write them in two lists on the board.
4. Review the meaning of *count* and *noncount nouns*. (See Language Note on LP page 127.)

 work book For more practice, use *Grammar Dimensions 2* Workbook page 53, Exercise 3.

EXPANSION [20 minutes]

You may want to use Activity 7 on page 135 after this exercise. This activity asks students to write a list of their food (possibly in their journals) for one day.

FOCUS 2 [10 minutes]

Building on Focus Chart 1, this focus chart illustrates how measure words can be used to make noncount nouns countable.

1. **Lead-in:** Write the food items from Focus Chart 2 on the board and ask students to think of different measurement or container words for each of them. Some possible answers:

   water: a bottle, a glass, a spoon, a drop
   coffee: a can, a jar, a package, a cup, a mug, a pot
   ice cream: a scoop, a dish, a bowl, a carton, a package
   milk: a carton, a bottle, a glass, a cup, a spoon

2. Ask what all these foods have in common (they are noncount nouns).
3. Explain that when we want to measure noncount nouns, we can use measure words. Measure words can be counted, even though the thing they are measuring cannot be counted. Count nouns can be measured with numbers (ten apples) or with measure words (two pounds of apples).

Most measure expressions follow this pattern.*

A/An/One Two Three	+	Measure Word (Singular/Plural)	+	of	+	Noun (Noncount/Plural)
a		cup		of		milk
a		pound		of		apples
two		cups		of		milk
two		pounds		of		apples

*Exception: specific numbers (including *dozen*):
a dozen eggs NOT a dozen of eggs
ten strawberries NOT ten of strawberries

EXERCISE 3

These are the recipes that Jim finally used. Complete the missing parts. (The picture may help you.)

Jim's Super Salad

1 large (a) ___head___ of red lettuce
1 medium-sized (b) ___head___ of romaine lettuce
1 large cucumber, cut into (c) ___slices___
6 tomatoes, cut into quarters
¹/₂ (d) ___pound___ of Swiss cheese, cut into small strips
1 (e) ___cup of___ cooked chicken, shredded into small pieces
2 hard-boiled eggs, shelled and cut into quarters

1. Line a large salad bowl with red lettuce leaves.
2. Tear the romaine lettuce leaves into medium-sized pieces.
3. Place in the bowl in layers: slices of cucumber and tomato, cheese, lettuce, and chicken.
4. Add olives and eggs. Cover and refrigerate for one hour. Toss with Jim's Super Salad Dressing just before serving.

Jim's Super Salad Dressing

1 (a) ___tablespoon of___ Dijon mustard   ¹/₂ (d) ___teaspoon of___ salt
4 (b) ___tablespoons of___ red wine vinegar   ¹/₂ (e) ___teaspoon of___ pepper
1 (c) ___tablespoon of___ sugar   ¹/₂ (f) ___cup of___ olive oil

1. Put the mustard into a bowl. Whisk in vinegar, sugar, salt, and pepper.
2. Slowly add the oil while continuing to whisk the mixture.

8 LESSON PLAN 1

LANGUAGE NOTE

Count nouns are objects that can be counted. They have singular and plural forms. For example, *apples, grapes, carrots,* etc. Noncount nouns are objects that are too small to count (*rice, flour, sugar*), or are part of a mass that cannot be separated (*coffee, water, chocolate*). Sometimes a noun can be both count and noncount, depending on how we view it. For example,

a chocolate: an individual chocolate in a box
a piece of chocolate: a pi"ece of a bar of chocolate
a fruit: a variety of fruit
a piece of fruit: one part of a whole fruit
a paper: a newspaper, a conference speech
a piece of paper: a page of writing paper

In some cases, the measure word is understood from the context. We know that, for example, in a restaurant, *Two coffees* really means, *Two cups of coffee.* (Or: *Two spaghettis,* means *Two dishes of spaghetti.*)

For more practice, use *Grammar Dimensions 2* Workbook page 53, Exercise 4.

EXPANSION [20 minutes]

You may want to use Activity 6 (research on the web) on SB page 135 after this exercise. This activity asks students to research different recipes on the Internet and compare them in class.

EXERCISE 3 [20 minutes]

1. Look at the drawn picture and ask them to name the measure expressions for the different items.

2. Have students work in pairs to fill in the blanks of the three recipes they discussed in the Opening Task.

3. Circulate around the room to help with new vocabulary, paying special attention to people who are less familiar with cooking. Note: Possible new vocabulary: (*Super Salad*) *shredded, line, tear, toss,* (*Super Salad Dressing*) *whisk,* (*chocolate chip cookies*) *cream, fluffy, sift, rack.*

4. This activity can also be completed as a class by filling in the missing information on an overhead transparency or as a homework assignment.

5. If some students finish early, have them write their recipes on the board to provide the class with visual aids as they discuss the differences.

form

meaning

use

Common Quantifiers

AMOUNT	EXAMPLES	EXPLANATIONS
all	(a) **All** of the dishes at the potluck were delicious. (b) He spends **all** of his money on wine.	Some quantifiers (words that talk about quantity/number or amount) can be used with **both count and noncount** nouns. Use *all* to mean *everything* or *everyone*.
most	(c) **Most** of the people in North America take vacations in the summer. (d) **Most** people in my town work in tourism.	*Most* means *almost everyone* or *almost everything*. Use *most* of when there is an article before the noun. Use *most* when there is no article.
many/much	(e) We heard that **many** people were coming. (f) We don't have **much** time. (g) A: Were **many** people hurt? (h) B: No, not **many**.	*Many* is used only with count nouns to talk about a large number. Use *much* with noncount nouns to talk about a large amount. *Many* and *much* are usually used in questions or negative statements.
a lot of *lots of* *a great deal of*	(i) We make **a lot of** trips back and forth over the mountains. (j) I heard that there was **lots of** new snow. (k) A **great deal of** current information is available on the Internet.	Use *a lot of* or *lots of* with very large numbers or amounts, and with either count or noncount nouns. *Lots of* is used in informal situations. Use *a great deal of* in formal situations, and only with noncount nouns. It means the same as *a lot of* or *lots*.
some	(l) We needed **some** milk for the recipe. (m) We were glad that we had put **some** new snow tires on our car.	*Some* is a smaller amount or quantity than a *lot of/lots of*. *Some* is used with both count and noncount nouns.

Continued on next page

Jim's Granny's Old Time Chocolate Chip Cookies

½ (a) ___*pound of*___ butter   1 (e) ___*teaspoon of*___ baking soda
1 (b) ___*cup of*___ brown sugar   1 (f) ___*teaspoon of*___ vanilla extract
¾ (c) ___*cup of*___   1 (g) ___*teaspoon of*___ salt
granulated sugar

2 eggs   1½ (h) ___*cups of*___ chocolate chips
2 (d) ___*cups of*___ flour

1. Preheat the oven to 350°F. Grease a cookie sheet.

2. Cream the butter and both the sugars together until light and fluffy. Add the eggs and vanilla and mix well.

3. Sift the flour, baking soda, and salt. Mix thoroughly.

4. Add the chocolate chips.

5. Form into cookies. Place on a cookie sheet and put on the middle rack of the oven for 8–10 minutes.

6. Cool for 5 minutes.

7. Enjoy! (This recipe makes about 40 cookies.)

Turn back to the Opening Task on page 121 and look at the ingredients (and the amounts) you suggested for these dishes. How many differences can you find between your suggestions and Jim's recipes? Whose recipe do you think will taste better?

EXERCISE 4

Last week Matthew ate a delicious spaghetti sauce at his friend Nancy's house. He enjoyed it so much that Nancy lent him the recipe so that he could make a copy of it. However, Nancy has obviously used this recipe many times and it is quite difficult to read. Can you help Matthew figure out the recipe? Fill in the missing words below.

Spaghetti Sauce

(from Nancy's kitchen)

First, cut 3 ____ of bacon into small pieces and cook over a very low heat.
Stir in ½ a ____ of ground meat along with 4 ____ of garlic and 2 ____ of onion, very finely chopped. Add 1 ____ of salt, a ____ of cayenne pepper, and 2 ____ of dried herbs. Mix in two
8-ounce ____ of tomato sauce. Cook on low heat for about 30 minutes.
Serve over fresh pasta.

If you were making this recipe yourself, would you change or add anything? Share any changes or additions with your classmates. Try to be as precise as possible.

ANSWER KEY

Exercise 4   slices (of bacon)   pound (of ground meat)   cloves (of garlic)   cups of (onion)   teaspoon (of salt)   tablespoons (of fresh herbs)   cans/jars (of tomato sauce)   dash (cayenne pepper)

EXERCISE 4 [10 minutes]

This exercise provides further practice of the items presented in Focus Chart 1.

1. Read the introduction to the exercise.
2. Have students work on the exercise individually or in pairs.
3. Ask volunteers to come and write the recipe on the board.
4. Check the answers as a class. Refer to the answer key on LP page 128.

EXPANSION 1 [20 minutes]

You may want to use Activity 5 (listening) on SB page 134 after this exercise. This activity asks students to listen to a recipe and write the measurement words they hear.

EXPANSION 2 [20 minutes]

You may want to use Activity 4 on SB page 135 after this exercise. This activity involves planning a potluck dinner for your class.

LESSON PLAN 2

FOCUS 3 [15 minutes]

1. **Lead-in:** You may want to use Exercise 5 on SB page 130 as a lead-in to the chart in Focus Chart 3. The exercise can be assigned for homework, and checked in class by reference to the chart.
2. Have students look at the chart and cover the right-hand column of explanations.
3. Students can work in pairs to work out what the explanations are.
4. Circulate while students are working and note which quantifiers are most problematic.
5. Students can uncover their charts and check their explanations.
6. Select the most problematic points and ask students to provide further examples.

LANGUAGE NOTE

Students may ask about when to use of with *all* and *most*. The following are good rules to follow.

All of is usually used before a noun with a determiner—e.g., *all of the vegetables, all of these dishes, all of her money*. Although it is also possible to use *all* in these cases, it is not so common in American English. *Of* is **not** used before a noun with no determiner—e.g., *all visitors, all homework* (* *all of homework*). However, *of* **must** be used before a pronoun—e.g., *all of us, all of them*.

Similar rules apply to *most*. *Of* **must** be used before a noun with a determiner—e.g., *most of the vegetables, most of these dishes, most of her money* (* *most the vegetables*). *Of* is **not** used before a noun with no determiner—e.g., *most people, most information* (* *most of people*). *Of* **must** be used before a pronoun—e.g., *most of us, most of them*.

AMOUNT	EXAMPLES	EXPLANATIONS
several	(n) We couldn't travel on *several* days last winter because the mountain passes were closed.	*Several* is used only with count nouns. *Several* means more than a small number.
a few / a little	(o) In a *few* days, we'll be ready to go. (p) There was *a little* snow on the mountains. (q) Let's buy *a little* food and *a few* cans of soda.	A *few* means more than two, but not many more. A *few* and *a little* have similar meanings. *A little* is used only with noncount nouns and *a few* is used only with count nouns.
few/little	(r) We have *few* friends and *little* money. (s) *Few* people know that she has *little* time left.	*Few* and *little* refer to the same amounts or numbers as *a few* and *a little*; however, they have a negative meaning. They mean *almost none*. *Few* is used only with count nouns, *little* only with noncount nouns.
a couple (of)	(t) I'd like to get *a couple of* blankets to keep in the car. (u) Let's ask *a couple (of)* people to come with us.	A *couple of* means two, but it is sometimes used informally to mean two or more. A *couple of* is used only with count nouns. In informal English, *of* is sometimes omitted.
none/no	(v) *None of* the people went to the meeting. (w) We heard that there was *no* new snow.	*None* means *not any*, and is used with count nouns. *No* has the same meaning, and is used with noncount nouns.

EXERCISE 5

Choose the correct quantifier for each sentence.

1. There are _____ big supermarkets in my town.
   a. a lot   b. a little   c. much   (d) several

2. We usually get _____ of rain in the summer.
   a. a little   b. some   c. most   (d) a lot

3. There are _____ fast-food restaurants near my house.
   (a) a couple of   b. most   c. a little   d. a great deal of

4. _____ people have the Internet at home.
   a. None   b. Little   (c) Few   d. Much

5. _____ education at my university concerns the use of new technology.
   a. All of   b. None of   c. Many of   (d) A great deal of

EXERCISE 6

Find a partner and take turns asking each other questions about your native countries or countries you know about. Use the topics in (A) to ask general questions. In your answers to the questions, give specific examples to explain what you mean. You must use a quantifier (from Focus 3) in your answer. Column (B) gives you ideas for quantifiers you can use in your answers, but you may use others.

Example: Q: *Is clothing expensive in (Vietnam)?*
A: *No, not really. A lot of people go to the big cities to buy clothes. There are lots of factories in the cities, so you can usually find clothes that are pretty cheap.*

(A) Topic	(B) Quantifier
1. clothing	some lots of/a lot of
2. tourist attractions	a few a couple of
3. holidays	most some
4. climate	no/none a great deal of
5. fast-food restaurants	some several
6. technology	a few many
7. English speakers	most a lot of
8. entertainment	all much

UNIT 8 LESSON PLAN 2

EXERCISE 5 [10 minutes]

This exercise practices the quantifiers presented in Focus Chart 3 and gives students the opportunity to explain their choice of quantifiers by referring to the grammar explanations in the chart. You may want to use this exercise before studying the chart as suggested in the instructional remarks for Focus Chart 3. The topics in this exercise will also help prepare students for the topics they will discuss in Exercise 6.

1. Assign this exercise for homework, or set a time limit of 10 minutes for students to complete this exercise individually.

2. If you are doing this exercise before studying Focus Chart 3, go to the teacher's notes for Focus Chart 3.

3. If you are doing this exercise after studying Focus Chart 3, have students explain their answers to their partner by referring to the explanations in Focus Chart 3.

4. Check the answers as a class. Refer to the answer key on LP page 130.

METHODOLOGY NOTE

As multiple-choice questions are frequently found in tests, this might be a good time to go over some strategies for approaching multiple-choice questions. First, ask students to share any tips or suggestions they have. Since this is a test of grammar, they should not be concerned with whether the sentences are true or false, but should look for clues in the grammar of the sentence. Using the first question as an example, show how each incorrect choice can be eliminated. Continue with the next question, or ask students to continue.

1. There are _____ big supermarkets in my town.

   Explanation: *supermarkets* is a countable noun, so the answer cannot be *a little* or *much*. *A lot* needs the preposition *of*. So the correct answer must be *several*.

EXERCISE 6 [20 minutes]

This exercise shifts the topic away from the food theme, considering other expressions that take quantifiers.

1. Review the topics on the list to be sure that students are familiar with the vocabulary.

2. If all your students are from the same country, have them choose another country they know well.

3. Model the example with a student.

4. Ask two students to model two or three questions and answers.

5. Set a time limit for students to work in pairs, asking and answering questions. Every time they use a quantifier, they should cross it off the list.

6. Ask volunteers to repeat some of their questions and answers for the class.

7. Listen for errors and ask students to correct them.

VARIATION

Do this exercise as a mixer activity.

1. Explain that students will stand up and walk around the room until you signal them to stop.

2. Arrange a stop signal such as ringing a bell, or switching the lights on and off.

3. At the stop signal, they must talk to the student nearest them and ask them about their country.

4. The object of the activity is to find out as much information as possible about their partner's country in 3 minutes.

5. At the signal they must start walking again. Then repeat the activity with a new student.

6. When they finish, have some students share their information with the class, correcting only errors in quantifier use.

For more practice, use *Grammar Dimensions 2* Workbook page 54 and page 55, Exercise 5.

EXPANSION [20 minutes]

You may want to use Activity 3 on SB page 134 after Exercise 6.

EXPANSION [20 minutes]

You may want to use Activity 2 on page SB page 133 after this exercise. This activity asks students to use quantifiers to describe their ideal birthday party.

Use Your English

ACTIVITY 1 writing/speaking

This "recipe" was written by an English teacher:

"Recipe" for the Perfect Student

Ingredients:

1 cup of motivation	1 cup of imagination
1 cup of determination	1 $^1/_2$ cups of willingness to make a guess
$^1/_2$ cup of patience	1 cup of independence
$^1/_2$ cup of tolerance	1 $^1/_2$ cups of cooperation with others
1 cup of laughter	1 pinch of fun

Combine ingredients and stir gently to bring out the best flavor.

What do you think the teacher meant by this?

Get together with a partner and create a "recipe" of your own. Here are some ideas, but you probably have plenty of your own:

- Recipe for a long-lasting marriage
- Recipe for the perfect partner
- Recipe for the perfect teacher
- Recipe for the perfect house
- Recipe for the perfect mother-/father

Share your recipes with the rest of the class.

ACTIVITY 2 writing

Write a paragraph describing your perfect birthday party (real or imaginary). Before writing, make notes on the people, food, music, and activities. When you have written your paragraph, exchange it with another student. Underline the quantifiers. Were they used correctly?

Example: *My ideal birthday party would have a lot of food, many friends . . .*

EXERCISE 7

Some of the sentences in the following letter have errors with nouns and with quantifiers. Find the errors and correct them. When you have finished, check your answers with another student.

Dear Nell,

I think I'm going to like my new job. So far it's interesting, and I hope that it stays that way! There are several of people who work in the same office with me. At the moment I share a desk with Jessica, who just started a couple week ago, but our office manager just ordered new furnitures so that soon we will each have a desk of our own. There are lot of people in the building who share desks and computers, so I feel pretty lucky to have my own to work on.

Every morning Martha, the staff assistant, brings us each a cup of coffee. She already knows that I like sugars in my coffee but no milks. Martha also brings the mails to us, and she likes to give us many advice about how to be efficient. Two times a day I get at least fifty letter which I have to respond to, so I do listen to Martha's advices. A few her ideas have really been useful!

Some days I can do most of my business on the computer. Other days I need a little more informations from my customers, so I need to talk to them on the telephone. Every day there are some problem that I cannot handle. If there are only couple of problems, my coworker helps, but on the days when there are lot of problems, we call in Anna, the office supervisor. Already there have been several time when even Anna couldn't handle the problems, and so she has had to call in her supervisor.

So you can see that I'm busy, and at this point, I'm not bored.

Talk to you soon—

Love,

Elliott

ANSWER KEY

Exercise 7 Error is in parentheses; correction follows. **Paragraph 1:** (several of) several; (couple week) couple of weeks; (furnitures) furniture; (lot of) lots of/a lot of **Paragraph 2:** (sugars) sugar; (milks) milk; (mails) mail; (many advice) advice/a lot of advice; (fifty letter) fifty letters; (advices) advice; (A few) A few of **Paragraph 3:** (informations) information; (some problem) some problems; (couple of problems) a couple of problems; (lot of problems) a lot of

EXERCISE 7 [20 minutes]

This exercise can be assigned as homework or as in-class pairwork. It practices quantifiers from Focus Chart 3 while at the same time practicing editing skills.

1. The letter is from someone describing his new job to a friend. Introduce the topic. Ask how we can tell it is an informal letter (Dear Nell, . . . Love, Elliott).

2. Have students work in pairs to find the mistakes, or if they have already done this exercise at home, to compare their answers.

3. It may help to identify (or ask students to identify) how many mistakes there are in each paragraph.

4. Make a copy of the letter on an overhead transparency as a visual aid when reviewing the answers. Refer to the answer key on LP page 132.

For more practice, use *Grammar Dimensions 2* Workbook page 54, Exercise 5.

EXPANSION 1 [20 minutes]

1. Using this letter in Exercise 7 on page 132 or by bringing in other examples, ask students to discuss the differences between writing personal letters in their country and in North America. Are there different ways of beginning and ending the letter? Do English speakers appear to be more or less formal? In what way(s)?

2. As a follow-up to this discussion, have students write their own letter to a friend following this model. They can describe their job, or their school. To ensure they practice the structures in this unit, require that they use the same number of quantifiers as in this letter.

EXPANSION 2 [15 minutes]

The variation in Activity 3 on SB page 134 is a guessing game that could be a fun way to close this unit.

UNIT GOAL REVIEW [10 minutes]

1. Review the unit goals on SB page 120. Refer to the pages of the unit where information on each goal can be found.

2. Look at the illustration on SB page 120. Can students find examples of measure words and quantifiers in the picture?

3. Test their knowledge by writing a list of count and noncount nouns on the board and ask them to give the first quantity or measurement they can think of for each.

For assessment of Unit 8, use *Grammar Dimensions 2 ExamView®*.

USE YOUR ENGLISH

The Use Your English activities in this section at the end of the unit contain situations that should naturally elicit the structures covered in the unit. For a more complete discussion of how to use the Use Your English Activities, see To the Teacher, LP page xxii. When students are doing these activities in class, you can circulate and listen to see if they are using the structures accurately. Errors can be corrected after the activity has finished.

ACTIVITY 1 writing/speaking [20 minutes]

You may want to use this activity after Exercise 4 on SB page 128. This activity can be done as homework or in-class writing.

1. Introduce the topic by asking students to describe a perfect student.

2. Read the "recipe" together with your students.

3. Ask for examples of each characteristic in order to check comprehension.

4. Divide students into groups to work on their own "recipes." They can choose one from the list or make up their own topic.

5. Have groups read their recipes out loud. The other students can try to guess which topic they are about.

6. You can collect all finished recipes and compile them into a creative writing "cookbook."

ACTIVITY 2 writing/speaking [20 minutes]

You may want to use this activity after Exercise 5 on SB page 130.

1. Introduce the topic of a birthday party.

2. Set a time limit for students to make a list of at least ten items. These can include types of food, decorations, music, etc.

3. Have students share their lists with a partner or with the class.

4. Assign the writing task for homework.

ACTIVITY 3　speaking

Your class is scheduled for a weekend trip to a nearby national park or state forest. Transportation is provided, and a few small overnight cabins are available. But you will need to decide what food to bring, and also what other things you will need. Here are some ideas: sleeping bags, cooking pots, eating utensils (plates, cups, silverware), firewood, sports equipment, depending on the season (fishing poles? swimsuits? skis?).

Work in groups and come up with a list. Be specific about the quantities. Compare lists to make sure you haven't forgotten anything!

ACTIVITY 4　speaking/listening/writing

■ STEP 1

Organize an international potluck. Everyone in the class should prepare and bring a dish, preferably from his or her country. After the meal, have each person describe his or her recipe. If possible, record the descriptions.

■ STEP 2

Listen to the recording and write down the recipes. Collect all the recipes for an international cookbook. Make copies and distribute them to the class.

ACTIVITY 5　listening

CD Track 13

■ STEP 1

Listen to the audio of a person describing a recipe for a traditional North American dish.

1. What dish is the speaker describing?
2. When is this dish usually eaten?
3. What are the important ingredients in the dish?

■ STEP 2

Listen to the audio again, and this time write down the ingredients and amounts.

Work with a partner to make sure that you understand what each ingredient is, and then take turns reading each ingredient and the amount aloud. If you decide to make this dish, it is important that your recipe is accurate!

For each ingredient with a measure word, write the kind of measure word:

- If it is a **container**, mark it C.
- If it is a **shape/typical state**, mark it S.
- If it is a **portion**, mark it P.
- If it is a **measurement**, mark it M.

1. Do you recognize the measurements?
2. Do you know what teaspoon/tablespoon/cup is?

ACTIVITY 6　research on the web

On the Web: Go on the Internet using a search engine such as Google® or Yahoo® and find a recipe for one of these dishes: potato salad/cheesecake/apple pie/carrot soup. Make a list of the ingredients. Then compare your list with a partner. What differences in the ingredients did you find?

ACTIVITY 7　reflection

Make a list of food and drink you had today. Organize your list with the correct measure word for each item. Compare your list with a partner.

Example: *a teaspoon of sugar, a slice of bread*

ANSWER KEY

Activity 5 Check audio script on LP page S-3 for answers.

ACTIVITY 3 — speaking/listening/writing [25 minutes]

You may want to use this activity after Exercise 6 on page 131.

1. Set a time limit of 5 minutes for students to come up with a list of at least 20 items.
2. Compile a group list on the board.
3. Check the correct use of quantifiers with each item.

VARIATION

Put the class into a circle and conduct a chain exercise. The first person starts out with a statement like, "For our weekend trip, we'll need 10 pounds of rice." The second person restates the first part and adds their own item: "For our weekend trip, we'll need 10 pounds of rice and 4 pots." Each person repeats the previous information, adding more items as they go. If students are allowed to be creative, they come up with some funny lists that include great examples of the use of quantifiers and terms of measurement.

ACTIVITY 4 — speaking/listening/writing, [15 minutes for planning, 1 hour or more for eating!]

You may want to use this activity after Exercise 4 on SB page 128, or at the end of the unit as a grand finale! This can be done as an out-of-class activity and is a great way for students to socialize and get to know about each other's cultures. If there are people who do not feel comfortable cooking, you can have them work in pairs with more experienced cooks.

1. Explain the idea of a "potluck" dinner. (A dinner where everyone brings a dish to share with the others.)
2. Arrange a time and place to have your potluck.

3. Make a list of the different dishes people can prepare. Make sure everyone is involved either in preparing a dish or helping someone else.
4. Remind students to keep a record of their recipes.
5. Bring the dishes and the recipes to class. Take photos of the dishes.
6. It may be a good idea to have students label their dishes with the ingredients. Labels will prevent misunderstanding if there are people who do not eat, for example, pork or other meat for religious, cultural, or personal reasons.
7. Exchange recipes and talk about the ingredients while enjoying your potluck dinner! Make a recording of your conversation if possible.
8. Collect the recipes (or play the recording and have students write them) to make an international cookbook for the class.

ACTIVITY 5 — listening [20 minutes]

CD Track 13

You may want to use this activity after Exercise 4 on SB page 128.

1. Introduce the topic of someone asking for advice about a recipe.
2. Play the audio while students answer questions in Step 1.
3. Check the answers. See audio script on LP page S-3.
4. Play the audio again while students answer the questions in Step 2.
5. Check the answers. See answers in the audio script on LP page S-3.

ACTIVITY 6 — research on the web [20 minutes]

You may want to use this activity after Exercise 3 on SB page 126.

1. Assign one recipe to each group of students, or have all students research all four recipes.
2. Ask volunteers to report on their research and write the recipes on the board. They should have roughly the same ingredients, but may differ in the amounts of each one.
3. Share tips and suggestions for searching recipe websites.

ACTIVITY 7 — reflection [15 minutes]

You may want to use this activity after Exercise 2 on SB page 125.

1. Set a time limit for students to make their lists on a piece of paper or in their journals.
2. Have students compare lists in pairs.
3. Discuss the use of quantifiers and the difference between count and noncount nouns.

DEGREE COMPLEMENTS

Too, Enough, and Very

UNIT GOALS

- Understand the meaning of *enough*, *not enough*, and *too*
- Form correct sentences with *enough*, *not enough*, and *too*
- Know how to use *too much*, *too many*, *too little*, and *too few*
- Understand the difference between *too* and *very*

OPENING TASK

Looking for Somewhere to Live

What's your ideal home?

■ STEP 1

Get together with a partner and try to guess what these housing abbreviations mean. Read the classified housing ads below to help you work out the answers.

apt   kit   BR   DR   lg   furn   mo

For Rent

1 1200 SQ FT BASEMENT
2 BR APT
$700
Newly Painted. Walk to center.
Furn/unfurn. No pets.
Call owner before 9 P.M.
(718) 555-1320

2 EAST VILLAGE
Renovated lg studio apt
w/new wood flrs. High
ceilings: sunny: lg windows:
lg walk-in closet: mod kit
$650/mo
555-0479

3 GREENWICH VILLAGE
Charming 1BR;
new kit & bath.
Very quiet building
$875/mo.
555-4345

4 GREENWICH ST.
3 BR Bright: lge kit. Nice gdn.
full bath: lge closets:
Call Tim
555-8246
$1250/mo.

■ STEP 2

Read the classified ads about different types of housing rentals. Then match the ads with the descriptions of different home hunters. Explain which homes are NOT suitable for these people.

a. Maria is looking for an unfurnished house or apartment with lots of light and plenty of closet space. She cannot pay more than $900 a month.
Best home: ___2___

b. Sandra and Suzanne are looking for a two-bedroom apartment with at least 1000 square feet. They can pay $800 a month.
Best home: ___1___

c. Tony and Carla have two children and a dog. They need a garden and a big kitchen. They can pay around $1200 a month.
Best home: ___4___

d. Peter is looking for a sunny furnished studio apartment in good condition. He can pay $700 a month.
Best home: ___3___

■ STEP 3

Work with a partner and complete the sentences. Make similar sentences about the other people.

Maria likes apartment _____ because _____ because _____. She does not like _____. She does not like apartment _____

apartment _____ because _____. She does not like apartment _____ because _____.

■ STEP 4

Look back at all the ads. Which place would you choose? Why? Which places would you definitely NOT choose? Why?

(Solution to the Opening Task on page A-16)

ANSWER KEY

Opening Task   **Step 1:** *apartment, kitchen, bedroom, dining room, large, furnished, kitchen, month*

Step 2   Answers may vary. Possible answers are listed above.

Step 3   Answers will vary.

UNIT 9 LESSON PLAN 1

UNIT OVERVIEW

Unit 9 provides practice with words and phrases that show degree: *too*, *enough*, and *very*. It introduces infinitive structures with *too*—e.g., *It's too hot to go out*. It reviews the use of count and noncount nouns in order to present and practice structures with *too much/many*, *too little/few*.

UNIT GOALS

Some instructors may want to review the goals listed on this page after completing the Opening Task so that students understand what they should know by the end of the unit. These goals can also be reviewed at the end of the unit when students are more familiar with the grammar terminology.

OPENING TASK [30 MINUTES]

The purpose of the Opening Task is to create a context in which students will need to incorporate words and phrases that show *to what degree*: phrases with *very* + adjective, *too* + adjective, and *not* + adjective + *enough*. The task is intended to focus attention on meaning rather than form. The problem-solving format is designed to show the teacher how well the students can produce the target structures implicitly and spontaneously when they are engaged in a communicative task (especially in Steps 3 and 4). For a more complete discussion of the purposes of the Opening Task, see To the Teacher, Lesson Planner (LP) page xxii.

Setting Up the Task

Introduce the topic by telling students about your own experiences with house-hunting through the newspaper or by talking about where you currently live. Ask students about their experiences.

■ STEP 1

Have the students initially work with partners to read the For Rent newspaper clipping. Then discuss their guesses about the abbreviations as a whole class. Help students work out the meanings. This step introduces some of the vocabulary they will need to complete the rest of the task.

Conducting the Task

■ STEP 2

1. Check that students understand the instructions. They have to explain not only which person or family matches which ad, but also why the other ads are NOT suitable.

2. Set a time limit of 10–15 minutes for students to work in pairs and solve the problem. Encourage discussion of different possible answers as this may encourage use of the target structures.

3. Circulate and listen to students, taking note of possible errors in meaning, form, or use so that you can focus on them later in the unit. Do not correct errors at this stage.

4. Check the answers. Refer to the answer key on LP page 136.

■ STEP 3

1. Allow time for students to write their answers to this step.

2. Briefly discuss answers as a class. **Note:** Exercise 1 returns to the task and gives students the chance to review and revise these sentences.

Closing the Task

■ STEP 4

1. Have students respond to this in small groups.

2. Circulate and listen to students, taking note of possible errors in meaning, form, or use so that you can focus on them later in the unit. Do not correct errors at this stage.

GRAMMAR NOTE

Typical student errors (form)

• Errors with word order, e.g. * *The windows aren't enough big.* * *There aren't closets enough.*

• Confusion between adjective, noun, and verb structures, e.g. * *She eats not enough.*

• Error in word choice, e.g. * *He speaks much fast.*

• Confusion between count and noncount degree complements, e.g. * *They have too many work.* * *We have too few time.*

Typical student errors (use)

• Confusion between too and very, e.g. Is your tea hot enough? * *Yes, it's too hot.*

• Misunderstanding the difference in meaning between a few/too few and a little/too little, e.g. * *I have a few friends to talk to* (Instead of: I have too few friends to talk to.)

meaning

FOCUS 1

Enough, Not Enough, Too

EXAMPLES	EXPLANATIONS
(a) There are **enough** closets.	*Enough* shows something is sufficient.
(b) This apartment is big **enough** for both of us.	You have as much as you need and you do not need any more.
	Enough usually shows that you are satisfied with the situation.
(c) There are **not enough** windows in this apartment. (I want more windows!) OR: There aren't **enough** windows in this apartment.	*Not enough* shows that something is insufficient. In your opinion, there should be more.
(d) The bedroom is **not** big **enough**. (I want a bigger bedroom!) OR: The bedroom isn't **enough**.	*Not enough* usually shows that you are not satisfied with the situation.
(e) The rent is **too** high. (It is more than I want to pay.)	*Too* shows that something is **more** than you want or need OR that it is **less** than you want or need. It depends on the meaning of the word that follows.
(f) The kitchen is **too** small. (I want a bigger one.)	
(g) That coffee is **too** hot. (I can't drink it.)	
(h) He speaks **too** fast. (I can't understand him.)	
(i) She's **too** young to drink. (She has to be 21 to drink alcohol in this state.)	*Too* usually shows that you are not satisfied with the situation.

EXERCISE 1

Look back at Step 3 of the Opening Task on page 137. Did you use *too*, *not enough*, or *enough*? If not, rewrite your reasons and see if you can use *too*, *enough*, or *not enough* in them.

Choose one of the families listed on page 137. In your opinion, what would each family say about these apartments? Where possible, use *too*, *enough*, and *not enough*.

1. Tiny but charming studio apartment. Large skylights. Limited storage space. $700.
too small, not enough closets

_____

2. Gorgeous penthouse apartment. Fabulous views of Central Park. 3 bedrooms, 2 bathrooms. Dining room and roof garden. $1800.
too large, too expensive

3. Bright two-bedroom apartment. Big closets. Next to fire station. $825.
enough closets, big enough, too noisy

EXERCISE 2

In this exercise, people are talking about problems that they are having, and their friends are responding by saying what they think caused these problems. For example:

I'm tired all the time.

You don't get enough sleep.

Read the list of problems and the list of causes below. What do you think caused the problems? Work with a partner and match the problems and their causes.

PROBLEMS		CAUSES
1. My feet really hurt.	_d_	a. You don't go to the dentist often enough.
2. I'm broke!	_e_	b. Maybe you shouted too much at the ball game.
3. I failed my math test.	_j_	c. You didn't add enough salt.
4. I've gained a lot of weight recently.	_g_	d. Perhaps your shoes aren't big enough.
5. I never feel hungry at mealtimes.	_h_	e. You spend too much money.
6. I can't sleep at night.	_i_	f. Your stereo is too loud.
7. I have a sore throat.	_b_	g. You don't get enough exercise.
8. This soup is tasteless.	_c_	h. You eat too many snacks.
9. My neighbors are always angry with me.	_f_	i. You drink too much coffee.
10. My teeth hurt.	_a_	j. You didn't study enough.

FOCUS 1 [10 minutes]

This focus chart presents the meanings of *enough*, *not enough*, and *very*. The structure of these forms is presented in Focus Chart 2.

1. **Lead-in:** Introduce the main points of this focus chart by talking about your own or about an imaginary home and saying what you like and dislike about it. For example:

   There's a great view, but there aren't enough windows to see the view, and there are too many trees. It's too dark. It's not big enough for my family, and there aren't enough closets.

2. Then ask students to remember and repeat back some of your sentences. For example;

   You: *What did I say about the windows?*

   Students: *There aren't enough windows.*

3. Read the examples and explanations in the chart. Word order with adjectives and nouns is dealt with in Focus Chart 2.

4. Ask students to talk in pairs about their own homes using the structures from this box.

5. You may want to provide a short drill to practice the meaning of these structures. For example:

   You: *It's too small.*
   Students: *It's not big enough.*
   You: *It's too expensive.*
   Students: *It's not cheap enough.*
   You: *It's too dark.*
   Students: *It's not sunny enough.*
   Etc.

METHODOLOGY NOTE

When using drills it is important to make sure that students understand the language point being practiced. The drill described above, for example, requires students to come up with the opposite adjective, which helps to check understanding of the target structure. When practicing drills, you can ask

students to repeat in unison, or select individuals or pairs of students to provide the answer, or you can alternate. Try to avoid the singsong intonation that is often generated by group repetition. Aim for a more natural intonation by providing a clear model.

EXERCISE 1 [15 minutes]

This exercise allows students to reflect on and improve their sentences in the Opening Task.

1. Turn back to the Opening Task and the sentences they wrote in Step 3.

2. Rewrite or edit the sentences to use the structures from Focus Chart 1.

3. Have students work in pairs to discuss and complete the other examples.

4. Circulate to see if there are structures that are problematic for a number of students, and then review the relevant rules in Focus Chart 1.

5. Discuss the answers as a class. There may be a variety of answers for each one. Refer to the answer key on LP page 138.

(workbook) For more practice, use *Grammar Dimensions 2* Workbook page 56, Exercise 1.

EXPANSION [20 minutes]

Bring in (or have students bring in) classified ads for housing from the local newspaper. Have students work in pairs choosing which apartments or houses they like best and explaining why. Highlight opportunities to use the structures from Focus Chart 1.

EXERCISE 2 [15 minutes]

This exercise provides further practice of the target structures using a variety of contexts.

1. Explain the situation of one person with a number of problems, and the other giving advice.

2. Model the first example with a student. Read the problem and the student will give you advice. Then switch roles.

3. Have students work in pairs, taking turns to read either a problem or a piece of advice.

4. Encourage the use of appropriate intonation and expression!

5. Check the answers by selecting students to read each pair of sentences aloud. Refer to the answer key on LP page 138.

EXPANSION 1 [20 minutes]

1. Bring in examples of people's problems such as advice columns from magazines. Choose some examples for students to read.

2. Have students create example sentences based on the stories and read them out to the class. See examples below.

3. The other students can give some advice.

   Problems

   My credit card bill is too high.
   I failed my math test.
   I gained too much weight this summer.
   I feel tired all the time.
   I don't have enough time to study.
   My car has broken down again.
   My children watch TV all the time.
   I don't have any friends in this city (town).

EXPANSION 2 [30 minutes]

You may want to use activity 2 on SB page 146 after this activity. This activity asks students to write a letter to their local councilor about a problem in the community.

FOCUS 2

Enough, Not Enough, Too

form

EXAMPLES

(a) This house is big enough.
That apartment is not big enough.

(b) Po speaks clearly enough.
Tan does not speak clearly enough.

(c) She ate enough.
He did not eat enough.

(d) We have enough money.
They do not have enough money.

(e) She is (not) old enough to vote.

(f) They studied hard enough to pass the test, but they didn't study hard enough to get a good score.

(g) We (don't) earn enough to pay the rent.

(h) I (don't) have enough chocolate to make a cake.

(i) She is too young.

(j) They work too slowly.

(k) This tea is too hot to drink.

(l) We worked too late to go to the party.

(m) That book is too difficult for me to understand.

(n) He walked too fast for the children to keep up.

EXPLANATIONS

Place *enough* or *not enough*:
- after adjectives

- after adverbs

- after verbs

- before nouns

Notice how *enough* can be used with:
- an adjective + an infinitive
- an adverb + an infinitive

- a verb + an infinitive
- a noun + infinitive

Place *too* before adjectives and adverbs.

Too + adjective or adverb is often followed by an infinitive.

Too + adjective or adverb is often followed by *for* + noun/pronoun + infinitive.

EXERCISE 3

Nazmi has some problems in his English classes. Rewrite the sentences using *too, enough,* or *not enough.* Compare your answers with a partner.

1. The teacher speaks too quietly.
   She doesn't ___ speak loudly enough ___.

2. Her writing is too small.
   Her writing is ___ not big enough ___.

3. My seat is too far away from the board.
   My seat isn't ___ close enough ___.

4. The test time is too short and we never finish.
   There is ___ not enough time ___.

5. I am too busy to finish all my homework.
   I don't ___ have enough time ___.

6. Our grammar book isn't easy enough.
   Our grammar book is ___ too difficult ___.

7. Our lessons aren't long enough.
   Our lessons are ___ too short ___.

8. I have a lot of questions but I don't ask them.
   I don't ___ ask enough questions ___.

9. I want to take the exam but I need to study more.
   I do ___ not study enough ___.

10. I don't check my answers carefully enough.
    I check my answers ___ too quickly ___.

Think of some other problems you have or know about. Describe the problem using *too,* or *not enough.* Take turns with a partner saying the same things in a different way.

FOCUS 2 [10 minutes]

1. **Lead-in:** Write these examples on the board.
The windows aren't big enough.
The house isn't sunny enough.
There aren't enough closets.
There isn't enough space.

2. Ask students to identify which sentences use adjectives (*big, sunny*) and which sentences use nouns (*closets, space*).

3. Write the following sentences with errors on the board or on an overhead projector: * *The windows aren't enough big.* * *There aren't closets enough.*

4. Ask students to work in small groups to correct the sentences and then come up with a rule to repair the errors in word order.

5. Create a short drill based on the sentences given above to practice word order. For example:

You: *windows*
Students: *There aren't enough windows.*
You: *sunny*
Students: *It isn't sunny enough.*
You: *closets*
Students: *There aren't enough closets.*
You: *big*
Students: *It isn't big enough.*

6. Read the examples and explanations in the box.

7. Ask students to provide further examples of structures with the infinitive. For example,
I am not old enough to buy alcohol in the United States.
I don't know English well enough to teach it.
I don't study enough to get good grades.
I don't have enough time to see my friends.

8. Ask students to transform the examples (i) through (n) using alternative structures. This will help prepare students for Exercise 3.
She is not old enough.
They don't work quickly enough.

The tea isn't cool enough to drink.
We didn't finish work early enough to go to the party.
That book isn't easy enough for me to understand.
He didn't walk slowly enough for the children to catch up.

EXERCISE 3 [15 minutes]

This exercise provides practice in using the structures from Focus Charts 1 and 2 accurately. Explain the context of a student who has problems in her English class.

1. Go over the first example together.

2. Have students work in pairs to complete the other sentences.

3. Check the answers, asking students to identify in each case whether it is an adjective, an adverb, a noun, or a verb. Refer to the answer key on LP page 140.

For more practice, use *Grammar Dimensions 2 Workbook* page 57, Exercise 2.

METHODOLOGY NOTE

You can ask if the answer is correct or incorrect by taking a show of hands (*How many of you think that answer is OK? How many think that it's not OK?*). If it's incorrect, give the student who has read the answer the opportunity to correct it. If he or she needs help, ask for a volunteer.

EXPANSION 1 [20 minutes]

1. Ask students to discuss their own problems at school or in class (now, or in the past).

2. Each pair can make a set of sentences similar to those in Exercise 3.

3. Pairs can exchange questions to test each other.

4. Ask volunteers to read them to the class.

EXPANSION 2 [20 minutes]

You may want to use Activity 9 on SB page 149 after this exercise. This reflection task can form part of your students' learning journal.

FOCUS 3

Too Much and Too Many; Too Little and Too Few

form   meaning

EXAMPLES

(a) Walt has too much money.

(b) There are too many students in this class.

(c) There's too little time to finish this.

(d) The class was canceled because too few students enrolled.

EXPLANATIONS

Use *too much* with noncount nouns.

Use *too many* with count nouns.

Too much and *too many* show that there is more than you want or need. They show that you are not satisfied with the situation.

Use *too little* with noncount nouns.

Use *too few* with count nouns.

Too little and *too few* show that there is less than you want or need. They show that you are not satisfied with the situation.

EXERCISE 4

Read the following description of a wedding reception where everything went wrong. Underline all the words or phrases that show there was not enough of something. Where possible, replace these with *too little* or *too few* and change the verbs as necessary.

My sister's wedding was a disaster. First of all, she decided to get married very
                                                                            was too little time to
suddenly, so there wasn't enough time to plan it properly. Nevertheless, about fifty of her
friends came to the reception in her studio. Unfortunately, there wasn't enough room for
everyone, so it was rather uncomfortable. She only had a few chairs, and our ninety-six-
year-old grandmother had to sit on the floor. My father had ordered lots of champagne,
but there weren't enough glasses, so some people didn't get very much to drink. In
addition, we had several problems with the caterers. There wasn't enough cake for
everyone, but there was too much soup! We also had problems with the entertainment.
My sister loves Latin music, so she hired a salsa band; however, it was hard to move in
such a small space, and my sister got upset when not enough people wanted to dance. I
got into trouble too. I was the official photographer, but I didn't bring enough film with
me, so now my sister is mad because she only has about ten wedding photographs—and
all of them are pictures of people trying to find a place to sit down!

Exercise 4 Expressions of insufficiency underlined; replacement follows.

wasn't enough room   too little room for everyone   only had a few chairs   had too few chairs
weren't enough glasses   were too few glasses   didn't get very much to drink   got too little to
drink   wasn't enough cake   was too little cake for everyone   not enough people wanted to dance
too few people wanted to dance   didn't bring enough film   brought too little film   only has about
ten wedding photographs   has too few wedding photographs

EXERCISE 5

You and your friends decided to give a big party. You made lots of plans, but unfortunately everything went wrong and the party was a total disaster. Get together with one or two other students and make a list of all the things that can go wrong at parties. Use this list to make a description of your disastrous party, using *too, too much, too many, too little, too few,* or *not enough*. Share your description with the rest of the class and decide who had the "worst" possible party.

meaning

FOCUS 4

Too versus Very

EXAMPLES

(a) *This writing is small.*

(b) *This writing is very small.*

(c) This writing is too small.

EXPLANATIONS

Very adds emphasis, but *too* shows that something is more than is necessary or desirable.

In (b) the writing is small, but I can read it.

In (c) the writing is smaller and I cannot read it. In these situations, *too* shows that you are unable to do something, but *very* does not.

FOCUS 3 [10 minutes]

This focus chart presents the form and meaning of *too much/too many* and *too little/too few*. You may want to assign Exercise 4 as homework before starting this section.

1. **Lead-in:** Review the meaning of count and noncount nouns. Review the use of *little* and *few* from Unit 8, Focus Chart 3.

2. Have students create a count and noncount column in their notebooks. Dictate the following list of nouns and have students write each word in the correct column.

homework	coffee
tests	clothing
time	cars
money	problems
friends	
work	
information	
exercise	

3. Create a chart with a count and noncount column on the board or overhead projector. Ask volunteers to come and write the words on the board in the correct column.

4. Read the examples and explanations in the box.

5. Have students make sentences about their own lives, using *too much/too many* and *too little/too few* and the words from the list.

EXERCISE 4 [20 minutes]

This exercise provides practice in using *too much/too many* and *too little/too few* accurately.

1. Introduce the topic of a wedding party where everything goes wrong. Ask for some suggestions from the students about what might go wrong.

2. If you have already assigned Exercise 4 as homework, ask students to check their answers in pairs. If not, have them complete the exercise now.

3. While students are working, circulate to see if there are problems, and if there are students who are doing well and find this exercise easy.

4. When everyone is finished, choose two or three students to read a section of the revised passage aloud to the rest of the class.

5. Refer to the answer key on LP page 142.

For more practice, use *Grammar Dimensions 2* Workbook page 58, Exercise 3.

EXPANSION [30–40 minutes]

You may want to use Activity 4 (speaking) and Activity 5 (writing) on SB page 148 after this exercise. These activities encourage students to discuss and write about their opinions on various social issues using the structures from Focus Charts 1–3.

EXERCISE 5 [20 minutes]

This exercise is an optional expansion of Exercise 4. To get this exercise going, you can start by describing a disastrous party of your own, real or fictional! For example:

We had a party that I will never forget. We had invited **too many** *people, because I assumed that some of the people I invited wouldn't be able to come. Right before the party, several people called me up and asked me if they could bring friends. So of course I said 'yes', although I knew I wouldn't have* **enough snacks**—*I had to run to the store and get more. Several of the people who came didn't drink alcohol, so they thought there was* **too much beer** *served at our party (In their opinion, any alcohol was too much!), while a few of my friends, who liked to drink, thought that there* **wasn't enough** . . . . .*

FOCUS 4 [5 minutes]

1. **Lead-in:** Write these examples on the board. Ask students to explain the difference in meaning. (1) *It's very hot. It's too hot.* (2) *She's very thin. She's too thin.*

2. Read the examples and explanations in the box.

LANGUAGE NOTE

Very much sometimes sounds odd/too formal in North American conversation. When talking about amounts, Americans tend to use "a lot" in casual, spoken contexts rather than "very much"—e.g., *I ate a lot* rather than: *I ate very much.*

EXERCISE 6

Complete the following with *too*, *too + to*, or *very*, as appropriate.

A: Hi Pam! I haven't seen you for ages!

B: I'm sorry. I've been (1) _too_ busy _to_ call. I've been house-hunting.

A: Did you find anything yet?

B: Yes, I found a place downtown. It's (2) _very_ expensive, but I think I'll have enough money.

A: What was wrong with your old apartment?

B: I need a place where I can work on my art designs, and my old apartment was (3) _too_ dark _to_ work in. This apartment is
(4) _very_ large and sunny.

A: It sounds great. The problem with my apartment is that it's
(5) _very_ noisy. But it's also
(6) _very_ cheap, so I guess I'll stay there till I have some more money.
Do you need any help moving?

B: Oh yes, please. Could you bring your car? My car is (7) _too_ small
_to_ carry all my stuff. Afterwards we can go out for lunch together.

A: Yes, I'd like that (8) _very_ much.

EXERCISE 7

Complete the following with *very*, *too*, *too + to*, *enough*, *not enough*, or *too much/many/little/few*, as appropriate.

Dear Tom and Wendy,

I'm writing to answer your questions about life in New York. In fact, this is quite hard to do because my opinions keep changing!

My apartment is nice, but the rent is (1) _very_ high. Luckily, I earn a good salary and I can afford it. The main problem is that the apartment just is (2) _not/n't_ big _enough_. I had to sell about half my furniture because I didn't have (3) _enough_ room for everything. I can't invite people for dinner because the kitchen is (4) _too_ small _to_ eat in. Luckily, the apartment has lots of windows, so all my plants are getting (5) _enough_ light. I live (6) _very_ close to a subway station; it only takes me a couple of minutes to walk there. However, I never take the subway to work because it's (7) _too_ crowded. You wouldn't believe it! There are just (8) _too many_ people crammed in like sardines, and you can't breathe because there is (9) _not/n't enough_ air. I haven't had the courage to ride my bike yet because there's just (10) _too much_ traffic. Mostly I walk everywhere, so the good news is that I am getting (11) _enough_ exercise!

Despite all this, there are lots of wonderful things about living here. There are (12) _enough_ museums and art galleries to keep me happy for years! However, at the moment, I have (13) _too little_ time to enjoy them because my job is driving me crazy. It's impossible to get all the work done because there are (14) _too many_ projects and (15) _not enough_ good people to work on them. As a result, I am (16) _too_ busy to make new friends or meet people. I don't sleep (17) _enough_ and so I am always tired. Worst of all, I don't even have (18) _enough_ time to stay in touch with dear old friends like you!

Nevertheless, I'm certain things will get better soon. Why don't you come and visit? That would really cheer me up!

Love,
Mary

LESSON PLAN 2

EXERCISE 6 [10 minutes]

This exercise practices *too* and *very* and continues the theme of house-hunting from the Opening Task.

1. Look at the picture and ask students to guess what they are talking about.
2. Do the first example together.
3. Have students work individually or in pairs to complete the rest of the conversation.
4. Ask students to read the conversation aloud, concentrating on word-linking and using appropriate intonation.
5. Refer to the answer key on LP page 144.

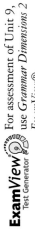

For more practice, use *Grammar Dimensions 2* Workbook page 59, Exercise 4.

METHODOLOGY NOTE

There are a number of ways you can deal with errors in written work. You can routinely set aside class time for students to self-edit or peer-edit their work. This may be difficult for students at first. Students may need guidelines and points to look out for in order to edit their own or each others' work. When you correct students' work you may want to use a coding system that allows students to correct their own work—e.g., *sp* for spelling, or *gr* for grammar. This saves time and generates more independent study. You will then probably receive somewhat improved second or third drafts. It is a good idea to set up a system where students know what kind of errors you intend to correct, how they will be corrected, and how many drafts they can do before receiving a grade.

EXPANSION 1 [40–60 minutes]

You may want to use Activity 6 (speaking) and Activity 7 (listening) on SB page 149 after this exercise. These activities ask students to interview each other (or a friend) and listen to a recording of people discussing world problems.

EXPANSION 2 [30 minutes]

You may want to use Activity 3 (speaking/writing) on SB page 147 after this exercise. This activity asks students to discuss the best ages at which people should be allowed to do certain activities. You can do just the speaking part and omit the writing, or assign the writing for homework.

EXERCISE 7 [15 minutes]

This exercise practices all the structures presented in this unit.

1. You may want to assign this exercise for homework, so that students can take their time reviewing the focus charts.
2. If you don't have time, assign this as homework and have students compare their answers in pairs. If not, set a time limit for students to do the exercise in class.
3. Have students ask questions about points they disagree on.
4. Check the answers as a class. Refer to the answer key on LP page 144.

UNIT GOAL REVIEW [10 minutes]

Ask students to look at the goals on the opening page of the unit again. Refer to the pages of the unit where information on each goal can be found.

EXPANSION [15 minutes]

1. Form two or three teams (depending on the size of the class).
2. Have each team design two or three sentences using the structure listed for each goal. For example, students make sentences with *enough, not enough,* and *too* (goal #1).
3. One person from a team reads their sentence (and/or writes it on the board).
4. Another team demonstrates their understanding of the sentence by paraphrasing it or describing it in terms of the target distinction (in this case, by contrasting *enough, not enough,* and *too*).
5. Assign points for each time a correct paraphrase is given; the team with the most points wins. Or, have the other teams judge whether or not the sentence is correct and if it communicated the meaning of the original sentence.

 ExamView Test Generator For assessment of Unit 9, use *Grammar Dimensions 2* ExamView®.

For a grammar quiz review of Units 7–9, refer students to pages 60-62 in the *Grammar Dimensions 2* Workbook.

Use Your English

ACTIVITY 1 speaking

Work with a partner or in teams to play this version of tic-tac-toe.

■ **STEP 1** Decide who will be "X" and who will be "O" and toss a coin to see who will start the game.

■ **STEP 2** For each round of the game, select a different topic from the list below.

■ **STEP 3** Choose the square you want to start with. With your team, agree on a meaningful sentence expressing the idea written in the square and relating to the topic of the round. For example: TOPIC: This classroom. *"This classroom is very small," "There aren't enough chairs in this classroom," "There are too few windows in this classroom,"* and so on. If your sentence is correct, mark the square with "X" or "O".

■ **STEP 4** The first team to get three across, down, or diagonally is the winner.

very	too + to	too
too few	not enough	too much
enough	too many	too little

ACTIVITY 2 writing

Write a letter to your local city councilor or mayor about a problem in your city or neighborhood. Describe the problem, and say why it is important. Be sure to use *too, enough,* and *very*. Suggest a possible solution.

TOPICS

1. This campus
2. Television
3. North America
4. This town or city

ACTIVITY 3 speaking/writing

■ **STEP 1** Look at the chart below. If you were responsible for making the laws in your community, at what ages would you permit the following activities? Write the ages in the column marked *Ideal Age.*

■ **STEP 2** Go around the room and collect information from your classmates about the ages at which these activities are permitted in the parts of the world (countries, states, provinces) that they know about. You can include information about this country (or state or province) as well. Write this in the last column.

ACTIVITY	IDEAL AGE	REAL AGE/WHERE
drive a car		
drink alcohol		
vote		
join the military		
get married		
own a gun		
leave school		

■ **STEP 3** When you have collected the information, prepare a report (oral or written) on the differences and similarities you found among different parts of the world. Include your own opinions about the ideal ages for these activities and give reasons to support them. Remember to announce the purpose of your report in your introduction and to end with a concluding statement. You can use these headings to organize your information: Introduction: Purpose of this report, Most interesting similarities among parts of the world, Most interesting differences among parts of the world, Your opinions on ideal ages, with reasons to support them, and Brief concluding statement.

■ **STEP 4** If you make a written report, remember to read it through carefully after you finish writing. Check to see if you were able to use any of the language in this unit. If you make an oral report, record your presentation and listen to it later. Write down any sentences that you used containing *too, very, not enough,* or *enough.*

USE YOUR ENGLISH

The Use Your English activities section at the end of the unit contain situations that should naturally elicit the structures covered in the unit. For a more complete discussion of how to use the Use Your English activities, see To the Teacher, LP page xxii. When students are doing these activities in class, you can circulate and listen to see if they are using the structures accurately. Errors can be corrected after the activity has finished.

ACTIVITY 1 speaking [30 minutes]

This activity reviews all the structures presented in this unit and can be used after Exercise 6 on SB page 144 or after Exercise 7 on SB page 145. You can also have students play this game in small groups.

1. Students may already be familiar with this game from Unit 2, Activity 3. If not, explain and demonstrate the game of tic-tac-toe on the board.
2. Play one round of the game as a whole class.
3. Divide the class into groups.
4. Have each group draw the chart in their notebooks. They can use small objects to show which squares they have "taken."
5. Have each group appoint a secretary to keep a note of the sentences made by the group.
6. At the end of the activity, discuss any disputed sentences as a class.

Suggestion: Play this game in teams of four or five, with a large poster-sized version of the chart from SB page 146 affixed to the wall, or an overhead transparency of the chart.

ACTIVITY 2 writing [30 minutes]

You may want to use this activity after Exercise 2 on SB page 139. This activity emphasizes accuracy in the written use of the structures presented in this unit.

1. Brainstorm problems in your local community. If possible, bring in a copy of the local newspaper and read some of the headlines.
2. Make a list of the problems on the board.
3. Have students work in groups. Each group should choose one problem.
4. Each group will write one letter.
5. Exchange letters for peer editing.
6. Read out loud interesting examples of the target structure.
7. Discuss which letters were most effective for their purpose and why.

ACTIVITY 3 speaking/writing [20 minutes]

You may want to use this activity after Exercise 6 on SB page 144.

■ STEP 1

1. Set a time limit of 5 minutes for students to complete Step 1. Emphasize that this is about their own opinions, not a test of their knowledge about the ages in any specific country. The purpose of this step is to start students thinking about what age is too young or old enough for each activity.

Suggestion: Have students compare opinions in small groups and try to agree. Then have one representative from each group present a short oral report to the class.

■ STEP 2 This is an extension of Step 1, requiring students to compare their ideal ages for each activity with actual ages in other countries and express their opinions about this.

1. Have students walk around the room and ask other students about the actual ages when these activities are allowed in other countries. If all your students are from one country, you can adapt Step 2 so that students complete the second column about their own country, or about the United States (as far as they know), or about any other country they know well.
2. If there is not enough room in the charts for students to record their answers, have them record answers in their notebooks.

EXPANSION 1 [30 minutes]

The following is an optional expansion of Steps 1 and 2.

■ STEP 3 When students have completed Step 2, have them prepare a short oral presentation on their findings. Ask volunteers to present their findings to the class.

Suggestion: Have students work in groups and present their findings to the group. (This can be less intimidating than presenting to the whole class.)

EXPANSION 2 [15 minutes/homework]

The following is an optional expansion of Step 3.

■ STEP 4 You can assign this for homework. Select a few of the richer examples of the target structures and present these to the class on an overhead transparency or on a handout.

ACTIVITY 4 speaking

The purpose of this activity is to share opinions on different social issues. Work with a partner and look at the issues listed below. For each one, think about what is sufficient (enough), what is insufficient (not enough), and what is excessive (too much) in this country and in other countries you and your partner know about. For example, you might think that public transportation in this country is too expensive and that there is not enough of it, but that public transportation in Egypt is very inexpensive but too slow. Record your opinions in your notebook. Be ready to share your ideas with the rest of the class.

Public Transportation   Housing

Health Care   Employment

Law and Order   Access for Disabled People to Public

Education   Buildings and Transportation

Care of the Elderly

ACTIVITY 5 writing

Choose one of the social issues you discussed in Activity 4. Review the information you collected on different countries. In your opinion, which country has the best solution? Which country, in your opinion, is the least successful in dealing with this issue? Write a short report, describing the best and worst solutions. Give reasons to support your opinions. Remember to introduce your topic; we have suggested one possibility below, but you can probably think of a better way. When you finish writing, read your report carefully and check to see if you were able to include any of the language discussed in this unit.

In the modern world, many countries are trying to find solutions to the same social issues, and it is interesting to see that different countries and cultures deal with these issues in different ways. In my opinion, some countries have better solutions than others. To illustrate this point, I will talk about _____ (social issue) and show how _____ (country) and _____ (country) both deal with it.

ACTIVITY 6 speaking/listening

STEP 1

Use the information from Activity 4. As a class, choose four topics that interest you. Then, by yourself or with another student, interview a friend or another student about these topics. Record your interview. Listen to your recording and make a brief summary of the person's opinions. Share your findings with others. What similarities and differences did your class find in these interviews?

STEP 2

Listen to your recording again and write down any sentences containing examples of language discussed in this unit.

ACTIVITY 7 listening

CD Track 14

STEP 1

List three serious problems facing the environment today.

STEP 2

Listen to the audio of two people discussing environmental problems. Which opinions do you agree or disagree with and why?

STEP 3

Listen to the audio again. Write down as many phrases containing *too*, *enough*, and *very* as you can.

ACTIVITY 8 research on the web

InfoTrac® College Edition: What are the causes of world hunger? Why do some countries have too much food, and others not enough? Go to *InfoTrac* and search using the keywords 'causes of hunger'. What are the different ways this topic can be understood and explained? Make notes and present your ideas to the class.

ACTIVITY 9 reflection

What do you like and dislike about your classroom or library? What do you have too much/many of? What do you have too little/too few of? Tell your partner.

ANSWER KEY

Activity 7   Step 2: Check audio script on LP page S-4.   *Step 3:* 1. *too many of them* 2. *too much noise and pollution* 3. *aren't enough playgrounds and parks to play in* 4. *enough room for another parking lot* 5. *too much oil and coal* 6. *aren't enough alternative forms of energy* 7. *too polluted to live in*

USE YOUR ENGLISH

ACTIVITY 4 speaking [30 minutes]

You may want to use this activity after Exercise 4 on SB page 142. This activity encourages students to use the target structures to talk about social issues. This activity provides a good way of gathering ideas for the writing activity in Activity 5.

1. Read the list of topics with your students and clarify the meaning of any new vocabulary.

2. Have students work in pairs and discuss each of the topics, comparing the situation in the United States (or in their country) with that in other countries.

3. Ask volunteers to report on their discussion.

4. You may want to write some key sentences on the board and discuss different ways of expressing them using the target structures.

EXPANSION [15 minutes]

A good pre-activity for this is for you or a guest speaker to provide a short lecture on one particular country, covering the topics in the list. Besides providing good listening comprehension practice, the material in the lecture could be used as the basis for comparison from country to country.

ACTIVITY 5 writing [30 minutes]

You may want to use this activity after using Activity 4.

1. Have students choose one of the issues they discussed in Activity 4.

2. Write the list of topics on the board, and write the student's name next to each one to make sure all the topics are covered.

3. Have students make notes of the key points of their report, using a chart or note-taking structure that they are familiar with.

4. Assign the writing for homework.

5. Have students peer-edit their work in class, then hand in their drafts.

6. If you feel your students would benefit from a concentration on writing, you can use this as a basis for a two- or three-step writing activity, having one rough draft and one or two revisions.

ACTIVITY 6 speaking/listening [30 minutes]

You may want to use this activity after Exercise 6 on SB page 144. This activity can be used as a follow-up to either Activity 4 or Activity 5.

1. Prepare this activity in class by asking students to choose their topics and write down the questions they will ask about each one.

2. Assign the interviews for homework. Students who do not have access to English-speaking friends, can carry out the interviews in their own language and report the results in English.

Suggestion: You may also use this as an in-class interviewing activity.

3. Discuss any examples of the target structures that came up in the interview or in the reports.

ACTIVITY 7 listening [20 minutes]

CD Track 14

This activity continues the theme of world problems and is a good follow-up to Activity 6.

■ **STEP 1** Brainstorm problems that have to do with the environment and write them on the board. Some possible ideas might be: pollution, energy, global warming, overpopulation.

■ **STEP 2**

1. Play the audio. See audio script on LP page S-4.

2. Have students discuss their opinions in pairs.

■ **STEP 3**

3. Play the audio again if necessary.

4. Gather opinions from the class. How many agree with the first speaker? How many agree with the second?

5. Play the audio again and have students write down examples of the target structures.

6. See Activity 8 as a possible follow-up to this activity.

ACTIVITY 8 research on the web [30 minutes]

You may want to use this activity after Activity 7. This activity continues the theme of world problems. The purpose of this activity is to provide a natural context for using comparisons. An additional purpose is to encourage students to learn to use InfoTrac® College Edition as a resource. See To the Teacher, LP page xxii for tips on how to use InfoTrac.

ACTIVITY 9 reflection [20 minutes]

You may want to use this activity after Exercise 3 on SB page 141. This activity provides an opportunity for students to use the target structures of the unit while reflecting on their language learning progress. You may have asked students to keep a record of their learning in a journal throughout this course as suggested in To the Teacher, LP page xxii. This reflection activity can form part of that learning record.

GIVING ADVICE AND EXPRESSING OPINIONS

Should, Ought To, Need To, Must, Had Better, Could, and Might

UNIT GOALS

- Use *must, had better, need to, should, ought to, could, might,* and imperatives to give advice appropriately

- Use *should, ought to,* and *should not* to express opinions

OPENING TASK

How to . . .

In North America, many "self-improvement" or "self-help" books are published every year. These books give people advice on how to improve their lives.

■ STEP 1

With a partner, look at the titles of the books below. What kinds of advice do you expect to find in each one? Make up short dialogs about each book, similar to the example below.

Example:

Student A: *I need to learn about a healthy diet.*

Student B: *You should read* Live Longer, Eat Better.

SELF-IMPROVEMENT

How to Dress for Success

Live Longer, Eat Better

LOSING 30 POUNDS IN 30 DAYS

How to Stay Married for a Long Time

Make More Friends

Ways to Save the Planet

■ STEP 2

Now read the sample passages from these books and match each one to the book you think it probably comes from.

A

As an important first step, you really ought to eliminate red meat. This may be hard at first, but you will be amazed to find that there are many healthy—and delicious—alternatives.

B

This is never as easy as it sounds, so you should be prepared to put time and effort into it. For example, doing volunteer work is one way to meet people who share your interests, and you may get to know them better as you work on projects together.

C

It's easier than you think. To really make a difference, you should starr slowly and establish a routine. Think about one thing that you can easily do (carpool? recycle paper, cans, and glass?) As soon as this becomes a habit, you should start to think about what to do next.

D

You should never settle into a regular, predictable routine. Surprise each other with fun activities, like picnics after work or moonlight barbecues on the beach.

E

You ought to make every effort to motivate yourself to stay on your diet! Buy a dress that is just a little bit too small for you and hang it in your closet. You should look at it every day and dream of the time when it will really fit you.

F

You shouldn't draw attention to yourself. Choose conservative but attractive styles. Navy blue is a good color choice. Remember that you ought to look competent and professional at all times.

■ STEP 3

With your partner, choose one of these self-help books. What advice would you give on the topic? Come up with at least three pieces of advice. Write these in your notebook.

ANSWER KEY

Opening Task **Step 2:** A. *Live Longer, Eat Better*   B. *Make More Friends*   C. *Ways to Save the Planet*   D. *How to Stay Married for a Long Time*   E. *Losing 30 Pounds in 30 Days*   F. *How to Dress for Success*

UNIT OVERVIEW

Unit 10 presents and practices structure with *should*, *ought to*, *need to*, and *must* for giving advice and expressing opinions. It also reviews imperative forms.

GRAMMAR NOTE

Modal verbs can be divided into two main groups: those that are connected with degrees of certainty (see Unit 5), and those that are concerned with obligation and permission. They add information about the speaker's attitude or opinion toward the topic. *Should* and *ought to* are both used to give advice (to say something is a good idea); *had better* and *need to* are stronger; *must* and imperative forms have the strongest meaning of very strong advice or obligation. *Should* is also used to express opinions, for example, about social issues.

UNIT GOALS

Some instructors may want to review the goals listed on this page after completing the Opening Task so that students understand what they should know by the end of the unit. These goals can also be reviewed at the end of the unit when students are more familiar with the grammar terminology.

OPENING TASK

The purpose of the Opening Task is to create a context in which students will need to use language for giving advice. The problem-solving format is designed to show the teacher how well students can produce the target structures implicitly and spontaneously when they are engaged in a communicative task. For a more complete discussion of the purpose of the Opening Task, see To the Teacher, Lesson Planner (LP) page xxii.

Setting Up the Task

1. Introduce the topic by asking students what they do when they have a problem in their lives. Do they ask friends or family for advice? Where else can they go to get advice on how to solve the problem?

2. Find out if your students are familiar with the self-improvement book industry. If it seems unfamiliar to them, you may need to spend more time setting up the task.

3. Bring in one or two self-improvement books, articles from magazines, or videos. Have students take a look at them and discuss what they are trying to achieve.

Conducting the Task

■ STEP 1

1. Have students work in pairs to read the titles of the books and discuss what kind of advice you would find in each one.

2. Have pairs share their ideas with the class. Do all groups have the same ideas?

■ STEP 2

1. Set a time limit for students to read the passages A-F and match the passages to the titles.

2. Circulate as they are reading and explain any new vocabulary.

3. Review answers together. See answers set on LP page 150.

VARIATION

Read passages out loud to the class as they read along silently, or ask students to read passages aloud. Students can match passages as they listen, or discuss as a class at the end.

Closing the Task

■ STEP 3

1. Point out that students will be using their advice in later exercises.

2. Have students share their advice with the class. Write some examples on the board.

3. As students are discussing advice, do not correct their grammatical errors at this stage but take notes of possible errors in form, meaning, or use for later in the unit.

4. Go back and underline some of the modal structures in the examples written on the board that students used to give advice. Point out that students will be studying these and other ways of giving advice.

GRAMMAR NOTE

Typical student errors (form)

- Using an infinitive *with to* after *should*, e.g. * *You should to do more exercise.*

- Omitting infinitive *with to* after *ought* or *need*, e.g. * *You ought drive more carefully.* * *You need go to the doctor.*

- Using third person '*s*' with *should*, e.g. * *She shoulds take a vacation.*

- Using the auxiliary *do* to make negatives or questions, e.g. * *He doesn't must go to work.* * *Do I should come to class tomorrow?*

- Using a subject with imperative forms, e.g. * *You go to the doctor immediately!*

Typical student errors (use)

- Using *had better* or *must* instead of *should* to show strong advice or opinion, e.g. *You'd better come to my house for dinner.* (Instead of: You should come to my house for dinner.)

- Using *must not* instead of *shouldn't*, e.g. * *You must not bring your sweater because it is warm.*

FOCUS 1 | Giving Advice with *Should, Ought To, Shouldn't*

meaning

EXAMPLES

	EXPLANATIONS
(a) A: I'm so tired. B: You **should/ought to** get more sleep.	*Should/should not* and *ought to* are often used to give advice (to tell someone what you think is a good or bad idea for him or her to do).
(b) A: I can't understand my teacher. B: You **ought to/should** talk to her about it.	Use *should* or *ought to* to show that you think something is a good idea.
	Ought to is often pronounced as *oughta* in spoken English.
(c) A: I have a terrible cough. B: You **should not (shouldn't)** smoke so much.	Use *should not (shouldn't)* to show that you think something is a bad idea.
	Ought to is not usually used in negatives or in questions in American English.
(d) Nami works too hard. She **should/ought to** take a vacation. (e) NOT: She shoulds/oughts to take a vacation.	*Should* and *ought to* are modal auxiliaries. They do not take third person *s*. For more information about the form of modals, see Unit 5.

EXERCISE 1

Look at the advice that you and your partner wrote in the Opening Task on page 151. Did you use *should, ought to, should not*? Check to see if you used them correctly. If you didn't use them at all, rewrite your advice to include them.

Share your advice with the rest of the class. Do not tell your classmates which book you were thinking about when you wrote the advice and see if they can guess correctly.

FOCUS 2 | Using *Need To* and Imperatives to Give Advice

use

EXAMPLES

	EXPLANATIONS
(a) A: My tooth hurts. B: You **need to** see a dentist.	*Need to* + base verb can also be used to give advice. It is stronger than *should* or *ought to*.
(b) A: My tooth hurts. B: You **should/ought to** see a dentist.	*Need to* is not a modal verb.
(c) A: My tooth hurts. B: **Go to** a dentist.	You can also use an imperative to give advice. An imperative is much stronger and much more direct than *need to*.
(d) A: I can't sleep. B: **Don't drink** so much coffee!	
(e) A: I can't sleep. B: You **shouldn't** drink so much coffee.	If you do not know the person you are addressing very well, it is usually better to use *should/shouldn't* or *ought to*.

EXERCISE 2

Thomson Heinle ELT,
A Thomson Learning Company

We are proud to announce an exciting new book, by language learners for language learners:

HOW TO BE A BETTER LANGUAGE LEARNER

Language learners from all over the world give you advice about ways to learn a second, third, or fourth language. This book will change the way you learn languages. . . .

THOMSON
HEINLE

Australia · Canada · Mexico · Singapore · Spain · United Kingdom · United States

You have been asked to contribute to this exciting new "self-help" book. First, think about your own experience as a language learner. Then, in your notebook write down at least three important things that you think someone who wants to learn **your** language should or should not do. Get together with a partner and compare your lists. How many similarities and differences can you find in your advice? Share your advice with the rest of the class.

FOCUS 1 [5 minutes]

All of the focus charts in this unit build on one another, comparing different forms.

1. **Lead-in:** Mention a few of your problems (real or imaginary) and ask your students for advice. See examples below.

   I can't sleep.
   I'm always tired.
   I don't have any friends.
   I get headaches all the time.

2. Use their advice to write examples using *should, shouldn't,* and *ought to* on the board.

3. Point out the difference between *should* (advice) and *must* (obligation). This is discussed further in Focus Chart 3.

4. You may want to add some examples of *yes/no* and *wh-* question forms. For example, *Should I go to the doctor? What should I do about it?* Point out that *ought to* and *must* are rarely used these days in American English question forms. See Language Note below.

LANGUAGE NOTE

To make advice sound more tentative, or more polite, you may want to teach the structures: *I think you should . . .* OR *Don't you think you should . . . ?* and the correlative question form, *Do you think I should . . . ?*

EXERCISE 1 [5 minutes]

This exercise gives students the opportunity to review the sentences they wrote in the Opening Task.

1. Ask students to turn back to the sentences they wrote for Step 3 of the Opening Task.

2. If they did not write their sentences at that time, they can do so now.

3. Have volunteers read aloud their advice (without mentioning the title of the book). The other students will try to guess which book it is from.

4. Discuss ideas for rephrasing or correcting their sentences using the structures from Focus Chart 1 and write them on the board.

For more practice, use *Grammar Dimensions 2* Workbook page 63, Exercise 1.

EXPANSION [20 minutes]

You may want to use Activity 1 on Student Book (SB) page 162 after this exercise.

FOCUS 2 [5 minutes]

This focus chart presents two structures for giving stronger advice.

1. **Lead-in:** Give some examples of situations where stronger advice might be needed. See examples below.

   Situation 1: You cut your arm on a piece of glass. It's bleeding a lot and won't stop. (You need to go to the hospital right away./Go to the hospital right away.)

   Situation 2: You have a fever and you feel sick. (You need to call the doctor right away./Call the doctor right away.)

   Situation 3: You just received a final payment notice for your phone bill. (You need to pay the bill right away./Pay the bill right away.)

2. Explain the difference in meaning; *need to* or an imperative is stronger and more urgent than *should* (but still not as strong as *must*; see Focus Chart 3. Modals of necessity will be presented in Unit 11.)

3. Explain the difference in form between *need to* and *should. Should* is a modal and does not take *to* or third-person *s. Need to* operates like a regular verb. It takes *to* and third-person *s.*

4. Review the form of imperatives (affirmative and negative forms). See typical errors on LP page 151.

5. You may want to add some examples of *yes/no* and *wh-* question forms with *need to.* For example, *Do I need to go to the doctor? What do I need to do about it?*

EXERCISE 2 [20 minutes]

This exercise provides an opportunity to practice structures from Focus Charts 1 and 2, depending on how urgent they think the advice is.

1. Introduce the topic by saying that you want to write a book about learning languages. Ask students to think about their own experiences and give you some advice about how to be a better language learner.

2. Read the description of the book and the introduction to the exercise.

3. Have students work individually to make a list of three pieces of advice.

4. Compare lists with a partner. What are the similarities and differences?

5. Circulate while they are working and make note of typical errors. Encourage use of all structures presented in Focus Charts 1 and 2.

6. Ask volunteers to come up to the board and write one suggestion each. Each student in turn can come and add to the list but they should not repeat a suggestion made by a previous classmate.

7. When the list is complete, have the class decide which advice is the most important. Do these items use *need to* or imperatives? Ask the class if they would modify some of the pieces of advice to make them stronger or weaker.

For more practice, use *Grammar Dimensions 2* Workbook page 65, Exercise 2.

FOCUS 3

Should and Ought To versus Must

use

EXAMPLES

(a) Alma: I can't sleep at night.
Bea: You **should** drink a glass of milk before you go to bed.

(b) Dora: Do I need to get a special visa to visit Taiwan?
Wen: Yes, you **must** go to the Taiwanese consulate here and get one before you leave. You **must not** try to enter the country without one.

EXPLANATIONS

Should and *ought to* shows that something is a good idea. In (a), Bea is giving advice, but Alma is not obliged to follow that advice; she is free to do what she pleases.

Must is stronger. In (b), it is obligatory for Dora to follow Wen's advice. She is not free to do what she pleases.
For more information about this use of *must*, see Unit 11.

EXERCISE 3

Oscar has just bought a used car. Complete the following, using *should*, *shouldn't*, *must*, or *must not* as appropriate. Different people may have different opinions about some of these, so be ready to justify your choices.

1. He ___should___ get insurance as soon as possible.
2. He ___should___ take it to a reliable mechanic and have it checked.
3. He ___must___ get it registered.
4. He ___must not___ drive it without insurance.
5. He ___must not___ drink and drive.
6. He ___must___ wear a seat belt.
7. He ___should___ lock the doors when he parks the car.
8. He ___should___ keep a spare key in a safe place.
9. He ___should not___ let other people drive his car.
10. He ___should not___ drive too fast.

FOCUS 4

Should and Ought To versus Had Better

use

EXAMPLES

(a) You **should** go to all your classes every day.
(b) You **had better** go to all your classes every day.

(c) You **should** see a doctor about that. (It's a good idea.)
(d) You'd **better** see a doctor about that. (It's urgent.)
(e) You **must** see a doctor about that. (It's obligatory.)

(f) *Teacher to student:* If you want to pass this class, you **had better** finish all your assignments.
(g) *Student to teacher:* If you come to my country, you **should** visit Kyoto.
(h) NOT: You **had better** visit Kyoto.

(i) You **had better** finish this tomorrow.
(j) I **had better** leave now.
(k) He **had better** pay me for this.

(l) She'd **better not** tell anyone about this.
(m) You'd **better not** be late.

EXPLANATIONS

You can also use *had better* to give advice. *Had better* is much stronger than *should* and *ought to*, but not as strong as *must*.

In (a), it is a good idea for you to do this.
In (b), if you don't go, something bad will happen.

Had better often shows that you think something is urgent.
Had better is often contracted to *'d better*.

Had better is often used in situations where the speaker has more power or authority (for example, boss to employee or teacher to student). In these situations, *had better* sounds like an order or a command. If you want to be sure that you sound polite, use *should* or *ought to*.

Had better refers to the present and the future. It does not refer to the past (even though it is formed with *had*).

Notice how the negative is formed.

ANSWER KEY

Exercise 3 *Answers may vary. Possible answers are listed above.*

FOCUS 3 [5 minutes]

1. **Lead-in:** Give examples to illustrate the difference in meaning between *should* and *must*. For example, *You must use a dictionary to check your work* (It's obligatory). *You should use a dictionary to check your work* (It's a good idea). Ask students for additional examples.

2. Read the examples and the explanations in the box. **Note:** The contracted form *mustn't* is rarely used in American English.

3. Explain that must and should are both modals and operate in the same way (not to and no third-person *s*).

LANGUAGE NOTE

Students may already be familiar with the use of *must* as a modal expressing necessity (Refer to Unit 11). They may not understand the finer distinction between *must* for necessity and *must* for advice. When we use *must* for advice, it usually means that there is some external reason that makes the action obligatory. For example, *I must go to the doctor because I have an appointment. You must pay the bill because it is overdue.* It is not simply a matter of my own opinion. If we wish to strengthen the meaning of *should*, we can use *bad better* (see Focus Chart 4).

EXERCISE 3 [10 minutes]

This exercise asks students to explain the reasons for their choices of stronger or weaker forms of giving advice.

1. Introduce the topic of buying a used car. What kinds of things should you look out for? Ask for some suggestions from the class.

2. Look at the picture and guess what kinds of questions they are asking about the car.

3. Have students work individually to complete the exercise.

4. When they finish, they can compare their answers in pairs.

5. Check the answers and ask students to justify their choices.

6. Answers may vary. Some of the differences may depend on the culture(s) in your classroom.

7. For example, wearing a seatbelt or having insurance may not be considered necessary in some cultures. Refer to the answer key on LP page 154.

 work book

For more practice, use *Grammar Dimensions 2* Workbook page 65, Exercise 3.

EXPANSION [30 minutes]

You may want to use Activity 3 on SB page 163 after this exercise.

FOCUS 4 [10 minutes]

1. **Lead-in:** Read the examples from the box, using intonation and tone of voice to emphasize the difference between *should* and *bad better*.

2. Ask for some example situations where someone in authority gives you advice (teacher, parents, boss, doctor, dentist, police officer, etc.)

3. Read the examples and explanations in the box.

4. Give students the following situations and ask them to think of two pieces of advice for each one, one using *should* and one using *bad better*.

   Teacher to student who is getting bad grades.

   Doctor to patient who won't stop smoking.

   Parent to child who does not do his/her homework.

   Boss to employee who is always late.

   Dentist to patient who needs to improve their home tooth care.

   Police officer to motorist who was parked in wrong place.

LANGUAGE NOTE

Had better is often used in similar situations with *should, ought to,* and *must,* but it tends to emphasize the negative consequences of an action. It is like adding "... *or else*" to the suggestion. This is why it is used with a sense of urgency or authority. For example, *You'd better leave* (or else I'm afraid we'll have an argument). *You'd better drink your milk* (or else you won't grow up strong).

EXERCISE 4

Angie is planning a trip to India and asks Sushila for some advice. Choose the most appropriate words from the box to complete the conversation. Use each word or phrase only once.

| should | should not | ought to | must | 'd better not | must not | 'd better |

Angie: I am planning a trip to India. Can you give me some advice?

Sushila: It's very hot there in the summer. You (1) _should_ go there in January or February when the weather is cooler.

Angie: Do I need a visa?

Sushila: Yes, if you have a U.S. passport, you (2) _must_ get a tourist visa. And you (3) _'d better_ get some vaccinations before you go. It's easy to get sick when you're not used to the food and water. You (4) _should/ought to_ take some insect repellant and some stomach medicine, too.

Angie: What about money?

Sushila: It's a good idea to change some money before you go and take your credit card, but you (5) _'d better not_ keep your credit card and passport together. If you lose both, you'll be in trouble!

Angie: What kind of clothes do I need?

Sushila: Take some light clothes for the day. But it can be cool at night, so you (6) _should not_ forget to take a sweater and jacket, too.

Angie: Are there any special customs I should know about?

Sushila: Yes, you (7) _must not_ wear shoes when you enter someone's home.

EXERCISE 5

Circle your choice in each of the following sentences.

1. You (should not/**must not**) smoke when you are in a movie theater in the United States.

2. While you are in Los Angeles, you (**had better**/should) try to visit Disneyland.

3. In the state of Michigan, people under the age of 21 (should not/**must not**) try to purchase alcohol.

---

4. You ('d better not/**must not**) talk on your cell phone while you are driving in New York City; it's against the law!

5. You (**'d better not**/must not) take your car into downtown New York, because you may not find a parking space.

6. Everybody who comes into the United States (**must**/should) show a valid passport or picture ID.

7. If you are interested in Egyptian art, you (**should**/had better) visit the Metropolitan Museum in New York. They have a fantastic collection.

8. It's difficult to find a hotel room in Boston. We (must/**should**) make a reservation before we go there.

9. You (had better/**should**) visit Washington DC in the spring because the cherry trees are very beautiful at that time of year.

10. You (**must**/should) have an appointment before you can visit the White House.

FOCUS 5   Should versus *Could* and *Might*

use

EXAMPLES	EXPLANATIONS
(a) A: I heard there's a new movie playing in town. B: Yeah, you should see that movie. It's great. (b) A: I don't know what to do on Friday night. B: You could see a movie.	You can also use *could* to give advice. *Could* is not as strong as *should* because it only expresses choices or possibilities. *Could* does not show that the speaker thinks that something is a good idea to do or that it is the right thing to do.
(c) If you want to improve your Spanish, you could take classes, you might listen to Spanish-speaking stations on the radio, you could find a conversation partner, or you might take a vacation in Mexico.	We often use *could* or *might* to express many different possibilities, without saying which one we think is best.

EXERCISE 4 [15 minutes]

This exercise gives students the opportunity to discuss the reasons for choosing *should/ought to*, *must*, or *bad better*.

1. Introduce the context of someone asking for advice on visiting another country. Ask for some suggestions for advice that students would give to someone visiting their country or the United States for the first time.

2. Ask students to predict what kind of questions they might ask about going to India.

3. Review the differences between *should/ought to*, *must*, and *bad better* from Focus Chart 4. Emphasize that these differences are a matter of how the advice is perceived by the speaker.

4. Have students complete the exercise on their own individually and compare answers in a group.

5. Discuss any examples where students disagreed with one another. In item 3, for example, it is possible to use either *should* or *bad better*, but the stronger form *bad better* is indicated by the fact that a bad result may follow from not doing this action (and similarly item 5).

6. Use an overhead transparency and do the exercise as a class. Ask students to give their answers and explain why they chose that form.

7. Have the rest of the class decide if they agree with each student's choice.

8. Refer to the answer key on LP page 156.

EXPANSION [10 minutes]

Have students create a similar conversation giving advice to someone visiting their country (or a country they know well) for the first time.

EXERCISE 5 [5 minutes]

This exercise continues the theme of giving advice on visiting another country. Students again have

to distinguish whether it is a rule and is therefore obligatory, a strong piece of advice (or something bad will happen), or just a suggestion.

1. This exercise can be done individually or in pairs.

2. Have students compare answers in pairs and justify their choices.

3. Check the answers as a class. Refer to the answer key on LP page 156.

work book

For more practice, use *Grammar Dimensions 2* Workbook page 66, Exercise 4.

EXPANSION [30 minutes]

You may want to use Activity 4 on SB page 163 after this exercise. Activity 4 asks students to write a report giving advice to someone visiting their country, hometown, or community. You can set this as homework after completing Exercises 4 and 5.

LESSON PLAN 2

FOCUS 5 [5 minutes]

This focus chart presents the use of *could* or *might* for giving advice. Students may be already familiar with the use of *could* and *might* for talking about possibilities (see modals of possibility in Unit 5).

1. Lead-in: Give one problem situation and ask students for a number of different possible solutions. Example: *I want to improve my English vocabulary.*

Possible advice: (1) *You could write down all the new words you hear every day.* (2) *You might want to keep a vocabulary notebook.* (3) *You could get a better dictionary.* (4) *You might buy a new vocabulary book.* (4) *You could use vocabulary cards to practice new words.*

2. Explain how these are all different options. The speaker is not suggesting that one action is better than the others.

3. Read the examples and explanations in the box. Emphasize the correct use of intonation with these examples. In example (a) the intonation is positive and *should* is stressed. In example (b) the intonation is more tentative and *could* is not stressed.

4. Provide further practice in using *could* and *might* by giving students the problem situations below. Ask them to come up with as many different solutions to each one as they can.

I can't sleep.
I'm always tired.
I don't have enough free time.
I can't save any money.

GRAMMAR NOTE

Could and *might* tend to be used to show options, stated or implied. The speaker is giving ideas on the situation, without making a judgment as to whether or not they are wise decisions.

A: I think Martin is really mad at me for what I said.

B: *You **should** call him to apologize. You know how he never forgets these things.* (B is judging the situation and thinks it is a good idea to call.) OR
*You could call him to apologize. Or you **could** just forget the whole thing. Martin is a pretty forgiving guy.* (B is giving choices, but doesn't think one idea is better than the other.)

EXERCISE 6

Your friends always come to you when they have problems because you usually have lots of great ideas about what to do.

STEP 1 For each problem, write down as many possible solutions as you can think of, using *could* and *might*.

STEP 2 Get together with two or three other students and compare your ideas. Decide who has the best solution to each problem and write it down, using *should*.

Example: Your neighbors play loud rock music all night.

Possibilities: You could talk with them. You could play very loud opera in the morning when they are still asleep. You might move. You might buy earplugs. You could call the police.

In our opinion, the best solution: You should buy earplugs.

1. Your friend's husband snores. Possibilities: _____

   In our opinion, the best solution: _____

2. Your friend's father is planning to come and visit for a few days. Unfortunately, he is a heavy smoker and your friend's roommates are nonsmokers who do not permit smoking in the house. Possibilities: _____

   In our opinion, the best solution: _____

3. A classmate has just spilled coffee on her favorite white shirt. She doesn't know what to do. Possibilities: _____

   In our opinion, the best solution: _____

4. Your friend can't sleep at night. She feels exhausted every morning and doesn't have enough energy to do anything all day. Possibilities: _____

   In our opinion, the best solution: _____

5. One of your classmates wants to learn more about American culture and customs and would really like to make friends with some Americans. He doesn't know how to start. You have lots of ideas. Possibilities: _____

   In our opinion, the best solution: _____

6. Your partner never has enough money. At the end of the month, he is always broke. He comes to you for some ideas about what to do. Possibilities: _____

   In our opinion, the best solution: _____

7. Two of your friends are taking a university class. The professor speaks very fast and they find it hard to follow the lectures. They are afraid that they are going to flunk the class. Possibilities: _____

   In our opinion, the best solution: _____

8. Your friend's fiancée has two dogs. She has had these dogs since she was a child and is very attached to them. Unfortunately, your friend is allergic to dogs. He loves his fiancée very much, but the dogs are making him sick. He doesn't want to upset her. Possibilities: _____

   In our opinion, the best solution: _____

EXERCISE 7

The following story is a well-known logic problem. Get together with some of your classmates and decide on the best solution.

A woman went shopping. First she bought a large piece of cheese. Next she walked to a pet store where she bought a white mouse for her nephew's birthday. Just as she was leaving the store, she saw an adorable black and white cat. She couldn't leave the store without it, so she bought the cat as well.

Unfortunately, her car is parked a long way from the pet store, and it's only possible for her to carry one thing at a time. What could she do in order to get everything to her car? How many solutions can you find?

She could _____

There are no parking areas near the pet store, so she cannot move her car, and there is nobody around to help her. Unfortunately, cats eat mice and mice eat cheese. This means that if she leaves the cat with the mouse, the cat will eat the mouse, and if she leaves the mouse with the cheese, the mouse will eat the cheese. What should she do? What is the best solution to her problem?

She could _____

You can find the solution to this problem on page A-17.
There are many different versions of this problem. Do you know one? Share it with the rest of the class.

ANSWER KEY

Exercise 7 First, the woman should take the mouse to the car, leaving the cat with the cheese. Next, she should return and pick up the cat and take it to the car. As soon as she gets to the car with the cat, she should remove the mouse and take it with her, leaving the cat in the car. When she gets back to the shopping area, she should pick up the cheese and leave the mouse. Then she should take the cheese to the car and leave it there with the cat. Finally, she should return to collect the

LESSON PLAN 2

EXERCISE 6 [20 minutes]

This exercise provides further practice in using *should/ought to* or *could/might* in real-life situations.

STEP 1   Have students complete this step for homework or set a time limit of 10 minutes for students to work individually to list as many solutions as they can.

STEP 2

1. Have students compare their solutions in pairs or groups and choose the best one for each situation.

2. Point out that there is no one correct answer to these situations as they depend on students' opinions.

3. As students work, circulate to listen to their ideas and help settle disputes. If a group is spending too much time on one decision, suggest they leave that one for the end so that they have time to discuss all eight situations.

4. Compare solutions as a class. Were some decisions more difficult than others? Why?

VARIATION

Have students read their solution, and other students will guess which situation it is for.

For more practice, use *Grammar Dimensions 2* Workbook page 67, Exercise 5.

EXPANSION [30 minutes]

You can make this topic more relevant to students' lives by asking them to come up with their own problem situations.

1. Divide students into groups. Have each group write a description of a problem that affects them or someone they know. They should not mention

any names or details that might identify who wrote the problem.

2. Collect the problems and redistribute them so that each group gets a different problem.

3. Each group should discuss the problem and come up with two or three different solutions. You may want to appoint one group member as a secretary.

4. When students have finished, they should pass their problem along to the next group.

5. Continue until all groups have discussed all the problems.

6. Compare all the solutions as a class and vote on the best solution.

EXPANSION [30 minutes]

You may want to use Activity 2 on SB page 162 after this exercise.

EXERCISE 7 [10 minutes]

Many students may be familiar with this logic problem.

1. Read the description of the problem with your students. You can read it aloud or ask volunteers to read the descriptions aloud.

2. After solving the problem, students may like to share other versions that they know about.

EXPANSION [30 minutes]

You may want to use Activity 5 on SB page 163 after Exercise 7.

FOCUS 6 — meaning

Should and Ought To versus Might, Could, Need To, Had Better, and Must

EXAMPLES

WEAK

might
could
should/ought to
need to
had better
must

STRONG

EXPLANATIONS

All these verbs can be used to give advice.
However, they express different degrees of
strength.

EXERCISE 8

Read the following situation and follow the instructions given:

Jennifer is an American student. As she is planning to major in international business, she decided that it would be important for her to know how to speak Japanese. She managed to get some money from her father and left for Japan for six months.

She has now been in Tokyo for three months, taking classes in Japanese language and conversation. When she first arrived, she missed home a lot, so she quickly made friends with other Americans she met. Instead of living with a Japanese host family, she decided to move in with two other American women, and now she spends all her time with her new friends. She takes Japanese classes every day, but she seldom spends any time with the students who do not speak any English. As a result, she rarely speaks Japanese and has not made much progress in the language. She hasn't learned much about Japanese culture either.

Jennifer is having a great time in Tokyo with her American friends, but now she's in a terrible panic. Her father has just called to tell her that he will be coming to Tokyo on business, and he wants her to help him while he is there. He wants her to help interpret for him, as well as advise him on Japanese culture and customs. She is feeling very anxious about meeting her father. . . .

First, make a list of all the possible solutions to Jennifer's problem that you can think of in two minutes. Get together with another student and role-play a conversation with Jennifer. Then switch roles.

Example: You must try to meet some Japanese people.

FOCUS 7 — use

Expressing Opinions with *Should*, *Ought To*, and *Should Not*

EXAMPLES

(a) Iryna believes that more people should drive electric cars.
(b) In Mune's opinion, more students ought to continue their education after high school.
(c) Most of my friends think that we shouldn't eat meat.

EXPLANATIONS

You can also use *should*, *ought to*, and *should not* to express your opinions about what you think is right or wrong.

EXERCISE 9

In your opinion, which of the following occupations should receive the highest salaries? Number the occupations in order of the highest to the lowest salaries (Number 1 is the highest salary).

____ TV news announcer   ____ CEO of a large company

____ firefighter   ____ bus driver

____ professional football player ____ politician

____ social worker   ____ elementary school teacher

____ attorney   ____ plastic surgeon

____ plumber   ____ police officer

____ emergency room doctor   ____ nurse

____ model

When you finish, compare your answers with a partner's. Be ready to share and justify your opinions with the rest of the class.

ANSWER KEY

Exercise 8 Answer will vary.

Exercise 9 Answer will vary.

UNIT 10 LESSON PLAN 2

FOCUS 6 [5 minutes]

This focus chart is a review of the different structures that have been discussed in this unit.

1. **Lead-in:** Read an example sentence (see examples below) and discuss the differences between the speaker's judgment when using each different structure. For example:

Before you go to the restaurant, . . .
. . . you **might** call first (= one idea is to call first)
. . . you **could** call first (= one idea is to call first)
. . . you **should** call first (= it's a wise idea to call first)
. . . you **ought** to call first (= it's a wise idea to call first)
. . . you **need** to call first (= it's necessary to call first)
. . . you'**d better** call first (there are negative consequences if you don't call first)
. . . you **must** call first (= it's absolutely necessary to call first)
. . . *to make a reservation.*

2. Ask students to make up their own examples using each structure.

EXERCISE 8 [20 minutes]

This exercise provides an opportunity to practice all forms presented in this unit. The context is one that students may easily relate to.

1. Read the passage aloud, or ask students to read it aloud or silently.
2. Ask a few questions to check comprehension. Some examples,
What is Jennifer studying? Why did she go to Japan? How long has she been in Japan? Why did she make friends with other Americans? Why doesn't she speak much Japanese in her daily life?
3. Set a time limit of 2 minutes for students to write a list of possible solutions.

4. Have students work in pairs to role-play the situation with Jennifer. Then switch partners.
5. Ask volunteers to role-play the conversation for the class.
6. After the exercise is finished, ask if anyone is having difficulties learning English that are similar to those experienced by Jennifer. Are there different suggestions that may apply to their situations?

For more practice, use *Grammar Dimensions 2* Workbook page 67, Exercise 6.

FOCUS 7 [5 minutes]

This focus chart presents a slightly different but related use of *should* and *ought* to express opinions.

1. **Lead-in:** Brainstorm a list of social problems in your country. Write the list on the board.
2. Ask students what they think a solution could be for each one. Encourage the use of *should/shouldn't* or *ought to* in their answers.
3. For some of these situations, the vocabulary may be rather difficult. You may want to take this opportunity to introduce some new vocabulary, which may also be useful to students when doing Activity (see below).
4. Read the examples and explanations in the chart. Point out that this meaning is consistent with that expressed in previous focus charts, as these structures are used to show the speaker's judgment of the situation.

EXERCISE 9 [30 minutes]

This exercise provides a free discussion activity for students to express their opinions using *should, ought to,* and *shouldn't.*

1. Read the list of occupations and check comprehension. (**Note:** CEO = Chief Executive Officer, usually the head of the company)

2. Set a time limit of 2 minutes for students to number the occupations individually.
3. Have students compare their answers in pairs.
4. Ask volunteers to present their opinions to the class, explaining why they hold them.
5. You may find that interesting cultural differences emerge from this discussion because of different attitudes as to whether salaries should be based on danger, education, or market forces.

VARIATION

Photocopy and cut the chart into individual "job cards." Be sure to make enough copies for each pair to work with.

6. In pairs, students arrange the strips of paper in a list, ranking the jobs from highest salary to lowest salary.
7. Have pairs compare their answers with each other, noting similarities and differences.
8. Discuss differences as a class.

For more practice, use *Grammar Dimensions 2* Workbook page 70, Exercise 7 and page 71, Exercises 8 and 9.

UNIT GOAL REVIEW [10 minutes]

Ask students to look at the goals on the opening page of the unit again. Help them understand how much they have accomplished in each area.

ExamView Test Generator — For assessment of Unit 10, use *Grammar Dimensions 2* ExamView®.

Use Your English

ACTIVITY 1 speaking/listening

STEP 1

Sometimes, for fun, people give each other advice on the best way to accomplish a negative goal—for example, the best way to lose your job or how to annoy your neighbors. Get together with another student and choose one of the following humorous topics. How many different ideas can you come up with?

- How to get a traffic ticket
- How to get rid of your boyfriend or girlfriend
- How to avoid learning English
- How to get an F in this class
- How to annoy your roommate

STEP 2

With your partner, make a poster presentation on the topic you chose. Display your poster and use it to explain your ideas to the rest of the class.

STEP 3

Record yourself as you make your poster presentation. Listen to your recording and write down all the sentences where you used *should, shouldn't, ought to, need to, must, bad better, might,* or *could.* Did you use them appropriately?

ACTIVITY 2 speaking

Many American newspapers have advice columns. People write to these columns for help with their problems. Three famous ones are "Dear Abby," "Ann Landers," and "Miss Manners." Clip any advice columns you can find in various newspapers and bring them to class. Cut off the answers to the letters and circulate the letters without their replies. (But do not throw away the replies.) In groups, try to come up with helpful advice. Share your responses with the rest of the class. Compare your advice with the advice the professionals gave.

ACTIVITY 3 writing

In groups, write a letter to "Dear Abby," asking for advice on a particular problem. Exchange your problem letter with another group and write solutions to their problem. Share both problem and solution with the rest of the class.

ACTIVITY 4 writing

Write a short report, giving advice to someone who is planning to visit your hometown, your country, or the community where you grew up. Advise him or her on places to visit, clothes to wear, things to bring, things to do, and how to act. Remember to start your report with an introductory statement.

Example: My hometown/country, (name), is very interesting, and if you follow my advice, I am sure that you will have an enjoyable and rewarding visit. . . .

When you finish writing, check and see if you have used *should, shouldn't, must, ought to, might, need to, could,* and *bad better.* It is not necessary to use one in every sentence, as this would sound very unnatural!

ACTIVITY 5 speaking

Is honesty always the best policy? Should we always tell the truth? Think about the following situations. Share your opinions on each one with your classmates. How many people share your point of view? How many have different ideas?

1. You saw your best friend's girlfriend out on a date with someone else. Should you tell your friend what you saw? Why? Why not?

2. A classmate cheated on the last test. Should you tell your teacher? Why? Why not?

3. Your friend has a new haircut. She is really happy with her new "look," but you don't like it at all. In fact, you think it makes her look quite ugly. She asks for your opinion. Should you tell her what you really think? Why? Why not?

4. You catch your 8-year-old son telling a lie. Should you tell him that it is wrong to lie? Why? Why not?

The Use Your English activities at the end of the unit contain situations that should naturally elicit the structures covered in the unit. For a more complete discussion of how to use the Use Your English activities, see To the Teacher, LP page xxii. When students are doing these activities in class, you can circulate and listen to see if they are using the structures accurately. Errors can be corrected after the activity has finished.

ACTIVITY 1

speaking/listening
[20 minutes]

You may want to use this activity after Exercise 6 on SB page 158. This activity is a fun way to review all the modals presented in this unit and encourages students to think creatively about problems.

▪ STEP 1

1. Read the problems with your students and check comprehension of the situations.
2. Divide your class into pairs of students or five groups and ask each pair/group to choose one situation.
3. Set a time limit for students to come up with as many suggestions as they can.

▪ STEP 2

4. Have each pair or group display their suggestions on a poster, and give a presentation to the class.

VARIATION

Ask one student from each pair or group to come up to the board and write a list of all the suggestions. Other groups can then add further suggestions.

▪ STEP 3

5. If you do not have access to recording equipment, assign other students to act as secretary, noting sentences where the speaker used the target structures.

ACTIVITY 2

speaking
[30 minutes]

You may want to use this activity after Exercise 1 on SB page 152. Activity 3 (writing) is a good follow-up to this speaking activity.

1. Bring in some examples of these "Dear Abby" letters from newspapers or from the Internet.
2. Hand out the problems (without the replies) and have students discuss them in pairs or groups.
3. Hand out the replies and compare answers to the problems.

ACTIVITY 3

writing
[30 minutes]

This activity is a good follow-up to Activity 2. As with Activity 2, this can also be done via e-mail.

1. Have students write the problem letters in class, or for homework.
2. If using e-mail, have students set up groups of three or four. They will arrange to send each other and answer each other's "problems."
3. Print out the replies and bring them to class.
4. Read out loud and discuss the answers, commenting on the use of modals for advice.

ACTIVITY 4

writing
[30 minutes]

You may want to use this activity after Exercise 5 on SB page 156.

1. Introduce the topic of giving advice to someone visiting your country, or another county you know well.
2. Write a list of subtopics on the board: places to visit, clothes to wear, things to bring, things to do, how to act. Add any more topics that your students can think of.
3. Have students make notes under each of these headings.
4. If all your students are from one country or culture, you can divide the paragraphs between different groups. Otherwise, assign the report for homework.
5. You can increase the formality of this writing exercise by creating a class travel magazine.
6. After their final edit, compile students' traveler's advice pieces into a booklet and distribute it to the class.

ACTIVITY 5

speaking
[30 minutes]

You may want to use this activity after Exercise 3 on SB page 154.

1. Read the situations and check comprehension of any new vocabulary.
2. Have students discuss each of the situations in small groups and come up with one piece of advice for each one.
3. Ask representatives from each group to report to the class and explain the reasons for their advice.
4. Encourage discussion and disagreement as this will enable students to see the target structures more freely.
5. After they finish, you may want to discuss cultural differences in attitudes towards lies or cheating. Are lies sometimes OK? or necessary? Is cheating always wrong?

ACTIVITY 6 speaking/writing

STEP 1

Read the following and circle *should* or *should not* to express the point of view that is closest to your own opinion on the topic.

1. School uniforms should/should not be obligatory.

2. Animals should/should not be used in laboratory experiments.

3. Doctors should/should not reveal the identity of an AIDS patient to the patient's employer or school.

4. Mothers should/should not work outside the home while their children are young.

5. A woman should/should not take her husband's family name when she marries.

6. Smoking should/should not be permitted in public places.

STEP 2

Choose the topic that interests you the most and then go around the room until you find one or two other students who share your opinion on that topic. Form a group with these students and brainstorm all the reasons and examples you can think of to support your point of view and then write them down. Choose the strongest ones, with the best examples, and use them to make a short report (oral or written) presenting your opinion. Share your report with the rest of the class and be ready to justify your position as necessary.

STEP 3

If you make a written report, read your report carefully and underline every example you can find of the modal auxiliaries from this unit.

If you choose an oral report, record your report. Listen to your recording and write down every sentence where you use one of the modal auxiliaries from this unit.

ACTIVITY 7 listening

CD Track 15

In this activity, you will hear an interview on the topic of smoking. Listen to the person's opinion. Does she think smoking should be banned in public places? What other ideas does she express? Check (✓) the statements you think the speaker agrees with.

✓ Smoking should be banned in public places.

___ People should not be able to buy cigarettes in drugstores and supermarkets.

✓ Parents should not smoke at home in front of children.

___ Teachers need to teach students about the dangers of smoking.

Listen to the audio again. Write down any sentences that contain examples of the verb forms in this unit.

ACTIVITY 8 speaking/listening

Many people have strong opinions about smoking. Ask five different people questions like these: "What's your opinion about smoking in public places?" "Do you think it's a good or bad idea to ban smoking in public places?"

Record their answers. Listen to your recording and be ready to share the information that you collect with the other people in your class. What do most of the people you interviewed think about this topic?

Listen to your recordings again. What are some of the words and the ways people used to express their opinions? Write down any sentences that contain examples of the verbs from this unit.

ACTIVITY 9 research on the web

InfoTrac® College Edition: Go to *InfoTrac* and search articles for advice on how to stop smoking. Type keywords "how to stop smoking." Take notes of the main points. What do you think should be done to stop people from smoking? Discuss this issue with your class.

ACTIVITY 10 reflection

What problems do you have studying English? Write down three problems. Tell your partner and ask for some advice.

GIVING ADVICE AND EXPRESSING OPINIONS *Should, Ought To, Need To, Must, Had Better, Could, and Might*

ANSWER KEY

Activity 7 *Check audio script on page S-4 of this book for answers.*

USE YOUR ENGLISH

ACTIVITY 6 — speaking/writing [20 minutes]

You may want to use this activity after Exercise 9 on SB page 161.

1. Read the list of topics with your students.

2. Have each student choose one topic and find two other students who agree with him or her.

3. Set a time limit for students to work on collecting ideas.

4. Ask representatives from each group to present their ideas to the class.

5. Ask the other students to comment, ask questions, or add additional arguments.

6. Assign the reports for homework.

7. Note that topic 6 is continued in Activity 7.

METHODOLOGY NOTE

It is important for students to receive feedback on their written work. This will help them to visualize a reader when they are writing, and it will also encourage them to see writing as a means of communication, not as a test. You can create opportunities for students to give and receive feedback from each other in the classroom by allowing classroom time for students to read each others' work. Encourage students to comment on the content of the work, not only on possible errors. When you give feedback, be sure to include a personal comment on the content of their report as well as on form, meaning, and use.

ACTIVITY 7 — listening [20 minutes]

CD Track 15

You may want to use this activity after Exercise 9 on SB page 161 or after Activity 6.

1. Introduce the topic by asking about rules about smoking in your city or school building.

2. Play the audio and have students write their answers individually. See audio script on LP page S-4.

3. Have students check their answers in pairs.

4. Play the audio again. Check the answers. Again, refer to the audio script for answers on LP page 164.

ACTIVITY 8 — speaking/listening [20 minutes/homework]

You may want to use this activity after Exercise 9 on SB page 161 or after Activity 7.

1. Read the instructions and have students create a list of questions. You may want to adapt this topic to one that is more relevant to your students than smoking.

2. Assign the interviews for homework.

3. Ask students to share the results of their interviews with the class, commenting on the types of modals used.

VARIATION

If your students have limited access to native speakers of English, invite people (friends, family, other teachers) who have strong English skills to participate in a panel discussion.

1. Record the discussion and have the class listen again and take notes of the different ways the speakers expressed their opinions.

2. When reviewing the language, draw a chart on the board with two columns, one for stronger opinions, one for weaker opinions.

3. Elicit from the students the different ways people expressed opinions, writing their answers in the appropriate column.

ACTIVITY 9 — research on the web

The purpose of this activity is to provide a natural context for using comparisons. An additional purpose is to encourage students to learn to use *InfoTrac® College Edition* as a resource. See To the Teacher, LP page xxii for tips on how to use InfoTrac. You can also do this activity on the Web. The main topic here is somewhat different from Activities 7 and 8 as it is about how to stop young people from smoking.

ACTIVITY 10 — reflection [30 minutes]

You may want to use this activity as a way of wrapping-up the unit after Exercise 9 on SB page 161. This activity provides an opportunity for students to use the target structures of the unit while reflecting on their language learning progress. If you have asked students to keep a record of their learning in a journal throughout this course as suggested in To the Teacher, LP page xxii, this reflection activity will form part of that learning record.

MODALS OF NECESSITY AND PROHIBITION
Have To/Have Got To, Do Not Have To, Must/Must Not, Cannot

UNIT GOALS

- Use *must, have to,* and *have got to* to show something is necessary

- Use *must not* and *cannot* to show something is prohibited

- Choose between *have to* and *have got to*

- Use *do not have to* to show something is not necessary

- Use *have to* for *must* the past

OPENING TASK

Customs and Immigration

■ STEP 1

Every country has rules about what you can bring with you when you enter the country. What is one rule you must follow to enter the United States? What is one rule you must follow to enter the country you are from?

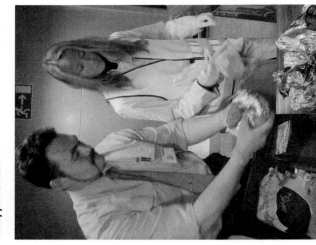

■ STEP 2

A friend of yours in Taiwan is planning a short vacation to California. He doesn't have much room to pack a lot of things because he's planning to travel with just a backpack. Here are some of the things he is thinking of taking with him:

a passport
a surfboard
fresh fruit
an international driver's
   license
traveler's checks
books about China
a return airline ticket

a map of the United States
fireworks
a laptop computer
a credit card
a tourist visa
California guide books
photographs of his
   hometown

an umbrella
a business suit
hiking boots
a cell phone
Chinese pop music CDs

■ STEP 3

Use the box below to help your friend organize the things he wants to take to the United States. Work with a partner and put them in the category where you think they belong.

1. It's necessary and obligatory: You can't enter the United States without this: You must take this with you.	3. It's a good idea to bring this: You should take this with you.
2. It's prohibited by law: You must not take this into the United States.	4. It's O.K. to bring this, but it isn't really necessary: You don't have to take this.

■ STEP 4

With your partner, write sentences about one or two items in each category, explaining why you think they belong there.

ANSWER KEY

Opening Task   **Step 3:** 1. a passport; a tourist visa   2. fireworks; fresh fruit (according to California law)   3. Answers will vary depending on individual points of view but may include: traveler's checks; a credit card; a return airline ticket; photographs of your hometown; Chinese pop music CDs (answers will definitely vary on this one); hiking boots (depending on the type of vacation)   4. Again, answers will vary, but may include: a cell phone; an international driver's license; an umbrella; a business suit; books about China; a laptop computer; a map of the U.S.; California guide books (can

UNIT OVERVIEW

This unit provides practice with modals and phrasal modals of necessity and prohibition: *have to/have got to, must/must not,* and *cannot.*

GRAMMAR NOTE

Must and *have to* are used to express requirements (actions that are necessary or obligatory) or to give strong advice. *Must not* and *cannot* are used to talk about prohibition (actions that are prohibited). *Don't have to* is used when there is no need or obligation to do something. The meanings of these modals of necessity should not be confused with the modals of probability and possibility presented in Unit 5.

UNIT GOALS

Some instructors may want to review the goals listed on this page after completing the Opening Task so that students understand what they should know by the end of the unit. These goals can also be reviewed at the end of the unit when students are more familiar with the grammar terminology.

OPENING TASK [30 minutes]

The purpose of the Opening Task is to create a context in which students will incorporate modals and phrases that express necessity and obligation: *have to/have got to/do not have to/must/must not,* and *cannot.* The problem-solving format is designed to show the teacher how well the students can produce the target structures implicitly and spontaneously when they are engaged in a communicative task. For a more complete discussion of the purpose of the Opening Task, see To the Teacher, Lesson Planner (LP) page xxii.

Setting Up the Task

The Opening Task uses the context of going through the Customs and Immigrations when entering the

United States in order to generate discussion that naturally uses modals of necessity and prohibition.

■ STEP 1

1. Ask students to look at the picture and try to work out what these people are doing. (They are customs officials examining food that has been brought into the country. It is not allowed to bring certain types of food into the United States—e.g., fruit.)

2. You may want to discuss the difference between customs and immigration, and ask students about any experiences they have had. What is the procedure for getting a visa to enter the U.S.? What kinds of substances are not allowed?

Conducting the Task

■ STEP 2

1. Check to see if everyone understands the vocabulary in the box. If not, ask other students to give definitions or describe the items.

2. Ask students: What things do you have to have on a vacation? Discuss as a class.

■ STEP 3

1. Have students work in pairs to do this step.

2. Circulate while they are working to see if they are using the target structure. Do not correct errors at this stage. Make notes of errors in meaning, form, and use which may help you later.

3. Encourage discussion and disagreement concerning the items as this will promote use of the target structures. Categories 1 and 2 are relatively straightforward because most of the items in this category are bound by U.S. law, so you can expect little disagreement here. Categories 3 and 4 are subjective, however, so you can expect some disagreement. There are no right or wrong answers; it depends on personal opinion. This is deliberately designed to focus attention on strong necessity/obligation and prohibition (Categories 1

and 2), and contrast this with weak necessity and absence of necessity (Categories 3 and 4).

Closing the Task

1. Compare answers as a class. Refer to the answer key on LP page 166. You can do this by drawing the chart on the board (or making an overhead transparency) and using student suggestions to fill in the categories.

2. Ask students to add items to each of the charts. Add their suggestions to the chart.

■ STEP 4

1. Here you will be able to see to what extent students are able to produce these forms when they are concentrating on meaning and not form. Don't worry about accuracy for now. Students will revise these sentences in Exercise 1.

2. You can use students' sentences as a bridge to Focus Chart 1.

GRAMMAR NOTE

Typical student errors (form)

- Using the infinitive *to* after *must,* e.g. * *You must to work harder.*

- Not using third-person form with *have to,* e.g. * *She have to go to the dentist.*

- Using the auxiliary *do* to make negatives or questions, e.g. * *He doesn't must go to work.* * *Do I must come to class tomorrow?*

- Confusing past and present forms, e.g. * *He has to go to the dentist yesterday.* (Instead of: *He had to go to the dentist yesterday.*)

Typical student errors (use)

- Using *mustn't* to mean absence of obligation, e.g. * *You mustn't pay any money because it is free for students.* (Instead of: *You don't have to pay any money.*)

- Misunderstanding *have to* as a form of the verb *have,* e.g. * *Q: Do you have to fill in a form?* A: *Yes, I have a form.*

FOCUS 1

Modals of Necessity, Prohibition, and Permission

EXAMPLES	EXPLANATIONS
(a) You **must** have a passport. OR	Use *must*, *have to*, or *have got to* to show something is necessary and obligatory (something that is strongly required, often by law).
(b) You **have to** have a passport. OR	
(c) You **have got to** have a passport.	
(d) You **must not (mustn't)** bring fresh fruit into the United States. OR	Use *must not (mustn't)* or *cannot (can't)* to show something is prohibited and absolutely not permitted (often by law).
(e) You **cannot (can't)** bring fresh fruit into the United States.	
(f) When I traveled to Iceland last year, I **couldn't** take any meat products.	In the past, use *couldn't*.
(g) If you go to live in Japan next year, you **won't be able to** take any pets with you.	In the future, use *will not (won't)* be able to.
(h) You **can** bring a surfboard.	Use *can* to show that something is permitted.
(i) About ten years ago, you **could** smoke on an airplane.	In the past, use *could*.
(j) In the future, you **will be able to** go to bed on an airplane.	In the future, use *will be able to*.
(k) You **should** bring a credit card.	Use *should* to show something is a good idea. For more information about this use of *should* see Unit 10.
(l) You **don't have to** bring a surfboard.	Use *do not (don't) have to* to show something is permitted, but not necessary. You can do this if you want to, but you are not required to.

EXERCISE 1

Look back at the sentences you wrote in Step 4 of the Opening Task. Did you use *must*, *have to*, *have got to*, *should*, *can*, *can't*, *mustn't*, and *don't have to*? If you did, check to see that you used them correctly. If you didn't use them, rewrite the sentences.

Example: *He must have a valid passport—it is required by law.*

In the rest of this unit, you will have the opportunity to practice all of these in more detail.

FOCUS 2

Modals and Phrasal Modals: *Must, Have To,* and *Have Got To*

EXAMPLES	EXPLANATIONS
(a) International students **must** get visas before they enter the United States.	*Must* is a modal and does not change to agree with the subject.
(b) My Taiwanese friend **must** get a tourist visa before he goes to the United States on vacation.	
(c) International students **have to** get visas before they enter the United States.	*Have to* is a phrasal modal. It changes to agree with the subject.
(d) My Taiwanese friend **has to** get a tourist visa before he goes on vacation in the United States.	*Have to* and *has to* are usually pronounced "hafta" and "hasta" in fast speech and informal conversation.
(e) International students **have got to** get visas before they enter the United States.	*Have got to* is a phrasal modal. It changes to agree with the subject.
(f) My Taiwanese friend **has got to** get a tourist visa before he goes to the United States on vacation.	*Have got to* and *has got to* are usually pronounced "'ve gotta" and "'s gotta" in fast speech and informal conversation.
(g) **Do** we **have to** go? **Does** she **have to** go too?	Notice how questions with *must*, *have to*, and *have got to* are formed. Use *do/does* with *have to*.
(h) **Have** we **got to** go? **Has** she **got to** go too?	Use *has/have* with *have got to*. Do not use *do/does*.
(i) **Must** we go? **Must** she go too?	Do not use *do/does* with *must*. However, *must* is rarely used in questions in American English.

ANSWER KEY

Exercise 1   *Answers will vary, depending on what students wrote in the Opening Task.*

FOCUS 1 [10 minutes]

This focus chart presents the range of modals of different strengths, reviewing *should* and *can* from Unit 10, and presenting the new modals *must*, *have to*, *have got to*, and *be able to*.

1. **Lead-in:** Review the sentences from the Opening Task. Ask students to explain the meanings of the various modals they used.

2. Write the following chart on the board and ask students to help you fill in the modals in the appropriate places according to their different degrees of strength. The answers are in italics in the chart.

	obligatory actions	prohibited actions
Strong →	(Answer: must/have to/have got to)	(Answer: must not/cannot)
	(Answer: should)	(Answer: shouldn't)
Weak	(Answer: can/be able to)	(Answer: don't have to)

3. Read the examples and explanations in the focus chart.

4. Discuss the meaning of the terms *obligatory/prohibited/permitted*, giving examples from your school or college. For example:

You must take an exam before you start. You must pay a fee.

You mustn't eat in the classroom. You mustn't use your cell pone during the lesson.

You should have a dictionary. You should check your homework carefully.

You shouldn't be late for class. You shouldn't come to class if you are sick.

You can ask the teacher questions. You can borrow books from the library.

Note: Uses of should/ought to/need to are dealt with in Unit 10, Focus Chart 6.

EXERCISE 1 [5 minutes]

This exercise, along with Focus Chart 1, can serve as a bridge from the Opening Task.

1. Have students turn back to the sentences they wrote in the Opening Task.

2. Students can work in pairs or small groups and then share sentences with the class.

3. The other students can check to see that the sentences are correct.

For more practice, use *Grammar Dimensions 2* Workbook page 72, Exercise 1.

EXPANSION 1 [20 minutes]

This exercise continues the theme of the Opening Task.

1. Ask students each to choose a country they know well.

2. Have them work in pairs to ask each other questions about rules in that country.

3. Ask volunteers to report on what they found out from their partner. For example: My partner knows a lot about Spain. He says that if you go to Spain you must . . . but you mustn't . . . , you can . . . but you cannot . . . , and you don't have to . . . .

EXPANSION 2 [20 minutes]

Ask students to write a paragraph or two on the *do's* and *don'ts* when visiting your home country. Remind them that a brief introductory statement or phrase is important in a descriptive paragraph. For example, "*If you want to visit* (name of country), *there are a few things you need to know* . . ."

FOCUS 2 [10 minutes]

1. **Lead-in:** Dictate some sentences using *bafta* and *basta* (see Pronunciation Note below) and have students write the full form of the sentence. Examples:

She *basta* do her homework.

They *bafta* go to work.

They've *gotta* get a visa.

My friends *gotta* go to the dentist.

I've *gotta* buy a new computer.

Do we *bafta* have an exam now?

2. Have students read the sentences back using full and reduced forms of pronunciation.

3. Read the examples and the explanations in the focus chart. Point out the difference in structure between modals like *must* and *should* that do not inflect or take *to*, and modals like *have to* and *need to* which take *s* in the third person and are followed by *to*.

4. In groups or as a whole class, have students make up sentences and read them aloud while others, including you, transcribe the full form.

For more practice, use *Grammar Dimensions 2* Workbook page 72, Exercise 2.

PRONUNCIATION NOTE

Hafta, basta, 've gotta and *'s gotta* are the reduced versions of *have to, has to, have got to* and *has got to* which all naturally occur in informal speech. For example: Do we *bafta* continue class today? Do you think Suzanna *basta* study every day? In rapid informal speech, the verb *have* is sometimes omitted in statements. For example, I *gotta* go home. = I *have got to* go home. Emphasize that this occurs only in informal settings.

EXPANSION [20 minutes]

You may want to use Activity 3 (writing) on Student Book (SB) page 182 after this focus chart. This activity asks students to write a letter to a friend about the requirements for applying to college in the United States.

EXERCISE 2

Many road signs are used internationally, but some used in the United States are confusing for tourists from other countries. What do you think the following road signs mean? Complete the sentences, using *have to* and *have got to* in your answers.

1. In the United States, drivers ___ have to turn right ___ when they see this sign.

2. Also, when they see this one, they ___ have got to stop.

3. This sign tells you that you ___ have to yield.

4. A driver who sees this sign ___ has to look out for pedestrians.

5. Be careful when you see this one. It means that you ___ have got to turn left.?

6. Q: What happens when there are two or three cars waiting at this sign?
A: The car that arrives last ___ has to wait until the other cars go.

How many of these road signs on page 170 are also found in your country? Are there are any road signs from your country that are not found in North America? Draw the signs and write sentences showing what you have to do when you see them.

EXERCISE 3

Work with a partner and decide which of the following are necessary and obligatory to do if you want to get a driver's license in the United States.

- speak English very well
- take driving lessons
- practice before the test
- take an eye test
- take a written test
- have a medical examination
- have a passport or birth certificate as ID

- pass a driving test
- have a high school diploma
- own a car
- study the information booklet from the DMV (Department of Motor Vehicles, the department that issues driver's licenses)
- have an international driver's license

EXERCISE 4

Role-play this situation with your partner. Your friend will ask you questions about how to get a driver's license. Answer the questions and explain what is necessary to get a driver's license in the United States; then explain what is necessary to get a driver's license in the country you are from. Then switch roles.

Example: A: *Do I have to take a written test?*
B: *Yes, you have to take a written test and a driving test.*

ANSWER KEY

Exercise 2 The use of *have to* and *have got to* may vary. Possible answers are listed above.

Exercise 3 Answers will vary from state to state and depending on students' opinions, but in general, states require that one takes an eye test, takes a written test, and passes a driving test to get a driver's license.

Exercise 4 Answers will vary.

EXERCISE 2 [5 minutes]

This exercise practices *have to* and *have got to*. It may be helpful to explain that there is only a slight difference in meaning between the two phrasal modals (see Focus Chart 3, SB page 172).

1. Introduce the topic of road signs. You may want to ask students about the meaning of signs that are found in your neighborhood.

2. Ask how many students in your class can drive a car. What road signs do they find most confusing? What signs are there for pedestrians? Ask for some examples.

   Suggestion: You may want to pair up drivers with nondrivers for this exercise.

3. Have students work in pairs to write sentences for each sign. They can compare answers with another pair.

4. Ask volunteers to write the sentences on the board.

5. Ask other students to comment on the sentences.

6. Check the answers. Refer to the answer key on LP page 170.

7. The questions on the top of SB page 171 are a potentially rich source for an interactive activity in a multicultural, multilingual setting.

VARIATION

Have students draw the signs on the board *without* telling others the meaning. Then have others guess the meaning in the form of a statement using *have to*, *have got to*, or other modals. Students may want to use international driving signs that aren't presented here!

EXERCISE 3 [10 minutes]

This exercise continues the driving theme to practice modals of necessity. If you are not teaching in the United States, you can adapt this to talking about

getting a driver's license in your country. This is not a test of students' knowledge about getting a driver's license; it is intended to encourage discussion using the relevant modals. Again, you may want drivers to pair up with nondrivers for this exercise.

1. Introduce the topic by looking at the picture and discussing what is happening. (He's taking driver education classes/driving lessons.)

2. Have students work in pairs to discuss which items are necessary or not necessary for getting a driver's license.

3. Ask a volunteer to come to the board and write the items in three columns:
   You must . . . You should . . . You don't have to . . . .

4. Refer to the answer key on LP page 170 for useful information.

5. If appropriate, you can bring in information (or ask students to bring) about getting a driver's license to show students. This could be useful for Exercise 4, too.

EXPANSION [10 minutes]

This is a good opportunity to share "driver's license stories." For example: Did you have to take the tests more than once? Did you take driver's education classes, and if so, what was your experience there? Did you or any one you know have a near-accident (or—hopefully not—an actual accident)? Did you or any one you know ever drive illegally (under age)? Or, if you have a driver's license and can remember your early driving experiences, tell your class about it. If you or some of your students have experiences of driving in the United States, they may want to tell the class about it.

EXERCISE 4 [15 minutes]

This exercise builds on Exercise 3 and provides practice in forming questions with modals of necessity.

1. Have students work in pairs, one student should know something about getting a license in the United States or refer back to their notes from Exercise 3.

2. Have students ask questions about the U.S. and about their country, or another country they know well.

3. Make a list of differences and tell the class.

4. For extra practice with writing, this topic is suitable for a two to three-paragraph (or more) comparison-contrast essay. This is also useful if you feel students need more practice with the structures covered in Unit 7.

Have To versus Have Got To

use

EXAMPLES	EXPLANATIONS
(a) Joe **has to** go on a diet.	Both *have to* and *have got to* show that something is necessary and obligatory. However, many people use *have got to* when they want to emphasize that something is **very** important and **very** necessary.
(b) Joe **has got to** follow a very strict diet because he has a serious heart condition. (If he doesn't follow the diet, he will die.)	
(c) You **have to** pay your phone bill once a month.	
(d) You **have got to** pay your phone bill immediately. (If you don't, the phone company will disconnect the phone.)	
(e) Hey Steve, you've **got to** (**gotta**) see this movie. It's really great.	In very informal conversation among friends, some people use *have got to* to show they think something is a really good thing to do. In (e), Steve's friend is not saying that Steve is obliged to see the movie; she is just strongly advising Steve to see it.

EXERCISE 5

Make a statement for each situation. Work with a partner and decide which you would use for each one: *have to* or *have got to*.

1. Your sister's 4-year-old son takes a nap every day and goes to bed at 8:00 every night. But today he didn't take a nap, and it's now 10:00 P.M.

    She says to her son, "You _____have got to_____ go to sleep now."

2. The last time your friend went to the dentist was four years ago. He doesn't think he has any problems with his teeth, but he feels he should probably go to the dentist for a checkup.

    He says, "I _____have to_____ make an appointment to see the dentist sometime soon."

3. You haven't been reading the assignments for your history class, and you did very badly on the first two quizzes. You are afraid that you'll fail the course.

    You tell your classmate, "I _____have got to_____ study every day if I don't want to fail my history class."

4. Your roommate is making dinner. She has just put a loaf of bread in the oven. Suddenly she realizes that she doesn't have an important item that she needs for dessert.

    She says, "I _____have to_____ go to the store. If I'm not back in ten minutes, can you take the bread out of the oven? It _____has got to_____ come out at 7:00 or it'll be ruined."

5. You are at a friend's house. You are feeling a little tired and want to go to sleep early.

    You say, "I _____have to_____ leave now. I'll see you after class tomorrow."

meaning use

Using Cannot (Can't) and Must Not (Mustn't) to Show Something Is Prohibited or Not Permitted

EXAMPLES	EXPLANATIONS
(a) You **cannot** (**can't**) bring fresh fruit into the United States. OR	Use *cannot* and *must not* to show that something is completely prohibited or not permitted (often by law). *Cannot* is more common than *must not* in American English. *Cannot* and *must not* are usually contracted to *can't* and *mustn't* in fast speech.
(b) You **must not** (**mustn't**) bring fresh fruit into the United States.	
(c) You **cannot** (**can't**) smoke in here. OR	
(d) You **must not** (**mustn't**) smoke in here.	
(e) Herbert, you **must not** (**mustn't**) eat any more of those cookies!	*Must not/mustn't* is also often used as a strong command in situations where you want someone to obey. In (e), eating cookies is not prohibited by law, but the speaker **really** wants Herbert to stop eating them.

ANSWER KEY

Exercise 5 Answers may vary, depending on students' perceptions of how important and how necessary the actions are. Possible answers are listed above.

FOCUS 3 [5 minutes]

This focus chart contrast the use of *have to* and *have got to*. Although some speakers of American English find little difference in meaning between the two, using *have got to* rather than *have to* expresses urgency, and is perhaps a bit more formal, sometimes reserved for situations of extreme importance and necessity.

1. **Lead-in:** Give some example situations using these structures and see if students can identify a difference. For example:

   Parent to child: *You have to eat your vegetables.* (It's a good idea)/*You have got to eat your vegetables.* (It's very important, otherwise you'll get sick.)

   Doctor to patient: *You have to watch your weight/salt intake.* (It's a good idea)/*You have got to watch your weight/salt intake.* (It's very important, otherwise your blood pressure will get dangerously high.)

2. Read the examples and explanations in the box.

3. Ask students for examples from their own lives.

PRONUNCIATION NOTE

As with Focus Chart 2, point out that the contraction *'ve* or *'s* with *got to* is sometimes omitted in informal situations. For example, rather than saying *You've gotta come with me,* speakers will sometimes say, *You gotta come with me.*

EXERCISE 5 [15 minutes]

This exercise provides a variety of contexts so that students can work out the factors in each situation that will affect the choice of structure.

1. Explain that in each situation students will have to consider factors such as relationship of speakers, urgency or importance, and that afterwards they will have to explain and justify their choices.

2. Set a time limit for students to read the situations and discuss them in pairs.

3. Select students to read aloud and justify their answers.

4. Compare answers as a class.

5. Answers may vary, depending on students' perceptions of how important and how necessary the actions are. Refer to the answer key on LP page 172.

For more practice, use *Grammar Dimensions 2* Workbook page 73, Exercise 3.

work book

FOCUS 4 [5 minutes]

1. **Lead-in:** refer back to the Opening Task and mention some rules about things you *mustn't* or *cannot* bring into the United States. Expand this to some other rules and laws in the U.S. For example:

   You must not/cannot drink alcohol if you are under 21.

   You must not/cannot smoke in restaurants or public places (in most U.S. states).

   You must not/cannot drive while talking on a cell phone.

2. Ask students for additional examples of things you *must not/cannot* do in your country or state.

3. Read the examples and explanations in the box.

LANGUAGE NOTE

1. Language learners who have had experience with speakers of British English (or dialects other than American English) may note that *must not* seems to be used more frequently than *cannot*.

2. The contraction *mustn't* is also used more often in other dialects, in comparison to *can't* in American English, although speakers of English will understand the meaning of both.

3. For many speakers of English, the use of *must not* may have a slightly stronger sense to it than the use of *cannot*.

4. The pronunciation of *can't* versus *can* may present a problem for some learners.

meaning

use

FOCUS 5

Must and Have To versus Must Not, Cannot, and Do Not Have To

EXAMPLES

EXPLANATIONS

(a) To enter the United States you must have a valid passport.

OR

(b) To enter the United States you have to have a valid passport.

Showing something is necessary and obligatory:

Use either *must* or *have to*. In this situation, they have the same meaning.

(c) You cannot bring fireworks into the United States.

OR

(d) You **must not** bring fireworks into the United States.

(e) NOT: You don't have to bring fireworks into the United States.

Showing something is prohibited:

Use *cannot* or *must not*. Do not use *do not have to*. In negative sentences, they do not have the same meaning. In this situation, *must not* means it is prohibited.

(f) You **don't have to** bring a surfboard to California because you can rent one there.

(g) NOT: You must not bring a surfboard to California because you can rent one there.

(h) There aren't any classes on Saturdays, so we don't have to come to school.

Showing something is not necessary:

Use *do not have to*. Do not use *cannot* or *must not*. In this situation, *do not have to* means you can do something if you want to, but you are not obliged to do it if you don't want to.

EXERCISE 8

Look back at the places and signs in Exercise 7. Can you use *don't have to* to describe any of these signs?

EXERCISE 9

With your partner, make a list of rules for your classroom, using *must, must not, cannot,* and *don't have to*. Take a vote to see which ones your classmates want to put on your classroom walls. Draw signs to go with your rules.

Example: *You cannot smoke in this room.*

EXERCISE 6

Look at the cartoon. Write statements in your notebook that use *cannot* and *must not* to describe each prohibited activity.

EXERCISE 7

Where would you see each of the signs below? Match the signs with the places. Say what you can, *must, cannot,* or *must not* do there. (Some signs may be found in more than one place.)

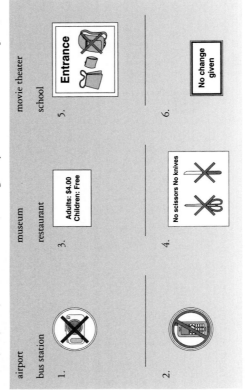

airport   museum   movie theater

bus station   restaurant   school

1.

2.

3. Adults: $4.00
   Children: Free

4. No scissors   No knives

5. Entrance

6. No change given

ANSWER KEY

Exercise 6 Answers will vary, but will probably include: You must not/cannot: walk on the grass; pick the flowers; park here; draw or write on the statue; throw bottles in this trash can; let your dog walk here/bring dogs here; smoke in the park; ride a bicycle here; climb the trees.

Exercise 7 1. Museum/movie theater: You can't/must not take pictures   2. Restaurant/movie theater/school: You can't/must not use a cell phone.   3. Museum: Adults must/have to pay $4.00. (Children don't have to pay.)   4. Airport/school: You cannot/must not carry any knives or scissors.   5. Museum: Leave backpacks at the front desk. (You don't have to leave purses or small bags.)

Exercise 8 Answers may include: Sign 3. You don't have to pay for children. Sign 5. You don't have to leave purses or small bags at the front desk.

Exercise 9 Answers will vary, depending on students' advice and opinions.

LESSON PLAN 1

EXERCISE 6 [10 minutes]

This exercise provides further practice of modals of prohibition.

1. Brainstorm ideas for interpreting these signs with the class.
2. Make a list on the board.
3. Refer to the answer key on LP page 174.
4. Ask students to suggest any additional signs they may have seen in parks or other public places. This will lead into Exercise 7.

EXERCISE 7 [10 minutes]

This exercise encourages students to use their general knowledge of rules in these public buildings. These may differ slightly from country to country.

1. Have students work in pairs to read the list of places and match them with the signs. They should write the name of the place(s) below each sign.
2. Check and compare answers as a class. Refer to the answer key on LP page 174.
3. Have students make sentences for each of the signs, saying what you *can*, *must*, *cannot*, or *must not* do. **Note:** Numbers 3 and 5 include an opportunity to practice *don't have to*. (Children don't have to pay. You don't have to leave your purse at the entrance.) This can serve as a bridge to Focus Chart 5 on the next page. Students will return to this in Exercise 8.

For more practice, use *Grammar Dimensions 2* Workbook page 74, Exercise 4.

FOCUS 5 [5 minutes]

This focus chart emphasizes the difference between necessity, prohibition, and absence of necessity. This can be confusing for students who may sometimes confuse *must not* and *don't have to*.

3. Award teams points for the funniest, most unusual, most "proper" (formal), etc., advice.

EXERCISE 8 [5 minutes]

This exercise focuses on the use of *don't have to* contrasted with *must not* and *cannot*.

1. Turn back to Exercise 7 to revisit situations where *don't have to* could be used.
2. If students need to rewrite their sentences, ask them to explain why.

1. **Lead-in:** Choose an example of *must* versus *don't have to* that will be clear and memorable for your students. For example:
   You must/have to take an exam when you graduate this college.
   You don't have to take an exam to enter this college.
2. Ask students for additional examples about their school or college.
3. Read the examples and explanations in the focus chart.

EXPANSION [20 minutes]

This additional exercise will help students make meaningful sentences that show their understanding of the target structures.

1. Choose a topic or have students choose a topic about what to do/what not to do when: giving a party, making friends, getting over the flu/a cold, inviting a potential boyfriend/girlfriend/partner out on a date, etc.
2. Write the different modals and phrasal modals from this focus chart on index cards: *must*, *have to*, *cannot*, *must not*, *don't have to*. Make an extra card for *don't have to* to allow extra practice with this.
3. Have students select a card from the pile and make statements using that modal or phrasal modal.
4. Let other students decide whether the statement is (grammatically or factually) correct. Sometimes this may be a matter of opinion!

VARIATION

1. Form teams and assign points to those that come up with statements that everyone agrees with.
2. Vote on who agrees/who doesn't agree, allowing alternate teams the opportunity to revise the initial statement, so that it is more acceptable to more students.

EXERCISE 9 [15 minutes]

This exercise encourages students to clarify their understanding of appropriate classroom behavior at the same time as they practice the new structures.

1. Have students work in pairs to make lists of rules.
2. Compile a list of rules on the board that everyone agrees on.
3. Divide the rules up for students to make signs.
4. Display them on the wall.
5. You may want to extend this activity by asking students to compare classroom rules in the United States and in their country. For example, *In Japan, you must stand when the teacher enters the classroom, but in the United States you don't have to.*

For more practice, use *Grammar Dimensions 2* Workbook page 75, Exercise 5 and page 76, Exercise 6.

■ EXERCISE 10

The magazine article below is about traffic laws in different European countries.

STEP 1   Before you read the article, look at the following statements. Do you think they are probably true or probably false? Circle T (for *true*), or F (for *false*). After you finish reading, look at the statements again and change your answers if necessary.

1. In Germany, you mustn't use bad language or make rude and insulting gestures if you get angry with other drivers.   (T)   F

2. You must be careful when you honk your horn in Greece.   (T)   F

3. You have to honk your horn when you pass another car in Gibraltar.   (T)   F

4. You cannot flash your lights at other drivers in Luxembourg.   T   (F)

5. In Scandinavian countries, you cannot drive with your headlights on during the day.   T   (F)

6. You have to drive more slowly at night in Austria.   (T)   F

7. In Romania, you don't have to keep your car clean.   T   (F)

How Not to Collide with Local Road Laws

If you are planning on driving in Europe, you should know that driving laws and customs vary greatly from country to country.

Be careful not to allow frustration with other drivers to develop into swearing or offensive gestures in Germany: They are illegal. Displays of anger are not welcome in Greece, either.

It is unlawful to honk your horn too loudly (although this may surprise many visitors to Athens!). In Gibraltar, using your horn at all is completely prohibited. In Luxembourg, the law says that drivers have to flash their lights each time they pass another car.

In Scandinavian countries, you have to drive with your headlights dimmed during the day, but in Poland, this is obligatory only in winter.

Make sure you fill your tank before you get on the Autobahn in Germany: It is illegal to run out of gas. Speed limits vary too, not just from country to country, but within countries as well. Beware of speed limits that change from one moment to the next. For example, in Austria, speed limits are lower at night and in France, the speed limit on the freeways drops from 130 kmh* to 110 kmh when it rains. (And if the French police catch you speeding, you have to pay a massive on-the-spot fine!)

But perhaps the strangest law of all is from Romania, where you must not drive your car if it is dirty.

Adapted with permission from *The European* (Magazine Section), 6/9/95

*kmh = kilometers per hour

STEP 2   Make statements using *must*, *have to*, *cannot*, *mustn't*, or *do not have to* about the following topics from the article.

1. Driving in Poland during the winter: _____
   You must/have to drive with your headlights dimmed during the day.

2. Driving on the Autobahn in Germany: _____
   You mustn't/cannot run out of gas.

3. Driving on the freeways in France: *You must/have to reduce your speed when it rains. You cannot/must not drive as fast as the "normal" speed limit when it rains.*

STEP 3   Are there any traffic laws that are sometimes confusing to visitors to the country you come from? Describe them to the rest of your class, using *must*, *have to*, *cannot*, *must not*, and *do not have to* where you can.

MODALS OF NECESSITY AND PROHIBITION *Have To/Have Got To, Do Not Have To, Must/Must Not, Cannot*

ANSWER KEY

Exercise 10   *Step 2: Answers may vary slightly but they are likely to be those listed above.*

EXPANSION [30–60 minutes]

You may want to use the sequence of Activities 4 (speaking/listening), 5 (speaking/listening), and 6 (research on the web) on SB pages 182–183 instead of or in addition to Exercise 10. These activities ask students to find out about rules and requirements for obtaining a green card, a social security number, a marriage license, a credit card, and U.S. citizenship.

EXERCISE 10 [20 minutes]

You may want to assign this reading for homework.

STEP 1

1. Remind students of some of the traffic signs they saw in Exercise 2 that were different in other countries.

2. Brainstorm (see Methodology Note below) any other traffic laws that might be different in other countries, or in other states. For example, in New York, you must not drive while using a cell phone.

3. Read the title and explain the literal and figurative meaning of *collide* (to crash into).

4. If you have set this exercise for homework, have students check their answers in pairs. If not, set a time limit of 10 minutes for students to complete the exercise.

5. Check the answers as a class. Refer to the answer key on LP page 176.

METHODOLOGY NOTE

Brainstorming is a way of generating and gathering ideas and is a good way to find out what students already know about a topic. It can be done individually, in pairs, groups, or as a class. All ideas, whether from individual or group work, are collected and written on the board, or on an overhead transparency. It is important to include **every** idea, and not to hinder creativity by labeling ideas as right or wrong. After the brainstorming is completed, you can ask students to categorize the ideas. Brainstorming works best if you record the ideas randomly, without categorizing them. This allows students the opportunity to later develop their own categories for organizing the ideas using, for example, a chart or a diagram.

STEP 2

1. Have students complete the sentences individually.

2. Ask volunteers to write them on the board.

3. Refer to the answer key on LP page 176.

STEP 3 Depending on the variety of your and your students' experience with and knowledge of international traffic laws, this step can be conducted as a whole-class discussion or, if there is less varied experience, as a written exercise.

EXPANSION [30 minutes]

If you feel students need more writing practice, assign a 1- or 2-paragraph description of the traffic laws of a country students are familiar with. Remind them to use the appropriate modals and phrasal modals covered in this unit. Use the descriptions students have written in a peer editing activity, in which a student exchanges his/her description with someone else's:

1. Students read each other's descriptions for content. Are all statements clear? If not, they can ask the writer of the description for clarification where necessary.

2. Students check each other's descriptions for the grammar targeted in this unit. Did they use the modals and phrasal modals *must, have to, cannot, mustn't,* or *don't have to* appropriately?

FOCUS 6

form

Talking about the Present, Past, and Future with *Have To* and *Must*

PRESENT	PAST	FUTURE
must	—	must
have to	had to	have to/will have to
do not have to	did not have to	do not have to/will not have to

EXAMPLES

(a) Students **have to** start school at 8:00 A.M.

(b) Students **must** start school at 8:00 A.M.

(c) Students **don't have to** go to school on Saturdays.

(d) We **had to** stay late after school yesterday.

(e) We **didn't have to** take the test last week.

(f) Ron **must** go to a meeting tomorrow.
OR

(g) Ron **has to** go to a meeting tomorrow.
OR

(h) Ron **will have to** go to a meeting tomorrow.

(i) He **doesn't have to** go to school next week.

(j) He **will not (won't)** have to go to school next week.

EXPLANATIONS

Use *must* (*not*), *have to*, and *do not have to* to show that something is (or is not) necessary in the present.

Notice that there is no past tense form of *must* when it shows necessity. Use *had to* to show that something was necessary in the past.

You can use *must*, *have to*, or *will have to* to talk about events that will be necessary in the near future.

You can also use negative forms *do not have to* or *will not have to* to talk about the near future.

EXERCISE 11

Maggie and her friend Jan are talking about jobs. Maggie is describing a job she had last summer. Complete their conversation with *have to*, and *do not have to* in the present, past, or future.

Maggie: The worst job I ever had was last summer, when I worked as a waitress in that tourist restaurant down by the aquarium.

Jan: Oh really? What was so terrible about it?

Maggie: For a start, I (1) __had to__ get up at 5:00 A.M. and, as I didn't have a car then, I (2) __had to__ walk.

Jan: Why didn't you take the bus?

Maggie: It doesn't start running until 7:00, and I (3) __had to__ be at the restaurant by 6:30 to set the tables for breakfast.

Jan: That's tough. Did they make you wear a silly uniform or anything?

Maggie: No, thank goodness. We (4) __didn't have to__ wear any special uniforms, except for hats. We all (5) __had to__ wear really stupid sailor caps. Mine was too small and it kept falling off.

Jan: So you're probably not planning on working there again next summer.

Maggie: Absolutely not. I'm earning twice as much at my present job, so with a bit of luck, I'll be able to save some money and I (6) __won't have to__ work at all next summer.

Jan: That sounds good. What's your present job like?

Maggie: It's much better. I start work at 11:00 A.M.

Jan: So you (7) __don't have to__ get up early. What about weekends?

Maggie: I (8) __don't have to__ work on weekends, but if I want to make some extra money, I can go in on Saturdays. It's ideal.

Jan: Maybe I should try to get a job there. Our landlord raised the rent last month and I just can't afford to stay there on my present salary.

LESSON PLAN 2

FOCUS 6 [5 minutes]

Lead-in: Ask students about rules they had in high school. If students cannot come up with the correct form of *had to* or *didn't have to*, tell students about your own experiences in high school. Introduce one or two model sentences to illustrate the past tense. For example, *When I was in high school I had to start school at 8:15 A.M. and we had to do two hours of homework every night.* Explain that *must* is not used in the past.

Note: Some students may ask about the use of *must have been* (presented in Unit 5) as a past form. Explain that this is only with the other use of must as a modal of probability.

1. Read the examples and explanations in the box.

2. Give some incorrect examples of these modals and ask students to correct them. For example:

He must go to the doctor yesterday.

Students change it to: *He had to go to the doctor yesterday.*

He doesn't have to study math last year.

Students change it to: *He didn't have to study math last year.*

He had to go to college next year.

Students change it to: *He has to go to college next year.* OR *He will have to go to college next year.*

EXERCISE 11 [15 minutes]

This exercise practices past, present, and future forms of *have to*.

1. Introduce the topic of someone doing a summer vacation job. Talk about working in a fast food restaurant. What could the advantages and disadvantages be? Ask for some suggestions.

2. Set a time limit for students to work with a partner and fill in the answers for each blank.

3. Check the answers. Refer to the answer key on LP page 178.

4. Have students read the conversation in pairs. Before they start, remind them to link words together smoothly, to use reduced forms/contractions, and to use appropriate intonation—falling intonation at the end of a statement, rising intonation at the end of a *yes/no* question, and louder volume, higher pitch for important or surprising information.

5. Model one or two sentences with a student.

6. Ask volunteers to perform the conversation for the class.

7. Have students create their own conversation using real information about themselves.

8. Ask volunteers to perform the conversation for the class.

work book

For more practice, use *Grammar Dimensions 2* Workbook page 77, Exercise 7, and page 78, Exercise 8.

EXPANSION [30 minutes]

You may want to use Activity 2 on SB page 181 after this activity. This activity asks students to compare their childhood memories about things they had to do with those of their classmates.

Use Your English

ACTIVITY 1 speaking

In Exercises 2, 6, and 7 you saw some examples of signs. The local tourist board has asked you and your classmates to create some signs for tourists visiting the area. Get together with two or three other students and draw at least three signs. For example: *You must not feed the ducks. You must have exact change for the bus. You must not drink this water.* Draw each sign on a different piece of paper. Do not write anything next to the sign—your classmates must guess what it is. Look at their signs and write down what you think they mean.

ACTIVITY 2 speaking

In this activity, you will be comparing your childhood memories with those of your classmates. Think back to when you were a child. Write down five things you had to do then that you do not have to do now. Example for Childhood: *I had to go to bed early.* Then write down five things you did not have to do then that you have to do now. Example for Now: *I can stay up late.*

Next, compare your list with those of two or three other classmates and be ready to report on your findings to the rest of the class.

YOU		YOUR CLASSMATES	
Childhood	Now	Childhood	Now
1	1	1	1
2	2	2	2
3	3	3	3
4	4	4	4
5	5	5	5

EXERCISE 12

Read the letter and choose the correct answer for each blank from the list below.

Dear Kimberley,

It's almost the end of the school year and we are in the middle of final exams. We (1) _____ take a lot of different tests and write essays. Luckily, my grades in English language are quite good, so I (2) _____ take any extra tests. Last year I (3) _____ go to summer school for two months because my grades were so bad, but I hope I (4) _____ go this year. My parents say I (5) _____ come to stay with you this summer unless I pass all my classes.

It's getting late now and I (6) _____ finish writing this letter. I have a history exam tomorrow morning and I (7) _____ go over all my notes tonight. In middle school, we (8) _____ take our notes into the exam, but here we (9) _____. I want to get a good average, so I (10) _____ fail this exam. I'm looking forward to seeing you again this summer. You (11) _____ write and tell me when I can come to visit you. There's a new Johnny Depp movie coming out in July and we (12) _____ go and see it together!

Love from,
Charlene

1. ○ (a) have got to   ○ (b) must not   ● (c) have to
2. ○ (a) must not   ○ (b) couldn't   ● (c) don't have to
3. ● (a) had to   ○ (b) should   ○ (c) must
4. ○ (a) can't   ● (b) won't have to   ○ (c) must not
5. ○ (a) must not   ● (b) can't   ○ (c) don't have to
6. ○ (a) can   ● (b) have to   ○ (c) had to
7. ● (a) have got to   ○ (b) had to   ○ (c) could
8. ○ (a) can   ○ (b) should   ● (c) could
9. ○ (a) couldn't   ○ (b) don't have to   ● (c) can't
10. ● (a) must not   ○ (b) don't have to   ○ (c) couldn't
11. ○ (a) had to   ○ (b) don't have to   ● (c) must
12. ○ (a) can't   ○ (b) had to   ● (c) have got to

EXERCISE 12 [15 minutes]

This exercise reviews most of the forms presented in this unit using a multiple-choice format that students may often find in tests. You may want to assign this exercise as homework.

1. Review some strategies for completing multiple-choice tests (see Methodology Note on LP page 131 in Unit 8).
2. Set a time limit for students to complete this activity individually (or set this as homework).
3. Check the answers as a class. Refer to the answer key on LP page 180.

EXPANSION [15 minutes]

You may want to use Activity 7 (reflection) on SB page 183 as a way of concluding this unit.

UNIT GOAL REVIEW [10 minutes]

Ask students to look at the goals on the opening page of the unit again. Refer to the pages of the unit where information on each goal can be found. You may test students by asking them, for example, to make sentences that contrast *have to* and *have got to* (as in Focus Chart 3 and Exercise 5) and have Students tell you what the difference in meaning is (goal #3).

ExamView® Test Generator For assessment of Unit 11, use *Grammar Dimensions 2 ExamView®*.

USE YOUR ENGLISH

The Use Your English section of activities at the end of the unit contain situations that should naturally elicit the structures covered in the unit. For a more complete discussion of how to use the Use Your English activities, see To the Teacher, LP page xxii. When students are doing these activities in class, you can circulate and listen to see if they are using the structures accurately. Errors can be corrected after the activity has finished.

ACTIVITY 1 speaking [20 minutes]

You may want to use this activity after Exercise 7 on SB page 174.

1. Refer students back to the signs in Exercise 6.
2. Brainstorm two or three ideas for signs that would be useful for tourists in your area.
3. Divide students into groups and have them work on drawing their signs using these or their own ideas. Remind students to use pictures and not too many words on their signs.
4. Have students show their signs to the rest of the class. The other students must guess what the signs mean.

VARIATION

This activity can also be turned into a competitive game.

1. Have students write down what they think the sign means *in silence*.
2. Hold up each sign, and ask students to hold up their written answers.
3. The student who got the most signs right (according to the intention of the sign-maker) wins.

 ACTIVITY 2 speaking [30 minutes]

You may want to use this activity after Exercise 11 on SB page 179.

1. Introduce the topic of talking about their childhood, and mention some rules of behavior that they may have had when they were children that they no longer have to obey. Give some examples from your own life.
2. Set a time limit for students to write their ideas about childhood. It is important to give students enough "thinking time" at this stage so the rest of the activity will be more lively and productive.
3. Have students compare their lists in groups and find out what was similar or different.
4. Ask volunteers to report their findings to the class.

EXPANSION [20 minutes]

For more writing practice, students can use the information to write about their childhood rules. Another possible topic would be to compare their own childhood rules with rules for children nowadays, at home or at school. Ask volunteers to read their reports aloud to the class, or select the reports to be read aloud. Have other students ask each other questions to get more details.

ACTIVITY 3 writing

A friend of yours is interested in studying at a North American university. Write him or her a letter explaining what he or she will have to do in order to enter a university.

ACTIVITY 4 speaking/listening

CD Tracks 16, 17, 18

STEP 1

Do you know what a person has to do in order to get any of the following?

- a green card (for permanent residence in the United States)
- a Social Security number
- a marriage license
- a credit card
- United States citizenship

With a partner, make a list of what you think a person must or has to do in order to get each of these.

STEP 2

Listen to the audio. You will hear somebody discussing three of the above topics. Which topics are the speakers talking about? What do they think you have to do to get these things? Make notes in the chart below or in your notebook.

TOPIC	WHAT YOU HAVE TO DO
1	
2	
3	

STEP 3

Now look at the list you and your partner made on the same topic. How many differences and how many similarities can you find?

STEP 4

Listen to the audio again. Write down any sentences containing examples of modals and phrasal modals expressing necessity and prohibition. Refer to Focus 1 and Focus 2 for review of these modals.

ACTIVITY 5 speaking/listening

STEP 1

Choose a topic from Activity 4 that you don't know anything about.

STEP 2

Interview three different people and ask them what they know about the topic. For example, you can ask: *What does somebody have to do if they want to get a green card?*

Record your interviews. Listen to your recording and take notes. Did all the people you interviewed tell you the same information? Or did they tell you different things? Share your findings with the rest of your class.

STEP 3

Listen to your recording again and write down any sentences containing *must, have to, must not, cannot, do not have to, have got to,* or *should.*

ACTIVITY 6 research on the web

On the Web: Use an Internet search engine such as Google® or Yahoo® to get more information about one of the topics in Activity 4. Take notes on what you read. Summarize your findings and tell the class. Be sure to make a note of which Web sites you used.

ACTIVITY 7 reflection

Make a list of helpful guidelines for a new student who is going to start studying English. Divide your list into things that are necessary and things that are not necessary. Compare lists with a partner. What things did you need to do in the past that you do not need to do now?

MODALS OF NECESSITY AND PROHIBITION *Have To/Have Got To, Do Not Have To, Must/Must Not, Cannot*

ANSWER KEY

Activity 4 Step 4: *Check audio script on LP page S-5 for answers.*

TOPIC	WHAT YOU HAVE TO DO
becoming a U.S. citizen	Be over 18, have a green card for 5 years, take a test in language and American history, swear an oath of allegiance
getting a social security number	Show birth certificate, passport, green card, or immigration status
getting a driver's license	Show photo ID, prove that you are resident in the state, show your social

USE YOUR ENGLISH

ACTIVITY 3 writing
[15 minutes]

You may want to use this activity after Focus Chart 2 on SB page 169. You can assign the writing part of this activity for homework.

1. Brainstorm some ideas for things you must, have to, or have got to do in order to enter a college or university in the United States.

2. Some useful vocabulary might be: TOEFL®, standardized tests (SAT), application form, application essay, academic records (transcripts), letters of recommendation, statement of purpose, visa.

3. You may want to discuss some of these requirements, and other kinds of advice, before assigning the letter for homework.

4. Have students peer-edit their work before handing in their assignments.

5. It may be helpful for students to do these revisions in pairs, since another student may have a "fresh" perspective.

ACTIVITY 4 speaking/listening
[60–90 minutes]

CD Tracks 16, 17, 18

You may want to use this activity, and the follow-up Activities 5 and 6 before Exercise 10 on SB page 176. This activity focuses on rules and regulations in the United States, but you may want to adapt these topics to ones that are more relevant and appropriate to your students.

STEP 1

1. If this class is conducted in the U.S., you may be able to invite a guest speaker to come and talk to your students about all of these and other topics. Some of your students may also have had long-term experiences in the U.S.

2. If you have several guest speakers, or several students who have experience of the U.S., students can conduct their interviews in pairs or small groups, asking the speaker to elaborate about important details.

3. Prepare some questions, and make sure students know they are to take notes and write a report afterwards.

4. Have them conduct the interviews and assemble as much information on these topics as they can.

STEP 2 Play the audio and allow time for students to take notes. See the audio script on LP page S-5.

STEP 3 Compare answers with those on the audio as a class. See answers on LP page 182.

STEP 4 Check to see if they used modals and phrasal modals expressing necessity and prohibition.

ACTIVITY 5 speaking/listening
[30 minutes/homework]

This activity asks students to interview *three* different speakers. The purpose of conducting these interviews is to listen for the natural use of modals of necessity and prohibition. This is a good follow-up to Activity 4.

STEP 1 Help students to choose a topic from Activity 4. It may help to divide the topics between groups so that every topic is covered. This will make it more interesting for students to share information with each other. As mentioned in the notes for Activity 4, you may want to adapt the topics to be more relevant to your context.

STEP 2 Assign the interviews for homework. If students do not have access to recording equipment, it is a good idea to conduct the interview in groups of two or three.

STEP 3 Have students present their results to the class. Adding their comments about the use of modals in their interviews.

Note: Activity 6 asks students to elaborate further by conducting research on the Web.

ACTIVITY 6 research on the web
[30 minutes]

This is a good follow-up to Activities 3 and 4. The purpose of this Internet search activity is to provide a natural context for using modals of necessity. An additional purpose is to encourage students to share strategies for finding information on the Internet. After they have shared information for their research, encourage students to share search tips. What Web sites were most useful? What keywords did they use?

ACTIVITY 7 reflection
[30 minutes]

You may want to use this activity after Exercise 12 on SB page 180. This activity provides an opportunity for students to use the target structures of the unit while reflecting on their language learning progress. You may have asked students to keep a record of their learning in a journal throughout this course as suggested in To the Teacher, page xxii. This reflection activity will form part of that learning record.

EXPRESSING LIKES AND DISLIKES

UNIT GOALS

- Express similarity with *too/either* and *so/neither*
- Express similarity with *so* clauses
- Use short phrases to show agreement and weak agreement
- Express likes and dislikes with gerunds and infinitives

OPENING TASK

What Kind of Food Do You Like?

■ STEP 1

Work in a group. Name the different foods in the pictures. Which ones do you like most? Which ones do you dislike?

■ STEP 2

Work with a partner. One of you is A, the other is B. Talk about food that you like and don't like, and complete the chart on the next page together.

■ STEP 3

In the top left-hand box, write three kinds of food that A and B both like. In the top right-hand box, write three kinds of foods that A does not like, but B does. In the bottom left-hand box, write three kinds of food that B doesn't like, but A does. In the last box, write three kinds of food that both A and B do not like.

	STUDENT A	
	LIKES	DOESN'T LIKE
LIKES	(A likes, and B does, too.)	(A doesn't like, but B does.)
DOESN'T LIKE	(B doesn't like, but A does.)	(B doesn't like, and A doesn't either.)

(Row labels at left: STUDENT B)

■ STEP 4

Share some of these findings with the class. Make a list of statements with *like* and *dislike* (or *doesn't/don't like*).

Example: *I like spicy food and Tina does too.*

ANSWER KEY

Opening Task   Answers will vary, depending on the information students have gathered.

UNIT OVERVIEW

This unit presents structures used to express likes and dislikes in English, including expressions such as *too, so,* and *(n)either.* Ways of expressing likes and dislikes using gerunds and infinitives are reviewed. Short phrases and hedges, as well as emphatic forms with *do* and *really,* are also presented.

GRAMMAR NOTE

The structures presented in this unit deal with ways of expressing similarities and differences using *so, too, either,* and *neither.* Learners sometimes have difficulty with recognizing affirmative or negative statements, using correct word order, and using the correct auxiliary. Since there are a number of structures available to express these ideas, it is also possible that learners may confuse or combine two or more structures when attempting to articulate these forms.

UNIT GOALS

Some instructors may want to review the goals listed on this page after completing the Opening Task so that students understand what they should know by the end of the unit. These goals can also be reviewed at the end of the unit when students are more familiar with the grammar terminology. Other instructors may want to discuss these at the end of the unit as students may not grasp the terms used at the start of the unit. Before you point out the goals of this unit, find examples of each goal as an illustration and put these examples up on the board or on an overhead transparency.

OPENING TASK [30 minutes]

The purpose of the Opening Task is to create a context in which students will need to use the present progressive to describe actions in progress. The problem-solving format is designed to show the teacher how well the students can produce the target structures implicitly and spontaneously when they are engaged

in a communicative task. For a more complete discussion of the purpose of the Opening Task, see To the Teacher, Lesson Planner (LP) page xxii.

Setting Up the Task

■ STEP 1

1. Introduce the topic of food by having students look at the pictures and name the different foods pictured.

2. Do a brainstorming activity, giving the class a minute to write down a list of the foods that they like and a minute to write a list of those that they don't like.

Conducting the Task

■ STEP 2

1. Look at the chart and explain how to fill it in.

2. Make an overhead projector transparency for a visual aid, if possible.

3. Model one short dialogue with a student and show how to fill in the chart. For example:

   You (student A): *Do you like pineapple?*

   Student (student B): *Yes, I do. Do you?*

   You: *No, I don't.* (Write pineapple in top right square.)

4. Have students decide who is A and who is B in their pairs.

5. Students can copy the chart in their notebooks.

■ STEP 3

1. Set a time limit of 10–15 minutes for students to discuss and fill in their charts.

2. Circulate while they are working and take notes of common errors. Do not correct errors at this stage.

■ STEP 4

1. Students should use the example sentence as a guide only. Encourage them to be creative in their statements.

2. Have students write their statements in their notebooks. They will return to these in later exercises.

Closing the Task

1. Collect various types of statements from different members of the class.

2. If you write some of their examples on the board, you can use and/or correct them in Exercises 1 and 2.

FOCUS 1

form | meaning

Expressing Similarity with *Too* and *Either*

EXAMPLES

(a) I like fruit, **and** Roberta **does too.**

(b) NOT: I like fruit, and Roberta likes fruit.

(c) Roberta doesn't eat meat, and I **don't either.**

(d) NOT: I don't eat meat, and Roberta doesn't eat meat.

EXPLANATIONS

To avoid repetition in affirmative sentences (sentences without *not*), use *and* (X) *do/does too.*

To avoid repetition in negative sentences (sentences with *not*), use *and* (X) *do/doesn't either.*

EXERCISE 1

Check the statements you made in Step 4 of the Opening Task on page 185. Did you use *too* and *either* correctly? If not, rewrite these statements using *too* and *either*.

FOCUS 2

form | meaning

Expressing Similarity with *So* and *Neither*

EXAMPLES

(a) I like fruit, **and so does** Roberta.

(b) Roberta doesn't eat meat, **and neither do I.**

EXPLANATIONS

Another way to avoid repetition is with *and so do/does* (X) in affirmative sentences, and with *and neither do/does* (X) in negative sentences.

Invert subject and verb after *so* and *neither.*

EXERCISE 2

Now work with a different partner and share the information on your charts in the Opening Task. Use this information to complete the following report. Make sure that your statements are not only grammatical but also true.

My classmates and I have strong opinions about the kinds of food we like and dislike. For example, _____ and so _____.

_____ and neither _____.

_____ too.

_____ either.

We also found other similarities in our taste in food. _____.

either. _____ so _____.

neither _____ too.

FOCUS 3

use

Expressing Similarity with *So*

EXAMPLES

(a) I speak French, and so **does** my mother.

(b) My mother exercises every day, and so **do** I.

(c) I **can** speak French, and so **can** she.

(d) I **have** studied it, and so **has** she.

(e) I **am** happy, and so **is** she.

EXPLANATIONS

Use *do* when you do not want to repeat the verb. Make sure that there is subject/verb agreement:

I do be/she does they/you do

Use an auxiliary verb (*can, have, should*) if the first verb uses one.

Use a form of *be* if the first verb is a form of *be.*

ANSWER KEY

Exercise 2 Answers will vary.

FOCUS 1 [5 minutes]

This Focus Chart presents structures that uses short forms to avoid repetition

1. **Lead-in:** Refer to the chart in the Opening Task and draw this chart on the board. If you wish, change the examples so they are true about you and one of your students, or about two of your students. Use check marks and Xs to indicate affirmative and negative statements.

Like	Dislike
✓ I like fruit.	I don't eat meat. (X)
✓ Roberta likes fruit.	Roberta doesn't eat meat. (X)

2. Ask students to try and complete each pair of sentences from the chart into one sentence starting with *I like fruit and . . .*; then, *Roberta doesn't eat meat and . . . .* **Note:** Students might come up with *so/neither* structures. If so, explain that this will come later in Focus Chart 2. For now, stick with *do/does + too/either.*

3. If students come up with the correct sentences, model and practice the pronunciation and write them on the board.

4. Read the examples and explanations in the focus.

LANGUAGE NOTE

To avoid sounding repetitious, the expressions *do too* and *don't either* replace the previous verb phrase. For example:

A: *I love really strong coffee.*
B: *Hey, I do too!* → (*Do too* replaces *love really strong coffee.*)
A: *I don't eat out very often.*
B: *Actually, I don't either. It's too expensive in this city.* → (*Don't either* replaces *don't eat out very often.*)

EXERCISE 1 [10 minutes]

This exercise allows students to rewrite their sentences in the Opening Task, using the new structures.

1. Direct the students to return to their statements in the Opening Task.

2. Return to previous examples on the board or generate a few new ones as a class.

3. Have students rewrite their sentences and check in pairs.

FOCUS 2 [5 minutes]

This focus chart builds on the information in Focus 1.

1. **Lead-in:** Look at the examples from Focus Chart 1 again. Ask students to rephrase these sentences using *so* or *neither.*

2. If students come up with the correct sentences, model and practice the pronunciation and write them on the board.

3. Read the examples and explanations in the chart. Provide more examples with student help.

GRAMMAR NOTE

Structures with *so* and *neither* sometimes cause problems because of the inversion of verb and subject. With the structures in Focus Chart 1 (*too* and *not. . . either*) the verb follows the subject, as is usual in statements. With the structures in Focus Chart 2 (*so* and *neither*), the verb comes before the subject.

EXERCISE 2 [15 minutes]

In this exercise, students have the opportunity to share information about likes and dislikes with a new partner while using the structures from Focus Charts 1 and 2.

1. Have students pair up with a new partner and tell their new partner about the chart they made with their previous partner.
Example: *I talked with (Enrico). He likes vegetables, and so do I.*

2. Students can work on their reports individually, and exchange reports for peer editing.

For more practice, use *Grammar Dimensions 2* Workbook page 79, Exercises 1 and 2.

[workbook]

FOCUS 3 [5 minutes]

This focus chart returns to the use of *so* in expressing similarity, focusing on the form of the verbs that accompany it.

Lead-in: You can ask students to complete Exercise 3 on SB page 188 before looking at this focus chart. This will introduce them to the various options available in this structure. While working out the solution, they will implicitly be working on the rules.

GRAMMAR NOTE

Because *do* is the auxiliary verb of all present simple verbs (except *be*), it replaces these verbs in the phrase that replaces the present simple verb phrase:

Jaro **writes** music and so **does** Wan.
Amanda **travels** a lot and so **do** Seamus and Myshka.

With all other auxiliaries, the auxiliary is repeated:

I'm going to a show tonight and so **is** Holly.
Steve **will** go back to school and so **will** Claire.

The same is true of *be* as a main verb:

Heidi and Mike **are** vegetarians and so **is** Catie.

EXERCISE 3

Read Lucille's story about her friend Barbara. Match the first half of the sentences in column A with the second half in column B. Draw an arrow to show the connection. The first one has been done for you.

A		B
1.	Barbara is 18 years old	a. and neither do we.
2.	Barbara went to Clarke High School	b. and so have I.
3.	I didn't study very hard	c. and so will I.
4.	She likes to travel	d. and so am I.
5.	I can't drive	e. and neither have I.
6.	Barbara's job isn't interesting	f. and so do my parents.
7.	She'll quit her job soon	g. and I did too.
8.	Barbara's parents want to go to California	h. and Barbara didn't either.
9.	They don't have much money	i. and Barbara can't either.
10.	Barbara has never been to California	j. and I do too.
11.	Barbara has studied Spanish	k. and they are too.
12.	We're excited about going to California	l. and neither is mine.

FOCUS 4

Showing Agreement with Short Phrases

use

EXAMPLES

(a) **Tina:** I love going to movies.
Rob: So do I.

(b) **Tina:** I never go to violent movies.
Rob: Neither do I.

(c) **Tina:** I can't stand watching violence.
Rob: I can't either.

(d) **Tina:** I prefer comedies.
Rob: Really? I do too.

EXPLANATIONS

Short phrases such as *so do I*, *neither do I*, *I can't either*, and *I do too* are used to show agreement with somebody else's opinions and ideas. They are very common in informal conversation.

EXERCISE 4

Read the comic strip. Can you find the missing parts of the conversation in the list below? Write the letters in the appropriate cartoon bubble.

1 I'm getting too old for this kind of thing.

2 My back is killing me.

3 I can't keep this going for much longer.

4 I'll certainly sleep well tonight.

5 I really don't know why I'm doing this.

6 Actually I think people who run marathons are crazy.

7 I certainly won't do this again.

8 Great race! I loved every minute!

9 I can't wait for the next one.

A I don't either!	B I do too!	C Neither can I!
D So did I!	E Neither will I!	F So is mine!
G I will too!	H So am I!	I I can't either!

ANSWER KEY

Exercise 3   2. g   3. h   4. j   5. i   6. l   7. c   8. f   9. a   10. e   11. b   12. k

Exercise 4   Answers C and I can be used interchangeably.

UNIT 12 LESSON PLAN 1

EXERCISE 3 [10 minutes]

This exercise allows students to see the range of options available when using structures with *so* and *neither*. **Suggestion:** You may decide to use this exercise before looking at Focus Chart 3.

1. Read the introduction to the topic.

2. Do the first example together with the class. Ask students how they know these two sentence halves match up. (The verb *be* is the same, and it is in the present tense.)

3. Have students continue in pairs with the rest of the exercise.

4. Check the answers as a class. Refer to the answer key on LP page 188.

5. Wrap up the exercise by asking students to think of three things that are the same about themselves and a partner, or someone in their family.

6. Ask volunteers to read their sentences to the class.

For more practice, use *Grammar Dimensions 2* Workbook page 80, Exercise 3.

EXPANSION [30 minutes]

You may want to use Activity 3 on SB page 194 after this exercise.

FOCUS 4 [10 minutes]

This focus chart builds on Focus Chart 3 by showing how these same forms can be used as short answers.

1. **Lead-in:** You can illustrate these short forms by making statements about your likes and call on students who (as you remember from their earlier exercises) share the same taste.

2. Model an example on the board, using the format of the examples in this focus chart but substituting actual information from your class.

3. Make a statement that you know one of your students would agree with. The student responds with a short answer.

4. Write the exchange on the board, calling on the class to suggest words as you go.

5. Read the examples and explanations in the chart, contrasting the word order in examples (a) and (b) (verb-subject), with examples (c) and (d) (subject-verb).

6. You may want to provide further practice with a short drill. Instruct students that they have to agree with everything you say. Then use the following (or similar) prompts.

> You: *I love movies.*
> Students: *So do I.*
> You: *I don't like opera.*
> Students: *Neither do I.*
> You: *I can't stand video games.*
> Students: *Neither can I.*
> You: *I am crazy about opera.*
> Students: *So am I.*
> You: *I am not crazy about rap music.*
> Students: *Neither am I.*
> You: *I never go to the cinema.*
> Students: *Neither do I.* (Note that verb is affirmative, but adverb is negative.)
> You: *I hate quiz shows.*
> Students: *So do I.* (Note that verb has a negative meaning but an affirmative form.)

METHODOLOGY NOTE

It is sometimes a good idea to do the exercises *before* presenting the material in the focus chart (as suggested in the teacher's notes for Exercise 3 and Focus Chart 3). There are a couple of reasons for doing this. One is that students have different learning styles, and although some learners will understand better if the rule is presented first, others may benefit from working out the rule by

themselves. Another reason is that working on the exercises, engages students more actively. It may take them longer to do the exercise, and they may make more errors, but it will be more memorable and, in the long term, result in more effective learning.

EXERCISE 4 [10 minutes]

This exercise provides an opportunity to see how the structures from Focus Chart 4 are used in conversation.

1. Make a copy of the comic on an overhead transparency and model the first square of the comic strip.

2. Have students do this activity for homework, or in-class pair work.

3. Check the answers as a class. Refer to the answer key on LP page 188.

For more practice, use *Grammar Dimensions 2* Workbook page 80, Exercise 4.

EXPANSION [5 minutes]

Follow up the activity with a discussion of humor. Since different cultures often have conflicting ideas about what is and isn't funny, lead the discussion with specific questions:

Do the students think this comic strip funny? What makes it funny? Would people in your students' country(s) find this type of humor funny? If not, how could they change this one to make it funnier?

EXPANSION [20 minutes]

You may want to use Activity 6 (listening) on SB page 195 after this exercise.

FOCUS 5

Short Phrases or Hedges and Emphatic *Do*

use

EXAMPLES

(a) Sue: I love ballet. What about you?
Tien: **Kind of.**

(b) Sue: Do you like opera?
Tien: **Sort of.**

(c) Tien: You **really are** a good swimmer.

(d) Sue: Thanks! I **do love** swimming.

(e) Tien: You know, I **really do** enjoy our conversations, Sue.

EXPLANATIONS

If you do not agree strongly with the speaker's opinions, you can use hedges (*sort of*, *kind of*) in informal conversation. In fast speech, *sort of* sounds like "sorta" and *kind of* sounds like "kinda."

You can add emphasis to a sentence by stressing the auxiliary or the *be* verb.

In sentences where there is no auxiliary or *be* verb, you can add *do* and stress it for emphasis.

You can add extra emphasis by adding *really* or *certainly* before the auxiliary verb.

EXERCISE 5

Claire and Chris have just met at a party and are finding out how much they have in common. Look at the chart showing their likes and dislikes.

✓ ✓ ✓ = really a lot   ✓ ✓ = a lot   ✓ = a little

Use the information from the chart to complete the conversation. Use agreement phrases with *so* or *neither*, hedges, or emphatic structures with *really* or *certainly* where appropriate. The first one has been done for you.

	LIKES		DISLIKES	
Chris	swimming ✓✓✓	hiking ✓✓	TV ✓✓	getting up in the morning ✓✓✓
	cats ✓✓✓	music ✓		country music ✓✓
	cooking ✓✓	Chinese food ✓✓		
Claire	cats ✓	cooking ✓	country music ✓✓✓	
	eating in ✓	music ✓✓✓	getting out of bed ✓✓	
	Chinese food ✓✓✓	swimming ✓✓	staying home ✓✓	
		hiking ✓	watching TV ✓✓	

Chris: Well, let me see . . . what are some of my favorite things? The ocean . . . I (1) ___really do___ love swimming in the ocean.

Claire: (2) ___So do I___ . Maybe we should go for a swim sometime.

Chris: Yes, that'd be great! Do you like hiking too?

Claire: (3) ___Sort of/Kind of___ . In general, I prefer to be active. I mean I don't like sitting at home and watching TV.

Chris: (4) ___Neither do I___ . But I (5) ___really don't___ like getting up in the morning.

Claire: Well, (6) ___neither do I___ . Most people don't like getting out of bed in the morning! What about music? Do you like music?

Chris: (7) ___Sort of/Kind of___ . I don't know too much about it, actually.

Claire: Really? I love all kinds of music, except for country. I hate country!

Chris: (8) ___I do too/So do I___ . We (9) ___certainly___ do agree on that one! What else? I love cooking, don't you?

Claire: (10) ___Sort of/Kind of___ . I really prefer eating out in restaurants, especially in Chinatown. I (11) ___really___ love Chinese food.

Chris: (12) ___So do I/I do too___ . I've heard that the new Chinese restaurant on Grant Avenue is supposed to be really good.

Claire: (13) ___So have I/I have too___ . Why don't we give it a try?

Chris: That sounds good. By the way, I have six cats. Do you like cats?

Claire: Well, (14) ___kind of/sort of___ . —as long as you don't *hate* them. . . .

Chris: That's O.K.—as long as you don't *hate* them. . . .

EXERCISE 6

One way to meet people is through personal ads in newspapers or magazines. These personal ads appeared in a local newspaper. Read them quickly and then read the statements that follow. Circle T (true) if you think the statement is true and F (false) if you think it is false.

(A) COULD THIS BE YOU?
You are attractive, slim, and athletic. You like dancing, eating candlelit dinners, and walking on the beach by moonlight. Like me, you also enjoy camping and hiking. You love dogs and you don't smoke. If you are the woman of my dreams, send a photo to Box 3092.

(B) BEAUTY & BRAINS
Warm, humorous, well-educated SF loves walking on the beach, dancing, cycling, and hiking. Seeks intelligent life partner with computer interests. P.S. —I'm allergic to cats, dogs, and smoking. Box 875.

(C) I'VE GOT YOU ON MY WAVELENGTH
Athletic, professional, DF, animal lover seeks active man who knows how to treat a lady. Box 4021.

(D) A FEW OF MY FAVORITE THINGS:
Cooking for my friends, cycling, walking on the beach with my dog, wise and witty women. I can't stand: snobs, cheap wine, jogging, people who smoke, women who wear makeup. DM looking for a special woman. Box 49.

1. A likes walking on the beach, and so do D and B. (T) F
2. B does not like smokers, and neither do A and C. T (F)
3. Cooking for friends is one of B's favorite pastimes. T (F)
4. D does not like women who wear a lot of makeup. (T) F
5. D likes dancing, and A does too. T (F)
6. A wants to find someone who likes hiking, and so does D. T (F)
7. Jogging and cycling are two of B's favorite sports. T (F)

Do you think any of these people would make a good couple? If so, why? If not, why not?

ANSWER KEY

Exercise 5   Answers will vary. Possible answers are listed above.

LESSON PLAN 2

FOCUS 5 [10 minutes]

This focus chart presents different ways of agreeing or disagreeing.

1. **Lead-in:** Draw a chart on the board.

	no	a little	yes
rock music			
opera			
rap music			
classical			
country			

2. Ask for a volunteer to answer questions about each type of music.

3. Have students ask the volunteer questions, and have another student fill in the answers on the chart.

4. You may repeat this with another student, writing the answers in a different color pen.

5. Review some of the answers given by the students. For the *no* column, did they say *no*, or did they also use other phrases such as *not really* or *not too much?* For the *a little* column, did they say *kind of* or *sort of* or *maybe?* For the *yes* column, did they say *I love it, I really love it,* or *I really do love it!?*

6. Refer students to the chart and read the examples and explanations using appropriate intonation.

7. Model the intonation and have students repeat.

8. Have students practice in pairs using the chart to ask and answer questions.

LANGUAGE NOTE

It is not always necessary to agree with the speaker in English (this may need to be emphasized in some cultures where it is considered impolite not to agree). *Hedges* are ways of avoiding a direct agreement without completely disagreeing. *Kind of* and *sort of* mean "a little bit" or "in a way." These expressions are less formal than the previously mentioned structures; the result is that they usually are reserved for spoken English and are, therefore, often pronounced in reduced form as *sorta* and *kinda*.

EXERCISE 5 [20 minutes]

This exercise provides practice with the structures in Focus Chart 5. Students have to use context clues to work out which type of answer is most appropriate.

1. Direct students to look at the chart. Ask some simple questions about the chart to check comprehension. For example:
   Does Chris like swimming? (Yes, he likes it a lot.)
   Does Claire like country music? (No, she hates it.)

2. Have students work in pairs to complete the exercise. Check the answers, asking students to justify their reasons for each choice. Refer to the answer key on LP page 190.

3. Have students practice reading the conversation aloud in pairs, using the appropriate stress and intonation.

4. Ask volunteers to perform the conversation for the class. The class can decide who read the conversation in the most interesting and natural way.

5. Students can then improvise a similar conversation from their own experience, using the one in the book as a model.

work book For more practice, use *Grammar Dimensions 2* Workbook page 81, Exercise 5.

EXPANSION [20 minutes]

You may want to use Activity 5 (speaking/listening) on SB page 195 after this exercise.

EXERCISE 6 [20 minutes]

This exercise uses short readings to review structures with *so* and *neither* from Focus Charts 2 and 3. It also introduces the forms discussed in Focus Chart 6 (gerunds and infinitives) on SB page 192.

1. Introduce the topic of personal ads in newspapers or magazines.

2. Explain the abbreviations:
   SF (= single female)
   DF (= divorced female)
   DM (= divorced male)

3. Set a time limit for students to read the ads and answer the questions.

4. You may want to allow use of dictionaries (monolingual or bilingual) or pair up stronger with weaker students so they can help each other with difficult words.

5. Check the meaning of new vocabulary.

6. **Suggestion:** Give some synonyms for some words in the readings and ask students to find the matching words. For example:
   Someone who likes to make jokes: humorous, (B)
   Someone who says clever and interesting things: witty (D)
   Someone who is friendly: warm (B)
   Etc.

7. Check the answers as a class. Refer to answer key on LP page 190.

8. Ask for suggested answers to the final question.
   Note: This exercise is revisited in Exercise 7.

FOCUS 6

Likes and Dislikes with Gerunds and Infinitives

use

EXAMPLES	EXPLANATIONS
(a) **Cooking** is my favorite hobby. (b) I love **cooking**. Do you? (c) My favorite hobby is **cooking**.	*Gerunds* (nouns formed from verb + *-ing*) can be used as: • the subject of a sentence • the object of a sentence • the complement of a sentence (something needed to complete the sentence)
(d) I like **to cook**. (e) I don't like **to swim**. (f) I hate **to go** to the dentist. (g) AWKWARD: **To cook** is my favorite hobby.	*Infinitives* (*to* + verb) are also used in talking about likes and dislikes. In this context, infinitives are usually used as objects of sentences or as complements, but they sound awkward as subjects.
(h) I don't like **swimming**. (i) I hate **going** to the dentist	When talking about likes and dislikes, you can usually use infinitives or gerunds. The verbs *hate*, *like*, and *love* can be followed by either a gerund or an infinitive.

EXERCISE 7

Look back at numbered list in Exercise 6.

1. Underline all the gerunds.

2. Check (✓) all the gerunds that are subjects and circle the gerunds that are objects or complements.

3. Replace the gerunds with infinitives where possible.

4. Rewrite sentences 2 and 4, using a gerund or an infinitive.

Sentence 2: _____ *B does not like smoking, and neither do A and C.* _____

Sentence 4: _____ *D does not like women wearing a lot of makeup.* _____

Use Your English

ACTIVITY 1 speaking

The purpose of this activity is to share information with one other person and then to report what you find to the rest of the class. While sharing information with your partner, try to find out **how many things you have** in common. Some ideas for starting your conversation are given below. When you have nothing more to say on this topic, decide on another one and find out what you have in common on that topic. Use the chart for your notes.

TOPIC	NOTES
family	Examples: any brothers and sisters?/grandparents alive?/father older than mother?

ACTIVITY 2 speaking

Form teams. Your job as a team is to find as many similarities as possible among the pairs of things listed below. The team that finds the most similarities is the winner.

1. an apple and an orange

2. tennis and golf

3. hiking and jogging

4. learning a foreign language and learning to ride a bike

You have to practice every day!

ANSWER KEY

Exercise 7 1. *Gerunds: walking, cooking, dancing, hiking, jogging, cycling* 2. *Gerunds as Subjects: cooking, jogging, cycling Gerunds as Objects: walking, dancing, hiking* 3. *Sentences 1, 5, and 6 can be rewritten using infinitives.*

Activity 1 Answers will vary.
Activity 2 Answers will vary.

FOCUS 6 [5 minutes]

This focus chart reviews the use of gerunds and infinitives in expressing likes and dislikes.

1. **Lead-in:** Review the meaning of the terms *gerund* (a noun made from a verb with the ending *-ing*) and *infinitive* (the base form of the verb preceded by *to*).

2. Refer back to Exercise 6 and ask students to find as many gerunds and infinitives as they can.

3. Ask students to cover the right-hand side of the chart and look at the examples in the first chart. Can they explain the difference between the uses of the word *cooking* in these sentences?

4. Have them check their answers by uncovering the right-hand side of the chart.

LANGUAGE NOTE

Gerunds (*singing, running, snowboarding*) and infinitives (*to sing, to run, to snowboard*) are not contrasted in *Grammar Dimensions 2* because the difference in their meaning is not particularly important when expressing likes and dislikes.

Gerunds and infinitives are nouns that are formed from verbs. They "act" like nouns in the sentence:

Karen likes coffee in the morning.
Karen likes dancing in the evening. OR Karen likes to dance in the evening.

Gerunds are generally used when talking about activities, while infinitives often express *intentions*:

If Wan has time, mountain-biking is his favorite activity.

Jeff plans to mountain-bike with Wan next weekend.

EXERCISE 7 [15 minutes]

This exercise allows students to check their understanding of the use of gerunds and infinitives.

1. Refer students back to Exercise 6.

2. Have them work through the different steps of the activity, either together as a class, or in pairs.

3. Check the answers. Refer to the answer key on LP page 192. The answers to Step 4 will challenge students' ability to use infinitives with a change of subject.

 For more practice, use *Grammar Dimensions 2* Workbook page 82, Exercise 6 and page 83, Exercises 7 and 8.

UNIT GOAL REVIEW [10 minutes]

Ask students to look at the goals on the opening page of the unit again. Refer to the pages of the unit where information on each goal can be found.

 For a grammar quiz review of Units 10–12, refer students to pages 84–86 in the *Grammar Dimensions 2* Workbook.

 ExamView Test Generator   For assessment of Unit 12, use *Grammar Dimensions 2 ExamView®*.

USE YOUR ENGLISH

The Use Your English section of activities at the end of the unit contain situations that should naturally elicit the structures covered in the unit. For a more complete discussion of how to use the Use Your English activities, see To the Teacher, LP page xxii. When students are doing these activities in class, you can circulate and listen to see if they are using the structures accurately. Errors can be corrected after the activity has finished.

 **ACTIVITY 1** **speaking** [30 minutes]

You may want to use this activity after Exercise 2 on SB page 187. The purpose of this activity is to provide a natural context for students to use the structures *So do I, I do too, Neither do I,* etc.

1. Check that all students are familiar with the term *in common* (things which are the same about both people).

2. Tell students to focus more on having a natural conversation than on filling in the chart. Circulate while students are talking and take notes of the most interesting examples.

   Suggestion: After pairs have finished talking, you can ask them to find a new partner and tell their new partner about their conversation with their first partner.

3. Ask volunteers to report their findings to the class. They can use their notes from the chart to help in their report.

 ACTIVITY 2 **speaking** [30 minutes]

You may want to use this activity after Exercise 7 on SB page 192. This is a fun activity and a change of context to practice the structures *. . . and (name) does too. And neither does (name).* etc.

1. Help the class to form two teams.

2. Assign the first topic and set a time limit.

3. Have teams make their lists directly on the board.

4. The whole class can check and review answers together.

ACTIVITY 3 speaking

Form pairs or groups of three.

■ **STEP 1**
Think of fifteen to twenty statements using *so/too/either/neither*. Make sure they are meaningful. Write each statement on two cards, like this:

> A My parents live in Paris
> B and so does my sister

> A I don't like broccoli
> B and they don't either

Therefore, if you have twenty statements, you will have forty cards.

■ **STEP 2**
Get together with another pair or threesome. Place all the A cards in one pile and all the B cards in another pile. Shuffle each deck of cards carefully.

■ **STEP 3**
Put the A pile facedown on the table. Then distribute the B cards among the players. Do not look at the cards; place them facedown on the table in front of you.

■ **STEP 4**
The first player turns the first card from the A pile on the table and puts the first card from his or her B pile beside it. The player must not look at his or her card before putting it down on the table. The object of the game is to create meaningful sentences. If the two cards on the table do not make a meaningful match, the next player puts his or her B card down. The game continues in this way until a meaningful match is created. The first player to spot a match shouts "Match" to stop the game. If the match is acceptable, he or she collects all the B cards on the table. The next A card is then turned over and the game continues.

■ **STEP 5**
The player with the most cards at the end is the winner. This game should be played as quickly as possible.

ACTIVITY 4 writing

Who are you most similar to in your family? Write a description of your similarities and differences. If you wish, think of someone in your extended family—for example, a cousin, aunt, or grandparent.

ACTIVITY 5 speaking/listening

■ **STEP 1**
Make a list of five popular musicians that you like or dislike. Or you can choose movies, movie stars, types of music, sports, writers, or books. Walk around the classroom and ask other students their opinions about your list. Find out how many students agree or disagree with you. Record your conversations or interviews.

■ **STEP 2**
Make a report on your findings. Listen to the recording to make sure your report is accurate. Did your classmates use short phrases such as *I do too, so do I, I don't either, neither do I, sort of,* and *kind of*? If not, what did they use instead to agree and disagree with each other?

ACTIVITY 6 listening

■ **STEP 1**
Listen to the audio of people talking about what they like and dislike. What general topic are they talking about? What specific topics do they mention?

 CD Track 19

■ **STEP 2**
Number the statements below in the order that you hear them. Mark the first statement as number 1 and so forth.

_1_ I do too.	_5_ I don't either.	_6_ Sort of.
_2_ So do I.	_3_ Neither do I.	_4_ Kind of.

■ **STEP 3**
Which statements do you agree and disagree with?

ACTIVITY 7 research on the web

 InfoTrac® College Edition Option: Go to *InfoTrac* to look up a review of your favorite movie or music. Do you agree with the reviewer? Tell the class.

ACTIVITY 8 reflection

Work with a partner. Complete a chart like the one in the Opening Task on page 185 with things you both like and don't like about learning English. Then tell your class.

ANSWER KEY

Activity 6 **Step 1:** Check audio script on LP page S-5 for answers.

ACTIVITY 3 — speaking [30 minutes]

You may want to use this activity after Exercise 3 on SB page 188. This activity reviews and practices the structures from Focus Charts 1, 2, and 3.

1. Go over the rules of the game before you begin and help students to form groups.
2. Set a time limit for students to prepare their cards. Encourage them to use a variety of different verbs. (Refer to Exercise 3 on SB page 188 for ideas.)
3. Reiterate that each half of the statement goes on a separate card. Have students mark "A" or "B" on the backs of the appropriate cards.
4. Circulate around the room to help settle disputes.
5. You may want to appoint a secretary in each group to take notes of disputed sentences.
6. If your class is large enough to have several groups, they can exchange piles of cards with each and play the game over again with the new set of cards.

ACTIVITY 4 — writing [20 minutes]

You may want to use this activity after Exercise 7 on SB page 192. This activity allows students to focus on accuracy in written work when using structures from this unit.

1. Talk about someone in your family and say how you are similar and different. You might talk about personality, hobbies and interests, and appearance.
2. Brainstorm a list of personality words, perhaps reviewing some of those from Exercise 6.
3. Have students choose a person to write about and make a list of characteristics they might mention in their descriptions. Have students organize the list before writing the paragraph.
4. You can assign the writing in class or as homework. Ask volunteers to read aloud their descriptions to the class.

ACTIVITY 5 — speaking/listening [20 minutes]

You may want to use this activity after Exercise 5 on SB pages 190–191. This activity allows students to practice the short answers from Focus Charts 4 and 5 in a natural context.

■ STEP 1

1. Help students to choose a topic they are interested in. Then, each student can make his or her own list.
2. Taking their notebooks and pens with them, they should walk around the room and ask as many students as they can about their opinions. Set a time limit.

■ STEP 2

Have students report their findings to the class, using the alternative structures from Focus Charts 1, 2, and 3. Which hedges or phrases were most common?

ACTIVITY 6 — listening [20 minutes]

CD Track 19

You may want to use this activity after Exercise 4 on SB page 189.

■ STEP 1

1. Introduce the topic of people talking about their likes and dislikes.
2. Play the audio and ask for the general topic. See audio script on LP page S-5.

■ STEP 2

1. Play the audio again and have students write their answers.
2. Compare answers in pairs and play the audio again if necessary. See the audio script on LP page S-5 for answers.

■ STEP 3   Ask for students' own opinions.

ACTIVITY 7 — research on the web [homework/15 minutes]

The purpose of this Internet search activity is to provide a natural context for *too, either,* and *so.* An additional purpose is to encourage students to learn to use *InfoTrac® College Edition* as a resource. See To the Teacher, page xxii for tips on how to use InfoTrac. After searching for reviews of their favorite movies or music, encourage students to share search tips.

ACTIVITY 8 — reflection [25 minutes]

This activity provides an opportunity for students to use the target structures of the unit while reflecting on their language learning progress. You may have asked students to keep a record of their learning in a journal throughout this course as suggested in To the Teacher, LP page xxii.' This reflection activity will form part of that learning record. Refer students back to the chart on SB page 185 and have them create a similar chart about learning English.

PRESENT PERFECT
WITH *SINCE AND FOR*

UNIT GOALS

- Use present perfect to show a connection between past and present situations
- Form correct sentences with present perfect
- Know how to use *for* and *since* correctly
- Know which verbs not to use with present perfect

OPENING TASK
Personal Information

■ STEP 1

Look at the picture. Where are they? What are they talking about?

■ STEP 2

Work in pairs. Student A, look at this page. Student B, look at page A-17.

Student A: Complete the information on the medical history form by asking your partner questions about Michael Menendez. Your partner will answer your questions by looking at page A-17. Use complete questions.

Example: Student A: *Does he smoke?*
Student B: *Yes, he does.*
Student A: *How long has he smoked?*

MEDICAL HISTORY

Name	Michael Menendez				
Date of birth 08/24/75	Cigarettes? (Yes)/No	Alcohol? (Yes)/No	Glasses? (Yes)/No	Serious Injuries? *Broken ankle*	Health Problems? *Headaches*
Height 5ft 11in Weight 185 lbs.	How long? 5 years *Started* 1995 *Stopped* 2000	How much? A glass of wine with dinner every night	How long? Since 2003	When? In 1992	How long? For 2 months

■ STEP 3

Use the information above to make sentences about Michael Menendez. Write complete sentences.

PAST:
1. He was born in 1975./He started smoking in 1995.
2. He stopped smoking in 2000. / He broke his ankle in 1992.

PRESENT:
1. He weighs 185 lbs./He is 5 feet 11 inches tall./He doesn't smoke.
2. He drinks a glass of wine with dinner./He wears glasses./He has headaches.

PAST AND PRESENT:
1. He has worn glasses since 2003.
2. He has had headaches for 2 months.

ANSWER KEY

Opening Task   Step 3: *Answers may vary. Possible answers above. Students may not yet be familiar with this grammar structure.*

UNIT 13

LESSON PLAN 1

UNIT OVERVIEW

Unit 13 provides practice with the present perfect used with *since* and *for*. It contrasts the use of the present perfect with the simple present and the simple past.

GRAMMAR NOTE

The present perfect is one of the most difficult tenses for learners, not only because of its name (it says *present* but is really about the past), but also because a few other languages have a tense with the same meaning (though several languages—e.g., French and German, have a tense that is formed in a similar way but used differently). The present perfect is used to describe past events viewed from the perspective of the present. It is used to talk about past events that have a connection with the present, started in the past and continue up to the present, or have happened just recently.

UNIT GOALS

Some instructors may want to review the goals listed on this page after completing the Opening Task so that students understand what they should know by the end of the unit. These goals can also be reviewed at the end of the unit when students are more familiar with the grammar terminology.

OPENING TASK [30 minutes]

In general, the purpose of the Opening Task is to create a context in which students will need to use present, simple past, and present perfect tenses. The problem-solving format is designed to show the teacher how well the students can produce the target structures implicitly and spontaneously when they are engaged in a communicative task. For a more complete discussion of the purpose of the Opening Task, see To the Teacher, Lesson Planner (LP) page xxii.

Setting Up the Task

The purpose of the task in this unit is to generate talk about different periods in Michael Menendez's medical history, using different verb tenses to talk about different time frames.

STEP 1

1. Introduce the topic by looking at the picture and the medical form. Talk about going to the doctor.
2. What kinds of information do doctors usually ask about? This may elicit many of the headings on the chart in Step 2.

Conducting the Task

STEP 2

1. Divide students into pairs, and tell all Student Bs to look at the chart on Student Book (SB) page A-17.
2. Explain that both students have information about the same man, but some information is missing. They will have to ask each other questions in order to complete the information.
3. Ask two students to model the example dialogue. If necessary, extend this to another example by asking Student B to ask Student A: *How tall is Michael?* (Student A answers: *He's 5 feet, 11 inches.*)
4. Circulate and listen for students' current use of the simple past tense (example: *be broke bis ankle*), the simple present tense (example: *be weighs*), the present perfect with *for* and *since* (example: *be bas worn glasses for reading since 1987/for 13 years*).
5. Do not correct errors at this stage. Note the structures that seem to be problematic. You can use them to focus your teaching points later in the unit.
6. Check the answers. Refer to the answer key on LP page 196.

Closing the Task

STEP 3

1. This step asks students to identify the meanings of the different tenses. Once they have recognized these different meanings, it will be easier for them to map meaning onto form when they come to the use of the present perfect in Focus Chart 1.
2. Students will probably have difficulty with the last category: Past and Present. Don't give the answers away; allow them to try and work out what it could mean.
3. Use this task as a bridge to the information in Focus Chart 1.

GRAMMAR NOTE

Typical student errors (form)

- Confusing *since* and *for*, e.g. * *I have lived here since two years.* (See Focus 3.)
- Errors with past participles, e.g. * *I haven't saw her today.* (See Focus 2.)

Typical student errors (use)

- Using present tense with *for* and *since*, e.g. * *I am here for three years.* (Instead of: *I have been here for three years.*) (See Focus 1.)
- Using present perfect instead of simple past with finished time expressions, e.g. * *I have seen him yesterday.* * *I have lived here three months ago.*
- Using *for* with the present perfect form of verbs that denote past completed actions, e.g. * *They have begun to study English for three years.* (See Focus 5.)

FOCUS 1

Present Perfect: Connecting Past and Present

use

EXAMPLES

EXPLANATIONS

PAST
(a) **I moved** to New York in 2002.
(simple past)

Use the simple past for completed action in the past.

PRESENT
(b) **I live** in New York now.
(simple present)

Use the simple present for facts about present situations.

PAST AND PRESENT
(c) **I have lived** in New York since 2002.
(present perfect)

(d) It is now 2006. **I have lived** in New York for four years. (present perfect)

Use the present perfect (*have* + past participle) to connect the past and present. One use of the present perfect is to tell us about something that began in the past and continues to the present. (For other uses of the present perfect, see Unit 14.)

EXERCISE 1

Use the information about Michael Menendez from the Opening Task on page 197 and page A-17 to complete the doctor's report below. Circle the simple present, simple past, or present perfect.

Medical Report on Michael Menendez

Michael Menendez spoke with me yesterday about serious headaches. He (1) has/had/(has had) these headaches for two months. His previous medical history is good. He (2) doesn't have/didn't have/(hasn't) (had) any serious illnesses. In 1992, he (3) is/(was)/has been in the hospital for three weeks, when he (4) breaks/(broke)/has broken his ankle in a skiing accident. He (5)(doesn't smoke)/didn't smoke/hasn't smoked: he (6) stops/(stopped)/has stopped six years ago, and he (7) doesn't smoke/didn't smoke/(hasn't) (smoked) since that time. He (8)(wears)/wore/has worn glasses when he reads and he (9) wears/wore/(has) (worn) them since 2003. He (10) works/(worked)/has worked with computers since 1998. I examined Mr. Menendez and did several tests. I asked him to return next week.

Signed: *Dr. Roberts*

LESSON PLAN 1

FOCUS 1 [5 minutes]

This focus chart presents the use of the present perfect with *since* and *for*, contrasting it with the simple past and the simple present.

1. **Lead-in:** Ask students simple questions to elicit sentences similar to the examples. *When did you move here, Elanos? How about you, Maria? How long have you lived here?*

2. Use the information to write sentences similar to those in the chart. As you write, ask students to help you with the correct tenses.

3. Read the explanations and examples in the chart.

4. Have students ask each other questions using these three different tenses. *Where do you live now? When did you move there? How long have you lived there?*

5. Have students listen to each other's answers for errors (see Language Note below).

6. The correct formation of the present perfect will be presented in Focus Chart 2.

LANGUAGE NOTE

Learners may have a tendency to use the present tense with *for* and *since*, either because it parallels the use in their own language, or because they are focused on the present tense meaning of the utterance. For example, the sentence, *I am here for three years*, may be understood by native speakers from the context, especially if it is given in reply to the question, *How long have you lived here?*, but it really has a future meaning (I am going to be here for three years).

EXERCISE 1 [5 minutes]

This exercise asks students to carefully consider the choice of tenses in each sentence and justify their answers by reference to the explanations in Focus Chart 1.

1. Refer students back to the information in the Opening Task, which will help them when completing this task.

2. Allow students to work individually to complete their answers.

3. Have students compare answers in pairs, justifying their choices.

4. Select students to read sentences aloud.

5. Ask students whether or not they think it is correct and ask them to explain why.

6. Review the answers. Refer to the answer key on LP page 198.

For more practice, use *Grammar Dimensions 2* Workbook page 87, Exercise 1 and page 88, Exercise 2.

EXPANSION 1 [15 minutes]

You may want to use Activity 1 on SB page 206 after this exercise.

EXPANSION 2 [15 minutes]

Have students make a list of things that they have owned, people they have known, and subjects they have studied. All must be things, people, and subjects that they still own, know now, and study now.

In pairs, they can use their lists to ask and answer questions using *How long* and continue the conversation about each one using simple past or simple present tenses. Examples:

Student A's list: *1989 Volkswagen, my best friend Sarah, yoga.*

Student B: *How long have you owned your 1989 Volkswagen?*

Student A: *For five years.*

Student B: *When did you buy it?*

Student A: *In 2003.*

FOCUS 2 — Forming the Present Perfect

form

To form the present perfect use *have/has* + past participle.*

STATEMENT

I You We They	have gone. ('ve)
She He It	has gone. ('s)

NEGATIVE

I You We They	have not gone. (haven't)
She He It	has not gone. (hasn't)

QUESTION

Have	I You We They	gone?
Has	She He It	gone?

* See Appendix 5 on page A-13 for the past participles of some common irregular verbs.

EXERCISE 2

Write the questions that the doctor probably asked Mr. Menendez in order to get these responses.

Example: _Do you drink?_
Yes, a little. I drink a glass of wine with dinner every night.

1. _Do you wear glasses?_
Yes, I do. I wear them when I read.

2. _When did you start wearing them?_
I started wearing them in 1987.

3. _Have you worn them for some time?_
I've worn them since 1987.

4. _Do you smoke?_
No, I don't smoke now.

5. _When did you stop?_
I stopped ten years ago.

6. _Have you smoked since then?/since that time?_
No, I haven't smoked since that time.

7. _Have you had these headaches for some time?_
Yes, I have had these headaches for two months.

EXERCISE 3

Work with a partner. Ask and answer questions about each other's medical history. Feel free to make up information on the following topics, or use the information about Michael Menendez on pages 197 and A-17 to answer questions.

Example: A: Have you had any serious illnesses?
B: Yes, I once had pneumonia when I was ten years old.

serious illnesses	time in hospital
smoking	drinking
eyesight	allergies
present health problem(s)	when problem(s) started

EXERCISE 4

Go back to Exercises 1 and 2. Look for the words *for* and *since*. In the boxes below, write down the word or words that directly follow *for* or *since*. The first example is *two months* with *for*, from Exercise 1.

SINCE	FOR
that time	two months
2003	
1998	three weeks

What does this tell you about the use of *since* and *for*? What kinds of words or phrases follow *since* and *for*?

ANSWER KEY

Exercise 3 *Questions and answers will vary, depending on what students choose to talk about. Possible answers are listed above.*

FOCUS 2 [10 minutes]

1. **Lead-in:** Check to see that students can form the present perfect correctly. You can do this by writing a list of verbs on the board and making up questions for each one. (You may want to check first that students know the past participle for each one.) See examples below. For further ideas, and to review the forms of common irregular verbs, see Appendix 5 on page A-13.

   How long have you . . . known (name of student)?
   How long have you . . . lived in (name of city or state)?
   How long have you . . . studied (name of subject)?
   How long have you . . . worked as a (name of job)?
   How long have you . . . owned (name of object— e.g., cell phone)?
   How long have you . . . been a student/in this class?

2. Have students ask each other questions. To practice third-person forms, ask them about previous answers given by students—e.g., *How long has (Natalie) lived in (California)?*

3. Read the examples in the focus chart. Model the pronunciation of contracted forms. And ask students to repeat after you.

4. You may want to add your own examples with *Wh-* questions

EXERCISE 2 [10 minutes]

This exercise practices using *yes/no* and *Wh-* questions with a variety of tenses.

1. Refer students back to the information in the Opening Task, which will help them complete this task.

2. Read the example question and answer.

3. Allow students to work individually and complete the exercise.

4. Have students compare their answers in pairs.

5. Review the answers as a class. Refer to the answer key on LP page 200.

work book For more practice, use *Grammar Dimensions 2* Workbook page 88, Exercise 3 and page 89, Exercise 4.

EXPANSION [20 minutes]

You may want to use Activity 2 on SB page 207 after this exercise.

EXERCISE 3 [15 minutes]

Answering these types of questions is useful practice for real-life doctor-patient situations. The kind of information used in this exercise is personal, so make sure students know they can make up the answers.

1. Explain that students will practice asking and answering questions similar to the ones about Michael Menendez on SB page 197. If they wish, they can role-play the conversation between Michael and his doctor, or they can use real information about themselves.

2. Model the first example with a student, and add a couple more questions if necessary.

3. Circulate while students are working to check that they are forming and using the present perfect accurately, and make note of the structure(s) that continue to be challenging for more than one or two students.

4. Review Focus Charts 1 and 2 if you feel it would be helpful for students to hear the rules stated again.

5. Ask students to restate the rules in their own words. Ask leading questions such as, *When do you use the present tense? Can you give me an example? When do you use the present perfect?*

EXERCISE 4 [5 minutes]

This is an example of presenting grammar through an inductive approach (see Language Note on LP page 199). In this exercise, students have to find the example and try to work out the rules. The rules are presented in Focus Chart 3 on SB page 202.

1. Refer students back to Exercises 1 and 2.

2. Have them find all the words that follow *since* and *for.*

3. Check the answers by writing them on the board or on an overhead transparency. Refer to the answer key on LP page 200.

4. Students' answers to the last questions in this exercise will serve as a bridge to Focus Chart 3, and, with luck, will resemble the Explanations in Focus Chart 3.

EXPANSION [30 minutes]

You may want to use Activity 3 on SB pages 207 and 208 after this exercise.

FOCUS 3 | *For and Since*

meaning

EXAMPLES

(a) for two weeks
(b) for ten years
(c) for five minutes

(d) since 1985
(e) since my birthday
(f) since I turned 40
(g) since Monday
(h) since April

EXPLANATIONS

For is used to show length of time (how long the period of time was).

Since is used to show when a period of time began.

EXERCISE 5

What difference in meaning (if any) is there in each pair of statements? Discuss with a partner.

1. a. Anthony and Eva lived here for ten years.
   b. Anthony and Eva have lived here for ten years.

2. Anthony and Eva met in 1998.
   a. They have known each other for over ten years.
   b. They have known each other since 1998.

3. a. They have worked for the same company for a long time.
   b. They worked for the same company for a long time.

4. It is May. Eva started studying Italian three months ago.
   a. Eva has studied Italian for three months.
   b. Eva has studied Italian since February.

5. It is July.
   a. Anthony hasn't drunk any coffee for six months.
   b. Anthony stopped drinking coffee in January.

form

FOCUS 4 | *For and Since*

EXAMPLES

(a) She's worked here (for) several years.
(b) (For) how long have you lived here?
(c) Since when have you lived here?
(d) NOT: When have you lived here?
(e) I've lived here since January.
(f) NOT: I've lived here January.

EXPLANATIONS

The word *for* can be omitted in statements.

For can also be omitted in questions.

Since cannot be omitted. "*How long . . .*" is more common than "*Since when . . .*" in questions.

EXERCISE 6

Look at the hotel register below. How many people are staying in the hotel right now? Who has stayed there the longest? Use the information from the register to make statements with the words given below.

Example: *Mr. and Mrs. Gordon stayed in the hotel for six nights.*

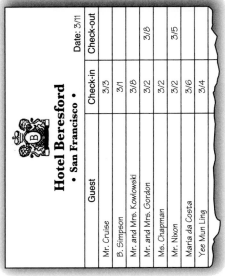

Hotel Beresford
• San Francisco •

Date: 3/11

Guest	Check-in	Check-out
Mr. Cruise	3/3	
B. Simpson	3/1	
Mr. and Mrs. Kowlowski	3/8	
Mr. and Mrs. Gordon	3/2	3/8
Ms. Chapman	3/2	
Mr. Nixon	3/2	3/5
Maria da Costa	3/6	
Yee Mun Ling	3/4	

1. Mr. and Mrs. Gordon/for
2. Maria da Costa/since
3. Yee Mun Ling/since
4. B. Simpson/for
5. Mr. and Mrs. Kowlowski/for
6. Ms. Chapman/since
7. Mr. Cruise/for
8. Mr. Nixon/for

ANSWER KEY

Exercise 5

1. (a) They don't live here now. (b) They still live here. 2. No difference. 3. (a) They still work for the same company. (b) They don't still work for the same company. 4. No difference. 5. No difference.

Exercise 6

There are seven people staying in the hotel right now. B. Simpson has stayed there the longest.
2. . . . has stayed in the hotel since March 6. 3. . . . has stayed in the hotel since March 4. 4. . . . has stayed in the hotel for 10 nights. 5. . . . have stayed in the hotel for three nights. 6. . . . has stayed in the hotel since March 2 7. . . . has stayed in the hotel for eight days/just over a week.

FOCUS 3 [10 minutes]

1. **Lead-in:** You can use the summary of students' answers from Exercise 4 as a lead-in to this focus chart.

2. Read the examples and explanations. See if they match the explanations developed by students in Exercise 3.

3. Ask students to add more examples to each box.

4. To review this you may give students a short dictation. Have students draw a two-column chart in their notebooks, with columns labeled *since* and *for*. Dictate the following time phrases, and students will write them in the correct column.

one week	three days	yesterday	Friday	2001
September	my birthday	20 years	a long time	a couple of hours

for		since	
one week	a long time	yesterday	September
three days	a couple of hours	Friday	my birthday
20 years		2001	

EXERCISE 5 [15 minutes]

This exercise emphasizes students' ability to explain grammatical differences in meaning.

1. Divide the class into groups to discuss the exercise.

2. When they are ready, appoint one student as a discussion leader to collect the answers from all the groups in the class and write them on the board.

3. The class must try to reach a consensus on each one. Limit discussion time.

4. At the end, evaluate the answers. Refer to the answer key on LP page 202.

For more practice, use *Grammar Dimensions* Workbook page 89, Exercise 5.

LESSON PLAN 2

FOCUS 4

If students are not having any problems with the formation of *for* and *since*, you may decide to omit this focus chart and go straight to Exercise 6.

1. For continued practice with *for* and *since*, use the information from Exercise 3 about students' own medical history (real or fictional) to ask and answer questions.

2. Note that omitting *for* in sentences is in informal speech only, though more usual in questions.

EXERCISE 6 [15 minutes]

This exercise provides practice with *since* and *for*, as well as distinguishing simple past from present perfect.

1. Check to make sure that students can interpret the chart by asking questions. For example, *What is today's date?* (Answer: *March 11th.*) *When did Mr. Cruise check in?* (Answer: *On March 3rd.*) *When did Mr. Cruise check out?* (Answer: *He hasn't checked out yet.*)

2. Have students work in pairs or small groups so that each student has the opportunity to give at least two or three answers. Circulate to check for accuracy.

3. Check the answers as a class. Refer to the answer key on LP page 202.

4. If you wish to extend this exercise, have students make true/false sentences about the chart. The other students will decide if they are true or not. If false, they must correct the error.

LANGUAGE NOTE

You might have to explain that it is the norm in the United States to put the month first, and then the day, while in some countries it is the other way around. Thus 3/1 is the 3rd of March or March 3rd in the U.S., but would be the 3rd of January or January 3rd in many other countries.

EXPANSION [10 minutes]

Have students use the hotel reservation chart in Exercise 6 to make true and false statements about the guests. The other students should say *true* or *false* and correct the statement if false. Some examples:

1. *Mr. Cruise has stayed at the hotel for five nights.* (False: eight nights)

2. *Ms. Chapman has stayed at the hotel for nine nights.* (True)

3. *Mr. and Mrs. Gordon have stayed at the hotel for seven nights.* (False: They checked out three days ago)

For more practice, use *Grammar Dimensions 2* Workbook page 90, Exercise 6.

FOCUS 5

Verbs Not Used with Present Perfect and For

EXAMPLES	EXPLANATIONS
(a) Shin arrived in the United States three years ago.	Some verbs talk about an action that happens all at once, an action that doesn't continue for a period of time.
(b) NOT: Shin has arrived in the United States for three years.	
(c) Shin has lived in the United States for three years.	In (c) we understand that it is the living in the United States that continues, not the arriving.
begin arrive meet end leave stop	For the same reason, these verbs are not usually used with present perfect and *for*.

EXERCISE 7

Rewrite these sentences. Be sure to use the present perfect and *since* or *for*.

Example: Karen wears glasses. She started to wear glasses when she was a child.
Karen has worn glasses since she was a child.

1. He works for the TV station. He started working there eight years ago.
He has worked for the TV station for eight years.

2. They are married. They got married in 1962.
They have been married since 1962.

3. She knows how to fix a car. She learned how to do it a long time ago.
She has known how to fix a car for a long time.

4. Tom rides his bike to work. He started to do it when his car broke down.
Since his car broke down, Tom has ridden his bike to work.

5. I wanted to go to China several years ago. I still want to go now.
I have wanted to go to China for several years.

6. My brother started painting when he was in college, and he still paints now.
My brother has painted since he was in college.

7. I was afraid of bats when I was a child, and I am afraid of them now.
I have been afraid of bats since I was a child.

8. My mother is in France. She went there last week.
My mother has been in France since last week.

9. My sister runs two miles every morning before breakfast. She started to do this when she was fifteen years old.
My sister has run two miles every morning since she was 15 years old.

10. They go to Cape Cod every summer. They started to do this twelve years ago.
They have gone to Cape Cod every summer for 12 years.

EXERCISE 8

Fill in the blanks with *since* or *for* OR the appropriate form of the verb in parentheses.

Leroy and Paula are having a party. Two of their guests, Lee and Bob, have just met.

Lee: (1) _____ Have you known Leroy and Paula (2) _for_ a long time?

Bob: I (3) _have known_ (know) Paula (4) _since_ my senior year in college. I first (5) _met_ (meet) Leroy at their wedding two years ago. What about you?

Lee: I'm a colleague of Leroy's. We (6) _have worked_ (work) together (7) _for_ several years.

Bob: Oh, Leroy (8) _showed_ (show) me some of your work last week. It's great.

Lee: Thanks. What do you do?

Bob: I (9) _taught_ (teach) French (10) _for_ ten years, but I (11) _quit_ (quit) a couple of years ago. Now I'm an actor.

Lee: An actor! I thought you looked familiar.

Bob: Well, not really. I (12) _haven't worked_ (not work) as an actor (13) _since_ last October. In fact, last night I (14) _started_ (start) to work as a waiter at the Zenon. *That's*

Lee: Really? I (15) _ate_ (eat) there last night. *That's* why you look familiar!

LESSON PLAN 2

FOCUS 5 [10 minutes]

1. **Lead-in:** Write incorrect and correct statements on the board using the verbs on the bottom left of the chart. Ask students to explain why they think these sentences are incorrect and/or correct. Some example sentences are below.

   * I've begun to study English for three years.

   I began to study English three years ago. OR I've studied English for three years

   * I have ended my relationship with him for two years. (incorrect)

   I ended my relationship with him two years ago. OR I haven't had a relationship with him for two years.

   * I've met her for three months. (incorrect)

   I met her three months ago. OR I've known her for three months.

   * I have stopped smoking for ten years. (incorrect)

   I stopped smoking ten years ago. OR I haven't smoked for ten years.

   * I have left Europe for 20 years. (incorrect)

   I left Europe 20 years ago. OR I haven't been in Europe for 20 years.

2. Read the examples and explanations in the chart.

3. Ask students to come up with their own examples, if they can.

EXERCISE 7 [15 minutes]

This exercise provides students with the opportunity for practice both in using the target structures and in explaining and defending their answers.

1. Have students work in pairs or small groups.

2. Circulate while students are working to check for accuracy. Encourage discussion of *why* the present perfect can or cannot be used.

3. Note items students disagree on (if any), or ask students to raise questions on those items that they couldn't agree on.

4. Review the answers as a class. Refer to the answer key on LP page 204.

EXPANSION [30 minutes]

You may want to use Activity 5 (listening) on SB page 210 after this exercise. This activity practices the use of the present perfect in the context of a job interview.

EXERCISE 8 [15 minutes]

This exercise combines practice of *since* and *for* with choice of correct tense.

1. Read the introduction to the exercise and read the first example.

2. Set a time limit for students to complete the answers individually.

3. Have students compare answers in pairs.

4. Check the answers as a class. Refer to the answer key on LP page 204.

5. You might want to review items 2 and 7 and ask students: Can *for* be omitted?

For more practice, use *Grammar Dimensions 2* Workbook page 91, Exercise 7.

EXPANSION 1 [30 minutes]

You may decide to use this conversation for pronunciation practice.

1. Give students a few minutes to work with a partner, and check to make sure they have the same answers for each blank.

2. Remind students to link words together smoothly and to use appropriate stress and intonation—falling intonation at the end of a statement, rising intonation at the end of a *yes/no* question, and louder volume/higher pitch for important or surprising information.

3. If appropriate, re-read each statement to demonstrate and then have students repeat.

EXPANSION 2 [30 minutes]

You may want to use Activity 6 (speaking/listening) on SB page 211 after this exercise. This activity practices the use of the present perfect in the context of a job interview.

EXERCISE 9

Look for mistakes in the following passage. Correct any mistakes that you find. One mistake has been corrected for you.

1. My sister is very good at languages. She studies

2. Italian at the language institute. She started studying

3. Italian in 1993, so she ~~studies~~ studied Italian several years. When

4. she was a child, she wanted to learn Russian and she still

5. wants to learn it. She has wanted to learn Russian

6. since a long time, but Russian courses are not offered

7. at the language schools near her home. Two years ago

8. she has found out that the local community college offers

9. courses in Chinese, so she started learning Chinese.

10. Unfortunately, she doesn't have a car, so she takes the bus

11. to school since two years.

Use Your English

ACTIVITY 1 speaking

Work in pairs or groups of three. Complete the following with information about your partner(s). Make a list of appropriate questions and then ask your partner(s) the questions. Here are some sample questions:

How long have you studied English?   *How long have you lived in this town?*

1. _____ for _____ hours.

2. _____ since _____ .

3. _____ for _____ .

4. _____ for _____ years.

5. _____ since _____ .

ACTIVITY 2 speaking

Work individually. Respond to this survey. Each response is a number.

____ The number of people you have talked to today

____ The number of weeks, months, or years you have known your oldest friend

____ The number of weeks, months, or years you have studied in this school

____ The number of hours or minutes since you last ate something

____ The number of minutes you have been in this classroom

Work in pairs. Say one number to your partner (in random order). Your partner has to guess what each number means.

Example:
A: *Five*
B: *Is that the number of weeks you have studied in this school?*

ACTIVITY 3 speaking/listening

■ **STEP 1** Work with a partner. Read the statements in the chart on page 208 and try to match each statement to someone in your class. Write the name in the column marked Guesses.

■ **STEP 2** Next, ask your classmates questions using *How long have you . . . ?* in order to find out who has done each thing the longest and shortest amounts of time. Fill in the answers in the column marked Facts.

Continued on the next page

ANSWER KEY

Exercise 9 Error in parentheses. **3.** (several years) *for several years* **6.** (since) *for* **8.** (has found out) *found out* **10.** (takes) *has taken* **11.** (since) *for*

EXERCISE 9 [10 minutes]

This exercise reviews the main grammar points presented in this unit.

1. You may want to assign this exercise for homework and review the answers in class.

2. If you think it will be helpful for students to gain more practice in talking about grammar, ask them to explain why they rewrote the statement the way they did: What was wrong with the original statement? Why is the rewritten statement better/correct?

EXPANSION [30 minutes]

You may want to use Activity 4 (speaking/listening/writing) on SB page 208 after this exercise, followed by Activity 7 (research on the web) on SB page 211.

UNIT GOAL REVIEW [10 minutes]

Ask students to look at the goals on the opening page of the unit again. Refer to the pages of the unit where information on each goal can be found.

ExamView® Test Generator   For assessment of Unit 13, use *Grammar Dimensions 2 ExamView®*.

USE YOUR ENGLISH

This Use Your English section of activities at the end of the unit contain situations that should naturally elicit the structures covered in the unit. For a more complete discussion of how to use the Use Your English activities, see To the Teacher, LP page xxii. When students are doing these activities in class, you can circulate and listen to see if they are using the structures accurately. Errors can be corrected after the activity has finished.

ACTIVITY 1 speaking [10 minutes]

You may want to use this activity after Exercise 1 on SB page 199. The purpose of this activity is for students to ask questions that will enable them to complete the sentences about their partner. The topics are up to them.

1. Give students 2 or 3 minutes to come up with questions that will enable them to fill in the sentences.

2. Circulate to listen for errors as well as creative and interesting examples.

3. Select students to read their sentences out loud.

EXPANSION

Invite a native speaker visitor, or several visitors, to your class if possible. Have students interview these people and record these interviews if people are comfortable with this. You can listen more closely for the use of simple present tense, simple past tense, present perfect, *since* and *for*.

ACTIVITY 2 speaking [10 minutes]

You may want to use this activity after Exercise 2 on SB page 200. This is a guessing game using real information about students.

1. Explain that students will write a list of five numbers.

2. Each number represents one of the items in the list.

3. Model the activity by writing a few numbers for yourself on the board.

4. Students will try to guess what they mean.

5. Allow 2 minutes for students to write their list of numbers. They should not show them to their partner.

6. Then, working in pairs, each student will say a number in turn. The other student will try to guess what it means.

ACTIVITY 3 speaking/listening [30 minutes]

You may want to use this activity after Exercise 4 on SB page 201.

■ STEP 1

Have students work in pairs to try to fill out the "Guesses" column of the chart on SB page 208. They may ask each other questions such as: How long do you think Gina has worn glasses?

Note: It is a good idea if you can tell students to include you in their guesses if they want.

■ STEP 2

1. Now students can walk around and ask questions to see if their guesses were correct. They will ask questions such as: *How long have you worn glasses?* They will be able to fill out the "Facts" column of the chart.

2. Review the answers together as a class.

(Continued on LP page 209.)

TYPE OF LEADERSHIP

COUNTRY	President	Monarch*	Prime minister	Military	Other
Great Britain		✓	✓		

* King, queen, emperor, etc.

HOW CURRENT LEADER CAME INTO POWER

COUNTRY	Election	Succession**	Coup**	Other
Great Britain	✓ (Prime Minister)	✓ (Queen)		

* *Succession:* the act of a position or title passing from one person to another, usually a relative
** *Coup:* a sudden or violent seizure of power by a group that has not been elected

WHAT CURRENT LEADER HAS DONE

COUNTRY	Length of time the current leader has been in power	Best thing he or she has done while in power	Worst thing he or she has done while in power***

*** Talk about the leader of your country or another country for which you've listed information in the blank

---

ACTIVITY 3 continued

GUESSES	WHO......	FACTS
	has studied English the longest time?	
	has been married the longest time?	
	has owned his or her watch the longest time?	
	has known how to drive the longest time?	
	has known how to drive the shortest time?	
	has had the shoes he or she is wearing today the longest time?	
	has worn glasses the longest time?	
	has worn glasses the shortest time?	
	has had the same hair style the longest time?	

ACTIVITY 4 speaking/listening/writing

In this activity, you will find out how different countries are governed.

STEP 1 Get together with a group of classmates from different countries, if possible. First use the three charts on page 209 to note and list information about your own country or another country you are familiar with. We have done some for you, as examples.

STEP 2 When you have all filled in the charts, begin sharing your information. Then use the charts to take more notes on what your classmates tell you. In the first two charts, check (✓) the appropriate box or write in the box marked other. In the third chart, write notes.

STEP 3 Be ready to share this information with the rest of the class.

USE YOUR ENGLISH

VARIATION

This activity is also fun to do as an interview, with people new to your students. In this case, you wouldn't bother with Step 1 guesses (unless you don't mind getting apparently random answers). Instead, students' questions would concentrate on getting the facts (Step 2). If there are several people being interviewed, you will also be able to fill in the chart about who has done the various activities the longest.

ACTIVITY 4 speaking/listening/writing
[30 minutes]

You may want to assign the first part of this activity (filling out the charts) for homework.

You can introduce this activity with a brief discussion of the political system in Great Britain, based on the headings in the chart. Or if you are more familiar with another country's system, that would be appropriate.

■ STEP 1

Have students choose a country that they know well. They will fill out the charts on SB page 209 for this country, either using their general knowledge or, if you have assigned this as homework, by doing some research.

■ STEP 2

1. Divide students into groups, so that each member of the group represents a different country. It can be the country they come from, or a country they have visited or know well.

2. Students can share their information in groups and complete the charts about each other's countries.

■ STEP 3

1. Ask volunteers to present the information to the class.

2. You can ask students to write a description of one country based on the information in the charts for homework.

Suggestion: If time allows, Activity 7 can also be used as a follow-up to this activity.

ACTIVITY 5 listening

CD Track 20

STEP 1

You are going to hear a job interview with a man applying for a job as an office manager. Listen to the job interview carefully. Do you think the man will get the job? Why or why not? Discuss with a partner.

STEP 2

Match the first part of each sentence in column A with the second part in column B.

A	B
1. I've worked	a. being part of a team.
2. I've been	b. able to solve every problem.
3. I've enjoyed	c. there for about three years.
4. I have found out	d. in charge of training the new staff.
5. I've learned	e. more or less everything there is to know about the job.
6. I haven't always been	f. how to work with people.

STEP 3

Listen to the audio again. This time, listen to all the interviewer's questions. Write them in the chart.

INTERVIEWER'S QUESTIONS
1.
2.
3.
4.
5.
6.

STEP 4

Role-play the interview with a partner. Change any of the questions or answers if you want.

ACTIVITY 6 speaking/listening

STEP 1

Find a classmate, a friend, or an acquaintance who is studying the same field as you, or who has or wants a job like yours. Conduct a practice job interview. You can work together to come up with questions, which should include when things happened and for how long: work experience, job history, and education. Feel free to make up information!

STEP 2

Decide who will be the "employer" (the interviewer) and who will be the "employee" (the interviewee). Take turns if there is time. Record the interviews.

STEP 3

Listen to the recording. Write down all the sentences with the present perfect. In each case, was it used correctly? Were *since* and *for* used? Were there cases where the present perfect should have been used but wasn't?

ACTIVITY 7 research on the web/writing

STEP 1

Choose a country that you are interested in. Go on the Internet and use a search engine such as Google® or Yahoo® to find out about the political system in that country. What kind of government does it have? When and how did the current leader come into power? What has the current leader done while he or she has been in power?

STEP 2

Write a brief summary of the information you found. Exchange reports with a classmate and check to make sure that the present perfect was used correctly.

ACTIVITY 8 reflection

Write three things you have done that have helped you to learn English. Make a class list and display the results as a class poster.

ANSWER KEY

Activity 5 **Step 2:** 1. c 2. d 3. a 4. e 5. f 6. b
Step 3 *Check audio script on LP page S-5 for answers.*

USE YOUR ENGLISH

ACTIVITY 5 — listening [30 minutes]

CD Track 20

You may want to use this activity after Exercise 7 on SB page 204.

1. Ask students to predict what kinds of questions are usually asked at a job interview. Write their suggestions on the board.

2. Ask if any of your students have been through such an experience. Ask them what kinds of questions they were asked, what kinds of answers they gave (or would have liked to give!), and what questions they weren't especially prepared for.

■ STEP 1

1. Explain that students will listen to a job interview and that they should listen for the answers to the main question: Do you think the man will get the job?

2. Play the audio. See audio script on LP page S-5 for answers. Have students compare their answers in pairs and tell you their opinions.

■ STEP 2

1. Allow time for students to match up the sentence halves before listening again.

2. Play the audio again.

3. Check the answers. See the audio script on LP page S-5 for answers.

■ STEP 3

1. Play the audio again, pausing the recording if necessary to allow time for students to write the questions.

2. Ask volunteers to come and write the questions on the board.

3. See the audio script on LP page S-5 for answers.

■ STEP 4

1. Have students role-play the interview in pairs (using appropriate intonation).

2. Ask volunteers to perform the role-play for the class.

ACTIVITY 6 — speaking/listening [30 minutes]

This activity builds on Activity 5. You can do this as an in-class interviewing activity, or assign this as homework.

■ STEP 1

1. Have students choose a partner who is interested in the same field or job as they are. This is important because students will work in pairs to develop the questions, and both students should have an understanding of what is required.

2. Have students create questions and decide on who will play which role.

■ STEP 2

1. Allow at least 10 to 15 minutes for students to practice their job interviews.

2. Record interviews if possible.

■ STEP 3

If possible, have some students perform their interviews for the class. Other students can take notes of whether *since*, *for*, and the present perfect were used correctly. They can also give positive feedback on how well they did in their interviews!

ACTIVITY 7 — research on the web/writing

This activity could be used as a follow-up to Activity 4. The purpose of this Internet search activity is to provide a natural context for using the present progressive. An additional purpose is to encourage students to share strategies for finding information on the Internet. After finding about the political system in the country they have chosen, encourage students to share search tips. What Web sites were most useful? What keywords did they use?

ACTIVITY 8 — reflection [15 minutes]

This activity provides an opportunity for students to use the target structures of the unit while reflecting on their language learning progress. You may have asked students to keep a record of their learning in a journal throughout this course as suggested in To the Teacher, LP page xxii. This reflection activity will form part of that learning record.

14

PRESENT PERFECT AND SIMPLE PAST
Ever, Never, Already, and Yet

UNIT GOALS

- Use present perfect and simple past appropriately

- Understand the meaning of *ever* and *never* in questions and statements

- Use present perfect questions appropriately

- Understand the meaning of *already* and *yet*

OPENING TASK

Around-the-world trip

■ **STEP 1**

Look at these pictures. Do you know any of these places?

■ **STEP 2**

Tosh and Yumiko are on a trip around the world. The cities are marked on the map on the next page. Starting in Tokyo, they are going to visit eight cities in four weeks. Look at Tosh and Yumiko's travel souvenirs. With a partner, draw Tosh and Yumiko's route on the map. Which places have they already visited? Which places haven't they visited yet?

■ **STEP 3**

Write down one city you have visited (in the world or in your state), one city you haven't visited, and one city you would like to visit. Walk around the classroom and find three people who have visited the same place names for each category. Discuss why you chose to write down those places.

ANSWER KEY

Opening Task **Step 1:** Top picture: Sydney, Australia's Opera House; Second picture, left: London, England's Big Ben; Third picture, right: Moscow, Russia's St. Basil's Cathedral. **Step 2** They have already visited Sydney, Honolulu, San Francisco, New York, and Paris. They have not yet visited London, Singapore, or Hong Kong. **Step 3** Answers will vary.

14 LESSON PLAN 1

UNIT OVERVIEW

Using a travel and entertainment theme, this unit focuses on the contrast between the present perfect and simple past. The meaning and use of *ever, never, already,* and *yet* are also presented.

GRAMMAR NOTE

The present perfect is used to describe past events viewed from the perspective of the present. It is used to talk about past events that have a connection with the present, started in the past and continue up to the present, or have happened just recently. Although the use of the present perfect can be more easily explained by saying that it is used for nonspecific times in the past, it is the connection of the past with the present that makes this tense applicable. When we say *I haven't been to Paris,* for example, we mean that we have not been to Paris in our lives up to now. When we say *I've already eaten dinner,* we mean I'm not hungry now, or I don't need any dinner now.

UNIT GOALS

Some instructors may want to review the goals listed on this page after completing the Opening Task so that students understand what they should know by the end of the unit. These goals can also be reviewed at the end of the unit when students are more familiar with the grammar terminology.

OPENING TASK [20 minutes]

The purpose of the Opening Task is to create a context in which students will need to use the present perfect. The problem-solving format is designed to show the teacher how well the students can produce the target structures implicitly and spontaneously when they are engaged in a communicative task. For a more complete discussion of the purpose of the Opening Task, see To the Teacher, Lesson Planner (LP) page xxii.

Setting Up the Task

STEP 1

1. Get the students to start thinking about the travel theme by briefly brainstorming places they would like to visit, and interesting places they have already visited.

2. Look at the pictures on Student Book (SB) page 212 and see if students can identify these places. Would they like to visit them? Why? Have they already been there? Did they like it? Why/why not?

Conducting the Task

STEP 2

1. Make sure students understand the task by first reading the task description, then asking students to repeat the directions to you in short steps, in their own words.

2. Allow students time to work out the problem in pairs. Do not offer too much assistance at this stage (unless they do not understand the directions). In the course of trying to work out the problem, they should be trying to use the present perfect.

3. Circulate while students are talking and make notes of their use of the present perfect. Is anyone using *already,* or *not . . . yet?* Take notes of good examples.

Note: This can be very helpful when you review Unit Goals at the end of the chapter; you can put some "before and after" examples on the board to show them how much they have learned.

Closing the Task

STEP 3

1. This step returns to the questions you asked in Step 1. If you have kept a record of the cities your students have visited, or haven't visited yet, you may point to these on the board as an example.

2. Have students write three cities in their notebooks, and ask questions to find other people with three same cities. For example, if student A has written that she has visited Paris, she should find three other people who have also visited Paris.

3. Do not correct errors at this stage, but you may take note of errors to use as a bridge to Focus Chart 1.

GRAMMAR NOTE

Typical student errors (form)

- Errors with past participles, e.g. * *I haven't saw her today.*
- Errors with word order and *yet* and *already,* e.g. * *I not yet have seen her.* * *I have been already to Paris.*
- Error in short answers, * *No, I haven't ever.* (Instead of: *No, never.*)

Typical student errors (use)

- Using present perfect with time expressions that denote finished time, e.g. * *I have graduated last year.* Or with *When,* e.g. * *When have you been there?*
- Using simple present for time up to now, e.g. * *I go to Italy three times already.*
- Confusion between *yet* and *already,* e.g. * *I didn't eat dinner already.* * *I have yet seen it.*

FOCUS 1

Present Perfect versus Simple Past

use

EXAMPLES	EXPLANATIONS
(a) Last year, she **graduated** from high school.	Use the simple past to talk about something that happened at a **specific time** in the past.
(b) He **lived** in this house from 1880 to 1888.	Use the simple past to show when something happened.
(c) He **has been** to Mexico. (d) They **have run** a marathon.	Use the present perfect when you talk about something that happened in the past without mentioning the specific time it happened. The experience is more important than when it happened.
(e) I **have been** to Thailand. I **went** there about ten years ago and **traveled** all over. I **had** a great time. The Thai people **were** open and friendly to tourists.	Use the present perfect to introduce the general idea. Use the simple past to give specific details.

EXERCISE 1

There is a "classic" film festival in town featuring a number of famous American movies at several different movie theaters. Robert loves classic movies, and so he is planning to invite some friends to a movie on Saturday night. Naturally, he wants to suggest a movie that nobody has seen. Use the information below to help him choose.

FILM FESTIVAL SCHEDULE

BALBOA 38th & Balboa 555~8184	CORONET Geary & Arguelio 555~4400	METRO Union-Webster 555~1835
HIGH NOON 4:55 8:30 10:55	ON THE WATERFRONT 1:20 3:30 5:37 7:30	CASABLANCA 1:00 3:15 5:30 10:00
ROMAN HOLIDAY 6:50 10:25	GALAXY Van Ness & Sutter 555~8700	REGENCY Van Ness & Sutter 555~6773
PSYCHO 12:30 4:45 8:40 11:15	THE GODFATHER 6:10 8:30 10:55	THE GRADUATE 4:40 7:40 10:30

Ann has seen the movie at the Coronet.
Patty and Mark went to the Metro last night.
Karen went to the Balboa on Tuesday to see the movie that started at 8:30.
Tom went to the Galaxy last weekend.
Carolyn and Terry have seen the movie at the Regency.
A couple of days ago Robert went to the Balboa and saw the movie that started at 8:40.

1. Which movie should they see?
2. Have you seen any of these movies?
3. Find out how many of your classmates have seen these movies.

EXERCISE 2

Use the information from Exercise 1 to make questions that fit with the following answers. The first one has been done for you.

1. *Did Carolyn and Terry go to the movies yesterday?*

   Yes, they did. They went to see *The Graduate* yesterday.

2. Has Tom seen . . .

   Yes, Tom has seen *The Godfather*.

ANSWER KEY

Exercise 1   1. *Roman Holiday*   2. and 3. Answers will vary.

GRAMMAR NOTE

The simple past and the present perfect are two different ways of looking at past events from the point of view of the speaker. The simple past is used for events that are viewed as finished, and are therefore frequently used together with the specific time phrases (yesterday, last year, in 1980, etc.). The present perfect is used for events that occurred in that past but that have a connection to the present. For example, *I have been to Thailand* means *in my life up to now*. In this case we do not emphasize the exact time that event took place.

As was shown in Unit 13, however, the present perfect *can* be used with specific time phrases. For example, *I have lived in Texas for ten years*. In the sample dialogue previous about Paris, the time period begins in the past and includes the present. The difference is that the simple past is then used with time expressions that denote finished time, while the present perfect is used with time periods that are not viewed as finished.

FOCUS 1 [10 minutes]

This focus chart contrasts the use of the simple past for past finished events, and the use of the present perfect for past events at a nonspecific time.

1. **Lead-in:** Use true information about your students from the Opening Task to write examples on the board using simple past and present perfect. For example:

   Leon has been to Mexico.

   Elena hasn't been to Germany.

   Francisco went to Canada last winter.

   Yeo visited Florida two years ago.

2. Ask students if they can work out why the simple past is used in some examples and not in others. Why is it incorrect to say: * Yeo has visited Florida two years ago. (Answer: Because the time is not specified. See Grammar Note above.)

3. Read the examples and the explanations in the focus chart.

4. For the simple past examples, ask questions to emphasize the nonspecified time, such as: *When did she graduate?* (Last year.) *When did Benjamin Franklin live there?* (From 1880–1888.) *When did she go to Mexico?* (We don't know.) *When did they run a marathon?* (We don't know.)

5. Practice some short conversations about places students have visited (This type of conversation will be revisited in Focus Chart 2).

   Student A: *Have you ever been to (Paris)?*
   Student B: *Yes, I have. I went there last spring.*
   Student A: *How was it? Did you like it? etc.*

EXERCISE 1 [20 minutes]

This exercise practices the use of the present perfect in a natural context. The problem-solving format focuses attention on language use rather than grammatical explanation.

1. Introduce the topic of movies by asking students what famous movies they have seen. You may ask them to suggest several that they think are "classic" movies (to illustrate the meaning of *classic*).

2. Check that students understand the chart by asking some questions. For example, *At which cinema can you see the movie Roman Holiday? At what different times is Casablanca showing? What film is showing at the Coronet?* Have students ask and answer these and similar questions, too.

3. Have students work in pairs or groups to solve the problem.

4. When they have finished, they can move on to questions 2 and 3.

5. Check and compare answers as a class. Refer to the answer key on LP page 214 for question. Other answers will all vary.

EXPANSION [15 minutes]

Have students answer question 3 by doing a "Find someone who . . ." competition.

1. Have students walk around the room and poll their classmates to find one person who has seen each film.

2. Students ask, *Have you seen . . . (name of movie)?* Once they have found a person who can answer *yes* to one of the movies, they write their name next to that film and move on to another classmate and ask about another film.

3. Once students have found seven people for the seven films, they sit down. The first person to sit down is the winner.

4. If no one answers *yes* to some of the films, see who has the most names.

EXERCISE 2 [15 minutes]

This exercise returns to the information in Exercise 1 and focuses on the formation of questions in the simple past and the present perfect.

1. Do the first example together as a class.

2. Have students complete the exercise individually.

3. Check the answers by eliciting students' questions and writing them on the board (or asking a volunteer student to write them).

4. Don't correct errors yourself; instead, invite the class to determine if the question is accurate and correct the errors if not. Refer to the answer key on LP pages 214 and 216.

FOCUS 2

Ever and *Never* in Questions and Statements

EXAMPLES	EXPLANATIONS
(a) **Have** you **ever** eaten Mexican food?	Use *ever* in questions with the present perfect to mean "at any time before now."
(b) Yes, I **have** eaten it. (c) NOT: Yes, I **have ever** eaten it.	*Ever* is not usually used in affirmative statements (those that mean or use *yes*).
(d) I **haven't ever** eaten it.	*Ever* is used in negative statements.
(e) I **have never** eaten it.	Use *never* with the present perfect to mean "at no time before now."
(f) No, **never**.	You can also use *No, never* as a short answer.

EXERCISE 4

Read the conversation. Underline and correct any mistakes.

Mick: Have you ever ~~visit~~ _visited_ Europe?

Dave: Yes. I've been there several times, in fact. Three years ago I've gone to France.

Mick: Really? Where did you go?

Dave: I went to Paris, of course. And then I rode my mountain bike in the Pyrenees. Last year I've ridden my bike in Germany and Switzerland. Have ever you been there?

Mick: I've never been to Germany, but I've ever been to Switzerland.

Dave: When was that?

Mick: I've taken an international business course there about eight years ago.

---

3. _Have Patty and Mark seen . . . ?_

   No, Patty and Mark haven't seen *High Noon.*

4. _Did Karen see High Noon last weekend?_

   No, she didn't see it last weekend. She saw it on Tuesday.

5. _Did Patty and Mark see Psycho?_

   No, they didn't see *Psycho.* They saw *Casablanca.*

6. _Has Robert seen Psycho?_

   Yes, he has. He saw it a couple of days ago.

7. _Have Carolyn and Terry seen Roman Holiday?_

   No, they haven't seen *Roman Holiday,* but they have seen *The Graduate.*

8. _Did Tom see The Godfather last night/yesterday/on Tuesday?_

   No, he didn't. He saw it last weekend.

EXERCISE 3

Alice is on vacation in New York City. Complete her postcard written to her family choosing verbs from the list below (some of the verbs can be used more than once). Use either the simple past or present perfect form of the verb.

try	see	walk	eat
have	go	spend	take

Hi Folks!

Having a great time! I (1) _have walked_ at least 50 miles, but (2) _have seen_ lots of interesting things. Yesterday I (3) _took_ the Staten Island Ferry, and on Thursday I (4) _went_ to the top of the Empire State Building. I (5) _have seen_ several shows. Two nights ago I (6) _went_ to see "Chicago." I (7) _had_ great tickets. Wonderful food!!! I (8) _have eaten_ some delicious meals. Yesterday I (9) _tried_ sushi for the first time. See you next week.

Love, Alice

P.S. I (10) _have spent_ lots of money!

The Murphys
1403 Eastwood
Ann Arbor, MI
48103

ANSWER KEY

Exercise 4 Errors are in parentheses. (I've gone); I went (I've ridden); I rode (Have ever you been); Have you ever been (I've ever been); I've been (I've taken); I took

EXERCISE 3 [15 minutes]

This exercise requires students to distinguish when to use the simple past and when to use the present perfect.

1. Check that students understand the situation by asking questions. For example, Who is the postcard from? Where is she now? Who is she writing to? Where do they live?

2. Ask if students notice any aspects of informal language—e.g., Having a great time instead of I'm having a great time.

3. Have students complete this individually in class or as homework.

4. Instruct pairs or small groups to compare their versions of the postcard.

5. Discuss points with which groups had disagreements. Note: Because Alice has written this postcard while she is in New York City, the present perfect often makes the most sense. If she were writing after leaving NYC, we would expect all of the verbs to appear in the simple past.

6. Have students write a similar postcard from their favorite city for homework (with pictures if possible).

7. Display the postcards in the classroom.

For more practice, use Grammar Dimensions 2 Workbook page 92, Exercise 1.

METHODOLOGY NOTE

It can be very motivating for students to know that their work will be read by others in the class or program. One reason is that students may start to think more carefully about their audience and how well their writing will be understood. When writing for the teacher, students presume the purpose is just for the teacher to check their mistakes. A second reason is that students can feel proud of their work and accomplishments in English. They can get inspiration from each others' work. This can enhance creativity and learning in your classroom.

EXPANSION [20 minutes]

You may want to use Activity 3 on SB page 222 after this exercise. This can be followed by Activity 4 (writing) on SB page 223.

FOCUS 2 [15 minutes]

This focus chart presents the meaning of ever and never with the present perfect (see Language Note).

1. Lead-in: You may want to introduce this section with a quick review of irregular past participles. (See Appendix 5 SB page A-13). You can do this by "dictating" a list of verbs and having students listen and write the past participle of each one.

ride	be	do
forget	go	see
read	fly	eat
write	drive	drink

2. Then ask students to come and write their answers on the board.

3. Ask students to make Have you ever . . . questions with each verb.

4. Read the examples and explanations in the focus chart.

5. Note the position of (n)ever in front of the main (not auxiliary) verb in question and statement forms:

Q: Has she *ever* tasted Vietnamese food.
A: No, I don't think she has *ever* tried it.

LANGUAGE NOTE

Ever can also be used with the simple past and other tenses, so it is probably best to avoid saying it is *always* used with the present perfect.

1. It is possible to use ever and never with the simple past when referring to a specific (finished) time. For example, Did you ever eat alligator meat when you lived in Australia? I never saw any alligators when I lived in Australia.

2. You can also use ever with the past perfect. For example, It was the most beautiful house I had ever seen. I had never seen such a beautiful home. Or with the future, for example, When will you ever learn to be quiet? I will never forget her face.

In spoken colloquial American English, the simple past is often used with ever and never with no change in meaning. For example, *Did you ever try alligator meat?* (= Have you ever tried alligator meat?) *I never tried this kind of meat before.* (= I have never tried this kind of meat before.) While this is common in spoken English, students should be encouraged to use the present perfect for these cases in standard written English.

EXERCISE 4 [10 minutes]

This exercise practices the skill of editing while reviewing the use of the present perfect, *ever*, *never*, and word order.

1. You may want to assign this exercise for homework.

2. Have pairs come to a consensus on errors and corrections.

3. Copy the conversation on an overhead transparency and review the exercise as a class. Refer to the answer key on LP page 216.

For more practice, use *Grammar Dimensions 2* Workbook page 93, Exercise 2.

EXPANSION [20 minutes]

You may want to use Activity 1 on SB page 221 after this exercise.

FOCUS 3

Present Perfect in Questions

use

EXAMPLES	EXPLANATIONS
(a) A: **Have you ever eaten** frogs' legs? B: No, I haven't.	Use the present perfect with *ever* when you want to know **if** something has happened.
(b) A: **Have you ever been** to Sub-Saharan Africa? B: Yes, I have.	When you ask these questions, you usually expect the answer to be *Yes, I have* or *No, I haven't.*
(c) A: **When did you go** there? B: I went there last year.	Use the simple past in questions when you want to know **when** something happened.

EXERCISE 5

Complete the conversations, using the present perfect or the simple past of the verb in parentheses. The first one has been done for you.

1. A: Excuse me, sir, we're doing a survey. Can I ask you a few questions?
   B: Sure, go ahead.
   A: (1) <u>Have you ever used</u> (you/use/ever) WonderWhite detergent?
   B: No, (2) ——— (I/try/never)it.
   A: Why not?
   B: (3) ——— (I/do/never) laundry in my life. My wife always does it.
   A: What about you, sir? (4) ——— (you/wash/ever) your clothes with WonderWhite?
   C: Yes, (5) ——— (I/try) it.
   A: When (6) ——— (you/try) it for the first time?
   C: (7) ——— (I/use) it for the first time about six months ago.

2. A: (1) ——— (you/read/ever) any books by Latin American writers?
   B: Yes, I (2) ——— . I (3) ——— (read) a great novel by a Colombian writer a few years ago.
   A: Which one?
   B: I (4) ——— (forget) his name. He (5) ——— (win) the Nobel Prize several years ago.
   A: Oh, you mean Gabriel García Márquez.

3. A: My brother is coming to stay with us for a few days next week. Do you have any ideas about how we can entertain him?
   B: (1) ——— (he/be/ever) here before?
   A: Yes. He (2) ——— (come) once about three years ago.
   B: (3) ——— (he/go) to Chinatown then?
   A: No, (4) ——— (he/be/never) to Chinatown, but (5) ——— (he/travel) a lot in China and in the Far East.
   B: Maybe you'd better not take him to the Greek restaurant when he was here three years ago! (6) ——— (you/take) him to Chinatown then!
   A: No, and (7) ——— (he/visit/never) Greece.
   B: Great! Why don't you take him there?

4. A: ——— (you/go out) last night?
   B: Yes. (2) ——— (we/go) to that new Italian restaurant.
   A: What's it like? (3) ——— (I/be/never) there.
   B: It's O.K., but (4) ——— (I/eat) better Italian food in other restaurants.
   A: (5) ——— (you/try/ever) the one on Main Street?
   B: Yes. (6) ——— (we/have) great meal there last weekend.

FOCUS 4

Already and Yet

meaning

EXAMPLES	EXPLANATIONS
(a) I've **already** eaten. (b) I haven't eaten **yet**.	Use *already* to show that an event was completed earlier. Use *yet* when an event has **not** been completed before the time of speaking.
(c) Have you eaten **yet**? (d) Have you eaten **already**? OR (e) Have you **already** eaten?	*Yet* in questions is more neutral than *already*. The use of *already* in questions shows that the speaker expects that an event has happened before the time of speaking.

ANSWER KEY

Exercise 5   1. B: I have/I've never tried; B: I have/I've never done; A: Have you ever washed; C: I have/I've tried; A: did you try; C: I used   2. A: Have you ever read; B: have; read; B: have/I've forgotten; won   3. B: Has he ever been; A: came; B: Has he been; A: he has/he's never been; he has traveled; B: Did you take; A: he has never visited   4. A: Did you go out; B: We went; A: I have/I've never been there; B: I have/I've eaten; A: Have you ever tried; B: We had a

FOCUS 3 [10 minutes]

This focus chart continues with question-forming.

1. **Lead-in:** Write the example questions from the chart on the board and brainstorm possible answers to these questions. This may help students to see how grammar structures fit into the natural flow of conversations. For example:
Question: Have you ever eaten frogs' legs?
Possible answers: Yes, I have. No, I haven't. No, never. Yes, in 2005/when I went to Paris/last week. Yes, they were delicious OR they were disgusting. No, and I don't want to. Etc.

2. Read the examples and explanations in the chart and note whether students came up with similar explanations.

3. Point out how example (c) continues the conversation from example (b). This will help with Exercise 5. Also see Language Note below.

LANGUAGE NOTE

1. Because the present perfect is used to ask **if** something has ever happened, it is often used to start conversations. However, once the *if* has been established, the conversation usually shifts to the simple past, to find out more about the situation:
A: **Has** Amanda ever **visited** you in Washington?
B: Yeah, she **came** to visit 5 months ago.
A: **Did** she **come** for work or just for fun?
B: Just for fun. We **got** to see so many concerts while she was here. It **was** so cool!

2. *Never* is not commonly used in questions; in rare cases it can be used to express surprise at someone's statement. For example,
A: I don't know anything about computers.
B: **Have** you **never used one before?**
The more common response would be:
B: **Haven't** you **ever used one before?**

Have you finished your homework already? (= You finished earlier than expected.)
Have you seen Pirates of the Caribbean yet? (= I expect that you will.)
Have you seen Pirates of the Caribbean already? (= It has only been out for short time, and I am surprised that you have seen it.)
I haven't been to Paris yet. (= but I'm planning to visit some time in the future.)
I've been to Paris already. (= so I don't need to go there again.)
I haven't done the dishes yet. (= but I'm planning on doing them later.)
I've done the dishes already. (= earlier than you expected.)

2. You can further illustrate the use of *already* and *yet* by taking examples from the Opening Task or from information you've learned about your students. For example:
Max has **already** been to . . . , but he hasn't been to . . . **yet.**
  Q: Has Jaro's band recorded a CD **yet?**
  A: Uh-huh. They've **already** recorded two CDs, actually.

3. Read the examples and explanations in the focus chart.

4. Notice the different word order with these two expressions.

EXERCISE 5 [15 minutes]

This exercise practices conversations that transition from present perfect to simple past.

1. Do this activity as a class.

2. Copy this page onto an overhead transparency and invite students to volunteer answers.

3. If errors are made, refer students back to the explanations in the focus chart. Refer to the answer key on LP page 218.

4. Have students read the conversations aloud using appropriate word-linking and intonation.

 For more practice, use *Grammar Dimensions 2* Workbook page 94, Exercise 3.

EXPANSION [20 minutes]

You may want to use Activity 7 (listening) on SB page 224 after Exercise 5.

You may want to use Activity 2 on SB page 222 as a way of reviewing the present perfect before introducing the next phase of the unit.

LESSON PLAN 2

FOCUS 4 [10 minutes]

This focus chart introduces the present perfect with *already* and *yet*. *Yet* is used in negative sentences and questions. *Already* is used in affirmative sentences and questions.

1. **Lead-in:** Contrast some examples with *yet* and *already*. Ask students to try to identify the difference in meaning. For example:
Have you finished your homework yet? (= I hope you will finish it soon.)

Use Your English

ACTIVITY 1 listening/speaking/writing

■ STEP 1

In this activity, you will be finding out about some of the things that your classmates have done. Look at the list in the box below. Move around the class and ask questions to see if you can find anyone who has ever done any of these things.

First you need to find who has had the experience (name); then you need to get specific details about the experience (when) (where) (how/why). Take notes below; it is not necessary to write full sentences at this point. In the box marked ***, you can add an experience of your own if you want to.

Be ready to share your findings with the rest of the class.

HAVE YOU EVER ....?

Experience	Name	When	Where	How/Why
met a famous person				
climbed a mountain				
seen a shark				
felt really frightened				
flown in a hot-air balloon				
***				

■ STEP 2

Now use the information you collected to write a report on your findings. Here is one way you can start your report:

I have interviewed some of my classmates about things they have done before now, and I have learned some interesting things about their past experiences. For example,....

EXERCISE 6

Get information from your classmates about the following topics and add topics of your own. Use *already, yet, ever,* and *never* in your questions when appropriate.

1. study other languages (besides English)
2. receive an F in a class
3. receive an A in a class
4. give a speech
5. be a teacher/teach students
6. feel nervous about speaking another language
7. feel excited about studying/learning
8. earn a Bachelor's degree
9. forget about a test that was scheduled
10. finish studying this chapter
11. master the present perfect tense

EXERCISE 7

Sue and her roommate Betsy are discussing their evening plans. Fill in the missing parts of their conversation. Use *already, yet, ever,* and *never* when appropriate.

Sue: (1) _Have you eaten yet_ ?

Betsy: No, not yet. But I'm hungry. I didn't eat lunch.

Sue: Well, should we go out to eat? I'd love to try that new Mexican restaurant down the street. (2) _Have you ever eaten/been/gone there?_

Betsy: No, (3) _I never have/not yet_. I was going to go with Deb and Rebecca last week, but at the last minute they changed their minds. (4) _Have you ever gone_ out to eat with them? They have a hard time making decisions!

Sue: No, (5) _I never have_ . One time we made plans to, but at the last minute they canceled.

Betsy: I'd rather be invited to their house for dinner, anyway. Deb's a great cook. She went to a chef's school in Paris. (6) _Have you eaten a dinner that she cooked_

Sue: (7) _Yes, I have_ . She makes the best chicken curry. Yum! Which reminds me. . . . You're not the only one that's hungry! Do you need to stop at the ATM on the way to the restaurant?

Betsy: No, (8) _I already did/stopped there_

Sue: Well, good, let's go then.

ANSWER KEY

Exercise 6 Answers will vary.

EXERCISE 6 [20 minutes]

This exercise practices the use of present perfect and the use of yet and already. When talking about these topics, students should progress naturally from present perfect to simple past (see Focus Chart 3).

1. Model one of the topics with a student, or ask two students to model a conversation. For example:

   A: *Have you ever studied any languages besides English?*

   B: *Yes, I have studied Portuguese.*

   A: *Oh really? Was it difficult?*

2. Have students work in pairs to talk about all the topics.

3. Circulate to monitor their language use. The focus is on communication, but you can take notes of errors (as well as good examples) to review at the end of the exercise.

4. Ask pairs to repeat some of their conversations for the class.

5. Review common errors and good examples with the whole class. Allow students to correct their own errors and correct each others' errors before providing the correct version.

EXERCISE 7 [15 minutes]

This exercise practices the ability to recognize contexts where the target structures should be used.

1. As you go over the directions, point out that students will find clues to how to form the questions and answers from the context of the other sentences given.

2. Students can complete this exercise individually or in pairs.

3. Review the answers as a class. Refer to the answer key on LP page 220.

For more practice, use *Grammar Dimensions 2* Workbook pages 95–97, Exercise 4.

---

ask each person they encounter only one question and then move on to another person. You may want to join in the activity, too.

4. Arrange a signal for students to stop talking and sit down (May need to change if we cut Methodology Note.).

5. Have volunteers report back on some of the interesting facts they discovered about their classmates.

STEP 2

Have students start writing their reports in class and continue for homework.

VARIATION

You can use the experiences in the chart, or use them as a guide to create your own to match the interests of your class. Or have the class create their own experiences around a theme. Some thematic examples are: the law (*gotten a speeding ticket, jay-walked, taken supplies from your workplace*) or the truth (*told someone they looked nice when you thought they looked terrible, lied about their age*).

UNIT GOAL REVIEW [10 minutes]

Ask students to look at the goals on the opening page of the unit again. Refer to the pages of the unit where information on each goal can be found.

ExamView Test Generator — For assessment of Unit 14, use *Grammar Dimensions 2* ExamView®.

USE YOUR ENGLISH

The Use Your English activities at the end of the unit contain situations that should naturally elicit the structures covered in the unit. For a more complete discussion of how to use the Use Your English activities, see To the Teacher, LP page xxii. While students are doing these activities in class, you can circulate and listen to see if they are using the structures accurately. Errors can be corrected after the activity has finished.

ACTIVITY 1 listening/speaking/writing [30 minutes]

You may want to use this activity after Exercise 4 on SB page 217.

STEP 1

1. Model one of the topics with a student, or ask two students to model a conversation. For example,

   A: *Have you ever met a famous person?*

   B: *Yes, I have.*

   A: *Oh really? Who? What was his/her name? Where did you meet him/her?*

2. Ask students to copy the charts in their notebooks.

3. Have students stand up and walk around the classroom with notebooks and pens. They should

---

METHODOLOGY NOTE

A good way to encourage a relaxed atmosphere and to get shy students talking is to play soft background music while doing these walk-around activities. The music is relaxing and decreases inhibitions about making mistakes. It can also influence the speed of talking. Rather lively music, for example, can make the conversations more lively. It can also be used as way of starting and stopping the activity—when you turn off (or gradually fade out) the music, students will know it is time to stop talking and sit down again.

ACTIVITY 2 speaking/listening

Move around the class and ask questions to find out if the following statements are true or false. If the statement is true, write T beside it; if it is false, write F.

1. Somebody in this room has appeared on TV. _____
2. Everybody here has eaten tacos. _____
3. At least three people have never ridden a motorcycle. _____
4. Somebody has swum in more than two oceans. _____
5. Several people have seen a ghost. _____
6. At least three people have been to Disneyland. _____
7. Nobody has been to Paris. _____
8. Somebody has run a marathon. _____
9. Half the class has never played soccer. _____
10. Somebody has never driven a car. _____

ACTIVITY 3 speaking/listening

The purpose of this activity is to confuse your classmates. You will tell the class about three things you have done in your life. Two of these things are true, but one is false. Your classmates will try to guess which one is false. For example:

I have ridden a bicycle from San Francisco to Los Angeles.
I have traveled by boat down the Nile.
I have broken my leg twice.

Which statement is false?

In order to decide which one is false, your classmates can ask you questions about the specific details of each experience. For example: "When did you ride your bike to Los Angeles?" "How long did it take?" "Which leg did you break?" and so on. After they have listened to your answers, the class will vote on which experience is false.

Take turns talking about your true and false experiences until everyone has taken part.

ACTIVITY 4 writing or speaking/listening

STEP 1

Write down one of the true stories you told in Activity 3, this time providing lots of details. Read the story aloud and record it.
OR If you want practice in telling the story without writing it down first, take a few minutes to think about the details you want to include. Then tell the story to a classmate and record it.

STEP 2

Listen to your own or each other's recordings for verb tense usage. Was the present perfect used? If it wasn't, were there cases where it should have been used? Was the simple past used correctly? Did you use already, yet, ever, and never appropriately?

ACTIVITY 5 speaking/listening

You have probably had many different experiences since you came to this country, this city, or this school. In this activity you will be finding out the best and worst experiences your classmates have had since they came here. First, go around the room and get as much information as you can from at least three different people. Use the chart to take notes on the information your classmates give you.

NAME	LENGTH OF STAY	BEST EXPERIENCE	WORST EXPERIENCE

ANSWER KEY

Activities 2–5 All answers will vary.

ACTIVITY 2 — speaking/listening [25 minutes]

You may want to use this activity before Focus Chart 4 on SB page 219. This can be a good class warm-up activity a few days into the unit as it provides review of the use of present perfect and acts as a "getting-to-know-you" exercise.

1. In this activity, students must turn the statements into questions. Make sure students understand that they have to create *you* questions—e.g., *Have you ever appeared on TV?* (Not: Has somebody in this room appeared on TV?)

2. Set a time limit for students to find out whether all the statements are true or false. A longer time limit (20 minutes) will allow students to extend their conversations to find out more information. A shorter time limit (10 minutes) will limit the conversations to just one question and answer.

3. Model a conversation with one student, or ask two students to model a conversation. For example:

    A: *Have you ever appeared on TV?*
    B: *No, I haven't.*
    A: *Have you ever eaten tacos?*
    B: *Yes, I have.*
    A: *When did you last eat tacos?*

4. Ask individual students to report back on their results. For example, *Sentence number one is true because Antonio was on TV last year.* You may invite students to ask Antonio questions or ask Antonio to give more details to the class.

ACTIVITY 3 — speaking/listening [20 minutes]

You may want to use this activity after Exercise 3 on SB page 216. It provides good practice of the difference between present perfect and simple past. This activity can lead to further, written practice in Activity 4.

1. Model the activity by telling students three sentences about yourself, one of which is false. They must ask you questions to find out which sentence is false.

2. Allow 3 minutes for students to write three sentences about themselves.

3. Have students work in small groups, or if your class is small, have them tell the class.

4. Point out that students cannot directly ask if the statements are true or false. For example: "Have you ever ridden your bicycle from San Francisco to Los Angeles?" would not be permitted.

5. To make the activity more difficult, have students start by asking *yes/no* questions only (*Did it take 5 hours to ride your bicycle? NOT How long did it take you to ride to Los Angeles?*)

ACTIVITY 4 — writing or speaking/ listening [30 minutes]

This activity builds on Activity 3 and focuses on grammatical accuracy in using tenses.

STEP 1

1. Have students choose one of the true stories they told in Activity 3.

2. If you use this as a writing activity, you may want to assign the writing for homework.

3. If you use this as a speaking activity, allow 10 minutes for students to make notes of details to add to their stories. They can refer to the notes when telling the story, but should not read them.

4. Have individuals read their stories to the class.

5. If you do not have access to recording equipment, assign different students the task of listening for the present perfect, the simple past, *yet* and *already, never* and *ever.*

STEP 2

Review comments and possible errors as a class. Remember to balance positive comments with criticism.

METHODOLOGY NOTE

Step 2 of Activity 4 is an example of a peer editing activity that can help students focus on grammatical accuracy. If working with a recording, have students critique pronunciation as well as language form and use. They can note problem sounds or unusual intonation patterns, depending on what you have been covering in class. To help them structure their feedback, make a handout of specific points you want them to focus on. For example, list three different features they should focus on: grammar, pronunciation, and content.

ACTIVITY 5 — speaking/listening [30 minutes]

You may want to use this activity after Exercise 7 on SB page 220. This activity can lead to further, written practice in Activity 6.

1. Ask students to tell you what kinds of questions they would ask for each column in the chart.

    What's your name?
    How long have you been here?
    What is the best experience you have had?
    What is the worst experience you have had?

2. Have students copy the charts in their notebooks.

3. Have them stand up, walk around, ask three other students their questions, taking notes of the answers.

ACTIVITY 6 writing

You have been asked to write a short article for your college newspaper on the experiences of international students. Review the information you collected in Activity 5. Choose the two most interesting or surprising "best" experiences and the two most interesting or surprising "worst" experiences. Organize your article so that you talk first about the bad experiences and then about the good experiences. Start your article with a brief introduction to the topic and to the students you interviewed.

ACTIVITY 7 listening

CD Track 21

STEP 1 Listen to the audio of two people talking about their travels.

Take notes in the chart below, using information from their conversation.

	SPEAKER 1/THE MAN	SPEAKER 2/THE WOMAN
WHERE? area of the world countries (list them)		
WHEN? what year(s)? length of stay		
HOW? transportation hotels/guesthouses		
WHY? reasons for traveling types of experiences		

STEP 2 Discuss these questions with a partner: How would you describe each speaker's traveling style? In other words, what type of travel do they enjoy? What types of places do they stay in? Do they enjoy being tourists or residents? How does your own style of traveling compare or contrast with those described?

STEP 3 Now listen to the audio again for the way the speakers used verb tenses. List the phrases from the conversation where the speakers used the present perfect verb form in their questions or answers. Compare your list with your classmates' lists. Did the speakers use yet, ever, or never with the present perfect?

ACTIVITY 8 writing

Write a letter to a family member or a friend and tell him or her about the best and the worst experiences you have had since you left home. Review your letter for the use of the present perfect. If you feel comfortable sharing your letter with someone, you can review each other's letters. Was the present perfect used? If it wasn't, were there cases where it should have been used? Was the simple past used correctly? Did you use *already, yet, ever,* and *never* appropriately?

ACTIVITY 9 research on the web

Ask your partner if he or she has ever used the Internet for any of the following, or done any of the following on the Internet. Then choose one of the topics. Go on the Internet and use a search engine such as Google® or Yahoo® and find a Web site to recommend to your classmates.

An online dictionary   Grammar practice
An online grammar reference   A job search
Examination practice   A college program search

ACTIVITY 10 reflection

Which of these activities have you done this week in English? Check your answers. Then circle the activities you want to do but haven't done yet. Share your answers with a partner.

Have you written ...?	□ a check	□ a letter	□ an email	□ an essay
Have you read ...?	□ a grammar book	□ a newspaper	□ a novel	□ a magazine
Have you spoken to...?	□ a friend	□ a co-worker	□ a teacher	□ a counselor
Have you listened to...?	□ a radio program	□ a song	□ a story	□ the news

ANSWER KEY

Activity 7 *Check audio script, LP page S-10 for answers.*

USE YOUR ENGLISH

ACTIVITY 6 · writing [20 minutes]

This activity builds on Activity 5 and focuses on grammatical accuracy in using tenses. It can also be used to focus on the use of transition expressions (*however, first of all, on the other hand,* etc.) to create greater cohesion in their articles.

1. Have students make a short plan or outline for their article, choosing two "best" and two "worst" experiences from the interviews they carried out in Activity 5. If you did not do Activity 5, students can write an article based on their own "best" and "worst" experiences.

2. You could also brainstorm ideas with the class for ways to start off the article. For example, I interviewed several students about their best and worst experiences since coming to this country (or city, or school). Some of the most interesting responses I received were from Elvira, who is from Bolivia, and Alejandro, who is from Brazil. First I will mention some of their worst experiences. Then I will contrast these with some of their best experiences.

3. You may then assign the rest of the writing for homework.

4. Review the activity in your next class by having students read their articles, or displaying them on the wall of your classroom (see Methodology Note on LP page 217).

ACTIVITY 7 · listening [20 minutes]

CD Track 21

You may want to use this activity after Exercise 5 on page 219.

Introduce the topic by asking students about their preferred traveling style. Do they like to travel alone, or in a group? Do they like to stay in hotels, or in youth hostels, or go camping?

STEP 1

1. Read through the chart.
2. Play the audio and have students take notes. See audio script on page S-10.
3. Compare answers in pairs.
4. Play the audio again.
5. Check the answers as a class. See the audio script, LP page S-10, for answers.

STEP 2
Have students work in pairs to discuss the questions. Discuss the answers as a class.

STEP 3

1. Play the audio again. This requires students to listen more closely for examples of language use.
2. Invite some students to write their phrases on the board for the whole class to review together. You can also use this activity to review the unit goals.

ACTIVITY 8 · writing [10–20 minutes]

This activity encourages the use of present perfect with *best* and *worst*.

1. This topic can be adapted for younger and older students. For younger college students, leaving home may be interpreted to mean leaving their family. For older students, it may mean leaving their home country.

2. You can brainstorm ideas for this activity by asking students to complete the following sentence stems:

   The best thing that has happened to me since I left home is . . .

   The worst thing that has happened to me since I left home is . . .

3. Start writing the letters in class and assign the rest for homework.

4. Have students exchange letters with each other. Encourage students to comment on content as well as on language use.

ACTIVITY 9 · research on the web

The purpose of this Internet search activity is to provide a natural context for using the present perfect. An additional purpose is to encourage students to share strategies for finding information on the Internet. What Web sites were most useful? You may want to compile a list of useful Web sites for learning English, based on information from students, and post it on your Web site or in your classroom.

ACTIVITY 10 · reflection [10 minutes/homework]

This activity provides an opportunity for students to use the target structures of the unit while reflecting on their language learning progress. Ask students to make a list of sentences that respond to the questions in the chart. You may have asked students to keep a record of their learning in a journal throughout this course as suggested in To the Teacher, LP page xxii. This reflection activity will be part of that learning record.

UNIT GOALS

- Correctly use present progressive with *just*
- Form present progressive correctly
- Use present progressive to describe unfinished actions and new habits
- Correctly choose between present perfect and present perfect progressive

OPENING TASK

Recent Activities

■ **STEP 1**

Look at the picture. How does she feel? Why do you think she feels like this?

■ **STEP 2**

Work with a partner. Match the pictures with the words and phrases below.

1.

Alan

2.

Linda

3.

Melina

4.

Julia and Fred

5.

Sue

6.

Tom and Brian

Julia and Fred		Sue		Tom and Brian	
4	muddy boots	6	running a marathon	5	crying
1	baking bread	5	chopping onions	3	swimming
2	fixing a car	3	wet hair	2	covered in oil
6	exhausted	4	gardening	1	covered in flour

■ **STEP 3**

Work in pairs. Student A chooses a picture and asks student B a question about it. Student B responds.

Example: A: *Why are Alan's hands covered in flour?*
                      B: *He's been baking bread.*

LESSON PLAN 1

UNIT OVERVIEW

This unit provides practice with the present perfect progressive. It contrasts the present perfect with the present perfect progressive.

GRAMMAR NOTE

The present perfect progressive is used to talk about events and states that started in the past and are still continuing, or have just stopped. You can often still see or feel the result of the past event. It can also be used for regular events that started recently. In contrast to the present perfect tense, it does not express completion. With stative verbs such as *live*, *work*, or *study*, there is often no difference between the present perfect and the present perfect progressive, although the present perfect progressive tends to suggest that the activity will continue in the future. With dynamic verbs, use of the present perfect progressive indicates continuation or repetition. Verbs that indicate one-time events such as *start*, *begin*, *finish*, or *stop*, are not usually used in the present perfect progressive. In American English, the past perfect continuous is often used instead of the present perfect progressive for recent past actions with a present effect.

UNIT GOALS

Some instructors may want to review the goals listed on Student Book (SB) page 226 after completing the Opening Task so that students understand what they should know by the end of the unit. These goals can also be reviewed at the end of the unit when students are more familiar with the grammar terminology.

OPENING TASK [20 minutes]

The purpose of the Opening Task is to create a context in which students will need to use the present perfect progressive. The problem-solving format is designed to show the teacher how well the students can produce the target structures implicitly and spontaneously when they are engaged in a communicative task. For a more complete discussion of the purpose of the Opening Task, see To the Teacher, Lesson Planner (LP) page xxii.

Setting Up the Task

STEP 1

1. Start by looking at the picture. Ask students to suggest a list of adjectives to describe how this woman feels. Examples: *tired, exhausted, sleepy, bored, fed up*.

2. Elicit a list of reasons for feeling like this. Examples: *She has been working/studying a lot. She hasn't been sleeping enough.* At this stage, accept all answers including those in the past simple or other tenses.

Conducting the Task

STEP 2

1. Students can work in groups or pairs to match the pictures with appropriate words and phrases from the list. There are two words or phrases for each picture.

2. Bring the class together to review the answers. Refer to the answer key on LP page 226. Encourage students to present their answers as full sentences.

3. You can elicit or weave in the fact that the statements refer to something that is apparent in the present and was caused by something that occurred in the past. This can act as a springboard to Focus Chart 1.

Reviewing the Task

STEP 3

1. Model the example dialogue with the students.

2. Have students work in pairs to practice dialogues for each picture.

3. Do not correct errors at this stage. Circulate and take notes of errors in meaning or form that may help you focus the material in this unit.

4. Have a few students present their dialogues as a way of bridging to Focus Chart 1.

5. Exercise 1 returns to this task by asking students to write full sentences.

GRAMMAR NOTE

Typical student errors (form)

- Errors with verb-subject agreement of auxiliary, e.g. * *She have been working hard.* * *You has not been sleeping.* (See Focus 2.)

- Errors with the past participle, e.g. * *I have been exercise a lot.* * *They have not be studying.* (See Focus 2.)

- Errors with word order, e.g. * *They have been not living at home.* * *They have been recently eating out a lot.* (See Focus 4.)

Typical student errors (use)

- Using present tense for events that started in the past, e.g. * *I am living here for five years.*

- Using present perfect progressive for an activity that is completed, e.g. * *She has been leaving her old job (instead of: She has left her old job).* (See Focus 1.)

- Using present perfect progressive for a time period that is completed, e.g. * *She has been working there five years ago.* (instead of: She worked there five years ago.)

- Using present perfect for an activity that is still ongoing, e.g. * *I've waited 20 minutes.* (instead of I've been waiting twenty minutes.) (See Focus 3.)

- Using present perfect progressive for an event that happened only once, e.g. * *Jim has been starting a new job* (instead of: Jim has started a new job). (See Focus 5.)

meaning | form

FOCUS 1

Present Perfect Progressive and *Just*: Recent Activities

use

EXAMPLES

(a) A: Why are your hands greasy?
    B: I have been fixing my car.

(b) A: How come you're so thirsty?
    B: I've just been running.

EXPLANATIONS

Use the present perfect progressive to talk about an activity that was happening (in progress) very recently in the past.
In (a) the activity is so recent that you can still feel or see the effect or result.

To emphasize that the activity is recent, use *just*.

EXERCISE 1

Look at the Opening Task on page 227. Write sentences that give explanations for each situation. Check that you have formed the present perfect progressive correctly.

1. _____ Alan's hands are covered in flour *because he has been baking bread.*
2. _____ Linda is dirty because she has been fixing her car.
3. _____ Melina's hair is wet because she has been swimming.
4. _____ Julia and Fred have muddy boots because they have been gardening.
5. _____ Sue is crying because she has been chopping onions.
6. _____ Tom and Brian are exhausted because they have been running in a marathon.

FOCUS 2

Present Perfect Progressive

Use *has*/*have* + *been* + verb + *-ing* to form the present perfect progressive.

STATEMENT		NEGATIVE		QUESTION		
I You We They ('ve)	have been sleeping.	I You We They	have not been sleeping. (haven't)	Have	I you we they	been sleeping?
She He It ('s)	has been sleeping.	She He It	has not been sleeping. (hasn't)	Has	she he it	been sleeping?

EXERCISE 2

You are riding the subway in a big city late at night. There are several other people in the same car. You observe them carefully and try to figure out what they have been doing recently. Use the verb in parentheses to make sentences about what each person has, or hasn't, been doing.

1. A young man with a black eye and ripped clothing. (fight)
   He's been fighting with somebody.

2. Two young men wearing sweats and carrying tennis racquets. (play)
   They have been playing tennis.

3. Two young women with many bags and packages from well-known department stores. (shop)
   They have been shopping.

4. A couple wearing shorts and walking shoes and backpacks. They seem very tired. (hike)
   They have been hiking for a long time.

5. A man with dark shadows under his eyes who looks very tired. (sleep)
   He hasn't been sleeping.

6. A woman with ketchup on her T-shirt. (eat)
   She's been eating a hamburger (or a hot dog).

7. A man with a two-day beard. (shave)
   He hasn't been shaving.

15 LESSON PLAN 1

FOCUS 1 [10 minutes]

This focus chart introduces the use of present progressive for recent past activities where the effect or result is evident in the present.

1. **Lead-in:** Use the example situations and pictures from the Opening Task to lead in to the concept of using the present perfect progressive for recent activities. Review the dialogues for each picture, emphasizing the present result of the past event in each one.

2. If possible, bring in pictures of people from magazines and have students create similar dialogues about them.

3. Distribute one picture to each pair.

4. Have pairs exchange pictures until everyone has practiced with all the pictures.

5. Bring the class together and compare different ideas for dialogues for each picture.

6. This focus chart leads naturally into Exercise 1.

EXERCISE 1 [10 minutes]

1. Allow 5 minutes for students to review the Opening Task and write sentences.

2. Have students exchange sentences with a partner to edit their work.

3. Review the answers by having students come to the board and write the sentences.

4. Reinforce the connection with Focus Chart 1 by explaining (or asking students to explain) how a recent event in progress in the past has an effect or result that is noticeable in the present.

5. Review any errors in form, which will naturally lead you to Focus Chart 2.

 For more practice, use *Grammar Dimensions 2* Workbook page 98, Exercise 1.

GRAMMAR NOTE

Students may ask about the difference between the present perfect and progressive tenses. The present perfect focuses on actions or events that are complete. The present progressive focuses on actions or events that have only *recently finished* (see Focus Chart 1) or are *still continuing* (see Focus Chart 3). The emphasis is on the action or event, not on its completion. In American English, the use of the present perfect progressive for recently completed actions with a present result is often replaced by the past continuous.

EXPANSION [15 minutes]

You may want to use Activity 2 (speaking) on Student Book (SB) page 235 as a follow-up to this exercise.

FOCUS 2 [5 minutes]

1. **Lead-in:** Review any errors in form that came up in Exercise 1 or in the Opening Task. You may want to write the errors on the board and ask students to correct them.

2. Point out the third person singular distinction: *has*, rather than *have*.

3. Mention that contractions of *have/has* are almost always used in informal speech: *I've been sleeping*, rather than *I have been sleeping*.

4. Model and practice the pronunciation of contractions: *I've, You've, He's, She's, We've, They've.*

5. You may want to add some examples of *Wh-* questions, e.g. *What have you been doing? Why have you been sleeping?*

EXERCISE 2 [10 minutes]

This exercise practices the use and the form of the present perfect progressive for recent activities.

1. Read the introduction to the exercise and do the first example together with the class.

2. Allow students a few minutes to work in pairs and write their answers.

3. Ask for volunteers to provide the answers.

4. Try to elicit all the possible answers from the class. Ask: *Are there any other possible answers?*

5. Ask students to suggest other similar descriptions with "clues" for the rest of the class to guess.

6. Bring in pictures of people from magazines and ask students to suggest what they have been doing using clues from their appearance.

 For more practice, use *Grammar Dimensions 2* Workbook page 99, Exercise 2 and Exercise 3.

METHODOLOGY NOTE

An interesting, unusual, funny, or strange picture can have a greater impact than any verbal or written explanation. A picture can stick in your mind and act as a trigger to remind you of the grammar point. Using pictures for this unit will help students, especially those with a strong visual memory, to remember the grammar point. Choose three or four memorable pictures (being careful to avoid pictures that may be culturally insensitive) that can generate a number of different dialogues, and really work with them to make them stick in your students' memory.

EXPANSION [15 minutes]

You may want to use Activity 3 (speaking) on SB page 236 as a follow-up to this exercise.

FOCUS 3

Perfect Progressive: Unfinished Actions

use

EXAMPLE

(a) He **has been waiting** for twenty minutes. (He's still waiting.)

EXPLANATION

Use the present perfect progressive to describe situations or actions that started in the past and are still going on.

EXERCISE 3

For each conversation, complete the following sentences. The first one has been done for you.

1. **Lee:** What are you doing?
   Mary Lou: I'm waiting to make a phone call. This woman _has been talking_ (talk) on the phone for the last twenty minutes.

2. **Dan:** Haven't you finished writing that book yet?
   Heidi: No, we're still working on it.
   Dan: You _have been writing_ (write) it for almost three years!

3. **Steve:** What's up? You look miserable.
   Tom: I am. I want to go for a bike ride, but it _has been raining_ (rain) since eight o'clock this morning.

4. **George:** Excuse me, but is this your dog?
   Barbara: Yes. Is there a problem?
   George: I can't get to sleep because that dog _has been barking_ (bark) for hours! Please keep it under control, or I'll call the police.

5. **Martin:** Are these your glasses?
   Gin: Yes! Thank you so much. I _have been looking_ (look) for them everywhere!

6. **Sarita:** How are things going in New York?
   Anastasia: We don't live there anymore.
   Sarita: Really?
   Anastasia: Yes. We _have been living_ (live) Philadelphia since January.

7. **Diane:** Why are Kemal and Cynthia so depressed?
   Marianne: They _have been studying_ (study) grammar for ages, but they still don't understand how to use the present perfect progressive.

8. **Pam:** Aren't you ready yet?
   Andrew: No. I've lost my keys and I _have been trying_ (try) to find them for the last half hour.

FOCUS 4

Present Perfect Progressive for New Habits

use

EXAMPLES

(a) They've **been eating** out a lot recently.

(b) He's **been exercising** a lot lately.

(c) I've **been walking** to work recently.

EXPLANATIONS

Use the present perfect progressive to talk about a regular habit or activity that is still happening.

Add a time phrase or word to show that the activity started recently.

EXERCISE 4

Stan is talking with his old friend Janet. They have not seen each other for several months, and Janet is surprised by some of the changes in Stan's appearance. Complete their conversation, using the verbs from the list below.

happen	sail	cook	do
feel	take	go	study
eat	ride	date	ski
talk	think	see	spend

(Continued on next page)

FOCUS 3 [10 minutes]

1. **Lead-in:** Make statements that are true about your own life. For example, I've been teaching ESL for 15 years. I've been playing the piano for 20 years. Ask: Am I doing these things now? Am I going to continue doing them?

2. To elicit similar examples from students, ask: Nikko, how long have you been studying English? Michelle, how long have you been speaking English?

3. If you are aware of any of your students' current hobbies or activities, ask questions about these as well. For example, Maria, how long have you been playing tennis? Tinh, how long have you been studying chemistry?

EXERCISE 3 [15 minutes]

This exercise practices the use of present perfect progressive for unfinished actions.

1. Allow students a few minutes to read the dialogues silently and fill in the blanks.

2. Ask students to read the dialogues aloud with a partner. Remind students that for natural-sounding speech, it's important to link words together smoothly and to use appropriate stress and intonation—falling intonation at the end of a statement, rising intonation at the end of a *yes/no* question, and louder volume/higher pitch for important or surprising information.

3. Ask volunteers to read the dialogues out loud.

4. Ask for comments and feedback from the class on pronunciation and intonation.

5. Review the correct answers and the reason for this choice of tense in each case as a whole class. Refer to the answer key on LP page 230.

For more practice, use *Grammar Dimensions 2* Workbook page 99, Exercise 4.

EXPANSION [15 minutes]

As an extension to Exercise 3, you can ask students to create their own mini-dialogues using the same verbs.

FOCUS 4 [10 minutes]

1. **Lead-in:** Ask students to each write on a piece of paper something new they've been doing recently that is still happening. It can be a new way of going to school, a new hobby or sport, a new class they are taking. Instruct them **not** to say *I've been studying English* but to try to think of something that is new or unusual: *I've been living with an American family. I've been going to a lot of Chinese films. I've been losing things!*

2. Collect the statements and read each one aloud. Ask the other students to guess who wrote it.

3. If the present perfect progressive is not formed correctly, or if another verb tense is more appropriate, first give students the opportunity to find and correct the error.

4. Read the examples and explanations in the focus chart. Point out the similarity with the use presented in Focus Chart 3 (an activity that started in the past and is not yet finished).

EXPANSION [20 minutes]

You may want to use Activity 5 (speaking/listening) on SB page 237 as a follow-up to this focus chart. This activity asks students to talk about things they have started doing recently.

EXERCISE 4

Exercise 4 begins with the direction line and vocabulary box on SB page 231 with the actual exercise items on SB page 232.

Janet: Pat, you look great! You've lost a lot of weight, too.

Stan: Well, I (1) __'ve been riding__ my bike to school recently, and I (2) __'ve been taking__ an aerobics class.

Janet: Is that all? No special diets or anything?

Stan: Not really. I (3) __haven't been going__ (not) to any fast-food restaurants. I (4) __'ve been cooking/eating__ at home instead — a lot of fresh vegetables and salads and other healthy stuff like that. It really makes a difference. I (5) __'ve been feeling__ much better, with lots more energy.

Janet: Well, you seem to be very busy these days. You're never home when I call. What else (6) __have__ you __been doing__ ?

Stan: I (7) __'ve been seeing__ somebody special. She's got a boat, so we (8) __'ve been sailing__ a lot, and she also has a cabin in the mountains, so we (9) __'ve been spending__ time there, too. And also, we (10) __'ve been thinking__ about taking some longer trips together. So it's all pretty exciting. But what about you? What (11) __have you been doing__ ?

Janet: Nothing. I (12) __'ve been studying__ for my final exams, but when they're over, I'm going to start having fun!

FOCUS 5

Present Perfect versus Present Perfect Progressive

use

EXAMPLES

(a) Jim has worked here for ten years.

(b) Jim has been working here for ten years.

(c) Jim has started a new job.

(d) NOT: Jim has been starting a new job.

EXPLANATIONS

With verbs that show actions or states over time (example: *work, live, study*), there is often little difference between the present perfect and present perfect progressive.

However, if the verbs refer to one time only, then the present perfect should be used, not the present perfect progressive.

EXAMPLES

(e) They have painted their house.

(f) They have been painting their house.

(g) Jean has visited her grandmother.

(h) Jean has been visiting her grandmother.

(i) Geraldo has exercised.

(j) Geraldo has been exercising lately.

EXPLANATIONS

In other cases the present perfect progressive:

• shows that the action is incomplete (unfinished). In (e), the painting is complete. In (f), it is not complete (see Focus 3). OR

• emphasizes that the action was in progress recently. (g) tells us that the visit occurred earlier. (h) tells us that the visit occurred recently and perhaps is still in progress (see Focus 1). OR

• talks about a new habit. (i) tells us that Geraldo exercised at some time earlier. (j) suggests that he has started a new habit (see Focus 4).

EXERCISE 5

Read each situation and circle the statement that best describes the situation.

1. Sally ate frogs' legs in September 1998, and again in December 1999.
   a. Sally has eaten frogs' legs.
   b. Sally has been eating frogs' legs.

2. Bill started reading that book last week and he's not finished yet. He will probably finish it tonight.
   a. Bill has read that book.
   b. Bill has been reading that book.

3. I rode a motorcycle once when I was 16 and once last year.
   a. I've been riding a motorcycle.
   b. I've ridden a motorcycle.

4. We first studied English grammar in school, ten years ago. This year we have grammar class for one hour every day, five days a week.
   a. We've been studying English grammar.
   b. We've studied English grammar.

5. My brother just can't quit smoking, even though he knows it's a bad habit. He started smoking when he was seventeen, and now he's almost thirty.
   a. My brother has been smoking for a long time.
   b. My brother has smoked for a long time.

EXERCISE 4 [15 minutes]

This exercise practices the use of the present perfect progressive for regular events or actions that have started recently and are continuing now.

1. Introduce the idea of old friends meeting after a long time. What kinds of changes would you notice? Ask for some examples using the present tense and discuss cultural guidelines for commenting on physical appearance. For example: *You look thinner. You look happy/worried/tired.* Ask for suggested replies, e.g., *I've been (haven't been) exercising. I've been seeing a new girlfriend./worrying about my exam./working a lot.*

2. Ask students to fill in the blanks individually and then practice in pairs (reminding them about using contractions and natural intonation).

3. Invite volunteers to read each part of the dialogue aloud.

4. Encourage feedback from the class on whether the answers are appropriate.

5. Review the correct answers and the reason for this choice of tense in each case as a whole class. Refer to the answer key on LP page 232.

METHODOLOGY NOTE

When reviewing the answers to exercises, it is important for students to have the opportunity to discuss and develop their ability to *think critically* about their grammar choices. One way of doing this is to ask for a class vote (by taking a show of hands, for example) on each answer and have those students who either agree or disagree justify their answers.

EXPANSION [20 minutes]

You may want to use Activity 4 (listening) on SB page 236 as a follow-up to this exercise.

For more practice, use *Grammar Dimensions 2* Workbook page 100, Exercise 5 and page 101, Exercise 6.

FOCUS 5 [5 minutes]

1. **Lead-in:** Read each pair of examples from the focus chart and ask, *Is there a difference in meaning?* (The only *no* answer is for statements (a)–(b).)

2. Give other examples of this lack of distinction in meaning using the verbs *live* and *study*. Example: *How long have you lived here, Etsuko?* Answer: *I've lived here for 3 months.*

3. Ask: *Can you say that in a different way with the same meaning?* Answer: *I've been living here for 3 months.*

4. Continue with the other pairs (c)–(h) in the focus chart, asking *Is there a difference in meaning?*

5. Elaborate on and have students read the explanation given in the focus chart. This can serve as a bridge to the next exercise.

EXERCISE 5 [20 minutes]

This is a suitable exercise for group work or for a group discussion.

1. Divide students into pairs or groups.

2. Set a time limit of 10 minutes for them to discuss their answers.

3. Ask a representative from each group to choose one question and justify their answer.

For more practice, use *Grammar Dimensions 2* Workbook page 101, Exercise 7.

LANGUAGE NOTE

Because the present perfect progressive emphasizes continuation, it cannot be used with time phrases that refer to a past period of time. We can say *I've been playing the piano for five years* because the period of time extends up to and includes the present, and can continue into the future. We cannot say * *I've been playing the piano until I was 12 years old/until five years ago/yesterday* because these time periods are completed.

EXPANSION [30 minutes]

Write the following sentences on the board or on the overhead projector. Conduct a game where students in teams rush to label which sentences are correct and which are incorrect (one sentence at a time). Students must clearly explain their decision before they are awarded a point. Prizes are optional.

Sentences for Grammar Auction

1. I've been eating out five times this week. (incorrect)
2. My family has been living in Denver ten years ago. (incorrect)
3. Susan has been swimming since she was 5 years old. (correct)
4. I haven't been swimming for ages. (correct)
5. I've been phoning you ten times today already. (incorrect)
6. Sam has been studying Chinese last year. (correct)
7. We've been playing chess every evening. (correct)
8. Have you ever been playing the violin? (incorrect)
9. You haven't been exercising recently, have you? (correct)
10. It's been raining for three hours. (correct)

ACTIVITY 1 writing

You have just received a letter from the editor of your high school newspaper. She wants to include information about former students in the next edition of the paper. Write a letter to the editor, telling her what you have been doing recently. (Do not feel you have to use the present perfect progressive in every sentence! To make this letter sound natural think about all the other tenses you can use as well.)

ACTIVITY 2 speaking

The purpose of this game is to guess recent activities from their current results. Work in teams. Each team should try to think of four different results of recent activities.

Example: Recent Activity: *You have been exercising*
Present Result: *now you are exhausted*

When everyone is ready, each team takes turns acting out the results of the activities they have chosen. For example, Team A has chosen "being exhausted." Everybody in Team A gets up and acts out being exhausted. The rest of the class tries to guess what Team A has been doing. The first person to guess correctly, "You have been exercising, and now you are exhausted," scores a point for his or her team.

EXERCISE 6

What would Doug and Sandy say in each situation below? The words in parentheses will help you, but you will need to add some other words.

1. It's 4:00, and Doug's partner Sandy has been napping since 1:00. Doug is waiting for her to wake up. When she finally does, he says: (I/wait/three hours)

2. Sandy has promised to change the oil in Doug's car. While she is sleeping, Doug decides to try to do it himself, but he can't. When Sandy wakes up, he says: (I/try/forty-five minutes)

3. Sandy's mother calls to tell her that Sandy's sister has had another baby. Her mother asks, "When are you and Doug going to have kids?" Sandy tells her: (we/discuss/ten years)

4. After her nap, Sandy is hungry and she wants Doug to go out with her to eat pizza. Doug doesn't want to go because he bought fresh fish for dinner and wants to try out a new recipe. He tells Sandy, "I don't want to go out because (I/plan/dinner/all day)"

EXERCISE 7

Complete the dialogues below, using present perfect progressive, present perfect, or simple past. Be prepared to explain your choice.

Dialogue 1

Keven: What's the matter? You look frustrated.

Tsitsi: I am. I (1) _____ (try) to study all day, but the telephone never stops ringing. People (2) _____ (call) all day about the car.

Keven: That's great. I (3) _____ (hope) to sell that car for six months now. Maybe today's the day!

Dialogue 2

Maria: I'm sorry I'm so late. (4) _____ (you/wait) long?

Alex: Yes, I have! Where (5) _____ (you/be)?

Maria: I really am sorry. My watch is broken, and I didn't know what time it was.

Alex: Why didn't you ask somebody? I (6) _____ (stand) out here in the cold for at least forty minutes.

Maria: Oh, you poor thing! But we'd better hurry to get to the movie theater.

Alex: It's too late. The movie (7) _____ (start).

Maria: Really?

Alex: Yes. It (8) _____ (start) twenty minutes ago.

ANSWER KEY

Exercise 6 1. I've been waiting for you to wake up for three hours. 2. I've been trying to change the oil for 45 minutes. 3. We've been discussing it for ten years. 4. I've been planning dinner all day.

Exercise 7 have/'ve been trying have been calling have/'ve been hoping Have you been waiting have you been have/'ve been standing has started started

EXERCISE 6 [10 minutes]

This exercise practices the use of the present progressive for actions that are still going on.

1. Ask students to work in small groups or pairs to read the situations and think about the context.

2. Have each pair or group write their answers.

3. Circulate while students are working to check for accuracy.

4. Note the items that students disagreed on (if any), and/or ask them to raise questions on those items that they couldn't agree on.

5. Have each pair or group read their answers. Ask students to explain why an answer is correct or incorrect. Refer to the answer key on LP page 234.

6. Refer back to the explanations in Focus Chart 5.

EXERCISE 7 [15 minutes]

This exercise requires students to decide when to use one of three different tenses: present perfect progressive, present perfect, and simple past.

1. Allow students time to work in pairs to complete the dialogues.

2. Have students practice reading aloud in pairs.

3. Ask volunteers to read their dialogues aloud.

4. Ask for comments on accuracy and appropriateness.

EXPANSION [15 minutes]

You may want to use Activity 1 (writing) on SB page 235 as a way of closing this unit. This could be followed by Activity 7 on page 237 (reflection).

UNIT GOAL REVIEW [10 minutes]

Ask students to look at the goals on the opening page of the unit again. Help them understand how much they have accomplished in each area. One way to do this is to present contrasts between the present perfect progressive and the present perfect (Goal #4), and ask students to talk about the differences in meaning using sentences from Focus Chart 5 and Exercise 5.

For a grammar quiz review of Units 13–15, refer students to pages 102–104 in the *Grammar Dimensions 2 Workbook*.

 For assessment of Unit 15, use *Grammar Dimensions 2 ExamView®*.

USE YOUR ENGLISH

The Use Your English section of activities at the end of each unit contain situations that should naturally elicit the structures covered in the unit. For a more complete discussion of how to use the Use Your English activities, see To the Teacher, LP page xxii. When students are doing these activities in class, you can circulate and listen to see if they are using the structures accurately. Errors can be corrected after the activity has finished.

You may want to use this activity at the end of the unit after Exercise 7 on SB page 234.

ACTIVITY 1 writing [15 minutes]

1. Brainstorm some ideas for the content of this letter. Topics may include aspects of college life, a new job, a new hobby or sport. It might also cover differences between living at home and living alone or in a dorm.

2. Have students plan their letter by making an outline of what will be in each paragraph. If there is time, have them start writing the first paragraph in class and finish the letter for homework.

3. Decide how to handle errors in the letters. Students can exchange letters for peer-editing. You can copy selected errors onto an overhead transparency or onto the board and have students correct them

VARIATION

After students write their letters, read them aloud, anonymously, and have the other students guess whose letter it is. If you choose to do this activity in this way, you might want to warn students *before* they write their letters so as to not give too much away!

ACTIVITY 2 speaking [20 minutes]

You may want to use this activity after Exercise 1 on SB page 228.

1. Model the activity yourself by acting out the word *exhausted*. Students will have to guess how you are feeling and why you are feeling that way (because you've been exercising).

2. You may want to prepare cards or pictures to help students get started. The cards should contain sentences such as, *You've been digging snow; You've been singing very loudly; You've been laughing a lot. You've been cutting onions. You've been gardening; You've been having an argument*. Then students will have to mime *exhausted, sore throat, 'crying', backache*, etc.

3. If you think that particular students may not be comfortable doing this kind of activity in the classroom, ask each group to choose a volunteer to do the "acting."

ACTIVITY 3 speaking

This is another team game. Each team presents a series of clues, and the rest of the class tries to guess what situation these clues refer to. For example, Team A chooses this situation: *A woman has been reading a sad love story.* The team tries to think of as many clues as possible that will help the other students guess the situation. When everyone is ready, Team A presents the first clue:

Team A: *Her eyes are red. (The other teams now make guesses based on this first clue.)*

Team B: *She has been chopping onions.* **Team A:** *No. She feels very sad.*

Team C: *She's been crying.* **Team A:** *No. She's very romantic.*

Team D: *She's been fighting with her boyfriend.* **Team A:** *No. She was alone.*

Team C: *She's been reading a sad love story!*

You can choose one of the situations below or you can make up one of your own. The person who guesses the correct situation scores a point for his or her team.

1. He or she has been crying.
2. He or she has been watching old movies.
3. He or she has been working late every night.
4. He or she's been training for the Olympics.
5. He or she has been chopping onions.
6. He or she has been feeling sick.

ACTIVITY 4 listening

CD Track 22

■ **STEP 1**

Listen to the audio of a conversation between two old friends. These people haven't seen each other for several years, so they have a lot to talk about.

Make a list of the things that each speaker (Speaker 1 (man) / Speaker 2 (woman)) has been doing or has recently done (or the things their family members and friends have done). Compare your list with a classmate's.

■ **STEP 2**

Look at the lists that you and your partner made. Together, write a sentence about each thing on your lists using either the present perfect or the present perfect progressive.

ACTIVITY 5 speaking/listening

■ **STEP 1**

Choose a goal: get healthy, learn a new skill, save money, or become famous. Imagine that you are trying to do this. What things have you been doing (or not doing) to achieve this goal? Make a list.

■ **STEP 2**

Interview your partner about his or her recent goal chosen from Step 1. Find out as much information as you can. Record your interview.

■ **STEP 3**

Listen to the recording of your interview in Step 2. Write down all the sentences that use the present perfect progressive. In each case, was it used correctly? Were there any cases where the present progressive could have been used but wasn't?

ACTIVITY 6 research on the web

Go on the Internet and use a search engine such as Google® or Yahoo® to research some news stories about what people have been doing recently. Look at an online newspaper or an online magazine and do another search there. For example, you could choose a local or favorite sports team, a celebrity, or a politician. Choose one story and explain what people have been doing and why. Give a summary to your class.

ACTIVITY 7 reflection

Make a list of five things that you have been doing recently to improve your English and five things you have not been doing.

ANSWER KEY

Activity 4 See audio script on LP page 5–6. Answers may include: Man: Has lived here for 6 years (since 1991), has had two children, has been busy being a dad, has been running a dry cleaning business, wife has been working when she is not busy with the kids. Woman: has been here about 5 years, has been working as an editor, has taken sailing lessons, has been mountain climbing; Eddy has been working in a law firm, they have had a daughter.

USE YOUR ENGLISH

ACTIVITY 3 speaking [20 minutes]

You may want to use this activity after Exercise 2 on SB page 229.

1. Read the introduction to the activity.
2. Model the first situations with the class.
3. Divide the class into teams.
4. Play the game using the situations given.
5. Ask students to think of different situations to continue the game.

VARIATION

The following is an effective activity for a class lacking energy! Students almost always participate enthusiastically in this team game. However, if you prefer more order in the classroom, you might think of ways to control or organize how teams will respond by making rules such as:

1. Only one person from each team can respond after a short team conference.

2. Only one team can respond at a time (in varying order).

ACTIVITY 4 listening [20 minutes]

You may want to use this activity after Exercise 4 on SB pages 231 and 232.

1. Read the introduction for all steps of the activity.
2. Play the audio. You may want to look at the audio script on page S-6 for the list of activities.
3. Have students compare answers in pairs.
4. Play the audio again.

5. Review the answers as a class. Refer to possible answers in the answer key on LP page 236.
6. Have students work in pairs to write sentences.

ACTIVITY 5 speaking/listening [20 minutes]

You may want to use this activity after Focus Chart 4 on SB page 231. This activity can be done in class or as an out-of-class interviewing activity.

■ STEP 1   Read the goals and have students choose one. Make sure there is a good spread of goals within the class.

■ STEP 2   Have students interview each other, or if this is to be done out of class, assign Step 2 for homework. If recording equipment is not available, have two students interview one person, so that one can take notes of uses of the present perfect progressive.

■ STEP 3   Have students report back to the class on uses of the present perfect progressive.

ACTIVITY 6 research on the web [30 minutes/homework]

The purpose of this Internet search activity is to provide a natural context for using the present perfect progressive. An additional purpose is to encourage students to share strategies for finding information on the Internet.

ACTIVITY 7 reflection [10 minutes/homework]

You may want to use this activity at the end of the unit after Exercise 7 on SB page 234. This activity provides an opportunity for students to use the target language structures of the unit while reflecting on their language learning progress. You may have asked students to keep a record of their learning in a journal throughout this course as suggested in To the Teacher, LP page xxii. This reflection activity will form part of that learning record.

UNIT GOALS

- Make offers with *would you like*

- Choose correctly between *would you like* and *do you want*

- Use correct forms when accepting and refusing offers

OPENING TASK

At the Hotel Reception

■ **STEP 1**

Look at the picture. What do you think the hotel receptionist is saying to the guest?

■ **STEP 2**

Work in pairs. Chose your role as Student A or Student B. After each problem, switch roles as guest or receptionist. *Do not look at your partner's problems.* Student A look below. Student B turn to page 244.

Student A: You are a hotel guest. You have lost your voice, but you have some urgent problems. (See "Student A's Problems" below.) Go to the hotel reception and communicate your requests to the hotel desk clerk *without speaking or writing.*

Student B: Your job is to work out what Student A needs and to offer a solution. Close your book and guess what student A needs.

STUDENT A'S PROBLEMS	STUDENT B'S OFFER (STEP 3)
1. You are thirsty.	
2. You have a headache.	
3. You are hot. Your hotel room is very stuffy. You cannot open the window.	
4. You have lost your door key.	
5. You need a taxi right away.	

■ **STEP 3**

When you have finished, check the list to see if you correctly understood each other's problems. Then think of an appropriate offer for your partner's problems using *Would you like . . . ?* Write them in your notebook. Share your responses with your class.

Opening Task Step 3: *Answers will vary. Possibilities:*

Student A: 1. Would you like something to drink? 2. Would you like an aspirin? 3. Would you like me to open the window? 4. Would you like me to get you another door key? 5. Would you like me to call a taxi for you?

Student B (from p. 244): 1. Would you like me to call building maintenance? 2. Would you like another light bulb? 3. Would you like another blanket? 4. Would you like me to get you something

UNIT OVERVIEW

Unit 16 presents different forms of offers using *Would you like . . . ?* and contrasts the appropriate use of *Would you like . . . ?* with *Do you want . . . ?* It also presents a variety of ways to accept and refuse offers.

GRAMMAR NOTE

This unit presents differences between offers to do something for someone and offers to give something to someone using the modal *would*. These differences can result in confusion if misunderstood. This unit also focuses on differences in levels of formality when making offers. Failure to recognize such differences does not usually cause miscommunication of meaning but can sometimes result in more subtle misunderstandings of tone or intention.

UNIT GOALS

Some instructors may want to review the goals listed on Student Book (SB) page 238 after completing the Opening Task so that students understand what they should know by the end of the unit. These goals can also be reviewed at the end of the unit when students are more familiar with the grammar terminology.

IMPORTANT: Because the Opening Task, Focus Charts, and Exercises can be reviewed and studied in one class length of 1.5 hours this unit contains only one organized Lesson Plan. However, by using all activities and expansion ideas, as well as, the workbook suggestions, it will be possible for teachers to make two lessons out of Unit 16 if so desired.

OPENING TASK [30 minutes]

The purpose of the Opening Task is to create a context in which students will need to use language for making offers. The problem-solving format is designed to show the teacher how well the students can produce the target structures implicitly and spontaneously when they are engaged in a communicative task. For a more complete discussion of the purpose of the Opening Task, see To the Teacher, Lesson Planner (LP) page xxii.

Setting Up the Task

■ STEP 1

1. Ask students to describe what is happening in the picture. Where are they? Who are they? What are they saying?

2. Elicit as many different suggestions from the class as you can. Accept all suggestions, including those that do not use the target structures.

Conducting the Task

■ STEP 2

1. This is an information-gap task where students have to guess each other's problems and make an offer in response.

2. Read the instructions and the descriptions of each student's role. Make sure students understand that they are going to play the roles of hotel receptionist and a hotel guest who has lost his or her voice. Do not read Student A's problems (Student B is supposed to guess them).

3. Have students work in pairs and have student B turn to SB page 244.

4. Explain that students will switch roles after each problem, but will continue to look at the same page throughout the activity.

5. Monitor students as they try to solve the problem. Take notes of any problems with accuracy or appropriateness but do not correct at this stage. You may use your notes later to target the material in this unit.

6. Students who finish early can go on to Step 3.

Closing the Task

■ STEP 3

1. Instruct students to work together to write their offers. Answers will vary; refer to the answer key on LP page 238 for possible answers.

2. Gather ideas and suggestions from the whole class. Concentrate on the meaning rather than the form. It is not necessary to go into detailed error correction here as students will have a chance to come back to these sentences in Exercise 1 on SB page 240.

GRAMMAR NOTE

Typical student errors (form)

• Confusing Would you like . . . ? and Do you like . . . ? e.g. Would you like coffee? * *Yes, I do.* (See Focus 1.)

• Confusion between asking if you want to do something or offering to do something for you, e.g. Would you like to open the window? Would you like <u>me</u> to open the window? (See Focus 1.)

Typical student errors (use)

• Refusing offers without using a 'softener' which can sound rude, e.g. *Would you like me to help you?* * *No.* (See Focus 3.)

• Using inappropriate levels of formality or informality. (See Focus 2 and 3.)

FOCUS 1

Offers with *Would You Like*

form

EXAMPLES

(a) Would you like some coffee?
(b) Would you like some help?
(c) Would you like to sit down?
(d) Would you like to use the bathroom?

(e) Would you like me to open the window?
(f) Would you like me to take your coat?

(g) Would you like Sally to open the window?
(h) Would you like Auntie Bev to help you wash your hands?

EXPLANATIONS

There are several ways to make offers.
Use *Would you like* + noun phrase.
Use *Would you like to* + verb phrase.

Use *Would you like me to* + verb phrase to make an offer about yourself.

Use *Would you like* (person's name) *to* + verb phrase to make an offer about someone else.

EXERCISE 1

Think about the offers you made in the Opening Task on pages 239 and 244. Were your offers formed correctly? Change the ones that were not correct.

FOCUS 2

Would You Like . . . ? or *Do You Want . . . ?*

use

EXAMPLES

(a) Would you like a cup of tea?
(b) Do you want a cup of tea?

(c) **Want** me to help you with your bags?
(d) Would you like me to help you with your bags?

EXPLANATIONS

Use *Would you like . . . ?* if you want to be polite. Offers with *Do you want . . . ?* are usually used with close friends and family. Example (a) is more polite or formal than (b).

In informal situations "*Do you*" can be omitted from *Do you want . . . ?* Example (c) is less formal than (d).

EXERCISE 2

Your new friend is having her first party in North America. She has invited some of her classmates, her teachers and their partners, and her neighbors: two elderly women. She has asked you to help her because she is nervous and does not know English very well. Change her commands and questions into polite offers, using *Would you like . . . ?* or *Do you want . . . ?*

	Make an offer to . . .
1. Come in.	everyone
2. Sit down.	the neighbors
3. Give me your coat.	the teachers and their partners
4. Want a chair?	the classmates
5. Want something to drink?	everyone
6. Cream in your coffee?	the classmates
7. Want the window open?	the teachers and their partners
8. Give me your cup. I'll get more coffee.	the neighbors

EXERCISE 3

Choose an item from the list below, but don't tell your partner which one. Try to get your partner to make an offer by hinting that you need him or her to help you. Continue by switching roles until you have practiced all the items in the list.

Example: **Student A:** Oh no! I left my dictionary at home and I need it for today's test.
Student B: Would you like to borrow my dictionary?
Student A: Thank you!

1. borrow a book
2. eat something
3. drink something
4. drive to the train station
5. use a cell phone
6. close the window
7. help me study
8. carry some boxes
9. _____ (make up your own offer)

ANSWER KEY

Exercise 1 Answers will vary.

Exercise 2 1. Would you like to . . . 2. Would you like to . . . 3. Would you like to . . . coats? 4. Do you want/Would you like to . . . 5. Do you want/Would you like . . . 6. Do you want/Would you like . . . 7. Do you want/Would you like the window open? 8. Would you like more coffee?

UNIT 16 LESSON PLAN 1

FOCUS 1 [5 minutes]

1. **Lead-in:** A good way to present this structure is to contrast it with *Do you like . . . ?* Point out that *Do you like . . . ?* asks about likes and preferences in general, while *Would you like . . . ?* focuses on what the listener wants right now or in the future. You may contrast the following pairs of questions:

   a. Do you like coffee? b. Would you like coffee?

   a. Do you like to play soccer? b. Would you like to play soccer?

2. Read the examples and explanations in the focus chart.

3. Ask students to think of situations where you might hear each of these examples—e.g., at a friend's house, in a library, in your adviser's office.

EXERCISE 1 [5 minutes]

This exercise allows students to edit their sentences from the Opening Task using information from Focus Chart 1. Direct students to work with their partner to edit their solutions from the Opening Task on SB page 239.

FOCUS 2 [10 minutes]

Continuing with the structure addressed in Focus 1, this focus chart compares *would you like* with *do you want* to demonstrate the difference in meaning and use.

1. **Lead-in:** Some students may already have used this structure in their sentences from the Opening Task. If so, you can use these to demonstrate this alternative, more informal form. Alternatively, change some of the *Would you like . . . ?* examples from Focus Chart 1 and ask students to suggest contexts in which they might occur.

2. Read the examples and the explanations in the focus chart. See the Pronunciation Note.

3. For further discussion of the modal *would*, refer to Unit 10, Focus Chart 1 Grammar Note. Unit 17, on the other hand, looks at *would* from the point of view of requests.

PRONUNCIATION NOTE

Practice the pronunciation of the less formal expression *do you want . . . ?* Point out that this is not bad English; it is the normal sound pattern of natural spoken English in less formal situations. You might also point out how the auxiliary is abbreviated or blended with the following word.

Do ya wanna cuppa coffee?

Does she wanna come over?

Do they wanna leave a little bit earlier?

EXERCISE 2 [10 minutes]

This exercise provides practice in using *would you like* and *do you want* appropriately.

1. Read the introduction aloud while the class reads silently.

2. Point out that their relationships to the people they are addressing and the context will determine whether it is appropriate to use *would you like* or *do you want*.

3. Have students work individually to write their answers in their notebooks.

4. Have students compare answers in pairs and report back to the class.

5. Call on the class to determine if others agree or disagree: specifically if the questions are appropriate and the forms are accurate.

EXPANSION [30–40 minutes]

You may want to use Activity 1 on SB page 245 after this exercise.

EXERCISE 3 [15 minutes]

This exercise provides practice in using the target forms in mini-conversations. There is also a certain amount of guesswork involved as students try to work out what kind of offer they should make.

1. Read the instructions and make sure students understand that they should choose ideas from the list in random order. Also, that they should hint at the request, and not make a direct request.

2. Role play the example conversation with a student (or ask two students).

3. Set a time limit of 10 minutes.

4. Circulate while students are talking and make notes of interesting conversations as well as common errors.

5. Invite or select students to repeat their conversations for the class.

6. Students can offer corrections and vote on the best or funniest conversations.

7. Collect some examples of responses to offers as a bridge to Focus Chart 3.

work book For more practice, use *Grammar Dimensions 2* Workbook page 105, Exercise 1.

EXPANSION [15 minutes]

You may want to use Activity 2 on SB page 245 after this exercise.

FOCUS 3

Accepting and Refusing Offers

use

EXAMPLES

(a) A: Would you like something to drink?
B: **Yes, please.**

(b) A: Would you like me to help you?
B: **Yes, please. That's very kind of you.**

(c) A: Do you want the rest of my hamburger?
B: **Sure. Thanks.**

(d) A: Would you like some coffee?
B: **No, thank you.**
OR
No, thanks.

(e) A: Would you like some coffee?
B: **No, thank you. I've had enough.**

(f) A: Would you like me to help you?
B: **No, thanks. That's nice of you, but I can manage.**

EXPLANATIONS

ACCEPTING OFFERS

Use *please* along with *yes* to politely accept offers.

To be very polite, use an extra phrase to show that you appreciate the offer. (This is not usually necessary in informal situations.)

In informal situations, words such as *sure*, *yeah*, and *thanks* show that you accept the offer.

REFUSING OFFERS

Use *thank you/thanks* with *no* to politely refuse offers.

For polite refusals, you can tell why the offer cannot be accepted.

EXERCISE 4

Match the offers with the appropriate responses. Where do you think each offer and response was made? Are they polite, or not very polite?

1. _c_ Would you like to go to a movie?

2. _a_ Another slice of pie?

3. _e_ Would you like me to get you some more coffee?

4. _f_ Do you want to have lunch together?

5. _d_ Want some help with your homework?

6. _b_ Would you like me to open the door for you?

a. Yes, please. It's delicious!

b. Thank you, but I can manage.

c. No, thanks. I have to go home early tonight.

d. That's very kind of you. Do you have time?

e. Sure. Here's my mug.

f. Good idea! When is your lunch break?

EXERCISE 5

Look at the following responses. What offer was probably made? Write it down in the blank.

1. Offer: _Would you like some more (coffee/tea)?_
   Response: No, thanks. I've had enough.

2. Offer: _Would you like some more (soup/cake)?_
   Response: Yeah, sure. I haven't eaten a thing all day.

3. Offer: _Would you like to see . . . (a photograph of something/my new . . .)?_
   Response: Oh, no, thank you. I've seen it already.

4. Offer: _Would you like a blanket?/Would you like me to turn up the heat?_
   Response: No, thanks. I'm warm enough.

5. Offer: _Would you like me to help you with that?/Would you like me to carry that for you?_
   Response: Yeah, it's really heavy. Thanks.

6. Offer: _Would you like to . . . (have lunch sometime)?_
   Response: Thanks, I'd love to. That sounds great.

7. Offer: _Would you like to borrow . . . (my grammar book)?_
   Response: Thanks, but I've already got one of my own.

EXERCISE 6

For each of the following situations, write a short dialogue in which one person makes a polite offer (using *Would you like . . .*) and the other person either politely accepts or politely refuses the offer. Then find a partner and read your dialogues aloud, taking parts.

1. The English instructor, at the front of the classroom, is ready to show a video in class today. The switch to turn on the video player is right by Stefan, at the back of the room.
   Stefan says: _Would you like me to turn the video on_ ?
   The instructor says: _____.

2. The dinner at Mrs. Zimunga's house is almost finished. Mrs. Zimunga notices that some of the guests ate their dessert—cherry pie—very quickly, and she thinks they might want another piece.
   Mrs. Zimunga says: _Would you like some more pie_ ?
   A guest says: _____.

3. Alfredo has a seat at the front of the city bus. He notices that an elderly woman has just gotten on, but there are no more seats left.
   Alfredo says: _Would you like my seat?/ to sit here_ ?
   The elderly woman says: _____.

(Answer Key Continued on SB page 244)

ANSWER KEY

Exercise 5   Answers will vary. Possible answers are listed above.

FOCUS 3 [5 minutes]

1. **Lead-in:** Use some of the examples of responses to offers that you collected in Exercise 3. List them on the board under headings "accepting" and "refusing." Ask students to help you categorize them and add to the list.

2. Have students practice the example dialogues from the focus chart in pairs, paying special attention to polite intonation.

3. You may find it relevant to discuss any cultural differences in accepting or refusing offers (see Culture Note below).

4. Ask your students to create more examples using each of the phrases presented in the focus chart. For example:

Jorge: *Would you like some more coffee?*
Elda: *No, thanks. No more caffeine for me today!*
OR

Liliana: *Do you guys want to meet later to study?*
Riaz: *Actually, I'm meeting Noom, but thanks.*
Ichihiro: *That'd be great for me, Liliana. What time?*

CULTURE NOTE

In some cultures it is not polite to accept a generous offer of food or help the first time it is offered. It is usual to wait for the offer to be repeated a second or third time to be sure that it is really sincere. Have students compare their cultural experiences.

EXERCISE 4 [5 minutes]

This exercise provides practice in recognizing different possible responses to offers.

1. Copy this exercise onto an overhead transparency.

2. Complete the exercise as a class, or have students work in pairs and review their answers as a class. Refer to the answer key on LP page 242 as needed.

3. If there is time, ask students for suggested alternative responses to each of the offers.

For more practice, use *Grammar Dimensions 2* Workbook pages 106–107, Exercise 2.

EXPANSION [15 minutes]

You may want to use Activity 4 on SB page 246 after this exercise.

EXERCISE 5 [10 minutes]

This exercise asks students to guess what kinds of offers were made by looking at the responses.

1. You may want to assign this exercise for homework to give students more time to think about the offers and write accurate sentences.

2. Have students compare answers in pairs.

3. When students have finished, compare some of their dialogues as a class.

4. Answers will vary. Refer to the answer key on LP page 242 for possible answers.

For more practice, use *Grammar Dimensions 2* Workbook pages 108–109 Exercise 3, and page 109, Exercise 4.

EXPANSION [30 minutes]

You may want to use Activity 5 (speaking/writing) on SB page 247 after this exercise.

EXERCISE 6 [15 minutes]

This exercise allows students to use all the forms presented in this unit and distinguish when to use them appropriately.

1. You may want to assign this exercise for homework to give students more time to think about the offers and write accurate sentences.

2. If you do this in class, allow time for students to read the situations and write their answers.

3. Have students compare answers and read their dialogs with a partner.

4. When students have finished working with their partners, compare some of their dialogues as a class. Encourage a variety of possible answers.

5. Answers will vary. Refer to answer key on LP page 242 for possible answers.

GRAMMAR NOTE

You may want to focus attention on the context as a clue for how polite the requests should be. The level of politeness depends on the person to whom the offer is being made, as well as the importance of the offer. It may be necessary to point out that being **too** polite is not always a good thing; with friends, for example, using *do you want* may be more appropriate for showing closeness between them when making small offers:

Amanda: *D'ya wanna come over?*
Misha: *Yeah, great idea! See ya in a minute.*

EXPANSION [15 minutes]

1. You may want to use Activity 3 (listening/writing) on SB page 246 after this exercise.

2. You may want to use Activity 7 (reflection) on SB page 247 as a way of closing this unit.

UNIT GOAL REVIEW [10 minutes]

Ask students to look at the goals on the opening page of the unit again. Refer to the pages of the unit where information on each goal can be found.

 For assessment of Unit 16, use *Grammar Dimensions 2* ExamView®.

Use Your English

ACTIVITY 1 speaking/listening

How do native speakers of English behave at parties? Is their behavior at formal parties different from their behavior at informal parties where the guests are all close friends or relatives?

Use the chart below to interview native speakers (or people who have spent a long time in an English-speaking country). There are blanks at the bottom for other topics you might want to find out about. Record your interview if possible.

WHAT DOES THE HOST DO OR SAY WHEN HE OR SHE . . .	FORMAL PARTIES	INFORMAL PARTIES
(a) invites the guests to sit down		
(b) offers the guests something to eat		
(c) encourages the guests to eat/drink more		
(d) invites the guests to start some activity (dancing/playing a game)		
(e)		
(f)		

ACTIVITY 2 writing

Your friend is coming to visit you this weekend. Write a short letter offering to meet him or her at the train station, and asking what activities he or she would like to do. Exchange your letter with a partner. Write a reply, accepting or refusing each offer politely. Exchange letters again. Were you polite enough?

---

4. As Mary is about to leave for the post office, she sees that there are several envelopes on the desk, stamped and addressed by her roommate Judith.

Mary says: <u>Would you like me to mail these for you</u> ?

Judith says: _____

5. Just as Thomas starts to drive away to work, he sees that his neighbor Rob is walking down the sidewalk to the bus stop. Thomas knows that Rob's office is not far from where he works.

Thomas says: <u>Would you like a ride to work</u> ?

Rob says: _____

6. Nyaradzo is jogging in the park, and she is about to cross a road. A stranger is waiting in his car, and he offers her a ride.

The stranger says: <u>Would you like a ride</u> ?

Nyaradzo says: _____

It's not always necessary to refuse offers **politely**! Check with your classmates to see their answers for Nyaradzo's response in item 6.

Opening Task (continued from page 239)

STEP 2:

Student B: Your job is first to work out what Student A needs and to offer a solution. After that you become a hotel guest. You have lost your voice, but you have some urgent problems. (Look at "Student B's Problems" below.) Go to the hotel reception and communicate your requests to the hotel desk clerk (Student A) *without speaking or writing*.

STUDENT B'S PROBLEMS	STUDENT A'S OFFER (STEP 3)
1. There is no hot water in your bathroom.	
2. The light bulb is broken in your reading lamp.	
3. Your hotel room is very cold. You need an extra blanket.	
4. You are hungry. You would like some sandwiches sent to your room.	
5. You have a high fever. You need a doctor right away.	

USE YOUR ENGLISH

The Use Your English section of activities at the end of the unit contain situations that should naturally elicit the structures covered in the unit. For a more complete discussion of how to use the Use Your English activities, see To the Teacher, LP page xxii. When students are doing these activities in class, you can circulate and listen to see if they are using the structures accurately. Errors can be corrected after the activity has finished.

ACTIVITY 1 speaking/listening
[30–40 minutes]

You may want to use this activity after Exercise 2 on SB page 241.

1. This activity is a chance for your students to discuss some cultural differences in making, accepting, and refusing offers when inviting someone to their homes (for coffee, dinner, or for a party).

2. Introduce the topic by asking students about their experiences in the United States or in other countries. Discuss the differences and the definition of "formal" and "informal" parties.

3. Students can interview each other, or you can assign this for homework so that they can interview someone from outside the class (or see variation below).

4. Have students report to the class on the results of their interviews.

5. You may want to follow this exercise with Activity 3 on SB page 246 (listening/writing).

VARIATION

If students don't have the opportunity to meet native speakers of English in person, you can organize this activity as an e-mail pen pal questionnaire.

1. Arrange for pen pals ahead of time. Sometimes you can contact students of the same age range at a sister school to set up a short- or long-term pen pal arrangement.

2. Pair your students up with people from the other group.

3. Direct students to create their own questions, using the chart as a guide.

4. When students have finished "interviewing" their pen pal, they can either report back orally or in written form.

ACTIVITY 2 writing
[20 minutes]

You may want to use this activity after Exercise 3 on SB page 241.

1. Read the instructions and brainstorm ideas from the class about what kind of offers could be made.

2. Have students start writing in class and complete their letters for homework.

3. Collect the letters and redistribute them for peer-editing. Encourage students to give positive comments as well as criticism.

4. Return the letters to the original writers and ask for any questions or queries.

5. Collect the letters so you can read them and correct them again. You may find them to be a useful way of checking comprehension of the language in this unit, as well as a source of examples for error correction later in the unit.

ACTIVITY 3 — listening/writing

CD Track 23

STEP 1
Listen to the audio of two people talking about giving parties. Divide a page in your notebook into two columns. Write some of the problems the man talks about in the first column. Write the suggestions the woman makes about each problem in the second column.

STEP 2
Discuss the problems and suggestions with a partner. How did the man respond to the woman's suggestions?

STEP 3
Listen again once or twice. This time write down the exact words the woman suggested using for the three problems you listed in Step 1.

STEP 4
What might the people at the party say in response to each of these suggestions? Write down three sentences in your notebook.

STEP 5
Write three sentences they might use to refuse the offers.

ACTIVITY 4 — speaking/listening

STEP 1
How can your classmate help you?
Think of two things that a classmate could do for you that would be helpful. Take two pieces of paper and write down one of those things on each piece. Do not write down your name.

Your teacher will collect the papers.

STEP 2
Your teacher will mix up the papers and give you two papers that other students wrote. (Make sure that you don't get your own!) Your job now is to guess who wrote each request for help. Go around the room to find the person. Make an offer to help each student you talk to using Would you like . . . ? or Do you want . . . ?

STEP 3
You must accept an offer if it is about the help you requested (the thing you wrote down on your piece of paper). You must refuse all other offers for help, even if they sound good.

ACTIVITY 5 — speaking/writing

STEP 1
A good friend is at home in bed sick. You want to help out and make your friend feel better. Make a list of five things in your notebook that you might do to help. Then get together with a partner who will play the role of your friend. Make offers using Would you like . . . ? and Do you want . . . ? Your "friend" can accept or refuse your offers.

STEP 2
Copy the chart below in your notebook. Write down responses to the offers you made in Step 1. If your friend accepts your offer, the response will go in the Accept column. If your friend refuses your offer, the response will go in the Refuse column. For each column, rank the responses in order of politeness. (Which responses seemed most polite? Which seemed least polite?)

RESPONSE TO YOUR OFFERS

OFFER	Accept	Refuse

ACTIVITY 6 — research on the web

Have you ever been annoyed by an email message? What kind of message was it? Why did you feel annoyed? Although email seems a fast and easy mode of communication, it also has rules of politeness which emailers have to learn. Find out about email etiquette by going to InfoTrac® College Edition and searching with keywords "email etiquette". Make notes of different types of advice that could make your emails more polite. Share them with your classmates.

ACTIVITY 7 — reflection

Think of a situation where you offered to do something for someone. What was the person's response? Did you get the response you expected? Explain the situation to your partner and compare his or her response. Would you both have done the same thing in that situation?

Switch roles and listen to your partner's situation. Compare your offers to do something and the responses.

ANSWER KEY

Activity 3 Check audio script on LP page 5–7 for answers.

CD Track 23

ACTIVITY 3 listening/writing [20 minutes]

You may want to use this activity after Activity 1, SB page 245.

STEP 1
1. Read the instructions for Step 1 and draw the chart on the board so that students can copy it into their notebooks.
2. Play the audio. See audio script on LP page S-7.

STEP 2 Have students discuss their answers in pairs.

STEP 3
1. Play the audio again.
2. Check the answers. See the audio script on LP page S-7 for the answers. Discuss which expressions are most and least formal.

STEP 4 Have students work individually to write possible responses to these offers.

STEP 5 Brainstorm ideas for accepting and refusing the offers.

ACTIVITY 4 listening/writing [20 minutes]

You may want to use this activity after Exercise 4 on SB page 242.

STEP 1
1. Distribute pieces of paper for this activity, two for each student.
2. You can have students write down real requests for help, or have them be more creative and write their "dream" requests. For example:

Take my test for me.
Give me a million dollars.
Arrange for me to meet Madonna.

3. Remind them not to write their names on their papers. You may want to write your requests too.
4. Collect the papers.

STEP 2 Redistribute the papers. Model a possible dialogue with one student.

STEP 3
1. Offers can only be accepted if it is the request you originally wrote.
2. Circulate while students are talking and join in the activity.

ACTIVITY 5 listening/writing [30 minutes]

You may want to use this activity after Exercise 5 on SB page 243.

STEP 1
1. Read the instructions for Step 1.
2. Have students work individually to make a list of things they could do to help.
3. Have students work in pairs to make, accept, and refuse offers. You can suggest that students take note of which offers are accepted and which are refused by their friend.

STEP 2
1. Draw the chart on the board and use an example from one of your students to illustrate how to complete it.
2. Have students complete their charts and then compare them with other students.
3. Rank the responses in order of politeness.

4. For further discussion of politeness, have students consider how they would change their offers if they were speaking with their grandmother or their younger brother or sister.

ACTIVITY 6 research on the web [15 minutes/homework]

The purpose of this Internet search activity is to provide a natural context for talking about levels of politeness. An additional purpose is to encourage students to learn how to use *InfoTrac® College Edition®* as a resource. See To the Teacher, LP page xxii for more information on how to use InfoTrac effectively.

ACTIVITY 7 reflection [10 minutes/homework]

You may want to use this activity after Exercise 6 on SB page 243 as a way of closing the unit.

This activity provides an opportunity for students to reflect on the use of the target structures in their real life. Although this is a partner activity, students can keep a record of such situations in their learner diary.

REQUESTS AND PERMISSION
Can, Could, Will, Would, and *May*

UNIT GOALS

- Make polite requests
- Politely agree to and refuse requests
- Ask for permission
- Give or politely refuse permission

OPENING TASK
Babysitting

■ STEP 1

Your neighbors are going out for the evening and they ask you to babysit their two children, aged 4 and 7 years old. They have a list of things for you to remember. What kinds of things do you think you will have to do? Work with a partner and make a list.

■ STEP 2

Your neighbors have left you a note with instructions about what to do while they are gone. Unfortunately, their 4-year-old daughter drew all over the note after her parents left and you can't read all of it. Work with a partner and try to complete the missing parts of the note on the next page. The first one has been done for you.

We're so glad you're here to watch the kids while we're gone. Here are some tips to help you.

C Will you please

1. _____ put them to bed by 8pm?

2. If they are hungry, _____

3. _____ brush their teeth before they go to bed?

4. They sometimes have trouble falling asleep, so would you mind _____

5. If there are any phone calls, _____

6. My cell phone is 356-555-5644. Please phone me if _____

■ STEP 3

Now look at the choices for the missing parts of the note above. Write the appropriate letter in the spaces on the note. Were your "answers" to the missing parts similar to these?

a. . . . could you make them some toast—but no candy!

b. . . . there is an emergency.

c. Will you please . . .

d. . . . reading them a story before they go to sleep?

e. Please could you make sure they . . .

f. . . . would you take a message and say we'll call back tomorrow?

ANSWER KEY

Opening Task *Step 2: 2. a 3. e 4. d 5. f 6. b*

LESSON PLAN 1

REQUESTS AND PERMISSION

UNIT OVERVIEW

Unit 17 provides practice with making polite requests, agreeing to and refusing requests, asking for permission, and giving or politely refusing permission. The modals *can, could, will, would*, and *may* are introduced, as they are important elements in performing these functions.

GRAMMAR/CULTURE NOTE

Differences in levels of formality when making requests or requests for permission can sometimes cause confusion or misunderstanding, as can cultural differences concerning when it is appropriate to refuse or accept a request. Some languages are more direct about making requests, for example, using a statement with a rising intonation, *You will help me?* Other languages use a very indirect approach, preferring to hint at a request in order to avoid putting the listener on the spot, for example, *I don't have money for the payphone.* (= *Could you lend me some change?*) or using many hedges and "softeners" to make requests more polite. This unit also presents opportunities to discuss the cultural differences in speech as it relates to linguistic communication.

UNIT GOALS

Some instructors may want to review the goals listed on Student Book (SB) page 248 after completing the Opening Task so that students understand what they should know by the end of the unit. These goals can also be reviewed at the end of the unit when students are more familiar with the grammar terminology.

OPENING TASK [20 minutes]

The purpose of the Opening Task is to create a context in which students will need to use requests. The problem-solving format is designed to show the teacher how well the students can use the target

structures implicitly and spontaneously when they are engaged in a communicative task. For a more complete discussion of the purpose of the Opening Task, see To the Teacher, Lesson Planner (LP) page xxii.

Setting Up the Task

STEP 1

1. Introduce the topic by looking at the picture. How old are these children? What are they doing?

2. Ask if anyone has ever had to babysit for a neighbor or friend. Have they asked anyone to babysit for them?

3. What kind of instructions would they get or give to a babysitter? Ask for some examples and make a list on the board. (This may depend on the age of the children, so you might have to specify the ages first.)

Conducting the Task

STEP 2

1. Read the description of the task. It's a good idea to have students cover up the answers listed under Step 3 while they work on Step 2.

2. Have students work in pairs or small groups to read the note and try to guess what could go in the illegible parts. They can write the guesses in their notebooks.

3. After this step, it's helpful to bring the class together in order to provide an opportunity for students to compare their guesses thus far.

Closing the Task

STEP 3

1. In pairs, students read the actual missing parts and decide where they should go in the note.

2. As a class, check how much students agree. Refer to the answer key on LP page 248. Bring to the

attention of the class that the writer is making a request. As a bridge to Focus Chart 1, you could write on the board or make an overhead transparency of the requests. Underline—or have students underline—the parts of the sentence that show that the speaker is making a request.

GRAMMAR NOTE

Typical student errors (form)

- Errors in short answers e.g. *Could you help me?* * *Yes, I could.* (See Focus 3.)

- Using infinitive after you *Would you mind . . . ?* e.g. * *Would you mind to open the window?* (instead of: *Would you mind if I opened the window?*) (See Focus 4.)

- Answering *yes* when agreeing to requests with *Would you mind . . . ?* e.g. *Would you mind helping me?* * *Yes.* (See Focus 5.)

Typical student errors (use)

- Using inappropriate levels of formality when making requests. (See Focus 1.)

- Refusing requests impolitely by not giving a reason, or not using polite phrases to soften the refusal, e.g. *Could you help me?* * *No.* (See Focus 2.)

- Confusing a request to do something with a request for permission, e.g. *Could you open the window?* and *Could I open the window?* (See Focus 4.)

FOCUS 1

use

Making Polite Requests

EXAMPLES

I left my notes at home.

(a) **Would you mind** lending me your notes?
(b) **Would you (please)** lend me your notes?
(c) **Could you** lend me your notes (please)?
(d) **Will you** lend me your notes (please)?
(e) **Can you (please)** lend me your notes?
(f) **Please** lend me your notes.

EXPLANATIONS

Most polite

↕

Least polite

The degree of politeness depends on who you are talking to and the type of request you are making.

EXERCISE 1

Below are some situations in a supermarket. For each situation, make a polite request.

1. You want to know what time it is. You see another customer who is wearing a watch and you say: _Could you please tell me what time it is?_

2. You want to buy some tomato sauce but you cannot find the right aisle. You see a store assistant and you say: _Could you tell me where the tomato sauce is, please?_

3. You want to get a box of tissues from the top shelf, but you are not tall enough to reach it. You see another customer nearby and you say: _Excuse me, would you mind helping me get this box of tissues?_

4. You cannot read the ingredients on a jar of jelly because you forgot your glasses. You find a store assistant and you say: _Would you please help me read this list of ingredients?_

5. You are shopping with a friend but when you get to the checkout line, you suddenly remember that you forgot to get some milk. You turn to your friend and say: _Will you keep my place in line? I have to get some milk._

6. When you are paying for your groceries, you remember that you need some change for the parking meter. You hand the cashier a dollar and say: _Can you give me some change for the parking meter, please?_

7. After paying for your groceries, you think there is a mistake on your bill. You go to the store manager and say: _Excuse me, would you mind checking this bill for me? I think there's a mistake._

FOCUS 2

use

Politely Refusing Requests

EXAMPLES

Can you lend me your notes?

(a) I'm sorry, but I need them to study for the test.
OR
(b) I'm afraid that I didn't take any notes.
OR
(c) I'd like to, but I left mine at home, too.

EXPLANATIONS

If you have to refuse a request, it is polite to say why you are refusing.

Phrases such as *I'm afraid that* or *I'm sorry* help to "soften" the *No*, and make it more polite.

EXERCISE 2

Walk around the classroom and ask a few classmates for the following things. If a classmate says *no*, write down the reason for refusing your request. Remember to write your classmates' names (or initials) in order to remember who you asked.

REQUEST		REASON FOR SAYING NO
1. lend you some money		
2. buy you a cup of coffee		
3. help you study for a test		
4. lend you a cell phone		
5. give you a ride home after class		
6. teach you how to dance		

ANSWER KEY

Exercise 1 Answers will vary. Possible answers are listed above.

Exercise 2 Since answers are dependent on the reason that students think up, they will vary.

LESSON PLAN 1

FOCUS 1 [5 minutes]

1. **Lead-in:** Have students begin the study of this page by closing their books. Start by making a variety of different requests. Use more polite language for the larger requests, more informal language for the smaller requests. Ask students to explain why you used different language for each one. Examples:

   Please lend me a pen.

   Can you lend me a piece of paper?

   Could you please let me use your cell phone?

   Would you mind lending me a dollar?

2. Explain that the difference in politeness depends on the type of request and also on the person you are addressing.

3. Write the examples from the focus chart on the board or on an overhead transparency in mixed-up order. Ask students to number them in order of politeness.

   Have students open their books and compare their answers with the focus chart.

4. Read the examples, varying your tone of voice to demonstrate distinctions between tone and the words used. For example, you could read (f) in a gruff, flat-toned voice and (b) in a clearly more polite, questioning voice.

5. Point out that between some of the questions— (b) as compared to (c), for example—the distinction is very slight, and some native speakers might consider them relatively "equal" in terms of degree of politeness. But the difference between (a) and (e), for example, is noticeable to most native speakers, especially if the *please* in (e) is omitted.

6. Refer to Grammar Note on LP page 257 for how to respond to *Would you mind . . . ?*

EXERCISE 1 [10 minutes]

This exercise provides practice in choosing the appropriate degree of politeness for a request.

1. Introduce the situation of shopping in a supermarket. Ask for some suggestions for requests you might need to make in a supermarket.

2. Have students work in pairs or small groups to read the situations and write their answers.

3. Ask volunteers to write their answers on the board. Each student should stand next to their sentence and explain why they chose that form of request.

4. The other students can agree or disagree.

5. Various answers are possible. Refer to the answer key on LP page 250.

 Use *Grammar Dimensions 2* Workbook page 110, Exercise 1.

EXPANSION [20 minutes]

You may want to use Activity 2 (speaking) on SB page 258 for a fun change of pace after this exercise.

FOCUS 2 [5 minutes]

1. **Lead-in:** Ask a student to ask you for something and respond with a simple *No*. For example, *Can you lend me a pen? No*. Explain that a lack of elaboration on **why** you are refusing a request is often interpreted as rudeness.

2. Ask for suggestions for how to make this refusal more polite.

3. Compare the suggestions with those in the chart.

4. Ask for comparative examples in other cultures and languages. Is the same strategy required? In other words, is it acceptable/polite to just say *no* and give no reason for your refusal?

EXERCISE 2 [15 minutes]

This exercise provides many opportunities for students to make and respond to requests.

1. Have students copy the chart into their notebooks.

2. Students will stand up and walk around the room. They should take their notebooks with them and write down the reasons for refusals.

3. Some students may need a little reassurance that it is okay to refuse a request, that there are polite ways to do this, and that the practice they will get in Exercise 2 may be very useful!

4. Circulate while students are talking and take notes of any errors, and also of different ways of agreeing to a request, which can be used to introduce Focus Chart 3.

5. Bring the class together to discuss the variety of different responses to their requests. What was the most creative or convincing reason for a refusal?

CULTURE NOTE

Remind students that it *is* acceptable to refuse requests and, in fact, some native English speakers are confused if they suspect that a response of "yes" is insincere, that the person doesn't actually want to respond positively to a request but is compelled, for some reason, to answer positively. Again, it may be helpful for students to give information about their own cultures and languages. Are there situations in the students' home cultures where, no matter the circumstance, it is rude to refuse a request?

Use *Grammar Dimensions 2* Workbook page 111, Exercise 2.

EXPANSION [20 minutes]

You may want to use Activity 1 (listening/speaking) on SB page 257 after this exercise. This activity involves research and observation in an out-of-class context.

FOCUS 3

Responding to Requests

EXAMPLES

Can you lend me your notes?

(a) I'd be glad to.

(b) Sure, why not?

(c) Yeah, no problem.

(d) Yeah, I guess so.

Could you loan me five dollars?

(e) Yes, I can.

(f) NOT: Yes, I could.

Would you go to the store with me?

(g) Yes, I will.

(h) NOT: Yes, I would.

EXPLANATIONS

You can respond to requests with short answers.

Examples (b) and (c) are very informal.

Example (d) shows that the speaker is uncertain.

Could and *would* are **not** used in responses to requests.

EXERCISE 3

Make polite requests for the following situations. Use *can, could, will, would,* or *would you mind* in these requests.

What is the response? How is the request politely accepted or refused?

1. You are carrying a large pile of books and aren't able to open the classroom door. You ask another student to open it.

You say: _Could you please open the door for me?_

What does the student say? _____.

2. You are at a restaurant, and the people at the next table are talking loudly on a cell phone.

You want them to stop, so you say: _Would you mind not talking so loudly_ ?

What do they say? _____.

3. Your friend is helping you hang a picture on your wall. She is holding it up while you decide where it should go.

You say: _Can you move it a little more to the left/right_ ?

What does your friend do or say? _____.

4. You are visiting a famous tourist spot, and a couple wants you to take their photograph together.

One person of the couple says: _Would you please take our picture?_

What do you do or say? _____.

5. You are trying to study for a test, and your neighbors are playing very loud music. You can't concentrate, so you say, _Would you mind turning down your music_ ?

What do your neighbors do or say? _____.

ANSWER KEY

Exercise 3 *Answers will vary. Possible answers are listed above.*

LESSON PLAN 1

FOCUS 3 [5 minutes]

1. **Lead-in:** Use some examples of agreeing to requests that you noted in Exercise 2. Write them on the board and ask students to rank them in order of formality.

2. Model and practice the intonation and pronunciation of the examples in the focus chart. It is helpful to model the word *Yeah* and have students repeat. Occasionally, there are students who have never actually uttered this word themselves (they are likely to say *yes* but not the more informal *yeah*), though they may have heard it.

3. Point out that it's acceptable to just use *Yes* or *Yeah* rather than following it with *I can* and *I will*.

EXERCISE 3 [15 minutes]

This exercise provides practice in making, accepting, and refusing requests, using all the forms presented so far, and deciding the appropriate level of politeness for each situation.

1. This exercise can be done individually or in pairs.

2. One way of doing this exercise is to assign pairs one particular dialogue (one pair is assigned #1, another #2, etc.) so that they are able to focus and practice "their" dialogue.

3. Allow students a few minutes to come up with answers and practice.

4. These situations can be performed as role-plays, with students standing up and speaking "ad lib" or from notes, rather than reading their answers word for word.

5. Have the audience "rate" the role-play on a 1–5 scale: 5 is appropriate (polite enough but not too polite), 1 is inappropriate (impolite or much too polite, given the circumstances). If there is a lot of variety in the ratings, ask raters to explain and defend their rating, using evidence from the context.

EXPANSION 1 [30 minutes]

You may want to use this writing exercise after Exercise 3.

1. Have students think of a situation where they have to make an important request (see the example).

2. Each student will write a short note on a rather small piece of paper to a friend making the request and explaining the reason for it. They should sign the letter with their name.

3. Collect all the folded papers and put them in a bag.

4. Have each student pick out a request (not their own!) and write a reply. They can accept or refuse the request. The reply must contain about three sentences (see example below) but should not mention the request explicitly. Students deliver their replies to the appropriate person.

5. Ask volunteers to read their replies to the class. The others should guess what the original request was.

Example request:

Dear Janni, Could you please help me move to my new apartment on Saturday? I have so many boxes of books and I can't manage it by myself. And could you bring your car too please? Thanks! Suzie

Example reply:

Dear Suzie, I'd like to help you but I am afraid that I am busy this weekend. I am going shopping with my parents on Saturday. Anyway, I have a bad back and I can't lift anything heavy. Janni

 Use *Grammar Dimensions 2* Workbook page 112, Exercise 3.

EXPANSION 2 [20 minutes]

You may want to use Activity 4 (writing) on SB page 259 after this exercise.

EXERCISE 4

Below are some questions you might ask in the classroom. Copy the question in the appropriate box in the chart below. The first one has been done for you.

SOMETHING THE SPEAKER WANTS TO DO (REQUEST FOR PERMISSION)	SOMETHING THE SPEAKER WANTS SOMEBODY ELSE TO DO (GENERAL REQUEST)
1. Do you mind if I turn on the lights?	2. Can you open the window?
3. May I ask you a question?	4. Could you speak more slowly?
6. Can I speak to you about the assignment?	5. Would you mind lending me your dictionary?
8. May we leave class early today?	7. Would you tell me the answer?
10. Could I borrow your textbook?	9. Could you show us how to find the answers?
11. Would you mind if I handed in my assignment a day late?	12. Will you help me with my homework?

1. Do you mind if I turn on the lights?
2. Can you open the window?
3. May I ask you a question?
4. Could you speak more slowly?
5. Would you mind lending me your dictionary?
6. Can I speak to you about the assignment?
7. Would you tell me the answer?
8. May we leave class early today?
9. Could you show us how to find the answers?
10. Could I borrow your textbook?
11. Would you mind if I handed in my assignment a day late?
12. Will you help me with my homework?

FOCUS 4

Asking for Permission

use

(a) Would you mind if I left early?	Most polite	↕
(b) Do you mind if I leave early?		
(c) May I leave early?		
(d) Could I leave early?		
(e) Can I leave early?	Least polite	

EXERCISE 5

For each answer, what was probably the question?

1. Question: _Would you mind if I handed in my assignment late_ ?

   Teacher to student: No, I'd like you to hand it in on Friday. I announced the due date two weeks ago, so I'm afraid I won't be able to make any exceptions.

2. Question: _May I close the window_ ?

   Friend to friend: Sure, it is a little cold in here.

3. Question: _Can I ask a question, please_

   Lecturer to member of the audience: Sorry, but I'm going to have to ask you to hold your questions until the end of my talk. We'll have fifteen minutes for questions.

4. Question: _May I speak to . . ._ ?

   Secretary (on phone): Yes, may I tell him who's calling?

5. Question: _May I talk to . . ._ ?

   Twelve-year-old child (on phone): Yes, hold on and I'll go and get him.

6. Question: _Could I have a cookie_ ?

   Mother (to child): OK, you can have one more. But only _one_, because we're going to eat soon, and I don't want you to spoil your appetite.

7. Question: _May I have another . . ._ ?

   Hostess to guest: Oh, of course, please help yourself. I'm glad you like them.

8. Question: _May I help you_ ?

   Customer to salesperson: Yes, I want to look at the sweaters that are on sale—the ones that were advertised in the newspaper?

REQUESTS AND PERMISSION *Can, Could, Will, Would, and May* **255**

ANSWER KEY

Exercise 5 Answers will vary. All general requests and requests for permission should include *Can . . . ? Could . . . ?, Will . . . ?, Would . . . ?, May . . . ?, and possibly please or Would you mind . . . ?* Possible answers are listed above.

EXERCISE 4 [10 minutes]

This exercise reviews the difference between asking if you can do something and asking someone to do something. It prepares students for Focus Chart 4 where this distinction is explained in more detail.

1. Review requests by asking what kind of requests students might make in a classroom. Or ask which requests are most commonly made in your class.

2. If any requests for permission come up, use this as a way to present the difference between a request and a request for permission.

3. Give two examples to illustrate the difference between asking someone to do something and asking if you can do something. For example:

Could you help me carry some books, please?
Could I borrow this book, please?

4. Have students complete the exercise individually or in pairs. They can write the numbers of the questions in the chart, or copy the questions.

5. Review the answers by asking a different student to read each question aloud. You can elicit answers from that student, from the one sitting next to the speaker, or from any one in the class.

PRONUNCIATION NOTE

Point out how these question phrases are reduced in natural, informal speech: *Do you mind* sounds like *D'ya mind. Can you* sounds like *Can ya. Could you* sounds like *Could'ja. Would you* sounds like *Would'ja.* Model and practice these questions. Emphasize that it is not necessary for students to sound like this, but that they are likely to hear native speakers reduce these phrases in this way.

EXPANSION [20 minutes]

You may want to use Activity 8 (reflection) on SB page 261 after this exercise. This activity encourages students to share ideas on ways to help each other improve their study skills.

FOCUS 4 [5 minutes]

1. **Lead-in:** Have students begin with closed books. Remind students of the use of *would you mind* for requests from Focus Chart 1. You can contrast these two examples:

Would you mind lending me your notes?
Would you mind if I opened the window?

2. Ask students to identify the difference in function between these two questions. One is a request asking someone else to do something. The second is a request for permission.

3. Ask students to identify the grammatical difference. See Grammar Note below for use of past tense and appropriate responses to *Would you mind . . . ?*

4. Read the examples from the focus chart in random order and have students number them in order of politeness.

5. Have students open their books and check the answers by looking at the chart. Point out the similarities between this focus chart and Focus Chart 1: *would you mind* questions are considered most polite; *could* questions somewhere in the middle; and *can* questions least polite/most informal. As with Focus Chart 1, the distinctions between (a)–(b) and (c)–(d), for example, aren't particularly strong, but the difference between the two extremes (a)–(e) is.

GRAMMAR NOTE

Would you mind . . . ? can be used for requests and for asking for permission. For requests, it is followed by a gerund, for example, *Would you mind carrying these books for me?* When asking for permission, it is followed by an *if* clause with the past tense—for example, *Would you mind if I left early today? (Do you mind if . . . ?* is followed by the present tense.) See Focus Chart 5 and the Grammar Note on LP page 257 for correct responses to *Would you mind . . . ?*

EXERCISE 5 [15 minutes]

In this exercise, students use the answers to work out what the question is.

1. Do the first question together as a class.

2. Explain to the students that they will need to look at the relationship between the people to work out the degree of politeness. They will need to look at the response to work out what kind of request was made.

3. Have students work in pairs to write their answers.

4. Ask volunteers to read their answers. Ask if the rest of the class agrees or disagrees or if they can provide alternative answers.

5. Answers may vary. Refer to the answer key on LP page 254 for suggested answers.

For more practice, use *Grammar Dimensions 2* Workbook page 113, Exercise 4.

EXPANSION [20 minutes]

You may want to use Activity 5 (reading/speaking) on SB page 259 after this exercise.

Use Your English

use

FOCUS 5

Responding to Requests for Permission

EXAMPLES

Would you mind if I left early?
(a) No, not at all.
(b) Sorry, but I need you to stay until 5:00.

May I leave early?
(c) Yes, of course.
(d) Sorry, but I'd rather have you stay until 5:00.

Could I leave early?
(e) Yes, you can.
(f) NOT: Yes, you could.

EXPLANATIONS

Use short phrases to answer requests for permission.

If you refuse a request, it is polite to give the reason.

Could is not usually used in responses to requests for permission.

EXERCISE 6

For each of the following situations, work with a classmate to make general requests or requests for permission, and then respond to these requests. Decide how polite you need to be in each situation and whether *can, could, will, would, may, would you mind,* or *do you mind* is the most appropriate to use. Use a variety of different possible responses.

1. You are at a friend's house, and you want to use the phone.

2. Your teacher says something, but you do not understand, and you want her to repeat it.

3. Your friend has asked you to pick her up at the airport. You want to know if her flight, #255 from Denver, is on time, so you call the airline.

4. You want to borrow your roommate's car.

5. Your roommate is going to the store, and you remember that you need some aspirin.

6. You are the first one to finish the reading test in class. You want to find out from your teacher if you are allowed to leave the room now.

7. It is very cold in class, and the window is open.

8. You see that your teacher is in her office with the door partly open. You want to go in to talk to her.

9. You are on the phone with the dentist's secretary because you want to change your appointment time.

10. You are at a close friend's house, and you would like a cup of tea.

ACTIVITY 1 listening/speaking

STEP 1

Go to a restaurant or cafeteria and pay attention to the different kinds of requests that are used. Try to observe five different requests. Take notes on these, using the chart below.

OBSERVATION SHEET

PLACE:

TIME:

DAY:

REQUEST:	WHO MADE IT:	RESPONSE:

STEP 2

Discuss the results of your observations with other classmates. Were their observations similar? What words were used most often in requests: *can, could, will, would,* or *would you mind?*

ANSWER KEY

Exercise 6 *Answers will vary. Possible questions are:* 1. May I use the phone? 2. Could you repeat that, please? 3. Could you please tell me if Flight 255 from Denver is on time? 4. May I borrow your car? 5. Would you mind buying me some aspirin? 6. May I leave the room now? 7. Can I/Would you shut the window, please? 8. Can you spare some time to talk with me? 9. Could I please change my appointment? 10. Can I have some tea, please?

LESSON PLAN 2/USE YOUR ENGLISH

FOCUS 5 [5 minutes]

1. **Lead-in:** Read the requests from the focus chart and brainstorm ideas for responding to them. Write all the suggestions on the board.

2. Refer back to Focus Chart 1 and the different ways of responding to *Would you mind . . . ?* versus *Could you . . . ?* Relate this to responding to requests for permission.

3. Read the examples and explanations in the focus chart.

4. Refer back to Focus Chart 3, pointing out that it's acceptable to just use *Yes* or *Yeah* for positive responses; it's not always necessary to use the short answers: *Yes, you can.* or *Yes, you may.* As with Focus Chart 3, informal responses such as *Yeah, sure,* and *No problem,* are also acceptable.

GRAMMAR NOTE

When agreeing to a request or a request for permission with *Would you mind . . . ?* the correct response is *No.* Because this can be confusing, it is usually elaborated by a further statement—for example, *"No, I don't mind"* or *"No, that's fine",* and sometimes replaced by an affirmative response. *Okay* or *Yes, of course you can* in order to make the meaning quite clear.

EXERCISE 6 [15 minutes]

This exercise reviews all the different language forms presented in this unit.

1. Remind students of all the different language forms they have practiced in this unit. Encourage them to use all of these forms in this exercise (or as many as they can).

2. Have students work in pairs or groups to complete the exercise.

3. While students are working in pairs, circulate and listen, noting questions and responses that strike you as either very good and natural sounding, or as inappropriate.

4. Read some of the questions and responses you heard, asking them what their reactions are.

5. Review and compare answers for each situation. Refer to the answer key on LP page 256 for possible answers.

Note: All requests and requests for permission include *Can . . . ? Could . . . ? Will . . . ? Would . . . ? May . . . ?* and possibly *Would you mind . . . ?* Responses can be nonverbal (as in #7—the person simply shuts the window) or they can include short answers such as *Yes, sure . . . * If requests for permission are refused, they should include a reason and/or *Sorry, but . . . * or another "softening" phrase.

For more practice, use *Grammar Dimensions 2* Workbook page 114, Exercise 5.

EXPANSION [20 minutes]

You may want to use Activity 6 (listening/writing) on SB page 261 after this exercise.

USE YOUR ENGLISH

The section of activities at the end of the unit contain situations that should naturally elicit the structures covered in the unit. For a more complete discussion of how to use the Use Your English activities, see To the Teacher, LP page xxii. When students are doing these activities in class, you can circulate and listen to see if they are using the structures accurately. Errors can be corrected after the activity has finished.

ACTIVITY 1 listening/speaking [20 minutes]

You may want to use this activity after Exercise 2 on SB page 251.

1. Students may want to redraw these charts on a larger piece of paper so that there is more room for notetaking.

2. Discuss with your class places where they might go to make these observations.

3. Have students complete the observation for homework (see Methodology Note below).

4. Each research team can present samples of their data as a role-play. They can perform for the rest of the class a few of the short interactions that they observed.

METHODOLOGY NOTE

If your class hasn't yet done this kind of observation/research activity, it's good to work in teams of two or three, each choosing a different site or a different post at one site (for example, in one cafeteria, students go to different places—one near the check stand/cash register, one where the food is served, etc.). This way students can check with each other and give support and suggestions, if they are experiencing problems. It's helpful to have more than one student involved, in order to increase the validity of the observation. Compiling notes will help to ensure the accuracy of what was said.

UNIT GOAL REVIEW [10 minutes]

Ask students to look at the goals on the opening page of the unit again. Refer to the pages of the unit where information on each goal can be found. One way is to present the goals as a checklist, having students create examples for each.

ExamView Test Generator — For assessment of Unit 17, use *Grammar Dimensions 2* ExamView®.

ACTIVITY  2　speaking

Play this game in a group of five or six students or with the whole class.

■ STEP 1

Pick a letter from the alphabet. Ask a classmate to buy you something at the mall that begins with that letter.

■ STEP 2

Your classmate must think of something to buy that begins with the letter you chose and then he or she must tell you what it is.

■ STEP 3

Your classmate then chooses another student.

Examples: Sara: *Bruno, would you please buy me something that begins with the letter S?*

Bruno: *Sure. I'll buy you sneakers. Sue, could you buy me something that begins with the letter M?*

Sue: *Ok. I'll buy you a magazine. Hartmut, would you mind buying me something that begins with the letter P?*

ACTIVITY　3　listening

How do people request permission to speak with someone on the telephone? Are these ways different depending on the situation?

Interview people about what they say in different situations. Some examples are: speaking with a doctor, speaking with a teacher, speaking with a close friend, and speaking with a family member.

SETTING	RELATIONSHIP	WHAT THEY SAY

ACTIVITY　4　writing

Congratulations! You have just won a certificate for Easy-Does-It Housecleaning Services. This entitles you to four hours of housecleaning service for your home. First make a list of what you want the housecleaner to do in your home (clean the windows, do the laundry, mop the floor, etc.). Then write these requests in a polite note to your housecleaner.

ACTIVITY　5　reading/speaking

■ STEP 1

What would you say in each of the following situations? Respond to each situation. Then compare your results with other students' results.

1. You are in the bookstore with a friend, standing in line to buy a textbook you need for class later that day. You realize you have left your wallet at home and you want your friend to lend you twenty dollars to pay for the book.

   You: _____

   Your friend: Sure. You can pay me back next week.

2. You have just heard about a new job and you feel that you are qualified. You need to ask your teacher for a letter of recommendation.

   You: _____

   Your teacher: I'd be happy to. When do you need it?

3. You are visiting a close friend at her house. You realize you are thirsty, but your friend hasn't offered you anything to drink.

   You: _____

   Your friend: Sure. Help yourself. You know where everything is, right?

ANSWER KEY

Exercise 5　Step 1: *Answers may vary slightly, but all should include a polite request and/or a request for permission.*

USE YOUR ENGLISH

ACTIVITY 2 speaking [15 minutes]

You may want to use this activity after Exercise 1 on SB page 250.

1. Demonstrate the rules of the game to the whole class.

2. If your class is small, continue playing as a whole class. If not, then divide into smaller groups to continue the activity.

3. You may add further rules to the game, for example, setting a time limit for each student to answer or make a request. If they do not manage, they are "out".

4. Remind students that their requests should be polite.

ACTIVITY 3 listening [20 minutes]

You may want to use this activity after Exercise 6 on SB page 256.

1. Read the description of the activity. Ask for suggestions for requests in these different situations.

2. Have students interview each other or someone outside the class. Students should find out what kind of requests their interviewees make, and also what kind of language they use.

3. You may want to assign different situations to different students.

4. Have students present their information to the class.

■ STEP 2 Students can do this part of the activity outside of class. If recording is a problem, students can do this step in research teams of two or three and take detailed notes. See Methodology Note on LP page 257.

METHODOLOGY NOTE

One way of increasing the potential for pooling and discussing ideas is to reorganize groups for the second round of discussion. You can do this in the following way. For the first step, organize your class into groups of four and assign each student in the group a letter A, B, C, or D. For the second stage, have all A students, all B students, all C students, and all D students stand up and regroup to sit together. If you have 16 students, you will then have four new groups and students can share the ideas from their first group in their second group.

ACTIVITY 4 writing [20 minutes]

You may want to use this activity after Exercise 3 on SB page 252.

1. Review some features of writing a polite note. It should include the date, a salutation, and perhaps an introductory or closing sentence such as *Thank you for coming to clean up my house today.*

2. Assign the writing as homework, or set a time limit in class.

3. Select (anonymous) extracts from some of the letters for discussion in class. How polite were they?

ACTIVITY 5 reading/speaking [20 minutes]

You may want to use this activity after Exercise 5 on SB page 255. This activity leads into Activity 6 (listening/writing).

■ STEP 1

1. Do the first situation together with your class. Have students write down their answers. Then compare the answers all together. This is to illustrate that there is no single correct answer.

2. Have students work in pairs to discuss and complete the rest of the activity.

3. Have students change partners and compare their answers. See Methodology Note.

4. Ask volunteers to perform a question and response sequence for the whole class. (If possible, record these for Activity 6.)

5. For each role-play, ask: *Was the request polite enough? If not, what is a better way of making the request?*

4. You just made plans to study for a big test with your classmates, but suddenly you realize that you have a doctor's appointment at the same time—at 2:00 tomorrow. You decide that you want to change your doctor's appointment, so you call the doctor's secretary.

You: _____

The secretary: *I think* it's possible. When would you be available?

5. It's time to leave the house to meet your friend for a dinner date. But you can't find your car keys anywhere, and your friend has already left her house to meet you. You want to borrow your roommate's car and look for your car keys later.

You: _____

Your roommate: Yeah, no problem.

6. You are visiting a close friend's mother. She has made peach pie, and you'd love to have a second piece. Your friend has told you that her mother loves to feed people, so you know that it wouldn't be rude to ask for another piece.

You: _____

Your friend's mother: Oh, of course! Let me get it for you.

 STEP 2 Ask at least three different people to respond to each situation. Record their answers.

 **ACTIVITY 6 listening/writing**

Now listen to the audio to hear what other speakers said in response to questions 1, 2, and 6 in Activity 5.

CD Track 24

 STEP 1 Compare the responses of the speakers on the audio with your responses in Activity 5, and also to the responses of the speakers you interviewed. Were you surprised at anything they said? Do you consider these polite responses? Do you think any of their requests would be refused?

STEP 2 For each situation, write down the exact requests that Agnes or Eliza made (if there were any). Then rate each request in terms of politeness on a 1 to 5 scale (1 = most polite; 5 = least polite/most informal). Are there any requests that are "off the scale" (not at all polite, or even rude)? Compare your ratings to other classmates' ratings, and discuss your results.

ACTIVITY 7 research on the web

Go on the Internet and use a search engine such as Google® or Yahoo® to find a site that can help you with writing a request letter. Type in keywords: "Writing a request letter". Use the information to write your own request letter.

ACTIVITY 8 reflection

Think of three ways your classmates could help you to improve your study skills. Write three requests to ask for help.

Example: *Could you show me how to organize my notes?*

In small groups, share your three requests and discuss the answers. What were the best ideas? Which ones can you use?

ANSWER KEY

Exercise 6   Step 2: *See audio script, LP page S-7.*

Step 2, exact requests:

Agnes: Please give me some money.

Eliza: Would you be able to lend me some money?

Agnes: Could you please write me a letter of recommendation?

Eliza: Would you be so kind as to write me a letter of recommendation?

USE YOUR ENGLISH

CD
Track
24

ACTIVITY 6 listening/writing
[20 minutes]

You may want to use this activity after Exercise 5 on SB page 255. This activity is a follow-up to Activity 5.

■ STEP 1

1. Explain that students will hear speakers responding to the task they completed in Activity 5. Have students refer back to their answers to that activity.

2. Play the audio. See audio script on LP page S-7.

3. Check the answers. See the audio script for answers, LP page S-7. Play the audio again if necessary.

4. Compare the answers with the students' answers.

■ STEP 2

1. Play the audio again. Have students write the exact requests and rank them in order of politeness.

2. Compare answers as a class.

VARIATION

If Activity 5, Step 2 was recorded, then this activity can be conducted with the Step 2 responses as well. Students transcribe the exact requests and then rate these on a 1–5 point scale. This is helpful for further listening comprehension practice, since it allows the opportunity for detailed listening. It also helps in "fine tuning" in that students can further check their insights about the degree of politeness (or impoliteness) in requests.

ACTIVITY 7 research on the web

The purpose of this Internet search activity is to provide a natural context for using requests. An additional purpose is to encourage students to share strategies for finding information on the Internet. What websites were most useful? This activity may tie in well with rules and formats for writing a formal or informal letter.

ACTIVITY 8 reflection
[15 minutes/homework]

You may want to use this activity after Exercise 4 on SB page 254. This activity provides an opportunity for students to use the target structures of the unit while reflecting on their language learning progress. After asking each other for advice, students can summarize the best ideas in their journal. You may have asked students to keep a record of their learning in a journal throughout this course as suggested in To the Teacher, LP page xxii. This reflection activity will be part of that learning record.

UNIT 18

USED TO WITH STILL AND ANYMORE

UNIT GOALS

- Use *used to* to compare past and present situations
- Form statements and questions with *used to*
- Use *still* and *anymore* correctly

OPENING TASK

Famous People Then and Now

■ STEP 1

Work with several other students. Look at the photographs of these movie stars. Which ones do you know? What kind of movies do you think they are in?

4.

1.

5.

2.

6.

3.

■ STEP 2

Look below at the photographs of the same people before they were famous. Match the old photographs with the current ones. Write the number and name next to each photo below.

e. (4) Morgan Freeman

c. (2) Nicole Kidman

f. (5) Brad Pitt

a. (3) Arnold Schwarzenegger

b. (6) Julia Roberts
d. (1) Jennifer Lopez

■ STEP 3

In your opinion, who has changed a lot? Who hasn't changed much? Explain why you think so.

Example: I think Brad Pitt has changed a lot.
Why?
Because he used to _____ but _____ now he _____ .

ANSWER KEY

Opening Task   Step 1: 1. Jennifer Lopez   2. Nicole Kidman   3. Arnold Schwarzenegger   4. Morgan Freeman   5. Brad Pitt   6. Julia Roberts

LESSON PLAN 1

UNIT OVERVIEW

In this unit, the structure *used to* is introduced to talk about past facts and habits, contrasting with *still* and *anymore*.

GRAMMAR NOTE

It can be difficult for learners to understand the distinction between the use of this tense and other past tenses. Other problems can occur because of confusion with two other similar structures: *be used to something/doing something* and *get used to something/doing something*. A further problem can be caused by similarity with the synonym *used* (past tense of the verb *use*), which has a different pronunciation.

UNIT GOALS

Some instructors may want to review the goals listed on Student Book (SB) page 262 after completing the Opening Task so that students understand what they should know by the end of the unit. These goals can also be reviewed at the end of the unit when students are more familiar with the grammar terminology.

OPENING TASK [20 minutes]

The purpose of the Opening Task is to create a context in which students can use the forms *used to* or *didn't use to*. The problem-solving format is designed to show the teacher how well the students can use the target structures implicitly and spontaneously when they are engaged in a communicative task. For a more complete discussion of the purpose of the Opening Task, see To the Teacher, Lesson Planner (LP) page xxii.

Setting Up the Task

■ STEP 1

1. Introduce the topic of movie stars by looking at the pictures and trying to guess who they are. If your students are not familiar with these faces, put the list of names on the board and ask students to match them up.

2. You may want to have students work in groups to share what they know about each movie star and then pool the information as a class.

3. Prepare students for Step 3 by asking them to describe the appearance of the people in the pictures. They can describe hair color, hairstyle, and facial features.

4. If students struggle with descriptions, write the following vocabulary words on the board as reminders: **hair**: *long, short, medium-length, blond, dark, brown, crew cut, wavy, curly, straight, bald or shaved*; **face**: *round, oval, square, pointed chin, square jaw, high forehead*.

Conducting the Task

■ STEP 2

1. In their groups, students match these older photos with the more current ones.

2. Review their answers before moving on to Step 3.

■ STEP 3

1. Groups decide who has changed the most, using the model sentence as a guide. They may use some of the vocabulary from Step 1.

2. Do not correct errors at this stage. Circulate and listen to students' language to evaluate their current knowledge of the target structures. Take notes of errors in form, meaning, and use in order to focus the material in the unit.

3. Invite volunteers to make sentences about the pictures.

4. Many answers are possible. Refer to the answer key on LP page 262.

Closing the Task

1. Review vocabulary to describe differences in appearance, such as hairstyles and color.

2. If you have a high school yearbook, bring it to class. Since many cultures do not have yearbooks, students may want to find out more.

3. Using your yearbook, have students describe how you have changed.

4. You may want to ask students to bring in pictures of themselves when they were younger for use later in the unit (see Activity 1 on SB page 269).

GRAMMAR NOTE

Typical student errors (form)

- Using the verb *be* with *used to*, e.g. * *She is used to have long hair. They were used to live in New York.* (See Focus 2.)

- Errors with *used* and *use*, e.g. * *I didn't used to like soccer.* (See Focus 2.)

- Errors in word order with adverbs of frequency, e.g. * *She always is late for class.* (See Focus 5.)

- Errors in word order with *still*, e.g. * *He lives still at home with his parents.* (See Focus 4.)

- Repeating the verb when it is unnecessary and better to use ellipsis, e.g. * *He used to drive to work, but now he doesn't drive to work.* (See Focus 3.)

- Pronunciation of *used* [juːzd] versus *used* [juːst].

Typical student errors (use)

- Using *used to* to talk about present situations, e.g. * *We used to live here since 1998.* (See Focus 1.)

- Confusion between *used to* do something and *be used to* doing something, e.g. * *I was used to learning the piano.* (See Focus 1.)

FOCUS 1

Comparing Past and Present with Used To

meaning
use

EXAMPLES

(a) Julia Roberts used to have curly hair (but now she doesn't).

(b) Arnold Schwarzenegger used to make movies (but now he doesn't).

EXPLANATIONS

Used to can be used to show that something was true in the past, but now it isn't.

Used to can also show that something happened regularly (often) in the past, but now it doesn't.

EXERCISE 1

Make statements with *used to* about Jennifer Lopez and Brad Pitt. Use the words in parentheses. You can add other ideas of your own.

1. Jennifer Lopez

a. (live in New York City / Long Island) _She used to live in New York City but now_ _she lives in Long Island._

b. (have dark hair / light brown hair) _She used to have dark hair but now she has_ _light brown hair._

c. (be on TV / make movies) _She used to be on TV but now she makes movies._

2. Brad Pitt

a. (have long hair / short hair) _Brad Pitt used to have short hair but now he has_ _long hair._

b. (live in Missouri / Hollywood) _He used to live in Missouri but now he lives_ _in Hollywood._

c. (drive limousines / is a movie star) _He used to drive limousines but now he is a_ _movie star._

Now make statements with *used to* about the other people in the Opening Task.

FOCUS 2

Used To

form

	STATEMENT	NEGATIVE	QUESTION
I / You / We / They	used to work.	did not **use to** work. (didn't)	Did I / You / We / They **use to** work?
She / He / It	used to work.	did not **use to** work. (didn't)	Did She / He / It **use to** work?

FOCUS 3

Anymore

use

EXAMPLES

(a) Jennifer Lopez used to live in New York, but she doesn't live there **anymore.**

(b) Jennifer Lopez used to live in New York, but she doesn't **anymore.**

(c) Jennifer Lopez doesn't live in New York **anymore.**

(d) We don't go there **anymore.**

(e) They **never** talk to me **anymore.**

(f) **No one** likes him **anymore.**

(g) Does he live there **anymore?**

EXPLANATIONS

Use *anymore* to show a change in a situation or activity.

If the second verb phrase has the same verb, you can omit it.

You can use *anymore* without *used to*. In (c) we understand that she used to live there.

Use *anymore* only with a negative statement or question.

EXERCISE 2

Interview your classmates about the changes in their lives. Then write short statements about these changes, using *anymore* and *used to*. (The word *but* may be helpful.)

Example: *Teresita used to live in Guam, but she doesn't anymore. She used to be single, but now she lives with a partner.*

UNIT 18 LESSON PLAN 1

FOCUS 1 [5 minutes]

1. **Lead-in:** Refer back to the sentences which students made in the Opening Task. Include one sentence with a stative verb and one with a dynamic verb.
2. Read the examples and the explanations in the focus chart.
3. Add further examples that students created in the Opening Task.

EXERCISE 1 [10 minutes]

This exercise provides practice with *used to*, using extra information about the movie stars in the Opening Task.

1. Refer back to the pictures of Jennifer Lopez and Brad Pitt.
2. Read the example sentence item 1 in Exercise 1, SB page 264 with the class.
3. Have students complete the sentences individually.
4. Students who finish early can compare answers in pairs.
5. Have students add sentences with information they know. For example:
Nicole Kidman used to be married to Tom Cruise.
Arnold Schwarzenegger used to be a bodybuilder.
Jennifer Lopez used to record music.

For more practice, use *Grammar Dimensions 2* Workbook page 115, Exercise 1.

EXPANSION [20 minutes]

To make this exercise more relevant to students' interests, ask them to choose a movie, music, or sports star that they like.

1. Have each student present one or two facts about their favorite movie, music, or sports star. Or have students work in groups to share information about their favorite stars.

2. Assign this topic for homework and have students research facts about their favorite stars. You may want to assign Activity 8 (research on the web) on SB page 271 as homework after this exercise.

FOCUS 2 [5 minutes]

1. **Lead-in:** You may want to start with the most difficult part of this structure, which is when to use *used to* or *use to*. Write the following sentences on the board. Ask students to fill in *used* or *use* in each one.

    She _____ to be a waitress.
    She didn't _____ to live in New York.
    Did she _____ to live in Brooklyn?
    Where did she _____ to live?

2. From these examples students may be able to work out the rule: *used* is in positive statements, *use* is in negative statements and questions. *Use* is the infinitive form and *used* is the regular past form.
3. Read the examples in the chart. You may want to add further examples of *Wh-* questions—e.g., *Where did you use to work? What did you use to do?*

For more practice, use *Grammar Dimensions 2* Workbook page 115, Exercise 2.

FOCUS 3 [5 minutes]

This focus chart presents the use of *anymore* used with negative statements or questions. It also presents the use of ellipsis (omitting the verb and the following phrase when they are repeated).

1. **Lead-in:** To introduce the idea of ellipsis, write this example on the board:

    Jennifer Lopez used to live in New York City, but now she doesn't live in New York City.

2. Ask students which words could be omitted (live in New York City) and why (to avoid unnecessary repetition).

3. Then ask if any words could be added to make the meaning clearer (anymore).
4. Read the examples and explanations in the chart.
5. You may want to mention that *Not anymore* can be used alone as a short answer

    A: *Does Sonia live with her parents?*
    B: *Not anymore. She's married now.*

EXERCISE 2 [15 minutes]

This exercise provides personalized practice of *used to* and *anymore.*

1. You may start by eliciting a few questions. For example, *Where did you use to live? What did you use to study?*
2. Set a time limit for students to ask each other questions and come up with three statements about their partner.
3. Ask volunteers to tell the class what they found out about their partner.
4. Encourage students to use ellipsis and *anymore.* Or ask other students to listen and suggest ways of improving the sentences using these structures.

For more practice, use *Grammar Dimensions 2* Workbook page 116, Exercise 3.

EXPANSION [20 minutes]

You may want to use Activity 6 (speaking) on SB page 270 after this exercise.

FOCUS 4

form   meaning

Still

EXAMPLES	EXPLANATIONS
(a) She **still** lives in New Mexico. (She lived in New Mexico fifteen years ago; she lives there now.)	Use *still* to show that something or someone has NOT changed.
(b) He **still** runs five miles a day. (He ran five miles a day in the past; he runs five miles a day now.)	Use *still* to show that an activity or habit has NOT changed.
(c) He **still** lives in New Orleans.	Use *still* before the main verb.
(d) He is **still** crazy after all these years.	Use *still* after the verb *be*.
(e) She can **still** play the piano.	Use *still* after an auxiliary verb such as *can, may, should,* etc.

EXERCISE 3

Write statements using *still* about the people in the Opening Task on page 262 who have not changed very much. The following items will get you started, but you can add ideas of your own. Work with your classmates if you need more information.

1. Julia Roberts (very slim)   *Julia Roberts still has long hair. She is still very slim*

2. Morgan Freeman (a beard) *Morgan Freeman still has a beard. He still wears an earring.*

3. Jennifer Lopez (long hair)   *Jennifer Lopez still has long hair*

4. Arnold Schwarzenegger (very strong) *Arnold Schwarzenegger still looks very strong*

5. Nicole Kidman (very pretty) *Nicole Kidman is still very pretty. She still has the same smile.*

6. Brad Pitt (handsome)   *Brad Pitt is still handsome. He still has blond hair.*

EXERCISE 4

Look at the two descriptions of Jack in the past and in the present. Describe how his life has changed. Use *used to, still,* and *anymore.*

1996	2006
• lived in Canada	• lives in the United States
• worked for a newspaper in Toronto	• works for a newspaper in Washington, DC
• went swimming every day	• goes running every day
• weighed 190 pounds	• weighs 190 pounds
• was single	• is married

EXERCISE 5

Look at the maps of the island of Madalia. Work with a partner and use the information from the maps to complete the report below. Use *used to, didn't use to, still,* and *anymore* as appropriate. Use the verbs in parentheses. The first one has been done for you as an example.

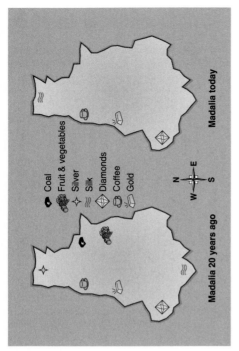

Coal
Fruit & vegetables
Silver
Silk
Diamonds
Coffee
Gold

Madalia 20 years ago   Madalia today

N W E S

Madalia is a small country that is rich in natural resources, and Madalians have exploited those resources for many years. However, it is possible to note some changes in those resources in the last twenty years. For example, twenty years ago, Madalians

(1) *used to mine* (mine) _____ coal _____ in the northeast. In addition, they

(2) _____ (grow) _____ in the east. Also, they (3) _____ ,

but today, they (4) _____ (not + mine) it _____ . Furthermore, in the

past, they (5) _____ (not + produce) _____ in the north; they

(6) _____ (produce) it in the _____ .

On the other hand, some things have not changed. They (7) _____ (mine)

_____ in the southwest, and they (8) _____ (grow) _____

in the northwest. Finally, they (9) _____ (mine) _____ in the west.

ANSWER KEY

Exercise 4 Answers will vary. Some sample responses are:

- Jack used to live in Canada but now he lives in the United States.
- He used to work for a newspaper in Toronto but now he works for one in Washington, D.C.
- He used to go swimming every day but now he goes running.
- He still weighs 190 pounds.

Exercise 5 2. still grow, fruit and vegetables   3. used to mine silver in the north   4. don't mine, anymore   5. did not/didn't use to produce silk in the north   6. used to produce, south   7. still mine, diamonds   8. still grow, coffee   9. still mine, gold

LESSON PLAN 1/LESSON PLAN 2

FOCUS 4 [5 minutes]

This focus chart presents the use of *still* with affirmative statements and questions.

1. **Lead-in:** Contrast *still* with *anymore* to emphasize the difference in form and use. *Still* can be used in questions, but is not used with negative statements.

   A: *Does Sonia **still** live with her parents?* OR A: *Does Sonia live with her parents **anymore**?*

   B: *I think she **still** does, but I'm not sure.* OR B: *Not **anymore**. Didn't you know she got married?*

2. Read the examples and explanations in the focus chat.

3. Point out the different word order with the verb *be* and other main verbs.

EXERCISE 3 [10 minutes]

This exercise provides practice with *used to* and *still*.

1. Refer back to the pictures in the Opening Task and ask which of these people they think have not changed very much. Use their responses to make examples using *still*.

2. Do the first example together with the class.

3. Allow students time to write their answers individually.

4. Compare answers as a class. Refer to the answer key on LP page 266.

EXERCISE 4 [20 minutes]

This exercise provides further practice in using *used to*, *anymore*, and *still* when describing people and changes in their lives.

1. Have students look at the pictures and the information about Jack. Ask for one or two sentences verbally.

2. Have students work in pairs to write as many sentences as they can, using *used to*, *anymore*, and *still*.

3. Have students read the sentences aloud.

4. You can do this as a game. Have each student or pair of students read one sentence. They must not repeat one that has been said before, although they can say it in a different way. If they are unable to make a new sentence, they are "out." The last one to read a new sentence is the winner. Note that you, or a student, will have to keep careful note of previous sentences to be sure that none is repeated.

5. Answers will vary. Refer to the answer key on LP page 266 for suggested answers.

EXPANSION [20 minutes]

You may want to use Activity 1 (writing) on SB page 269 after this exercise. This activity asks students to bring in photos of themselves when they were young and write statements about how they have (or have not) changed.

For more practice, use *Grammar Dimensions 2* Workbook page 117, Exercise 4.

LESSON PLAN 2

EXERCISE 5 [15 minutes]

You can use this exercise to review the use of *still* and *anymore* with *used to* from the previous lesson. This exercise moves away from the theme of describing people to describing countries.

1. Start by asking students to discuss the differences they see on the maps. This will allow them to discuss unfamiliar vocabulary and get an understanding of the map.

2. Have students work in pairs to complete the description.

3. Circulate around the room to help out during this activity.

4. Discuss the answers as a class. Refer to the answer key on LP page 266.

EXPANSION 1 [20 minutes]

You may want to use Activity 2 (writing) on SB page 269 after this exercise. This activity asks students to talk or write about a place they knew when they were younger.

EXPANSION 2 [20–30 minutes]

You may want to use Activity 3 (speaking/listening) on SB page 269 followed by Activity 5 (listening) on SB page 270 after this exercise. These two activities ask students to interview and listen to interviews with older people about how life has changed.

For more practice, use *Grammar Dimensions 2* Workbook page 117, Exercise 5.

Use Your English

EXERCISE 6

The words below tell how often something happens. Arrange these words in a list with **most frequent** at the top and **least frequent** at the bottom. Add any other similar words you can think of and put them in the appropriate place on the list.

often	always	never	seldom
sometimes	hardly ever	usually	rarely

Check your answers with Unit 1, Focus 3.

FOCUS 5

Adverbs of Frequency

EXAMPLES

(a) I **usually** get up at 6:00 A.M.

(b) They were **rarely** happy.

(c) You will **sometimes** hear from them.

(d) I have **seldom** spoken to her.

(e) They **never** used to dance.

(f) He **always** used to call her.

(g) **Sometimes** I go to bed at 9:00 P.M.

EXPLANATIONS

Adverbs of frequency (*always*, etc.) can appear in different positions in a sentence:

• before the main verb.

• after the verb *be*.

• after auxiliary verbs (*will, can, have,* etc.).

• before *used to.*

Sometime can appear at the beginning or at the end of a sentence.

EXERCISE 7

Write a short article for your old high school magazine, reporting on your life and habits and how they have changed (or not) over the years since you left high school. Also describe your present life and habits and compare them with your past.

Try to include the following:

• something you used to do but don't do anymore

• something you used to do and still do

• something you didn't use to do but do now

• something you never, sometimes, often, or usually do

Don't forget to include changes (or not) in your physical appearance. We have begun the article for you:

I left high school in _____ (year). As I look back on my life since then, I realize that some things have changed, and some things have stayed the same. Let me start by telling you about some of the changes . . .

ACTIVITY 1 writing

STEP 1

If possible, find an old photograph of yourself (as a baby, a child, or one taken several years ago). If you cannot find a photograph, draw a picture. Attach the photo or picture to a large piece of paper and write several statements about yourself, showing things you used to do and don't do now, things you didn't use to do, and things you still do. Do not write your name on the paper. Your teacher will display all the pictures and descriptions.

STEP 2

Work with a classmate and try to guess the identity of each person. Who in the class has changed the most and who has changed the least?

ACTIVITY 2 writing

Think of a place you know well—the place where you were born or where you grew up. Write about the ways it has changed and the ways it has not changed.

ACTIVITY 3 speaking/listening

STEP 1

Interview a senior citizen. Find out about changes in the world or in customs and habits during his or her lifetime. What does he or she think about these changes? Record your interview, and then report on your findings to the class.

STEP 2

Listen to the recorded interviews. Did the speakers use *used to, still,* or *anymore* when talking about changes? If not, what did they use instead?

ANSWER KEY

Exercise 6   always, usually, often, sometimes, seldom, rarely, hardly ever, never

18 LESSON PLAN 1

EXERCISE 6 [10 minutes]

This exercise reviews adverbs of frequency from Unit 1. It will prepare students for Focus Chart 5 and will be combined with the topic of *used to* in Exercise 7.

1. Remind students of the meaning and function of adverbs of frequency.
2. Have students order the list individually.
3. Ask a volunteer to write them on the board in the correct order or check the answers on page 4 of the Student Book.

EXPANSION [15 minutes]

You may want to use Activity 7 (speaking/listening/writing) on SB page 271 after this exercise. This gives students extensive opportunity to practice adverbs of frequency

FOCUS 5 [5 minutes]

This focus chart presents the word order used with adverbs of frequency.

1. **Lead-in:** Ask students to make up some sentences about themselves, using the adverbs from Exercise 6.
2. Emphasize the importance of the word order by providing extra examples about your class:
   Roberto rarely arrives late to class.
   Fabiola always sits in between Fernando and Satomi.
   Nabi, Juan, and Ribo never used to eat dinner so early, but now they have to because they live in a dorm.

EXERCISE 7 [15–30 minutes]

1. Introduce the topic of how your students have changed since leaving high school.
2. Brainstorm a list of topics that might be mentioned in an article on this topic. For example, daily routine, study habits, sports, friends, opinions.

3. Read the instructions for the exercise.
4. Have students make notes or an outline before they start writing.
5. Set a time limit in class or assign this writing for homework.

workbook For more practice, use *Grammar Dimensions 2* Workbook page 119, Exercise 6.

UNIT GOAL REVIEW [10 minutes]

Ask students to look at the goals on the opening page of the unit again. Refer to the pages of the unit where information on each goal can be found.

workbook For a grammar quiz review of Units 16–18, refer students to pages 121–122 in *Grammar Dimensions 2* Workbook.

 For assessment of Unit 18, use *Grammar Dimensions 2* ExamView®.

USE YOUR ENGLISH

ACTIVITY 1 writing [30 minutes]

You may want to use this activity after Exercise 4 on SB page 266.

■ STEP 1
1. Ask students to bring their old photos or a sketch of themselves as children to the next class.
2. Have students write sentences about themselves

■ STEP 2
1. Collect the writing and pictures and give each set a number.

2. Put each set on the wall in random order. Or mix them up and lay them out on a large table.
3. Students will write the numbers and their guesses as to the names of the students.
4. If students are unable to bring in pictures, you can also do this activity with the sentences and no pictures.

ACTIVITY 2 writing [20 minutes/homework]

You may want to use this activity or Activity 3 after Exercise 5 on SB page 267.

1. As a pre-writing activity, have students brainstorm their ideas. First have them list places they know well.
2. After they choose one to focus on, have them list ways it has changed and ways it has not changed in two columns on their paper.
3. Assign the writing for homework.

ACTIVITY 3 speaking/listening [20 minutes/homework]

You may want to use this activity after Exercise 5 on page 267 (instead of or in addition to Activity 2).

■ STEP 1
1. Start by brainstorming ideas for topics and questions. For example, transport, communication, work, clothes, food, music, etc.
2. Assign the interview task for homework.

■ STEP 2
Have students report back on the information learned from the interviews (and the type of language used) in the next class.

Suggestion: If students do not have access to a large group of native speakers of English, invite someone who has strong English language skills to class for all to interview. Record if possible.

ACTIVITY 4 — listening

CD Track 25

STEP 1

Listen to the audio of two senior citizens talking about the changes during their lifetimes. In your notebook, list each change that they discuss. Count the number of changes on your list.

Compare answers with your classmates.

STEP 2

Listen to the audio recording again, and pay attention to the way the senior citizens talk about changes. Did the speakers use *used to*, *still*, or *anymore* when talking about changes? If not, what did they use instead? Compare your findings again with another student.

ACTIVITY 5 — speaking/writing

The women's movement has helped change the lives of many women in different parts of the world. However, some people argue that things have not really changed and many things are still the same for most women. Think about women's lives and roles in your mother's generation and the lives of women today in your country. Make an oral or written report on what has changed and what has stayed the same.

ACTIVITY 6 — speaking

This activity gives you the opportunity to "become" a different person. Choose a new identity for yourself. Choose a new name, age, sex, profession, habits, occupation, personality, and appearance? How does your new person differ from the "real" you?

Create a full description of this person and introduce the "new" you to the class, comparing him or her with the person you used to be.

Example: *I want to introduce the new me. I used to be a college student, but now I am a movie star. I never used to leave home, but now I often travel to distant and exotic places. I used to wear practical clothes that I bought on sale. Now I wear designer clothes and expensive jewelry. . . .*

ACTIVITY 7 — speaking/listening/writing

Write a profile of one of your classmates.

STEP 1

Interview your partner and find out something that he or she . . .

1. never does
2. seldom does
3. sometimes does
4. often does
5. usually does
6. always does

STEP 2

Write a report of your interview, without using your classmate's name. Begin with an introduction: (for example) "I am going to tell you some things about one of our classmates." End your report with a question: "Can you guess who this is?"

STEP 3

Read your report out loud, or display it along with all the other reports written by your classmates. Can you identify the people described?

ACTIVITY 8 — research on the web

Go on the Internet and use a search engine such as Google® or Yahoo® to find out what famous stars used to do before they were famous. Type in keywords: "before they were famous" and the star's name. Collect some interesting facts to tell your classmates.

ACTIVITY 9 — reflection

Think about how your learning styles and habits have changed since you were in high school. Write three sentences about how you used to study and learn then compared to now.

ANSWER KEY

Activity 4   *Check audio script, LP page S-7, for answers.*

USE YOUR ENGLISH

ACTIVITY 4 — listening [20 minutes]

You may want to use this activity as a follow-up to Activity 3.

STEP 1

1. If you have previously done Activity 3, review some of the topics that came up in those interviews.

2. Explain that students will hear a recording of two senior citizens talking about changes. They should take notes while they listen.

3. Play the audio. Then, Check the answers. See the audio script on LP page xx for the answers.

STEP 2

Play the audio again, this time asking students to notice the language the answers as a class.

ACTIVITY 5 — speaking/writing [30 minutes]

You may want to use this activity after Exercise 7 on SB page 268.

1. Introduce the topic of the women's movement and some notable changes that have been brought about in improving women's rights.

2. Brainstorm ideas for some of these changes and write them on the board. For example, salaries, childcare, education.

3. Have students work in groups and come up with a list of things that have changed, and things that have not changed much.

4. Have group representatives give a presentation to the class. You may want to videotape the presentations. Then review the presentations, providing feedback on presentation skills such as body language, topic organization, and language use.

ACTIVITY 6 — speaking [20 minutes]

You may want to use this activity after Exercise 2 on SB page 265.

1. Start by asking: If you could change one thing about yourself, what would you change?

2. Collect a few ideas. Then introduce the idea of creating a new imaginary personality.

3. Read the instructions for the activity and the example.

4. Have students fill out a checklist of their new characteristics.

5. Invite volunteers to tell the class about their new personality.

ACTIVITY 7 — speaking/listening/writing [30 minutes]

You may want to use this activity after Exercise 6 on SB page 268.

STEP 1

1. Have students work in pairs. It's a good idea to get students to stand up and move to another part of the room to sit with a new partner, perhaps someone they don't know very well. (They can move back to their original seat later in the activity.)

2. Read the instructions for the activity.

3. Set a time limit for students to interview their partner and find out as much as they can. If you set a short time limit of say 5 minutes, this will make the activity more of a contest.

STEP 2

Students then go back to their original seats and use their notes to write about their partner.

STEP 3

1. Invite students to read the reports to the class.

2. After students have read, their partners can correct them if anything is not correct.

3. The class can provide feedback on grammar.

VARIATION

1. Pair students up and have them conduct their interviews by e-mail.

2. After their interviews, they can post their reports to the whole class.

3. Remember to set a time limit by which all reports should be identified.

METHODOLOGY NOTE

It is not really necessary to correct every mistake when students are speaking or giving presentations, as long as the meaning is clear. In written work, however, accuracy is far more important. Students who are very fluent verbally may be disappointed when they get their work back with lots of corrections, so it is a good idea to explain these different standards of accuracy for verbal and written communication.

ACTIVITY 8 — research on the web [15 minutes/homework]

You may want to use this activity after Exercise 1 on SB page 264. The purpose of this Internet search activity is to provide a natural context for using the present perfect. An additional purpose is to encourage students to share strategies for finding information on the Internet.

ACTIVITY 9 — reflection [5 minutes/homework]

This activity provides an opportunity for students to use the target structures of the unit while reflecting on their language learning progress. You may have asked students to keep a record of their learning in a journal throughout this course as suggested in To the Teacher, LP page xxii. This reflection activity will form part of that learning record.

PAST PERFECT
Before and After

UNIT GOALS

- Correctly use past perfect and simple past in a single sentence
- Correctly form past perfect sentences
- Understand the meanings of *before*, *after*, *by the time*, and *by*
- Use past perfect and the present perfect in the right situations

OPENING TASK
Family Changes

STEP 1

Family Tree A shows Tom's family when he left home in 1985 to travel around the world. Work with a partner to study *Family Tree A*. Note that ⚭ = married.

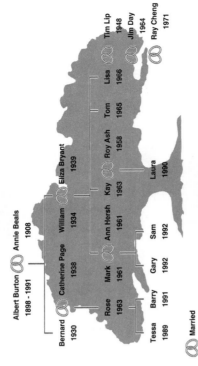

Family Tree A

⚭ Married

STEP 2

Now look at *Family Tree B*, which shows Tom's family after he returned home from his world travels in 1993. What changes do you notice in Tom's family?

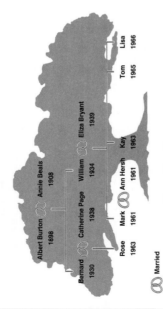

Family Tree B

⚭ Married

STEP 3

Make at least five statements about changes that had taken place when Tom returned from his travels. Start these statements with:

When Tom returned, ...

OR   *Tom returned after. . . .*

OR   *By the time Tom returned, ...*

ANSWER KEY

Opening Task   Step 2: Answers will vary. Possible answers include:
• Rose had two children.   • Mark and Ann had two sons.   • Kay got married and had a daughter.   • Lisa was married three times.

UNIT OVERVIEW

Unit 19 provides practice with the past perfect and with words/phrases commonly used with the past perfect: *before, after, by the time,* and *by.* It contrasts the past perfect with the simple past and present perfect.

GRAMMAR NOTE

The past perfect tense is used to talk about a past event that occurred before another past event. Therefore, it is mainly found in sentences combined with other tenses in order to clarify the sequence of two or more past events. However, the use of this tense is rarely obligatory, as sequence of events can usually be clarified by time markers such as *before* and *after* used alongside the simple past tense. The main problem for learners is to learn when to use this tense effectively. As it is more often used in writing than in speaking, it can also help to improve their writing fluency.

UNIT GOALS

Some instructors may want to review the goals listed on Student Book (SB) page 272 after completing the Opening Task so that students understand what they should know by the end of the unit. These goals can also be reviewed at the end of the unit when students are more familiar with the grammar terminology.

OPENING TASK [20 minutes]

The purpose of the Opening Task is to create a context in which students will need to use the past perfect. The problem-solving format is designed to show the teacher how well the students can use the target structures implicitly and spontaneously when they are engaged in a communicative task. For a more complete discussion of the purpose of the Opening Task, see To the Teacher, Lesson Planner (LP) page xxii.

Setting Up the Task

■ STEP 1

In order to do this task, students will first need to know how a family tree works and also some of the key vocabulary used in family trees.

1. Look at Family Tree A and make sure everyone can locate Tom.
2. Briefly elicit or introduce vocabulary for family relationships by asking, for example: What relationship is Bernard to Tom? (Answer: *Bernard is Tom's uncle/Tom's father's brother.*) What relationship is Tom to Catherine Page? (Answer: *Tom is Catherine's nephew; Catherine is married to Bernard, Tom's father's brother.*) and so on.
3. Students can work in pairs to further discuss the relationships in Family Tree A.

■ STEP 2

1. Explain that Tom left home to travel overseas and returned eight years later. Family Tree A shows Tom's family when he left, and Family Tree B when he returned.
2. Ask students to compare and discuss the changes in the family trees.
3. Circulate while students are talking to see if they are using the past perfect. Do not correct errors at this stage. Take note of errors in meaning, form, or use for later use in this unit.

■ STEP 3

1. Have students report to the class about these changes using the sentence stems provided.
2. Reach a group consensus on how many changes there are.
3. Refer to the answer key on LP page 272.

Closing the Task

1. Write (or have students write) some of the sentences on the board or an overhead transparency and use this as a bridge to Focus

Charts 1 and 2 by reformulating statements where the past perfect was incorrectly formed.
2. It is not necessary to go through all the statements as students will return to these sentences in Exercise 1 on SB page 275.

GRAMMAR NOTE

Typical student errors (form)

- Errors with formation of the past participle, e.g. * *We had read two chapters by yesterday.*
- Confusion of *had* with *had to,* e.g. * *They had finish their homework by today.*
- Using simple past instead of past perfect with *by the time* and *by* (+ day or date).

Typical student errors (use)

- Not distinguishing past perfect from simple past, e.g. What had they done when you came home? * *They cooked dinner.* (instead of: They had cooked dinner.)
- Unclear sequence of past events (especially in writing).

FOCUS 1

meaning

Past Perfect and Simple Past

EXAMPLE

When I got there, he **had eaten** all the cookies.

1   2

First, he ate the cookies; **then**, I got there. (I didn't see him eat the cookies.)

EXPLANATIONS

When two events both happened in the past:

- use the past perfect for the first (earliest) event.
- use the simple past for the second (most recent) event.

FOCUS 2

form

Past Perfect

To form the past perfect, use *had* + past participle (*-ed* for regular verbs; see Appendix 5, p. A-13 for forms of irregular verbs).

STATEMENT		NEGATIVE		QUESTION		SHORT ANSWER
I You We They	had arrived. ('d)	I You We They	had not arrived. (hadn't)	Had	I you we they } arrived?	Yes we had.
She He It	had arrived. ('d)	She He It	had not arrived. (hadn't)	Had	he she it } arrived?	No, she had not (hadn't).

EXERCISE 1

Look at the family trees in the Opening Task on page 272–273 to complete the statements. If there is a verb in parentheses, use it; otherwise, use any appropriate verb. The first one has been done for you.

1. When he returned home, Tom found that his grandfather (die) _had died_ .
2. When Tom returned, he learned that his cousin _had had two children_ .
3. Tom arrived home to find that his sister Lisa _had (gotten) married three times_ .
4. When _Tom got/arrived/returned home_ , his sister Kay _had gotten married_ ; in addition, she and her husband _had had a daughter_ .
5. On his return home, Tom found that his brother and sister-in law _had had twin boys_ .
6. Tom learned that his great grandmother had experienced both sorrow and joy. On the one hand, she (lose) _had lost her husband_ , but on the other hand, she (gain) _had gained five great-grandchildren_ .
7. Sam and Gary have never met their grandfather, because he _had died_ before they _were born_ .
8. By the time Tom got back home, his parents and his aunt and uncle (become) _had become grandparents_ .
9. Tom also found that Rose _had had_ children, but she (not) _had not/hadn't (gotten) married_ Lisa, on the other hand, _had (gotten) married_ three times, but she (not) _had not/hadn't had_ any children.

FOCUS 1 [5 minutes]

1. **Lead-in:** Have students begin with books closed. Write the example sentence from the Focus 1 chart on the board. Ask students which event happened first. How do they know?

2. Have students open books and look at the picture, reading the explanations in the chart. Emphasize that both events happened in the past, but one happened before the other. When the two events are combined into one sentence, the earliest event uses the past perfect, and the most recent event uses the simple past.

3. Use the statements elicited from students in Step 3 of the Opening Task to elaborate on the information presented here. Example: *When Tom returned, his brother Mark and Mark's wife Ann had had two children.* Ask: *Which event happened first?* (Answer: *Tom returned.*) Ask: *Which event happened second?* (Answer: *Mark and Mark's wife Ann had two children.*) See Language Note below.

4. Ask similar questions about some of the students' other statements.

LANGUAGE NOTE

Some students may not know that the more formal *give birth* or *bear children* is rarely used; it's more common to say *have a baby* or *have a child/children.* When *have* is the main verb, it becomes *had* + past participle = *had had* in the past perfect. For example, *When Tom came home, Mark and Ann had had two children.*

FOCUS 2 [10 minutes]

1. **Lead-in:** Review the past participles of some common verbs (see Appendix 5 on SB page A-13).

2. Read the examples in the focus chart.

3. Review the pronunciation of contracted forms.

4. You may want to add some examples of *Wh-* questions with the past perfect—e.g., *Had you ever eaten octopus before you went to Brazil? Had they ever seen snow before?*

GRAMMAR NOTE

The past perfect is especially common with the conjunction *when.* This is because *when* has several different meanings and the use of the past perfect can help to clarify which meaning is intended. For example, *When I came home, be ate the cookies.* (First I came home and then he ate the cookies.) *When I came home, be had eaten the cookies.* (First he ate the cookies, and then I came home.) The past perfect can also be used with the conjunctions *before* and *after,* but this is optional. However, it must be used with the time expressions *by the time* and *by* (+ day or date) when referring to the past (see Focus Chart 3).

EXERCISE 1 [15 minutes]

This exercise returns to the sentences created by students in Step 3 of the Opening Task and focuses on accurate use and formation of the past perfect.

1. If you did not manage to complete this step of the Opening Task, you may want to assign this exercise for homework. Otherwise, allow time for students to go over the family trees in the Opening Task and complete the sentences in pairs or individually.

2. Copy this exercise onto an overhead transparency and compare answers as a class. Refer to the answer key on LP page 274.

workbook For more practice, use *Grammar Dimensions 2* Workbook page 122, Exercise 1.

EXPANSION [30 minutes]

You may want to use Activity 3 (speaking/listening) on SB page 281 after this exercise. This activity asks students to interview each other about their family history (see Methodology Note).

METHODOLOGY NOTE

Grammar can be made more memorable if it is directly related to the learner's own personal information, background, interests, and needs. Activities that use personalization help learners to apply abstract language rules to concrete meaningful situations. This enables students to try out hypotheses about new language and helps them to learn and remember it. Personalization exercises have a drawback, however. Some students are reluctant to talk about themselves, their families, or their past. They may have unhappy memories of the past or have family problems that are too painful to talk about. Therefore, it is a good idea to provide an alternative topic, allow students the opportunity to use a fictional identity, or allow them to opt out by "accompanying" a partner who is willing to share their personal information.

EXERCISE 2

In the following pairs of statements, decide which event probably happened first. Write 1 beside the event you think happened first and 2 beside the one you think happened second. Then combine the statements to make one sentence using because. The first one has been done for you.

Example: My legs ached. 2
I played tennis. 1
My legs ached because I had played tennis.

1. His car broke down. 1
He took the bus. 2
He took the bus because his car had broken down.

2. Charlotte was depressed. 2
She failed her English exam. 1
Charlotte was depressed because she had failed her English exam.

3. Tanya sat in the sun all afternoon. 1
Her skin was very red. 2
Tanya's skin was very red because she had sat in the sun all afternoon.

4. We didn't eat all day. 1
We were really hungry. 2
We were really hungry because we hadn't eaten all day.

5. Brenda's clothes were too tight. 2
She didn't exercise for several months. 1
Brenda's clothes were too tight because she hadn't exercised for several months.

6. Neville couldn't sleep. 2
He drank several cups of very strong coffee. 1
Neville couldn't sleep because he had drunk several cups of very strong coffee.

7. We studied hard for three weeks. 1
We thought the test was easy. 2
We thought the test was very easy because we had studied hard for three weeks.

8. I felt very tired yesterday morning. 2
I didn't sleep well. 1
I felt very tired yesterday morning because I hadn't slept well.

form

meaning

FOCUS 3

Before, After, By the Time, By

EXAMPLES

First Event	Second Event
(a) She had left	before I arrived.
(b) She had left	by the time I arrived.
(c) After she had left,	I arrived.
(d) She left	before I arrived.
(e) After she left,	I arrived.
(f) He had finished all his shopping	by Christmas.
(g) After I had left,	he arrived.

EXPLANATIONS

Before, after, and *by the time* show the order of events.

You can use the past perfect with *before* and *after,* but it is not necessary. You must use the past perfect in sentences with *by the time.*

By + a noun phrase can also show order of events.

Punctuation note: Use a comma after a clause with *before* or *after* if the clause comes first.

EXERCISE 3

Look at the following sentences; each one uses the past perfect. First, underline the event that happens first. Then check (✓) the sentences where it is **necessary** to use the past perfect to show the order of events.

1. Cathy went to her high school reunion ten years after she had graduated.
2. She had checked the map carefully before she started her journey.
✓ 3. She lost her way because so many things in her hometown had changed.
✓ 4. By the time she arrived, the party had almost finished.
5. Many of her old school friends had left before she got there.
6. She didn't recognize some of her friends because they had changed so much.
7. After she had talked to them for a while about the old days, she started to feel quite sad.
✓ 8. By the time she got home, she had decided not to go to any more high school reunions.

EXERCISE 2 [20 minutes]

This exercise provides practice in the meaning and formation of sentences with the past perfect and the simple past.

1. Explain that for each pair of sentences, students will have to decide which event happened first. Then combine them into one sentence.

2. Look at the example together with the whole class. Check comprehension of the example by asking questions. For example, Which event happened first: my legs ached, or I played tennis? Did I play tennis because my legs ached? or did my legs ache because I played tennis?

3. Allow time for students to complete the sentences individually or in pairs.

4. Invite volunteers to write their sentences on the board.

5. For each sentence, ask: *Which event happened first? Which event happened second?*

6. Ask the class for feedback on accuracy of meaning and form.

Note: During this exercise, students sometimes ask about the ordering of events in a sentence. *Do we have to put the earliest event first?* Explain that we understand the order of events because of the verb tense used, not because of the position in the sentences. This grammar point can serve as a bridge to Focus Chart 3.

EXPANSION 1 [20–30 minutes]

You may want to use this speaking activity to provide further practice of the form and meaning of the past perfect.

1. Hand out some blank strips of paper, one for each student.

2. Each student will write one interesting true fact about something they have done in the past—e.g., *I climbed Mount Everest. I swam with a dolphin.*

3. Collect the papers and mix them up. Hand them out again. (Students shouldn't take back their own sentences.)

4. Students will walk around the room and try to find the person who wrote the sentence.

5. Then they will ask questions about events previous to the event on the paper—e.g. *Had you ever climbed a mountain before? What kind of mountains had you climbed? Had you always wanted to swim with a dolphin?*

Use *Grammar Dimensions 2* Workbook page 123, Exercise 2 and page 124, Exercise 3.

EXPANSION 2 [20 minutes]

You may want to use Activity 5 (speaking) on SB page 282 after this exercise.

FOCUS 3 [5 minutes]

1. **Lead-in:** Have students cover or turn over their books.

2. Read the examples (a)–(f) in random order—some of them as is, some of them with the clauses shifting positions.

3. For each sentence, ask: *Which event happened first? Which event happened second?*

4. Read the examples and explanations in the chart.

Point out that you can shift the two clauses (parts of the sentence) around. Example: *Before I arrived, she had left. By the time I arrived, she had left.*

5. Draw attention to the punctuation note. Have students go back to their sentences in Exercise 1 and check their punctuation.

GRAMMAR NOTE

The past perfect is not always used by native speakers in informal situations, as is the case with *after* and *before* in this focus chart—(d) and (e). One of the reasons why it's acceptable to omit the past perfect with *after* and *before* sentences is that the order of events in these sentences is clear. However, formal language tests will certainly address this grammar point. In addition, the past perfect is naturally used when the order of events is important for the meaning of the sentence.

EXERCISE 3 [10 minutes]

This exercise provides practice in recognizing the sequence of events in sentences that use both simple past and past perfect.

1. Read the instructions and check that students understand there are two tasks: First, to underline the event that happened first. Second, to check the sentences where it is necessary to use the past perfect.

2. Do the first sentence together with the class.

3. Allow time for students to complete the exercise individually.

4. Use a copy of the exercise on an overhead transparency to check the answers as a class. Refer to the answer key on LP page 276.

EXPANSION [30–40 minutes]

You may want to use Activity 1 on SB page 280 after this exercise to introduce some more personalized practice of this grammar point. This can be followed by Activity 2 on SB page 281.

Use *Grammar Dimensions 2* Workbook page 125, Exercises 4 and 5.

EXERCISE 4

Rewrite the following sentences in your notebook. Omit the underlined words and use the word in parentheses. Use the past perfect where necessary.

Example: First, Sue saw some photos of her grandmother's village, and then she decided to visit Italy. (after)

After Sue saw/had seen some photos of her grandmother's village, she decided to visit Italy.

1. Sue did some research on the Internet, and then she planned her trip. (after)
2. She bought an airline ticket, and then she booked a hotel in Palermo. (after)
3. She bought a guidebook and a map, and next she packed her bags. (before)
4. She arrived in Palermo, and next she called her mother's school friend. (after)
5. She walked around the city, and then she met her mother's friend in the main square. (before)
6. They drove to her grandmother's village, and then they visited her grandmother's old home. (after)
7. They spoke to many family members, friends, and other villagers, and then they returned to the city. (before)
8. Sue learned a lot about her grandmother's life before she got back at the end of the day. (by the time)
9. She went back to her hotel, and next she wrote some notes about her experience. (after)
10. She returned home, and six months later she wrote a successful book about her trip. (by the end of the year)

Were there any sentences where you **had** to use the past perfect?

FOCUS 4 | Past Perfect versus Present Perfect

use

EXAMPLES	EXPLANATIONS
(a) She **was** tired yesterday because she **had taken** a long bike ride.	Use the past perfect to **contrast two** events in the past.
(b) She **is** tired (now) because she **has taken** a long bike ride.	Use the present perfect to **connect the** past with the present.

EXERCISE 5

Underline the mistakes in the following sentences and correct as necessary.

Example: *I wasn't tired yesterday because I ~~have~~ slept for ten hours the night before.*
(had, above "have")

1. Nigel wasn't hungry last night because he has eaten a large sandwich for lunch.
2. Jan is really confused in class last Tuesday because she hadn't read the assignment.
3. Graham had gone home because he has a terrible headache today.
4. Howard is a lucky man because he had traveled all over the world.
5. Martha went to the hospital after she has broken a leg.
6. Before he has left the house, George locked all the doors and windows.
7. Professor Westerfield always returns our papers after she had graded them.
8. I didn't see you at the airport last night because your plane has left before I got there.
9. Matthew and James were late because they have missed the bus.

EXERCISE 6

In the story below, use the appropriate verb tense (simple past, past progressive, past perfect, present perfect) for the verbs in parentheses.

Richard (1) __hasn't had__ (have, not) a vacation for several years. But last month he decided to go Florida for a week. He (2) __was driving__ (drive) to the airport when he realized that he (3) __had forgotten__ (forget) his passport. He immediately turned back. But when he (4) __arrived__ (arrive) home, he found that he (5) __didn't have__ (have, not) his door keys. He (6) __had left__ (leave) them inside the house! He (7) __had hidden__ (hide) under a plant pot in the backyard. But the keys that he (8) __climbed__ (climb) over the wall to get the keys (9) __weren't__ (be, not) there because he (10) __hadn't put__ (put, not) them back last time. He (11) __was opening__ (open) the kitchen window, when a neighbor (12) __saw__ (see) him from her yard. "(13) __Have/Did__ __have locked/ did you lock__ (lock) yourself out again?" "Yes, and I you (14) __left/have left__ (leave) my passport inside!" The neighbor (15) __helped__ (help) Richard to get into his house. Finally, he (16) __drove__ (drive) back to the airport with his passport, but of course by then his plane (17) __had left__ (leave). Since then, Richard (18) __hasn't tried__ (try, not) to go on vacation again.

Exercise 4 1. After Sue had done/did some research on the Internet, she planned her trip.
2. After she had bought/ bought an airline ticket, she booked a hotel in Palermo.
3. She had bought/ bought a guidebook and a map before she packed her bags.
4. After she had arrived/arrived in Palermo, she called her mother's school friend.
5. She had walked/walked around the city before she met her mother's friend in the main square.
6. After they had driven/drove to her grandmother's village, they visited her grandmother's old home.
7. They had spoken/spoke to many family members, friends, and other villagers, before they returned

(✓) 8. Sue had learned a lot about her grandmother's life, by the time she got back at the end of the day. 9. After she (had gone) went back to her hotel, she wrote some notes about her experience.
(✓) 10. She returned home, and by the end of the year she had written a successful book about her trip.
To the teacher: (✓) = must use past perfect with "by the . . ." time expressions

Exercise 5 1. because he had eaten 2. Jan was really confused 3. Graham has gone home OK: because he had
4. he has traveled OK: was a lucky man 5. she had broken her leg 6. Before he had left/ left the
house 7 after she has graded them OK Professor Westerfield always returns 8. your plane had left

EXERCISE 4 [15 minutes]

You can use this exercise to review the use of time conjunctions with the past perfect.

1. You may want to assign this exercise for homework.
2. Explain that students will have to rewrite the sentences, changing the tenses as required, and using the time conjunctions provided in parentheses.
3. When students have completed the exercise, invite volunteers to come and write their sentences on the board.
4. Ask the class for feedback on grammatical accuracy and punctuation.
5. Refer to the answer key on LP page 278.

EXPANSION [20 minutes]

You may want to use Activity 6 (listening) on SB page 282 after this exercise.

FOCUS 4 [10 minutes]

This focus chart reviews the use of the present perfect for present results of a past event, contrasting this with the use of the past perfect for describing two past events.

1. Write the two example sentences on the board, leaving blank the spaces for *bad* and *has*.
2. Ask students to explain the differences between these two sentences.
3. Compare their explanations with the chart.
4. Give students a few more contrasting sentences, as in (a) compared to (b). For example: *I had fixed the flat tire and then it broke again.* (two events in the past are contrasting) versus *I've fixed the flat tire and now it's okay.* (event in the past connected to the present).

5. The exercises following this focus chart work further on the present perfect–past perfect distinction.
6. For a review on the use of the present perfect—and how it connects the past to the present, see Units 13 and 14.

EXERCISE 5 [15 minutes]

This exercise provides practice in distinguishing when to use present perfect or past perfect.

1. Do the example sentence together with the class.
2. Because this exercise can be beneficial for students in editing their writing, it's a good idea to have them first work individually, and then compare answers with a partner.
3. Circulate while students are working individually and make note of any items that seem to cause problems.
4. Go over these items when you regroup as a whole class, or ask for questions on those items that students disagreed on or had trouble with. Refer to the answer key on LP page 278.
5. Ask students to explain their revisions: What was wrong with the original statement?

EXERCISE 6 [20 minutes]

This exercise provides practice with a variety of past tenses. Some answers may vary.

1. Ask students to read the whole story first to get a sense of the narrative.
2. Have students work in pairs to choose the correct tense.
3. Have volunteers read one sentence each, defending their answers in terms of time frames.
4. For each sentence, ask if the rest of the class agrees or disagrees.

5. The following questions may help students to decide:
   (1) Did two events happen in the past—one happened first; one happened second? (= past perfect – simple past)
   (2) Did the event happen in the past and have an effect on the present? (= present perfect)
   (3) Did the event happen at a particular time in the past? (= simple past)
   (4) Was the event in progress in the past while another event happened? (= past progressive – simple past)
6. Check the answers. Refer to the answer key on LP page 278.

Use *Grammar Dimensions 2* Workbook page 126, Exercise 6.

EXPANSION [20 minutes]

You may want to use Activity 7 (research on the web) on SB page 283 after this exercise.

UNIT GOAL REVIEW [10 minutes]

Ask students to look at the goals on the opening page of the unit again. Refer to the pages of the unit where information on each goal can be found.

 **ExamView** Test Generator — For assessment of Unit 19, use *Grammar Dimensions 2 ExamView®*.

Use Your English

ACTIVITY 1 speaking/listening writing

The purpose of this activity is to compare different events and achievements at different times in our lives. You will need to get information from five of your classmates to complete this activity.

■ STEP 1 The left-hand column in the chart below shows different ages; your job is to find one interesting or surprising thing each classmate had done by the time he or she reached those ages. If you don't want to talk about your life with other students, feel free to invent things that you had done at those ages. Be ready to report on your findings. Copy this chart into your notebook so you have enough room to write.

	NAME	NAME	NAME	NAME	NAME
By the time, he or she was 5 years old . . .					
By the time he or she was 10 years old . . .					
By the time he or she was 15 years old . . .					
By the time he or she was 18 years old . . .					
By the time . . .*					
By the time . . .*					

* You choose an age.

■ STEP 2 Now choose the three most surprising pieces of information you found for each age. Tell the class what you found out.

ACTIVITY 2 speaking

■ STEP 1 Use the information from Activity 1 for a poster presentation. Take a large poster-sized sheet of paper and use this to make a poster that communicates the information you found. You can use graphics, pictures, and diagrams to make your poster interesting and eye-catching.

■ STEP 2 Display your poster so that your classmates can enjoy it and be ready to answer any questions they might have about it.

ACTIVITY 3 speaking/listening

■ STEP 1 Find out about someone's family history, preferably from someone 60 or older. You can help that person construct a family tree (as in the Opening Task), or you can use a chart like the one below to get information. Record your interview.

BIRTHS, DEATHS, MARRIAGES, DIVORCES	
1980–present	
1960–1980	
1940–1960	
1920–1940	

■ STEP 2 Report your findings to the class, either in a written or an oral report. (Record the report if it's done orally.) Be sure to use the past perfect and before, after, by, or by the time to contrast past events.

ACTIVITY 4 listening

Listen to the recordings of your oral reports from Activity 3 or from the actual interviews. Was the past perfect used? Were the time words *before*, *after*, *by*, or *by the time* used? Were there occasions where the past perfect or time words could have been used, but weren't?

USE YOUR ENGLISH

The Use Your English section of activities at the end of the unit contain situations that should naturally elicit the structures covered in the unit. For a more complete discussion of how to use the Use Your English activities, see To the Teacher, LP page xxii.

ACTIVITY 1 speaking/listening/writing [30–40 minutes]

You may want to use this activity after Exercise 3 on SB page 277.

■ STEP 1

1. Students can redraw this chart in their notebooks so that there is more room for notes.
2. Practice the first question with two or three students first. Or have them ask you the first couple of questions.
3. Allow time for students to read through the remaining questions and think about their answers without speaking.
4. Have students stand up and walk around, asking and answering questions, and filling in their charts.
5. Circulate and join in the activity. Take note of any errors.

■ STEP 2

1. Signal for students to sit down.
2. Ask volunteers to report to the class on the most surprising or interesting facts they found out.

VARIATION

Ask students to write a written report for homework. The report can focus on one question (Example 1) or on one person (Example 2).

Example 1

The age of 15 is very interesting. By the time Roberto, Ali, and Tina were 15, they had done quite different things. Roberto had worked in his father's office, Ali had lived in ten countries, and Tina had won several prizes for swimming.

Example 2

By the time, X was 15, he/she had traveled to three countries. Before this, X had lived with his/her older sister, since his/her parents' had moved to China for business purposes.

ACTIVITY 2 speaking [20–30 minutes]

This activity is a follow-up to Activity 1.

■ STEP 1

1. Bring in a sample of this kind of poster. If you are doing this for the first time, you might want to make one poster together, as a whole class, or keep one of your student's posters (with his/her permission) as a sample for your next class.
2. Although it's nice to have lots of different kinds of materials available for this, a large sheet of paper is really all that's necessary. If students seem a little intimidated by such a project, assign them to work in teams (with at least one "artistic type" per team), making this truly collaborative.

■ STEP 2

1. Give half the class an opportunity to circulate and ask questions about the posters made by the other half.
2. Then switch positions where the students who circulated first now answer questions about their posters.

ACTIVITY 3 speaking/listening [30 minutes /homework]

You may want to use this activity after Exercise 1 on SB page 275.

■ STEP 1

1. Help your students to think of a person they could interview and brainstorm possible questions together.
2. Have students work in groups.

■ STEP 2

1. Have students make presentations to the class about their interviews.
2. Ask the class to ask further questions to elicit more details.

ACTIVITY 4

This activity is a follow-up to Activity 3.

1. If you have a pool of recordings from Activity 3, do some prelistening outside of class. This way you can select one or two tapes where there are a number of examples of past perfect usage. Many native speakers often use the simple past, with very few cases of past perfect usage. But it has been our experience that this context—talking about family history—rarely fails: there are at least a *few* cases of the past perfect that are naturally used.
2. If there are few uses of the past perfect, concentrate on the last step of this activity: Analyze the oral report or interview for cases where the past perfect or time words *could have been used*, but weren't.
3. Have students revise these sentences so that the past perfect and time words *are* used.

ACTIVITY 5 speaking

Form groups of three or four students. Each student will think of a place that you visited in the past. It can be a place in your town or city, or in another country. Think of something special or interesting that happened to you there. Start the story with one sentence. Your group will interrupt your story with questions using *before* or *after*.

Example: A: *I went to Spain two years ago.*

B: *Had you been to Spain before?*

ACTIVITY 6 listening

STEP 1

CD Track 26

Listen to the audio of a senior citizen talking about her family history. Each time the speaker talks about an important family event—births, deaths, marriages, divorces—record the date (or the approximate date) on the chart below and write down who the event happened to. The first one is done for you.

BIRTHS	DEATHS	MARRIAGES	DIVORCES	RELATIONSHIP TO SPEAKER
	1941			mother

STEP 2

Work with a classmate to list the speaker's important family events in chronological order.

STEP 3

Listen to the audio for each usage of the past perfect. Write down the sentences in your notebook. Were the time words *before*, *after*, *by* or *by the time* used?

Then complete these sentences.

1. The speaker used the past perfect _____ times.

2. The interviewer used the past perfect _____ times.

3. The time words *before*, *after*, *by*, or *by the time* were used _____ times altogether (by both speakers).

Do your classmates agree with your answers?

ACTIVITY 7 research on the web

STEP 1

Choose a country that you know or would like to find out more about. Go on the Internet and use a search engine such as Google® or Yahoo® to find three or four important dates in the history of that country. These dates should mark important changes or turning points in the history of the country.

Here are some examples from American history:

DATE / EVENT	WHY IT WAS IMPORTANT
1492: Discovery of America by Europeans	Before 1492, Europeans had believed that the earth was flat.
1776: Independence from Great Britain	Before 1776, America had been a colony of Great Britain.
1920: Women got the right to vote.	Before 1920, American women had not been able to vote.

STEP 2

Work with a partner. Tell him or her about the dates and events you chose. Your partner will try to imagine what life was like before and after those events.

ACTIVITY 8 reflection

Think of one thing that changed your ideas about learning English. Was there a teacher, another student, or a book that helped you to see things differently? Talk with a partner. Explain how your ideas changed before and after this experience.

ANSWER KEY

Activity 6 *Step 3:* Check audio script on LP page 5–8 for answers.

USE YOUR ENGLISH

ACTIVITY 5 speaking [20 minutes]

You may want to use this activity after Exercise 2 on SB page 276.

1. Model the activity by starting off a story about a place you have visited.

2. Prompt students to ask you questions using the past perfect.

3. Have students work in groups to continue the activity.

4. Circulate and take note of any problems and also of good questions.

5. Regroup as a class and read some of the good examples and some of the errors.

6. Have students correct the errors, or think of possible alternatives.

ACTIVITY 6 listening [20 minutes]

You may want to use this activity after Exercise 4 on SB page 278.

CD
Track
26

■ STEP 1

1. Have students copy the chart into their notebooks.

2. Explain that they will hear a senior citizen talking about her family history. They will listen and take notes in the chart.

3. Play the audio. See audio script on LP page S-8.

■ STEP 2

1. Have students work in pairs to compare answers and list the events in chronological order.

2. Compare answers as a class. See audio script on LP page S-8 for answers.

■ STEP 3 Play the audio again. Have students listen and take notes of the language.

ACTIVITY 7 research on the web [20 minutes/homework]

You may want to use this activity after Exercise 6 on SB page 279.

■ STEP 1   You may want students to complete this section as homework. Review the examples of American history before assigning the task.

■ STEP 2   The purpose of this Internet search activity is to provide a natural context for using the past perfect. An additional purpose is to encourage students to share strategies for finding information on the Internet. Ask: *What Web sites were most useful?* You may want to have students present their information in the form of a poster or chart and display them in the classroom in addition to the partner work.

ACTIVITY 8 reflection [10 minutes]

This activity provides an opportunity for students to use the target structures of the unit while reflecting on their language learning progress. You may have asked students to keep a record of their learning in a journal throughout this course as suggested in To the Teacher, LP page xxii. This reflection activity will be part of that learning record.

ARTICLES
The, A/An, Some, and Ø

UNIT GOALS

- Understand the meaning of the articles *the, a, an,* and *some*

- Use articles correctly for first and second mentions of an item

- Know which articles to use with singular, plural, and noncount nouns

- Understand when to use *Ø* (no article)

OPENING TASK
Looking for the Perfect House

◾ STEP 1

Look at the pictures. Describe each one. What is your ideal type of house?

1.

2.

3.

4.

5.

◾ STEP 2

Put the following sentences in order so that they make a story. When you have finished, check to see if other students have the story in the same order.

a. ___2___ Esinam found a real-estate agent to help them.

b. ___8___ They finally decided to buy the little house and remodel the kitchen.

c. ___5___ The second place they saw was a pretty brick house by a lake, but the house was too expensive.

d. ___7___ Finally they saw a little one-bedroom house surrounded by trees at the end of a dead-end street.

e. ___9___ When I last talked to them, they had finished remodeling the kitchen, and they liked the house a lot.

f. ___1___ Esinam and Sunita decided to buy a house.

g. ___6___ The real-estate agent then showed them a house near some apartment buildings, but the house was too big, and the apartment buildings were too ugly.

h. ___4___ First they looked at a nice house in the suburbs, but there were no trees, and the house was too far away from work.

i. ___3___ They told the real-estate agent that they wanted to live in a quiet neighborhood. They also said that they preferred small houses.

◾ STEP 3

Write the numbers of the pictures in Step 1 in the correct story order.

___1___   ___2___   ___5___   ___4___   ___3___

20 LESSON PLAN 1

UNIT OVERVIEW

Unit 20 looks at the English articles in detail. The form, meaning, and use of *the*, *a/an*, *some*, and Ø (no article) are contrasted.

GRAMMAR NOTE

Although most students will have studied the use of articles before, this area of grammar is one of the most difficult for students to learn, especially if their first language does not use articles—for example, Russian, Arabic, or Chinese. There are four articles in English: *a/an*, *some/any*, *the*, and zero article. Articles are used to show whether we are talking about things in general, or in particular. They are also used to show whether we are speaking about things that are known to both speaker and listener, or not. The use of articles also depends on whether the noun is a count noun or a noncount noun.

UNIT GOALS

Some instructors may want to review the goals listed on Student Book (SB) page 284 after completing the Opening Task so that students understand what they should know by the end of the unit. These goals can also be reviewed at the end of the unit when students are more familiar with the grammar terminology.

OPENING TASK [20 minutes]

The purpose of the Opening Task is to create a context in which students will need to use articles. The problem-solving format is designed to show the teacher how well the students can use the target structures implicitly and spontaneously when they are engaged in a communicative task. For a more complete discussion of the purpose of the Opening Task, see To the Teacher, Lesson Planner (LP) page xxii.

Setting Up the Task

STEP 1

1. Introduce the topic of housing by looking at the pictures. Describe the main features of the houses.

2. How do they differ from houses in their country or in other countries they know? Does this house conform to their idea of "the perfect house"?

3. Ask for some tips or suggestions on looking for a home to rent or buy. Where can you get information? What are the different steps in looking for a home to rent or to buy?

Conducting the Task

STEP 2

1. Have students work individually or in pairs to order the sentences in the story.

2. You can also copy the sentences onto strips and have students arrange the strips in the correct order.

3. While they are working, circulate to see whether they are using articles as clues in working out the puzzle.

4. Have students compare their versions of the story.

5. Students will return to this story in Exercise 11 on SB page 296.

STEP 3

1. Have students discuss in pairs which houses match which part of the story.

2. Ask volunteers to give and justify their answers.

3. Monitor the use of articles, but do not explain or correct at this stage. Use the information to help determine where you should spend more time later.

Closing the Task

1. Choose one or two examples of students' sentences to illustrate the meaning of definite, indefinite, and zero article.

2. You may use these sentences as a bridge to Focus Chart 1.

GRAMMAR NOTE

Typical student errors (form)

- Using *a* before nouns that start with a vowel sound, e.g. * *a orange*, * *a hour*. (See Focus 3.)
- Using *an* before words starting with a vowel letter but with a consonant sound, e.g. * *an university*, * *an European*. (See Focus 3.)

Typical student errors (use)

- Using indefinite article for nouns that are known to both speaker and listener, * *Where did you park a car?* (See Focus 1.)
- Omitting the article or using *some* with singular count nouns, e.g. * *I need new notebook.* * *I'd like to buy some new CD.* (See Focus 3.)
- Using indefinite articles with noncount nouns, e.g. * *Please give me an advice.* (See Focus 3.)
- Using *some* to talk about all members of a group of things, e.g. * *Some spiders have eight legs.* (See Focus 4.)
- Using *the* for nouns in general statements, e.g. * *The rice is eaten in Asia.* (See Focus 6.)
- Using *a* for unique nouns, nouns that have already been mentioned, or nouns with superlatives, e.g. * *It is a best movie I've ever seen.* (See Focus 7 and 8.)

form meaning

FOCUS 1

Definite and Indefinite Articles: *The, A/An, Ø* (no article), *and Some*

EXAMPLES

(a) *Father to Son:* Where did we park the car?

(b) Which car are they talking about?
The family car.

(c) Al needs a new notebook.

(d) What does Al need?
A new notebook.

(e) Al needs **a** new computer, new software, and new instructional manuals.

(f) Al needs **some** new software and some new instruction manuals.

EXPLANATIONS

Use the definite article *the* to talk about a specific noun. In (a), the father and son are thinking about the same car—a car that they both can identify.

With *the,* you can answer the question *Which . . . ?*

Use the indefinite article *a* or *an* to talk about one of a group of similar things, not about a specific thing.

In (c), Al is thinking about notebooks in general. He's not thinking about a specific notebook that he can identify.

With *a/an,* you can answer the question *What . . . ?* (d) Use *a* or *an* with singular count nouns.

Use the indefinite article *Ø* (no article) with noncount nouns or plural count nouns.

Use the indefinite article *some* to talk about a nonspecific number or quantity with plural nouns or noncount nouns.

EXERCISE 1

Fill in the blanks in the story below with *the, a, an, Ø* (no article), or *some.*

1. I recently found ___a___ new job in New York City.

2. We spent the weekend looking at ___Ø___ apartments for rent.

3. Many apartments were very small, but ___some___ older apartments were quite large.

4. We finally chose ___an___ apartment in Brooklyn.

5. ___The___ apartment building we chose was made of wood and was about 100 years old.

6. We had lived in a new house before, but ___Ø___ old houses have more character.

7. One night, our daughter Sarah said she could hear ___some / Ø___ voices in the room upstairs.

8. She thought there were ___some / Ø___ ghosts up there.

9. But when we went to look, ___the___ room was empty.

10. We told ourselves it was our imagination playing ___Ø___ tricks on us.

11. Later we realized that ___the___ walls were very thin.

12. ___The___ voices that we heard were from the people next door.

---

use

FOCUS 2

Using Articles: First and Second Mention

EXAMPLES

(a) I read a great book yesterday.

(b) Martha just bought a new backpack.

(c) I found **an** old dress of my mother's in the attic.

(d) I found an old dress of my mother's in the attic in the trunk. **The** dress was beautiful, with pearl buttons and lace sleeves.

EXPLANATIONS

A /*an* is generally used to talk about a noun for the first time (first mention). Since the noun is introduced for the first time, it is not yet identified as a specific thing.

Use *the* when the noun has been introduced and is now identified (sometimes called "second mention").

20 LESSON PLAN 1

FOCUS 1 [5 minutes]

1. **Lead-ines 1:** Use some examples of sentences created by students in the Opening Task. Ask them why they chose *a* or *the* in these sentences.

2. Read the example and explanations in the focus chart to see if any of their explanations are the same.

3. In English, singular count nouns **must** have an article. You may want to review the idea of count and noncount nouns, or select certain nouns that you have noticed cause the most difficulty. See below for a possible list of nouns that can cause difficulty. For a review of the difference between count and noncount nouns, see the Grammar Note for Exercise 2, Unit 8 on LP page 127.

Noncount nouns	Count nouns
accommodation	advertisement
advice	apartment
equipment	building
furniture	house
information	job
money	journey
news	meal
time	newspaper
travel	problem
work	weekend

EXERCISE 1 [10 minutes]

1. Read the instructions and do the first sentence together with the class.

2. You may need to explain that Ø = no article.

3. Have students read through all the sentences first to get an idea of the story, rather than treating each sentence in isolation.

4. Students can work in pairs to complete the exercise. Encourage them to explain their answers to each other if they disagree.

5. Review the answers as a class; refer to the answer key on LP page 286. Refer students back to the

---

relevant point in Focus Chart 1 when errors are made.

6. Students will refer back to this exercise in Exercise 2 and Exercise 5.

EXPANSION [20 minutes]

You may want to use Activity 1 (speaking) on SB page 299 after this activity.

GRAMMAR NOTE

1. If students are having trouble grasping the basic difference between *the* and *a/an*, you may wish to point out that, historically, *a/an* had the same meaning as *one*, while *the* used to be a different form of *this*. Mentioning this historical distinction often helps students grasp the difference between one of a group (*a/an*) and one in particular (*the*).

2. *Some* is used **instead of** *the* or *a/an*:

   *I'd like **some** more coffee, please.*

   NOT: * I'd like **the some** more coffee, please.

   When *some* is used as a quantity, count nouns must be plural:

   *Milo takes **some** vitamins every morning to stay in good health.* NOT: * Milo takes **some** vitamin every morning to stay in good health.

[work book]

For more practice, use *Grammar Dimensions 2* Workbook page 127, Exercise 1.

FOCUS 2 [5 minutes]

1. **Lead-in:** To illustrate the concept of first and second mention, use the first example sentence as the start of short dialogue. For example:

   A: *I read **a** great book recently.*

   B: *Oh yeah, what's **the** book called?*

   A: *White Teeth by Zadie Smith. Have you heard of it?*

---

2. Read the examples and explanations in the focus chart.

3. Have students make up dialogues using the other examples.

4. This concept is further discussed in Focus Chart 8 on SB page 295.

form

FOCUS 3

Indefinite Articles with Singular, Plural, and Noncount Nouns

EXAMPLES	EXPLANATIONS
(a) I'd like to buy a piano and **an** organ.	Use *a* and *an* with singular count nouns. Use *a* before consonant sounds and *an* before vowel sounds. It is the **sound**, not the letter, that tells you whether to use *a* or *an*.
(b) **a** youngster	
(c) **a** university	
(d) **an** energetic woman	If there is an adjective before the noun, then the first sound of the **adjective** tells you whether to use *a* or *an*, not the first sound of the noun.
(e) **an** unusual doll	
(f) I'd like to buy **some** new CDs and tapes, and then I'd like to listen to **music** all day.	Use *some* or Ø (no article) with plural count nouns and noncount nouns.

EXERCISE 2

Now look back at Exercise 1 and tell your partner why you used each article (*a/an*, *some*, *the* or Ø). Did you complete the exercise correctly? If not, go back and rewrite the sentences you missed.

EXERCISE 3

Read the following paragraph. For each underlined noun phrase, is the article usage correct? If the article usage is not correct, write the correct usage above the underlined words. These questions will help you:

- Is the writer talking about a noun for the first time?
- Is the writer talking about a specific noun?
- Is the writer talking about one of a group of similar things—**not** an identified/specific noun?

Since 1988, (1) a herd of deer has come to Pedro's apple orchard each October just after apple harvest for a feast. (2) An orchard is bordered by a forest, and Pedro and his family are able to watch (3) the herd come out of (4) a forest and walk directly to the nearest apple trees. Within minutes after the deer enter (5) the orchard, (6) the apples are gone, and (7) the deer return to the forest with their stomachs full. Watching the deer has become (8) an annual event for Pedro and his family. If Pedro could predict (9) the annual apple-eating event, he would invite his friends and have (10) the deer-watching party.

EXERCISE 4

Fill in the blanks with *a*, *an*, or Ø (no article).

1. If I won the lottery, first I would buy ___a___ piece of land in the country.

2. Then I would build ___an___ unusual house and ___a___ huge barn.

3. Of course I would build ___a___ long fence, too.

4. Then I would buy ___Ø___ horses, ___Ø___ cows, and maybe ___a___ llama.

5. I would make sure to buy ___Ø___ hay for the winter, so that the animals would have plenty to eat.

6. I would probably hire ___Ø___ people to take care of the horses.

7. People say that you can't buy ___Ø___ happiness, but I think my ranch would certainly make me happy!

ANSWER KEY

Exercise 2 1. a—singular count noun; talking about it (a job) for the first time; answers the question What? 2. Ø—plural count noun; talking about a group of things (apartments), not a specific apartment; answers the question What? 3. some—plural count noun; talking about quantity; answers the question What? 4. an—singular count noun; talking about it (an apartment) for the first time; answers the question What? 5. The—singular count noun; second mention; answers the question Which? 6. Ø—plural count noun; talking about a group of things (old houses)

be used with a plural count noun. 9. the—singular count noun; second mention; answers the question Which? 10. Ø—plural count noun; talking about a group of things (apartments), not a specific apartment; answers the question Which? 11. the—singular count noun; answers the question Which? 12. the—singular count noun; second mention; answers the question Which?

Exercise 3   Correct: 1, 3, 5, 6, 7, 8, 9

Incorrect: (2) should use the *the* because *orchard* has already been mentioned (4) should use the *the* because *forest* has already been mentioned (10) should use *a* because this is the first time *deer-*

LESSON PLAN 1

20

EXERCISE 2 [10 minutes]

1. Refer students back to Exercise 1 on SB page 287.
2. Ask them to review their answers and find any articles that may be explained by the rules in Focus Chart 2.
3. Invite volunteers to present their answers to the class.

EXERCISE 3 [10 minutes]

1. Copy the exercise onto an overhead projector transparency so you can make corrections directly on the page.
2. Have students work in pairs to complete the exercise.
3. Discuss their answers as a class. Refer to the answer key on LP page 289. For each noun phrase, ask the three questions in order to come up with the final answer.

For more practice, use *Grammar Dimensions 2* Workbook page 128, Exercise 2.

EXPANSION [20–40 minutes]

You may want to use Activity 2 (speaking/listening) and Activity 3 (writing) on SB page 299 after this exercise. These activities ask students to bring in pictures (from magazines or other sources) and describe them in order to practice the use of articles.

FOCUS 3 [5 minutes]

1. **Lead-in:** Write the following words on the board and any others that might present a challenge. Ask students to determine if they use *a* or *an*.

umbrella	uniform
hour	orange
university	honest person
European	older person
herb	difficult operation
year	Etc.
week	

2. Use their answers to work out the rule that *an* comes before a vowel *sound* (not a vowel *letter*). See Pronunciation Note below.
3. Read the examples and explanations in the focus chart.
4. The difference between *some* and Ø is discussed further in Focus Chart 4 on SB page 290.

PRONUNCIATION NOTE

Sentences (b) and (c) illustrate the point that *a* comes before a **consonant** sound, as the phonetic transcription demonstrates:

(b) a youngster [yʌŋ stər]
(c) a university [ˌyu nə'vɜr 'sɪ ti]

Contrast (c) with:
an uncle ['ʌŋ kəl]

Other examples:
a hotel [hou'tel]
an hour [auər, au ər]
an honest living [ɒn ɪst]

EXERCISE 4 [5 minutes]

1. Encourage students to read through all the sentences first to get an idea of the story.
2. Have students work individually.
3. Ask students to read aloud and defend their choices.
4. Ask the class if they agree or disagree. Refer to LP page 288 for answers.

EXPANSION [20 minutes]

You may want to use Activity 4 (speaking/listening/writing) on SB page 300 after this exercise. This activity practices the use of articles when using abstract nouns.

For more practice, use *Grammar Dimensions 2* Workbook page 129, Exercise 3.

FOCUS 4

Some Instead of Ø (No Article)

EXAMPLES	EXPLANATIONS
(a) Al needs **some** new clothes.	Use *some* with plural count nouns and noncount nouns when you want to talk about quantity (amount).
(b) I'd like to get **some** tickets to the concert on Friday.	
(c) I'd like to listen to **some** jazz. (s'm jazz)	When *some* is used instead of Ø (no article) in conversation, it is not stressed.
(d) Can we get **some** cookies at the bakery? (s'm cookies)	
(e) I'd like to listen to (some) jazz.	Usually *some* is optional (you **can** use it, but it's not necessary).
(f) Al needs (some) new clothes.	
(g) Cookies are called biscuits in England.	Do not use *some* when you are talking about all members of a group of similar things.
(h) NOT: Some cookies are called biscuits in England.	
(i) Spiders have eight legs.	
(j) NOT: Some spiders have eight legs.	

EXERCISE 5

Look at your answers in Exercise 1. Mark with a check (✓) all the answers where Ø (no article) was used with either a plural count noun or a noncount noun. Could you use *some* instead? Discuss your answers with a partner.

1. _____
2. _____
3. _____
4. _____
5. _____
6. _____
7. _____
8. _____
9. _____
10. _____
11. _____
12. _____

FOCUS 5

The with Singular, Plural, and Noncount Nouns

EXAMPLES	EXPLANATIONS
(a) *Son to Father:* Where did you put **the** keys?	Use *the* with all nouns that can be specifically identified:
 • plural count nouns: In (a) both speakers can identify which specific keys are being talked about.
(b) *Son to Friend:* Turn on **the** light, please.	• singular count nouns: In (b) they can both identify which specific light is being talked about.
(c) *Housemate to Housemate:* I can't find **the** sugar. Where did you put it?	• noncount (mass) nouns: In (c) they can both identify which sugar is being talked about.

EXERCISE 6

Fill in the blanks in the following story with *a/an, some, the,* or Ø (*no article*).

1. Last fall Anita worked in ___an___ apple orchard, picking apples.

2. ___The___ work was not easy.

3. She had sore muscles ___the___ first week of work, and every night she slept very soundly.

4. ___The___ first orchard she worked in was considered small, with only fifty trees.

5. It was owned by ___an___ old, retired couple, who worked in the orchard as ___a___ hobby.

6. ___The___ next orchard Anita worked in was much larger, about twenty acres.

7. In this orchard, ___some/the___ trees had yellow apples, which were called "Golden Delicious."

ANSWER KEY

Exercise 5 From Exercise 1: **2.** can use *some* with apartments since a nonspecific quantity is being referred to **6.** can't use *some* because it is talking about all old houses (all members of a group of similar things) **7., 8.** same as **2. 10.** same answer as **6.**

LESSON PLAN 1

FOCUS 4 [5 minutes]

1. **Lead-in:** Give students some contrasting examples where *some* is used with the same meaning as zero article, and where *some* is used to contrast with *many*. (See Language Note below.) For example:

    Cats are very intelligent. (= all cats)

    Some cats are very intelligent. (= not all cats)

    I want to buy some books. (= an unspecified quantity)

    I am going to buy books. (= an unspecified quantity)

2. Read the examples in the chart aloud and ask students to identify the meaning of *some*.

3. If you read the incorrect sentences (h) and (j), ask students to explain why they are wrong.

LANGUAGE NOTE

Note that *some* is used when we want to stress the quantity aspect of the noun phrase; otherwise, it can be omitted.

For example, *She has some friends.* (contrasted with *many*)

She has friends. (= she is not alone in the world, contrasted with *none*)

When the word *some* is stressed, it emphasizes the meaning of *some* as opposed to *many*.

EXERCISE 5 [5 minutes]

1. Refer students back to Exercise 1 on SB page 287.

2. Have pairs discuss their ideas on when *some* can be used.

3. As a class, review their answers and reach a consensus on when to use *some*. Refer to the answer key on LP page 290.

EXPANSION [20–40 minutes]

You may want to use Activity 5 (listening) followed by Activity 6 (speaking/listening) on SB page 300 after this exercise. These activities center on the theme of people describing their home.

For more practice, use *Grammar Dimensions 2* Workbook page 130, Exercise 4.

FOCUS 5 [5 minutes]

1. **Lead-in:** Introduce this grammar point by asking some questions about things in the classroom about which both you and the students have shared knowledge (use examples of both singular and plural nouns). For example, *Where is the light switch? Could you come to the board please? Are the markers on my desk? Are the windows open? Has the lesson started?*

2. Ask students why they think *the* is used in each case? Could it be replaced by *some* or by zero article?

3. Continue with contrasting examples if students cannot work out the rule. For example, *Could you lend me a pen? Do you have a cell phone?*

4. Read the examples and explanations in the focus chart to confirm or clarify students' guesses.

LANGUAGE NOTE

Another way to explain this aspect of using the definite article *the* is that these are shared resources. Outside of the group in which they are speaking, they would need to be identified more clearly. The notion of shared resources explains why we can say *the hospital, the bank, the movies,* even when the exact hospital, bank, or movie theater is not identified. This explanation is related to the point in Focus Chart 7 on SB page 293.

EXERCISE 6 [10 minutes]

1. Encourage students to read through the whole exercise to get a sense of the story.

2. Set a time limit for students to complete the exercise (or assign the exercise for homework).

3. Prepare and use an overhead transparency to review the answers. Refer to the answer key on LP page 290 and 292.

For more practice, use *Grammar Dimensions 2* Workbook page 130, Exercise 5.

8. Every day Anita ate ___*some*/Ø___ apples for breakfast and for lunch.
9. Even though ___*the*___ weather was beautiful, and ___*the*___ hard work made her feel very healthy, Anita was relieved when ___*the*___ apple-picking season was over.

Now work with a classmate and explain your choices.

meaning

use

FOCUS 6

Making General Statements with Ø (No Article)

EXAMPLES	EXPLANATIONS
(a) A1: I need new **clothes**. 	Use Ø (no) article to make general statements. In (a), A1 is not thinking about specific clothes that he and his listener can identify. Use Ø (no article) to talk about plural count nouns that are not specific.
(b) I'd like to get **flowers** for my birthday.	In (b), you can't identify **which** flowers; you and the listener are not thinking about specific flowers.
(c) He is hoping to find **love**. (d) I like **jazz**.	Use Ø (no article) when you make a general statement using noncount (mass) nouns.
(e) Pencils are made with **graphite**. (f) **Rice** is eaten in Asia.	Use Ø (no article) when you make a general statement about a whole group or category.
(g) **Medical care** is very expensive in the United States.	Statements that use Ø (no article) can usually be paraphrased with *in general*. In (g): *In general*, medical care in the United States is expensive. (There may be some exceptions to the fact stated.)
(h) Most people like **vacations**.	
(i) The university offers excellent classes in **art** and **music**.	

EXERCISE 7

Circle the errors in article usage in the sentences below. Specifically, should you use *the* or Ø (no article)?

1. The love is a very important thing in our lives.
2. Without the love, we would be lonely and confused.
3. I believe that the money is not as important as love, although some people don't feel this way.
4. If the money is too important, then we become greedy.
5. When we get old, the health becomes as important as love.
6. My grandmother says, "Just wait and see. Work you do and the money you earn are important now, but when you're old . . ."
7. ". . . love that you feel for your family and friends, health of your loved ones—these are the things that will be most important."

meaning

FOCUS 7

The with Unique/Easily Identified Nouns

EXAMPLES	EXPLANATIONS
(a) In June, **the sun** doesn't set until 9:30.	The definite article *the* is used with nouns that are easily identified. Use *the* with nouns that are **universally** known (everyone in the world can identify it). In (a), everyone knows **which** sun they're talking about, since there's only one.
(b) Mary went to **the coast** on her vacation.	*The* is also used when the noun is **regionally** known (everyone in the region can identify it). In (b), everyone knows **which** coast they're talking about, since there's only one in the region.
(c) Did you feed **the cats**?	We can also use *the* when the noun is **locally** known (everyone in the immediate location can identify it). In (c), everyone in the immediate location knows **which** cats they're talking about, since they live together in the same house.

ANSWER KEY

FOCUS 6 [5 minutes]

1. **Lead-in:** Review some of the rules for articles presented in this unit so far. Introduce the idea of making general statements by playing this game. Write the following topics on the board, and ask volunteers to come to the front of the class and speak for 30 seconds on the topic without pausing.

2. Other members of the class will monitor if they pause or not. If they pause more than 5 seconds they are "out."

3. While they are speaking, take notes of correct and incorrect general statement using articles. Possible topics may include Vacations, Nature, Cell phones, Happiness, Cats, Music, or Health.

4. Check comprehension of specific versus general statements by asking for examples of each for each topic. For example,

Count nouns

Vacations are good for your health. (general)
I will never forget the vacations I had when I was a child. (specific)

Noncount nouns

Nature is being destroyed by pollution. (general)
The nature outside of New York City is quite beautiful. (specific)

5. Read the examples and explanations in the focus chart.

6. Have students work in pairs to think of other sentence pairs of contrasting examples.

METHODOLOGY NOTE

This note reviews the concept of deductive versus inductive learning and how they are used or applied in the classroom. Although some students prefer to see and understand a grammar rule first before trying out an exercise or an activity, other students learn better by looking at examples first. The first method is known as the deductive approach. Students learn the rule and then apply it to specific examples. The second method is known as the inductive approach. Students look at examples and work out the rules. It is a good idea to vary these approaches in order to facilitate different learning styles in your class. It may also be a good idea to explain which approach you are using and why. Although the deductive approach may seem to be more rational and save time, the inductive approach requires more engagement from the student. Inductive work may be more memorable in the long term as it encourages peer work.

FOCUS 7 [5 minutes]

1. **Lead-in:** Refer back to the examples you gave in Focus Chart 5 for nouns that everyone has shared knowledge of. Explain that this also explains the use of *the* for nouns that are unique or easily identified in the world.

2. Examples of unique nouns in the world include *the sun, the earth.* Nouns that are unique in the country or region you are in might include *the capital, the coast, the mountains,* or more locally, *the train station, the hospital, the library.*

3. Read the examples and explanations in the focus chart.

4. Have students make a list of unique nouns. Divide the list into three columns: global, regional, local.

5. You can make this into a competition by setting a time limit of 5 minutes. The first person to have 20 nouns is the winner.

EXERCISE 7 [10 minutes]

This exercise provides practice in distinguishing *the* or zero article when talking about general or specific nouns.

1. Emphasize the importance of editing skills when correcting one's own written work.

2. Set a time limit for students to work individually to find the errors.

3. Have them compare answers with a partner.

4. Review the answers, referring back to the relevant explanations in Focus Chart 6. Refer to the answer key on LP page 292.

For more practice, use *Grammar Dimensions 2* Workbook page 131, Exercise 6.

EXERCISE 8

For sentences 1–10 below, answer these three questions (answers may vary):

a. Where would you hear this sentence spoken?
b. Who do you think the speaker is?
c. What do you think happened or what was the conversation about **before** or **after** the sentence was spoken?

1. Please turn on *the* TV.
2. Could you change *the* channel?
3. We need some more chalk. Would you mind checking *the* blackboard in *the* back?
4. *The* rosebushes are lovely.
5. Could you pass *the* salt, please?
6. Excuse me, where's *the* women's restroom?
7. *The* sky is so blue today. I don't think you'll need *the* umbrella.
8. Have you seen *the* dog?
9. It's so romantic. See how bright *the* moon is?
10. Let's go to *the* mountains for our vacation instead of to *the* beach.

Use your answers to the three questions above to discuss in class why *the* was used in each sentence.

EXERCISE 9

Tell why *the* is used in each of the following sentences. (Some of these you will recognize from Exercise 8.) In the space at the left, write down **where** you think this statement was made. Then, on the right:

• If it is **universally** known, circle **U.**
• If it is **regionally** known, circle **R.**
• If it is **locally** known (because of the immediate location), circle **L.**

Setting

a living room	1. Please turn on *the* TV.	U R (L)
a living room	2. Could you change *the* channel?	U R (L)
a classroom	3. We need some more chalk. Would you mind checking *the* blackboard in *the* back?	U R (L)
a garden	4. *The* rosebushes are lovely	U R (L)
at dinner	5. Could you pass *the* salt, please?	U R (L)
any public place	6. Excuse me, please. Where's *the* women's restroom?	U (R) L
in or outside of someone's home	7. *The* sky is so blue today. I don't think you'll need *the* umbrella.	(U) R L

in someone's home or outside in the yard	8. Have you seen *the* dog?	U R (L)
outside	9. It's so romantic. See how bright *the* moon is?	(U) R L
anywhere	10. Let's go to *the* mountains for our vacation, instead of to *the* beach.	U (R) L
in a family's house	11. Son: Hey Dad, can I borrow *the* car? Dad: Sure, if you can find *the* keys!	U R (L)
anywhere	12. I like your dress. Did you buy it at *the* mall?	U (R) L

meaning

FOCUS 8

Using *The:* Second Mention, Related Mention, and Certain Adjectives

EXAMPLES	EXPLANATIONS
(a) She used to have a cat and a dog, but **the** cat died.	Sometimes we use *the* with a noun because the noun has been talked about before (second mention).
(b) Last year I bought a guitar and a banjo. I decided to sell **the** banjo since I rarely play it.	We can identify the cat in (a) and the banjo in (b) because they have been talked about before.
(c) He bought a suit, but **the** jacket had a button missing, so he had to return it. (d) I had a lock, but I lost **the** key for it.	In other situations we can identify a noun because it is *related* to something that has been talked about before (related mention). In (c), we know which jacket they're talking about, since *jacket* is part of *suit.*
(e) She had started to read a book when she noticed that **the** first chapter was missing. (f) She's **the** first person I met here and the only friend I have. (g) That's **the** hardest test I've ever taken. (h) You made **the** right choice.	Adjectives or phrases like *last, next, first, only,* and *right,* and superlatives like *best, hardest,* and *happiest* usually use the definite article *the* because they describe something that is "one of a kind." There's only one "first chapter" (in e), only one "first person" (in f), and only one "hardest test" (in g).
(i) It's **the** same old story. (j) We are taking **the** same class.	The definite article is always used with the adjective *same.*

Exercise 8

1. (a) In a family's living room. (b) A parent or older sibling speaking to a younger child. (c) Before—the listener was near the TV. After—he or she turned on the TV. 2. (a) In a family's living room. (c) Before—the listener was near the TV or was holding the remote. After—he or she changed the channel. 3. (a) In a classroom. (b) The teacher. (c) Before—the teacher ran out of chalk. After—a student did what was requested 4. (a) In a garden. (b) A guest/visitor. (c) Before—they were taking a tour of the garden. After—they continued the tour. 5. (a) At dinner. (b) One of the people at the table. (c) Before—they were serving themselves. After—someone honored the request. 6. (a) In any public place.

After—the person she asked gave her directions. 7. (a) In or outside of someone's house. (b) One family member to another (or roommate). (c) Before—they were discussing the weather while looking out the window. After—the person said good-bye and left the house (without the umbrella). 8. (a) In someone's home or outside in the yard. (b) One family member to another. (c) Before—the person noticed the dog was gone. After—the other person answered the question and/or helped look for the dog. 9. (a) Outside (b) Probably two people who are romantically involved, but not necessarily (c) Before and after—they made small talk and/or kissed. 10. (a) Anywhere (b) A family member (c) Before and after—they were discussing vacation plans and destinations.

LESSON PLAN 2

■ EXERCISE 8 [15 minutes]

This exercise provides practice in recognizing clues of context provided by the use of articles.

1. Read the instructions with your students.
2. Do the first example together.
3. Have students complete the exercise in pairs.
4. While students are working, draw a 3-column chart on the board, labeling columns "where," "who," and "what happened."
5. When reviewing their answers, fill out the chart on the board.
6. Answers will vary. Refer to the answer key on LP page 294 for suggested answers.

■ EXERCISE 9 [15 minutes]

This exercise connects the relevance of setting to the meaning and use of articles.

1. Do the first example together with the class.
2. Have students work individually to complete the exercise, or assign this for homework.
3. Review the answers as a class. Refer to the answer key on LP page 294.

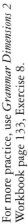

For more practice, use *Grammar Dimensions 2* Workbook page 132, Exercise 7.

EXPANSION [20 minutes]

You may want to use Activity 8 (research on the web) on SB page 301 after this exercise. Alternatively, have students bring in newspaper articles and underline uses of the definite article that are examples of universal, regional, or local reference. See Methodology Note on LP page 297.

FOCUS 8 [10 minutes]

This focus chart continues with the issue raised in Focus Chart 2 SB on page 287.

1. **Lead-in:** Have students cover the right-hand side of the chart and read the examples. Ask for suggestions for reasons why *the* is used in these cases.
2. Uncover the right-hand side of the chart and compare the suggested reasons with the ones in the chart.

For more practice, use *Grammar Dimensions 2* Workbook page 133, Exercise 8.

EXPANSION [20 minutes]

If you feel that students need further practice with using articles with adjectives like *first, next, best,* etc., you may want to use the following questionnaire to help them practice and remember this rule.

Work in pairs to ask and answer these questions.

1. *What is the best book you have ever read?*
2. *Have you ever read the same book twice? What was it?*
3. *What is the last movie you saw in a movie theater?*
4. *What is the next place you want to visit on vacation?*
5. *What is the only food or drink you cannot give up?*
6. *Who was your first English teacher?*
7. *What is the hardest grammar point we have studied in this book so far?*
8. *What is the most important thing in your life?*

EXERCISE 10

Read the story below. Decide why the *the* is used each time it is underlined. If it is used because it has been talked about before, circle **S** (for **second mention**). If it is used because a **related** noun has been talked about before, circle **R** (for **related mention**).

Jerry was late for his appointment, so he went into a telephone booth near the bus stop to make a phone call. It looked like someone was living in the telephone booth.

1. Jerry was late for his appointment, so he went into a telephone booth near the bus stop to make a phone call. It looked like someone was living in <u>the telephone booth</u>. Ⓢ R

2. There was a small blanket covering <u>the window</u> of the telephone booth like a curtain. S Ⓡ

3. <u>The floor</u> of the telephone booth was swept clean with a broom. Ⓢ R

4. <u>The broom</u> was hung on a hook in the corner of the telephone booth. S Ⓡ

5. By <u>the telephone</u>, there was a pen and a notepad with a short list of names and telephone numbers. S Ⓡ

6. Jerry also noticed that there was a coffee mug and a toothbrush sitting neatly by <u>the telephone directory</u>. S Ⓡ

7. <u>The coffee mug</u> looked like it had recently been rinsed. There were still drops of water in it. Ⓢ R

8. Jerry had such a strong feeling that he was in someone's living space that he decided to find another place to make <u>the phone call</u>. Ⓢ R

EXERCISE 11

Look at the story in the Opening Task on page 285, making sure that it is in the right order. How many times is *the* used? Underline each *the* and explain why it was used.

	Reason *the* is used
Example: i. *the* real-estate agent	*second mention*

EXERCISE 12

Underline and number each use of *the* in the following story. Then tell why each is used. The possible reasons for the use of *the* with a noun are:

a. It's universally known.

b. It's regionally known.

c. It's locally known—the immediate location makes it clear.

d. Second mention.

e. Related mention.

f. The adjective or phrase makes it "one of a kind."

Vocabulary:

levee—raised bank or wall to stop flooding

Hurricane Katrina, which hit Louisiana, Mississippi, and Alabama in

1   August 2005, was the costliest and most destructive natural disaster the United

2   States had ever seen. The hurricane resulted in damage to *levees* that protect

3   New Orleans from Lake Pontchartrain and most of the city was flooded by the

4   lake's waters. Large sections of the city lie at or below sea level, and over a

5   million people lost their homes. Federal and state emergency services were

6   criticized for their slow response to the disaster and nongovernmental agencies

7   such as the Red Cross as well as many private individuals from all over the

8   country volunteered their time and money to organize aid for the disaster

9   victims. Oil-refining in the region was also severely hit, causing job losses and

10 higher fuel prices. The government estimated that around $200 billion would be

11 needed to rebuild New Orleans and other towns in the region.

12

1.	f
2.	a
3.	d
4.	d
5.	e
6.	d
7.	d
8.	b
9.	a
10.	e
11.	e
12.	a
13.	d

mention c. The second place—because of the adjective *second;* the house—*second mention* g. the real estate agent—*second mention;* the house—*second mention;* the apartment buildings—*second mention* d. the end of a dead-end street—*related mention (dead-end streets have an "end")* and uniqueness because there is only one end of a dead-end street, which is regionally known b. the little house—*second mention;* the kitchen—*second mention* e. the kitchen—*second mention;* the house—*second mention*

Exercise 12   Answers may vary, since it may be possible to justify the choice of *the* for more than

one reason. Possible answers are listed above.

EXERCISE 10 [15 minutes]

This exercise helps students distinguishing second mention from related mention references.

1. Read the instructions with the class.
2. Do the first examples together.
3. Circulate while students are working to listen for problem areas.
4. Review the answers as a class. Refer to the answer key on LP page 296.

EXERCISE 11 [5 minutes]

Students must have completed the Opening Task in order to do this exercise.

1. Refer back to the Opening Task.
2. If you have an overhead transparency of the sentences in the correct order, it may be easier to do this as a class.
3. This activity can be done as written homework.
4. Refer to the answer key on LP page 296.

EXPANSION [20 minutes]

You may want to use Activity 7 (speaking/listening) on SB page 301 after this exercise.

EXERCISE 12 [20 minutes]

1. Have students look at the picture on SB page 297. Ask them to make predictions about the topic and events in the article before they read it. Later, find out if any of their predictions were correct.
2. Before students read, decide if you would like them to use dictionaries or not. If they complete the reading in class, circulate to help with vocabulary questions. Encourage them to consult each other as well.

3. Review the directions on SB page 296. Refer back to Focus Charts 2, 5, and 7 if needed.
4. Direct students to read through the passage before they start to get a sense of the overall meaning and context.
5. Ask some easy comprehension questions about the article. Examples:

    What are the main ideas in the article? (the damage caused by Hurricane Katrina)

    What kind of damage did Hurricane Katrina cause? (flooding, homes were destroyed, oil-refineries were damaged or destroyed)

    Why was New Orleans so badly hit? (Because it is mostly below sea level, because damage to the levees caused flooding)

    Think of a title for the article. (Answers will vary. Examples: Nature's Deadly Force)
6. Then have them go through again and identify examples of *the*.
7. Students can work in pairs to identify and explain uses of *the*, writing the relevant letters and numbers in the lines provided.
8. Review any problematic answers as a class.
9. You may want to assign Exercise 13 for homework after this exercise.

METHODOLOGY NOTE

This unit uses articles adapted from newspapers to illustrate the use of articles. Using authentic material from newspapers, magazines, advertisements, or other sources can be beneficial for a variety of reasons. First, it helps students to bridge the gap between language studied in class and language all around them. Second, it develops a critical approach to language study that students can use in their independent study. Third, it encourages students to have confidence in reading and using such materials outside of class.

EXERCISE 13

In the following newspaper article, circle each *the* and *a*. Then explain why those articles are used.

Vocabulary:

relief—help for victims of a disaster
shelter—temporary accommodation
cot—temporary bed
disturbing—shocking
trailer—mobile home

Volunteers Head South to Help Victims of Hurricane Katrina

1　Matthew Toledo spent several days in Louisiana helping with relief efforts following Hurricane Katrina. Here are some of his observations of the experience.

　　"I felt I had to get on a plane and help in any way that I could. So I decided to buy a plane ticket and go down to Baton Rouge. I asked the Red Cross to place me where they

5　had the greatest need. I told them I could do anything. They asked me if I had been trained as a shelter manager, and I said yes.

　　"I worked through the day getting people cots, blankets, and food, and then spent the evening sorting clothes and shoes that had been donated. One thing that impressed me was how compassionate the local residents were to the new 'residents' of their

10　community. There was a constant stream of local people sorting clothes, serving meals, offering jobs—even their homes.

　　"Everybody had a story of survival. There were many disturbing stories, but there were also several stories of hope. A grandmother with three young children crawled out of their second story window to escape the rising waters. Just then, an empty fishing boat

15　was floating towards them. They got on the boat and reached safety.

　　"Then there were two young men who drove their red Toyota pickup from New Orleans to Baton Rouge. They arrived at the shelter seeking food and a place to sleep. The next day they went out into the community and got jobs with a local building contractor. The next day they asked to be awakened by 5:30 so they could report to work on time. The

20　day after that they went out and signed a two-year lease on a trailer to move into.

　　"These guys, along with hundreds of volunteers that I was with, are the images that will stay with me—folks looking out for each other and committed to making things better."

Source: Adapted from Info/Trac® College Edition Article A137146366 Los Angeles Business Journal, September 12, 2005 v27 i37 p10 (1). http://infotrac-college.thomsonlearning.com (accessed 10/06/05).

Exercise 13 Line 2: the experience—identified　Line 3: a plane—first mention　Line 4: a plane ticket—first mention　Line 4: the Red Cross—unique noun/name　Line 5: the greatest need—unique noun　Line 6: a shelter manager—not specific, first mention　Line 7: the day—specific (the day of the story)　Line 7: the evening—specific (the evening of the story)　Line 9: the local residents—specific　Line 9: the 'new residents—specific　Line 12: a story of survival—not specific　Line 13: a grandmother—first mention　Line 15: the rising waters—specific (the waters caused by mention　Line 17: the shelter—second mention　Line 17: a place to sleep—not specific　Line 17: The next day—specific (the day of the story)　Line 18: the community—specific (the community of that area)　Line 18: a local building contractor—first mention　Line 18: The next day—specific (the day of the story)　Line 19: the day after that—specific　Line 20: a two-year lease—first mention　Line 20: a trailer—first mention　Line 21: hundreds of volunteers—not specific　Line 21: the images—identified

---

Use Your English

ACTIVITY 1 speaking

TIC-TAC-TOE/Arranging Objects

Choose a small common object that can be moved around. It can be something that you are wearing (a ring, a watch) or carrying with you (a pencil, a book). It is all right if some people choose the same object. All of you will give your objects to one student. This student will then draw a big tic-tac-toe chart on the chalkboard

Now form two teams. Each team tells the student who has all the objects on a desk or table to arrange them according to their directions, one sentence at a time. (For example, "Put a book under the ring. Put the red pencil next to the book.") If the article usage in the sentence is correct (and the person is able to follow the directions), then the team gets to put an X or O in any of the tic-tac-toe squares. If it is not correct, then the team must pass. The first team to get three X's or three O's in a row or diagonally wins the game.

ACTIVITY 2 speaking/listening

Find a photograph or drawing to bring to class. Work in pairs. You have two minutes to look at your partner's picture. After the two minutes are up, give back the picture. Your partner can ask you ten questions about the picture to test your memory. The winner has the most correct answers. Concentrate on using articles correctly.

Example:　Student A:　What is the man wearing?
　　　　　　　Student B:　He's wearing a coat and a hat.

ACTIVITY 3 writing

Now without the help of your partner, write a short description of the picture that you described in Activity 2. Again try to use the articles correctly.

EXERCISE 13 [30 minutes]

This exercise attempts to apply the rules for article use presented in this unit to a semiauthentic text.

1. Because this exercise uses semiauthentic language, it will take considerable time to do in class. It is therefore advisable to assign this for homework and go over the answers in class.

2. Start by asking some easy comprehension questions about the article. Examples:

    Look at the headline. What is the main topic of the article? (volunteers who helped victims of Hurricane Katrina)

    Who is Matthew Toledo? (a volunteer)

    How did he help volunteers? (He helped to organize a shelter.)

    Was his experience positive or negative? Why? (Positive, because he saw so many people helping each other.)

3. Use an overhead transparency to identify all the examples of *the* and *a*.

4. Invite volunteers to choose one and explain the reasons for its use. Ask the class to agree or comment.

5. Suggest that students look for a newspaper article on a topical theme and analyze the use of articles in a similar way. This could be assigned as an optional extra written exercise for homework. See Methodology Note on LP page 297.

EXPANSION [20–30 minutes]

You may want to use Activity 9 (reflection) on SB page 301 as a way to close this unit.

UNIT GOAL REVIEW [10 minutes]

Ask students to look at the goals on the opening page of the unit again. Refer to the pages of the unit where information on each goal can be found.

Or you may want to start your own collection of pictures.

1. This activity is designed to lead students to use the "first mention/second mention" concept in article choice.

2. Arrange the class in a circle to complete this activity. See Methodology Note below.

3. While they are working do not correct their article use directly; instead, note errors you hear in context and discuss them at the end of the activity.

ACTIVITY 3 writing [20 minutes]

This activity is a good follow-up to Activity 2 and may be assigned for homework.

METHODOLOGY NOTE

Use Your English activities provide many opportunities for students to move around, regroup, or pair up with students they have not worked with before. This is useful for a number of reasons. Some students learn better when they are moving around the classroom. It also provides a change of pace from the routine of the class. Working with the same students all the time tends to reinforce the same mistakes, so changing partners can provide fresh input for new hypotheses and for questions.

ExamView Test Generator

For assessment of Unit 20, use *Grammar Dimensions 2 ExamView®*.

USE YOUR ENGLISH

This Use Your English section of activities at the end of the unit contain situations that should naturally elicit the structures covered in the unit. For a more complete discussion of how to use the Use Your English activities, see To the Teacher, LP page xxii. When students are doing these activities in class, you can circulate and listen to see if they are using the structures accurately. Errors can be corrected after the activity has finished.

ACTIVITY 1 speaking [20 minutes]

You may want to use this activity after Exercise 1 on SB page 287.

1. Most students will be familiar with this game, but they may not know it by the name "tic-tac-toe." Do a quick model of the game as it is usually played before playing this modified game.

2. Instead of reading the instructions, it may be easier to demonstrate the game yourself.

3. Rather than using the board for the tic-tac-toe chart, make a "life-size" chart on paper that can be placed on a desk or the floor. This way the original items can be placed in the chart.

ACTIVITY 2 speaking/listening [20 minutes]

You may want to use this activity after Exercise 3 on SB page 288. Students will need to bring in pictures from magazines or other sources for this activity.

ACTIVITY 4 speaking/listening/writing

Here are some things that people say contribute to their happiness: love, romance, success, wealth/money, fame, popularity, health, religion. Interview three people about what they think is most important for their happiness. If possible, record their answers. Be sure to get information about the people you are interviewing, such as age group, gender, and occupation.

In an oral or written summary, give the results of your interviews and see if there is agreement in people's answers.

ACTIVITY 5 listening

CD Track 27

■ STEP 1

Listen to the audio of two people (Speaker 1 and Speaker 2) describing their homes. Write as many nouns as you can hear in your notebook.

■ STEP 2

Listen to the audio again and check which of these nouns are mentioned with definite or indefinite articles.

■ STEP 3

Compare your list with a partner. Discuss the reasons for the speakers' choice of articles.

ACTIVITY 6 speaking/listening

Ask a speaker of English and/or a classmate to describe their house, apartment, or other living space (for example, a dormitory) to someone who has never seen it. If possible, record their descriptions. How many rooms are there? Where are they located? How many doors and windows are there in each room? What kind of furniture is there? Are there curtains, or are there pictures on the wall?

After you share these descriptions with the rest of the class, listen carefully to the recording for article usage.

ACTIVITY 7 speaking/listening

A lot of people like to have nice quality or expensive possessions. What would you like? Describe five items to put on your "wish list" to someone. Explain how you would use each thing or how it would change your life. (Some examples are: a house, a swimming pool, a sports car, etc.) Record your description.

Listen carefully to your recording. Did you use articles correctly?

ACTIVITY 8 research on the web

Go on the Internet and use a search engine such as Google® or Yahoo® to find at least four headlines from recent online newspapers. Copy them or print them out and bring them to class. Put in articles (*the*, Ø article, *a/an*, or *some*) wherever you think they are appropriate in order to make the headlines into more complete statements. (Note: You might need to add main verbs or auxiliaries too, such as a form of *be* or *do*.)

Example: Powerful Storm Threatens Gulf Coast

Adding articles: A powerful storm threatens *the* Gulf Coast.

Explanation: *A* is used with *storm* because it is not a specific storm. It has not been mentioned before. *The* is used with *Gulf Coast* because this is the name of a specific identifiable region of the United States.

ACTIVITY 9 reflection

Look back at the rules for using articles in this unit. Compare the use of articles in English with another language that you know. Explain the differences to a partner or your class. Can you identify any common errors that you or a speaker of that language might make when using articles in English?

Activity 5 Speaker 1:

First mention a	Second mention the	Other uses of the
house	rug	the ground floor (shared knowledge: the house I live in)
living room	living room	the floor (shared knowledge: the study I just mentioned)
study	kitchen	the window (shared knowledge: belonging to the house I live in)
kitchen	study	the garden (shared knowledge: belonging to the house I live in)
table	rug	
	view	
	desk	

Speaker 2:

living room	bed	kitchen (2)	the second floor (shared knowledge: of the building I live in)
bedroom	chest (of drawers)	bedroom	the best room ("one of a kind")
kitchen	lamp	living room (2)	the table (related mention)
bathroom	sofa		
kitchen table	armchair		
cup (of coffee)			

USE YOUR ENGLISH

ACTIVITY 4 · speaking/listening/writing
[30 minutes]

You may want to use this activity after Exercise 4 on SB page 289.

1. You can use this as an in-class or as an out-of-class interviewing activity.
2. Have students work in groups to create questions that will elicit people's opinions on what brings happiness.
3. Use students' questions to create a class questionnaire. Write the questions on the board and have students copy them into their notebooks.
4. Alone or in pairs, students ask at least five people their questions.
5. After conducting the poll, have students compile the results as a class and make generalizations about what makes people happy based on their results.

ACTIVITY 5 · listening
[20 minutes]

You may want to use this activity after Exercise 5 on SB page 290.

CD Track 27

■ STEP 1

1. Read the directions and have students draw a chart with two columns labeled "Speaker 1/ Man" and "Speaker 2/Woman" in their notebooks.
2. Play the audio. See audio script on LP page S-8.

■ STEP 2

Play the audio again and have students mark which nouns use definite and indefinite articles.

■ STEP 3

1. Have students compare answers in pairs.
2. Review the answers. Refer to the answer key on LP page 300.

ACTIVITY 6 · speaking/listening
[20 minutes]

You may want to use this activity after Activity 5.

1. Students can interview each other or someone from outside of class.
2. Have students present a summary of what they heard and some comments on the use of articles.

ACTIVITY 7 · speaking/listening
[15 minutes]

You may want to use this activity after Exercise 11 on SB page 296.

1. Introduce the idea of a "wish list" and brainstorm ideas from the class.
2. Set a time limit of 3 minutes for each student to write his or her own wish list.
3. Have students work in pairs to talk about their wishes.
4. Or have students record themselves at home and report back on their use of articles.

VARIATION

Have the class create a class wish list through an e-mail discussion list.

1. After all members of the class make their proposals, compile a list of their ideas and post them again, asking each person to vote on the top three items.

2. Use the results to rank the items on the class wish list.
3. Discuss language issues afterwards in class, bringing examples of errors and calling on students to correct the errors.

ACTIVITY 8 · research on the web
[20 minutes/homework]

You may want to use this activity after Exercise 9 on SB page 294. The purpose of this Internet search activity is to provide a natural context for using the present perfect. An additional purpose is to encourage students to share strategies for finding information on the Internet.

1. Encourage students to provide explanations of their article changes to the class (See the example on SB page 301).
2. If time allows, make overhead slides of the articles and have students suggest article changes on each others articles.

ACTIVITY 9 · reflection
[15 minutes]

You may want to use this activity after Exercise 13 on SB page 298. This activity provides an opportunity for students to use the target structures of the unit while reflecting on their language learning progress. You may have asked students to keep a record of their learning in a journal throughout this course as suggested in To the Teacher, LP page xxii. This reflection activity will be part of that learning record.

UNIT GOALS

- Use articles with names of places
- Use articles with names of institutions

OPENING TASK

Geography Quiz

■ STEP 1

Look at the pictures. How many of these places can you identify?

Mount Everest

Amazon River

Sahara Desert

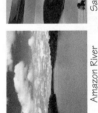

Greenland

Lake Superior

Jupiter

■ STEP 2

Form groups of five. In your group, complete the chart. If you have different opinions in your group, write down all the different answers. Which ones can you match with the photos from Step 1?

WHAT IS . . . ?	ANSWER
the largest continent in the world	Asia
the longest river	the Amazon
the largest country (in size, not population)	Russia
the biggest island	Greenland
the highest mountain range	the Himalayas
the highest mountain	Mt. Everest
the biggest desert	the Sahara
the largest ocean	the Pacific Ocean
the largest lake	Lake Superior
the largest planet	Jupiter

■ STEP 3

When you have finished, compare your answers with those of other groups. Write the final answers on the board. (If you cannot agree, you may want to research the answer for homework.)

■ STEP 4

Take turns making complete statements based on the information in your chart.

Example: *The Amazon is* _____ *the longest river in the world.* _____ .

ANSWER KEY

Opening Tasks *Answers may vary.*

ARTICLES WITH NAMES OF PLACES

UNIT OVERVIEW

Unit 21 provides practice with articles that occur with names of places and with names of institutions. You may want to bring in a world atlas, map, or globe so that students can look up the many place names used in this unit.

IMPORTANT: Because most of this unit and its exercises can be completed in one lesson plan of 90 minutes, Lesson Plan 2 is abbreviated and only 40 minutes long. To extend the Lesson Plan into a full 90 minutes or more, use all of the suggested activities as well as the accompanying *Grammar Dimensions 2* Workbook exercises.

GRAMMAR NOTE

The use of articles with place names can be quite confusing. Why do we say *America* (no article), but *The United States*? Why do we say *Mount Everest* (no article), but *The Himalayas*? Why do we say *Times Square* (no article), but *the Statue of Liberty*? These and other rules will be presented and practiced extensively in this unit.

UNIT GOALS

Some instructors may want to review the goals listed on Student Book (SB) page 302 after completing the Opening Task so that students understand what they should know by the end of the unit. These goals can also be reviewed at the end of the unit when students are more familiar with the grammar terminology.

OPENING TASK [20 minutes]

The purpose of the Opening Task is to create a context in which students will need to use names of places. The problem-solving format is designed to show the teacher how well the students can use the target structures implicitly and spontaneously when they are engaged in a communicative task. For a

more complete discussion of the purpose of the Opening Task, see To the Teacher, Lesson Planner (LP) page xxii.

Setting Up the Task

■ STEP 1

Introduce the topic by looking at the pictures. Ask students to guess where and what they are. Use this opportunity to go over some vocabulary they will need in Step 2. For example, *continent, desert, mountain range, planet.*

Conducting the Task

■ STEP 2

1. Start by asking students the first question. Elicit as many suggestions as you can and write them on the board. Ask students to justify their answers, but do not provide the correct answer.

2. Explain that the purpose of this task is to encourage discussion using place names. They should write down all the suggestions made by their group. It is not a test of their knowledge.

3. Circulate while students are working and take note of possible problem areas with article usage.

4. Groups that finish early can try to match their answers with the pictures in Step 1.

■ STEP 3

1. Ask a volunteer to come to the board and write the answers.

2. The class should try to reach a consensus.

3. Check the answers. Refer to the answer key on LP page 302.

Closing the Task

■ STEP 4

1. Ask different groups to make sentences about the answers.

2. Students can write their answers as full sentences if there is time. These sentences can serve as a bridge to Focus Chart 1.

3. Students will return to these answers in Exercise 1.

GRAMMAR NOTE

Typical student errors (use)

- Using articles with names of continents, countries, cities, mountains, lakes, etc, e.g. * *He lives in the New York City.* (See Focus 1.)
- Omitting articles with names of rivers, deserts, oceans, etc., e.g. * *Andes Mountains are in South America.* (See Focus 1.)
- Using articles with names of institutions, e.g. * *The Boston University* (See Focus 2.)
- Omitting articles with names of tourist attractions, e.g. * *Empire State Building.* (See Focus 2.)

FOCUS 1

Articles with Names of Places

form

EXAMPLES

South America
Zimbabwe
New York
First Avenue
Interstate 90

Mars
Jamaica
Mount Shasta
Lake Champlain
Yosemite National Park

the Yellow River
the Gobi Desert
the Arctic Ocean
the Caspian Sea
the Andes
the Hawaiian Islands
the Great Lakes
the Middle East
the United States

EXPLANATIONS

Use **Ø** (no article) with names of:

- continents
- countries
- cities
- streets and highways

- planets
- islands
- single mountains
- lakes
- parks

Use **the** with names of:

- rivers
- deserts
- oceans
- seas
- mountain ranges
- groups of islands
- groups of lakes
- most regions
- countries that are collections take **the**

EXERCISE 1

Look at the categories below. For each category (1–10), put the correct answers from the Opening Task on pages 302–303 in either Column A or B. For example, the largest continent is Asia, which does not use *the*, so this would go in Column B for #1.

CATEGORY	(A) USE *THE*	(B) DON'T USE *THE*
1. the largest continent in the world		Asia
2. the longest river	the Amazon	
3. the largest country (in size, not population)		Russia
4. the biggest island		Greenland
5. the highest mountain range	the Himalayas	
6. the highest mountain		Mt. Everest
7. the biggest desert	the Sahara	
8. the largest ocean	the Pacific Ocean	
9. the largest lake		Lake Superior
10. the largest planet		Jupiter

EXERCISE 2

Read the conversation. Underline all the names of places. Explain why *the* is used or **not** used in each case.

A: Have you ever been to Canada?

B: Yes, I went there with my friend a couple of years ago during the winter vacation.

A: Where did you go?

B: Well, we stayed in Vancouver most of the time and went skiing on Mount Whistler. Then we took a train up to Lake Louise. It's really high up in the mountains and the train ride is spectacular. Oh yes, and we also visited Victoria, which is the capital of British Columbia.

A: I thought Vancouver was the capital?

B: Vancouver is the largest city, but the capital is actually a smaller city on Vancouver Island. It's very pretty there.

A: Did you like Vancouver?

B: I think it's an amazing place—wherever you go you can get marvelous views of the Pacific Ocean and of the Rockies. Next time I want to take a boat trip to the Queen Charlotte Islands or maybe up the western coast to Alaska.

Write and practice a conversation with your partner about a place that you have visited. Include as many names of countries, islands, cities, mountains, lakes, and other places as you can.

ANSWER KEY

Exercise 2 *Canada (—no article—with name of country), Vancouver (with cities), Mount Whistler (with name of a single mountain), Lake Louise (with names of lakes), Victoria (with cities), British Columbia (with provincial names); the Pacific Ocean, the Rockies, Queen Charlotte Islands (use the with name of oceans, mountain ranges, and groups of islands); Alaska (with states).*

21 LESSON PLAN 1

FOCUS 1 [20 minutes]

1. **Lead-in:** Continue the geography quiz theme by asking students to think of a continent, a country, a city, an island, a lake, an ocean, a mountain range, and a mountain. Ask them to write down the names of one of each.

2. Then have students work in pairs to describe each one without saying the name. Their partner will guess what it is. This can also be done as a class team activity.

3. Take notes of errors as well as correct examples during this activity.

4. Ask students to identify which of them use articles and which ones do not.

5. Compare their answers with the information in the focus chart.

6. To ensure that students understand each point, elicit additional examples for each category. Examples:

   Question: *Can you give me another example of a continent?*

   Possible answers: *Africa, Asia*

   Question: *What is the rule for using articles?*

   Answer: *Continents use Ø (zero article) and so on.*

Note: Students will occasionally come up with examples that don't follow the rules. Point out that these are exceptions (See "countries" in the lower section of the chart) and that most of the place names do follow these rules for article usage. Another rule for North American English is that political partitions such as state and provincial names as well as counties and parishes generally do not use *the*.

EXERCISE 1 [5 minutes]

1. If you have already checked the answers to the Opening Task, students can simply fill in the chart, applying the information learned from Focus Chart 1. If not, you can review the correct answers while filling out the chart. Refer to the answer key on LP page 304 and review them as a class.

2. Ask if there are any of these examples that students find especially difficult to remember. Ask for suggestions or tips for how to remember the rules. See Activity 8 (reflection) on SB page 311.

For more practice, use *Grammar Dimensions 2* Workbook page 134, Exercise 1.

EXPANSION [20 minutes]

You may want to use Activity 1 (speaking/writing) on SB page 309 after this exercise.

EXERCISE 2 [10 minutes]

1. Have students work individually to underline all the place names.

2. Students can work in pairs or groups to explain each article usage.

3. They can refer back to Focus Chart 1 to explain the reason for the use (or nonuse) of the article with each place name.

4. Refer to the answer key on LP page 304 and check the answers as a class.

5. Ask two volunteers to read the dialogue aloud. (If you want, you can ask them to read the dialogue with mistakes in the use of articles and have the class call out and correct them.)

6. Have students work in pairs to make up and write their own dialogues.

7. Invite volunteers to read the dialogue aloud for the class.

8. Ask the class to provide feedback on the use of articles.

For more practice, use *Grammar Dimensions 2* Workbook page 135, Exercise 2.

EXPANSION [20 minutes]

You may want to use Activity 2 (speaking) on SB page 309 after this exercise.

form

use

FOCUS 2

Articles with Names of Institutions

EXAMPLES

(a) Summit Elementary School
(b) Children's Hospital and Medical Center
(c) Boston College
(d) Louisiana State (University)

(e) **the** Eiffel Tower
(f) **the** University of Northern Iowa

EXPLANATIONS

Use Ø (no article):
- for schools, hospitals, and prisons
- when the place name comes **before** *College* or *University*

Use **the**:
- for most tourist attractions
- when *University of* comes before the place name

EXERCISE 4

The following conversation is between Sheryl Smith, a real estate agent, and the Joneses, who want to buy a house. Fill in the blanks with *the* or Ø (no article).

Sheryl Smith: I'm sure you'd like the area. It borders (1) ___Ø___ Discovery Park, which has free outdoor concerts at (2) __the__ Rutherford Concert Hall, and also there's (3) __the__ Whitehawk Native American Art Museum, which you've probably heard of. It's quite well known.

Mike Jones: Yes, yes.

Donna Jones: What about schools?

Sheryl Smith: Well, there's (4) __the__ Smith College of Architecture, of course . . .

Donna Jones: I mean public schools for our children.

Sheryl Smith: Oh, well, (5) ___Ø___ Golden Oaks Elementary School is only a few blocks away, on (6) ___Ø___ First Avenue. And there's a high school about a mile north of the park.

Mike Jones: (pointing) Aren't those (7) __the__ White Mountains?

Sheryl Smith: Yes. On clear days, you can even see (8) ___Ø___ Mt. Wildman, the tallest mountain in the range.

Mike Jones: Oh, yes. I heard about a good fishing spot there, on (9) ___Ø___ Blue Lake.

Sheryl Smith: Yes, my husband goes there and to (10) __the__ Nooksack River to fish. He could tell you all about it.

Mike Jones: Ms. Smith, I think you might have made a sale today.

EXERCISE 3

Fill in the blanks with *the* or Ø (no article).

(1) ___Ø___ Burma is sandwiched between (2) ___Ø___ India and (3) ___Ø___ Bangladesh on one side and (4) ___Ø___ China, (5) ___Ø___ Laos, and (6) ___Ø___ Thailand on the other. To the south is (7) __the__ Andaman Sea and (8) __the__ Bay of Bengal. Burma has several important river systems including (9) __the__ Irrawaddy, which runs almost the entire length of the country and enters the sea in a vast delta region southwest of (10) ___Ø___ Rangoon, the capital. (11) __The__ Mekong River forms the border between Burma and Laos. (12) __The__ Himalayas rise in the north of Burma, and (13) ___Ø___ Hkakabo Razi, on the border between Burma and Tibet, is the highest mountain in southeast Asia, at 5881 meters (19,297 feet).

Adapted from *Burma, A Travel Survival Kit*, by Tony Wheeler. Lonely Planet Publications, 1982

21 LESSON PLAN 1

EXERCISE 3 [15 minutes]

1. Look at the map and ask students if they are familiar with any of these places and what they know about them.

2. Students can work individually or in pairs to fill in the blanks.

3. Check the answers by reading (or having students read) each sentence one by one.

4. Look at the map to find the places. If they are not marked, fill them in according to the description.

5. Refer to the answer key on LP page 306.

6. To encourage further discussion of these place names, ask students to try to work out the meaning of *sandwiched between, river system, delta region, border.*

For more practice, use *Grammar Dimensions 2* Workbook page 135, Exercise 3.

EXPANSION [20 minutes]

1. Have students choose a country they know and write a similar description for homework, leaving a blank before each place name as in Exercise 3.

2. In class, students can exchange descriptions and try to fill in the articles.

3. They can exchange back again to have their answers corrected.

4. Discuss any problems that arise as a class.

FOCUS 2 [5 minutes]

1. **Lead-in:** Ask students to think of names of schools, colleges, universities, hospitals, and local tourist attractions in your town or city.

2. Try to work out the rules presented in Focus Chart 2 from these examples.

3. Read the examples and explanations in the focus chart.

EXERCISE 4 [15 minutes]

1. Give students a few minutes to work with a partner, and check to make sure they have answers for each blank.

2. Ask volunteers to read the dialogue aloud, as naturally as possibly, paying attention to intonation, word-linking, and stress.

3. Because this dialogue is so long, you can switch speakers halfway through.

4. Refer to the answer key on LP page 306.

EXPANSION [20–40 minutes]

You may want to use Activity 4 (listening) on SB page 310 and/or Activity 6 (reading) on page 311 after this exercise.

For more practice, use *Grammar Dimensions 2* Workbook page 136, Exercise 4.

Use Your English

ACTIVITY 1 speaking/writing

Form groups of five students. Think of five famous places in the world—for example, mountains, lakes, islands, or buildings. With your group, write a quiz to find out how many people in your class know where these places are. Your quiz should have five questions and each question should have three possible answers. Exchange quizzes with the other groups in your class and answer their questions.

Example: Where is Madagascar?

a. in the Pacific Ocean   b. in the Atlantic Ocean   c. in the Indian Ocean

ACTIVITY 2 speaking

With the help of your teacher, form two teams. Each team will have five minutes to think of as many names of islands, mountains, and lakes as possible and write them on a sheet of paper (or on the blackboard). Each name with correct article use will be worth one point. The team that has the most correct names and articles wins.

ACTIVITY 3 writing

Think of a city or region you know and like. What places are the top tourist sights for first-time visitors? Write a short description of the tourist attractions and special features. Draw a map showing the locations of these places. Display your work in the classroom

---

EXERCISE 5

Fill in the blanks with *the* or Ø (no article). The first two have been done for you.

1. Ø   Hawaii
2. the   Hawaiian Islands
3. Ø   Saudi Arabia
4. Ø   Harvard University
5. the   Himalayas
6. the   Museum of Modern Art
7. Ø   First Avenue
8. the   Mississippi River
9. the   University of Miami
10. Ø   Turkey
11. the   United States
12. the   Pyramids
13. the   West
14. Ø   Africa
15. Ø   Lake Wenatchee
16. Ø   Saturn

EXERCISE 6

For each underlined place name, check to see if the article is used correctly. If it is wrong, correct it: Add *the* or cross out *the*. The first one has been done for you.

WHERE TO GO IN SAN FRANCISCO

Situated on (1) ^{the} West Coast of the United States, (2) the city of San Francisco is a popular tourist destination with a variety of unique sightseeing opportunities for every visitor. No visit to San Francisco is complete without crossing (3) the Golden Gate Bridge. You can walk, cycle, or drive across this 1.7-mile-long bridge, which offers a fantastic view of the city on one side and (4) Pacific Ocean on the other. Try a taste of Chinese food in (5) the Chinatown, the largest Chinese community outside (6) the Asia. A short ferry ride will take you to (7) the island of Alcatraz, the famous island prison in the middle of (8) the San Francisco Bay. Visit (9) the Golden Gate Park for more exciting views of the city and across the Bay to (10) Marin Headlands. Other places of interest around the city include (11) Asian Art Museum and (12) California Academy of Sciences, which has a planetarium and an aquarium.

ANSWER KEY

Exercise 6   1. the   2. the   3. the   4. the   5. Ø   6. Ø   7. the   8. Ø   9. the   10. Ø
11. the   12. the

UNIT 21 — LESSON PLAN 2/USE YOUR ENGLISH

EXERCISE 5 [10 minutes]

1. If you want to make this exercise into a game or competition, form teams and give 1 point for each correct answer.

2. You can give an extra point for each time a student (or someone from the team) can say *why* their answer is correct. In other words, what is the rule? (You can decide whether or not to have students check their answers by looking them up in the focus charts.)

VARIATION

A faster way to use this exercise is to simply call out each place name and have the class raise their hands in response: left hand for *the* and right hand for *no article*.

EXERCISE 6 [20 minutes]

This exercise provides practice in editing skills that are useful for students in editing their own writing.

1. Introduce the topic of sightseeing in San Francisco. Ask students if they know of any famous places in the city. Bring pictures of famous landmarks and ask students to name them as best they can.

2. Have students work individually to read the article and correct as necessary.

3. Students can compare answers in pairs and explain the reasons for their choices, referring back to the relevant focus charts.

4. Circulate and monitor any problems.

5. Go over any problematic areas with the whole class. Refer to the answer key on LP page 308.

EXPANSION [20–40 minutes]

You may want to use Activity 3 (writing) on SB page 309 and/or Activity 5 (speaking/writing/listening) on page 310 as a way to close this unit. Or use Activity 7 (research on the web) on SB page 311 as a homework research activity.

USE YOUR ENGLISH

The Use Your English section of activities at the end of the unit contain situations that should naturally elicit the structures covered in the unit. For a more complete discussion of how to use the Use Your English activities, see To the Teacher, LP page xxii. When students are doing these activities in class, you can circulate and listen to see if they are using the structures accurately. Errors can be corrected after the activity has finished.

ACTIVITY 1 — speaking/writing [30 minutes]

You may want to use this activity after Exercise 1 on SB page 305.

1. In this activity, students test each other's knowledge of geography and also learn how to develop multiple-choice questions.

2. You may want to have a world atlas or a globe on hand for reference during this activity.

3. As a variation, you can have groups include at least one city, one lake, one mountain, etc. in their lists.

4. Have students exchange quizzes with each other (noting their answers on a separate paper). Then check the answers to the quizzes as a class.

UNIT GOAL REVIEW [10 minutes]

Ask students to look at the goals on the opening page of the unit again. Refer to the pages of the unit where information on each goal can be found.

For a grammar quiz review of Units 19–21, refer students to pages 137–139 in the *Grammar Dimensions 2* Workbook.

ExamView Test Generator — For assessment of Unit 21, use *Grammar Dimensions 2 ExamView*®.

ACTIVITY 2 — speaking [20 minutes]

You may want to use this activity after Exercise 3 on SB page 306.

1. Organize your class into two teams.

2. Allow 5 minutes for each team to write as many place names as they can.

3. Have teams exchange papers and check each others' work. This may take 10–15 minutes.

4. If possible, look up the different places in a world atlas or on a globe.

ACTIVITY 3 — writing [30 minutes]

You may want to use this activity after Exercise 4 on SB page 307.

1. You can do this activity in class or assign it for homework.

2. If you feel students need more practice with writing and editing, have them exchange their written descriptions with another student, who will

   (a) first read through the paper for general content. Is there anything that he or she can't understand? If so, they can ask the writer for clarification or elaboration.

   (b) edit the description for accuracy in terms of article usage (and other errors, if you choose). Was *the* or zero article used correctly?

3. If students need more practice with listening, ask them to read their descriptions aloud, with other students taking notes. When each student has finished reading his or her description, review the place names for accuracy in article usage.

4. Display the written descriptions with pictures around your classroom, or collect them into a portfolio that can be passed around the class. Make sure each description is signed by the author(s) so students can ask further questions if they want.

ACTIVITY 4 — listening

CD Track 28

Listen to the audio of a person talking about where she lives.

1. Work with a partner. Discuss the place the woman is talking about. Where is it? Why does she like it?

2. Listen again. Circle the names of the places the woman mentions.

~~Leblon Beach~~	— North America	— Pacific Ocean
— Sugar Loaf Mountain	— Santa Marinha Street	— South America
the — City Historic Museum	— City Park	— Rio de Janeiro
— Museum of Brazil		— Ipanema Beach

3. In front of the names of the places you wrote, write the word *the* or leave the space blank. Compare your answers with a classmate's and discuss why Ø (no article) or *the* was used with each place name. If you disagree on any answers, look back at Focus 1 and Focus 2 for help in deciding on the correct answer.

ACTIVITY 5 — speaking/writing/listening

STEP 1

You have been asked by a travel company to design a poster to attract overseas visitors to the region where you are living. Or, if you prefer, you can make a poster about another place you know and like (See Activity 3), especially if there are other students interested in the same place.

Get together with a group of students to brainstorm local areas of interest. Your poster should have pictures and labels about the area and also short written descriptions. Display and compare your posters.

STEP 2

The poster that you made in Step 1 in Activity 5 was so successful that you have been asked to talk about the region to a group of tourists and travel guides. Record your short talk. Listen to the recording and check to see if you used *the* and Ø (no article) correctly.

ANSWER KEY

Activity 4 *See audios script on LP page S–8.*

1. The woman is talking about Rio de Janeiro, in Brazil. Rio de Janeiro is in South America. The woman likes it because the people are nice and there's a lot to see. 3. The only article used is **the** Santa Marinha Street.

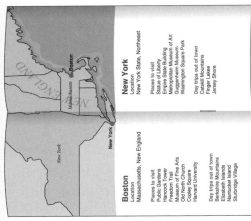

Boston
Location
Massachusetts, New England

Places to visit
Public Gardens
Hancock Tower
Freedom Trail
Museum of Fine Arts
Old North Church
Copley Square
Harvard University

Day trips out of town
Berkshire Mountains
Elizabeth Islands
Nantucket Island
Sturbridge Village

New York
Location
New York State, Northeast

Places to visit
Statue of Liberty
Empire State Building
Metropolitan Museum of Art
Guggenheim Museum
Washington Square Park

Day trips out of town
Catskill Mountains
Finger Lakes
Jersey Shore

ACTIVITY 6 — reading/speaking

Read the information about two vacation destinations. Work with a partner.

Student A will ask questions about each place. (Example: Where should I go for the weekend?)

Student B will use the information to help Student A decide where to spend the vacation.

Example: Well, I just went to Boston, Massachusetts. There's a lot to see there. . . .

ACTIVITY 7 — research on the web

InfoTrac® College Edition Option: What are the seven wonders of the world? What are some different ways of interpreting this title? Go to *InfoTrac* to find the answers. Search for the keywords 'seven wonders of the world'. Compare your answers with a group and make a list of your choices for the top seven most amazing sights in the world.

ACTIVITY 8 — reflection

Which rule for using articles with place names do you find most difficult to remember? Is there a name of a place that you often get wrong? Think of a memory tip that will help you to remember the correct article usage for this place. Share your ideas with a partner.

Example: No article needed with names of three things that begin with 'c': continents, countries, cities.

Activity 6

Boston	Massachusetts	New England	the Public Garden
Copley Square	the Hancock Tower	the Museum of Fine Arts	the Old North Church
Harvard University	the Berkshire Mountains	the Elizabeth Islands	Nantucket Island
Sturbridge Village	New York	New York State	the Northeast
the Statue of Liberty	the Empire State Building	the Metropolitan Museum of Art	the Guggenheim Museum
the Catskill Mountains	the Finger Lakes	the Jersey Shore	

USE YOUR ENGLISH

ACTIVITY 4 **listening** [20 minutes]

CD Track 28

You may want to use this activity after Exercise 3 on SB page 306.

1. Explain that students will listen to someone describing a place. They will listen first for the general meaning.

2. Play the audio. Review the audio script on LB page S-8 while students listen.

3. Play the audio again while students circle the place names.

4. Students work in pairs to decide which place names have articles, referring back to the relevant focus charts in the unit.

5. Check the answers as a class. Refer to the answer key on LP page 310.

ACTIVITY 5 **speaking/writing/ listening** [30 minutes]

You may want to use this activity after Exercise 6 on SB page 308.

STEP 1

1. Bring in samples of similar posters to show your students (see Methodology Note). You could also bring in a map of your local region so that students can refer to it and draw sections of it for their posters.

2. Assign students to work in teams (with at least one "artistic type" per team), making this a truly collaborative activity.

3. Students can collect pictures from the Internet or from tourist information materials and add them to their posters for homework.

4. Display the posters in the classroom and allow time for students to walk around and read the posters.

STEP 2

1. Give students time to ask each other questions about the posters.

2. Students may prepare and record a "talk" about their own posters.

3. Have students play the recordings for each other. Have other students listen for proper article use.

You may want to follow this activity with Activity 6.

METHODOLOGY NOTE

1. It's helpful to bring in a sample of this kind of poster. You could bring in one from a travel agency. Or bring in one made by a previous student (with his or her permission, of course).

2. Although it's nice to have lots of different kinds of materials available for this, a large sheet of paper, magazines, and/or newspapers (that can be cut up) are all that's necessary.

4. Circulate while students are talking and listen for errors in article usage.

5. As a class, go over the article usage for each place name.

VARIATION

Bring in tourist information about other places in the United States and have students role-play similar conversations about them.

ACTIVITY 7 **research on the web** [15 minutes/homework]

The purpose of this Internet search activity is to provide a natural context for using articles with place names. An additional purpose is to encourage students to explore the use of InfoTrac® College Edition as a language learning resource. See To the Teacher, LP page xxii. for more information on how to use InfoTrac effectively.

ACTIVITY 6 **reading** [20 minutes]

You may want to use this activity after Exercise 4 on SB page 307.

1. In this activity, students will role-play two friends talking about places to visit for a vacation. Student A is asking Student B for some advice.

2. Have students work in pairs. Both students can read the information in the pamphlet. Students should decide with which names of places they should be using *the*. Refer to the answer key on LP page 310 as needed.

3. Allow 10 minutes for students to role-play the conversations together. Ask a few pairs to perform their role-play.

ACTIVITY 8 **reflection** [10 minutes/homework]

This activity provides an opportunity for students to use the target structures of the unit while reflecting on their language learning progress. You may have asked students to keep a record of their learning in a journal throughout this course as suggested in To the Teacher, LP page xxii. This reflection activity will be part of that learning record.

UNIT GOALS

- Know when to use passives
- Correctly form *be* and *get* passives
- Know the difference between the *be* passive and the *get* passive
- Know when to include the agent in the sentence

OPENING TASK

The Island of Campinilea

You are gathering information for a book on the fictional island of Campinilea, an island located somewhere off the west coast of South America. The first chapter will be called "The Products and Natural Resources of Campinilea."

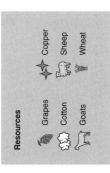

Resources

Grapes   Copper

Cotton   Sheep

Goats   Wheat

STEP 1

Use the key to interpret the information on the map on the next page. Discuss the island's resources with a partner.

Examples: Where are grapes cultivated? . . . in the north.
Where is cotton grown?

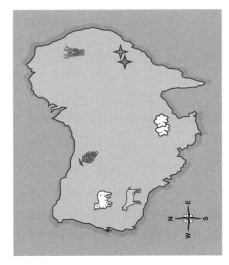

STEP 2

Use the map to match the activities to the appropriate location. The first one has been done for you.

ACTIVITIES	LOCATIONS
cultivate grapes	in the east
raise sheep	in the southeast
grow cotton	in the northwest
grow wheat	in the north
mine copper	in the west
raise goats	in the south

STEP 3

Using this information, make five sentences about the products and natural resources of Campinilea for the first chapter of your book.

UNIT OVERVIEW

In this unit, students look in depth at the passive voice.

GRAMMAR NOTE

The grammatical feature of *voice* pertains to who or what serves as the subject in a clause. In the active voice, the subject of a clause is usually the agent or doer of some action. In the passive voice, the receiver of the action is in the subject position. The informational emphasis is on the action that is being done to someone or something. The agent of the action can be mentioned by adding a phrase with *by*. If students are not familiar with the term "agent," you can tell them it's the "doer" of the action (which is not the subject in the passive). The form of the passive can be confusing as it uses the auxiliary *be* and the past participle, both of which are used in different ways to form other tenses in the active voice. It can also be problematic for learners to decide when the use of the passive is appropriate.

UNIT GOALS

Some instructors may want to review the goals listed on Student Book (SB) page 312 after completing the Opening Task so that students understand what they should know by the end of the unit. These goals can also be reviewed at the end of the unit when students are more familiar with the grammar terminology.

OPENING TASK [20 minutes]

The purpose of the Opening Task is to create a context in which students will need to use the passive. The problem-solving format is designed to show the teacher how well the students can use the target structures implicitly and spontaneously when they are engaged in a communicative task. For a more complete discussion of the purpose of the

Opening Task, see To the Teacher, Lesson Planner (LP) page xxii.

Setting Up the Task

1. Introduce the idea of a fictional island.
2. Look at the symbols on SB page 312 and match them with their meanings.
3. Discuss what these various resources could be used for and how they might be cultivated, raised, grown, or mined.
4. Review vocabulary that will be needed in later steps of the Opening Task: *cultivate, raise, grow, mine.*

Conducting the Task

STEP 1

1. Look at the map and practice talking about the points of compass.
2. Ask students to discuss the location of the resources in pairs or groups, using the example as a guide.
3. Circulate while students are talking and take notes of any language problems, but do not correct at this stage.

STEP 2

When students have finished Step 1, they can move on to Step 2. Refer to the answer key on LP page 312.

Closing the Task

STEP 3

1. Direct pairs/groups to write at least five sentences about the activities, describing where they take place.
2. Have each group write its sentences on the board, or on an overhead transparency.
3. Bring the class together to share and compare answers.

4. Point out that Exercises 1–4 (SB pages 314–317) build on this task.
5. Ask students about the resources and industries of their country or another country they know well.

FOCUS 1   Active and Passive

EXAMPLES	EXPLANATIONS
(a) Farmers cultivate grapes in the north.	Use the active to focus on the person who performs the action.
(b) Grapes **are cultivated** in the north.	Use the passive to focus on the result of the action, not the person who performs it.
(c) NOT: Sheep are lived in the northwest.	Passives are only used with transitive verbs (verbs that take an object in the active voice).

EXERCISE 1

Look at Step 3 of the Opening Task on page 313. Did you use the passive or the active? Write each statement both ways. Which statement sounds better? Why?

1. a. *They cultivate grapes in the north*

   b. *Grapes are cultivated in the north.*

2. a. _____

   b. _____

3. a. _____

   b. _____

4. a. _____

   b. _____

5. a. _____

   b. _____

FOCUS 2   Forming the *Be* Passive

To form the passive, use the appropriate tense of be, followed by the past participle (pp):

EXAMPLES		TENSE	FORM	
(a)	Wool **is produced** here.	Simple Present	am/is/are	+ PP
(b)	Wool **is being produced** here right now.	Present Progressive	am/is/are being	+ PP
(c)	Wool **was produced** here.	Simple Past	was/were	+ PP
(d)	Wool **was being produced** here ten years ago.	Past Progressive	was/were being	+ PP
(e)	Wool **has been produced** here since 1900.	Present Perfect	have/has been	+ PP
(f)	Wool **had been produced** here when the island was discovered.	Past Perfect	had been	+ PP
(g)	Wool **will be produced** here next year.	Future (*will*)	will be	+ PP
(h)	Wool **is going to be produced** here.	Future (*be going to*)	am/is/are going to be	+ PP
(i)	Wool **will have been produced** here by the year 2025.	Future Perfect	will have been	+ PP

EXERCISE 2

The second chapter of the book on Campinilea is called "The People of Campinilea and Their Customs." Look at the following statements about Campinilea; write 1 beside those you think belong to Chapter 1 (Products and Resources) and 2 beside those you think belong to Chapter 2 (People and Customs).

__2__ 1. In the west, unmarried women leave their family homes at the age of 25 and raise goats in the mountains.

__1__ 2. Miners mined silver throughout the island during the last century.

__1__ 3. They will plant the first crop of rice in the south next year.

__2__ 4. In the southeast, fathers take their oldest sons to the copper mines on their twelfth birthday in a special ceremony to teach them the legends and rituals associated with Campinilean copper.

__2__ 5. Easterners are more traditional than southerners; for example, farmers in the east have harvested wheat in the same way for hundreds of years, while those in the south are constantly exploring new techniques for growing cotton.

__1__ 6. They have produced grapes in Campinilea for only a few years.

ANSWER KEY

Exercise 1 The passive voice is preferable throughout as it focuses on the result of the action: *Sheep are raised . . . , Cotton is grown . . . , Wheat is grown . . . , Copper is mined . . . , Goats are raised . . . .*

LESSON PLAN 1

FOCUS 1 [5 minutes]

1. **Lead-in:** Use the sentences students created in the Opening Task to illustrate the explanations in this focus chart, which introduces the difference between the active and passive.
2. Ask students to make further examples using information about their own countries or about the United States.

LANGUAGE NOTE

The key difference between the active and the passive voice is **focus**. Since the subject is seen as the key noun in the sentence, the passive is used to focus attention on the result or "receiver" of the action by placing it as the subject; the "doer" (or agent) of the action can be mentioned, but is often not included.

Although they are presented here together, the passive is not simply a transformation of the active. There are situations where the passive is far more common or appropriate than the active. For example:

She was born in South Africa but is an Australian citizen now.
(NOT: Her mother bore her in South Africa but
. . . .)

[To her boss]: *I'm sorry, but I was told there would be no meeting today.*

(Having missed the meeting, this person does not want to point out who is to blame, for reasons of kindness or diplomacy.)

EXERCISE 1 [5 minutes]

1. This exercise can be done orally or in written form.
2. If students have already written passive sentences in Step 3 of the Opening Task, you may ask them to write or say the equivalent active sentences and talk about the difference in focus (see Language Note above).

3. When discussing whether the active or passive sounds better for these sentences, ask students to consider whether the product or the producer is more important. It is likely that the passive will sound better since it is obvious who is performing the action (farmers, miners, etc.).

 For more practice, use *Grammar Dimensions 2* Workbook page 140 Exercise 1.

FOCUS 2 [10 minutes]

1. **Lead-in:** Use examples of errors that you noticed in the Opening Task to highlight difficulties with the formation of the passive.
2. Emphasize that the passive is not a tense, but it occurs with almost all tenses. This form is used to stress the importance of the product or result, not the person doing the production.
3. Read the examples in the focus chart.
4. Ask students to work in pairs. Student A will look at the chart and say "simple present." Student B will close the book and say "Wool is produced here." Student A will check the answer.
5. Students can test each other on the formation of the passive in each tense. Then they switch roles.

EXERCISE 2 [5 minutes]

1. Students can work individually to decide which sentences belong in each chapter.
2. They can work in pairs to discuss the appropriateness of using the passive and active voices.
3. Ask students to justify their choices.
4. In Chapter 1 (Products and Resources), the passive is more likely, while in Chapter 2 (People and Customs), the people—or producers of these products—deserve greater focus and, thus, the active is more appropriate.
5. If there is time, have students write out the two paragraphs, or assign this for homework.

EXPANSION [20 minutes]

To provide further practice with the passive, students can choose one of the resources listed in the Opening Task and describe how a product is made from it—for example, wine, goat's cheese, or a wool sweater. The description should include at least three or four steps. For example:

First, the wool is cut off. Then it is washed in soap and water. After that, it is combed and rolled into long strings. Then the wool is dyed in different colors. Finally, it is used to knit sweaters.

For more practice, use *Grammar Dimensions 2* Workbook page 141, Exercise 2.

FOCUS 3

use

The Passive

EXAMPLES	EXPLANATIONS
(a) All the cookies **were eaten** last night.	Use the passive when you don't know who performed the action.
(b) Wheat **is grown** in the east.	Use the passive when the person who performed the action is obvious. In example (b), it is obvious that farmers are the people who grow the wheat.
(c) A mistake **was made.**	Use the passive when you don't want to tell who performed the action.
(d) The computer **is protected** from electrical damage by a special grounding plug.	The passive is more formal than the active. It is more common in writing, especially in scientific and technical reports, and in newspaper articles. It is less common in conversation.
(e) The proposal **was rejected** by the people of King County in last night's vote.	

EXERCISE 4

The Campinilean police are currently investigating a robbery that took place in a hotel room a few nights ago. Work with a partner. One of you should look at Picture A below; the other should look at Picture B on page A-18. One of you has a picture of the room **before** the robbery, and the other has a picture of the room **after** the robbery. Seven different things were done to the room. **Without looking at your partner's picture,** ask each other questions and find what these seven things were and complete the report below.

ROBBERY AT HOTEL PARAISO

Last night the police were called to investigate a robbery that took place at the Hotel Paraiso. The identity of the thief is still unknown. The police took note of several unusual occurrences. For example,

_____

_____

_____

The public has been asked to contact the police with any information about the identity of the thief. Any information leading to an arrest will be rewarded.

Picture A

Do you think it would be appropriate to use the passive in any of these statements from Exercise 2 on page 315? Why do you think so? Rewrite those statements here:

Yes, because it is not important to know who performed the act (mining, planting, producing). Rewritten statements: **2.** *Silver has been mined throughout . . . .* **3.** *The first crop of rice will be planted in . . . .* **6.** *Grapes have been produced in . . . .*

EXERCISE 3

Complete the following, using the verb tense that fits best.

Adventurous tourists are beginning to discover Campinilea, and the island is hard at work getting ready to welcome more visitors. A new airport (1) _____*was built*_____ (build) last year, and at the moment, hotels (2) _____*are being constructed*_____ (construct) along the southern beaches. A new road (3) _____*will be finished*_____ (finish) next year so visitors will be able to reach the northern region. Five years ago, very little (4) _____*was known*_____ (know) about Campinilea; but last year, three books (5) _____*were written*_____ (write) about the island, and several guide books (6) _____*were published*_____ (publish). At the moment, these books (7) _____*are being translated*_____ (translate) into different languages. English (8) _____*is (being) taught*_____ (teach) in schools so many Campinileans know a little English, but not many other foreign languages (9) _____*are spoken*_____ (speak).

Tourism has brought many changes to this small island, and people are afraid that it will have a negative effect on the traditional customs and culture of the people. For example, last month in the capital, several young Campinileans (10) _____*were arrested*_____ (arrest) for being drunk in public, and some tourists (11) _____*were robbed*_____ (rob) near the beach. However, if you leave the tourist areas and go up to the mountains, you will find that life is still the same as it was hundreds of years ago. For example, since the sixteenth century, the same tribal dances (12) _____*have been performed*_____ (perform) to celebrate the Campinilean new year, and the same type of food (13) _____*has been served*_____ (serve). For centuries, visitors (14) _____*have been invited*_____ (invite) to join Campinileans in the celebration of festivals, and you will find traditional Campinilean hospitality in these regions has not changed at all.

ANSWER KEY

Exercise 4 *The flowers were moved. The door was opened, and a windowpane from the door was broken. The vase was taken from the top of the dresser. The dresser drawer was opened, and a jewelry box was moved to the top of the dresser. Jewelry was stolen from the box. The suitcase was moved and partially unlocked. The telephone was unplugged/disconnected.*

EXERCISE 3 [20 minutes]

This exercise provides practice with different tenses using the passive. You may want to assign this exercise for homework and go over the answers in class.

1. Allow time for students to read the story and try to fill in the answers. The passive is required in all cases, but the tenses will vary. Students may want to refer back to the chart in Focus Chart 2 to remind them of how different tenses are formed in the passive.

2. Have students compare answers in pairs.

3. Circulate while students are talking and take notes of problem areas.

4. Go over the answers as a class. Refer to the answer key on LP page 316. You may find it easier to use an overhead transparency of the story.

5. Ask some general questions about the content of the passage to highlight the fact that although the agent is sometimes obvious, we do not always know who the agent is. Use these questions as a bridge to Focus Chart 3. For example:

Who built the airport and hotels? (Campinilean islanders? Companies?)

Who wrote the guidebooks? (Foreigners? Campinileans?)

Who arrested some people for being drunk? (the police)

Who robbed some tourists? (Campinileans thieves? Or foreigners?)

Who performs tribal dances? (Campinileans)

Who serves the food? (Campinileans?)

Who eats the food? (Campinileans and foreigners?)

EXPANSION 1 [10 minutes]

1. Ask students to explain who is doing the action (who is the "agent") in each example in Exercise 3.

2. If you have time, you can ask students to turn each passive into an active sentence. How does this change or add to the meaning? (This may not always be possible if the agent is unknown.)

EXPANSION 2 [20 minutes]

You may want to use Activity 7 (speaking or writing) on SB page 327 after this exercise.

For more practice, use *Grammar Dimensions 2* Workbook page 143, Exercise 3.

FOCUS 3 [5 minutes]

1. **Lead-in:** Refer back to Exercise 3. Have students match the explanations in this box with the examples you discussed in Exercise 3.

2. Use more examples to illustrate the explanations:

(a) The reason for his disappearance was never discovered.

Karen's purse was stolen while she was riding the bus.

(b) When he was arrested, he used his one phone call to contact his wife.

I can't believe it! I've been fired!

(c) I've been informed that one of you has been stealing from me!

I have to rewrite my report because I was given the wrong information.

(d) The results of this project will be used to make important advances in cancer research.

First, the sample is placed in a container.

At this moment, the president is being advised on which action to take.

EXERCISE 4 [10 minutes]

This exercise uses a pair-work information gap that provides many opportunities to use the passive.

1. Be sure students know they should only look at one of the two pictures.

2. If there is a group of three, two people can look at Picture B and take turns offering information.

3. Do one example together with the class.

4. While students are working, circulate around the room and help with verb forms (active or passive). If students tend to use the active form—e.g. *Someone broke the window* encourage them to use the passive instead, *The window was broken.*

5. Have students make a list of differences and either write them on the board (one student can compile answers from the class), or hand them in for correction.

EXPANSION [20 minutes]

To provide further practice with information of questions and answers in the passive, have students turn the information from Exercise 4 into role-play. One student will role-play a newspaper reporter or a police detective. The other will report what they saw at the scene of the robbery. If students prefer, they can make up their own crime scene and role-play a similar conversation, which they can then turn into a written report.

FOCUS 4

use

Including the Agent in Passive Sentences

EXAMPLES | **EXPLANATIONS**

(a) Wheat is grown in the east. (b) NOT: Wheat is grown in the east by farmers.	In most situations where the passive is used, the *by*-phrase (the agent) is understood and therefore is *not* used.
(c) Wheat is grown in eastern Campinilea. It is planted by men, and it is harvested by **women and children**.	You can include the agent (the person who performs the action) with a *by*-phrase if that information is important.
(d) *Hamlet* was written by **William Shakespeare**. (e) Several South American countries were liberated by **Simon Bolivar**. (f) I can't believe it! This novel was written by a **14-year-old**.	It is important to include the agent: • when new information is added, (Example c, second sentence) • with proper names or famous people (Examples d and e) • when the agent's identity is surprising or unexpected (Example f)

EXERCISE 5

Decide if each italicized phrase (*by* + agent) is necessary in the sentences below. Cross out the *by*-phrases that you think are unnecessary.

Passage 1

Campinilea was described (1) *by Jules Verne* in one of his early novels. It was seen (2) *by people* as an exotic yet stable society. Recently, it was rated (3) *by Travel Magazine* as one of the top ten tourist spots in the world. One of the reasons for the country's popularity is that the products produced (4) *by Campinileans* in Campinilea are excellent.

For example, rugs have been produced (5) *by Campinilean people* for centuries. They are woven (6) *by women from the mountain tribes* and are then transported to the capital (7) *by mule* and are sold in the markets (8) *by relatives of the weavers*.

Another excellent product is the mineral water of Campinilea. In restaurants in the capital city, bottled water is served (9) *by waiters*. It is interesting that this water is rarely drunk (10) *by Campinileans*, but it is much appreciated (11) *by foreign tourists*.

Passage 2

Dear Janette,

I've been working hard this whole week on my book. In some ways, I wish that I hadn't gotten paid an advance (1) *by the publishers*, since now I feel a lot of pressure to finish quickly. I guess that's the purpose of an advance! I really hope, though, that when the book is finally finished (2) *by me*, it will be appreciated (3) *by people*. I am hoping that I can finish soon, because it means that I will soon be paid in full (4) *by the publishers*! Even if it's done soon, the book won't actually be published (5) *by the publishers* until at least six months after the manuscript is received (6) *by them*.

Did I tell you that Scout got hurt (7) *by another dog*? She was playing with Patches, the neighbor's dog, like she always does, and her ear got bitten pretty severely (8) *by Patches*. I had to take her to the vet's and get it stitched up (9) *by the vet*. The vet asked me if Scout got attacked (10) *by Patches*, and I had to explain that no, she and Patches just like to play rough. Luckily, Scout's fine. And of course she and Patches are playing together again, just as hard as ever, so it's clear that their friendship hasn't been damaged (11) *by the experience*.

Gotta run! Back to work on the book . . .

Love,
Dean

FOCUS 5

form

Forming the *Get*-Passive

To form the *get*-passive, use the appropriate tense of *get*, followed by the past participle (pp):

EXAMPLES	TENSE	FORM	
(a) Her cookies always **get eaten**.	Present Simple	*get/gets*	+ PP
(b) Her cookies **are getting eaten**.	Present Progressive	*am/is/are getting*	+ PP
(c) Her cookies **got eaten**.	Past Simple	*got*	+ PP
(d) Her cookies **were getting eaten**.	Past Progressive	*was/were getting*	+ PP
(e) Her cookies **have gotten eaten**.	Present Perfect	*have/has gotten*	+ PP
(f) Her cookies **had gotten eaten**.	Past Perfect	*had gotten*	+ PP
(g) Her cookies **will get eaten**.	Future (*will*)	*will get*	+ PP
(h) Her cookies **are going to get eaten**.	Future (*be going to*)	*am/is/are going to get*	+ PP
(i) Her cookies **will have gotten eaten** by the time we get home.	Future Perfect	*will have gotten*	+ PP

ANSWER KEY

Exercise 5 **Passage 1:** Unnecessary *by*-phrases: 2, 4, 5, 9
Passage 2: Unnecessary *by*-phrases: 1, 2, 3, 4, 5, 6, 8, 9

FOCUS 4 [10 minutes]

Note that there is no hard and fast rule about whether to include the agent in passive sentences. However, constant use of the agent in such sentences will sound unnatural, as the choice of the passive usually means that the agent is less significant than the result or recipient of the action.

1. **Lead-in:** With student books closed, contrast examples where the agent needn't be mentioned and examples where including the agent adds interesting information.

For example:

(does not add extra information) *Our car was stolen by some thieves. The man was arrested by the police.*

(adds extra information) *The telephone was invented by Alexander Graham Bell. Our dog was run over by a motorbike.*

2. Ask students to explain why the agent is not needed in some of these examples and ask the students to make a rule to explain this.

3. Have students open their books and read the examples and explanations in the focus chart.

4. Ask students to think of further examples to illustrate each point.

LANGUAGE NOTE

Students may sometimes get confused by the use of the past participle with *be* to describe finished results. For example, *The lesson is finished.* This can mean (a) The lesson is over or (b) The lesson has been finished by someone. There are many past participles that can be used as adjectives in this way. This grammar point is discussed in Unit 24.

EXERCISE 5 [15 minutes]

This exercise encourages students to discuss the appropriate use of the agent in passive sentences and provides practice in editing skills.

1. Do the first example together with the class.
2. Have students work individually to read Passage 1 and mark their answers.
3. Students can compare answers in pairs.
4. Check the answers as a class. Refer to the answer key on LP page 318.
5. You can assign Passage 2 for homework in order to review this grammar point at the beginning of the next class.

EXPANSION [40–50 minutes]

You may want to use Activity 6 (reading) on SB page 326 after this exercise. Students will make up their own version of the card game "Snap" using information about famous people and their achievements. Allow time for making the cards (about 20 minutes) and for playing the game (20–30 minutes).

For more practice, use *Grammar Dimensions 2* Workbook page 144, Exercise 4.

My car got stolen!
All my computer files got destroyed!
I got eaten alive by mosquitoes!

2. Have students use their examples to practice the different tenses as well as question and negative forms.
3. If there are problems, refer students to the chart in Focus Chart 5. Note that question and negative forms do not follow the same pattern as *be*-passive.

LESSON PLAN 2

FOCUS 5 [5 minutes]

This Focus Chart presents the **form** of the *get*-passive. The **use** of the *get*-passive will be addressed in Focus Chart 6 (SB page 322).

1. **Lead-in:** Ask students if they have ever heard the passive used with *get*. Elicit some examples from the students and write them on the board. (You may notice how many of these examples will tend to be from situations where something bad has happened. This point will come up in Focus Chart 6.) Examples:

Questions: Simple present and past:

EXAMPLES

QUESTION FORM

(a) Do her cookies **get eaten**?

(b) Did her cookies **get eaten**?

Do/does + subject + *get* + PP

Did + subject + *get* + PP

Negative: Simple present and past:

EXAMPLES

NEGATIVE STATEMENT FORM

(a) Her cookies do not **get eaten**.

(b) Her cookies did not **get eaten**.

subject + *do/does* + *not* + *get* + PP (*don't/doesn't*)

subject + *did not* + *get* + PP (*didn't*)

EXERCISE 6

Read the following situations. What do you think probably happened before each one? Match the situation with one of the previous events in the box below.

Situation	Previous Event
1. Oh, no! Not my clean white shirt!	_d_
2. We're finally able to pay our bills.	_a_
3. It's so exciting to see my name in print.	_g_
4. I told you not to leave it outside at night!	_h_
5. When I came back to the parking lot, I found these dents on the side.	_b_
6. They took him straight to the hospital by ambulance.	_c_
7. Thank you for all your support. Now that I am mayor, I will work to improve our schools.	_f_
8. The packet's empty, and there are only a few crumbs left!	_e_

a. They got paid.

b. His car got hit.

c. Someone got injured.

d. Some coffee got spilled.

e. All the cookies got eaten.

f. She got elected.

g. His book got published.

h. Her bike got stolen.

EXERCISE 7

Complete the following with the *get*-passive and the appropriate tense.

A: You're late! What happened?

B: I had to take the bus, because my car (1) _is getting fixed_ (fix).

A: Oh? What's wrong with it?

B: It (2) _got broken into_ (break into) last week and a window on one of the doors (3) _got damaged_ (damage).

A: That's terrible! How did it happen?

B: Well, I went into the bank on Thursday and when I came out, I saw that the side window (4) _had gotten smashed_ (smash). Some thieves had broken into the car. Not only that, but I (5) _had gotten fined_ (fine) too, because I hadn't put enough money in the meter.

A: (6) _Did_ anything _get stolen_ (steal) from inside the car?

B: Yes, the CD player and some CDs. I reported it to the police.

A: (7) _Did_ anyone _get arrested_ (arrest)?

B: No, but they found the CDs later. They (8) _had gotten thrown_ (throw) into a trash can!

A: At least they found something! When will your car be ready?

B: I hope the work (9) _will get finished_ (finish) by next Monday. That's just as well because I (10) _am not going to get paid_ (pay) by the insurance company until next week and I can't afford to pay for it until then.

EXERCISE 6 [5 minutes]

This exercise allows students to recognize the variety of everyday situations where the *get*-passive might be used.

1. Have students cover the box at the bottom of the page.

2. Read the first situation together with the class and elicit suggestions as to what might have happened.

3. Have students continue in pairs.

4. When they have finished they can compare their answers with the previous events in the box.

5. Refer to the answer key on LP page 320 and ask the class for any other possible previous events for each situation.

LANGUAGE NOTE

Get-passives are often (but not exclusively) used to describe actions with negative effects (See Focus Chart 6).

EXERCISE 7 [15 minutes]

This exercise provides practice with various tenses of the *get*-passive.

1. Have students read through the dialogue first to get a sense of the story.

2. Do the first example with the class. Emphasize that although the *get*-passive is used in every case, students must think carefully about the correct tense. They can refer back to the chart in Focus Chart 5 if they need to.

3. Circulate while students are working and take note of any problem areas.

4. Refer to the answer key on LP page 320. Check the answers by asking two students to read the dialogue aloud using natural intonation and word-linking. You may want to switch speakers halfway through.

5. Discuss any problem areas.

EXPANSION [20–40 minutes]

You may want to use Activity 4 (listening) and Activity 5 (listening) on SB page 325 after this exercise.

For more practice, use *Grammar Dimensions 2* Workbook page 145, Exercise 5.

FOCUS 6

Be-Passive versus Get-Passive

use

EXAMPLES

(a) They are married.

(b) They got married last year.

(c) The answer was known.

(d) NOT: The answer got known. (know = an unchanging state)

(e) She was wanted by the police for shoplifting.

(f) NOT: She got wanted by the police for shoplifting.

(g) To a friend: Have you heard the news? Isao's car got stolen!

(h) In a police report: A white Honda Civic was stolen last night.

EXPLANATIONS

In most situations, the be-passive emphasizes a continuing state, while the get-passive emphasizes a change in the situation.

Because the get-passive emphasizes a change in a situation, it is only used with action or process verbs. It cannot be used with stative verbs (verbs that refer to situations, or "states," that do not change).

Some common stative verbs:

own	like	hate	love
know	feel	see	want

Get-passives are often used in conversation and rarely in writing or formal speaking.
Be-passives are more formal than get-passives.
Get-passives often describe actions with negative effects.

EXERCISE 8

Where possible, change the underlined verbs to get-passives. If it is not possible to use the get-passive, explain why.

Passage 1

Steve is usually very punctual, but yesterday was a really bad day. First, the elevator in his apartment building broke down, and he (1) was trapped on the 5th floor for 20 minutes. Next, his car (2) was hit by a motorbike on the way to work. Luckily, the driver (3) wasn't injured, but the back of his car (4) was damaged, so he had to stop and exchange insurance information. When he finally arrived at work, he found that his computer (5) was infected by a virus, and he wasn't able to prepare his report on time. A few minutes later, he (6) was called to the manager's office. The manager (7) was disliked by everyone for being so strict. Steve explained how he (8) had been delayed by the elevator, the motorbike, and the computer virus, but the manager was not amused. "How can we (9) be respected by our customers if our reports (10) are not delivered on time?" Steve thought he would (11) be fired on the spot, but instead the manager just told him to stay late until the report (12) was finished.

Passage 2

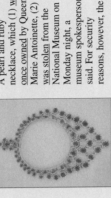

"Fake" Jewel Robbery

A pearl and ruby necklace, which (1) was once owned by Queen Marie Antoinette, (2) was stolen from the National Museum on Monday night, a museum spokesperson said. For security reasons, however, the jewels on display at the museum (3) had been replaced by copies. "Luckily, the real jewels (4) weren't taken," said a museum guard. "I guess we (5) were all fooled," said one visitor to the museum.

EXERCISE 9

Tabloid newspapers present sensational, but usually untrue, stories. Look at the following tabloid newspaper headlines and rewrite each one as a complete sentence. Use a be-passive wherever possible; use a be-passive where you cannot use a get-passive. Remember to add articles when necessary.

Example: *TEEN EATEN BY GIANT COCKROACHES*
A teenager got eaten by giant cockroaches.

1. ELVIS SEEN IN SUPERMARKET LINE
   Elvis was seen in a supermarket line.

2. VICE-PRESIDENT KIDNAPPED BY SPACE ALIENS
   The vice-president got kidnapped …

3. WORLD'S WORST HUSBAND MARRIED 36 TIMES
   The world's worst husband got married 36 times.

4. FALSE TEETH STUCK IN MAN'S THROAT FOR SIX MONTHS
   A man's false teeth got stuck in his throat for six months.

5. THREE-YEAR-OLD ARRESTED DRIVING TRUCK
   A three-year-old got arrested for driving a truck.

What do you think each headline is about? Why?
Find some of your own examples from other newspapers. Read them to your classmates. Your classmates will try to guess what the story is about.

ANSWER KEY

Exercise 8   Passage 1: 1. got trapped 2. got hit 3. didn't get hurt 4. got damaged 5. got infected 6. got called 7. had gotten delayed 10. don't get delivered 11. get fired 12. got finished. Sentences 7 and 9: The be-passive must be used with stative verbs such as the ones in these sentences.

Passage 2: 2. got stolen 3. had gotten replaced 4. didn't get taken 5. all got fooled
Sentence 1: The be-passive can only be used—it emphasizes a continuing state.

FOCUS 6 [10 minutes]

For this Focus Chart you may want to stress the difference in level of formality between *be*- and *get*-passives. The *get*-passive is used in speech and in informal contexts only.

1. **Lead-in:** Write these example sentences using the *be*-passive on the board and ask students which ones could be changed to use the *get*-passive.

   They were married last year. (yes)

   Our house was owned by a famous artist. (no)

   My car was stolen. (yes)

   This book is known by everyone in the country. (no)

   We were informed of the delay by email. (no)

2. Ask students to try and guess why some can use the *get*-passive and some cannot.

3. Check their guesses with the chart in the focus chart.

4. Read the examples and explanations in the focus chart. Review the meaning of stative and action verbs.

5. Refer back to Exercise 7 to see why *get*-passives were used in each case. (The conversation is informal, the verbs are action verbs, and many of the examples refer to negative events.)

LANGUAGE NOTE

Note that *get* is almost always associated with informality, whether in passive or in phrasal verbs: *get up* (awake), *get in* (enter), *get over* (recover), *get into* (become engaged in).

EXERCISE 8 [15 minutes]

This exercise requires students to distinguish when to use get-passives by applying the rules from Focus Chart 6.

Passage 1

1. Have students read the whole text to get a sense of the story.

2. Look at the first example together.

3. Explain that there are no mistakes (the text is correct as it is) but students have to determine when it would be possible to use the *get*-passive.

4. Students can work individually.

5. Then compare their answers in pairs, explaining their reasons in each case.

6. Appoint one discussion leader who will have the class come to a consensus on where *get* can be used in place of *be*.

7. Students should defend their decisions to the class. Refer to the answer key on LP page 322.

8. Ask students to suggest an appropriate title for the story (e.g. Steve's Bad Day).

EXPANSION [20–40 minutes]

You may want to use Activity 2 (speaking/listening) on SB page 324 and Activity 3 (writing or speaking/listening) on page 325 after this exercise.

For more practice, use *Grammar Dimensions 2* Workbook page 146, Exercise 6.

Passage 2

1. Read the title and ask students to guess what the article is about.

2. Ask if they think the language of a newspaper article will be formal and informal.

3. Have students work out the answers individually.

4. Compare answers as a class. Refer to the answer key on LP page 322.

5. Please note that the answer to number 5 requires a change in word order—i.e., *We all got fooled.* (This is because the adverb *all* follows auxiliary verbs and the verb *be*, but it precedes other verbs.)

EXERCISE 9 [15 minutes]

As this exercise requires some thought and creativity, you might want to assign this for homework in order to get more interesting results.

1. Remind students of the rules for newspaper headlines (articles and auxiliaries usually get dropped).

2. If possible, bring in some examples from newspapers and read them to the class, asking them to guess what they are about.

3. Read the first example with the students, noting the addition of the article and *got*.

4. Have students complete the exercise for homework or set a time limit for work in class.

EXPANSION [20–40 minutes]

1. As a follow-up to this activity, have students find additional headlines in newspapers or on Internet news sites.

2. Students can bring the headlines and read them aloud so the others can guess what the stories are about.

3. Or make a poster collage of all the headlines and display it in the classroom. You can use the poster later to review this grammar point.

4. Or use Activity 1 (reading/speaking/listening) on SB page 324; it continues the theme of newspaper headlines.

5. To extend this activity further, choose one of the newspaper articles and analyze examples of the passive. Which tenses are used? Is the *be*-passive or the *get*-passive used? Why?

UNIT GOAL REVIEW [10 minutes]

Ask students to look at the goals on the opening page of the unit again. Refer to the pages of the unit where information on each goal can be found.

 For assessment of Unit 22, use *Grammar Dimensions 2 ExamView*®.

Use Your English

ACTIVITY 1   reading/speaking/listening

Look at the following tabloid headlines and ask three friends to explain what he or she thinks each headline means. Record the conversation and then listen to the recording to see if he or she uses any passive forms in his or her explanations. Share your findings with the rest of the class.

WOMAN HYPNOTIZED BY ALIENS
MAN'S LIFE SAVED BY HITCHHIKING GHOST
SUITCASE DROPPED 5,000 FEET BY AIRLINE
BIGFOOT FOUND IN NEW YORK CITY
WOMAN PREGNANT WITH DAUGHTER'S BABY

ACTIVITY 2   speaking/listening

In this activity, you will make a chain story about somebody's bad day—a day when everything went wrong. One student will start the story and will continue until he or she uses a *get*-passive. When he or she uses a *get*-passive, the next person will continue.

Example: Student 1: *Andy had a really bad day. First, he overslept. When he got dressed, he forgot to put his pants on.*

> **Student 2:** *He ran out of the house, but was embarrassed to realize he had forgotten his pants. Before he could get back inside, he got bitten by the neighbor's dog.*

> **Student 3:** *The dog . . .*

ACTIVITY 3   writing or speaking/listening

Have you ever had a really bad day? A day when everything went wrong, through no fault of your own? Describe the day, either in an informal letter to a friend, or, if you prefer, out loud to a classmate. If you tell your story rather than write it, record it. Listen to the recording for the use of the passive, especially the *get*-passive.

ACTIVITY 4   listening

Ask someone (a native speaker of English, if possible) to tell you about a really frightening experience he or she has had. Find out what happened, and how it happened. Record the conversation.

Listen to the recording. Was the passive used? If so, was it the *be*-passive or the *get*-passive? Was the agent (the *by*-phrase) used?

ACTIVITY 5   listening

■ **STEP 1**   Listen to the audio of two people talking about bad experiences they have had. What experiences did the speakers have? What is similar and different about their experiences?

■ **STEP 2**   Listen to the audio again. Write down all the statements that use the passive. For each statement, was the *be*-passive or the *get*-passive used? Was the agent (the *by*-phrase) used?

CD Track 29

ANSWER KEY

Activity 5   Check audio script on LP page S-9 for answers.

USE YOUR ENGLISH

The Use Your English section of activities at the end of the unit contain situations that should naturally elicit the structures covered in the unit. For a more complete discussion of how to use the Use Your English activities, see To the Teacher, LP page xxii. When students are doing these activities in class, you can circulate and listen to see if they are using the structures accurately. Errors can be corrected after the activity has finished.

ACTIVITY 1 reading/speaking/listening
[20 minutes]

You may want to use this activity after Exercise 9 on SB page 323.

1. You can do this in class or as an out-of-class interviewing activity. Students can interview each person separately or three people in a group.
2. Have students make notes of the different interpretations and see who can come up with the largest number of different interpretations.
3. To shorten the activity, assign just one headline to each interviewer.
4. Follow up by asking students to find their own examples in newspapers or on the Internet if you have not already done so as part of Exercise 9.

ACTIVITY 2 speaking/listening
[10–15 minutes]

You may want to use this activity after Exercise 8 on SB page 322. Activity 3 is a good follow-up to this activity.

1. Review the instructions and make sure students understand the meaning of a "chain story".
2. Arrange the class in a circle, or in several small circles if you have a large class.
3. It helps the continuity of the story if next person to tell the story begins with the *get*-passive (starting their part of the story with the previous event).

ACTIVITY 3 writing/speaking/listening
[20 minutes]

You may want to use this as a follow-up to Activity 2.

1. You may want to start this off by having students mime some things that went wrong. Their partner will guess what happened.
2. Next, have students make notes about their "bad day" to prepare for the writing task.
3. Circulate around the room as they work and note examples of the *get*-passive.
4. Have students write or record the description for homework.
5. Select some examples from their work and discuss whether using the *be*-passive or the *get*-passive would be more appropriate.

ACTIVITY 4 listening
[30 minutes/homework]

You may want to use this activity after Exercise 7 on SB page 321.

1. You can do this in class or as an out-of-class interviewing activity.
2. If you do this in class, allow time for students to gather their ideas and make notes, or ask for any help with vocabulary.
3. If appropriate, gather students into a circle with the "storyteller" and have them ask questions at each stage of the story.
4. Then have students transcribe the interview from their notes for homework.

ACTIVITY 5 listening
[20 minutes]

You may want to use this activity after Exercise 7 on SB page 321.

CD
Track
29

STEP 1

1. Introduce the theme of someone talking about their bad day.
2. Have students make a chart in their notebooks so they can take notes about the two people.
3. Play the audio. See audio script on LP page S–9.
4. Check the answers, referring to the audio script.

STEP 2

1. Play the audio again, pausing the audio to allow time to write.
2. Once students have written down their passive statements, ask them to consider why the speaker chose passive and not active voice and why an agent was used.
3. Refer back to relevant focus charts in the unit as needed.

ACTIVITY 6 reading

ACHIEVEMENT SNAP

■ **STEP 1** a. Work in pairs. Try to think of twenty different achievements (discoveries, inventions, or works of art), as well as the name of the person(s) who created them. Here are a few examples:

ACHIEVEMENT	PERSON
The telephone	Alexander Graham Bell
Hamlet	William Shakespeare
Mona Lisa	Leonardo da Vinci
Psycho	Alfred Hitchcock

b. Write each name on an index card and then write each achievement on a different index card. You should have a total of forty cards. Now you are ready to play Achievement Snap. The object of the game is to make a correct match between Achievement and Person.

■ **STEP 2**

1. Get together with another pair. Put all your "People Cards" in one deck and all your "Achievement Cards" in another deck. Shuffle each deck carefully.

2. Put the deck of Achievement Cards face down on a table.

3. Deal the People Cards to the players. Each player should have several cards. Do not look at your cards.

4. The dealer turns over the first Achievement Card and puts down his or her first People Card.

5. Keep taking turns at putting down People Cards until a match is made. The first person to spot a match shouts "Snap" loudly and explains the match: "The telephone was invented by Alexander Graham Bell." If everyone agrees that the match is factually and grammatically correct, the player takes the pile of People Cards on the table.

6. The winner is the person who collects the most People Cards. Remember to use an appropriate verb in matching the person and the achievement. Common verbs include: *compose, write, discover, invent, direct, sing, paint.*

   NOTE: It is possible to continue playing after you lose your People Cards. If you correctly spot a "match," you can collect the cards on the table.

ACTIVITY 7 speaking or writing

Make a presentation (oral or written) about your country or a place that you know well. Bring in pictures or maps to illustrate your talk. Describe the resources and products, any changes over time, and any predictions for the future.

ACTIVITY 8 research on the web/writing

Choose one famous invention discovery, or creation such as one of those in Activity 6. Go on the Internet and use a search engine such as Google® or Yahoo® to search for information about your topic.

When, where, and how was it invented discovered, or created?

Who was it invented or discovered or created by?

Write a short summary of your research and tell the class.

What was the most interesting thing that you learned?

Which Web site was most useful in helping you with your research?

What kind of research could this Web site be useful for?

ACTIVITY 9 reflection

Choose one tense of the passive that you find difficult to remember. Choose a sentence from your story in Activity 3 that could use this tense. Draw a picture to illustrate your sentence.

USE YOUR ENGLISH

ACTIVITY 6 reading
[50 minutes]

Materials needed for this game: a pack of cards (for demonstration only), index cards or paper cut up into small squares or rectangles, 40 cards or pieces of paper for each pair of students.

1. As a warm-up, ask students if they know the game of "Snap".

2. Ask a student to explain the rules and see if everyone agrees.

3. Explain that this game is an adaptation of "Snap". Students will make two sets of cards. One set of cards will have names of famous people. The other set of cards will have their discoveries, inventions, or achievements.

4. Start off by brainstorming a few examples on the board.

5. Review Step 1 in the student book.

6. Then allow 15–20 minutes for students to create their sets of cards.

Note: In order to differentiate the two different packs of cards, you can use different colored cards. Or write "A" and "P" on the back of each card. Allow time for making the cards (about 20 minutes) and for playing the game (30 minutes).

1. When the cards are ready, have each pair sit with another pair and start playing the game.

2. Follow Step 2 in the Student Book.

3. To continue the game further, have groups exchange sets of cards with each other.

VARIATION

If you wish to prepare this game for your students (instead of having them prepare the cards), you can create two sheets of paper with squares already filled in with names and achievements, photocopy them, and cut them up. To make them last longer, paste them onto cardboard before cutting them up. This will shorten the preparation time for the game, but will reduce the creativity required from students.

You may want to use this activity after Exercise 5 on SB page 318.

ACTIVITY 7 speaking or writing
[60 minutes/homework]

You may want to use this activity after Exercise 3 on SB page 316.

1. Assign this activity for homework. Ask students to prepare a 5–8 minute presentation.

2. If you have access to video equipment, tell the students that you will videotape each student's presentation. Tell the students that you will be looking at the following: *organization of presentation, knowledge of topic, any pictures or maps or use of board, clarity of speech including speed and pronunciation.*

3. Have students run through the presentations with partners.

4. Students can make their presentations orally, or prepare written descriptions for display in the classroom or to be collected in a portfolio.

5. If you videotaped the presentations, schedule a one-on-one appointment to watch the tape together and discuss the strengths and areas for improvement.

ACTIVITY 8 research on the web/writing
[30 minutes/homework]

You may want to use this activity after Exercise 5 on SB page 318.

The purpose of this Internet search activity is to provide a natural context for using the passive. An additional purpose is to encourage students to share strategies for finding information on the Internet. What Web sites were most useful? Have students share successes and frustrations.

ACTIVITY 9 reflection
[15 minutes/homework]

This activity provides an opportunity for students to use the target structures of the unit while developing strategies for improving their learning. You may have asked students to keep a record of their learning in a journal throughout this course as suggested in To the Teacher, LP page xxii. This reflection activity will form part of that learning record.

PHRASAL VERBS

UNIT GOALS

- **Know when to use phrasal verbs**

- **Know which phrasal verbs take objects and which phrasal verbs do not take objects**

- **Correctly form sentences containing phrasal verbs and objects**

- **Know which phrasal verbs are separable and which are inseparable**

OPENING TASK

School Routines

■ STEP 1

Look at the pictures. What do you think is happening in each one?

■ STEP 2

Work with a partner. Read the clues and complete the crossword.

[Crossword puzzle with the following filled-in answers:]
- MAKE
- HAND
- LOOK
- CROSS
- FIND
- DIVIDE
- CLEAN
- TURN
- WRITE

Clues across:

1. Use the new words to _____ up your own story.

3. Please _____ up the new words in a dictionary.

4. Read the answers and _____ out the incorrect choices.

5. At the end of the lesson, please _____ up the classroom.

6. Look at the answer key and _____ out if your answers are correct.

Clues down:

2. At the end of the test, you must _____ in all your papers.

3. Don't _____ out any questions. Try to answer everything.

6. Use your pencil to _____ in the blanks.

7. You can use your calculator to _____ out the answers.

8. Please _____ up when the teacher says your name.

■ STEP 3

Check your answers with your classmates. How many of these things have you done today? Tell your partner.

(Solution to Opening Task Puzzle on page A-18)

LESSON PLAN 1

UNIT OVERVIEW

Unit 23 provides the grammar of transitive, intransitive, separable, and inseparable two-part phrasal verbs.

GRAMMAR NOTE

One difficulty with phrasal verbs is recognizing them. The main verb looks just like a normal verb—e.g., *get, put, take,* and the preposition might look like it is attached to a noun. Another problem is that although the meanings of some phrasal verbs are easy to guess—e.g., *stand up, put down*—other verbs have meanings that seem unrelated to the meaning of the individual parts—e.g., *put off, catch on, call off*. A third difficulty is that many phrasal verbs have more than one meaning. The meaning can only be identified by context.

UNIT GOALS

Some instructors may want to review the goals listed on Student Book (SB) page 328 after completing the Opening Task so that students understand what they should know by the end of the unit. These goals can also be reviewed at the end of the unit when students are more familiar with the grammar terminology.

OPENING TASK [15 minutes]

The purpose of the Opening Task is to create a context in which students will need to use phrasal verbs. The problem-solving format is designed to show the teacher how well the students can produce the target structures implicitly and spontaneously when they are engaged in a communicative task. For a more complete discussion of the purpose of the Opening Task, see To the Teacher, Lesson Planner (LP) page xxii.

Setting Up the Task

■ STEP 1

1. Use the pictures to encourage some discussion of what is happening in the photos so that students will use the verbs spontaneously—e.g., *He's putting on/taking off his jacket. He's handing in/giving back his homework. He's looking up something/logging on to the Internet.*

2. Talk further about daily activities connected with school routines, trying to incorporate phrasal verbs if possible.

Conducting the Task

■ STEP 2

1. Make sure students understand the meaning of *across* and *down* in this context. Do one example with the class if necessary.

2. Set a time limit for students to complete the crossword. They can work individually and then compare answers in pairs.

3. If some students finish early, have them check these phrasal verbs in the dictionary and find synonyms or see if they have any other meanings.

Closing the Task

■ STEP 3

1. Ask volunteers to share their answers with the class. Refer to the answer key on LP page 328.

2. You can review different tenses by having students ask each other questions. These questions will give students the opportunity to use phrasal verbs in conversation. For example:

   How many words have you looked up today?
   Have you handed in your homework today?
   Did you clean up the classroom yesterday?
   Do you usually stand up when the teacher says your name?

3. Circulate while students are speaking and make notes of any problems areas. This will help you target the material in this unit. Do not correct errors at this stage.

4. Ask volunteers to share information about their partner with the class.

GRAMMAR NOTE

Typical student errors (form)

- Errors with particles, e.g.,* *Could you look over my cat while I'm away?* (See Focus 2.)

- Not separating phrasal verbs when the object is a pronoun, e.g. * *He turned on it.* (See Focus 4.)

- Separating phrasal verbs that are inseparable, e.g. * *She ran her friend into.* (See Focus 5.)

- Separating phrasal verbs when the object is a long noun phrase, e.g. * *She threw all the clothes that were several years old out.* (See Focus 6.)

Typical student errors (use)

- Not recognizing that phrasal verbs form one lexical unit, i.e. interpreting them as two separate items: a verb and a preposition. (See Focus 1.)

- Interpreting phrasal verbs literally, e.g. not recognizing the difference between: *Look up the word in a dictionary* and *Look up the chimney.* (See Focus 2.)

- Misunderstanding phrasal verbs that are synonyms, e.g. *They got on the plane.* (= board) *They don't get on.* (= be friends)

FOCUS 1

Phrasal Verbs

form

EXAMPLES

	Verb	Particle	
(a) Please	take	out	your books.
(b) You can	look	up	the new words.
(c) Don't	hand	in	your papers until the end of the exam.

EXPLANATIONS

Phrasal verbs have two parts: a **verb** and **particle**. Common particles are *off, on, in, out, up.*

EXERCISE 1

With a classmate, use the phrasal verbs to make a list of instructions for each task.

Example: Take a test: put away/fill in/leave out/hand in
First, put away all your textbooks and notes.
Then fill in your name and student ID on the test sheet.
Don't leave out any questions.
Finally, hand in your papers at the end of the test.

1. Take out a library book: look up/take down/check out/give back

2. Use a CD player: take out/switch on/put in/turn up

3. Get cash from an ATM: put in/key in/take out/take back

4. Drive a car: get in/put in/switch on/press down

5. Your idea: ....

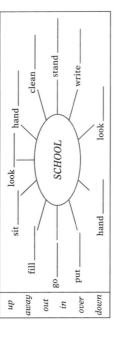

meaning

FOCUS 2

When to Use Phrasal Verbs and How to Learn Them

use

EXAMPLES

(a) **Look out!** There's a car coming!

(b) The movie starts at 8:00. Please don't **show up** late or we won't get good seats.

(c) You should **look over** your homework before you give it to the teacher.

(d) My friend David **looks after** my cats when I go on vacation.

EXPLANATIONS

Phrasal verbs are very common, especially in informal spoken English.

It is often difficult to guess the meaning of a phrasal verb, even when you know the meaning of each part. In some situations, however, the context can help you make a guess.

In (a), *look out* means be careful.

In (b), *show up* means arrive.

When you use the same verb with a different particle, the meaning usually changes.

In (c), *look over* means to check or examine something.

In (d), *look after* means to take care of.

To remember the meanings of phrasal verbs, learn the two parts together as one vocabulary item, in the same way that you learn new words.

EXERCISE 2

Get together with a classmate and match each verb in the diagram below with a particle from the list to the left of the diagram to create a set of phrasal verbs to describe typical school activities. (Notice that some verbs can take different particles to express different meanings.) Check that you understand the meaning of the phrasal verbs you create (your teacher or a good English/English dictionary can help). Remember, in this exercise, we are only thinking about phrasal verbs that are often used to talk about "school."

up
away
out
in
over
down

Diagram: **SCHOOL** — sit, look, hand, clean, stand, write, look, hand, put, go, fill

ANSWER KEY

Exercise 1 1. *Take out a library book:* First, look up the title of the book. Then take down the book from the shelf. Check out the book at the desk. Finally, don't forget to give back the book before the due date.
2. *Use a CD player:* First, take out the CD from its cover. Then switch on the CD player. Put in the CD. Finally, turn up the volume. 3. *Get cash from an ATM:* First, put in your ATM card. Then key/type in your PIN number (and the amount of cash you need). Take out your cash. Finally, take back your accelerator/gas pedal. 5. *Your idea. Example:* Do research on the Internet: Go on the Internet. Type in the keyword (s). Click on the website. Look up the topic.

Exercise 2 Clockwise: look up, look away, look out, look in, look over, look down; hand out, hand in, hand over; clean up, clean out; stand up, stand away, stand out, stand in; write up, write over; put up, put away, put in, put down; go up, go away, go out, go over; fill up, fill out, fill in; sit up, sit out, sit

LESSON PLAN 1

FOCUS 1 [10 minutes]

1. **Lead-in:** To continue the theme of phrasal verbs associated with classroom activities, you may want to start this lesson with a brief TPR (Total Physical Response) activity. Give a series of commands, such as: *stand up, sit down, turn around, turn on the light, turn off the light, pick up your pen, put down your pen, take out your book,* etc. Ask students what all of these commands have in common (to introduce the term *phrasal verbs* if they do not already know it). Alternatively, you may want to mime these actions and have students guess the verbs.

2. At this point, students may want to discuss further what difficulties they have with learning phrasal verbs. See Language Note below about phrasal verbs and prepositional verbs.

3. Make sure students understand the meaning of the terms *verb* and *particle* in relation to phrasal verbs.

EXERCISE 1 [20 minutes]

The theme of giving commands or instructions using phrasal verbs is continued in this exercise.

1. Ask students to close their books.

2. Write the four phrasal verbs from item 1 on the board.

3. Have students use the verbs to give instructions for taking a test.

4. Have students open their books and compare their answers with the example in the book.

5. Have students work in pairs to complete the exercise.

6. Refer to the answer key on LP page 330. When reviewing the answers, you may want to have one student read the instructions aloud while the other students mime the actions.

7. Gather a variety of ideas for item 5 and ask the class to help correct or improve the suggested directions.

For more practice, use *Grammar Dimensions 2* Workbook pages 147–148, Exercise 1.

LANGUAGE NOTE

Some students may ask about phrasal verbs with three parts. These are phrasal verbs that have a particle and a preposition—e.g., *put up with, get away with,* etc. They are always inseparable, but in other ways operate just like phrasal verbs.

EXPANSION [20 minutes]

You may want to use Activity 4 (listening) on SB page 345 after this exercise. This activity continues the theme of classroom instructions.

FOCUS 2 [5 minutes]

This focus chart explains that phrasal verbs are used in informal English and presents some strategies for learning them.

1. **Lead-in:** Read the examples in the focus chart and ask students (a) how they would work out the meaning of these phrasal verbs and (b) how they would try to learn and remember their meaning. You may use this opportunity to collect a list of useful strategies from the class in addition to the ones presented in this chart.

2. Contrast some examples of formal and informal English to illustrate that phrasal verbs tend to be used in informal spoken English. For example;

   *Please **give back** your books by Monday./Please **return** your books by Monday.*

   *They didn't **show up** until 8 P.M./They didn't **arrive** until 8 P.M.*

3. Read the explanations in the focus chart.

EXERCISE 2 [15 minutes]

This exercise continues the theme of phrasal verbs in the school context and helps illustrate the flexibility of phrasal verbs and particles. You may want to have dictionaries available for reference.

1. You can organize this as pairwork or a team competition. Set a time limit of 10 minutes for teams to make a list of verbs using the verbs and particles in the diagram.

2. Ask students to give example sentences for each phrasal verb they come up with. If you or other students don't understand the meaning, ask them to explain their answers, either by giving a definition or by miming/acting out the situation.

3. The team with the most correct sentences is the winner.

For more practice, use *Grammar Dimensions 2* Workbook page 148, Exercise 2.

EXPANSION [20 minutes]

You may want to use Activity 5 on SB page 346 after this exercise. This activity involves giving instructions for how to make a peanut butter and jelly sandwich.

form meaning

FOCUS 3 | Phrasal Verbs That Take Objects

EXAMPLES

(a) We had to **call off** the meeting because everyone was sick.

(b) We're trying to sleep. Please **turn down** that radio!

EXPLANATIONS

Like other verbs, many phrasal verbs take objects.

In (a), the object of the sentence is *the meeting*.

In (b), the object of the sentence is *that radio*.

Some common phrasal verbs that take objects:

PHRASAL VERB	EXAMPLE	MEANING*
Call off	We had to **call off** the meeting because everyone was sick.	Cancel
Put off	Let's **put off** our meeting until next week.	Change to a later time or date
Pick up	Please **pick up** your towel! Don't leave it on the bathroom floor.	Lift or take from a particular place
Set up	We need to **set up** a time to discuss this.	Arrange a meeting or appointment
Talk over	It's important for couples to **talk over** their problems and misunderstandings.	Discuss a problem

PHRASAL VERB	EXAMPLE	MEANING*
Throw out	I **threw out** all my old school books and papers when we moved.	Put in the garbage, get rid of
Turn down	We're trying to sleep. Please **turn down** that radio!	Lower the volume of radio, TV, etc.
Turn off	I'll **turn off** the TV as soon as this program ends.	Stop a machine, engine or electrical device
Turn on	She always **turns on** the radio to listen to the news.	Start a machine, engine or electrical device

*Some of these phrasal verbs may have different meanings in different situations.

EXERCISE 3

Use the phrasal verbs from Exercise 2 to complete the text below.

French Lessons

I will never forget my first French lessons many years ago in high school. Our teacher was very strict and rather old-fashioned, even for that time. When she entered the classroom, we all had to (1) stand _up_ and say "Bonjour, Madame Morel," and we couldn't (2) sit _down_ until she gave us permission. Every class followed exactly the same routine, with absolutely no variation. First, we always had "dictée."

The teacher read a passage, sentence by sentence, and we had to (3) write _down_ exactly what she said, word for word. We weren't allowed to use dictionaries in class, so we couldn't (4) look _up_ the meanings of any words we didn't know. Then, she always gave us precisely five minutes to (5) look _over_ our papers to check the spelling and punctuation. This was very important because if we (6) handed _in_ work that had more than one mistake in it, we had to stay behind after class. Next, she always (7) handed _out_ a list of vocabulary words for us to memorize. Then after exactly ten minutes, she gave us a quiz that always told us to (8) "fill _in_ the blanks with the appropriate vocabulary word." Finally, she (9) went _over_ the vocabulary words from the previous day's lesson to make sure that we hadn't forgotten them. How I hated French lessons! Even when the bell rang at the end of the day, we couldn't leave until we (10) had cleaned _up_ the classroom and (11) put _away_ all our books.

EXERCISE 4

Use as many of the phrasal verbs from Exercises 1, 2, and 3 as you can to describe a class you have taken or are taking now. Make a list and then describe the class to a classmate.

ANSWER KEY

Exercise 4 *Answers will vary.*

LESSON PLAN 1

EXERCISE 3 [15 minutes]

This exercise gives students the chance to use the phrasal verbs from Exercise 2 in context.

1. Allow several minutes for students to read the text and get a sense of the story.

2. To check the answers, have students read out the sentences in turn, asking the other students if they agree or not. Refer to the answer key on LP page 332.

3. To review the verbs used in this text, ask students if they like or dislike the method of teaching described here and why.

EXERCISE 4 [20 minutes]

This exercise reviews all the phrasal verbs studied so far.

1. You may want to do this exercise orally first and then assign the written description for homework.

2. Set a time limit for students to make their lists of verbs.

3. If students are in the same classes, ask them to read their descriptions without revealing which class they're talking about. Let other students guess.

4. Have students record their descriptions and then listen to the recording for phrasal verb usage.

EXPANSION [20 minutes]

You may want to use Activity 2 (speaking/listening) and Activity 3 (listening) on SB page 345 after this exercise. These activities develop the theme of talking about daily activities using phrasal verbs.

FOCUS 3 [15 minutes]

This focus chart presents transitive phrasal verbs (verbs that take objects).

1. **Lead-in:** Review the difference between transitive and intransitive verbs (this distinction will be important in Focus Chart 4 when explaining how to use separable phrasal verbs). Compare some of the verbs already used in this unit—e.g., *look up*, *take out* (transitive); *look out*, *show up* (intransitive).

2. Read the first two examples in the focus chart and ask students to work out the meaning. (*call* = cancel, *turn down* = reduce volume)

3. Cover the right-hand column in the lower chart and do the same for each example. First, ask students to guess the meaning, then to identify which word is the object.

   For the first example:

   What is the phrasal verb? (*call off*)
   What does call off mean? (*cancel*)
   What is the object of the phrasal verb? (*The meeting*)

4. Have students work in pairs to test each other on the meanings of the phrasal verbs presented in this chart. One student can look at the book and ask questions. The other students can close their book and try to remember the meaning. Then switch roles.

5. Ask students if they are familiar with other meanings for the phrasal verbs in Focus 3. If not, encourage students to check their dictionaries to check other meanings for all of the phrasal verbs in the chart. Explain the meanings and create sample sentences.

EXERCISE 5

Respond to the following situations using as many of the phrasal verbs discussed so far in this unit as possible. (Some of the language from Unit 10, *Giving Advice and Expressing Opinions*, and Unit 17, *Requests and Permission*, might also help you here.)

1. You are trying to talk on the phone but your roommate is listening to some very loud music.
   You say: _Please turn down that radio!_

2. A friend is applying for a job and has just written a letter of application.
   He asks you to check the letter for grammatical errors.
   He says: _Would you mind reading over my letter to see if there are any mistakes?_

3. A family member is sick and you need to leave town for a few days to take care of her. You call a colleague and explain the situation. Then you ask him to telephone your clients and delay all the meetings you had arranged with them until the following week.
   You say: _Could you please tell my clients that I need to put off all my meetings and reschedule them next week?_

4. It is the first class meeting of the school year. Your new teacher is explaining his policy about grading and homework. He expects students to give him their homework on time.
   He says: _I expect you to hand in your homework on time._

5. You have helped organize a foreign film festival on campus. You ask some of your classmates to help you distribute fliers about the movies to students in the cafeteria during the lunch break.
   You say: _Can you hand out these fliers to students in the cafeteria?_

6. Your friend's roommate leaves papers and clothes all over the floor. She asks for your advice.
   You say: _Tell him or her to pick up all the papers or clothes or you'll throw them away/out._

use

FOCUS 4

Separating Verbs and Particles

EXAMPLES

	subject	verb	particle	object (noun)	
(a)	She	turned	on	the light.	

OR

	subject	verb	object (noun)	particle	
(b)	She	turned	the light	on.	

	subject	verb	object (pronoun)	particle	
(c)	She	turned	it	on.	
(d)	NOT: She turned on it.				
(e)	He cleaned it up.				
(f)	NOT: He cleaned up it.				

EXPLANATIONS

Many phrasal verbs are **separable:** When the object is a noun, you can:

Put the object **after** the particle.

OR

Put the object **between** the verb and the particle.

When the object of a separable phrasal verb is a pronoun, you must put the object **between** the verb and the particle.

This is because the pronoun gives information that is known to both speaker and listener (here, the speaker and listener both know what *it* refers to). Known information does not usually come at the end of a sentence in English.

ANSWER KEY

Exercise 5 *Answers will vary. Possible answers are listed above.*

EXERCISE 5 [15 minutes]

This exercise practices the use of phrasal verbs in everyday contexts.

1. To prepare for this activity, ask students to keep a vocabulary log—a list (preferably alphabetical) of phrasal verbs they learned in this chapter and other phrasal verbs they are familiar with. As with any vocabulary list, along with the vocabulary item itself (in this case, the phrasal verb), they should write the meaning and a sample sentence or two that contains the phrasal verb.

2. Set a time limit for students to work in pairs and write their answers.

3. Ask volunteers to read their answers aloud. Encourage a variety of responses for each situation.

4. Ask the class to evaluate whether the phrasal verb was used correctly and also to comment on the type of language used. Was it polite enough, for example?

For more practice, use *Grammar Dimensions 2* Workbook page 149, Exercise 3.

EXPANSION [20 minutes]

This may be a good time to go over various strategies for learning and remembering phrasal verbs.

1. Ask students to suggest any strategies they have been using so far that they have found to be effective. These may include: using translations, synonyms, explanations, example sentences, and drawings.

2. Have students compare vocabulary notebooks to share ideas.

3. Ask for suggestions for abbreviations for transitive/intransitive/separable/inseparable. Compare them with those used in a dictionary.

4. Ask for suggestions on how to review the meaning of phrasal verbs.

5. You might find yourself and students also creating sentences like: *We looked the words in the dictionary up.* This can serve as a bridge to Focus Chart 6. (Example: *We looked the words up* sounds acceptable, but *We looked the words in the dictionary up* sounds a little strange, since the object is rather lengthy.)

LESSON PLAN 2

FOCUS 4 [10 minutes]

This focus chart presents separable phrasal verbs and the rules for word order with object pronouns. Inseparable phrasal verbs are presented in Focus Chart 5.

1. Lead-in: Write these sentences on the board. Ask if students notice any difference in meaning (there is none):

   She turned on the light.
   She turned the light on.

2. Ask students to find the object in the sentences (a) and (b) (that is, *the light*) and replace it with a pronoun. This will work in the first example, but not in the second. Use this to introduce the rule presented in this focus chart: "When the object of a separable phrasal verb is a pronoun, you must put the pronoun between the verb and the particle." Here are more examples for the students to change the object to an object pronoun:

   The boy took off his jacket.
   Samantha threw out the garbage.
   We took back the books to the library.

3. Discuss the example sentences in the focus chart, making sure that students understand that although the placement of the full noun phrase object is flexible—examples (a) and (b)—when the object of the phrasal verb is a pronoun, it must come between the verb and the particle—examples (c) through (f).

4. Go over the phrasal verbs used in the previous exercises and focus chart. Use each *separable* phrasal verb in a sentence (if it's not in a sentence already) and experiment with the placement of the full noun phrase object compared to the pronoun object. Example:

   We looked up the words in a dictionary. We looked them up. (NOT: * *We looked up them.*)

Some common inseparable phrasal verbs:

PHRASAL VERB	EXAMPLE	MEANING*
Come across	You never know what you'll find at a yard sale! Last week, I **came across** a valuable old Beatles record.	Find something or someone
Run into	Colleen was really surprised to **run into** her ex-boyfriend at the supermarket.	Meet someone unexpectedly
Get off	Don't **get off** the bus until it stops.	Leave a bus, train, or plane
Get on	You can't **get on** a plane without a boarding pass.	Enter a bus, train, or plane
Go over	Our teacher always **goes over** the main points in a unit before she gives us a test.	Review
Get over	Jeb has gone to bed early because he's still **getting over** the flu.	Recover from illness or sadness

*Some of these phrasal verbs may have different meanings in different situations.

EXERCISE 7

Replace the underlined words with phrasal verbs from the list below. Separate the verb and particle where necessary.

pass away   find out   came across   cheer up   put off   run into   call on   get on

came across
1. Yesterday Sally finally <u>found</u> Marie's phone number. She tried to call her, but the line was busy.

2. So, she decided to <u>visit her at home</u>.

3. Earlier that day, Sally <u>met</u> their friend Ron <u>unexpectedly</u> as he was leaving the apartment building.

4. He was ready to <u>enter</u> the bus to go to his sister's house.

5. He told Sally that his grandfather had <u>died last week</u>.

6. Of course, Sally was sorry to <u>hear</u> the sad news.

7. She suggested to Marie that the three friends should <u>postpone</u> the dinner party they had been planning.

8. Marie agreed, and she also thought they should visit Ron to help him <u>recover from</u> his loss.

PHRASAL VERBS

EXERCISE 6

Replace the underlined words with a phrasal verb from the list below. For now, only separate the verb and the particle when the object is a pronoun.

try on	find out	take off	throw out	set up	take back
go over	put on	call up	get off	put off	

taking your shoes off
Shirley: Why are you (1) <u>removing your shoes</u>? I thought you were going to go for a walk.

Julia: I decided to (2) <u>wear</u> my boots. It's raining outside.

Shirley: I thought those boots were too small. You said you wanted to (3) <u>return</u> them to the store. Did you (4) <u>discover</u> if they have a larger size?

Julia: I guess I (5) <u>delayed</u> it too long. When I (6) <u>phoned</u> the store, the salesperson said I'd have to wait at least a month for the next delivery, so I decided to keep these after all.

Shirley: That's crazy! Don't wear them if they're too small. Why don't you borrow my hiking boots?

Julia: I thought you (7) <u>put</u> those <u>in the garbage</u> when we moved.

Shirley: No, they're somewhere in my closet if you want to (8) <u>wear</u> them <u>to see if they fit you.</u>

Get together with a classmate. Compare your answers and then read the new dialogue aloud to each other. Change roles and read the dialogue again.

form   meaning

FOCUS 5   Inseparable Phrasal Verbs

EXAMPLES

(a) Yesterday I **ran into** my friend Sal.
OR

(b) Yesterday I **ran into** her.

(c) NOT: Yesterday I ran my friend into.

(d) NOT: Yesterday I ran her into.

EXPLANATIONS

Not all phrasal verbs can be separated. Some phrasal verbs are **inseparable**: With these verbs you cannot put the object between the verb and the particle, even when the object is a pronoun.

It is difficult to guess which phrasal verbs are separable and which are inseparable. It is a good idea to learn if a phrasal verb is separable or inseparable when you learn its meaning. A good dictionary will give you this information.

UNIT 23

ANSWER KEY

Exercise 6 2. put my boots on 3. take them back 4. find out 5. put it off 6. called up 7. threw those out 8. try them on

Exercise 7 2. call on her 3. ran into 4. get on 5. passed away 6. find out 7. put off 8. cheer him up

PHRASAL VERBS

EXERCISE 6 [15 minutes]

This exercise provides practice in recognizing when a phrasal verb should be separated from its particle.

1. Have students read through the dialogue first (aloud or silently) to get a sense of the context.

2. To make this exercise easier, you may want to start off by matching the phrasal verbs in the box with their synonyms (underlined verbs in the text).

3. Then ask students to replace the verbs with the appropriate phrasal verb, separating verb and particle if necessary.

4. Ask volunteers to read the revised dialogue aloud in pairs.

5. To check the answers, ask volunteers to read the dialogue for the class. Refer to the answer key on LP page 336.

6. Review any errors and discuss the reasons for them.

7. If students are keeping a log of the phrasal verbs used in this unit, remind them to make a note of the synonyms, too, as this is a useful way of reviewing and remembering phrasal verbs.

For more practice, use *Grammar Dimensions 2* Workbook page 150, Exercise 4.

FOCUS 5 [10 minutes]

1. Lead-in: Review the difference between transitive and intransitive verbs. Explain that these verbs are transitive, but they do not separate. (The separable/inseparable distinction does not apply to intransitive verbs because they have no object.)

2. Read the first example in the focus chart and try to guess the meaning of *run into* (= meet by accident).

3. Cover the right-hand column in the focus chart on the top of SB page 337 and do the same for each example. First, ask students to guess the meaning, then to identify the object.

For the first example:
What is the phrasal verb? (come across)
*What does **come across** mean? (find)*
What is the object of the phrasal verb? (Beatles record)

4. Have students work in pairs to test each other on the meanings of the phrasal verbs presented in this chart. One student can look at the book and ask questions. The other student can close the book and try to remember the meaning. Then switch roles.

5. Emphasize that to learn to use a phrasal verb in their speaking and writing, they should know both its meaning and its "rules"—whether or not it is separable. If students just want to know what a phrasal verb means when they hear it or read it, the meaning is most important.

EXERCISE 7 [15 minutes]

This exercise provides practice in distinguishing separable from inseparable phrasal verbs.

1. Have students read through the story first (aloud or silently) to get a sense of the context.

2. To make this exercise easier, you may want to start off by matching the phrasal verbs in the box with their synonyms (underlined verbs in the text).

3. Then ask students to replace the verbs with the appropriate phrasal verb, separating verb and particle if necessary.

4. To check the answers, ask volunteers to read the revised story for the class.

5. Review any errors. Refer to the answer key on LP page 336. Discuss which verbs are intransitive (*pass away*), which verbs are separable transitive verbs (*find out, cheer up, put off*) and which ones are inseparable transitive verbs (*come across, run into, call on, get on*).

6. If students are keeping a log of the phrasal verbs used in this unit, remind them to make a note of the synonyms too as this is a useful way of reviewing and remembering phrasal verbs.

For more practice, use *Grammar Dimensions 2* Workbook page 151, Exercise 5.

EXPANSION [20 minutes]

You may want to use Activity 8 (research on the web) on SB page 347 after this exercise. This activity develops students' knowledge about English learning websites and ways of using them as a learning tool.

FOCUS 6

When and When Not to Separate Phrasal Verbs

EXAMPLES	EXPLANATIONS
(a) Last week Sharifah organized her closet and **threw out** all her old clothes. OR	You can separate the verb and the particle when the object consists of just a few words.
(b) Last week Sharifah organized her closet and **threw** all her old clothes **out**.	
(c) Last week Sharifah organized her closet and **threw out** all the clothes that were several years old.	Do not separate the verb and particle when the object is longer than three or four words.
(d) NOT: Last week Sharifah organized her closet and **threw** all the clothes that were several years old **out**.	

EXERCISE 9

Are the underlined phrasal verbs correct in the following sentences? In sentences where the verb and the particle are incorrectly placed, circle the particle and draw an arrow to show its correct position.

Example: *I have a meeting at 4:00 tomorrow, but I'm trying to put off ⓘt until the next day.*

Put it off. Correct

1. Cherie always <u>shows up</u> for work on time. She has to <u>get</u> the bus <u>on</u> at 7:00 A.M., but yesterday she overslept and didn't <u>get up</u> until 8:00. She was late for work!

2. Last month, Sunny went through her file cabinets and <u>threw</u> all the papers she had been keeping since her time in graduate school <u>out</u>.

3. When Nina <u>ran</u> Tim <u>into</u>, he <u>pointed out</u> that they had not been in touch for over a year. They promised to <u>call</u> each other <u>up</u> more often in the future.

EXERCISE 8

STEP 1

Where do you think the following were probably said? Match the sentences with the pictures.

1.

2.

3.

4.

Example: ___4___ Please *hand* your papers in now.
Please hand them in now.

a. ___4___ Let's go over last week's quiz.
Let's go over it.

b. ___3___ Can I try on this shirt?
Can I try it on?

c. ___1___ Let's set up a meeting for next week.
Let's set it up for next week.

d. ___2___ You can't check out these books without a current ID.
You can't check them out without a current ID.

STEP 2

Underline the phrasal verbs. Rewrite each sentence using a pronoun, moving the particle if it is possible to do so.

STEP 3

Now think of other phrasal verbs that could be used in each context. Make sentences as in Step 2. Exchange sentences with your partner, and rewrite them using pronouns.

ANSWER KEY

Exercise 8 Step 2: a. —go over— b. —try on— c. —set up/set a meeting up— d. —check out—

Step 3 Answers will vary. Possibilities: Let's look at . . . Can I put on . . . Let's try for/ plan on . . . You can't take them out . . .

Exercise 9 Incorrect placements are: 1. *get on* is inseparable. 2. *threw out* should stay together since the object is too long 3. *ran into* should stay together since *run into* is inseparable.

(Continued on page 340.)

EXERCISE 8 [15 minutes]

This exercise provides practice in using phrasal verbs in everyday contexts.

STEP 1

1. Look at the pictures and discuss where they probably are and who is in them.
2. Explain that students will first match the sentences with the pictures.

STEP 2

1. Then they will rewrite the sentences using a pronoun for the object (and separating the phrasal verb if necessary).
2. Set a time limit for students to work in pairs to complete the exercise.
3. Refer to the answer key on LP page 338 and review the answers and explain any errors.

STEP 3

You may organize this as a competition to see who can come up with the most sentences, or the largest number of phrasal verbs for each picture. Alternatively, you may assign one picture to each group and have them read their sentences aloud to be checked by the rest of the class.

EXPANSION [20 minutes]

You may want to use Activity 6 (writing reading) on SB page 346 after this exercise. This activity uses students' creative skills to create conversations using phrasal verbs in context.

FOCUS 6 [2 minutes]

1. Lead-in: Use the separable phrasal verbs in Focus Charts 3 and 4 (and the exercises in this unit) to make up (or have students make up) sentences where the separable phrasal verbs should *not* be separated because of a lengthy object (more than

a few words). Alternatively, collect examples of these in students' earlier work in this unit. Examples (phrasal verbs from Focus Chart 3, SB page 333):

> She **called** the meeting for the secretaries and the new employees **off**. Acceptable: She called the meeting off.
> Nancy's mother **threw** all of Nancy's valuable vinyl rock and roll record albums from the 1970s **out**. Acceptable: Nancy's mother **threw** all of Nancy's record albums **out**.

2. Read the examples and explanations in the focus chart.

EXERCISE 9 [20 minutes]

This exercise provides practice in editing skills as well as reviewing the meaning of phrasal verbs already presented in this unit. Students will have to apply different rules for separating (or not separating) phrasal verbs presented in the unit so far.

1. Do the first example with the class. Remind students that some of the sentences are correct. Their task is to identify which ones are incorrect.
2. Have students work individually to read the sentences and remind themselves of the meaning of each verb. Answer any questions about meaning.
3. Then have students work in pairs to correct the sentences.
4. Ask volunteers to call out which answers they are sure of (these can be in any order). They must explain why the word order is incorrect, referring to the relevant grammar rule. Refer to the answer key on LP page 338.
5. Remind students to enter new phrasal verbs in their vocabulary book and to use a variety of strategies for remembering phrasal verbs such as writing synonyms, explanations, and example sentences.

For more practice, use *Grammar Dimensions 2* Workbook page 152, Exercise 6.

EXPANSION [20 minutes]

You may want to use Activity 9 (reflection) on SB page 347 after this exercise. This activity encourages students to develop a variety of strategies for learning phrasal verbs.

FOCUS 7

Phrasal Verbs That Do Not Take Objects

EXAMPLES	EXPLANATION
(a) My roommate's gone on vacation, and I have no idea when he's going to **come back**.	Some phrasal verbs do not take objects. Because they do not take objects, they are inseparable.
(b) Cyril waited for his friends for over an hour but they didn't **show up**.	

Some common phrasal verbs that do not take objects:

PHRASAL VERB	EXAMPLE	MEANING*
Break down	My car **broke down**, so I walked.	Stop working (machine, engine etc.)
Catch on	Some fashions **catch on** right away.	Become popular
Come back	Goodbye, please **come back** soon.	Return
Come to	When I **came to**, I was in the hospital.	Regain consciousness
Eat out	Darlene is too busy to cook, so she usually **eats out**.	Eat in a restaurant
Get by	He doesn't earn much, but he seems to **get by**.	Survive satisfactorily, with limited money
Grow up	His mother **grew up** in Vancouver.	Become an adult
Pass out	When Pat broke her leg in a skiing accident, she **passed out**.	Faint, lose consciousness
Show up	It isn't a good idea to **show up** late for a job interview.	Arrive, appear at a place

*Some of these phrasal verbs may have different meanings in different situations.

---

4. When Sandra called, Graham was out. He tried to <u>call back</u> her, but he couldn't get through because the line was busy.

5. Eli's mother <u>passed</u> last year <u>away</u>. Since she died, he has <u>put</u> the decision about what to do with her house in Brooklyn <u>off</u>.

6. When Sally and the other children arrived at camp, the camp counselor <u>went</u> the rules <u>over</u>. The boys had to wash the dishes and the girls had to <u>put away</u> them.

EXERCISE 10

Go over the sentences you wrote in Exercise 5 on pages 334 and 335. Underline the phrasal verbs you used and separate the particles where you think it is possible.

When you said put it out, did you mean the cat or the fire?

ANSWER KEY

Exercise 9 (cont.) 4. *call back* should be separated—*call her back*—since *her* is a pronoun.

5. *passed away* should stay together since *pass away* is inseparable, *put off* should stay together since the object is too long. 6. *go over* is inseparable, *put away, put away* should be separated - *put them - away- since them is a pronoun.

EXERCISE 10 [5 minutes]

1. Have students do this exercise individually.

2. Then have them pool their results and raise questions only on those items they disagree on.

3. You can also ask students to review and edit the example sentences they have been keeping in the notebooks.

EXPANSION 1 [20 minutes]

To help students learn to identify the grammar of phrasal verbs, it may be a good idea to bring in a set of English-English dictionaries and look up a few of the phrasal verbs presented in this unit.

If you cannot bring in a set of dictionaries, you can copy a page of a dictionary onto an overhead transparency. Ask students to answer these questions:

Is the verb transitive or intransitive? How is this shown?

Is the verb separable or inseparable? How is this shown?

How many meanings does this verb have?

How do you work out which meaning is relevant or important?

Does it have a one-word synonym?

Is it a formal or informal word? In what kinds of contexts is it usually found?

Note: Your dictionary may not provide the answers to all of these questions. Encourage students to get a good English-English dictionary and use reference dictionaries in the library or online to expand their knowledge of grammar and vocabulary.

EXPANSION 2 [20 minutes]

You may want to use Activity 7 (writing) on SB page 347 after this exercise. This activity asks students to write a letter about their recent activities using phrasal verbs.

FOCUS 7 [5 minutes]

1. Lead-in: Read the first two examples in the top of the focus chart. Ask students about the meanings of these verbs (*come back* = return, *show up* = arrive, appear). Ask what the object is (there is no object). Review the difference between transitive and intransitive verbs. Explain that the separable/inseparable distinction does not apply to intransitive verbs because they have no object.

2. Cover the right-hand column in the lower chart and do the same for each example. First, ask students to guess the meaning, then to identify the object. For the first example:

   What is the phrasal verb? (break down)

   *What does **break down** mean? (stop working)*

3. Have students work in pairs to test each other on the meanings of the phrasal verbs presented in this chart. One student can look at the book and ask questions. The other students can close their book and try to remember the meaning. Then they switch roles.

EXERCISE 11

Use phrasal verbs to complete the letter from Nancy to her housemate, Mary.

Replace the underlined words with phrasal verbs from the list below. You may need to change the form of the phrasal verb.

If the phrasal verb can or must be separated, put the particle in the appropriate position. (See the example.) You will need to use some of the phrasal verbs more than once; you may not need to use some of them at all.

run into	talk over	turn down	show up
come over	find out	pick up	get off
hang up	come back	grow up	put on
catch on	pass out	eat out	put off

Mary and Nancy have recently moved to a new city and have just bought a house together. Mary is currently overseas on a business trip, so Nancy has written her a letter, telling her all the news.

Dear Mary,

I miss you! Being alone in this new house is a good experience for me, but at the end of the day I wish you were here to (1) __discuss__ _talk_ ___over___ things ∧ with me. I've been very busy painting the kitchen—you won't recognize the place when you (2) __return__ _come back_ ! However, at the moment it's a terrible mess and there's no way I can cook here yet, so I (3) __eat in restaurants__ _eat out_ every night. You'll be glad to know that there are several excellent Thai restaurants in our neighborhood. It's amazing how Thai food has (4) __become popular__ _caught on_ everywhere in the last few years, isn't it?

Guess what? The other day I (5) __met unexpectedly__ _ran into_ Ruth and Maureen. What a surprise! They (6) __were leaving/departing__ _were getting off_ the bus at the bus stop right by our house. It turns out they were on their way to visit Ruth's grandmother, who lives just around the corner. Ruth's son, Sam, was with them. Actually it was a bit embarrassing because I didn't recognize him at first; you really won't believe how much he (7) __has matured/become an adult__ _has grown up_ since we last saw him.

I (8) __am discovering__ _finding out_ lots of new things about our neighborhood . . . and our neighbors! We'll have to (9) __lower__ _turn down_ the volume on our CD player by 7:30 each night. The neighbors in the green house (10) __arrived here/at this place__ _came over_ , to complain about the noise the other day. They have a 3-month-old baby, so they need it to be quiet so the baby can sleep. We (11) __discussed__ _talked it over_ it in a very "neighborly" way. I

---

told them, though, that you're a night owl, and that night time is the time you like to listen to music. Loud! We decided you'll have to start (12) __wearing__ _putting on_ headphones!

There's a lot more I could say. I can't wait for you to (13) __show up__ _come back_ on time at the airport. This time I promise (14) __I'll arrive__ _return_ on time at the airport. See you soon. . . .

Love,

Nancy

EXERCISE 12

STEP 1   Work with a classmate or a small group. Can you fill in the missing words in this word puzzle to create phrasal verbs? Sometimes the missing word is a particle that can combine with all the attached verbs to make different phrasal verbs; other times, the missing word is a verb that can combine with all the attached particles to make different phrasal verbs. (A good English/English dictionary may help you.)

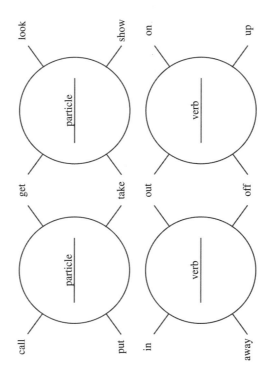

STEP 2   Use each phrasal verb in a sentence, showing that you understand its meaning. State whether the phrasal verb is separable or inseparable.

ANSWER KEY

Step 1 *There are different ways to fill in the puzzle:*

Upper left: *off/up/out* **Lower left:** *put/get/take*

Upper right: *on; up* **Lower right:** *look/put/get*

EXERCISE 11 [20 minutes]

1. Go over the instructions carefully as this exercise is slightly more complicated than the previous ones.

2. Have students read the letter silently first, then match up the verbs in the text and the phrasal verbs in the box.

3. Then have students work in pairs to replace the verbs.

4. Check the answers by having students read the sentences aloud. Refer to the answer key on LP page 342. After each item, ask the other students if they have other comments: *Did they choose another phrasal verb? Are there other ways to say this* (Should the verb + particle be separated/not separated)?

For more practice, use Grammar *Dimensions 2* Workbook page 153, Exercise 7.

EXPANSION [20 minutes]

You may want to use Activity 3 on SB page 343 after this exercise.

EXERCISE 12 [20 minutes]

This exercise is a puzzle that will help students expand and explore different possible combinations of verbs and particles in phrasal verbs.

STEP 1

1. Go over the instructions.

2. Have students work in small groups.

3. One student in each group can be the "secretary" taking note of questions.

4. Distribute an English-English dictionary to each group if possible.

5. Circulate while students are working and answer any questions.

STEP 2

1. Students can compile their sentences in their groups.

2. Regroup as a whole class and ask volunteers to read their sentences aloud (explaining in each case whether the phrasal verb is transitive or intransitive, separable or inseparable).

3. Other members of the class will decide if it is correct.

UNIT GOAL REVIEW [10 minutes]

Ask students to look at the goals on the opening page of the unit again. Refer to the pages of the unit where information on each goal can be found.

 ExamView Test Generator   For assessment of Unit 23, use *Grammar Dimensions 2 ExamView®*.

ACTIVITY 1 speaking

You can either play this game with a classmate or in teams. You need a die/dice to play.

STEP 1
Player (or team) 1 throws the die/dice and selects the verb from circle A that corresponds to the number thrown. For example, if she throws 3, then the verb is *turn*.

STEP 2
Player (or team) 2 throws the die/dice again and selects the particle from circle B that corresponds to the number thrown. For example, if she throws 1, the particle is *off*.

STEP 3
The first player (or team) to come up with a sentence containing the verb + particle, scores a point. For example, the player who comes up with a sentence using *turn off* correctly scores the point. If the combination of verb + particle does not create a meaningful phrasal verb, the first player to say "Impossible" scores the point.

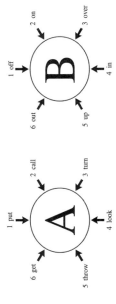

Variation: After you have played this game a few times, get together with some classmates to make your own version. Choose six verbs and six particles. Draw two circles and write the verbs and particles in each circle. Try out your game on your classmates.

If you are playing in a team, you could copy the two circles onto a big piece of paper and stick it on the wall so that everyone can see.

ACTIVITY 2 speaking/listening

STEP 1
Interview three different people. Ask them to describe their typical morning routines, from the moment they wake up until they leave the house to go to work or school. Record their responses.

STEP 2
Listen to what they say. What differences and what similarities do you find? Write down any phrasal verbs that they use. Share your findings with your classmates and your teacher.

ACTIVITY 3 listening

Listen to the audio of native speakers of English describing their early morning routines. What differences and similarities do you find among the speakers? Make a list of the phrasal verbs that the speakers used. Compare your list with a classmate.

CD Track 30

ACTIVITY 4 listening

Your teacher is going to give you a set of instructions. Listen to each instruction; if the instruction contains a phrasal verb, do what your teacher tells you to do. If the instruction does **not** contain a phrasal verb, do nothing. For example, if your teacher says "Stand up," you stand up because *stand up* is a phrasal verb. If your teacher says "Turn to your right," you do nothing at all because *turn* is not a phrasal verb.

Variation: Anyone who follows a command that does not contain a phrasal verb drops out of the game. The last person to remain in the game is the "winner." After a while, give your teacher a rest and take turns giving the commands to the rest of the class.

ANSWER KEY

Activity 3 *See audio script on LP page 6–9 for similarities and differences; answers may vary.*
Phrasal verbs used include: wake up, turn on, get up, put on, go out, get back, turn up, take off, jump in, go into, sit down, put away, turn off, go off, turn over, go back, get out, put off, get up, turn on, put on, run around, get on.

USE YOUR ENGLISH

The Use Your English section of activities at the end of the unit contain situations that should naturally elicit the structures covered in the unit. For a more complete discussion of how to use the Use Your English activities, see To the Teacher, LP page xxii When students are doing these activities in class, you can circulate and listen to see if they are using the structures accurately. Errors can be corrected after the activity has finished.

ACTIVITY 1 speaking [30 minutes]

This activity can be used at any point in the unit. You will need several dice for this game.

■ STEP 1 Demonstrate the game by rolling the dice and choosing a verb from circle A.

■ STEP 2 Then roll the dice again and choose a particle from circle B.

■ STEP 3 Make up a sentence using the phrasal verb you have created. Your sentence can be correct or incorrect. Ask the class to decide.

VARIATION

You can play this game as a whole class all together. Or have students play the game in pairs or in small groups divided into teams. The variation can be used to review this game in another lesson.

ACTIVITY 2 speaking/listening [20 minutes]

You may want to use this activity after Exercise 3 on SB page 332.

1. This activity can be done as an in-class or out-of-class interviewing activity.

2. Start by asking students to come up with questions they could ask.

3. If there are difficulties getting access to an audio-recorder, conduct this activity in small "research teams" (of three to five people): one or two people should ask the questions, designing a set of questions beforehand and/or asking the speaker to elaborate whenever more information is needed.

4. The other people in the team should take notes, writing down every phrasal verb used—and if it's unfamiliar, what the context/meaning is. Having more than one student do this helps to ensure that the data is "complete," since one student may catch what another student has missed.

5. If there isn't a pool of native speakers available in your area, have your students interview people who are proficient in English—people who have studied English for many years, for example, or those that have lived in English-speaking countries.

ACTIVITY 3 listening [20 minutes]

CD Track 30

This is a good follow-up to Activity 2.

1. Explain that students will listen to people describing their daily routines. They should listen first for general meaning and take notes of the main ideas.

2. Play the audio. See audio script on LP page S-9.

3. Students can compare answers in pairs.

4. Play the audio again and have students take notes of phrasal verbs.

5. Refer to the answer key on LP page 344 and review the answers as a class.

ACTIVITY 4 listening [15 minutes]

You may want to use this activity after Exercise 1 on SB page 330.

1. This game is a kind of competition. Students gradually drop out until there is one person left who is the winner.

2. Demonstrate the game first with a few easy examples.

3. Play the game quite slowly at first, speeding up as students get better.

4. After completing one or two rounds of the game, ask a student to be the "teacher" and read out the commands (see below).

5. The following are some instructions to read to students (or make up some of your own). Be sure to mix up the commands with phrasal verbs and those without!

Phrasal verbs: *Stand up. Turn around twice. Turn over that sheet of paper/book. Take off your watch/hat/earring/coat. Clean out/damp out your purse/backpack/pockets. Write down your name. Hand in your assignment for today/yesterday. Put away your (...). Turn on/off the lights. Talk over this activity with (...). and so on.*

<u>Not phrasal verbs:</u> *Say hello to (...). Write your name on the blackboard/that piece of paper. Discuss this activity with (...). Remove your watch/hat/earring/coat. Shut the door/window. Open the window/door.*

ACTIVITY 5   writing/reading

The purpose of this activity is to write a set of instructions for somebody who doesn't know how to make a peanut butter and jelly sandwich. First, look at the bag of supplies that your teacher has brought to class. Then, work with your group to write your instructions, trying to use as many phrasal verbs as possible. When you are ready, read the instructions to your teacher, one step at a time, and he or she will try to follow your instructions exactly as you give them.

ACTIVITY 6   writing/reading

STEP 1 Choose one of the contexts below. What phrasal verbs do you associate with these contexts? Think of as many phrasal verbs as you can for each context and write them in the outer circle around each context. Redraw these context circles with a larger white band in your notebook.

STEP 2 Exchange notebooks with a classmate. Choose one of the contexts and write a dialogue on a piece of paper. Include many of the phrasal verbs he or she has written down.

STEP 3 Exchange your paper with a different classmate. Read the dialogue. Can you guess the context he or she has chosen?

at a library

on an airplane

in a clothes store

at a doctor's office

ACTIVITY 7   writing

Think about everything you have done in the last week. Write a letter to your teacher, telling him or her about your week, **trying to use as many phrasal verbs as possible**. Before you hand your letter in, look it over carefully to find out how many phrasal verbs you were able to use. Write the number of phrasal verbs you used at the end of the letter.

ACTIVITY 8   research on the web

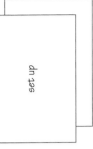

Go on the Internet and use a search engine such as Google® or Yahoo® to find a Web site where you can test your knowledge of phrasal verbs. Enter keywords "test phrasal verbs". Choose one Web site to recommend to your classmates.

ACTIVITY 9   reflection

Choose five phrasal verbs from this unit that you find difficult to remember. Think of a sentence that explains the meaning of each verb. Write each sentence on a card, using a blank instead of the phrasal verb. Write the verb on the back of the card. Use the cards to test yourself or a classmate.

Example:

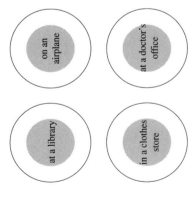

I called all the company directors to find out when they were free so that I could ⸺ a meeting.

set up

USE YOUR ENGLISH

ACTIVITY 5 · writing/reading [20 minutes]

You may want to use this activity after Exercise 2 on SB page 331. You will need to bring the ingredients for a peanut butter and jelly sandwich for this activity (sliced bread, peanut butter, jelly, knife, plate).

1. Lay out the ingredients on your desk, asking students to name each one.

2. Have students work in groups to write their instructions.

3. Set a time limit of 10 minutes.

4. When they are ready, ask a representative from each group to read the instructions aloud.

5. Follow the instructions exactly in order to show whether they are correct or not. This activity can be very funny if you follow your students' instructions to the letter. They are likely to leave out important details. For example: They may say *Put some peanut butter on the bread* but forget to say: *Put the knife in the peanut butter jar.*

ACTIVITY 6 · writing/reading [30 minutes]

You may want to use this activity after Exercise 8 on SB page 338.

■ STEP 1

1. Look at the four circles and ask students to suggest one or two phrasal verbs for each context.

2. Have students continue working individually, writing as many verbs as they can for each circle.

■ STEP 2

Have students exchange books and write dialogues. You can have students perform their dialogues orally, as "real," natural-sounding conversation; the other students can guess the context (in this case you can omit Step 3).

■ STEP 3

Have students exchange dialogues with a different students and guess the context.

ACTIVITY 7 · writing [20–30 minutes]

You may want to use this activity after Exercise 11 on SB page 342.

1. Brainstorm suggestions for what might be included in this letter. Suggest phrasal verbs if appropriate.

2. Have students write a brief outline for the letter and ask them to complete the activity for homework.

3. Use the letters for a peer-editing activity as follows:

   (a) Have students exchange papers with a partner.

   (b) Make sure that they read the description for general meaning: Can they understand everything? Are there points that need clarification or elaboration?

   (c) Then have students check their partner's paper for the number of phrasal verbs used to see if their counts correspond.

   (d) Have students check that the phrasal verbs are used appropriately in terms of both meaning and grammar.

ACTIVITY 8 · research on the web [homework/10 minutes]

You may want to use this activity after Exercise 7 on SB page 337.

The purpose of this Internet search activity is to provide a natural context for using the present perfect. An additional purpose is to encourage students to share strategies for finding information on the Internet. What websites were most useful? You may want to compile a list of useful websites for learning English, based on information from students, and post it on your website, or in your classroom.

ACTIVITY 9 · reflection [15 minutes]

You may want to use this activity after Exercise 9 on SB page 347.

This activity provides an opportunity for students to develop learning strategies for remembering phrasal verbs. You may have asked students to keep a record of their learning in a journal throughout this course as suggested in To the Teacher, LP page xxii. Reflecting on the effectiveness of these and other learning strategies can form part of that learning record.

ADJECTIVE CLAUSES AND PARTICIPLES AS ADJECTIVES

UNIT GOALS

- **Form correct adjective clauses with *who* and *that* to describe people**

- **Use adjective clauses with *which* and *that* to describe things**

- **Understand how to use participles as adjectives**

- **Know the difference between -*ed* and -*ing* participles**

OPENING TASK

Who Do They Love?

■ **STEP 1**

Look at the people in the picture. What are their relationships? Who likes whom?

■ **STEP 2**

Lee, Tracy, Sid, and Kit are in love. Can you find who belongs together? Get together with a partner to read the clues, complete the chart, and solve the puzzle.

CLUES:

1. Lee loves the person who speaks Swahili. O
2. Tracy loves the person who tells amusing stories. O
3. The teacher loves the writer. O
4. The pilot loves the person who is interested in history. O
5. Sid loves the person that plays the piano. O
6. The person who tells amusing stories is a pilot. S
7. The person that runs three miles a day is a doctor. S
8. The person who plays the piano is a teacher. S
9. The person who is interested in history is a doctor. S
10. The doctor loves the person who tells amusing stories. O
11. The person who speaks Swahili is a writer. S
12. The pilot loves the person who runs three miles a day. O

Information about Lee:
- plays the piano _____
- is a teacher _____

LEE
loves...

- the person who speaks Swahili _____
- the writer _____
Name _Sid_

Information about Kit:
- tells amusing stories _____
- is a pilot _____

KIT
loves...

- the person who runs 3 miles a day _____
- the doctor _____
Name _Tracy_

Information about Tracy:
- is interested in history _____
- runs 3 miles a day, is a doctor _____

TRACY
loves...

- the person who tells amusing stories _____
- the pilot _____
Name _Kit_

Information about Sid:
- speaks Swahili _____
- is a writer _____

SID
loves...

- the person who plays the piano _____
- the teacher _____
Name _Lee_

■ **STEP 3**

Complete the sentences. Read them to a partner. Compare answers.

The person ___who___ loves Lee is ___Sid___. The person ___who___ loves Kit is ___Tracy___.

The person ___whom___ Sid loves is ___Lee___. The person ___whom___ Tracy loves is ___Kit___.

(Opening Task, Step 3 solution found on page A-18)

LESSON PLAN 1

UNIT OVERVIEW

Unit 24 introduces the grammar of adjective clauses. In addition, it addresses the difference between past (*bored, tired*) and present (*boring, tiring*) participles when used as adjectives.

UNIT GOALS

Some instructors may want to review the goals listed on Student Book (SB) page 348 after completing the Opening Task so that students understand what they should know by the end of the unit. These goals can also be reviewed at the end of the unit when students are more familiar with the grammar terminology.

GRAMMAR NOTE

Adjective clauses (also known as relative clauses) are a way of adding information about the subject or object of a sentence and embedding it into the original sentence structure. Using such clauses will help students become more descriptive than they can be using only simple adjectives like *nice, tall,* and *unusual.* The grammar of adjective clauses includes using the correct word order, the correct relative pronoun, and agreement between the subject of the main clause and the verb in the adjective clause. Some languages (e.g., Japanese) place adjective clauses before the relevant noun. Other languages (e.g., Arabic) repeat the pronoun in the adjective clause. Such differences can interfere with fluency and accuracy in the use of adjective clauses.

OPENING TASK [20 minutes]

The purpose of the Opening Task is to create a context in which students will need to use the adjective clauses. The problem-solving format is designed to show the teacher how well the students can use the target structures implicitly and spontaneously when they are engaged in a

communicative task. For a more complete discussion of the purpose of the Opening Task, see To the Teacher, Lesson Planner (LP) page xxii.

Setting Up the Task

▪ STEP 1

1. Have students look at the photograph and ask them to decide what relationship the people have to each other.
2. Explain that there are four people: Lee, Tracy, Sid, and Kit. The problem is to figure out who loves whom.

Conducting the Task

▪ STEP 2

1. Quickly read the clues aloud.
2. Model how to complete the chart. Read the first clue and have the students look at Lee's box and read: "the person who speaks Swahili" on the line below "LEE loves . . . ."
3. Put students into pairs or groups of three to solve the problem.
4. While they are working, circulate around the room and make sure they understand the task. Also, note problems they have using the structures that will be practiced in this unit.
5. Before students finish, draw the chart on the board.
6. Refer to the answer key on LP page 348. Bring the class together and have the students tell you where to fill in the information.

Closing the Task

▪ STEP 3

1. Point out the grammatical structures used to describe the people who are loved.

2. If they have a question about *who* or *that plays the piano,* note that both of these expressions can refer to people, as they will learn in Focus Chart 1.
3. Have students complete the sentences.
4. Check the answers as a class on page A-18 of the student book.
5. Students will return to the task in Exercise 1 on SB page 350.

GRAMMAR NOTE

Typical student errors (form)

- Using *which* in clauses about people, e.g. * *He's the man which plays the piano.* (See Focus 1.)
- Repeating the subject in adjective clauses, e.g. * *He's the man who he plays the piano.* * *This is the book which I wanted to read it.* (See Focus 1.)
- Lack of agreement between subject and verb in adjective clause, e.g. * *He's the man who play the piano.* (See Focus 1.)
- Using *who* in clauses about things, e.g. * *This is the book who I wanted to read.* (See Focus 2.)

Typical student errors (use)

- Not using adjective clauses especially in written work, e.g. * *My sister plays the piano. The piano is in our living room.* (instead of: My sister plays the piano which/that is in our living room.) (See Exercise 5.)

FOCUS 1

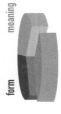

form   meaning

Adjective Clauses: Using *Who* and *That* to Describe People

EXAMPLES	EXPLANATIONS
(a) The person **who speaks Swahili** is a writer.	Restrictive adjective clauses (also known as relative clauses) give identifying information about a noun.
(b) The pilot loves the person **who runs three miles a day.**	
(c) The person **who plays the piano** is a teacher. OR	Adjective clauses begin with a relative pronoun. To refer to people, you can use the relative pronouns *who* or *that*. *That* is more commonly used in informal conversation than in writing.
(d) The person **that plays the piano** is a teacher.	
(e) Sid loves the person **who plays the piano.** OR	Every adjective clause contains a verb.
(f) Sid loves the person **that plays the piano.**	
Subject (g) **The person** who tells amusing stories is a pilot.	An adjective clause can describe the subject or object of the main clause.
Object (h) Lee loves **the person** who speaks Swahili.	

EXERCISE 1

Go back to the clues in the Opening Task on page 348.

a. Underline every adjective clause you find.

b. Circle every relative pronoun.

c. Draw an arrow to connect the relative pronoun with the noun it describes.

d. Write "S" if the adjective clause describes the subject of a sentence. Write "O" if it describes the object.

Example: The pilot loves the person ⟶ who runs three miles a day. O

EXERCISE 2

Get together with a partner and look over the information in the chart below. The owners of the houses on this block of Upham Street are all women.

HOUSE	HABITS	LIKES	DISLIKES	PLACE OF BIRTH	OCCUPATION
1.	swims three times a week	dogs	TV	Manchester	lawyer
2.	eats out every night	fast cars	baseball	Madrid	marketing manager
3.	lifts weights	music	politics	Miami	marketing manager
4.	drinks five cups of coffee a day	cats	ballet	Mexico City	lawyer
5.	sings in the shower	art	baseball	Montreal	marketing manager
6.	walks to work	movies	basketball	Moscow	lawyer

Use the information in the chart to make as many true statements as you can about the owners of these houses, using adjective clauses. We have started the first ones for you.

1. The woman who ___*likes dogs*___ lives next to the woman who ___.

2. The lawyer that ___*dislikes ballet*___ lives between the marketing manager who ___ and the marketing manager who ___.

3. The marketing manager who ___ lives between the lawyer that ___ and the marketing manager who ___.

4. The woman ___.

ANSWER KEY

Exercise 1   *See answers on LP page 348.*
Exercise 2   *Answers will vary.*

24 LESSON PLAN 1

FOCUS 1 [10 minutes]

1. **Lead-in:** Write the first example sentence on the board. "The person who speaks Swahili is a writer." Ask: What is the subject of this sentence? (the person) What information do we know about the subject? (He or she speaks Swahili and he or she is a writer.) What is the main information? (He is a writer.) What is the extra additional information? (He speaks Swahili). Underline the adjective clause (who speaks Swahili). Explain that adjective clause adds extra information about the subject—example (a)—or the object —example (b).

2. Students can be confused about the difference between the main verb of the sentence and the verb in the clause.

3. Pay special attention to the focus chart examples (g) and (h). Give them extra examples of difference between subject and object clauses from the class, circling or underlining the main verbs of the sentences:

Subject:

The student that is from Spain can dance flamenco beautifully.

Your classmates who have lived in the United States for a short time may be experiencing culture shock.

Object:

Jorge helped the student who/that sits next to him with her homework.

Do you know anyone who is from Singapore?

EXERCISE 1 [10 minutes]

This exercise allows students to return to the sentences in the Opening Task and analyze them by applying the information from Focus chart 1.

1. Allow time for students to work individually.

2. Ask volunteers to write a few examples on the board. Be sure to include some object and some subject clauses.

3. If necessary, further model this exercise with some of the examples from the focus chart.

work book

For more practice, use *Grammar Dimensions 2* Workbook page 154, Exercise 1.

LANGUAGE NOTE

This unit deals only with restrictive adjective clauses. The grammar of nonrestrictive clauses is presented in Book 3, Unit 12. Relative pronouns *which, who,* and *that* are presented in this unit. There are two additional relative pronouns, *whom* and *whose. Whose* is used instead of *his, her,* or *its.* For example, *That is the girl whose sister went to Egypt.* (= That is the girl. Her sister went to Egypt.) *Whom* is used as an object pronoun for people. For example, *She is the girl whom I love. Whom* is used in formal English; *who* is more common in everyday speech and in written English. The grammar of *whose* and *whom* is also presented in Book 3, Unit 12.

EXERCISE 2

1. This exercise is a logic-solving puzzle similar to the one in the Opening Task.

2. Copy this exercise onto an overhead transparency.

3. Complete the first example together with the class.

4. Have students complete the exercise in pairs.

5. When they are finished, have them compare answers with another pair.

6. Answers will vary. Refer to the answer key on LP page 350 for suggested answers.

7. The last part of the exercise can also be done as a peer-editing task.

EXPANSION [20 minutes]

At this point it may be helpful to provide some further practice in distinguishing subject from object adjective clauses (see Language Note on LP page 353).

Have students work in pairs to combine the following sentences using relative pronouns. Then identify which ones are subject and which are object pronouns.

1. *He's the teacher. He taught us last year.*
2. *This is the dictionary. It helps me with my phrasal verbs.*
3. *Where's the book? I gave it to you yesterday.*
4. *Isabel and Rita are the women. They are going to Argentina.*
5. *Francisco is the man. He works in a computer store.*
6. *Where are the keys? I left them on the desk this morning.*
7. *This is the man. I met him in the coffee shop last week.*
8. *That is the car. I sold it to Alberto last year.*

LANGUAGE NOTE

A point which may come up when asking students to combine sentences in this way is that nouns may not be defined twice in the sentence. For example, *He is our teacher. He taught us last year.* When these two sentences are combined, the word *our* must be replaced by *the,* since the adjective clause now defines the word *teacher.*

5. The lawyer _____

6. The marketing manager _____

7. _____

8. _____

9. _____

10. _____

Look back at the sentences you have written. Underline the adjective clauses, circle the relative pronouns, and draw arrows to the appropriate nouns (as you did in Exercise 1).

form

use

FOCUS 2 *Which and That*

EXAMPLES	EXPLANATIONS
(a) I bought a book **which** I really wanted to read. OR (b) I bought a book **that** I really wanted to read. (c) The book **which** he wrote is excellent. OR (d) The book **that** he wrote is excellent.	To refer to things in adjective clauses, you can use *which* or *that*. *That* is more common in informal conversation than in writing.

EXERCISE 3

Do this exercise with a group of five or six classmates. Complete the chart below. This chart is like the one in Exercise 2, except for the first category. Decide on who will be Student #1. Then use your positions in the group seating arrangement to finish writing your names in column 1.

STUDENT NAME	HABITS	LIKES	DISLIKES	PLACE OF BIRTH	OCCUPATION OR DESIRED OCCUPATION
1.					
2.					
3.					
4.					
5.					
6.					

STEP 1 Interview each other to fill in the blanks on the chart. Feel free to make up your answers, just for fun.

STEP 2 When you have filled in your charts, make clues about each person in the chart using adjective clauses in your statements. The other students will guess who you are talking about.

Example: *She is sitting between the person who likes ice cream and the person who wants to be a doctor.*

ANSWER KEY

Exercise 3   *Answers will vary.*

ADJECTIVE CLAUSES AND PARTICIPLES AS ADJECTIVES

EXPANSION [20 minutes]

You may want to use Activity 4 on SB page 360 (listening) after Exercise 2.

FOCUS 2 [5 minutes]

1. **Lead-in:** Write examples (a) and (c) on the board. Ask students to identify the subject, the verb, and the adjective clause. Is the adjective clause about the subject or the object? Which is better, *which* or *that*? (The answer is in the chart.)

2. As with Focus Chart 1, these adjective clauses can be in the subject or object position of the sentences.

EXPANSION [20 minutes]

1. To create examples of subject and object adjective clauses, display a map of the world or project one copied onto an overhead transparency.

2. Be sure students are close enough to see the map and that they are familiar with the points on the compass.

3. Tell students that they should guess which country you are talking about based on your description of the country.

4. For each country make a statement such as:

   I am looking at the country which is east of the Czech Republic.

   The country that is south of India is an island.

5. After students guess correctly, write each of your examples on the board.

For more practice, use *Grammar Dimensions 2* Workbook pages 155 and 156, Exercise 2.

LANGUAGE NOTE

It will be helpful later for students to be able to distinguish between subject and object adjective clauses. A more advanced grammar point (not mentioned in this unit) is that relative pronouns can be omitted in restrictive clauses if the pronoun refers to the object of the sentence. For example, *He's the man who (that or whom) I met yesterday.→ He's the man I met yesterday.* To understand this point, students need to be able to distinguish object from subject relative clauses and restrictive from nonrestrictive clauses.

EXERCISE 3 [20 minutes]

This exercise allows for some personalization of the grammar of adjective clauses.

1. Refer students back to Exercise 2 on SB page 351 for the format of this chart.

2. Have students work in groups of five or six.

3. Explain that they will fill in information about themselves and each other (it does not need to be true). All students in the group will fill in the same information.

4. Step 1: Students interview each other.

5. Step 2: Students use the information to make clues about each person.

EXPANSION [20 minutes]

You may want to use Activity 3 on SB page 360 (speaking) after this exercise.

EXERCISE 4

STEP 1 Complete the following to make true statements about yourself. Try to describe both people and things in your statements. Circle the appropriate relative pronouns. (More than one relative pronoun may be possible.)

1. I am bored by people that _____ which _____ .
who

2. I am interested in _____ which _____ .
that
who

3. I am frightened of _____ which _____ .
that
who

4. _____ which _____ are really annoying.
that
who

5. _____ that _____ is/are often interesting.
which
who

STEP 2 Get together with a partner and compare your statements. Be ready to share the most interesting or surprising statements with the rest of the class.

EXERCISE 5

Edit the following story. Use relative pronouns whenever possible to avoid repeating words, as in the example. After you have finished editing the passage, compare your suggestions for changes with a classmate's. (There is sometimes more than one way to make improvements and avoid repetition.)

1. It's interesting talking with women. ~~These women~~ have had experiences.
who
~~Their experiences~~ are similar to mine. There are a lot of things to talk about.
which

2. For example, *balance* is a topic. Most of my women friends are interested in this topic.

3. Achieving balance is a challenge for many women. Many women have jobs and family responsibilities.

4. Some women don't have jobs outside their homes. These women sometimes feel criticized. They feel criticized by other people.

5. These people think that women should have careers. This is an attitude. More and more people share this attitude.

6. Some women work at jobs and have young children. These women also feel criticized. They feel criticized by other people.

7. Other people think that all women should stay at home with their children. They should never be sent to a day care center. Day care is a business, not a loving home. This is a belief. This belief makes some women feel a lack of balance in their lives.

8. Some women never have children. These women may feel pressure from their own parents. Their own parents worry that their children won't provide them with grandchildren.

9. These are examples. These examples show how it can be difficult for women to feel sure they are doing the right thing for themselves and for their children.

form
meaning

Participles as Adjectives

EXAMPLES	EXPLANATIONS
(a) People who have traveled to many different countries are often very **interesting**.	*Interesting* and *amused* are participles formed by adding *-ing/-ed* to a verb. These participles act like adjectives when they modify nouns.
(b) We were very amused by the jokes that Bruce told us.	
(c) Professor Rand is very knowledgeable, but his lectures are **boring**. *(source/boring)*	Adjectives that end with *-ing* usually describe the source (the thing or person that makes us feel a certain way).
(d) Many students were bored during Professor Rand's lecture. *(emotion/bored)*	Adjectives that end with *-ed* usually describe the emotion (how we feel about something).

ANSWER KEY

Exercise 4 Answers will vary.

Exercise 5 There may be some variety in how this passage is rewritten. The following is one way:

1. It's interesting talking with women who have had experiences which are similar to mine since there are a lot of things to talk about. 2. and 3. For example, *balance* is a topic which/that most of my women friends are interested in, since achieving balance is a challenge for many women who have jobs and family responsibilities. 4. Women who don't have jobs outside of their homes sometimes feel

more and more people share. 6. Women who work at jobs and have young children also feel criticized by other people who think that all women should stay at home with their children. 7. Some people believe that children should never be sent to a day care center, which is a business, not a loving home. This is a belief which/that makes some women feel a lack of balance in their lives. 8. Women who never have children may feel pressure from their own parents, who worry that their children won't provide them with grandchildren. 9. These are examples that show how it can be difficult for women

EXERCISE 4 [20 minutes]

This exercise allows some more space for personalization of the grammar in this unit.

STEP 1

1. If possible, copy this exercise on an overhead transparency.
2. Model the first example with statements about yourself. Have students choose the relative pronoun for you.
3. Allow time for students to complete Step 1.
4. While they are working, circulate around the room to see if they need any help.

STEP 2

1. Have students compare their answers in pairs.
2. Ask volunteers to share the most interesting answers with the class.

EXERCISE 5 [20 minutes]

This exercise provides practice in editing skills essential for improving written work.

1. In class, have pairs—preferably of different language backgrounds—work without dictionaries.
2. Instruct them to read through the text first, helping each other with unfamiliar vocabulary.
3. After pairs edit the passage, review the exercise on an overhead transparency. Encourage alternative versions.

EXPANSION [20 minutes]

You may want to use Activity 2 (writing/reading) on SB page 360 after this exercise.

LESSON PLAN 2

FOCUS 3 [10 minutes]

1. Lead-in: Introduce this topic by bringing in pictures of people with different expressions on their faces (see Exercise 6 for a list of adjectives). Ask students to try to describe the different expressions using adjectives.
2. Ask students to try to describe the different expressions using adjectives.
3. Use student examples to introduce the grammar point.
4. Read the examples and the explanations in the focus chart.

GRAMMAR NOTE

The difference between *-ing* and *-ed* adjectives often causes trouble. Comparing these adjective forms with their verb counterparts can be a helpful illustration. For example:

Active present progressive → present participle:

Martin is interesting his classmates with stories of his trip to Belgium.

→ Martin is interesting.

Passive→ past participle:

Boukar was confused by the lecturer's use of technical terms.

→ Boukar was confused.

EXERCISE 6

STEP 1 In the pictures below, draw arrows that start at the source (the reason for the feeling) and that point to the emotion (the way the person feels).

STEP 2 Then use the word (on the right) to label the pictures with *-ing* adjectives (which describe the source) and *-ed* adjectives (which describe the emotion). The first one has been done for you.

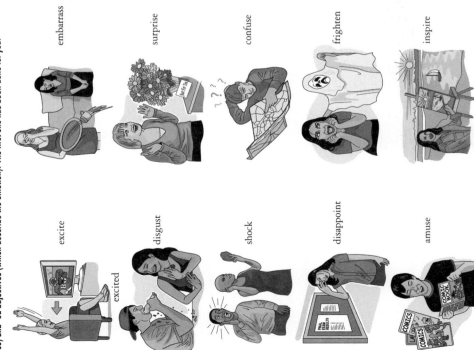

excite

excited

disgust

shock

disappoint

amuse

embarrass

surprise

confuse

frighten

inspire

ANSWER KEY

Exercise 6 *Step 2:* Order of answers: Left to right, down the page: <u>exciting</u> TV show, <u>excited</u> man ◆ <u>embarrassing</u> accident, <u>embarrassed</u> woman ◆ man's <u>disgusting</u> eating habits, <u>disgusted</u> woman ◆ <u>surprising</u> gift, <u>surprised</u> woman ◆ <u>shocking</u> haircut, <u>shocked</u> man ◆ <u>confusing</u> map, <u>confused</u> man ◆ <u>disappointing</u> exam results, <u>disappointed</u> woman ◆ <u>frightening</u> ghost, <u>frightened</u> woman ◆ <u>amusing</u> comics, <u>amused</u> man ◆ <u>inspiring</u> view, <u>inspired</u> woman

---

EXERCISE 7

Circle the correct adjective for each of the following sentences.

1. Melanie likes the family in the apartment above her, but sometimes she feels that their teenage boy is (annoying)/annoyed, especially when he plays his stereo too loudly.

2. However, she usually finds their presence upstairs very (comforting)/comforted.

3. Once she heard a (frightening)/frightened noise outside. She thought it was a prowler, so she called up her neighbors.

4. They invited her to their apartment for a (relaxing)/relaxed cup of tea and a (soothing)/soothed conversation.

5. This helped her to calm down until she was no longer frightening/(frightened).

6. Melanie especially likes Jane, the mother. Jane tells Melanie (amusing)/amused stories about herself and her family members' daily life.

7. Jane's husband Bob is a shoe salesperson. Even though this may sound like a (boring)/bored job, it's not.

8. Lots of (surprising)/surprised things happen to shoe salespeople. Just last week, for example, a real prince came into the store with his bodyguards and bought twenty pairs of Italian leather shoes.

9. The prince thought Bob was such a polite and (amusing)/amused person that he gave him a fifty-dollar tip.

10. Of course, Bob thought that this was very (exciting)/excited, and he took Jane and the family out to dinner that night.

11. Jane works part-time in a pet store as a dog groomer. She says that some of the customers never give their dogs baths. These dogs are sometimes so dirty and uncomfortable that it is (shocking)/shocked.

12. Jane's stories are so (entertaining)/entertained that Melanie usually doesn't mind the noise that Jane's teenage son makes.

13. In fact, Melanie was very disappointing/(disappointed) when she heard that Jane and her family might move.

EXERCISE 6 [15 minutes]

This exercise practices the difference between -ed and -ing adjectives using a variety of adjectives.

STEP 1

1. Go over the first example with the class.
2. Have students work in pairs to draw arrows.

STEP 2

1. Have students write the correct word under the picture.
2. Check the answers using an overhead transparency if possible. Refer to the answer key on LP page 356.
3. Extend this exercise by asking students for other examples of situations where these adjectives would be appropriate.

For more practice, use *Grammar Dimensions 2* Workbook page 156, Exercise 3.

EXPANSION [20 minutes]

You may want to use Activity 1 (speaking/ listening/writing) on SB page 359 after this exercise.

EXERCISE 7 [15 minutes]

1. Do the first sentence as a class.
2. Tell students to read though the whole exercise first to get a sense of the story.
3. Have students work independently or in pairs to complete the exercise.
4. Refer to the answer key on LP page 356 and review the answers as a class.

For more practice, use *Grammar Dimensions 2* Workbook page 157, Exercise 4.

EXPANSION [20 minutes]

You may want to use Activity 5 (listening/speaking) and Activity 6 (speaking) on SB page 361 after this exercise. These activities use guessing and miming to practice -ing and -ed adjectives.

EXERCISE 8

Circle all the *-ed* and *-ing* adjectives in the following passage. Then decide whether the correct form has been used. In other words, are there cases where the *-ing* adjective is used when the *-ed* adjective should be used (or vice versa)?

SHELLEY'S ANCESTORS

Shelley had an (interested) day yesterday. Three of her favorite cousins dropped in for an (unexpected) visit, and they had a very (stimulating) conversation. They told each other (surprised) stories about some of their relatives. Shelley was (shocked) by some of these stories. For example, when their great aunt—their grandmother's sister—was quite young, she traveled around the world, fell in love with a Dutch sailor, and had a baby but did not get married. Her (embarrassing) parents disowned her, but many years later they helped her raise the child. Another distant member of the family was a drug addict in New York in the thirties, and according to Shelley's cousins' mother, he was quite a rude and (disgusting) fellow. This man's brother was a horse of a different color, though. Apparently he was an (inspired) and (talented) artist, who also created (amused) illustrations for children's books. After hearing all of these stories, Shelley realized that her family history was certainly not (bored!)

Use Your English

ACTIVITY 1 speaking/listening/writing

CAN YOU TOP THAT?

- **STEP 1** Look at the list of adjectives below and choose one that describes an experience you have had (for example, an embarrassing moment, a boring day, an exciting date). Try to remember how you felt as a result.

embarrassing	disgusting	frightening	boring
horrifying	rewarding	exciting	entertaining
disappointing	surprising	relaxing	shocking
annoying	amusing	exhausting	inspiring

- **STEP 2** Circulate for fifteen minutes and exchange experiences with classmates to find out if they have had an experience that "tops" yours—that is, an experience that is even more embarrassing, more boring, or more exciting than yours.

- **STEP 3** Report to the rest of the class on what you found. Vote on who has had the most embarrassing, boring, exciting (etc.) experience.

- **STEP 4** Choose two of the experiences that your classmates told you about and describe them in writing.

- **STEP 5** When you finish writing, read your work and circle any participles used as adjectives. Underline any adjective clauses that you used.

ANSWER KEY

Exercise 8 *interested* should be *interesting*   *unexpected, stimulating*—OK   *surprised* should be *surprising*   *shocked*—OK   *embarrassing* should be *embarrassed*   *disgusting*—OK   *inspired, talented*—OK   *amused* should be *amusing*   *bored* should be *boring*

■ EXERCISE 8 [20 minutes]

1. Start this exercise as a class, looking at the first sentence for possible errors. The rest of this exercise can be done for homework.

2. Bring to class enough transparency pens and copies of the passage on overhead transparencies for each pair.

3. Distribute one pen and transparency to each pair, and have them complete the exercise on the transparency itself.

4. Call on different pairs to come to the front of the class and review two or three of their sentences at a time, working through the text. Three or four pairs will be needed to complete the whole text.

5. As one pair discusses their answers, the other students use their answers to determine if the sentences are correct or not. Refer to the answer key on LP page 358.

EXPANSION [20–40 minutes]

You may want to use Activity 7 (research on the web) and Activity 8 (reflection) on SB page 361 as a way to close this unit.

■ UNIT GOAL REVIEW [10 minutes]

Ask students to look at the goals on the opening page of the unit again. Refer to the pages of the unit where information on each goal can be found. Can they use the relative pronouns correctly? What is the difference between -ed and -ing forms of adjectives?

For assessment of Unit 24, refer to *Grammar Dimensions 2 ExamView®*.

■ STEP 5

Have students edit their own work or exchange stories in order to peer-edit. Collect students' work for teacher feedback (see Methodology Note below).

METHODOLOGY NOTE

To focus on the structure covered in this unit, separate your writing feedback into two sections. In one section, only provide specific correction and feedback on errors made on this unit's structures. Other repeated errors can be commented on in a "general feedback" section or paragraph.

USE YOUR ENGLISH

The Use Your English section of activities at the end of the unit contain situations that should naturally elicit the structures covered in the unit. For a more complete discussion of how to use the Use Your English activities, see To the Teacher, LP page xxii. When students are doing these activities in class, you can circulate and listen to see if they are using the structures accurately. Errors can be corrected after the activity has finished.

ACTIVITY 1   speaking/listening/writing [40 minutes]

You may want to use this activity after Exercise 6 on SB page 356.

■ STEP 1

Allow a few minutes for students to choose an adjective and think of a story. Allowing more time at this stage will make the stories more interesting.

■ STEP 2

Have students walk around and share stories. Play music in the background if you feel this will help make a more relaxed atmosphere.

■ STEP 3

Ask volunteers to share the most interesting or surprising stories with the class.

■ STEP 4

Allow a few minutes for students to write their descriptions.

ACTIVITY 2 writing/reading

STEP 1 Think of a person that everyone in your class knows (someone famous or someone in your class!). Or think of a thing or object that is familiar to everyone. Write three statements using adjective clauses that describe this person or thing.

I'm thinking of something that I drink every day. It's something that is more expensive now than it used to be. It's something that helps me feel more awake. (Answer: coffee)

STEP 2 Read your statements one at a time and have others guess what or who you are describing. Work in pairs or in teams if you prefer.

ACTIVITY 3 speaking

Think of someone that you know. Choose someone who is quite a character. In other words, think of someone who stands out in some way or is easy to remember. Describe this person, using some adjective clauses and some *-ed* or *-ing* adjectives to describe him or her.

ACTIVITY 4 listening

CD Track 31

STEP 1 Make a list of all the characteristics you would like to find in the ideal partner (spouse, girlfriend, boyfriend, companion).

STEP 2 Listen to the audio. You will hear three friends talking about their ideal partners. Take notes about their ideas.

STEP 3 Look at the list you made in Step 1 and compare it with the notes you made from the tape. How many differences and similarities can you find?

STEP 4 Listen to the audio again. Write down any examples of adjective clauses and participle adjectives that you hear in your notebook.

ACTIVITY 5 listening/speaking

First think of as many -ing adjectives as possible. Your teacher will write each of these on a separate sheet of paper. As your game goes on, your group may add more to the list as needed. You will use these words to play Password in teams or in pairs. In this game, one person (or team), the Clue-Giver, looks at the word on the piece of paper without letting the other person (or the other team) see it.

Then the Clue-Giver gives a one-word clue that describes this word to the other person (or the other team), the Clue-Guesser. The Clue-Guesser can continue to give as many clues as needed in order for the word to be guessed. The goal is to have the Clue-Guesser guess the word as soon as possible with as few clues as necessary.

ACTIVITY 6 speaking

Think of as many *-ed* adjectives as possible. Then "mime" (act out) these words and phrases, which are written on separate sheets of paper. You can use gestures and facial expressions, or you can invent a silent story, but you cannot speak. The goal is to have the other person (or the other team) guess the word or phrase as quickly as possible.

ACTIVITY 7 research on the web

InfoTrac® College Edition: Choose a pair of participle adjectives (an *-ed* adjective and an *-ing* adjective)—for example, *frightened / frightening* (see p. 356 for some other examples). Search *InfoTrac®* for articles containing these words in the title or in the article content. Choose five different examples. Write down the sentence where the adjective occurred and the topic of the article. Compare answers with your classmates.

ACTIVITY 8 reflection

Choose three pairs of participle adjectives (an *-ed* adjective and an *-ing* adjective) that you find difficult to remember. Make up one sentence using both adjectives.

Example: *The new movie was interesting and my friends were all interested in my opinion of it.*

ANSWER KEY

Activity 4 Check audio script on LP page S-9 for answers.

USE YOUR ENGLISH

ACTIVITY 2 writing/reading [20 minutes]

You may want to use this activity after Exercise 4 on SB page 354. This activity uses written work in order to focus on accuracy.

STEP 1

Read the example aloud and ask students to guess the answer. Then have students write their own clues.

STEP 2

1. Ask students to read their clues aloud so the class can guess.
2. If people are having trouble guessing correctly, the first person can provide hints in the form of other sentences (following the same structure).
3. Make notes of any errors for later discussion.
4. Keep some examples of this written work for use in your next class.

ACTIVITY 3 speaking [30 minutes]

You may want to use this activity after Exercise 3 on SB page 353. This can be done as either a speaking or as a writing activity or both.

1. Start this activity by brainstorming a number of adjectives to describe people. Or you may want to choose certain well-known personalities in the media and have students think of adjectives to describe them.
2. Allow time for students to make notes before telling the class about their chosen person.
3. If possible, have students record themselves for later analysis of their use of the targeted adjectives and adjective clauses.

ACTIVITY 4 listening [20 minutes]

CD
Track
31

You may want to use this activity after Exercise 2 on SB page 351.

STEP 1

Brainstorm adjectives or personal qualities for an ideal girl or boyfriend. Have students make their own individual lists or make a class list of the top five characteristics.

STEP 2

Play the audio. See audio script on LP page S-9.

STEP 3

Have students compare their notes from Step 1.

STEP 4

1. Play the audio again. Identify the target grammar structures.
2. Check the answers by referring to the audio script on LP page S-9.

ACTIVITY 5 listening/speaking [20 minutes]

You may want to use this activity after Exercise 6 on SB page 356.

1. You will need pre-cut blank pieces of paper.
2. Ask students to brainstorm -ing adjectives and write each one on a separate paper.
4. Model the game with you as the Clue-Giver and the whole class as Clue-Guessers to ensure they know what to do.
4. If using teams, assign one person on each team to keep score. This will help settle any disputes that may come up.

ACTIVITY 6 speaking [20 minutes]

You may want to use this activity after Exercise 7 on SB page 357.

1. You will need pre-cut blank pieces of paper.
2. Ask students to brainstorm -ed adjectives and write each one on a separate paper.
3. Model the activity with you as the Clue-Giver and the class guessing.
4. If using teams, assign one person on each team to keep score. This will help settle any disputes that may come up.

ACTIVITY 7 research on the web [20 minutes/homework]

You may want to use this activity after Exercise 8 on SB page 358.

The purpose of this Internet search activity is to encourage students to research natural contexts where participle adjectives are used. An additional purpose is to encourage students to learn how to use *InfoTrac®College Edition* as a resource. See To the Teacher, LP page xxii, for more information on how to use InfoTrac effectively.

ACTIVITY 8 speaking/listening [30 minutes]

You may want to use this activity after Exercise 8 on SB page 358.

This activity provides an opportunity for students to use the target structures of the unit to develop learning strategies. You may have asked students to keep a record of their learning in a journal throughout this course as suggested in To the Teacher, LP page xxii.

UNIT GOALS

- Know when to use hypothetical conditionals

- Form correct conditional sentences for present, past, and future situations

- Know the difference between future conditionals and hypothetical conditionals

- Understand the meaning of *would*, *might*, and *may* in conditionals

OPENING TASK

Imaginary Situations

■ STEP 1

Imagine you are on a desert island. What things would you need to survive? Discuss with a partner and make a list.

■ STEP 2

Get together with a partner and look at each object very carefully. What would you do with them on a desert island?

Example: *If I had a knife, I would......*

IF I ...	I WOULD ...
have / a knife	If I had a knife, I would use it to cut wood for a fire.
see / ship	If I saw a ship, I would try to make a fire so they would see the smoke.
find / human footprints	If I found human footprints, I would follow them to find out who it was/who they belonged to.
not have / water	If I didn't have any water, I would get juice from fruit or plants.
meet / another survivor	If I met another survivor, I would work with him or her to make a plan/escape/build a shelter/get help.

■ STEP 3

Share your ideas with the rest of the class. Vote on the most interesting and creative ideas.

(Opening Task Step 2 Solution found on page A-18)

ANSWER KEY

Opening Task Answer will vary. Possible answers are listed above.

25 LESSON PLAN 1

UNIT OVERVIEW

Unit 25 provides practice with future, hypothetical, and factual conditionals.

GRAMMAR NOTE

Conditionals are clauses that start with *If*, or sentences that include a clause starting with *If*. Traditional grammars teach four types of conditionals: factual conditionals (simple present in both clauses), future conditionals (simple present and will + verb), hypothetical conditionals (simple past and would + verb), and past hypothetical conditionals (past perfect and would + have + verb). The tenses of these different types of conditionals can also be mixed ('mixed conditionals"). The main difficulty for learners is to remember the sequence of tenses and to understand that the past tense in hypothetical and past hypothetical conditionals do not refer to real past events, but to imaginary situations. The use of the past tense indicates a distancing from reality, which makes these events less likely in the view of the speaker.

UNIT GOALS

Some instructors may want to review the goals listed on Student Book (SB) page 362 after completing the Opening Task so that students understand what they should know by the end of the unit. These goals can also be reviewed at the end of the unit when students are more familiar with the grammar terminology.

OPENING TASK [20 minutes]

The purpose of the Opening Task is to create a context in which students will need to use hypothetical conditionals. The problem-solving format is designed to show the teacher how well students can use the target structures implicitly and spontaneously when they are engaged in a communicative task. For a more complete discussion

of the purpose of the Opening Task, see To the Teacher, Lesson Planner (LP) page xxii.

Setting Up the Task

■ STEP 1

1. Use the picture to check understanding of the phrase *desert island* and to explain the task situation.
2. Brainstorm ideas in pairs or as a class about what things would be essential for survival on a desert island.
3. Pairs report back and have class try to reach a consensus on the ten most important items.
4. Write the list on the board.

Conducting the Task

■ STEP 2

1. Have students work in pairs to look at the pictures and discuss what they would do in each situation.
2. Circulate while students are working but do not correct errors at this stage.
3. Have students make notes of what they *would* do. Students may or may not write in complete sentences at this point.
4. Take notes of student errors for use later in the unit.

Closing the Task

■ STEP 3

1. Ask a few volunteers to tell the class their ideas.
2. You don't need to focus on any errors in form at this point.
3. Vote on the most interesting and creative ideas.

Note: Exercise 1 gives students the opportunity to review what they wrote in Step 2 and focus on accuracy.

GRAMMAR NOTE

Typical student errors (form)

- Errors in word order with question forms, e.g. * *What you would do if you were on a desert island?* (See Focus 1.)
- Errors in sequence of tenses, e.g. * *If I would be on a desert island, I need water.* (See Focus 1.) * *If you helped me, I would have passed the exam.* (See Focus 2.)
- Errors in use of commas, e.g. * *If we were on a desert island we would try to escape.* (See Focus 3.)

Typical student errors (use)

- Using a future conditional instead of hypothetical conditional, e.g. * *If I am on a desert island, I will build a shelter.* This situation is unlikely, therefore a hypothetical conditional is more appropriate. (See Focus 1.)
- Using a hypothetical conditional instead of a past hypothetical conditional, e.g. * *If you phoned me yesterday, I would come with you.* This situation is about the imaginary past, therefore a past hypothetical conditional is more appropriate. (See Focus 2.)
- Using a future conditional instead of a hypothetical conditional, e.g. * *If Hilary Clinton is a man, she will be President tomorrow.* This situation is imaginary, therefore a hypothetical conditional is more appropriate. (See Focus 3.)

FOCUS 1

form   meaning

Hypothetical Conditionals

EXAMPLES	EXPLANATIONS
(a) **Ann:** What **would** you do if you **were** on a desert island by yourself?	Use hypothetical conditionals to talk about an imaginary situation. This is not a real situation, but one that you are picturing in your mind.
(b) **Shin:** First, **I'd look** for food and water, and then **I'd build** a shelter.	Use *was* or *were* for verbs with *be* and the simple past for other verbs in the *if* clause.
(c) **Ann:** What if there **wasn't** any food on the island?	Use *would* + base form of the verb in the main clause.
(d) **Shin:** I think **I'd try** to make a signal for a boat or a plane.	Use an *if* clause to introduce the topic. After that, it is not necessary to repeat the *if* clause in every sentence. *Would* + base form of the verb shows that you are talking about a hypothetical situation that has already been introduced.

EXERCISE 1

Write the sentences from the Opening Task. Be sure to use *if* clauses and *would* correctly.

1. If I had a knife, I would use it to cut some wood for a fire.
   _____

2. If I saw a ship, I would
   _____

3. _____
   _____

4. _____
   _____

5. _____
   _____

EXERCISE 2

What would you do if you were in these situations? Which situation would you prefer to be in and why? Discuss with a partner. Write two or three sentences with *If*. Then share your ideas with the rest of the class.

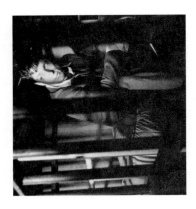

_____
_____
_____

EXERCISE 3

STEP 1   **Choose one of your classmates to be the "leader" for this exercise.**

STEP 2   **The leader will finish this sentence: "If I were a millionaire, ..."**

Example: *If I were a millionaire, I would buy a big house in the country and retire.*
     (*If* clause)   (Main clause)

STEP 3   **The next person will change the main clause into an if clause and add a new main clause.**

Example: If I bought a big house in the country and retired, I would write poetry all day long.

STEP 4   **Go around the room so that everyone has a chance to add to the "chain" of events.**

ANSWER KEY

Exercise 1   *Answers will depend on what students wrote in the opening task.*

Exercise 2   *Answers will vary. Main clauses should all use would.*

Exercise 3   *Answers will vary, but main clauses should all use would. If-clauses should be based on the main clause.*

25 LESSON PLAN 1

FOCUS 1 [10 minutes]

1. **Lead-in:** Use one or two correct examples from students' discussion in the Opening Task and write them on the board. For example:

   If I had a knife, I would cut down trees to make a shelter.

2. Identify the two clauses. Underline the verbs in each clause.

3. Explain that the *if*-clause uses the simple past tense to show unreality (hypothetical reality). The main clause uses *would* + verb.

4. The two clauses can also be in reverse order with no change in meaning (note the lack of a comma in this second example).

   I would cut down trees to make a shelter if I had a knife.

5. Next, ask students to make a question for this answer.

   What would you do if you had a knife? (or If you had a knife, what would you do?)

6. Read the examples and explanations in the focus chart.

7. Note that sequence of clauses and punctuation will come up again in Focus Chart 3.

8. Model and practice the contracted forms of *would* (*I'd, you'd, she'd,* etc.) Note that *had* cannot be contracted here as it is not an auxiliary verb.

EXERCISE 1 [5 minutes]

This exercise asks students to review and write their sentences from the Opening Task.

1. If students have already written their sentences from the Opening Task, ask them to go back and check them using the information in Focus Chart 1.

2. You can use this exercise to practice question forms by having students ask each other in pairs, *What would you do if you had a knife?* etc.

3. Review the questions and the many possible answers as a class. (See student book page A-18 for possible answers.)

EXPANSION [20 minutes]

You may want to use Activity 1 (speaking) on SB page 378 after this exercise. This can be followed by Activity 2 (writing) on SB page 379.

work book

For more practice, use *Grammar Dimensions 2* Workbook page 158, Exercise 1.

LANGUAGE NOTE

Students may ask about the use of *was* and *were* with the first person. Which is better, *If I was on a desert island* or *If I were on a desert island?* The answer is that both are correct. In the first person, the use of *were* is more formal, and still taught as more acceptable grammar in academic writing. However the use of *was* is more common nowadays, especially in informal spoken language, but also increasingly in written and formal contexts.

EXERCISE 2 [15 minutes]

This exercise provides a freer practice of question and answer forms using hypothetical conditionals.

1. Use the pictures to introduce the two different contexts: a desert island and a prison cell.

2. Ask a student to describe what is happening in the picture to the rest of the class. Example, left-hand picture:

   There's a man all alone on a really small desert island. It looks like the island is out in the middle of nowhere. There doesn't seem to be any food on the island, but . . . .

3. Let other students add information if you feel that the descriptions were incomplete.

4. Ask them to write a few sentences to answer the questions.

5. Ask volunteers to read them aloud to the class.

6. The rest of the class can listen for accuracy, pointing out any errors in form.

EXPANSION [20 minutes]

You may want to use Activity 3 (writing) on SB page 379 after this exercise.

EXERCISE 3 [15 minutes]

This is a group activity that practices sequence of tenses in hypothetical conditionals.

1. First demonstrate the activity with one or two students.

2. Organize the class into small groups. If your class is small, this can be played as a class.

STEP 1 Have each group choose a leader.

STEP 2 The leader will start off the activity.

STEP 3 The next person will continue the "chain."

STEP 4 Usually students catch on to this chain after one or two turns.

EXPANSION [20–40 minutes]

You may want to use Activity 4 (listening/speaking) on SB page 379 after this exercise. This can be followed by Activity 5 (speaking/listening) on SB page 380.

form meaning

FOCUS 2 | Past Hypothetical Conditionals

EXAMPLES	EXPLANATIONS
past perfect	Past hypothetical conditionals talk about imagined situations in the past. It is not possible for these situations to happen because they refer to the past. To express these situations, use past perfect in the *if* clause and *would* + *have* + past participle in the main clause.
(a) If you **had called** me last night, I *would* + *have* + past participle **would have come** to see you.	
(b) If we **had known** it was Marianne's birthday, we **would have had** a surprise party for her.	
(c) If Bonnie **hadn't robbed** a bank, she **wouldn't have gone** to jail.	We know that it is impossible to change the past, but we often think about how things might have been different in the past. In (a), I *didn't* come to see you because you *didn't* call me. In (c), Bonnie *did* go to jail because she *did* rob a bank.
past perfect	Some hypothetical conditionals make a connection between the past and the present. They show an imagined change in a present situation, caused by an imagined change in a past situation. These are untrue situations because it is impossible to change the past. You usually use past perfect in the if clause and *would* + base form of the verb or *would* + *be* + verb+ *-ing* in the main clause.
(d) If Dominica **had passed** her exam, she *would* + base verb **would be** a doctor now.	
(e) If Pia **hadn't been** born in Egypt, she **would not speak** fluent Arabic.	
past perfect	
(f) If we **had won** last week's lottery, we *would* + *be* + verb + *-ing* **would be lying** on a beach in the South of France today.	

EXERCISE 4

Read the following:

Ilene hates parties, so just over ten years ago, she was surprised to receive an invitation to a New Year's party from somebody that she didn't know very well. She didn't really want to go by herself, so she asked her friend Diana to go with her. Before the party, Ilene and Diana had a nice dinner together at Diana's house. It was a cold, snowy night and when it was time to leave for the party, all Ilene wanted to do was stay home and watch a video. Diana persuaded her to change her mind, however, and after they had driven all the way across town, Ilene realized that she had left the party invitation at home. Diana wanted to go back and get it, but Ilene thought she could remember the address. They found the right street, but Ilene wasn't sure about the number of the house, so they drove around until they came to a house where there was a party going on. They decided this was the right place. They didn't recognize anybody there and Ilene wanted to leave right away. However, Diana, who wasn't as shy as Ilene,

persuaded her to stay. Feeling very uncomfortable, Ilene stood in a corner by herself, watching Diana have a good time. After about an hour, she decided to go home. As she was leaving, she tripped and fell down some icy steps outside the house. Luckily just at that moment, somebody was coming up the steps on his way to the party and he caught her in his arms. And that's how Ilene met her husband. . . .

Ilene and Jeff have now been together for ten years, and they are still amazed at the way they met. For a start, Ilene had gone to the wrong party. The one she had been invited to was a couple of blocks away. And then it turned out that Jeff hadn't been invited to that party either. In fact, he was only in town because his sister was very sick and he had flown in from out of state to visit her. His sister lived next door, and when he ran into Ilene, he was on his way to ask the neighbors if they could turn the music down. Jeff, who is an anthropologist, was supposed to leave the next day to spend two years in West Africa, but that night, there was a terrible snowstorm and the airport was closed for three days. It was during those three days that Jeff and Ilene first got to know each other. But that's not all; when Jeff got to West Africa, there was a great deal of political unrest in the region where he was working. After two months, he was forced to abandon his research project. The first thing he did when he got back to the United States was call Ilene.

Now, every New Year's Eve, Jeff and Ilene laugh about how they almost never met. "What if . . . ?" Jeff always asks. "Don't even think about it," Ilene always replies.

Get together with a partner and think about how Jeff and Ilene met (and how they almost didn't meet). How many statements containing hypothetical conditionals can you make about their story? For example: *If Ilene hadn't received a party invitation, she wouldn't have gone out on New Year's Eve. If Jeff had been gay, he wouldn't have been interested in Ilene.*

Share your statements with the rest of the class. Who was able to make the most?

form

FOCUS 3 | Word Order in Conditionals

EXAMPLES	EXPLANATIONS
(a) If we were on a desert island, we would use string to make a fishing line. OR We would use string to make a fishing line if we were on a desert island.	Differences in word order do not change the meaning.
(b) If we had known how to build a boat, we would have escaped. OR We would have escaped if we had known how to build a boat.	Use a comma after the *if* clause when it comes first.

ANSWER KEY

Exercise 4 Answers are likely to include the following, but students may find even more than these. **Examples:** If Ilene hadn't received a party invitation, she wouldn't have gone out on New Year's Eve. If Jeff had been gay, he wouldn't have been interested in Ilene. If Diana hadn't persuaded Ilene to change her mind, she wouldn't have gone to the party. If Ilene hadn't left the party invitation at home, she wouldn't have ended up at the party where she met Jeff. If Ilene had remembered the right address, she

party, she might have left before she met Jeff. If Ilene hadn't tripped down the steps, she wouldn't have been caught in Jeff's arms. If Jeff hadn't been visiting his sister next door, he wouldn't have gone next door to the party at all. If Jeff hadn't gone next door to tell people to turn the music down, he wouldn't have met Ilene. If there hadn't been a terrible snowstorm that night, he would have left for West Africa the next day. If Jeff had stayed in West Africa longer he might have forgotten about Ilene.

25 LESSON PLAN 1

FOCUS 2 [10 minutes]

1. **Lead-in:** Describe a situation (true or imaginary) where you wish something different had happened. For example:

   You didn't help me with my homework, so I didn't pass my exam.

2. Ask questions about this situation to check comprehension. For example:

   Did you help me with my homework? (no) Did I pass my exam? (no)

3. Now ask students to imagine if this situation had been different. Ask them to make a sentence starting with *If*. They may try to use the past tense form from Focus Chart 1. In this case, explain that this situation happened in the past and is even more unreal because there is no chance of changing it.

   If you had helped me with my homework, I would have passed the exam.

4. Underline the verbs and identify the tenses. (past perfect and would + have + verb)

5. Read the examples and explanations in the focus chart.

6. For each example, ask comprehension questions as above.

EXERCISE 4 [20 minutes]

This exercise practices recognizing situations when past hypothetical conditionals can be used. (The majority of sentences will be past hypothetical conditionals, though some mixed conditionals may also be possible.)

1. If you and your class enjoy competitive activities, have students work in small teams of four or five rather than in pairs.

2. Set a time limit of 10 minutes for students to read the story and write as many hypothetical conditionals that they can.

3. The team with the most sentences, or a representative from each team, can write down

their hypothetical conditionals on the board or on an overhead transparency.

4. The team with the most *accurate* hypothetical conditionals—accurate in terms of meaning and form—wins. Or you can score each sentence, awarding one point for accuracy in form, one point for accuracy in meaning. Let the class be the judges!

 For more practice, use *Grammar Dimensions 2* Workbook pages 159–160, Exercise 2 and/or 3.

PRONUNCIATION NOTE

Model and practice the contracted forms of the past hypothetical conditional.

If you had (you'd) called me last night, I would have (would've) come to see you.

What would you have (woudyuev) done, if I had (I'd) called you?

EXPANSION [20 minutes]

You can provide further practice with past hypothetical conditionals with the following exercise.

1. Hand out blank strips or squares of paper.

2. Have each students write down one mistake they have made in the past. It should be a true sentence. For example, *I didn't learn to drive when I was younger.*

3. Collect the papers and redistribute them so everyone has a different paper.

4. Have students stand up and walk around the room, asking questions to find the author of their sentence.

5. When they find the author, they should use past hypothetical conditionals to explain why this was a mistake and what could have been done differently.

6. Have students report to the class on what they found out about their partner.

FOCUS 3 [2 minutes]

1. **Lead-in:** Review the information about verb sequence covered in Focus Chart 2.

2. Read the examples and explanations in the focus chart. Focus on comma use in particular.

3. Review students' sentences from Exercise 4 and check them for correct use of punctuation.

EXERCISE 5

How would **your** life be different now if things had been different in the past? Use the headings below to make a list of important events in your life.

Example: *If I hadn't gone to the ballet when I was 5 years old, I wouldn't have studied dancing. I wouldn't be a dancer now if I had studied art instead of ballet.*

1. Something you did when you were young

_____

2. Something you didn't study when you were young

_____

3. A person you met or a place you visited

_____

4. An opportunity you decided not to take

_____

5. A book that you read

_____

6. An important decision that you made

_____

When you have made your list, get together with another student and tell him or her how your life would be different if these things had (or hadn't) happened. Then tell the rest of the class what you found out about your partner.

ANSWER KEY

Exercise 5 *Answers will vary. Some students may start out with answers similar to the model/example.*

EXERCISE 6

For each situation, complete the following hypothetical conditionals, using the given verb in your answers.

Situation A

Example: 1. Eloise's husband has always been a thin man in good physical condition. If he suddenly _____ (become) fat, Eloise _____ (be) shocked.

This is a hypothetical situation which will probably **not** happen because Eloise's husband has always been a thin man.

Answer: Eloise's husband has always been a thin man in good physical condition. If he suddenly _became_ (become) fat, Eloise _would be_ (be) shocked.

2. Eloise started seeing a doctor about her cholesterol problem three years ago. If she _had known_ (knew) about her problem earlier, she _would have changed_ (change) her diet years earlier.

Situation B

3. Ali's doctor says that one of the reasons Ali has high blood pressure is that he never expresses his anger. His doctor says that it is not healthy to "bottle it up." He says that if Ali _got_ (get) angry once in a while, his blood pressure _would not be_ (not + be) so high.

4. Ali never gets angry with his family. His children _would run away_ (run away) from him if he ever _yelled_ (yell) at them.

Situation C

5. Dan, who doesn't earn very high wages, has been shopping at discount stores for years. Even if he _had_ (have) a lot of money to shop with, he _would buy_ (buy) from discount stores.

6. When Dan graduated from college, his father gave him a used truck. Together they worked on the truck until it was in excellent condition. If Dan _had not learned_ (not + learn) how to repair trucks, he _would have been_ (be) more enthusiastic about new trucks.

25 LESSON PLAN 1

EXERCISE 5 [15 minutes]

This exercise can be used to practice both types of clause sequence for past hypothetical conditionals.

1. Read the headings and model one example. For example, under item 1 you may write, *I went to the ballet when I was 5 years old.*

2. Allow 5 minutes for students to write an event under each of the headings. (A bit of silent time at this stage will make the discussion more interesting later as students will have come up with more interesting ideas.)

3. When they have finished, have them work in pairs to make *If*-sentences about their "events."

4. Then change partners and tell the new partner what they found out about the previous partner.

VARIATION

You can do this exercise as a guessing game.

1. Have students write their *If*-sentences anonymously on a piece of paper.

2. Circulate to see if students' *If*-clauses are satisfactory to them. Does it say what the student wants it to say? If not, help them to rephrase this statement.

3. Collect students' papers and read them aloud, letting the class guess the identity of the writer.

4. To focus on accuracy, have students review their work, either individually or exchanging their papers with a partner. They can then rewrite sentences that are inaccurate.

EXERCISE 6 [20 minutes]

This exercise practices the formation and use of all types of hypothetical conditionals presented so far. This exercise can be assigned for homework if you are short on time in class.

1. Look at the examples together with the class.

2. Decide whether the events happened in the past or not.

3. Discuss why each tense is appropriate.

4. Read the example explanation.

5. Have students work in pairs or small groups to complete the rest of the exercise.

6. Ask volunteers to report to the class. They can use the explanation in the example as a model to say why they chose their answers. Refer to the answer key on LP page 368.

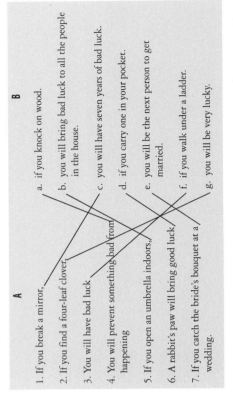

meaning

form

FOCUS 4 | Future Conditionals

EXAMPLES

simple present   *will/be going to* + base verb

(a) If you **study hard**, you **will get** a good grade.

(b) If it **rains** tomorrow, I'm **going to bring** my umbrella.

(c) **Steve will give** you a ride if you ask him.

EXPLANATIONS

Future conditionals make predictions about what will happen in the future. You usually use simple present in the *if* clause and *will be* or *be going to* + base form of the verb in the main clause.

EXERCISE 8

Most countries have superstitions. Here's a common North American superstition: If a black cat crosses your path, you will have bad luck.

Match A and B below to create some other common North American superstitions. Check your answers with other students and with your teacher.

A

1. If you break a mirror,
2. If you find a four-leaf clover,
3. You will have bad luck
4. You will prevent something bad from happening
5. If you open an umbrella indoors,
6. A rabbit's paw will bring good luck,
7. If you catch the bride's bouquet at a wedding,

B

a. if you knock on wood.
b. you will bring bad luck to all the people in the house.
c. you will have seven years of bad luck.
d. if you carry one in your pocket.
e. you will be the next person to get married.
f. if you walk under a ladder.
g. you will be very lucky.

Do you have any of these superstitions in your country? Do any of these superstitions have a different meaning in your country? (For example, in Great Britain, if a black cat crosses your path, you will have **good luck**.) Think of some common superstitions from your country and tell them to the rest of your class. How many people in your class believe in these superstitions?

Situation D

7. People who live in this area have forgotten how to conserve water. If it __had not rained__ (not + rain) so much last year, people__would have remembered__ (remember) water conservation practices.

8. People __will be able__ (be able) to water their lawns every day if it __rains__ (rain) more this summer. However, the forecast is that this area is going to experience a drought this summer.

(*#8: point out that the answer uses the future conditional—see Focus Chart 4*)

EXERCISE 7

STEP 1   On one sheet of paper, write the following words and complete the hypothetical *if* clause.

If I were _____

Now, on another sheet of paper complete the main clauses.

I would _____

STEP 2   Your teacher will collect and scramble your *if* clauses and your main clauses, and then you will take one of each. Read your sentence aloud to the rest of the class. Does it make sense?

STEP 3   After hearing everyone read their sentences, find the person who has the main clause that matches the *if* clause you have now.

STEP 4   Now find the person who has the *if* clause that matches your main clause.

ANSWER KEY

Exercise 7   *Answers will vary, and will depend on what students wrote in Step 1.*

Exercise 8   1. *c*   2. *g*   3. *f*   4. *a*   5. *b*   6. *d*   7. *e*

25 LESSON PLAN 1

EXERCISE 7 [20 minutes]

This is a creative game-like exercise that allows time and space for a bit of humor and fun!

1. You will need some small strips or pieces of paper for this activity, two for each student.

STEP 1
Give two pieces of paper to each student. Each student will write two clauses, one on each piece of paper.

STEP 2

1. Collect the papers and mix them up. Hand them out again, two to each student.
2. Students will read their new "sentences" aloud.

STEPS 3 and 4
Students stand up and walk around, trying to find the missing half of their sentences. They may find more than one match.

For more practice, use *Grammar Dimensions 2* Workbook pages 160–162, Exercises 4 and/or 5.

FOCUS 4 [10 minutes]

1. Review the answers to Exercise 6 if you assign this for homework.
2. Lead-in: Write two example sentences on the board, one hypothetical conditional and one future conditional. For example:

   (a) *If you study harder, you will get a good grade.*
   (b) *If you studied harder, you would get a good grade.*
3. Ask: Which is possible? (both) Which one is less likely? (b)
4. Underline the verbs and identify the tenses in the future conditional (present tense and will + verb).
5. Explain that the future conditional is used for situations that we think are quite likely and possible. The past tense conditional—as mentioned in Focus Chart 1—is used for situations that we think are less likely. Emphasize that the difference

is in attitude to the situation, not necessarily in the situation itself.

6. Read the examples and explanations in the focus chart.
7. Notice the use of commas and the clause order in the examples.

EXERCISE 8 [10 minutes]

This exercise practices future conditionals in the context of talking about superstitions.

1. Introduce the topic of superstitions with the example given or another superstition that you are sure your students are familiar with.
2. Allow a few minutes for students to match up the sentences in the box.
3. Refer to the answer key on LP page 370 and check the answers as a class.
4. If you have a multicultural/multilingual class, the second part of this exercise—where students think of common superstitions from their own cultures—can create an entertaining and informative discussion.

For more practice, use *Grammar Dimensions 2* Workbook page 162, Exercise 6.

EXPANSION [20 minutes]

You may want to extend the discussion of superstitions by having students work in groups to create halves of sentences as in Exercise 8. Groups can exchange sets of sentences with each other and work on putting them together correctly.

FOCUS 5

Future Conditionals or Hypothetical Conditions?

EXPLANATIONS

Future conditionals talk about possible situations and show what you think will happen in those situations.

Hypothetical conditionals talk about improbable situations: situations that are not likely to happen (b), or impossible situations (c and d).

EXAMPLES

Future Conditional:
(a) If a woman **runs** for president of the United States one day, more women **will go** into politics.

Hypothetical Conditionals:
(b) If I **ran** for president, nobody **would** vote for me.
(c) If Elvis **had run** for president, a lot of his fans **would have voted** for him.
(d) If Al Gore **had become** president in 2000, American politics **would be** quite different today.

EXERCISE 11

Say whether the situations in the *if* clauses are future (possible) or hypothetical (improbable). Compare your answers with a partner's.

1. If it rains, I will not have to water the garden. _future (probable)_

2. If it rained, I would be very happy. _hypothetical (improbable)_

3. Marcy would quit her job if she got pregnant. _hypothetical (improbable)_

4. If I won the lottery, I would travel around the world. _hypothetical (improbable)_

5. Aunt Shira will give us a wedding shower if we decide on a wedding date. _future (probable)_

6. If Laurel gets hurt again, her father will make her quit the girl's soccer team. _future (probable)_

7. If the baby slept through the night without waking up, his parents would finally get a good night's sleep. _hypothetical (improbable)_

8. Jasmine would buy a big house if she were rich. _hypothetical (improbable)_

EXERCISE 9

Go around the room and ask the other students the questions in the chart below. Change partners after every question. Write the answers you receive in your notebook.

When your chart is complete, compare your answers with your classmates. In your opinion, what was the most interesting or surprising answer to each question? Write it in the chart.

Example: *Question:* What will you do if you get an A in this class?
Answer: I'll hug my teacher and say, "Thank you! Thank you!"

WHAT WILL YOU DO . . .

QUESTION	ANSWER	MOST INTERESTING ANSWER
1. . . . . if you get an A in this class?		
2. . . . . if your pants rip in tomorrow's class?		
3. . . . . if I give you $10 right now?		
4. . . . . if there is a fire drill?		
5. . . . . if you don't see me tomorrow?		
6. . . . . if our teacher is sick tomorrow?		
7. . . . . if it's raining when class is over?		
8. . . . . if you lose this book?		

EXERCISE 10

Think of five ways in which you would like to change your life.

Example: *I'd like to exercise more.*

Tell your partner how your life will change if these things happen.

Example: *If I exercise more, I'll be fitter and healthier.*

HOW WOULD YOU LIKE TO CHANGE YOUR LIFE?	WHAT WILL HAPPEN?
1.	
2.	
3.	
4.	
5	

ANSWER KEY

Exercise 9 *Answers will vary, depending on students' creativity (and/or energy level that day).*
Exercise 10 *Answers will vary.*

LESSON PLAN 2

EXERCISE 9 [15 minutes]

This exercise is a fun walk-around activity that can produce some unexpected answers!

1. Ask two students to read the example question and answer.
2. Explain that students will have to stand up, walk around, and ask each other questions to fill in the chart.
3. They must change partners after every question.
4. Review the answers by having students read their most interesting answers aloud.

EXERCISE 10 [20 minutes]

This exercise allows students to personalize their use of the future conditional. The hypothetical conditional is also possible, depending on how realistic and likely they think their changes will be.

1. Read the example with the class.
2. If necessary, model some other examples that are true for you.
3. Allow 5 minutes for students to write five things they would like to change in their lives.
4. Have students work in pairs to tell each other about what will happen using the future conditional.
5. Ask volunteers to share their sentences with the class.

FOCUS 5 [2 minutes]

If you have already discussed the difference between the meanings of these conditionals, this focus chart and the following exercise can be omitted.

1. **Lead-in:** Review some of the sentences from Exercise 10 and discuss with students how likely they think they are and whether hypothetical or future conditionals would be more appropriate.
2. Read the examples in the focus chart and discuss why each tense is used in each case. Past tenses are used to show that the event is seen as more distant from the present, or in other words, as more unlikely.

EXERCISE 11 [10 minutes]

This exercise practices recognizing the difference between hypothetical and future conditionals.

1. Use item 1 as an example. Ask: *Does the writer/speaker think that this situation (1) will or might happen?* (= possible = future conditional) or (2) *probably won't happen?* (= improbable = hypothetical conditional).
2. To give students more time to come up with and discuss their answers, do this exercise in small groups or pairs.
3. Refer to the answer key on LP page 372. Re-group as a class and discuss differences of opinion for particular items, asking students to defend their answers in terms of likelihood/probability. Why do they think a situation will or might happen, or probably won't happen?

work book

For more practice, use *Grammar Dimensions 2* Workbook page 163, Exercise 7.

form   meaning

FOCUS 6

Factual Conditionals

EXAMPLES	EXPLANATIONS
simple present	Factual conditionals talk about what is always true or what usually happens in certain situations. You really expect these things to happen. Use simple present in the *if* clause and simple present in the main clause.
(a) If you **leave** milk in the sun, **it turns** sour.	
(b) I **eat** yogurt and fruit for breakfast if I **have** time	
(c) **When you leave** milk in the sun, it turns sour.	Because you expect these situations to happen, you can use *when* or *whenever* (every time that) instead of *if*. The meaning does not change.
(d) I **eat** yogurt and fruit for breakfast **whenever** I have time.	

EXERCISE 13

Get together with a partner and complete the following statements to make factual conditionals with *if*, *when*, and *whenever*. Check your answers with your classmates and your teacher.

Example: If you heat water, _____ it boils _____ .

1. An ice cube melts if _____ it is warm _____ .

2. If you heat metal, _____ it expands _____ .

3. Red wine stains when _____ you spill it _____ .

4. Cats purr if _____ you stroke/pet them _____ .

5. Rain changes to snow if _the temperature is below 0 degrees Centigrade/32 degrees Fahrenheit_ .

6. If you press the "Power" button on a computer, _____ it will turn on _____ .

7. Wool shrinks _if you put it in boiling water_ .

8. At the end of a play, people usually applaud _____ if they like it _____ .

Discuss each of the sentences above with your partner. Decide if they are always true or usually true.

EXERCISE 12

Work with a partner to complete the following. In each sentence, decide if the situation is possible or hypothetical and write an appropriate form of the verb.

Situation A

1. Gao is a doctor, but if he _____ were _____ (be) a truck driver, he _____ would have _____ (have) very different skills. This situation is hypothetical *because Gao is not a truck driver.*

2. Gao's wife is a doctor, too, but she is planning to change her career. If she _____ changes _____ (change) her career, she _____ will study _____ (study) to become a lawyer.

Situation B

3. Antonieta is Brazilian, but she has lived in the United States and New Zealand, so she speaks excellent English. If she _____ stayed _____ (stay) in Brazil, her English _____ would not be _____ (not) (be) so good.

4. However, Antonieta _____ will speak _____ (speak) French too if she _____ moves _____ (move) to France next year.

Situation C

5. Mary's car is old. If it _____ breaks down _____ (break down), she _____ will buy _____ (buy) a new one.

6. Because Mary has a car, she has driven to school every day this term. But if she _____ did not have _____ (not) (have) a car, she _____ would take _____ (take) the bus.

Situation D

7. Marcia has applied to graduate school. She _____ will start _____ (start) school next fall if she _____ gets accepted _____ (get) accepted.

8. When Marcia was 21, she quit school for several years to get married and raise a family. If she _____ had continued _____ (continue) her studies instead of raising a family, she _____ would have begun _____ (begin) graduate school a long time ago.

ANSWER KEY

Exercise 12 The appropriate form of the verb is listed above.   2. (possible; she is planning to change her career) 3. (hypothetical; she did not stay in Brazil—past fact that can't be changed) 4. (or would speak/moved) (possible; it is likely that living in France will enable Antonia to learn French. However, we could say it is hypothetical because we don't have clear evidence that Antonia will move to France) 5. (possible; the car is old and could break down) 6. (hypothetical; she does in...

Exercise 13 Answers may vary. Possible answers are listed above.

EXERCISE 12 [20 minutes]

This exercise can also be omitted if you feel students are confident in distinguishing when to use future or hypothetical conditionals. Like Exercise 6 on SB page 369, each pair of items in this exercise talks about one story.

1. Read the example with the class.

2. Have students work in pairs or small groups.

3. To speed up the exercise, ask each group to focus on just one story (for example, one pair/group looks at Situation A; another looks at Situation B, another at Situation C, another at Situation D).

4. Refer to the answer key on LP page 374 and review the answers.

5. If you think it will be useful to continue to focus on meaning—and to give students practice in talking "about" grammar, ask students to defend their answers in terms of likelihood/probability. Is the situation likely to happen? Is it improbable/not likely to happen? Or is it impossible? (i.e. It can't happen because the situation is in the past, which cannot be changed).

For more practice, use *Grammar Dimensions 2* Workbook page 164, Exercise 8.

FOCUS 6 [5 minutes]

1. **Lead-in:** Write example sentences (a) and (b) on the board. Ask students to underline the verbs and identify the tenses (both are present tense). Ask if these are "real" or "hypothetical" (they are real). Ask what happens if you replace *if* with *when* (the meaning is the same). Ask about the rules for commas (the same as for other conditionals).

2. Read the examples and the explanations in the focus chart.

3. Practice rephrasing all the sentences in (a) through (d), replacing *if* with *when* or *whenever*, and vice versa, and reversing the clause sequence.

EXERCISE 13 [10 minutes]

1. Read the example with the class.

2. Set a time limit for students to complete the exercise individually.

3. Refer to the answer key on LP page 374 and review the answers as a class.

4. Allow time for students to give feedback on the form and the meaning of each one.

5. Point out that if, when, and whenever can usually replace each other with little or no change in meaning (as in Focus Chart 6).

6. Point out that the word order is flexible: It doesn't matter which comes first—the main clause or the if-clause (as in Focus Chart 3).

For more practice, use *Grammar Dimensions 2* Workbook page 165, Exercise 9; pages 166–167, Exercise 10; and page 168, Exercise 11.

EXERCISE 14

Complete the following conversations with *will, would, may, might, would have, might have,* or *may have*.

Conversation A

Abel: Have you and Ken decided what you're going to do over Labor Day weekend?

Miles: Not really. It all depends on the weather. If it's nice, we (1) ___will/'ll go___ (go) camping, that's for sure. But if it rains, we (2) ___might visit___ (visit) my folks in Oakland or we (3) ___might stay___ (stay) here and catch up on our reading. I'm really not sure yet. I guess we'll just wait and see.

Conversation B

Mother: Don't drop that glass!

Child: Why not?

Mother: If you drop something made of glass, it (4) ___will/'ll break___ (break).

Child: Oh.

Mother: Watch out! Don't turn it upside down.

Child: Why not?

Mother: Because if you do that, it (5) ___will/'ll spill___ (spill).

Conversation C

Janette: Did you hear about the guy who found an old Lotto ticket in a trash can?

Dean: Yeah, the guy who won eight million dollars? The guy with four grown kids and a bunch of grandchildren?

Janette: Yeah. He bought the ticket six months ago and he found it just two days before it was due to expire.

Dean: If he had found it two days later, he (6) ___wouldn't have won___ (not) (win) the eight million dollars.

Janette: Yeah, and his children (7) ___wouldn't be___ (not) (be) rich now.

Dean: And his grandchildren (8) ___wouldn't have___ (not) (have) college funds.

Janette: And the eight million dollars (9) ___would have gone back___ (go back) into the next Lotto!

Dean: And we (10) ___would have won___ (win) it!

ANSWER KEY

Exercise 14 *There may be some variation in answers. Likely answers are listed above.*

meaning

FOCUS 7

Would, Might, May, and *Will* in Conditionals

EXAMPLES	EXPLANATIONS
Hypothetical Conditions:	
(a) If I were on that desert island, **I would** definitely try to get away as soon as possible.	Use *would* in the main clause to show the most probable result of the *if* clause.
(b) If I were on that desert island, **I might** try to get away or **I might** wait for someone to rescue me.	Use *might* in the main clause to show other possible results of the *if* clause. When you use *might,* you are less certain of the result.
(c) If Americans got more exercise, they **might** be healthier.	
Past Hypothetical Conditionals:	
(d) If John Lennon hadn't died, the Beatles **might have** reunited.	In past hypothetical conditionals, you can use *might have* + past participle or *may have* + past participle. The meaning does not change.
OR	
If John Lennon hadn't died, the Beatles **may have** reunited.	
(e) If we had arrived at the airport ten minutes earlier, we **might have** caught the plane.	
OR	
If we had arrived at the airport ten minutes earlier, we **may have** caught the plane.	
Future Conditionals:	
(f) If it rains tomorrow, we **will** stay home.	In future conditionals, use *will* in the main clause to show that you strongly expect this result to happen.
(g) If it rains tomorrow, we **might** stay home or we **might** go to the movies.	Use *might* or *may* in the main clause to show that this result is possible, but you are not so certain that it will happen.
OR	
If it rains tomorrow, we **may** stay home or we **may** go to the movies.	

25 LESSON PLAN 2

FOCUS 7 [5 minutes]

This is a review of all the conditionals covered in this chapter except factual conditionals.

1. **Lead-in:** Read aloud one sentence from (a) to (g) at random for students (with books closed) or write it on the board. Elicit from them what the meaning is in each sentence. Is the situation likely to happen? Not likely to happen? Impossible? What type of conditional it is—Hypothetical? Past hypothetical? Future?

2. The new information here is the use of modals *might* and *may*. If you think it is helpful, you can review Units 5 and 10, which treat the relative "strength" of the prediction—how likely the situation is and how certain the speaker/writer is of the result.

EXERCISE 14 [15 minutes]

This exercise reviews all conditionals presented in this unit.

1. Give students a few minutes to work with a partner to complete the exercise.

2. Give students a few more minutes to rehearse the dialogues aloud. Remind them to link words together smoothly, to use reduced forms/contractions when appropriate, and to use intonation effectively—falling intonation at the end of a statement, rising intonation at the end of a *yes-no* question, and louder volume, higher pitch for important or surprising information.

3. Have pairs perform the dialogues for the class.

4. Encourage feedback on form, content, and presentation.

For more practice, use *Grammar Dimensions 2* Workbook page 168, Exercise 12.

EXPANSION [20 minutes]

You may want to use Activity 8 (research on the web) and / or Activity 9 (reflection) on SB page 381 after this exercise.

UNIT GOAL REVIEW [10 minutes]

Ask students to look at the goals on the opening page of the unit again. Refer to the pages of the unit where information on each goal can be found.

For a grammar quiz review of Units 22–25, refer students to pages 169–171 in the *Grammar Dimensions 2* Workbook.

ExamView® Test Generator   For assessment of Unit 25, refer to *Grammar Dimensions 2 ExamView®*.

Use Your English

ACTIVITY 1 speaking

■ STEP 1　Work in groups of four.

■ STEP 2　Read the following questions. Without showing anyone else your paper, write down what you think you would be and what each person in your group would be in the following situations:

a. If you were an animal, what would you be?

b. If you were a color, what would you be?

c. If you were food, what would you be?

Example: *If I were an animal, I would be a cat. If Terri were an animal, she would be a deer. I also think that Rachel would be a mouse, and Peter would be a flamingo.*

■ STEP 3　When you have all finished, share your ideas and compare what you think your group members would be with what **they** think they would be.

	a. ANIMAL	b. COLOR	c. FOOD
You			
Name:			
Name:			
Name:			

Remember that it is not necessary to repeat the *if* clause in every sentence.

ACTIVITY 2 writing

In a paragraph or two, describe the most interesting results about **yourself** from Activity 1. First tell why you described yourself the way you did. Then tell why you think your group members described you the way they did.

For example, if you said, "If I were a color, I would be purple," but everyone else said you would be yellow, give us the possible reasons for these opinions. Remember that it isn't necessary to repeat the *if* clause in every sentence.

ACTIVITY 3 writing

Form teams. Together write an imaginary future situation on a piece of paper. For example, *What would happen if . . . everyone in the world were ten feet taller? . . . everyone lived the same number of years? . . . all children studied at home?*

After you write down one situation, work together to describe the results. Then your team will tell some of your ideas to the other teams. They will try to guess the situation and tell what the *if* clause is. The team that guesses the situation most often wins.

ACTIVITY 4 listening/speaking

Your school is about to build a new library. The president of the student union wants to celebrate the event by placing a time capsule inside the walls of the new building. (A time capsule is a box containing a number of objects that represent the culture of a community at that point in time. You put into the time capsule objects that you feel reflect the ideas, culture, and values of the community. If people find the time capsule one hundred years from now, they will have an idea of what life was like in the past.)

If the president asked you about what to put in the time capsule, what would you say? Get together with two or three other students and decide on a list of five objects that you would put in the time capsule because you believe they represent American culture now. Share your ideas with the rest of the class and explain why you chose these objects. When you have heard everybody's ideas, vote on the five objects that you, as a class, would put in a time capsule to represent current American culture.

USE YOUR ENGLISH

The Use Your English section of activities at the end of the unit contain situations that should naturally elicit the structures covered in the unit. For a more complete discussion of how to use the Use Your English activities, see To the Teacher, LP page xxii. When students are doing these activities in class, you can circulate and listen to see if they are using the structures accurately. Errors can be corrected after the activity has finished.

ACTIVITY 1 speaking [20 minutes]

You may want to use this activity after Exercise 1 on SB page 364. This is a popular psychology game for people to find out what their image of themselves is, and what other people's images of them are.

1. Students can redraw this chart on a larger piece of paper so that there is more room.

2. Read the questions and the example with the students. Please note that some cultures may find it offensive to be compared to animals, and they can agree in their group to omit this question if it is inappropriate.

■ **STEP 1** Have students form small groups.

■ **STEP 2** Allow 5 minutes for students to write their answers.

■ **STEP 3** Have students share their answers in groups.

VARIATION

1. Make this activity into a competitive game by awarding points for correct matches of guesses and answers. For a little extra pressure, points can be deducted for incorrect use of conditionals.

2. To speed up this activity, just choose one question.

ACTIVITY 2 writing [5 minutes]

This activity is a follow-up to Activity 1.

1. Ask: *What did you learn about yourself from Activity 1?* Ask volunteers to talk about why they chose their images and whether they were different from those of their classmates.

2. Have students write a few sentences about what they learned. You may want to set this as a journal task for homework.

ACTIVITY 3 writing [5 minutes]

You may want to use this activity after Exercise 2 on SB page 365.

1. Choose one of the example questions and brainstorm ideas with the class. Write them on the board.

2. Have students form teams and think of their own imaginary future situation.

3. In groups, discuss the situation and write the results (but not the situation) on a piece of paper. For example, if the situation is *What would happen if all children studied at home?* The results would be: *There wouldn't be enough jobs for teachers. All schools would close. Children wouldn't make any friends. Children would be isolated.* Etc.

4. Teams exchange results and try to guess what the situations were.

5. Display the most interesting ones in the classroom.

ACTIVITY 4 listening/speaking [20 minutes]

You may want to use this activity after Exercise 3 on SB page 365.

1. Introduce the concept of a "time capsule." Suggest a few of your own ideas on what you would put in a time capsule as examples.

2. Allow a couple of minutes for students to read the description of the activity.

3. Set a time limit of 10 minutes for students to come up with five objects.

4. Appoint one class leader to take suggestions from the class and vote on the top five objects.

5. Each person must justify why they chose that particular item.

VARIATION

Use this activity as the source for a writing activity. Students describe each of the items they would put in a time capsule and defend their choice. This can be an exercise in argumentation. Effective argumentation leaves the reader convinced of the writer's opinion.

ACTIVITY 5 — speaking/listening

The purpose of this activity is to find out what Americans would put in a time capsule like the one in Activity 4.

STEP 1
Interview three different native speakers of English by asking the question: If you had to put three things in a time capsule to reflect American culture right now, what would you choose and why? Record your interviews.

STEP 2
Listen to your recording and report your findings to the rest of your class. As a class, make a list of the objects that everyone interviewed would put in the time capsule. What does this tell you about American culture today? Compare this list with the one that your class made in Activity 4. How many differences and similarities are there in these lists? Do your ideas about what represents American culture differ from Americans' ideas?

STEP 3
Listen to your recording again. How many times do the speakers use *would*? Write down any sentences containing *would*. How many times do the speakers use full *if* clauses? Why do you think this is so? Write down any sentences containing *if* clauses. What does this tell you about the use of *if* clauses in real conversations?

ACTIVITY 6 — listening

CD Track 32

Listen to the audio of three different Americans talking about what they would put in a time capsule.

STEP 1
What would they put in the capsule? List the objects.

STEP 2
Listen to the audio again. How many times do the speakers use *would*? Write down any sentences containing *would*. How many times do the speakers use full *if* clauses? Why do you think this so? Write down any sentences containing *if* clauses. What does this tell you about the use of *if* clauses in real conversations?

ACTIVITY 7 — speaking/listening or writing/reading

If you had to put five objects representing your culture into a time capsule, what would you choose and why? Make a report (either written or oral) on your choices. If you make a written report, read your or another student's work carefully and check to see if you or he or she were able to use any of the language from this unit. If you choose an oral report, record yourself as you make the report. Listen to your recording and write down any sentences containing language from this unit.

ACTIVITY 8 — research on the web

Peter, Paul, and Mary were a popular folk group in the sixties. The title of one of their famous songs was, "If I had a hammer . . ." Go on the Internet and use a search engine such as Google® or Yahoo® to find the words to this song. Find a recording online if possible. Can you sing it? What do you think the words mean?

ACTIVITY 9 — reflection

Think of three ways in which you could make more time to study English. Write your ideas as sentences starting with '*If* . . .' Example: *If I stopped watching TV, I'd read more English books or newspapers.*

ANSWER KEY

Activity 6 *See audio script on LP page 5-10.*

Step 1 *The man would include a copy of* The New York Times, *a laptop computer, an autographed major league baseball. The woman would include Levi's jeans, a Big Mac, and a copy of* TV Guide.

USE YOUR ENGLISH

ACTIVITY 5 — speaking/listening
[15 minutes/homework]

This activity is a follow-up to Activity 4.

STEP 1

1. This can be done as an out-of-class interviewing activity. Or you can invite a guest speaker to come and be interviewed by the class.

2. If you don't have access to a pool of native speakers, have students interview people in their own language about their own culture.

STEP 2
Present the results to the class. The results of the time capsule object poll may produce some interesting cross-cultural discussion.

STEP 3
Have students report on if clauses and use of would. Do they have any interesting observations about use of the conditional in spoken language as a result?

ACTIVITY 6 — listening
[20 minutes]

This activity is a follow-up to Activities 4 and 5.

STEP 1

CD Track 32

1. Explain that students will hear three speakers talking about what they would put into a time capsule.

2. Play the audio. See audio script on LP page S-10. Students will take notes.

3. Have students compare answers in pairs.

STEP 2

4. Play the audio again.
5. Check the answers.
6. Play the audio and listen for examples of conditionals.

ACTIVITY 7 — speaking/listening or writing/reading
[20 minutes]

You may want to use this activity after Exercise 4 on SB page 366.

See notes for Variation on Activity 4. If you adapted Activity 4 to serve as a written activity, you can focus here on spontaneous speech. In this case, allow students to make notes but not full sentences so that they don't read their report but "say it" more ad lib, referring to notes if necessary.

ACTIVITY 8 — research on the web
[10 minutes/homework]

You may want to use this activity after Exercise 14 on page SB 377.

The purpose of this Internet search activity is to encourage students to share strategies for finding information on the Internet.

Have students share resulting Web sites in class.

ACTIVITY 9 — reflection
[15 minutes/homework]

You may want to use this activity after Exercise 14 on SB page 377.

This activity provides an opportunity for students to use the target structures of the unit while reflecting on their language learning progress. You may have asked students to keep a record of their learning in a journal throughout this course as suggested in To the Teacher, LP page xxii. This reflection activity will be part of that learning record.

APPENDICES

Appendix 1A   Simple Present (verb/verb + –s)

Statement	Negative	Question	Short Answers
I / You / We / They } work.	I / You / We / They } do not/ don't work.	Do { I / you / we / they } work?	Yes, { I / you / we / they } do.
He / She / It } works.	He / She / It } does not/ doesn't work.	Does { he / she / it } work?	Yes, { he / she / it } does.
			No, { I / you / we / they } don't.
			No, { he / she / it } doesn't.

Appendix 1B   PRESENT PROGESSIVE (*am/is/are* + verb + *–ing*)

Statement	Negative	Question	Short Answers
I am (I'm) working.	I am not (I'm not) working.	Am I working?	Yes, I am. No, I'm not.
You are (you're) working.	You are not (aren't) working.	Are you working?	Yes, you are. No, you aren't. OR You're not.
She/He/It is (She's/He's/It's) working.	She/He/It is not (isn't) working.	Is she/he/it working?	Yes, she/he/it is. No, she/he/it isn't. OR She's/He's/It's not.
We are (We're) working.	We are not (aren't) working.	Are we working?	Yes, we are. No, we aren't. OR We're not.
They are (They're) working.	They are not (aren't) working.	Are they working?	Yes, they are. No, they aren't. OR They're not.

Appendix 1C   Simple Past (verb + −ed or irregular form)

Statement	Negative	Question	Short Answers
You We They He She It } worked.	I You We They He She It } did not/ didn't work.	Did { I you we they work? he she it	Yes, { I you we they did. he she it No, { I you we they didn't. he she it

Appendix 1D   Past Progressive (was/were + verb + −ing)

Statement	Negative	Question	Short Answers
he He } was sleeping. It We You } were sleeping. They	I She } was not sleeping. He (wasn't) It We You } were not sleeping. They (weren't)	Was { I she sleeping? he it Were { we you sleeping? they	Yes, { I she } was. he it No, { we you } weren't. they

Appendix 1E Present Perfect (*has/have* + verb + past participle)

Statement	Negative	Question	Short Answers
I You We They } have gone. ('ve) She He It } has gone. ('s)	I You We They } have not gone. (haven't) She He It } has not gone. (hasn't)	Have { I you we they } gone? Has { she he it } gone?	Yes, { I you we they } have. Yes, { he she it } has. No, { I you we they } haven't. No, { he she it } hasn't.

Appendix 1F Present Perfect Progressive (*has/have* + *been* + verb + *–ing*)

Statement	Negative	Question	Short Answers
I You We They } have been ('ve) sleeping. She He It } has been ('s) sleeping.	I You We They } have not been (haven't) sleeping. She He It } has not been (hasn't) sleeping.	Have { I you we they } been sleeping? Has { she he it } been sleeping?	Yes, { I you we they } have been. Yes, { he she it } has been. No, { I you we they } haven't been. No, { he she it } hasn't been.

Appendix 1G   Past Perfect (*had* + verb + past participle)

Statement	Negative	Question	Short Answers
I You We They She He It } had ('d) arrived.	I You We They She He It } had not (hadn't) arrived.	Had { I you we they she he it } arrived?	Yes, { I you we they he she it } had. No, { I you we they he she it } hadn't.

Appendix 1H   Future: *will* (*will* + verb)

Statement	Negative	Question	Short Answers
I You We They he He It } will leave. ('ll).	I You We They She He It } will not (won't) leave.	Will { I you we they she he it } leave?	Yes, { I you we they he she it } will. No, { I you we they he she it } won't.

Appendix 1I   Future: *be going to* (*am/is/are* + verb)

Statement	Negative	Question	Short Answers
I am going to leave. ('m)	I am not going to leave. ('m)	Am I going to leave?	Yes, I am.
You We They } are going ('re) to leave.	You We They } are not going (aren't) to leave.	Are { you we they } going to leave?	Yes, { you we they } are.
She He It } is going ('s) to leave.	She He It } is not going (isn't) to leave.	Is { she he it }	Yes, { he She it } is.
			No, I am not. ('m not.)
			No, { you we they } are not. (aren't)
			No, { he she it } is not. (isn't)

Appendix 2A   The *Be* Passive

To form the passive, use the appropriate tense of *be*, followed by the past participle (pp).

	Tense	Form of *Be*	
a) Wool **is produced** here.	Simple Present	*am/is/are*	+ pp
b) Wool **is being produced** here right now.	Present Progressive	*am/is/are being*	+ pp
c) Wool **was produced** here.	Simple Past	*was/were*	+ pp
d) Wool **was being produced** here ten years ago.	Past Progressive	*was/were being*	+ pp
e) Wool **has been produced** here since 1900.	Present Perfect	*have/has been*	+ pp
f) Wool **had been produced** here when the island was discovered.	Past Perfect	*had been*	+ pp
g) Wool **will be produced** here next year.	Future (*will*)	*will be*	+ pp
h) Wool **is going to be produced** here.	Future (*be going to*)	*am/is/are going to be* + pp	
i) Wool **will have been produced** here by the year 2010.	Future Perfect	*will have been*	+ pp

Appendix 2B   The *Get* Passive

	Tense	Form of *Get*	
a) Her cookies always **get eaten**.	Simple Present	*get/gets*	+ pp
b) Her cookies **are getting eaten**.	Persent Progressive	*am/is/are getting*	+ pp
c) Her cookies **got eaten**.	Simple Past	*got*	+ pp
d) Her cookies **were getting eaten**.	Past Progressive	*was/were getting*	+ pp
e) Her cookies **have gotten eaten**.	Present Perfect	*have/has gotten*	+ pp
f) Her cookies **had gotten eaten**.	Past Perfect	*had gotten*	+ pp
g) Her cookies **will be eaten**.	Future (*will*)	*will get*	+ pp
h) Her cookies **are going to get eaten**.	Future (*be going to*)	*am/is/are going to get* + pp	
i) Her cookies **will have gotten eaten** by the time we get home.	Future Perfect	*will have gotten*	+ pp

APPENDIX 3   Forming Conditionals

Appendix 3A   Factual Conditionals

If Clause	Main Clause
[*If* + simple present] If you heat water,	[simple present] it boils.

Appendix 3B   Future Conditionals

If Clause	Main Clause
[*If* + simple present] If you study hard,	[*will/be going to* + base verb] you will get a good grade.

Appendix 3C   Hypothetical Conditionals

If Clause	Main Clause
[*If* + simple past] (a) If we had lots of money, [*If* + Be very → subjunctive *were*] (b) If I were rich,	[*would* (*'d*) + base verb] we'd travel around the world. [*would* + base verb] I'd travel around the world.

Appendix 3D Past Hypothetical Conditionals

If Clause	Main Clause
[*If* + past perfect] If you had called me,	[*would* + *have* (*'ve*) + *verb* + past participle] I would have come to see you

Appendix 4A   Probability and Possibility (Unit 5)

Possible (less than 50% certain)	Probable (about 90% certain)	Certain (100% certain)
less certain ↑ He *could* play golf. He *might* play golf. ↓ He *may* play golf. more certain	He *must* play golf.	He plays golf.
less certain ↑ She *could* be a doctor. She *might* be doctor. ↓ She *may* be a doctor. more certain	She *must* be a doctor.	She is a doctor.
less certain ↑ *Could* he play golf? ↓ *Might* he play golf? more certain	—	*Does* he play golf?
less certain ↑ *Could* she be a doctor? ↓ *Might* she be a doctor? more certain	—	*Is* she a doctor?
less certain ↑ He *might not* play golf. He *may not* play golf. ↓ He *couldn't* play golf. more certain	He *must not* play golf.	He *does not/doesn't* play golf.
less certain ↑ She *might not* be a doctor. She *may not* be a doctor. ↓ She *couldn't/can't* be a doctor. more certain	She *must not* be a doctor.	She *is not/isn't* a doctor.

Continued on next page

Continued from previous page

Possible (less than 50% certain)	Probable (about 90% certain)	Certain (100% certain)
less certain ↑↓ He *could have* played golf. He *might have* played golf. He *may have* played golf. **more certain**	He *must have* played golf.	He played golf.
less certain ↑↓ She *could have* been a doctor. She *might have* been a doctor. She *may have* been a doctor. **more certain**	She *must have* been a doctor.	She *was* a doctor.
less certain ↑↓ *Could* he *have* played golf? *Might* he *have* played golf? **more certain**	—	*Did* he play golf?
less certain ↑↓ *Could* she *have* been a doctor? *Might* she *have* been a doctor? **more certain**	—	*Was* she a doctor?
less certain ↑↓ He *could be* playing golf. He *might be* playing golf. He *may be* playing golf. **more certain**	He *must be* playing golf.	He *is* playing golf.
less certain ↑↓ He *could have been* playing golf. He *might have been* playing golf. He *may have been* playing golf. **more certain**	He *must have been* playing golf.	He *was* playing golf./ He *has* been playing golf.
less certain ↑↓ It *could* rain tomorrow. It *may (not)* rain tomorrow. It *might (not)* rain tomorrow. **more certain**	It *will probably* rain tomorrow. It *probably won't* rain tomorrow.	It *will/will/not/won't* rain tomorrow.

Past Forms (rows 1–4)

Progressive Forms (rows 5–6)

Future Forms (row 7)

ppendix 4B   Giving Advice and Expressing Opinions (Unit 10)

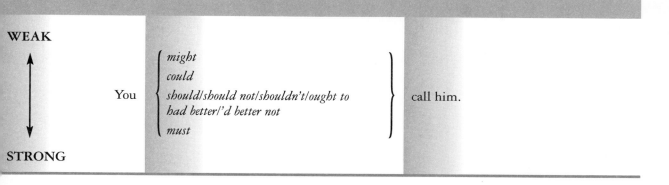

WEAK

STRONG

You

{
might
could
should/should not/shouldn't/ought to
had better/'d better not
must
}

call him.

Appendix 4C Necessity and Obligation (Unit 11)

PRESENT	PAST	FUTURE
Necessary and Obligatory		
She *must* go.	—	She *must* go.
She's/*has got to* go.	—	She's/*has got to go.*
She *has to* go.	She *had to* go.	She *has to* go./ She'll/*will have to* go.
Not Necessary and not Obligatory		
She *doesn't/does not have to* go.	She *didn't/did not have to* go.	She *doesn't/does not have to* go.
		She *won't/will not have to* go.

Appendix 4D Probihition and Permission (Unit 11)

PRESENT	PAST	FUTURE
Prohibited and not Permitted		
We *can't/cannot* smoke in here.	We *couldn't/could not* smoke in here.	We *will not/won't be able to* smoke in here.
We *mustn't/must not* smoke in here.	—	
Permitted		
We *can* smoke in here.	We *could* smoke in here.	We *will be able to* smoke in here.

BASE FORM	PAST-TENSE FORM	PAST PARTICIPLE	BASE FORM	PAST-TENSE FORM	PAST PARTICIPLE
be	was	been	leave	left	left
become	became	become	lend	lent	lent
begin	began	begun	let	let	let
bend	bent	bent	lose	lost	lost
bite	bit	bitten	make	made	made
blow	blew	blown	meet	met	met
break	broke	broken	pay	paid	paid
bring	brought	brought	put	put	put
build	built	built	quit	quit	quit
buy	bought	bought	read	read*	read
catch	caught	caught	ride	rode	ridden
choose	chose	chosen	ring	rang	rung
come	came	come	run	ran	run
cost	cost	cost	say	said	said
cut	cut	cut	see	saw	seen
dig	dug	dug	sell	sold	sold
do	did	done	send	sent	sent
draw	drew	drawn	shake	shook	shaken
drink	drank	drunk	shoot	shot	shot
drive	drove	driven	shut	shut	shut
eat	ate	eaten	sing	sang	sung
fall	fell	fallen	sit	sat	sat
feed	fed	fed	sleep	slept	slept
feel	felt	felt	speak	spoke	spoken
fight	fought	fought	spend	spent	spent
find	found	found	stand	stood	stood
fly	flew	flown	steal	stole	stolen
forget	forgot	forgotten	swim	swam	swum
get	got	gotten	take	took	taken
give	gave	given	teach	taught	taught
go	went	gone	tear	tore	torn
grow	grew	grown	tell	told	told
hang	hung	hung	think	thought	thought
have	had	had	throw	threw	thrown
hear	heard	heard	understand	understood	understood
hide	hid	hidden	wake	woke	woken
hit	hit	hit	wear	wore	worn
hold	held	held	win	won	won
hurt	hurt	hurt	write	wrote	written
keep	kept	kept			
know	knew	known			
lead	led	led			

* Pronounce the base form: /rid/; pronounce the past-tense form: /red/.

ANSWER KEY
(for puzzles and problems only)

UNIT 1

Answers to Exercise 10 (page 12)

- Horses sleep standing up.
- Bats use their ears to "see."
- Scorpions have twelve eyes.
- Elephants sometimes go for four days without water.

- Swans stay with the same mates all their lives.
- Antelopes run at 70 miles per hour.
- Bears sleep during the winter months.
- Spiders live for about two years.

UNIT 2

Student B Opening Task (page 18)

Picture B

Answers to Exercise 5 (page 25)

1. (example) See you later
2. I hear you
3. Know what I mean?
4. I love you
5. I don't think so
6. I don't know
7. Believe it or not
8. You are (You're) welcome

UNIT 4

Answers to Exercise 10 (page 62)

1.	A	5.	M	9.	E	13.	O	17. K
2.	P	6.	R	10.	B	14.	F	18. D
3.	G	7.	Q	11.	I	15.	C	19. S
4.	J	8.	N	12.	L	16.	H	

UNIT 5

"Official" Answers to Activity 1 (page 84)

A giraffe passing a window.   2. A pencil seen from the end.   3. A cat climbing a tree.

UNIT 6

Solution to the Opening Task
(pages 88–89)

Mrs. Meyer killed her husband. She entered the bathroom while he was brushing his teeth, and she hit him over the head with the bathroom scale. Then she turned on the shower and put the soap on the floor. *How do we know this?*

- From the toothbrush: He was brushing his teeth, not walking out of the shower.
- From the footprints: The shoe prints indicate a woman's high heeled shoes leading from the shower.
- From the bathroom scale: The scale does not indicate zero.

Pair Work Task: Activity 1 (page 99)

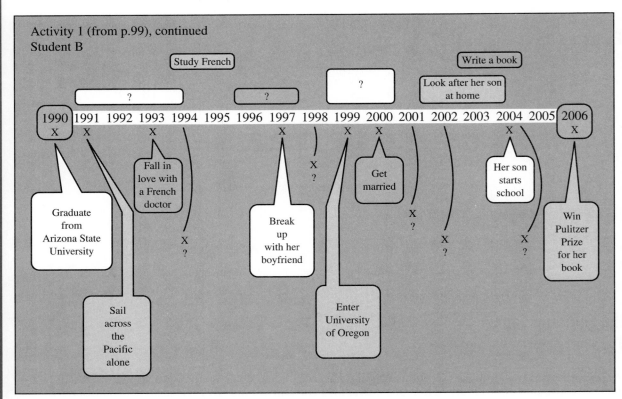

Activity 1 (from p.99), continued
Student B

Study French · Write a book

? · ? · ? · Look after her son at home

| 1990 | 1991 | 1992 | 1993 | 1994 | 1995 | 1996 | 1997 | 1998 | 1999 | 2000 | 2001 | 2002 | 2003 | 2004 | 2005 | 2006 |

1990 X — Graduate from Arizona State University

X — Sail across the Pacific alone

1993 X — Fall in love with a French doctor

X ?

1997 X — Break up with her boyfriend

X ?

1998 X — Enter University of Oregon

2000 X — Get married

X ?

X ?

2004 X — Her son starts school

Her son starts school

X ?

2006 X — Win Pulitzer Prize for her book

UNIT 7

Solution to the Opening Task (pages 104–105)

Linda   Bob   George
Susan   **Diana**   Frank
                 Carla

UNIT 9

Solution to Opening Task (page 137)

a. 2, b. 1, c. 4, d. 3

MEDICAL HISTORY					
Name	*Micheal Menendez*				
Date of birth _/_/ 75	Cigarettes? Yes/No	Alcohol Yes/No	Glasses? Yes/No	Serious Injuries ? _____	Health problems? *Headaches*
Height _____	How long? *For 5 years* Started *1995*	How much?	How long? *Since 2003*	When? *In* _____	How long? *For 2 months*
Weight 85 lbs	Stopped *2000*				

UNIT 10

Solution to Exercise 7 (page 159)

First, the woman should take the mouse to the car, leaving the cat with the cheese. Next, she should return and pick up the cat and take it to the car. As soon as she gets to the car with the cat, she should remove the mouse and take it with her, leaving the cat in the car. When she gets back to the shopping area, she should pick up the cheese and leave the mouse. Then she should take the cheese to the car and leave it there with the cat. Finally, she should return to collect the mouse and bring it with her to the car.

UNIT 13

Student B Opening Task (page 197)

Student B: Complete the information on the medical history form by asking your partner questions about Michael Menendez. Your partner will answer your questions by looking at page 197. Use complete questions.

Example: Student A: *Does he smoke?*
Student B: *Yes, he does.*
Student A: *How long has he smoked?*

UNIT 22

Student B Solution to Exercise 4 (page 317)

Picture B

UNIT 23

Student B Opening Task (page 329)

UNIT 24

Solution to the Opening Task (page 349)

The person _who_ loves Lee is _Sid_. The person _who_ loves Kit is _Tracy_.
The person _whom_ Sid loves is _Lee_. The person _whom_ Tracy loves is _Kit._

Unit 25

Opening Task (page 364) Possible answers

- If I had a knife, I would use it to cut wood for a fire.
- If I saw a ship, I would try to make a fire so they would see the smoke.
- If I found human footprints, I would follow them to find out who it was.
- If I didn't have any water, I would get juice from fruit or plants.
- If I met another survivor, I would work with him or her to make a plan / escape / build a shelter / get help.

CREDITS

Text Credits

88: From *Crime and Puzzlement* by Lawrence Treat, Illustration by Leslie Cabarga. Reprinted by permission of David R. Gordine, Publisher Inc. Copyright 1981 by Lawrence Treat, Illustrations by Leslie Cabarga.

176: Adapted with permission from "How not to collide with local road laws," *The European* (Magazine Section) June 9, 1985.

298: Adapted with permission from "Volunteers Head South to Help Victims of Hurricane Katrina" *Los Angeles Business Journal*, Sept 12, 2005 v27 i37 p.10(1).

306: Adapted with permission from "Burma: A Travel Survival Kit" by Tony Wheeler. Lonely Planet Publications 1982.

Photo Credits

Page 0: Top: © Photos.com/RF, Bottom: © Photos.com/RF

Page 5: Top Left: © ImageState/Alamy, Bottom Left: © Design Pics Inc./Alamy/RF, Top Right: © Henning von Holleben/Photonica/Getty, Bottom Right: © Erik Dreyer/Stone/Getty

Page 11: Photos.com/RF

Page 15: © Stockbyte Platinum/Alamy/RF

Page 18: © Photos.com/RF

Page 25: © Nick Koudis/Photodisc Red/Getty/RF

Page 34: © A. Inden/zefa/Corbis

Page 43: © IndexOpen/RF

Page 48: © Julia Fullerton-Batten/Stone+/Getty

Page 49: © Photos.com/RF

Page 59: © BananaStock /Alamy/RF

Page 62: Left: © Jon Feingersh/zefa/Corbis, Right: © Rick Gomez/Corbis

Page 70: © Photos.com/RF

Page 76: © Marsi/Photodisc Red/Getty/RF

Page 86: Left: © Andrew Holt /Alamy, Left Center: © Charles Gullung/Photonica/Getty, Right Center: © Comstock Premium / Alamy/RF, Right: © NASA / Photo Researchers, Inc

Page 96: © Getty Images

Page 98: © Charlotte Thege / Peter Arnold, Inc.

Page 99: © Photos.com/RF

WORKBOOK ANSWER KEY

Unit 1

Simple Present: Habits, Routine, and Facts

EXERCISE 1 [page 1]

like; study; listen; raise; have; try; helps; rewrite; ask; helps
doesn't participate; interrupts; whispers; eats; drinks; pays attention; does

EXERCISE 2 [page 1]

Sentences will vary.
1. A good student works hard to improve his/her writing.   2. He/she studies hard.   3. She/he listens carefully to the directions.   4. He/she raises his/her hand when he/she has a question.   5. She/he tries to encourage other students.   6. A poor student doesn't participate in class.   7. He/she interrupts the teacher.
8. She/he whispers to other students.   9. He/she never pays attention.   10. She/he hardly ever does her/his assignments.

EXERCISE 3 [page 2]

2. Suzette writes . . .   3. Keiko doesn't read . . .
4. Yaniv doesn't discuss . . .   5. Yaniv doesn't watch . . .
6. Jean Marc and Wan-Yin speak . . .   7. Maria goes . . .

8. Roberto practices . . .   9. Mohammed watches . . .
10. Wan-Yin doesn't listen . . .

EXERCISE 4 [page 3]

Add "Do you. . ." to make questions with the ideas from Exercise
3. Answers will be "Yes, I do./No, I don't." Record of answers: "Yes, he/she does./No, he/she doesn't.

EXERCISE 5 [page 4]

2. changes   3. lives   4. swims   5. eats   6. builds
7. flies   8. washes   9. catches   10. breathes   11. sits

EXERCISE 6 [page 5]

Answers will vary.

EXERCISE 7 [page 5]

Answers will vary. Possible answers:
1. I sometimes . . .   2. I never . . .   3. I always . . .
4. I hardly ever . . .   5. I usually. . .   6. I seldom . . .
7. I rarely . . .   8. I often . . .   9. I sometimes . . .
10. I usually . . .

Unit 2

Present Progressive and Simple Present: Actions and Styles

EXERCISE 1 [page 6]

Mohammed is an exchange student from Kuwait who's living in Toronto this academic year. His teachers and classmates are worried about him because he looks tired and is acting differently from the way he usually acts. He's usually very outgoing, and he talks and laughs with the other students, inside the classroom and out. But these days he isn't smiling much. Normally Mohammed has lunch in the cafeteria, but today he isn't there eating. He often goes outside to smoke a cigarette, but he's not there smoking today.

Finally someone asked Mohammed what was wrong. He explained that he is a Muslim (i.e., a follower of Islam). In the lunar calendar, it's now the month of Ramadan, so he's fasting*. This month he isn't eating, drinking, or smoking during the daylight hours. The purpose of Ramadan is to teach discipline, and the fasting teaches compassion for people who are hungry and thirsty.

Everyone at Mohammed's school is glad that he's all right and that he's just trying to be a good Muslim.

EXERCISE 2 [page 6]

1. __Is__ someone __typing__ those letters for me? I need them right now. Yes, Marcia __is__.
2. Who __is using__ my computer? (OR the contraction Who's using . . .) Dave __is__.
3. Jody, __are you filing__ those papers for

Ms. Baxter? No, ___I'm not___ (OR I am not.)___.
Jim ___is___. 4. That poor plant ___is dying___.
(or the contraction *plant's*) I know. That's why
I ___am watering___ it. (OR the contraction *I'm*)
5. ___Are you checking___ in or out, sir? I'm
___checking___ in. (OR *I am* . . .) 6. Why ___are they
standing___ in line? It's 7:00, time for the morning
shift to begin. They ___are punching___ in. (OR the
contraction *They're punching*) 7. Where ___is___ Fanaye
___filling___ out her application form? (OR the
contraction *Where's*) In Human Resources.
8. What ___are you wearing___ for the job interview
today? (OR the contraction *What're* . . .)
___I'm wearing___ a pantsuit. (OR *I am* . . .)
9. Why ___is he taking___ off his tie? (OR the
contraction *Why's* . . .) It's 5 o'clock, time to go home.
10. Why ___is he quitting___ his job? (OR the
contraction *Why's* . . .) Because he hates working in that
company.

EXERCISE 3 [page 9]

Maria is an athlete who ___is representing___ her
country in the Olympic Games. She *is running* in the
marathon, a 26.2-mile race. She usually ___competes___
in the triathlon, which means she ___has___ to run 6.2 miles,
swim 1/4 mile, and ride a bicycle 25 miles. There's
only a month to go before the Olympics, so Maria
is training hard to prepare. During regular training,
she *swims* 1500 meters and *runs* 5 miles, but during
this pre-Olympic training, she ___is swimming___ less and
(*is*) *running* more. She usually ___works___ out in the
weight room an hour a day; however, this month she
___is lifting___ weights for two hours a day—double her
normal time. Whereas cross-country skiing is part of
her winter training, now the weather is warmer and she
is bicycling and roller-blading, so that different muscle
groups are exercised. Normally Maria *is* careful about
her diet; she ___eats___ very little fat and a lot of fruits
and vegetables. Now she *is making* extra sure that she
eats/is eating a lot of carbohydrates for energy. In
addition, she ___is trying___ to get plenty of sleep. She
___is___ confident that she'll be prepared, mentally and
physically, for the Olympics, and she ___is___ proud to be a
part of this great event.

EXERCISE 4 [page 9]

This exercise really encourages the students to listen if
all of their photographs are similar in theme (e.g., tell
them to bring a picture of two women/men/children,
two people on the telephone, or two people playing
a sport).

EXERCISE 5 [page 10]

Stewart and Annie *are* college professors. Right now
it *is* spring break and they *are* on vacation. They
usually *travel* , but this year they *are staying* home.
They can't take a trip because they ___have___ too much

to take care of. They have to fix things around the
house and besides, they *think* it *is* cruel to leave
their pets home alone. They have three indoor cats.
They *don't own* a dog, but their next-door neighbor
moved away and abandoned her dog, an Alaskan
Malamute named Keno. They *are taking* care of him,
which *isn't* easy because he *is* a big dog and he *is*
afraid of people. Their former neighbor, Theresa,
abused the dog. As a result, every time Stewart or
Annie *tries* to pet Keno or touch him, he jumps away
and puts his head down. He *thinks* that they're going
to hit him; he *doesn't understand* kindness; he *knows*
only cruelty. Stewart and Annie *are trying* to be
patient; they *are treating* him with love, hoping that
someday he will trust human beings again. They *take*
Keno for a walk every morning and night, and they
play with him in the yard every day. Out on the
street, he *doesn't know* how to behave, so the couple
is training him. He *is learning*, little by little, and he
is beginning to trust them. They say that they *are
looking* for a home for him, a place where he would
have lots of room to run and people who *love* him. It
seems to me that Keno already *belongs* to someone who
loves him.

EXERCISE 6 [page 11]

	state/ possession/ quality	action/ experience
1. Mark <u>looks</u> terrible today.	✓	
2. <u>Do</u> you <u>think</u> he has the flu?	✓	
3. Joe <u>is looking up</u> a word in the dictionary.		✓
4. I <u>think</u> this apartment is too small.	✓	
5. I'm <u>thinking</u> about moving to a bigger place.		✓
6. Daniel <u>has</u> a brand-new bicycle.	✓	
7. I'm <u>having</u> trouble with my car.		✓
8. Pew! Something in the refrigerator <u>smells</u> awful.	✓	
9. Alonzo's at the perfume counter <u>smelling</u> the colognes.		✓
10. <u>Are</u> you <u>having</u> a good time on your vacation?		✓
11. <u>Do</u> you <u>have</u> time to help me?	✓	
12. Thank you. I <u>appreciate</u> your help.	✓	
13. Another girlfriend?! Who's he <u>seeing</u> now?		✓
14. I <u>don't see</u> the logic of that argument.	✓	
15. Cynthia's <u>having</u> problems with her daughter.		✓

EXERCISE 7 [page 12]

ACROSS

2. ensemble   8. opera   10. or   12. baaa   13. be
14. GE   15. SOS   16. echo   19. tete   20. torn
21. beta   22. HRS   23. nor   24. ed   25. cana
29. MC   30. finito   32. teachers

DOWN

1. together   2. sob   4. EPA   5. MEA   6. bra   7. LA
9. research   11. record   13. bottom   15. seen
17. HRS   18. on   19. TB   25. CIA   26. ANC
27. NIH   28. ate   30. FE   31. OR

Unit 3

Talking About the Future: *Be Going To* and *Will*

EXERCISE 1 [page 14]

Nancy's mother: Now, I have it all planned, honey.
We<u>'re going to go shopping</u> for your wedding dress
<u>this weekend</u>. Oh, you<u>'ll look</u> so beautiful in a long,
white dress!
Nancy: Mom, I<u>'m not going to spend</u> hundreds of
dollars on a dress that I<u>'ll never wear</u> again.
Mother: But your father and I <u>will pay</u> for it!
Nancy: No, Mother. I<u>'m going to wear</u> a simple dress.
Tim: And I<u>'m going to wear</u> a suit. No rented tuxedoes
for me!
Mother: Your friend Carrie has a wonderful video of her
wedding. I<u>'ll call</u> her mother <u>this afternoon</u>; maybe we
can hire the same videographer.
Nancy: Mother! Uncle John is a photographer. I'm sure
he<u>'ll take</u> pictures, and he <u>won't charge</u> anything.
Mother: Now, what about the reception? We<u>'re going
to have</u> a big party with music and dancing, aren't we?
We<u>'ll hire</u> a band, and . . .
Nancy: No, Mom. Tim and I want to have something
more simple. <u>Will you and Dad have</u> the reception at
your house?
Mother: Well, it *is* traditional that the bride's parents
pay for the reception . . . I'm sure it<u>'ll be</u> OK with your
father. I<u>'ll ask</u> him <u>tonight</u>.
Nancy: Thanks, Mom!

EXERCISE 2 [page 15]

Questions and answers will vary.

EXERCISE 3 [page 15]

1. will   2. will   3. won't (will not)   4. will   5. will
6. won't (will not)   7. will   8. won't (will not) (Note:
In these first two paragraphs, #1–8, the tone is fairly
formal and the actions will not happen immediately.
The last paragraph, #9–16, is much more informal.)
9. 'm going to (am going to)   10. 'm going to (am
going to)   11. 'm going to (am going to)   12. 'm going
to (am going to)   13. 'm going to (am going to) /will
14. will   15. are going to   16. 'm going to (am
going to)

EXERCISE 4 [page 16]

Answers will vary.

EXERCISE 5 [page 17]

1. I'll get it right away.   2. I'll be on time from now
on./It won't happen again.   3. I'm going to go in
July.   4. I'll help you.   5. I'll call her as soon as I can.
6. I won't tell anyone.   7. It'll be better next year.
8. It won't happen again.

EXERCISE 6 [page 18]

Crossword puzzle:

ACROSS

1. Fortune   6. Al   7. OK   9. AC   11. Do   13. In
14. Oh   15. Saw   17. Pie   18. Spend   19. Shelf
20. Never   24. Sweet   27. Dad   28. ICU   29. RR
30. Tu   31. Ad   33. Or   34. Men   35. Mom
37. Sandnes

DOWN

1. FA   2. Old   3. Non   4. EK   5. Cassandra
8. The future   10. Cap   12. Odd   13. ITS   14. Oil
16. We   17. PE   21. Ear   22. VD   23. Round
24. Shame   25. EI   26. Eco   30. Tea   32. Dos
34. MS   36. MS

TEST PREP • UNITS 1–3 [page 20]

1. b	9. b	17. b	25. a
2. b	10. d	18. a	26. a
3. a	11. a	19. d	27. c
4. c	12. c	20. c	28. a
5. b	13. d	21. c	29. c
6. a	14. a	22. d	30. b
7. b	15. b	23. a	
8. c	16. b	24. a	

Unit 4
Asking Questions: *Yes/No*, *Wh-*, Tag Questions, and Choice Questions

EXERCISE 1 [page 23]

2. Do; study   3. Is; living   4. Will; study   5. Would; eat   6. Is   7. Are; working   8. Am   9. Were; working   10. Was   11. Did; take   12. Do; sing

EXERCISE 2 [page 24]

Questions and answers will vary.

EXERCISE 3 [page 24]

2. You usually study on Saturday?
3. Your mother is living in the United States right now?
4. You'll study English next year?
5. You would eat meat?
6. English is a difficult language for you?
7. You're working right now?
8. I'm taller than you?
9. You were working last night?
10. Mathematics was your favorite subject in elementary school?
11. You took a vacation last summer?
12. You sometimes sing in the shower?

EXERCISE 4 [page 25]

Questions will vary.

EXERCISE 5 [page 26]

Questions may vary.

What do you think your strong points are? Are you looking for a full-time or part-time position? Where do you come from? When did you leave your last job? Why did you leave it? What kind of computers do you know how to use? When will you be available to work? How will you get to work? When can you start working? How much do you expect to earn?

EXERCISE 6 [page 27]

Questions will vary.

EXERCISE 7 [page 27]

2. Who is the oldest? Ken. . .
3. Who played basketball in high school? Ken. . .
4. Who visited Korea last year? Joy. . .
5. Who will start college next year? Bill is entering. . .
6. Who is the youngest? Bill. . .
7. Who likes Chinese food? Joy. . .
8. Who has children? Ken. . .
9. Who likes sports? Ken. . .
10. Who is the middle child? Joy. . .
11. Who is married? Ken. . .
12. Who is single? Joy and Bill are. . .
13. Who is a pilot? Ken. . .
14. Who is artistic? Bill. . .
15. Who sings? Bill. . .
16. Who is the shortest? Joy. . .

EXERCISE 8 [page 28]

3. When will he start. . .
4. What will he start in two months?
5. Who went with his uncle. . .
6. Who(m) did he go with. . .
7. Who found a nice apartment?
8. What did they find near the university?
9. Who needs a roommate?
10. What does Glenn need?
11. Who called several friends?
12. Who(m) did Glenn call?
13. Who else needs a roommate?
14. What does Sean need?
15. Who will share his apartment with Sean?
16. Who(m) will Glenn share his apartment with?

EXERCISE 9 [page 29]

Oral practice; intonation.

EXERCISE 10 [page 30]

Dialogue 1 Jim: I am
Catherine: isn't she?   Jim: she is
Catherine: don't you?   Jim: we do.
Catherine: won't you?   Jim: I will/we will.
Catherine: aren't you?   Jim: I am.
Guillermo: do you?   Chris: I don't; are you?

Dialogue 2 Chris: did you?   Guillermo: isn't it?
Chris: it is.   Guillermo: shouldn't it?

EXERCISE 11 [page 30]

Oral practice; intonation.

Unit 5

Modals of Probability and Possibility: *Could, May, Might, Must, Couldn't,* and *Can't*

EXERCISE 1 [page 31]

Some answers may vary.
1. is 2. must be 3. must work 4. must like 5. must be
6. could be . . . might be (or vice-versa) 7. may . . .
could (or vice-versa) 8. doesn't have . . . could have
9. must not . . . must 10. could . . . might (or vice-versa)

EXERCISE 2 [page 32]

1. She must like chocolate. 2. She might be a nurse.
3. He must ride a motorcycle. 4. They must be related.
5. Natalya couldn't be Oleg's mother. 6. They may not
because Lin is sick. 7. He may not know that that's
rude. 8. She must be married. 9. She might not know
how to drive. 10. She could be in the wrong class.

EXERCISE 3 [page 33]

Gladys: They couldn't make enough money to afford
that car. They must be drug dealers.
Norman: They could/might/may have inherited the
money, or they could might/may have won the car in a
contest.
Gladys: There must have been a dozen wine bottles.
They must be alcoholics.
Norman: The Riccios could/might/may have had a
party, or they could/might/may have invited friends
over for dinner.
Gladys: Kathy must have gone to one of those AA
meetings. . .

Norman: She could/might/may have been at a store
near the church.
Gladys: Tim must have gotten drunk and hit him.
Norman: Gladys, the boy could/might/may have fallen
off his bike.
Norman: Gladys, you must be crazy.
Gladys: You could/may/might be right.

EXERCISE 4 [page 34]

1. He could/may/might be taking a nap.
2. He must not/couldn't be taking a nap.
3. My sister must be grocery shopping.
4. My sister must not/couldn't be grocery shopping.
5. Everybody must be walking the dog.
6. She must have been drinking coffee.
7. They may/might/could have been playing chess.
(We can't conclude that they were playing right
before Jonathan arrived.)
8. He may/might/could have been reading. (An
argument could be made for *must have been.*)
9. My sister may/might/could have been roller-
blading. (Again, we can't conclude that she was
roller-blading right before Jonathan arrived.)
10. Someone must have been smoking.

EXERCISE 5 [page 37]

1. 'll probably go 2. may 3. 'll probably 4. must have
hurt 5. might have left 6. could be 7. must be 8. might
9. 'll probably 10. must

Unit 6

Past Progressive and Simple Past with Time Clauses: *When, While,* and *As Soon As*

EXERCISE 1 [page 38]

Answers will vary slightly, according to students'
interpretations of the pictures

Case #1 Veronica Rio
2. He was short and thin. He was clean-shaven and had
curly hair. 3. I ran after him.

Case #2 Eva Galor
4. I was on Rodeo Drive (and I was) shopping.
5. Yes, he was tall and thin. He was wearing a hat and
sunglasses.

6. No, he didn't./No, he didn't have a mustache.
7. I shouted/yelled/screamed.

Case #3 Ruth Rox
8. We were playing cards/bridge.
9. He was of medium build. He had a beard.
10. He was wearing a suit/tuxedo.
11. No, he didn't./Yes, he did. (We have no
indication of how he spoke.)
12. We shouted/yelled/screamed/called the
manager.

EXERCISE 2 [page 40]

Answers will vary slightly. Possible sentences include:

1. There was a man with a mustache talking on the telephone.
   A man with a mustache was talking on the telephone.
2. A/The security guard was watering the plants.
   There was a security guard watering the plants.
3. There was a line of customers/people waiting.
   A lot of people were waiting in line.
4. Two tellers were taking care of/waiting on customers.
   There were two tellers taking care of/waiting on customers.
5. A lady/woman wearing slippers and carrying a little dog in her purse was (standing) in line.
   There was a lady/woman wearing slippers and carrying a little dog in her purse (standing in line).
6. A young couple was holding hands and kissing.
   There was a young couple holding hands and kissing.
7. A bald man with glasses and a mustache was reading the newspaper.
   There was a bald man with glasses and a mustache reading the newspaper.
8. A young woman was talking on her cell phone.
   There was a young woman talking on her cell phone.
9. A young mother with a baby carriage was holding her baby.
   There was a young mother with a baby carriage holding her baby.
10. Just outside the door, a man was smoking.
    Just outside the door, there was a man smoking.
11. Another man was outside washing/cleaning the windows.
    There was another man outside washing/cleaning the windows.

EXERCISE 3 [page 41]

Again, answers will vary slightly. Possible answers include:

1. He was (sitting) at his desk (and he was) talking on the telephone.
2. Yes, he was. He was watering the plants.
3. Yes, there were. Another teller was talking to/taking care of/waiting on a customer. OR There was another teller talking to/taking care of/waiting on a customer.
   A man/An employee was outside cleaning/washing the windows. OR There was a man/an employee outside washing the windows.
4. Yes. A lot of/six customers were standing in line.
5. It was a man. He was wearing shorts and a T shirt. He had sandals on.
6. It was a young mother. She was pushing a baby carriage holding her baby. She was wearing a dress/skirt.

7. Yes, the man at the door was just standing there. He was smoking.
8. It was 10:30/ten-thirty/half past ten.
9. He was wearing a T shirt and bell bottoms/bell-bottomed pants. He wasn't wearing a hat or glasses.
10. I was talking to/taking care of/waiting on a customer.

EXERCISE 4 [page 42]

1. False - Veronica Rio ran after the thief when/as soon as he stole her purse.
2. False - Ms. Rio was having a drink when the thief took her purse. OR Ms. Rio ran after the thief as soon as/when he took her purse.
3. True
4. False - While Eva Galor was shopping, the thief took her purse.
5. True
6. False - As soon as/When the thief took her purse, Eva shouted, "Stop, thief!"
7. True
8. False - As soon as/When the Gentleman Jewel Thief took their jewels, the ladies shouted/yelled/screamed/called the manager. OR When the Gentleman Jewel Thief took their jewels, the ladies were playing bridge.
9. True
10. False - When/While the Gentleman Jewel Thief was committing his crimes, he was polite to his victims. OR . . . he wasn't rude . . .

EXERCISE 5 [page 43]

1. When/As soon a the thief stole her purse Veronica Rio ran after him.
2. When the thief took her purse, Ms. Rio was having a drink. OR As soon as/When the thief took her purse, Ms. Rio ran after him.
4. The thief took Eva Galor's purse while she was (window) shopping.
6. Eva shouted, "Stop, thief!" as soon as/when the thief took her purse.
8. The ladies shouted/yelled/screamed/called the manager as soon as/when the Gentleman Jewel Thief took their jewels. OR The ladies were playing bridge when the Gentleman Jewel Thief took their jewels.
10. The Gentleman Jewel Thief was polite to his victims when/while he was committing his crimes.

TEST PREP • UNITS 4–6 [page 44]

1. d	6. c	11. b	16. d
2. d	7. d	12. c	17. d
3. a	8. b	13. b	18. c
4. c	9. a	14. d	19. a
5. a	10. b	15. b	

Unit 7

Similarities and Differences: Comparatives, Superlatives, *As . . . As, Not As . . . As*

EXERCISE 1 [page 46]

1. less . . . than
2. more . . . than
3. more . . . than
4. most
5. neater . . . than
6. more than
7. more . . . than
8. more . . . than
9. less . . . than
10. more . . . than
11. more than
12. most

EXERCISE 2 [page 48]

Answers will vary.

EXERCISE 3 [page 49]

1. the most . . . the least 2. higher 3. worse than; the best 4. the most expensive; the least expensive 5. lighter than 6. heavier than; safer 7. easier 8. more fun than; more dangerous 9. healthiest; the least expensive 10. more . . . than

EXERCISE 4 [page 50]

1. F	4. T	7. F	10. F
2. F	5. T	8. T	
3. T	6. T	9. T	

EXERCISE 5 [page 50]

1. less . . . than 2. as . . . as 3. as many . . . does/takes 4. as . . . as 5. the most . . . the least 6. as . . . as 7. as many . . . as 8. as . . . as . . . does 9. as . . . as . . . does/talks 10. more than . . . does

EXERCISE 6 [page 51]

1. Mr. and Mrs. Callahan, Johnny is not doing as well. . . 2. Johnny doesn't seem to study as much. . . 3. Johnny doesn't concentrate as much. . . 4. Johnny's spelling isn't as good. . . 5. When learning new lessons, Johnny isn't as fast . . . 6. Johnny isn't quite as cooperative . . . 7. Johnny doesn't read as fast . . . 8. Johnny isn't as polite . . . 9. In music class, Johnny doesn't sing as well . . . 10. All in all, Johnny isn't doing quite as well . . .

Unit 8

Measure Words and Quantifiers

EXERCISE 1 [page 52]

2. a loaf   3. a carton of/a dozen   4. a head   5. a jar
6. a can/a bag   7. a box   8. a bunch   9. a bottle
10. a carton/a pint/a quart

EXERCISE 2 [page 53]

Sentences will vary.

EXERCISE 3 [page 53]

1. bananas C   2. bread NC   3. eggs C   4. lettuce NC
5. mayonnaise NC   6. dog food NC   7. cereal NC
8. radishes C   9. white wine NC   10. ice cream NC

EXERCISE 4 [page 53]

Avocado Ice Cream
2 cups of milk
1/2 cup of granulated sugar
1/4 teaspoon of salt
2 eggs
1 cup of heavy cream
2 teaspoons of lemon extract
1 cup of mashed avocado

Cheese Enchiladas
1 dozen corn tortillas
1 pint of heated enchilada sauce
1 tablespoon of chopped onion
1 pound of shredded cheddar cheese
8 ounces of sour cream

EXERCISE 5 [page 54]

2.—5. There is a little /some juice in the glass.
6.—7. There is a lot of juice in the glass.
8. There is a great deal of/ lots of juice in the glass.
Sentences may vary.
1. All of the children are in the swimming pool.
2. Most of/a lot of/the children are in the swimming pool.
3. A few children are diving into the pool.
4. There are a lot of/lots of children in the pool.
5. Several/Some children are lying next to the pool.
6. Most of/a lot of the children are out of the pool.
7. There are a few children in the pool.
8. There are a couple of children in the pool.
9. There are no children in the pool.

Unit 9

Degree Complements: *Too, Enough,* and *Very*

EXERCISE 1 [page 56]

1. too 2. not enough 3. not; enough. 4. too
5. enough 6. enough 7. enough. 8. enough.
9. enough. 10. enough. 11. too 12. too 13. too

EXERCISE 2 [page 57]

Answers will vary greatly.

At the caterer's
1. No, ice cream isn't sophisticated enough, and it has too many calories. 2. No, it's too rich and not unusual enough. 3. No, they're too heavy for dessert.

At the department store
4. No, it's too tight. 5. No, it's too long, and I couldn't move easily enough. 6. Definitely not, it's too sexy and has too many spots. 7. Yes, it's perfect. It's not too short, and it's loose enough to be comfortable.

Auditioning musicians
8. No, they play too wildly, and there's not enough space for their equipment. 9. No, they play too quietly and seriously. 10. No, they sing too loudly, and they're not sophisticated enough. 11. Perfect. They play softly enough, and the room isn't too small for four musicians.

EXERCISE 3 [page 58]

(1) too many (2) too few (3) too much (4) too much (5) too little (6) too little (7) too many. (8) too much (9) too much (10) too few

EXERCISE 4 [page 59]

Sentences will vary.

TEST PREP • UNITS 7—9 [page 60]

1. c	8. c / 9. d	19. b	26. d
2. d	10. c	20. c	27. c
3. d	11.–12. d	21. b	28. d
4. c	13. b / 14. a	22. d	29. c
5. b	15. b / 16. d	23. d	30. b
6. b	17. c	24. c	31. c
7. a	18. d	25. a	

Unit 10

Giving Advice and Expressing Opinions: *Should, Ought To, Need To, Must, Had Better, Could,* and *Might*

EXERCISE 1 [page 63]

Sentences will vary.
On Thin Ice
2. You should explain that your heritage is important to you. 3. You should take her to a game with you.
4. You shouldn't do things just "to be like the other kids."
Worn Out in Waukegan
1. You should sit down with your husband and tell him what's on your mind. 2. If you both have jobs, he ought to do half of the housework. 3. You should take turns making dinner and washing the dishes.
4. You shouldn't pick up or wash his clothes if he drops them on the floor.
Dissatisfied in Dallas
1. First of all, you shouldn't listen to your friends but should decide what's important to you. 2. You ought to talk to someone at your local community college

about careers in nursing   3. You should try to talk to a nurse about his or her work.   4. You should definitely change jobs if you're very dissatisfied.

EXERCISE 2 [page 65]

Sentences will vary.
1. He ought to practice conversation with English speakers.   2. He shouldn't expect to understand all the dialogue right away.   3. He needs to calmly think about what he wishes to say.   4. He should listen carefully to others.   5. He ought to try to relax.
6. She doesn't need to carry on very long conversations, usually.   7. She needs to get a good dictionary.
8. She should always study the words her teacher marks for correction.   9. He needs to get more sleep at night.
10. He shouldn't stay up late listening to music.

EXERCISE 3 [page 65]

1. must   2. should   3. must   4. should   5. should
6. must not   7. should   8. must   9. must   10. must

EXERCISE 4 [page 66]

Answers may vary.
1. had better/should   2. had better   3. shouldn't
4. should/ought to   5. had better not   6. had better
7. should/ought to   8. had better   9. ought to/should   10. had better not

Sentences with *should, ought to, had better*, or their negative forms will vary. Suggested answers are:
1. You should be more careful with your allowance. I can't give you more money every time you need some.   2. Do you think I ought to major in chemistry?   3. You had better quit smoking if you want to live much longer.   4. You shouldn't drive this care on the freeway. It's too old to go that fast.

EXERCISE 5 [page 67]

Migalie: should; could; **Victoria:** could; **Migalie:** could; **Victoria:** could; **Migalie:** should; should; **Victoria:** should; might; **Migalie:** might; **Victoria:** should; **Migalie:** should

EXERCISE 6 [page 67]

Sentences will vary greatly.
1. He must bring a . . . to the Bureau of Motor Vehicles. *Explanation:* Identification is required. "Must" implies that it is absolutely necessary.
2. He might fail the . . . if he doesn't learn all the rules of the road. *Explanation:* It's a real possibility but not a certainty.
3. He shouldn't be nervous if he's studied enough for the test. *Explanation:* It's normal to be nervous

before a test, but if he feels prepared for it, it will probably go well. A simple modal verb is used.
4. He ought to . . . before the test. *Explanation:* Its a good idea to practice parallel parking. This is simple, friendly advice.
5. Angelica must get . . . *Explanation:* This is required for registration.
6. She ought to . . . *Explanation:* It's a good idea to register early so she can get the classes she wants.
7. She should find . . . *Explanation:* It's not necessary, but it's a good idea.
8. She needs to buy . . . *Explanation:* This may be a matter of some urgency if the books are likely to sell out quickly. "Need" is slightly stronger than "should."
9. I must remember to buy her . . . *Explanation:* It's not obligatory, and I am free to do what I choose, but I will feel terrible if I don't, so a strong modal is used.
10. I could bake . . . *Explanation:* It's a possibility or option.
11. I'd better remind my father about it. *Explanation:* My mother would be seriously hurt if he forgot about it, so it's very important that I remind him.
12. They ought to start . . . *Explanation:* It's always a good idea.
13. They mustn't turn . . . *Explanation:* They are required to turn it in on time or take a lower grade.
14. They must type . . . *Explanation:* It's obligatory. The teacher will not accept handwritten papers.
15. They need to go . . . *Explanation:* They can't do research without consulting reference materials. This is not just a good idea, but a necessity.
16. Diego ought to call . . . *Explanation:* It's a good idea, especially if he's not sure what's wrong.
17. He should go . . . *Explanation:* It's a good idea.
18. He could take . . . if he has a headache or fever. *Explanation:* It's one possibility or option.

EXERCISE 7 [page 70]

Answers will vary.

EXERCISE 8 [page 71]

Discussions will vary.

EXERCISE 9 [page 71]

Sentences will vary.
1. . . . should work outside the home if they want to.
2. Men should wash clothes as often as women do.
3. Boys ought to learn . . .   4. Girls ought to learn . . .
5. Boys and girls should go . . .   6. Women should participate . . .   7. Women should become . . .
8. Teenagers shouldn't be able . . .   9. Students shouldn't study . . .

Unit 11

Modals of Necessity and Prohibition: *Have To, Have Got To, Do Not Have To, Must/Must Not, Cannot*

EXERCISE 1 [page 72]

A check mark (✓) next to 1, 2, 6, 8, 9, 11 and 12

EXERCISE 2 [page 72]

1. you do
2. Does she have to
3. she doesn't
4. Do we have to
5. must
6. do we have to
7. mustn't/must not
8. have got to/'ve got to
9. Do we have to
10. mustn't/must not
11. have to
12. must
13. have to

EXERCISE 3 [page 73]

2. have to 3. 's/has got to 4. does Irene have to . . . has to 5. 've/have got to 6. 's/has got to 7. 's/has got to 8. have to 9. have to 10. have to/have got to (It depends on how important or necessary the speaker feels about the vaccinations.)

EXERCISE 4 [page 74]

2. You mustn't dive in the shallow water.
3. You mustn't go in the deep water until you pass a swimming test. 4. You mustn't take beach balls in the pool. OR You can't take beach balls in the pool.
5. You mustn't push. 6. You mustn't bring/have radios in the pool area. OR You can't bring have radios in the pool area. 7. You mustn't break the rules. 8. You mustn't have/bring pets/dogs here. OR You can't have/bring pets/dogs here. 9. You mustn't eat or drink in the pool area. OR You can't eat or drink in the pool area. 10. You mustn't hit that little boy.

EXERCISE 5 [page 75]

2. must not/mustn't 3. have to . . . must not/mustn't 4. doesn't have to 5. don't have to 6. have got to/'ve got to/have to 7. mustn't/must not/can't 8. has to 9. doesn't have to 10. have to

EXERCISE 6 [page 76]

Answers will vary.

EXERCISE 7 [page 77]

1. didn't have to 2. have to/must 3. had to 4. did you have to 5. had to 6. had to 7. didn't have to 8. did you have to 9. had to 10. have to/must 11. have to/must 12. mustn't / must not 13. do I have to/will I have to 14. have to/will have to/'ll have to/must

EXERCISE 8 [page 78]

Answers will vary.

Unit 12

Expressing Likes and Dislikes

EXERCISE 1 [page 79]

1. does too
2. don't either
3. doesn't either
4. do too
5. do too
6. doesn't either
7. do too
8. don't either
9. do too
10. doesn't either

EXERCISE 2 [page 79]

1. Ramón studies math, and so does María José
2. I don't understand Greek, and neither do my friends.
3. Ann doesn't like liver, and neither does her sister.
4. Cheryl loves animals, and so do her children.
5. Elizabeth loves the English language, and so do my students. 6. Maria doesn't like to write in English, and neither does Dora. 7. Kim listens to classical music, and so do I. 8. She doesn't listen to hip-hop, and neither do I. 9. I like the teacher's new haircut, and so do the other students. 10. SoYoung doesn't like it, and neither does HyungGue.

EXERCISE 3 [page 80]

1. Scott lives in Iowa, and so *does* Debbie. 2. I don't know how to windsurf, and my brother doesn't *either*. 3. Sung can't type and neither *can* Fathi. 4. Mark went to the wrong restaurant, and so *did* Alonzo.

5. Bob didn't go sailing, and *neither* did Irene. 6. Mayumi hasn't been here long, and Sato *hasn't* either. 7. Cynthia was in class yesterday, and you *were* too. 8. You were sick last week, and *so* was Sheila. 9. Lee won't come with us, and *neither* will Kim.10. Maureen has a cute boyfriend, and so *does* Patty.

EXERCISE 4 [page 80]

1. b	4. g or e	7. k	10. h
2. e or g	5. d	8. a	11. i
3. c	6. j	9. f	

EXERCISE 5 [page 81]

1. sort of / kind of 2. I did too./So did I. 3. I don't either./Neither do I. 4. I am too./So am I. 5. Sort of./Kind of. 6. I don't either./Neither do I. 7. So am I./I am too. 8. So am I./I am too! 9. Sort of./Kind of. 10. Kind of./Sort of.

EXERCISE 6 [page 82]

Answers will vary in the checklist. The **gerunds** to circle are:
LEFT-BRAIN: doing, sewing, working, writing, doing, meeting, buying, speaking, competing
RIGHT-BRAIN: swimming, skiing, bicycling, thinking, dancing, making, fishing, running, meeting, shopping, rearranging, decorating
The **infinitives** to underline are:
LEFT-BRAIN: to plan, (to) arrange, to collect, to read
RIGHT-BRAIN: to relax, (to) do, to paint, (to) sketch, to sing

How many gerunds did you circle? 21
How many infinitives did you underline? 9

EXERCISE 7 [page 83]

Individual answers will vary. The following parts of speech should be used.
1. Gerund 2. Gerund / Gerund
3. Gerund or Infinitive. 4. Gerund or Infinitive.
5. Gerund 6. Gerund 7. Gerund or Infinitive.
8. Gerund. 9. Gerund. 10. Gerund / Gerund.

EXERCISE 8 [page 83]

Group activity.

TEST PREP • UNITS 10–12 [page 84]

1. a		16. d	
2. c		17. a	
3. d		18. d	
4. c		19. a	
5. c		20. b	
6. a		21. d	
7. c		22. d	
8. c		23. a	
9. c		24. d	
10. c		25. c	
11. c		26. b	
12. a		27. a	
13. b		28. d	
14. c		29. c	
15. d		30. d	

Unit 13

Present Perfect: *Since* and *For*

EXERCISE 1 [page 87]

Past:
1. She wanted to be . . . when she was a child.
2. She moved. . .
3. She began. . .

Present:
1. She is studying. . .
2. She wants. . .
3. She is volunteering. . .

Began in the past and continues now:
2. She has studied. . .
3. She has wanted. . .

EXERCISE 2 [page 88]

Sentences will vary.

EXERCISE 3 [page 88]

Donor: haven't eaten
Interviewer: Have you given
Donor: have given
Interviewer: has it been
Donor: haven't donated
Interviewer: Have you had
Donor: haven't had
Interviewer: Have you been
Donor: haven't been
Interviewer: Have you traveled
Donor: have been; have lived

EXERCISE 4 [page 89]

Answers will vary.

EXERCISE 5 [page 89]

Count Dracula: since
Stoker: for
Stoker: since
Count Dracula: since; since
Stoker: since
Count Dracula: since
Stoker: since
Stoker: for

EXERCISE 6 [page 90]

Sentences may vary slightly.
1. Dr. Moreau has worked at Mercy Hospital for_____years.
2. Dr. Jekyll has worked at the hospital since 1978.
3. Dr. Zhivago and Nurse Nightingale have worked at the hospital for_____years.
4. Dr. Faust has worked at the hospital for_____years.
5. Nurse Ratchet has worked at the hospital for_____years.
6. Dr. Doolittle has worked at the hospital since 1973.
7. Dr. Spock has worked at the hospital for_____years.

8. Nurse Candystripe has worked at the hospital for_____years.
9. Nurse Shark has worked at the hospital since 1984.
10. Dr. Livingston has worked at the hospital since 1969.
11. Dr. Freud and Dr. Spock have worked at the hospital since 1988.

EXERCISE 7 [page 91]

1. Lisa has taken that medicine since 2004.
2. Have you wanted to be a surgeon since . . .
3. Larry has been . . . since 1989.
4. My stomach hasn't hurt since . . .
5. Joe has delivered flowers to the hospital for two years.
6. Sylvia has known my doctor since they met . . .
7. It hasn't rained since 5:00.
8. The doctor has been in the room with Doug for 30 minutes.
9. Medical technology has been improving since the last century.
10. She hasn't taken the medicine since it made her sick.

Unit 14

Present Perfect and Simple Past: *Ever* and *Never*, *Already* and *Yet*

EXERCISE 1 [page 92]

1. began
2. flew
3. told
4. has flown
5. has met
6. has seen
7. went
8. saw
9. has done
10. jumped
11. rode
12. hasn't been
13. crashed
14. had
15. had
16. fought
17. won
18. has been
19. have

EXERCISE 2 [page 93]

Students' answers to these questions will vary. (*Yes, I have.* or *No, I haven't.*)
1. Have you ever found a wallet in the street?
2. Have you ever flown in a helicopter?
3. Have you ever shot a gun?
4. Have you ever broken a bone?
5. Have you ever given blood?
6. Have you ever met a famous person?
7. Have you ever had a car accident?
8. Have you ever worn snowshoes?

9. Have you ever ridden a camel?
10. Have you ever seen a penguin?

EXERCISE 3 [page 94]

Answers will vary.

EXERCISE 4 [page 95]

1. Have you already bought your (air)plane ticket?
2. Have you ever lost a plane/an airplane ticket on a trip?
3. Have you already made your hotel reservations?
4. Have you checked out the weather forecast?
5. Have you packed your suitcase yet?
6. Have you found a pet/cat sitter yet?
7. Have you already gotten your passport?
8. Have you already applied for a visa?
9. Have you changed your money yet?
10. Have you read any travel books yet?
11. Have you ever missed a flight/plane?
12. Have you ever taken someone else's suitcase/bag/luggage at the airport?

Unit 15
Present Perfect Progressive

EXERCISE 1 [page 98]

2. He has been sleeping.
3. He has been dreaming.
4. He has been lifting boxes.
5. She has been unpacking dishes.
6. They have been moving furniture.
7. They have been moving into a new house.
8. They have been sitting in the sun.
9. They have been swimming.
10. They have been looking for shells.

EXERCISE 2 [page 99]

Questions and answers will vary.
1. How long has he been sleeping?/He's been sleeping for a couple of hours.
2. What has he been dreaming about?/He's been dreaming about his final exams.
3. Why has he been having a nightmare?/Because he's been studying all week.
4. What have they been doing?/They've been moving into a new house.
5. How long have they been moving furniture./They've been moving furniture all day.
6. Who has been lifting heavy boxes?/The man has been lifting heavy boxes.
7. What has the woman been doing?/She's been unpacking dishes.
8. How long have they been sitting in the sun?/They've been sitting in the sun for three hours.
9. What have they been doing at the beach?/They've been swimming.
10. What have they been looking for?/They've been looking for shells.

EXERCISE 3 [page 99]

Answers will vary. The pattern will follow "Have you been speaking only English/talking to your classmates?" and so on. The answers will include "Yes, I've been speaking. . ./She's been speaking. . ." and so on.

EXERCISE 4 [page 99]

Sentences will vary.

EXERCISE 5 [page 100]

Jimmy: haven't been sleeping
Joel: Have you been feeling
Jimmy: haven't been feeling; have been bothering
Joel: Has something been happening; has been worrying
Jimmy: have been thinking; have been studying
Joel: Have you been studying; asking
Jimmy: have been memorizing; have been trying

EXERCISE 6 [page 101]

Sentences will vary.

EXERCISE 7 [page 101]

(1) have been reading
(2) have been reading
(3) have; realized
(4) has been
(5) have been collecting
(6) has been waking up
(7) has had
(8) has been
(9) has been working
(10) has been setting up

TEST PREP • UNITS 13–15 [page 102]

1. c	17. d
2. d	18. d
3. a	19. d
4. b	20. b
5. c	21. d
6. a	22. a
7. b	23. d
8. d	24. d
9. c	25. b
10. a	26. d
11. d	27. b
12. b	28. a
13. b	29. a
14. c	30. d
15. b	31. c
16. d	32. a

Unit 16
Making Offers with *Would You Like*

EXERCISE 1 [page 105]

Would you like a table by the window? Would you like some coffee? Would you like sugar or cream in your coffee? Would you like to order now? What would you like? How would you like your eggs? Would you like me to tell the cook to make them over easy? Would you like eggs, too? Would you like anything else?

EXERCISE 2 [page 106]

Sentences will vary.
First Date
2. Yes, thank you. I'd like that very much.
3. What kind of restaurant would you like to go to?
4. I prefer French or Italian restaurants.
5. What movie would you like to see?
6. I'd really like to see_____.

One Year Later
7. Want to stay home and watch the football game?
8. I'd really rather go country-western dancing.
9. Want to order out for pizza?
10. No, I'd rather have Chinese food.
11. Well, do you want to go bowling and eat at the bowling alley instead?
12. Sure.

EXERCISE 3 [page 108]

Sentences will vary.
1. No, thank you, but I would like something to drink.
2. Want me to help you with your homework, son? Yeah, that would be great. *Explanation*: Both the offer and acceptance are quite informal because the speakers are father and son.

3. Would you like me to go over the directions with you? Thanks. *Explanation*: The exchange might be fairly formal if the two people don't know each other.
4. Would you like me to help you with those packages? Yes, please. That's very kind of you. *Explanation*: This is a polite, formal exchange between strangers.
5. Would you like me to phone someone for you? No, thank you. I'm waiting for my son. He'll be here soon. *Explanation*: The man offering help is concerned for the older man and speaks to him respectfully.
6. Want some lemonade? Sure. Thanks. *Explanation*: This is a very informal exchange between friends.
7. This is a great city. Let me show you around. That would be great, but I'm going to be tied up in this meeting all day. *Explanation*: This is a polite, fairly informal exchange between two people who don't know each other well.
8. Want an aspirin? Yes, please. *Explanation*: This an informal exchange between husband and wife.

EXERCISE 4 [page 109]

Sentences will vary.
1. Would you like me to call a doctor for you? No, thanks. I think I'll be OK.
2. Would you like me to show you around? Thanks, but I think I can manage.
3. Would you like some more coffee? No, thank you. We'd like the check, please.
4. Would you like me to see if we have your size in the back? Yes, please. That's very kind of you.
5. Do you want another hot dog? Sure. Thanks.
6. Would you like to see our video of the Greek islands? Yes, thanks. That would be great.

Unit 17
Requests and Permission: *Can, Could, Will, Would, and May*

EXERCISE 1 [page 110]

Sentences will vary.
1. Would you please tell me which bus goes to the beach?
2. Could you tell me how often the bus stops here?
3. Would you mind opening the door for me? I've got my hands full here.
4. Will you please wake me up half an hour early.

5. Could you please show us where our seats are.
6. Will you please pick up some milk on your way home.
7. Can you lend me some eggs? I've run out, and I'm making a cake.
8. Could you please tell me where the immigration building is?
9. Would you mind handing me that box of cake mix on the top shelf, please?

EXERCISE 2 [page 111]

Answers may vary.
1. I'd like to, but I don't understand it myself.
2. I'm sorry, but I don't have any money with me.
3. I'm sorry, but I can't help you. I'm scared of heights.
4. I'm sorry, but I've never changed a tire, and I'm not very good with tools.
5. I'm sorry, but we're all out of orange juice.
6. I'd like to, but I have to finish this report.
7. I'm sorry, but my care is in the garage, too.
8. I'd like to, but I have to be downtown in ten minutes.
9. I'm sorry, but I don't know how this copier works.

EXERCISE 3 [page 112]

Answers will vary.
1. Sure, I'd be glad to.
2. Yes, I will.
3. Of course, I'd be happy to.
4. Certainly, no problem.
5. Yes, I will.
6. I'd be happy to.
7. Sure, why not?
8. Yes, I will.
9. I'd be glad to.
10. Yeah, I guess so.

EXERCISE 4 [page 113]

Questions will vary.
1. May I spend the night at Suzy's?
2. Would you excuse me for a moment?
3. Do you mind if I smoke?
4. Would you mind if I brought a friend to class?
5. May I put one of these posters in your window, please?
6. Do you mind if I leave work early today?
7. May I open the window a little, please?
8. May I check this out?
9. May I park here?
10. May I please visit my counselor?

EXERCISE 5 [page 114]

1. I'm sorry, but you can't sleep at Suzy's on a school night
2. Certainly.
3. I'm sorry, but I'm allergic to cigarette smoke.
4. Certainly. I'd like to meet your friend.
5. Sure, go right ahead.
6. I'm sorry, but I need you to finish this project today.
7. Yes, you may.
8. I'm afraid not. Magazines may only be read in the library.
9. Sorry, but there's no parking on this block.
10. Yes, you may.

Unit 18
Used To with *Still* and *Anymore*

EXERCISE 1 [page 115]

1. True	6. True
2. True	7. False
3. False	8. True
4. False	9. False
5. True	10. True

EXERCISE 2 [page 115]

Answers will vary, but all will include *used to /didn't use to* + verb. Questions are:
1. Where did you use to live?
2. When you were a little boy/girl, what did you use to play?
3. When you were in elementary school, what did you use to do after school?
4. When you were very young, did your parents use to read to you?
5. What bad habit did you use to have?
6. What did you use to look like?
7. Who used to be your best friend?
8. Did you use to live in the city or the country?
9. Where did you use to go on vacation?
10. Did you use to wear glasses?

EXERCISE 3 [page 116]

1. used to	10. used to
2. used to	11. anymore
3. anymore	12. used to
4. used to	13. anymore
5. anymore	14. used to
6. anymore	15. anymore
7. anymore	16. used to
8. used to	17. anymore
9. anymore	

EXERCISE 4 [page 117]

1. True
2. False. There is still a city called Moscow in Russia.
3. True
4. False. The Golden Gate Bridge is still in San Francisco.
5. True
6. False. Anthony and Cleopatra used to float down the Nile River. OR Anthony and Cleopatra don't float down the Nile River anymore.
7. False. They still don't speak Icelandic in Ireland. OR They still speak Icelandic in Iceland. OR They still speak Irish/English in Ireland.

8. True
9. True
10. False. The Taj Mahal is still in India.
11. True
12. False. Tanzania is still in Africa.

EXERCISE 5 [page 117]

1. isn't anymore
2. still is
3. Does he still wear
4. Does he still play
5. doesn't play rock and roll anymore
6. doesn't anymore
7. Does she still look
8. doesn't have long brown hair anymore
9. is still
10. still has
11. still does
12. still are

EXERCISE 6 [page 119]

1. She always used to go dancing on weekends./She used to go dancing very often.
2. No, she never used to have children. OR No, she didn't (use to have children).
3. Yes, she sometimes helps them/the kids with their homework.
4. She often used to travel.
5. No, she seldom/hardly ever used to cook and clean. OR Yes, she used to cook and clean, but hardly ever/seldom/not very often.
6. Yes, she often cooks and cleans now.OR Yes, she still cooks and cleans.

7. No, she doesn't. (She doesn't go dancing anymore. OR She never goes dancing anymore.)
8. Yes, she does./Yes, she still goes to the beach./Yes, she still goes to the beach sometimes.
9. No, she seldom/hardly ever goes out to eat anymore.
10. She (often/usually) does the laundry every day.

TEST PREP • UNITS 16–18 [page 120]

Answer Key

1. c	11. c
2. b	12. b
3. d	13. c
4. a	14. b
5. c	15. a
6. b	16. b
7. c	17. d
8. c	18. d
9. d	19. b
10. a	20. a

Unit 19

Past Perfect: *Before* and *After*

EXERCISE 1 [page 122]

BEFORE ACCIDENT

1. *Jerry had never been in the hospital*.
2. He had never seen so many doctors.
3. He had never felt so much pain.
4. He had played tennis.
5. He had sailed.
6. He had always had a dog.
7. He had been engaged to Debbie.

AFTER ACCIDENT	NOW
1. *Jerry was in the hospital.*	1. *He's in a wheelchair.*
2. He had a lot of operations.	2. He's learning to play table tennis.
3. He had to learn to get around in a wheelchair.	3. He sails.
4. He needed a specially trained dog.	4. He competes in races.
5. He got Connie.	5. He's engaged to Patty.

EXERCISE 2 [page 123]

1. How many times had you been in the hospital before the accident?
   Never. (I had never been in the hospital.)
2. What sports had you played before the accident?
   I had played tennis and (I had) sailed.
3. Had you run in races?
   No, I hadn't.
4. Before Connie, had you had a dog?
   Yes, I had. (I had always had a dog.)

EXERCISE 3 [page 124]

2. He slept late because nobody had set the alarm. OR Because nobody had set the alarm, he slept late.
3. Nobody had done the laundry, so Allen didn't have any clean underwear.
4. There wasn't any coffee because nobody had gone grocery shopping. OR Because nobody had gone grocery shopping, there wasn't any coffee.

5. There wasn't any gas in the car because Allen had forgotten to go to the gas station. OR Because Allen had forgotten to go to the gas station, there wasn't any gas in the car.
6. His boss had told him not to be late anymore, so he was very worried.
7. While he was driving, he looked in the mirror and saw that he hadn't combed his hair.
8. He realized that he hadn't cashed his paycheck when he got to the gas station.

OR When he got to the gas station, he realized that he hadn't cashed his paycheck.
9. As soon as he got to work, Allen found that he had left his wallet at the gas station. OR Allen found that he had left his wallet at the gas station as soon as he got to work.
10. When he noticed there were no cars in the parking lot, he realized that he had forgotten it was Saturday. OR He realized that he had forgotten it was Saturday when he noticed there were no cars in the parking lot.

EXERCISE 4 [page 125]

2. _____ He locked the doors, turned off the lights, and went upstairs.
   ₁ _____ ₂ _____ ₃

3. __✓__ When he got upstairs, he realized that he had forgotten to take out the garbage.
   ₂ _____ ₃ _____ ₁

4. _____ He went back downstairs and took out the garbage.
   ₁ _____ ₂

5. _____ When he went upstairs to brush his teeth, he heard a noise.
   ₁ _____ ₂

6. __✓__ By the time Mr. Wilson got to the door, the noise had stopped.
   ₂ _____ ₁

7. _____ He went back upstairs and heard the noise again. It sounded like someone crying.
   ₁ _____ ₂ _____ ₃

8. __✓__ He went back downstairs, and again, before he reached the door, the noise had stopped.
   ₁ _____ ₃ _____ ₂

9. __✓__ By that time, Mr. Wilson had gone up and down the stairs so many times that he was dizzy. He went to bed.
   ₁ _____ ₂ _____ ₃

10. __✓__ The next morning when Mr. Wilson went outside to get the newspaper, he saw what had caused the noise the night before.
    ₂ _____ ₃ _____ ₁

11. __✓__ He was surprised to see that the cat had had kittens.
    ₂ _____ ₁

EXERCISE 5 [page 125]

2. He had walked the dog and let the cat out.
3. He was going upstairs (to brush his teeth when he first heard the noise).
4. He went (back) downstairs (when he heard the noise). OR He went to the door.
5. To take out the garbage./He first went back downstairs to take out the garbage. OR Because he had forgotten to take out the garbage.
6. After he went upstairs./He heard the noise after he went upstairs.
7. (He felt dizzy) because he had gone up and down the stairs so many times.
8. He had walked up the stairs four times (by the time he went to bed).
9. The/His cat had. OR The/His cat had caused the noise.

EXERCISE 6 [page 126]

2. went
3. went
4. had never worn
5. (had) been
6. has learned
7. has also learned
8. visited
9. was
10. had ever seen
11. was
12. was
13. stayed
14. fished/had fished
15. grew
16. fell
17. got

18. is
19. is
20. has
21. has/has had

22. is teaching/has taught
23. is learning OR has learned
24. isn't/hasn't been
25. has written

Unit 20

The, A/An, Some and *Ø*

EXERCISE 1 [page 127]

1. Ø
2. the
3. an
4. the/some
5. a
6. the
7. a
8. Ø
9. Ø
10. a
11. Ø

EXERCISE 2 [page 128]

(1) no change
(2) the
(3) no change
(4) the
(5) a
(6) no change
(7) the
(8) the
(9) a
(10) the
(11) the
(12) the
(13) the
(14) the
(15) the
(16) a
(17) the
(18) The

EXERCISE 3 [page 129]

1. a
2. A
3. Ø
4. an
5. a
6. a
7. An
8. Ø
9. an
10. Ø
11. a
12. a
13. Ø
14. Ø
15. Ø
16. Ø

EXERCISE 4 [page 130]

(1) some/ Ø
(2) some
(3) some
(4) Ø
(5) Ø
(6) some
(7) some/ Ø
(8) some/ Ø
(9) some/ Ø
(10) Ø

EXERCISE 5 [page 130]

(1) a
(2) Ø
(3) some
(4) Ø
(5) the
(6) the
(7) the
(8) the
(9) Ø
(10) a
(11) a
(12) some/ Ø
(13) a

EXERCISE 6 [page 131]

(1) the
(2) Ø
(3) Ø
(4) Ø
(5) the
(6) The
(7) Ø
(8) The/ Ø
(9) the
(10) Ø
(11) Ø
(12) Ø
(13) Ø
(14) Ø
(15) Ø
(16) Ø
(17) the
(18) Ø

EXERCISE 7 [page 132]

Sentences will vary.

EXERCISE 8 [page 133]

(2) The
(3) the
(4) the
(5) the
(6) the
(7) A
(8) the
(9) An
(10) a
(11) a
(12) the
(13) the
(14) the
(15) The
(16) the
(17) The
(18) The
(19) an

Unit 21

Articles with Names of Places

EXERCISE 1 [page 134]

Words to be circled are in parentheses; names that take articles are underlined.
(North America); (Canada); the United States; the Arctic Ocean; the Atlantic Ocean; the Pacific Ocean; (Alaska); (Canada); (Quebec); (Prince Edward Island); (Canada); (Montreal); (Toronto); (Canada); (Mount Logan); (Mount St. Elias); (Canada); the Rocky Mountains. The Great Lakes; (Lake Huron); (Canada); the St. Lawrence River; the Mackenzie River

EXERCISE 2 [page 135]

Individual writing practice.

EXERCISE 3 [page 135]

Answers will vary.

EXERCISE 4 [page 136]

(2) Ø
(3) Ø
(4) the
(5) the
(6) the
(7) the
(8) Ø
(9) Ø
(10) The
(11) Ø
(12) the

TEST PREP • UNITS 19–21 [page 137]

1. d
2. a
3. b
4. b
5. d
6. d
7. a
8. d
9. b
10. c
11. b
12. b
13. a
14. b
15. c
16. d
17. d
18. a
19. a
20. d
21. d
22. c
23. c
24. a
25. d
26. a
27. a
28. a
29. b
30. a

Unit 22

The Passive

EXERCISE 1 [page 140]

✓ Focus on subject: # 1, 2, 3, 8, and 9
✓ Focus on result: # 4, 5, 6, and 7

EXERCISE 2 [page 141]

1. was made
2. was bought
3. (was) moved
4. were drawn up
5. was limited
6. was designed
7. was built
8. was covered
9. were cut
10. were visited
11. was named
12. was called
13. was nicknamed
14. was named
15. was finished
16. wasn't painted
17. was/had been sent
18. were moved
19. were seen
20. has been sold/was sold
21. have been notified/were notified
22. had just been promoted
23. were both employed/are both going to be employed/will both be employed
24. have been allowed/will be allowed/are going to be allowed
25. haven't been bothered/weren't bothered

EXERCISE 3 [page 143]

2. The boy's father, Donald Derby, hit a bus at the intersection of 1st Avenue and Spencer Street.
3. Derby had run a stop sign.
4. The boy was thrown through the car window.
5. Derby's daughter, Debbie, 3, was also in the car, but she was not cut by the broken glass.
6. The father was taken to St. Christopher Hospital.
7. The driver of the bus, Joe Barta, was also injured.
8. He was taken to Cedars Hospital, where he was treated.

9. The Derbys were not wearing seat belts.
10. Derby will be charged with running a stop sign and driving without a license.

EXERCISE 4 [page 144]

Paragraph 1:   by the turtles
Paragraph 2:   by them
               by the people
               by the people
Paragraph 3:   by them
Paragraph 4:   by officials (Responses may differ regarding *this* agent.)
               by someone
               by the government
               by them

EXERCISE 5 [page 145]

2. The meals get cooked.
3. The dishes get done.
4. Parks are getting designed.
5. Historic buildings are getting renovated.
6. Housing for poor people is getting built.
7. Classrooms got painted.
8. Trees got planted.
9. The cafeteria got remodeled.
10. Salaries will get cut./Salaries are going to get cut.
11. Employees will get laid off./Employees are going to get laid off.
12. New employees will not get hired./New employees are not going to get hired.

EXERCISE 6 [page 146]

Paragraph 2:   got laid off
               got poisoned/was poisoned
               was served/had been served
Paragraph 3:   did not get delivered/were not delivered
               got lost
               got confused
               got torn/was torn
               was interrupted/got interrupted
               got scared
Paragraph 4:   was going to be held/was held
               got put/was put

Unit 23
Phrasal Verbs

EXERCISE 1 [page 147]

Answers may vary.
2. didn't put on
3. sat down
4. put down
5. cleans up
6. picks up
7. writes out
8. turns out/turns off

EXERCISE 2 [page 148]

1. put off
2. look up
3. write up
4. put on
5. help out
6. find out about
7. hand in
8. met up with
9. go out
10. woke up
11. got out

EXERCISE 3 [page 149]

2. cleans up; room; takes out
3. turn down; music
4. turns off; turns on; television
5. set up; put off; meeting
6. call off; meeting; set up

EXERCISE 4 [page 150]

2. . . . cleans her room up and takes the trash out.
3. . . . turn that music down!

4. . . . turns the radio off and turns the TV on.
5. . . . set a meeting up . . . put the meeting off . . .
6. . . . call the meeting off . . . set another meeting up

EXERCISE 5 [page 151]

1. . . . to cheer her up.
2. I called her up . . .
3. . . . turned it on . . .
4. . . . take it back . . .
5. . . . get by with it.
6. No change possible.
7. . . . went over it . . .
8. . . . to throw it out.
9. He found it out.
10. . . . came across it

EXERCISE 6 [page 152]

Answers will vary.
1. They forgot to turn them off.
2. . . . turn off all the electrical appliances before . . .
3. I called my family up on Sunday.
4. I called them up.
5. He quickly got off the horse.
6. He quickly got off it.
7. I took off my wet . . .
8. I took my shoes off.
9. I looked it up in the phone book.
10. I looked up the new address of the movie theater in the phone book.
11. She ran into her parents at the movies.
12. She ran into them at the movies.

EXERCISE 7 [page 153]

Answers will vary.

Unit 24
Adjective Clauses

EXERCISE 1 [page 154]

1. A gossip is a person that likes to talk about other people.
2. Teenagers are young people who are between the ages of thirteen and nineteen.
3. Pickpockets are thieves who steal money from your pocket or purse.
4. Snobs are people that think they're better than everyone else.

5. A teetotaler is someone who doesn't drink alcohol.
6. A know-it-all is someone that thinks (s)he knows everything.
7. A private is a soldier that has the lowest rank in the army.
8. A couch potato is an individual who spends a lot of time watching TV.
9. Senior citizens are people who are elderly.
10. A celebrity is a person that is famous.

EXERCISE 2 [page 155]

Conversational definitions:
2. Dogs are pets that we call "man's best friend."
3. Piranhas are fish that people are afraid of. OR Piranhas are fish that we see in hot climates.
4. The monkey is a wild animal that we see in the jungle, swinging through the trees.
5. The parrot is a colorful bird that we see in hot climates.
6. The polar bear is a big wild animal that we see living in ice and snow. OR The polar bear is a big wild animal that people are afraid of.

Written definitions:
7. Cockroaches are insects which exterminators are constantly trying to eradicate.
8. Dogs are domestic animals which scientists classify as the canine species. OR Dogs are domestic animals which we call carnivores, or meat-eating animals.
9. Piranhas are fish which we call carnivores, or meat-eating animals.
10. The monkey is a primate which scientists have determined to be related to human beings.
11. The parrot is a multi-colored bird which we find inhabiting tropical jungles.
12. The polar bear is a mammal which we find inhabiting the arctic regions.
   What differences—besides the use of *that* and *which*—do you see between the formal and informal definitions?

Conversational definitions: shorter than the written definitions
vocabulary is easier

Written definitions: longer than the conversational definitions
vocabulary is more difficult/scientific/technical

EXERCISE 3 [page 156]

1. experienced
2. obsessed
3. disciplined
4. disappointed
5. surprising
6. covered
7. shocked
8. frustrated
9. annoying
10. exhausted
11. worried
12. relieved

EXERCISE 4 [page 157]

Answers will vary, with the following *-ed/-ing* forms for each verb:
1. surprised
2. frustrating
3. confused
4. exciting
5. worried
6. frightening
7. fascinating
8. embarrassed
9. annoyed
10. relieved

Unit 25
Conditionals

EXERCISE 1 [page 158]

1. were . . . wouldn't have
2. would live/would be living . . . didn't have
3. would have . . . were living
4. knew . . . would work/could work/would be working . . . wouldn't work/wouldn't be working
5. went . . . would learn/could learn (It's understood that he doesn't go to school.)
6. would live/could live/would be living/could be living . . . had
7. would be . . . didn't have
8. were . . . would bring/could bring
9. would be . . . brought/could bring
10. were . . . would have

EXERCISE 2 [page 159]

1. Constantine wouldn't have to live in another country if politics were different.
2. If he didn't have to live abroad, he would live in his apartment in Bucharest. (OR *would be living*)
3. If he lived in Bucharest, he would have a comfortable life.

4. Constantine could work as an engineer if he knew more English; he wouldn't work as a taxi driver. (*could work* or *would work/would be working*; *wouldn't work* or *wouldn't be working*)
5. He would learn more English, especially how to read and write, if he went to school.
6. If he had a decent job, he would live in a nice apartment. (OR *would be living / could live*)
7. If he didn't have to wait for political asylum—it's been three years—his life would be easier.
8. He would bring his family to the United States if he were a resident. (OR *could bring*)
9. If he brought his family to live here, he would be happier. (OR *could bring*)
10. She would have Constantine's help if she were here.

EXERCISE 3 [page 159]

Answers will vary.

EXERCISE 4 [page 160]

In all of these answers, the main clause can come first, followed by the *if* clause (comma deleted). The following contractions are used: *would've (would have), hadn't (had not),* and *wouldn't (would not).*

1. If Mary hadn't met Gordon, she would've married her high-school sweetheart.
2. If Gordon hadn't gone to medical school, he would've gone to law school.
3. If Gordon hadn't become a doctor, he would've become a lawyer.
4. If Claudia hadn't had Mr. Stack for algebra, she wouldn't have passed math and (she wouldn't have) graduated from high school.
5. If Mr. Stack hadn't been Claudia's teacher, she would've quit school.
6. If Barb hadn't married Tom, she wouldn't have moved to Toronto.
7. If Barb hadn't known how to speak French and Spanish, she wouldn't have gotten a job with an airline. (OR *hadn't spoken*)
8. If Jan hadn't gotten pneumonia, she wouldn't have moved to Arizona.
9. If Jan hadn't moved to Arizona, she wouldn't have learned to ride a horse.
10. If there had been birth control years ago, my grandmother wouldn't have had twelve children.

EXERCISE 5 [page 161]

In all of these answers, the main clause can come first, followed by the *if* clause (no comma). The same contractions as those in Exercise 4 are used in these answers, plus *'d (would* and *had)*

1. If I had seen her, I would've given her the message./I would've given her the message if I had seen her.
2. If I'd had some money, I would've gone with you last weekend. (OR *would've been able to go*) / I would've gone with you last weekend if I'd had some money.
3. If I had known you were in the hospital, I would've visited you./I would've visited you if I had known you were in the hospital.
4. If we hadn't broken the law, we wouldn't have gotten into trouble./We wouldn't have gotten into trouble if we hadn't broken the law.
5. If I had known we were going to be so late, I would've called you./I would've called you if I had known we were going to be so late.
6. If the cookies hadn't been there, I wouldn't have eaten them./I wouldn't have eaten the cookies if they hadn't been there.
7. If you had been careful, you wouldn't have made a lot of mistakes./You wouldn't have made a lot of mistakes if you had been careful.
8. If Lexi had been at the meeting, we would've been able to solve the problem./We would've been able to solve the problem if Lexi had been at the meeting.
9. If I had had a car, I wouldn't have taken the subway./I wouldn't have taken the subway if I had had a car.
10. If you hadn't told me the news, I wouldn't have known./I wouldn't have known the news if you hadn't told me.

EXERCISE 6 [page 162]

In all of these answers, the main clause (with the name, Eva) can come first, followed by the *if* clause (comma deleted). For example, for #1, the alternative answer is *Eva will have to learn Japanese if she moves to Tokyo.*

1. If Eva moves to Tokyo, she'll have to learn Japanese.
2. If Eva learns Japanese, she'll be the first one in her family to learn another language.
3. If Eva marries Mack, she'll stay in Fremont, her hometown.
4. If she lives in Fremont, she won't have to learn another language.
5. If she doesn't leave Fremont, her life won't change very much.
6. If Eva marries Travis, she'll be rich.
7. If she lives in a mansion, she'll feel like a princess.
8. If she doesn't feel like herself, she'll lose control over her life.
9. If she marries Sato or Travis, her life will be more exciting.
10. If she doesn't get married, she won't have to worry about this.

EXERCISE 7 [page 163]

Answers will vary.
future hypothetical

✓		1. If the rain stops soon
	✓	2. What would you do if
✓		3. If you ever do that again
	✓	4. If I were in her shoes
	✓	5. I wouldn't do that if
	✓	6. He wouldn't say that if
	✓	7. If you gave me a million dollars
✓		8. I will leave the tip if
✓		9. If I never see you again
✓		10. If you go barefoot
✓		11. I will say "You're welcome" if
	✓	12. If you really loved me
✓		13. My teacher will become angry if
✓		14. If people stop fighting wars
	✓	15. I would be very happy if
✓		16. Oh, darling. If you leave me

EXERCISE 8 [page 164]

1, 3, 5, 6, and 10 should have a checkmark

EXERCISE 9 [page 165]

1. make a reservation
2. don't eat your food in the restaurant
3. order another round
4. want more coffee
5. order an appetizer
6. like it cooked very little
7. ask for the check
8. ask for a doggy bag

9. the service is all right
10. ask for the manager

EXERCISE 10 [page 166]

ACROSS
1. Lightning
9. FAA
10. uno
12. ow
14. shins
15. PR
16. mew
18. lei
19. eden
21. sued
22. bad
23. hike
25. okay
27. ins
30. yet
31. NC
32. spill
33. RH
34. tie
36. horseshoe

DOWN
2. if
3. gas
4. haha
5. nuns
6. ins
7. no
8. something
11. Friday the
13. wed
15. pee
17. weeks
18. lucky
20. cat
24. Inc
26. aer
28. apes
19. ale
32. sir
34. to
35. to

EXERCISE 11 [page 168]

1. g   If you make something up, you're lying.
2. e   When you make believe, you pretend.
3. h   If you make dinner, you cook.
4. c   You talk when you make a speech.
5. f   If you make off with something, you steal.
6. d   Something is logical when it makes sense.
7. a   If you make something over, it's renovated, or like new.
8. b   When you're successful, you made it.

EXERCISE 12 [page 168]

1. I felt a lump in my breast
2. he might have died
3. I see anything out of the ordinary
4. I call the doctor today
5. I hadn't quit smoking years ago
6. I might have gotten seriously ill
7. I had the flu
8. you have the chills
9. the doctors hadn't cured her cancer

TEST PREP • UNITS 22–25 [page 169]

1. b	16. b
2. d	17. b
3. c	18. a
4. d	19. b
5. c	20. c
6. d	21. a
7. b	22. b
8. a	23. d
9. a	24. c
10. b	25. a
11. b	
12. c	
13. d	
14. c	
15. d	

AUDIO SCRIPT

(CD Tracks 1, 2, 3) Unit 1, Page 15, Activity 4

(CD Track 1) Conversation 1
Speaker 1: I love the smell of apples, cinnamon, and sugar because my mom always makes caramel apples and popcorn balls on this holiday. And then children go around from door to door and we always give candy and usually they dress up as witches and ghosts. It's quite scary!
Speaker 2: Do you dress up?
Speaker 1: Me? No! It's just the children! But we decorate the house with jack o' lanterns and spider webs and things like that. It's fun.

(CD Track 2) Conversation 2
Speaker 3: Well, I like the holiday when the whole family gets together, and we have a huge feast—usually there's turkey with cranberry sauce, sweet potatoes, and cornbread, and lots of other things. Everyone usually eats too much!
Speaker 2: Is it a bit like Christmas?
Speaker 3: Yes, But we don't usually give each other gifts or cards so it's not really too commercial, and I like that.

(CD Track 3) Conversation 3
Speaker 2: Are there any holidays you dislike?
Speaker 3: Yes, there is one holiday I don't like. I dislike all those pink "I love you" cards. Lots of my students get cards and chocolates. But I feel sorry for the students who don't get any. It's not fair.

(CD Track 4) Unit 2, Page 30, Activity 1

Nicola: Thanks so much for letting me visit today.
Marie: It's a pleasure to have you here. Let's see what's going on in our study center today. OK, this is the job corner. Su-Lin and Adam are filling out job applications and practicing job interviews. And . . . . that's the computer corner. Melina and Tam are using the Internet to do some research for their project. This is where we keep all the exam practice papers. Students often come here to prepare for exams.
And this corner is where we keep all the grammar books and dictionaries. What are you doing, Sam?
Sam: I'm checking the mistakes in my homework.
Marie: Good idea! As you can see, we're all very busy …. Do you have any questions?
Nicola: Do you ever have any classes here?
Marie: Yes, every day at 10 A.M. for one hour. Students learn English and get help with writing and grammar, or exams.
Nicola: Do students come here every day?
Marie: Some students do, but the average is about once a week. Usually when they need help with an assignment!

(CD Track 5) Unit 3, Page 46, Activity 4

Speaker 1: Do you have any plans for the future?
Speaker 2: Oh sure. Once I graduate from college, I'm going to take a trip to Europe.
Speaker 1: Any country in particular?
Speaker 2: Well, I was thinking of going to Prague maybe in the Czech Republic. I'm going to stay for a while. And I'll write to my friends back home. And I thought while I was there from Prague I'm going to get one of those train tickets. I'm going to get a Eurail Pass.
Speaker 1: Mm-hmm, a Eurail. . .
Speaker 2: Uh-huh, and in order to make it affordable I'm going to try to get a job.
Speaker 1: Oh, that's great. Any idea of uh, what kind of job you might be looking for?
Speaker 2: Well, I was an English major; I was thinking maybe I'd get a job teaching English.
Speaker 1: Great. That's nice. Thank you; thanks. Now my next student is a high school graduate and I'd like to ask her if she has any special plans following her graduation.
Speaker 3: Yes I do; I have lots of plans. But I can also tell you one thing I won't do—I won't stay home this summer. I'm not going to study or work this summer either.
Speaker 1: Well, do you have any idea what you want to do this summer?

Speaker 3: Yes, I'm going to go to summer camp. Yeah, I'm going to relax a lot. It's really great because I go back every summer. I've gone to the same camp for like 10–12 years and, all my friends are there and it's great because you get to be outside all the time and play sports, I really like to play sports. And it's also very social because it's a coed camp. It's really, really fun. It's going to be terrific.
Speaker 1: That's a great way to spend the summer. Have you had any thought in terms of what you're going to do about your career?
Speaker 3: When September comes next year I'll go back to school and I'll probably study liberal arts in college because I'm not sure exactly what it is I want to do and I think liberal arts is a great overall education.

Speaker 1: Yes, that will give you a good overview. OK, well thank you, that's very good. Thanks for sharing those thoughts about college, and liberal arts, and your future. Now my next guest here is a young fellow and I'd like to ask him what his plans are for his education, college and career.
Speaker 4: I'll probably be a lawyer like my dad. I'll get married, have a couple kids—a girl and a boy. And we'll have a good life together. I'm not going to make *any* decisions for my kids. They're going to make all their own decisions.
Speaker 1: Well, that's great. I think they'll really appreciate that. Thank you very much!

(CD Track 6) Unit 4, Page 68, Activity 6 *without interviewer's questions*

Lisa: Hello? (*pause*)
Lisa: Yes, this is she. (*pause*)
Lisa: Oh, hi. (*pause*)
Lisa: Yeah, I speak three, actually: Spanish, German, and Italian. (*pause*)
Lisa: Yes, that's right. I'm currently teaching English for international business here at Perry College. (*pause*)
Lisa: Ah, from Asia, mostly. Most of them come from Japan and China. (*pause*)

Lisa: Ah, well, they usually stay between three and six months. (*pause*)
Lisa: Before this job? I taught English in a private language school in Italy, in Milan. (*pause*)
Lisa: No, I didn't teach any business classes there. Mostly conversation classes and classes in American culture. (*pause*)
Lisa: Um, that was from 2001 to 2003.

(CD Track 7) Unit 4, Page 68, Activity 6 *with interviewer's questions*

Lisa: Hello?
Gary: Yes, hello. Is this Lisa Hartman?
Lisa: Yes, this is she.
Gary: Hi, Lisa, this is Gary Berman with Riga Language Academy calling about the job you applied for.
Lisa: Oh, hi.
Gary: Hi. Lisa, as you know we'd like a little more information about your background and experience—questions we ask everybody. OK. First of all, do you speak any foreign languages?
Lisa: Yeah, I speak three, actually: Spanish, German, and Italian.
Gary: Oh, great. And right now you're teaching at Perry College, aren't you?
Lisa: Yes, that's right. I'm currently teaching English for international business here at Perry College.

Gary: Mm-hmm, interesting. Where do your students come from?
Lisa: Ah, from Asia, mostly. Most of them come from Japan and China.
Gary: Mm-hmm. And how long do they stay?
Lisa: Ah, well, they usually stay between three and six months.
Gary: And what did you do before this job?
Lisa: Before this job? I taught English in a private language school in Italy, in Milan.
Gary: Oh. So did you teach business English there, too?
Lisa: No, I didn't teach any business classes there. Mostly conversation classes and classes in American culture.
Gary: Mm-hmm. And when was this, when did you work there?
Lisa: Um, that was from 2001 to 2003.

(CD Track 8) Unit 5, Page 86, Activity 4

Speaker 1: Well, first a woman goes into a jewelry store. She must be very rich because she's wearing a fur coat. In the next picture, she might be pretending to buy that diamond necklace. Then while the owner was busy, some thieves got away around the back. There could be jewels or money or in those briefcases.

Then the owner realized what happened. He might be calling for help. Then he goes inside again. Perhaps he's calling the police. I guess the woman must have gotten away somehow.

Speaker 2: I think the jewelry store owner might have gotten a phone call that a famous movie star was going to come to his store. Then when the movie star arrived, she might want to buy that necklace. Next she's getting into the car to go home, so she must have bought the necklace. The owner is waving goodbye. But while he was outside, there was a robbery. The thieves must have stolen the jewels while the owner was busy talking to the movie star. I guess the movie star might have been part of the plan.

(CD Tracks 9, 10, 11) Unit 6, Page 102, Activity 5

(CD Track 9) Conversation 1
Interviewer: What were you doing when you heard the news about the Tsunami?
Speaker: I was at home in Florida with my family. It was the day after Christmas and we were sitting down to lunch when I heard the news on the radio. We turned on the TV and there were these terrible pictures. I just felt so sorry for all those people who got swept away by the water.
Interviewer: What did you do then?
Speaker: Well, after we got over the shock, we talked about it in our family and discussed what we could do to help. We decided the best thing to do was to send money to the Red Cross. Each of our children contributed and we sent them a check.

(CD Track 10) Conversation 2
Interviewer: What were you doing when you heard the news about the Tsunami?
Speaker: I was working as a volunteer at the local church in New York. We provide free dinners for the homeless. I go there every year around the holidays. We were all feeling quite cheerful and then, while we were clearing up after dinner, we heard the news. It seemed so devastating, that something like that could happen so suddenly without any warning. I think we were all in shock. And then we all started to ask if anyone had any friends or family over there. One man said his brother was on his honeymoon with his wife in Thailand, and he called his dad. I heard later they were OK, but it was really frightening.

(CD Track 11) Conversation 3
Interviewer: What were you doing when you heard the news about the Tsunami?
Student: I was at my parents' house in California. We were getting ready to drive to my sister's apartment for lunch. Then my dad heard it on the news and he ran outside to tell us. We all went inside to see what was happening. We couldn't believe it. People lost their homes. People on vacation died. We sent some money to help the victims, and later we packed up some clothes to send over there. We just felt we had to do something, however small. It's something that could happen anywhere. It could happen here.

(CD Track 12) Unit 7, Page 118, Activity 6

Robin: So how's your new job, Terry? Is it better than working here with us?
Terry: Oh, you know I really miss you guys . . . but there are a lot of pluses to working in a large company, I get a bigger expense account for one thing!
Robin: Yeah, and the pay's probably better, too, right?
Terry: Yeah, the pay's better, but we have to work harder. It's busier and we have to work longer hours.

Robin: What's your manager like?
Terry: The manager's OK, but there are so many employees. It isn't as friendly as it can be in a smaller company.
Robin: Don't worry. You'll make friends soon.
Terry: I hope so . . . more money isn't always the most important thing . . . a good atmosphere is important, too.

(CD Track 13) Unit 8, Page 134, Activity 5

Jeff: Hello.
Eliza: Hi, Jeff?
Jeff: Yeah.
Eliza: It's Eliza.
Jeff: Hi, how are you?
Eliza: Hi, I need your help desperately.
Jeff: What's the matter?
Eliza: Well, I'm cooking Thanksgiving dinner for the first time for my entire family, and I don't know how to make stuffing, and I know that you make a great stuffing.
Jeff: Oh, yeah. Let me tell you—it's really easy.
Eliza: OK.
Jeff: First, put in as little oil as possible, like a tablespoon, sauté a pepper, an onion, and about a pound of diced mushrooms.

Eliza: OK. . .
Jeff: Let them reduce. Throw in a tablespoon of tarragon and some ground black pepper.
Eliza: Uh-huh.
Jeff: Then when it cools throw it in a bowl with your cubed bread, the stuffing.
Eliza: Right.
Jeff: Um, then add one beaten egg.
Eliza: Mm-hmm.

Jeff: And a little bit of ground parmesan cheese.
Eliza: Oh, sounds delicious.
Jeff: It's really good, and it's fat-free except for the oil.
Eliza: Wow, great!
Jeff: Good luck!
Eliza: Thank you.
Jeff: Let me know how it goes.
Eliza: OK!
Jeff: OK.

(CD Track 14) Unit 9, Page 149, Activity 7

Speaker 1: I think that cars are our biggest environmental problem. There are simply too many of them! They cause too much noise and pollution . . . they're also dangerous. There aren't enough playgrounds and parks for our children to play in, but there's always enough room for another parking lot, or a highway!

Speaker 2: I just don't think cars are the most important issue. The main problem is energy—we use too much oil and coal and it's causing serious damage to the environment. There aren't enough alternative forms of energy like solar or wind energy. In a few years, our environment will be too polluted to live in and we'll have to live in artificial capsules underground!

(CD Track 15) Unit 10, Page 165, Activity 7

Man: So you think that smoking should be banned in all public places?
Woman: Yes, that's right, all public places. That means restaurants, places of business, public bathrooms. I just feel that people need to feel that they can enjoy a meal in surroundings where people are not likely to smoke.
Man: You think that restaurants ought to be smoke-free?
Woman: That's right; restaurants definitely should be smoke-free.
Man: And people need to feel that they can have an enjoyable meal where there's no smoking?
Woman: That's exactly what I feel. And I also feel that drug stores and restaurants shouldn't sell cigarettes and that there should be special stores where cigarettes are sold and that way they can be strictly controlled.
Man: You mean like the government should set up a special group of stores, chain of stores, which are controlled by the government.
Woman: That's right; I think the government should do that.
Man: What about education, do we need to educate young people about the dangers of smoking?
Woman: Oh, absolutely we need to educate young people about the dangers of smoking; particularly I think it's the parents' responsibility, not the schools' and teachers'. They shouldn't do this. The parents should teach their children that smoking is dangerous.
Man: So you believe that the school and the teacher shouldn't do this, but the parents should?

Woman: That's what I believe. I think it starts in the home.
Man: What about advertising? Do you think that cigarette companies should be able to, you know, advertise or should not be able to advertise?
Woman: Oh, absolutely. I think it's very important that cigarette companies shouldn't sponsor any kind of sporting event. I think this is particularly bad for young people.
Man: So there should be a law, in your opinion, that cigarette companies should not be able to sponsor sporting events?
Woman: Yes, I think you could go that far. The government should get involved.
Man: Mm-hmm. What about medical research, should there be more medical research on the dangers of smoking?
Woman: Yes, once again, I think the government ought to spend more money on helping people to stop smoking, and that means they should do much more medical research and they need to research particularly I think the addiction and how people become addicted to smoking. I think banning smoking is not enough. I think we need to think about how to treat the problem.
Man: So, in your opinion, we need to understand how to help people learn how to fight this addiction . . . and banning smoking isn't enough.

(CD Tracks 16,17,18) Unit 11, Page 182, Activity 4

(CD Track 16) Topic 1
Speaker 1: Let's start with this topic. Do you know how to get it?
Speaker 2: Well, I'm not too sure, but I think you have to be over 18. Then you have to live here and have your green card for at least five years. After that you have to fill out some forms and apply and then you need to take a test in language and American history—the Constitution and things like that. And then you go to the court and take the oath of allegiance. I think that's it.

(CD Track 17) Topic 2
Speaker 1: And what do you know about getting this?
Speaker 2: Hmm that's an interesting question. I think you can just apply for one with the government. I'm pretty sure you have to show your birth certificate and your passport, and something to show your immigration status, like if you're allowed to work here or not. You don't have to have a green card. I think they check everything and then . . . they send you a number.

(CD Track 18) Topic 3
Speaker 1: How about this topic? Do you know much about it?
Speaker 2: Yes, in fact, I do. But check out your city's requirements too. You definitely need some photo ID, like your passport or license or birth certificate and you don't have to be a citizen. But in many places you have to prove that you live in the state. So, for example, a utility bill addressed to you at your home, or something like that. You might need to take blood tests or wait a period of time to prove you are serious. Something like that. Some states even require couples classes to discuss problems you both might encounter. Good luck!

(CD Track 19) Unit 12, Page 195, Activity 6

Speaker 1: I love to go to baseball games.
Speaker 2: Oh yeah, I do too. You know, I get so hungry I always eat about three hot dogs when I go to a ball game.
Speaker 1: So do I. Ketchup, mustard. . .
Speaker 3: Three hot dogs? Wow! You guys!
Speaker 1: Well, do you play any sports? Like do you play baseball?
Speaker 3: No, I never play baseball.
Speaker 2: Neither do I.
Speaker 1: Huh. . .
Speaker 2: Oh! You know, do you like watching soccer on TV?
Speaker 1: Well, kind of. But I'd rather watch a football game. American football, that is. Not soccer.

Speaker 2: But you know what I have to say? I really don't like to watch football on TV.
Speaker 3: Oh, I don't either.
Speaker 1: Why not? It's the best.
Speaker 3: It's so boring! Oh it takes forever! I don't even understand first and ten, all these downs.
Speaker 2: I know; I don't get that either. I don't understand that at all.
Speaker 3: No, it's silly.
Speaker 2: Bill, how about personally, do you like jogging?
Speaker 1: Well, sort of . . . I'd rather play tennis, at least you get to hit a ball back and forth.
Speaker 2: Yeah, that's fun; I like that too!
Speaker 3: Me too! We should play sometime.

(CD Track 20) Unit 13, Page 210, Activity 5

Interviewer: Where do you work now?
Martin: I work in the sales department of Computeam Electronics. I'm their chief sales representative.
Interviewer: Oh yes? And how long have you worked there?
Martin: For about three years. At first I was on the telesales side, but then I got promoted about two years ago, and since then I've been in charge of training the new staff and maintaining quality in customer service.
Interviewer: What do you like about your job?
Martin: I've enjoyed being part of a team—my sales team is really great!
Interviewer: Why do you want to change your job?

Martin: Well, as I mentioned, I've worked there for three years now and I have found out more or less everything there is to know about the job, so think it's time to make a change and try something new.
Interviewer: What experience have you gained from your job that would help you to be an effective manager?
Martin: Well, I've learned how to work with people and how to solve problems.
Interviewer: What kind of problems have you had . . . for example?
Martin: Well . . . I haven't always been able to solve every problem, but I know how to get people working on a problem together.

(CD Track 21) Unit 14, Page 224, Activity 7

Speaker 1: So it sounds like you've traveled a lot. Where? France . . . ?

Speaker 2: I've traveled mostly in Europe, western Europe.

Speaker 1: Wow!

Speaker 2: France, Italy, Spain. And where have you traveled?

Speaker 1: I've traveled a lot in Italy and a little bit in France and a lot of, you know, backpacking and that kind of thing. That's how I traveled.

Speaker 2: When? In the summer, fall, winter—

Speaker 1: Well, mostly in the spring and summer when I was in my 20s, you know, late 20s.

Speaker 2: And as far as transportation, did you ever use a train or plane or was it always on foot?

Speaker 1: No, I'd fly over there. I certainly couldn't walk.

Speaker 2: You couldn't swim the Atlantic, no.

Speaker 1: But I, yeah, mostly backpacking but, you know, I'd take the train, sure. You, what did you do? How did you travel?

Speaker 2: Well, I'm lazy, and I drove when I was out in the countryside, and of course I flew over to Europe, but then I would taxi in the big cities and get a car and drive where I wanted to go.

Speaker 1: How much time did you spend in these countries?

Speaker 2: I would try to get at least three weeks so I didn't feel rushed.

Speaker 1: Oh, that's great.

Speaker 2: I like to do it sort of on the spur of the moment. Did you stay in hostels—

Speaker 1: Yeah, and sometimes just, you know, under the stars. And you?

Speaker 2: So in good weather you'd actually camp out and sleep out in some farmer's field?

Speaker 1: Yeah. That's right, in a barn somewhere, We'd knock on the door and ask if that was OK. You know, in Europe they're pretty hospitable too—

Speaker 2: Yeah, they understand that, that they're welcoming to the backpacker and—

Speaker 1: Yeah, they're pretty used to us. And you, where did you stay? Did you ever—I bet you never backpacked?

Speaker 2: Oh, no, no, no, no. I love my comfort.

Speaker 1: So have you ever stayed in a hostel or inexpensive hotel?

Speaker 2: No, I never have.

Speaker 1: Wow.

(CD Track 22) Unit 15, Page 236, Activity 4

Peter: Amy, it is so good to see you. I can't believe we haven't run into each other before.

Amy: I know. How long have you lived here?

Peter: Six years.

Amy: My God.

Peter: Yeah, since 1990 I moved here.

Amy: I've been here for about five years.

Peter: That's amazing. And you work just around the block?

Amy: Yes, I do.

Peter: Wow. What have you been doing?

Amy: Well, I work as an editor.

Peter: Uh-huh.

Amy: So, that's really been going really well.

Peter: Good.

Amy: It's a lot of long hours. I've also been on—I took sailing lessons.

Peter: Oh, terrific. Good, good, good . . . , Are you still mountain climbing, too?

Amy: I am. I do mountain climb.

Peter: That's great, oh, that's terrific. How's Eddy?

Amy: Eddy is great. Eddy is really terrific.

Peter: Good. What's he up to?

Amy: He is working in a law firm. He works really, really long hours, and we have a daughter.

Peter: Oh, congratulations! I had no idea.

Amy: Thank you.

Peter: How old is she now?

Amy: Her name is Sarah. She's five, and she's beautiful.

Peter: Oh, gosh, I haven't seen you for so long.

Amy: I know. What are you doing?

Peter: Well, I have two children.

Amy: You do? Oh, that's great!

Peter: I've been busy being a dad, yes, when I'm not you know, doing the dry cleaning thing.

Amy: So, are you still doing the dry cleaning thing?

Peter: Yeah, I'm up to four stores now. We just opened one in Somerville.

Amy: Is your wife working with you?

Peter: Yeah, yeah, when she can, you know, when she's not with the kids.

Amy: Oh, I know—

Peter: Yeah, Michael and Katie. Michael's four and Katie's about to turn one.

Amy: Oh, that's great. Well, I'm literally running to a PTA meeting, so—

Peter: Great to see you. I know where you work now, I'll call you.

Amy: OK, great.

Peter: Good to see you. Bye.

Amy: Bye.

(CD Track 23) Unit 16, Page 246, Activity 3

Annie: Hi.

Jim: Hi; thanks for coming early and helping me set up.

Annie: No problem.

Jim: I really want this to be a good party.

Annie: Oh, don't worry, it will be.

Jim: Well, I'm kind of nervous about it. Can I ask your advice?

Annie: Sure.

Jim: What should I do if I run out of coffee?

Annie: Oh, well why don't you say, "Would you like some tea instead? We have plenty."

Jim: What should I do if I run out of food?

Annie: Well, you could say, "Would you like me to order pizza? It's no trouble."

Jim: Thank you; those are good ideas.

Annie: Sure! Is there anything else I can help you with?

Jim: You know what I have a problem with sometimes? Getting people to get up to dance. They just sit there. What can I do if no one dances?

Annie: Well, you know a lot of times the problem is the music. You could just say, "Do you want me to change the music? What would you like to hear?"

Jim: Oh, that's a great idea. Hey, what can I do if *Jim* starts playing the piano?

Annie: Oh, Jim! Well, you can ask people, "Would you like me to stop playing?"

Jim: Good thinking, Annie. Thanks!

Annie: You're welcome! Now relax; let's just enjoy the party!

(CD Track 24) Unit 17, Page 261, Activity 6

Interviewer: Question No. 1: Agnes, you are in the bookstore with a friend standing in line to buy a textbook that you need for class later that day. You realize that you've left your wallet at home and you want your friend to lend you $20 to pay for the book. What do you do?

Agnes: Oh, I would say, "Oh, my God, I left my wallet home. Please give me some money."

Interviewer: Eliza, same question.

Eliza: I would say, "I left my wallet at home. Would you be able to lend me some money?"

Interviewer: Great. Question No. 2: Agnes, you've just heard about a new teaching position in your field and you feel that you're qualified. You need to ask your teacher for a letter of recommendation. How do you do that?

Agnes: I would say, "I heard there's a teaching position in the next district and I really would like this job. I'm qualified. Could you please write me a letter of recommendation? I need one."

Interviewer: Good. Eliza, same question.

Eliza: I think I would do the same thing. I'd explain how much I wanted the teaching position, and then I would ask him or her if they would be so kind as to write me a recommendation.

Interviewer: Good. Question No. 6: Eliza, you are visiting a close friend's elderly mother. She has made a peach pie, and you'd love to have a second piece. Your friend has told you that her mother loves to feed people, so you know that it wouldn't be rude to ask for another piece. What do you do?

Eliza: I would say, "This is the best peach pie I have ever eaten. Could I have a second piece?"

Interviewer: Flatter her into a second piece. Agnes, same question.

Agnes: Oh, I love peach pie, and knowing she loves to feed people, I wouldn't hesitate to ask for a second piece.

(CD Track 25) Unit 18, Page 270, Activity 4

Speaker 1: Since you have decades more experience of the world than I have, can you tell me in your lifetime what changes have you seen?

Speaker 2: Well, I think the computer has changed things more since I was a young man than anything else. It's amazing how fast you can get information. You go to the doctor's office and they press a couple of buttons and they find out when you were last there and what medication you're on and stuff like that.

Speaker 3: When I first got married, using the telephone was too expensive. I used to write my family.

Speaker 1: Really?

Speaker 3: Yes, of course. Absolutely.

Speaker 1: Do you think people don't write letters anymore?

Speaker 3: Ah, no, but I believe that it's probably sent by, you know, what is that called?

Speaker 1: Email?

Speaker 3: Yes, electronic mail.

Speaker 1: Well, it's the computer again.

Speaker 3: Yes, yes.

Speaker 1: What other changes?

Speaker 2: Well, I think things have sped up kind of generally; my children fly to California or to Europe for the weekend!

Speaker 3: Oh, yes.

Speaker 1: And there are high-speed trains.

Speaker 2: Right. In Japan and France. High-speed trains from Boston to New York.

Speaker 3: And even everyday things, you know, like going shopping. I didn't go shopping in big supermarkets. I went from store to store. I went to the

butcher and the produce man and the butter and egg man.
Speaker 2: And there's less use of cash these days, you know, you give them a credit card and push it through a slot—
Speaker 3: Absolutely.
Speaker 2: And they know what your account balance is.
Speaker 3: Right. And I had a running bill at my grocer's. Really, I mean—

Speaker 1: You mean you bought groceries on credit?
Speaker 3: Oh, absolutely. He knew everyone in the neighborhood.
Speaker 2: If I don't have the cash, the lady at my corner store knows I'll get her the money. She trusts me even today.

(CD Track 26) Unit 19, Page 282, Activity 6

Man: So Harriet, tell me about your life.
Harriet: Oh, gosh. Well, my mother was always sick when I was little. By the time I was in the third grade, my mother had died.
Man: Oh, so young.
Harriet: Yeah, I think it was in 1941 when she passed away. And then I finished high school in 1950.
Man: Was high school a very important part of your life?
Harriet: Well, you know, I was still getting over my mother's death actually. It was rough. But, then after I finished high school, Ralph and I got married. That was a very special time in my life, and that was in 1952.
Man: So you got married just two years out of high school.
Harriet: Right, right, Ralph wanted to go to college, so I got a job in an office and then I worked and he went to college.

Man: So you supported him throughout that time.
Harriet: I sure did, I did indeed and by the time he finished college, I was 25 years old. Yes, and you know, by then, I was ready to have children. Yes, so we did. Our first child, little Annie, was born in 1955. By the time she was two years old, we had a second child. Little Richard—he's a doll! He was born in 1956. And then Ralph got a new job in 1958. And actually that wasn't such a good thing because he started working day and night.
Man: So you didn't see very much of him.
Harriet: Not at all. The kids were asleep by the time he got home at night. And so they never saw him and I never saw him either. And we got a divorce in 1960. And you know at that time, divorces were not as common as they are now.
Man: Oh, I know, that's true.

(CD Track 27) Unit 20, Page 300, Activity 5

Speaker 1: We live in a small house. There's a living room, a study, and a kitchen on the ground floor. The living room is quite large. We eat in the kitchen so we have a table and two chairs in there. The study is my favorite room. It's not very large but it has a nice rug on the floor. I bought the rug on a visit to Turkey five years ago. There's an old desk in there. My computer's on the desk facing the window, which has a lovely view of the garden.
Speaker 2: Well, there are six apartments in my

building. I live on the second floor. My apartment has two rooms, a living room and a bedroom, and also a kitchen and a bathroom. The kitchen is the best room. It has two large windows, so it's very sunny. There's a large kitchen table and I love to sit at the table with a cup of coffee and read or just daydream. The bedroom is quite small. There's a bed, a chest of drawers, and a lamp. The living room has a sofa and an armchair. But I don't spend much time in the living room. I prefer the kitchen.

(CD Track 28) Unit 21, Page 310, Activity 4

Paul: Maria, where are you living these days?
Maria: I've been in South America for three years. I live in Rio de Janeiro.
Paul: No kidding! Do you like living in Rio?
Maria: Sure! The people are so nice and there's so much to see!
Paul: I've always heard it's beautiful there. Can you tell us about some of the places you really love?
Maria: There are a lot of places. Well, there's City Park. It's on Santa Marinha Street.
Paul: What's special about City Park?
Maria: It has a beautiful view of Leblon Beach. You can

also visit the City Historic Museum in City Park.
Paul: What else is there to see?
Maria: Let me see. Everyone wants to go to Sugar Loaf Mountain. There's a beautiful view of the city from there, too.
Paul: Sugar Loaf Mountain. That's the mountain with the cross on top.
Maria: Yes, exactly. How did you know?
Paul: Oh, I've seen pictures. What's your favorite beach?
Maria: Well, I love swimming at Ipanema Beach. I think it's the most beautiful beach on the Atlantic Ocean.

(CD Track 29) Unit 22, Page 325, Activity 5

Irene: So Larry, Paul told me you got ripped off a couple of weeks ago. What happened?
Larry: You won't believe this. I was actually in a bank making out a deposit slip, and I had a briefcase between my legs on the floor, and I was concentrating on what I was doing, right? And I felt something moving against my, my pants, and I wasn't terribly aware, until I looked down and my briefcase was gone.
Irene: Wow, that's terrible!
Larry: . . . which contained important papers. It contained my cell phone, and I looked around. . .
Irene: So that was all taken?
Larry: It was entirely taken. I looked around and the thief had left. I don't know whether this person was hiding somewhere in the bank or handed off the briefcase to somebody that left out on the street, but I was absolutely panic-stricken.
Irene: Sure.
Larry: And important things were taken. And. . .

Irene: So what did you do?
Larry: Well, first I went to the bank guard who hadn't seen anything. Then I went to the bank manager, I filed a report, and then I had to go back to work.
Irene: Well, Larry, the reason I'm asking you about this is because my house was broken into last week.
Larry: I heard about that. I'm sorry, Irene.
Irene: Oh, it was. . .
Larry: What got taken?
Irene: Everything got taken. I mean, everything. We were gone maybe—
Larry: Nothing got left? I mean, all the valuables got taken?
Irene: Television, stereo, jewelry, money, you know, just everything was taken.
Larry: Was the back door broken into or. . .
Irene: No, I think they got in through a fire escape in the window, and we were only gone, I don't know, an hour and a half, and in that time they took everything.

(CD Track 30) Unit 23, Page 345, Activity 3

So Jeff, what's your morning routine? What do you do from the moment you wake up?
Jeff : Um, I usually wake up around the same time every morning, around 5:30, and I turn on the radio and listen to the news for a bit and then I get up. And I usually put on an old pair of sweats and a tee shirt, sweatshirt and I go out and run.
Woman: Oh.
Jeff: I leave the house around 6:00, so I get back around 6:30 or so, and then I put on some real loud music. I turn it up really loud.
Woman: Oh. . .
Jeff: Well, I don't have any neighbors close by so it doesn't matter. Take off my running clothes and jump in the shower and sing along with the music.
Woman: Oh, that must be pretty.
Jeff: Like I said, there are no neighbors. And after my shower I get dressed and I go into the kitchen and make breakfast. I always make myself a pot of tea and then have a bowl of cereal and some fruit and when my tea is ready I sit down and I read the paper for about

ten minutes. And then I put all the breakfast stuff away and I go and brush my teeth, make sure that I've turned off all the lights, and put on my coat and walk to the station.
Woman: Well, that's a pretty full morning. What about you, Agnes, what do you do?
Agnes: Well, I set my alarm for 7:00. I don't like it, but I do. And as soon as it goes off, I usually turn over and go right back to sleep for another 20 minutes or so.
Woman: That's just like me.
Agnes: Oh, really, I hate to actually get out of bed, and I put it off until the last minute. But I usually get up around 7:30, sometimes even later. So the first thing I do is go into the kitchen and make myself a cup of coffee, and then I turn on the TV. I watch the news or a breakfast show for a few minutes. And then I take a shower, very quick one, and then I get dressed, I put on my make-up, do my hair, and if I have time I grab something to eat, but usually I don't. I'm just running around too much because I have to get to the bus stop and get on the bus at 8:15.

(CD Track 31) Unit 24, Page 360, Activity 4

Lee: Oh, here's a good one. Pat, what would you say your ideal partner would be like?
Pat: Hmmm, oh, God. Well, let me see. My ideal partner would be someone who is amusing, definitely

amusing. I mean, he has to be someone who would be funny. That's important for me. That's the most important thing. I mean, not that, you know, I don't want him to be ugly, but. . .

Lee: Right.

Pat: But he should be someone who has a sense of humor, who likes to laugh, who likes to be silly. Someone who's silly. What about you?

Lee: My ideal partner? Just like me. No, I'm kidding. No, I think someone who is pretty attractive, I mean, I have to admit it, it sounds shallow, but looks are important to me. But I think intelligent and a sense of humor and a real dedication to the relationship I think is important, but yeah, humor helps get through a relationship.

Pat: Oh, yeah.

Lee: Yeah, so that's my story and I'm sticking to it. What about you, Chrissy?

Chrissy : My ideal mate would have to be a person that is taller than I am, and when you're six-one that's not easy, and he'd have to be dark, I don't want a person who's blond or a red-head. I just don't find them attractive. And someone who makes me laugh. That's the most important.

Pat: That's the key.

Chrissy: Yeah, a commonality.

(CD Track 32) Unit 25, Page 380, Activity 6

Student 1: If you had to choose three objects to represent American culture at the end of the twentieth century, which ones would you choose?

Student 2: Well, I think I'd choose a copy of the *New York Times* and a laptop computer, and I think an autographed major league baseball.

Student 1: Why would you choose the baseball?

Student 2: Well, baseball is the American national game; it's played everywhere.

Student 1: Right, right.

Student 2: And the baseball is the symbol, and I'd have some famous baseball players autograph it, sign it.

Student 1: Well, if you had to choose one, of all three, which one would you choose if you had to make a decision?

Student 2: Oh, I'd have to choose I think a copy of the *New York Times*, the most read paper, in terms of importance, in the country.

Student 1: Mm-hmm.

Student 2: Definitely include that.

Student 1: Good. What would you choose to represent American culture at the end of the twentieth century if you had to choose three objects?

Student 3: I guess I'd choose a pair of jeans: Levi's, a Big Mac, and a copy of the *TV Guide*.

Student 1: And which do you think is like the most important if you had to choose?

Student 3: I guess the *TV Guide* would give the most information. So I guess if I could only put one object in the time capsule I would choose that.

Student 1: Yeah, that sounds good. I agree.